PREMODERN JEWISH BOOKS, THEIR MAKERS AND
READERS IN AN ERA OF MEDIA CHANGE

BIBLIOLOGIA

ELEMENTA AD LIBRORUM STUDIA PERTINENTIA

Collection publiée sous les auspices de l'Institut
de recherche et d'histoire des textes, Paris.

VOLUME 67

Comité de rédaction
André Binggeli, CNRS, Institut de recherche et d'histoire des textes, Paris
Paola Degni, Università Ca'Foscari Venezia
Michele C. Ferrari, Friedrich-Alexander-Universität Erlangen
Françoise Fery-Hue, CNRS, Institut de recherche et d'histoire des textes, Paris
Xavier Hermand, Université de Namur
Marilena Maniaci, Università degli studi di Cassino e del Lazio meridionale
Donatella Nebbiai, CNRS, Institut de recherche et d'histoire des textes, Paris
Judith Olszowy-Schlanger, École Pratique des Hautes Études, Paris
Teresa Webber, Trinity College, Cambridge

Premodern Jewish Books, Their Makers and Readers in an Era of Media Change

edited by
KATRIN KOGMAN-APPEL AND
ILONA STEIMANN

BREPOLS

A note on transliteration:
Given that this volume is concerned with the cultural history of books,
a simplified transliteration key without diacritics was applied.

© 2024, Brepols Publishers n.v., Turnhout, Belgium.

All rights reserved. No part of this publication may be reproduced, stored in a retrieval system, or transmitted, in any form or by any means, electronic, mechanical, photocopying, recording, or otherwise without the prior permission of the publisher.

D/2024/0095/216
ISBN 978-2-503-60463-3
E-ISBN 978-2-503-60465-7
DOI 10.1484/M.BIB-EB.5.132304
ISSN 1375-9566
E-ISSN 2565-9286

Printed in the EU on acid-free paper.

Table of contents

Introduction
Katrin Kogman-Appel and Ilona Steimann
9

Part One
Media Change

Changes in Bookmaking
Joel ben Simeon's Manuscripts in the Transition from Customized to Mass Production
Rodica Herlo-Lukowski
19

Joel ben Simeon in Transition
Evelyn M. Cohen
49

Jewish Books from Portugal to the Early Sefardi Diaspora
Débora Marques de Matos
65

The Emergence of the Printing Self
Egodocuments and Micro-Egodocuments in Jewish Paratexts from Manuscript to Print
Avriel Bar-Levav
87

From Manuscript to Print and Back Again
Two Case Studies in Late Sixteenth-Century Jewish Book Culture
Pavel Sládek
97

***Lishmah Qedushat Sefer Torah* or the Impossibility of Printing a Kosher Torah Scroll from Rabbinic Perspectives**
Annett Martini
133

Part Two
The Craft of Editing

The 1514 'Grace after Meals, Sabbath Hymns and *Qiddush*' and the Experimental Beginnings of Woodcut Illustration in Prague
Sarit Shalev-Eyni
151

Hayyim Shahor and Jewish Life in Sixteenth-Century Ashkenaz
Lucia Raspe
175

Of Roots and Signs
Printing Ashkenazi Responsa in Sixteenth-Century Venice
Tamara Morsel-Eisenberg 193

Part Three
Reading

The Masorete and His Readers
A Relationship Obscured Now Rediscovered
Dalia-Ruth Halperin 227

Early Hebrew Printing and the Quality of Reading
A Praxeological Study
Hanna Liss 251

Hegemonies of Reading
Layout, Materiality, and Authorship in Early Hebrew Prints
Federico Dal Bo 275

Part Four
Confiscation and Destruction

Burning the Talmud
Before and After Print
David Stern 301

The Bookless Talmud and the Talmud Book: The Loss of Books in the Medieval and the Early Modern World
Yakov Z. Mayer 339

Part Five
Christian Collections

A Medieval Hebrew Psalter with Latin Glosses (MS Paris, BnF hébr. 113) and Its Cambridge Connection
Judith Olszowy-Schlanger 353

A Forced Journey between Two Faiths
The Hebrew Manuscripts of the University of Vienna
Ilona Steimann 369

'Ben Hacane Liber qui dicitur Pelia'
Egidio da Viterbo's Kabbalistic Excerpts
Saverio Campanini 393

Alfonso de Zamora and Hebrew Manuscripts on Grammar and Exegesis in Sixteenth-Century Spain
Javier DEL BARCO   409

On the Beginnings of Christian Hebraist Bibliography in the Sixteenth Century
Maximilian DE MOLIÈRE   429

Manuscript Index   447

General Index   449

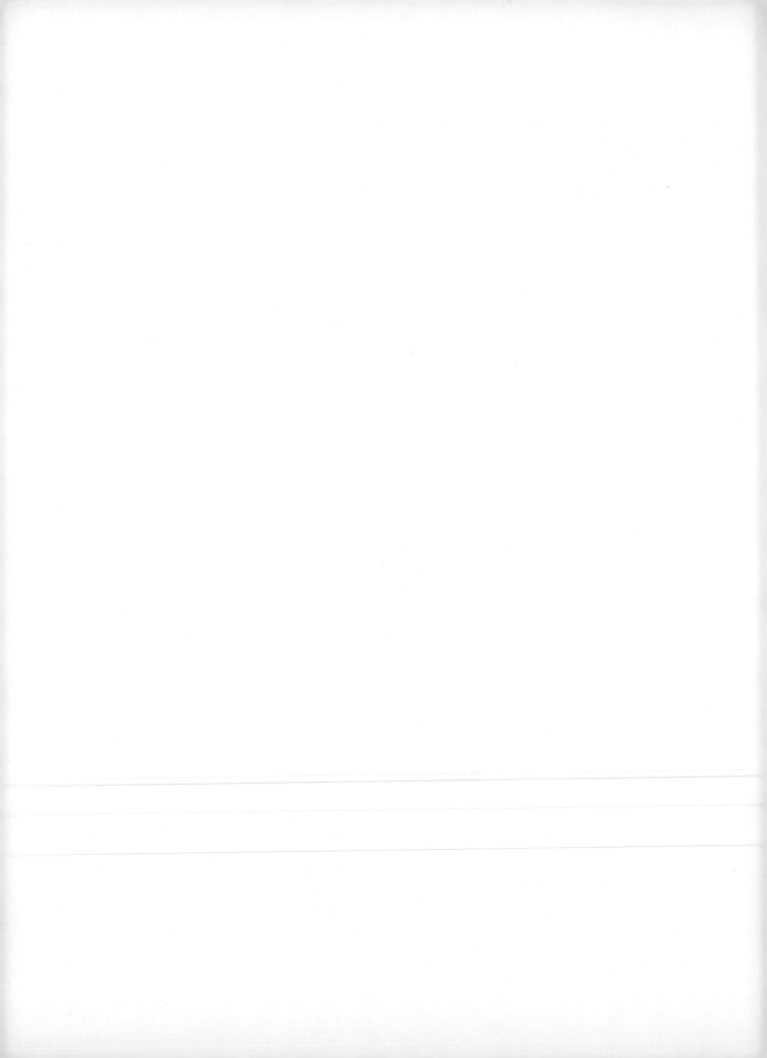

KATRIN KOGMAN-APPEL AND ILONA STEIMANN

Introduction

On some unknown date, perhaps before 1500, Gershom Soncino, who nicknamed himself *ger sham* ('a foreigner elsewhere'), set out on one of his many journeys, this time to France, to acquire suitable manuscripts for the production of good printed editions.[1] Although the history of the book traditionally focuses on printed books, this episode, reported by Gershom himself, demonstrates vividly the close interdependence between handwritten and printed media. Research on this interdependence still leaves significant lacunae concerning, for example, the role of the book, both handwritten and printed, as a material object and the complex developments associated with the editing and publishing of texts in an age of media change.

Even though material features of medieval manuscripts have been studied intensively in a field that is commonly defined as codicology, these studies have been geared primarily to attribution and dating — the coming to grips with the technological progression of book production. The study of texts has always been at the core of research in the humanities, and content-focused research can approach texts as completely abstract phenomena. However, very little attention has been paid to the actual artefacts that contain these texts and their cultural and sociological implications.

Early historians of the book, associated with the so-called 'Bibliography School', were concerned with the materiality of the book in general and manuscripts in particular. Codicology and the study of book production was an auxiliary discipline to literary history and, later, also to art history (research involving illuminated manuscripts). In the study of manuscripts, codicology was complemented by palaeography, another analytical tool developed to assist

---

1 The pun *ger sham* appears, e.g., on the title page of Gershom Soncino's 1533 edition of David Qimhi's *Sefer Mikhlol* ('Book of Completeness') printed in Istanbul, https://www.nli.org.il/en/books/NNL_ALEPH002060901/NLI (accessed May 2022). For Gershom's appreciation of French scholarship mentioning his sojourn there, see the last page of his edition of Rashi's commentary, printed in Rimini, c. 1525, https://www.nli.org.il/en/books/NNL_ALEPH002082292/NLI [accessed in May 2022]; on his trip to France, see also Abraham M. Habermann, 'The Printers of the Soncino Family [in Hebrew]', in *Chapters in the History of Hebrew Printers and Other Matters of the Book*, ed. by Abraham M. Habermann (Jerusalem: Rubin Mass, 1978), p. 19.

Katrin Kogman-Appel • University of Münster
Ilona Steimann • Hochschule für Jüdische Studien, Heidelberg

scholarly efforts towards attribution and dating.[2] To these, one can add stylistic analysis, most often employed in the attribution or the dating of illuminated manuscripts. At the same time, bibliographical research governed the study of printed books. In this field, it was the study of typography that addressed the material aspects along with that of watermarks, which revealed information about the origin of the paper used in the various printshops. Apart from those concerns and taking a distance from the material aspects, the biographies of printers, the history of certain printshops, and information about the when and where of specific printed editions were the issues that attracted the interest of scholars.

In the 1960s, the book history field took a turn towards cultural studies. Scholars, among them several members of the French *Annales* school, shifted the focus away from production and began to consider the various roles books play(ed) in the societies that use them. The new discipline of book culture focused on such matters as reading practices; (il)literacy; publication and marketing strategies; cultural tastes and fashions; the ways the physical presentation of a text affects its reception; collecting strategies; and the development of libraries, books, and communication studies.[3] Not only did these endeavours centre on print culture, but the strong sociological interest in book culture also channelled the study away from material aspects, two trends that left the materiality of the premodern book at the periphery of the relevant scholarship.

Interest in the materiality of books reappeared only recently and has been linked to the development of material culture studies since the 1980s when the exploration of artefacts was introduced in historical research. At the core of these new interests in the materiality were artefacts with a strong potential for revealing patterns of daily life. The book as a material object was not of immediate concern, and it is only very recently that the materiality of the book aroused the interest of book historians. Originally, this new focus was concerned with printed media,[4] but more recently scholars have realized that the study of manuscripts is a crucial aspect of book history and cannot be set apart.[5] The material qualities of the premodern containers of text (inscriptions, papyri, codices, scrolls) and the role of these qualities in the mediation and uses of texts has since attracted significant scholarship. There is now particular interest in studying how books were handled and used in an approach that was recently described in terms of praxeology and reception theory. Markus Hilgert

---

2 The pioneer in this field, as far as Hebrew manuscripts are concerned, is Malachi Beit-Arié. His method is described in great detail in Malachi Beit-Arié, *Hebrew Codicology: Historical and Comparative Typology of Medieval Hebrew Codices Based on the Documentation of the Extant Dated Manuscripts until 1540 Using a Quantitative Approach* (Jerusalem and Hamburg: The Israel Academy of Sciences and the University of Hamburg, 2021), online edition <https://doi.org/10.25592/uhhfdm.9349> [accessed in May 2022].

3 Examples of discussions about the early school of book culture are: Donald McKenzie, *Bibliography and the Sociology of Texts (The Panizzi Lectures)* (Cambridge et al.: Cambridge University Press, 1985); Marshall McLuhan, *The Gutenberg Galaxy: The Making of Typographic Man* (Toronto: University of Toronto Press, 1962); Walter J. Ong, *Orality and Literacy: The Technologizing of the Word* (London and New York: Routledge, 1982); Lucien Fèbvre and Henri-Jean Martin, *The Coming of the Book: The Impact of Printing, 1450–1800* (London and New York: Verso, 1976); Roger Chartier, *The Order of Books: Readers, Authors, and Libraries in Europe between the Fourteenth and Eighteenth Centuries* (Stanford: Stanford University Press, 1994).

4 Robert Darnton, 'What Is the History of Books?', in *The Kiss of Lamourette: Reflections in Cultural History*, ed. by Robert Darnton (New York: Norton, 1990), pp. 107–35.

5 See Jessica Brantley, 'The Prehistory of the Book', *Publications of the Modern Language Association* 124/2 (2009), pp. 632–39. For a useful introduction to the field, see Thomas Meier, Michael R. Ott, and Rebecca Sauer, *Materiale Textkulturen. Konzepte – Materialien – Praktiken* (Berlin: de Gruyter, 2015).

speaks of 'practices and agents of reception' and argues that in the historical perspective, when we lack actual contact with the material features as agents of reception, the material condition of a book (or any other artefact that contains text) is crucial as a source of information.[6] This material-focused approach is thus designed to determine the cultural and social roles these objects played in the societies that produced and used them.

Another significant development in book history in recent decades challenges the notion of a print revolution and looks instead at this history in terms of a gradual transition from the late Middle Ages into the early modern period. The observation that manuscript culture did not cease to exist immediately after the invention of the printing press and that manuscripts and printed books coexisted for several centuries yielded a reappraisal of the two media as entangled rather than dichotomously separate cultural phenomena.[7] How contemporaneous makers of books and their readers experienced these changes has been only scantily addressed thus far, and there are numerous open questions in regard to the way these experiences determined early modern book editing processes.

Recent approaches that tackle these questions have guided the approach of the *Encyclopedia of Jewish Book Cultures*, edited by Emile Schrijver and currently being published by Brill. Among other considerations, the work is designed to direct attention to those features of Jewish book culture that appear to be intrinsic to the *Jewish* context. At the same time, however, it also integrates this Jewish book culture within the broader context of what its editors refer to as 'general book culture'. Thus, it looks at the Jewish book afresh from the perspectives that govern the recent discourse on book history while, at the same time, points specifically to the crucial complexities that the Jewish context implies.[8]

Based on these premises and faithful to the methodological standards the recent discourse has set, the present volume has a relatively clear goal: it considers manuscripts and prints as stations in a continuum bringing together studies about books as artefacts within transitional zones. The history of the book from the handwritten to the printed medium is understood as a process marked by innovation and social change, but also by disorientation and bewilderment. Interreligious circulation of books (not only in the sense of read texts but also, and primarily, as handled objects) was marked by deep tensions between Jewish and non-Jewish attitudes towards knowledge, scholarship, and treatment of the book as a material object. Professionals of the book trade who migrated from one Jewish culture to another functioned among different cultural spheres. The journey of a book from production to use was determined by a complex set of factors: communication among authors,

---

6 Markus Hilgert, '"Text-Anthropologie": Die Erforschung von Materialität und Präsenz des Geschriebenen als hermeneutische Strategie', *Altorientalistik im 21. Jahrhundert. Selbstverständnis, Herausforderungen, Ziele = Mittelungen der Deutschen Orientgesellschaft*, 142 (2010), pp. 85–124; Markus Hilgert, 'Materiale Textkulturen. Textbasierte historische Kulturwissenschaften nach dem *material culture turn*', in *Materialität. Herausforderungen für die Sozial- und Kulturwissenschaften*, ed. by Herbert Kalthoff, Torsten Cress, and Tobias Röhl (Paderborn: Wilhelm Fink, 2016), pp. 255–67.

7 See, e.g., *The Uses of Script and Print, 1300–1700*, ed. by Julia Crick and Alexandra Walsham (Cambridge, UK, and New York: Cambridge University Press, 2004); Roger Chartier, 'Crossing Borders in Early Modern Europe: Sociology of Texts and Literature', *Book History*, 8 (2005), pp. 37–50; *Public Lettering: Script, Power, and Culture*, ed. by Armando Petrucci (Chicago: Chicago University Press, 1993); David McKitterick, *Print, Manuscript and the Search for Order, 1450–1830* (Cambridge, UK, and New York: Cambridge University Press, 2005), chapter 1.

8 Emile Schrijver and David Finkelstein, 'Book History and Jewish Book History', in *Encyclopedia of Jewish Book Cultures*, ed. by Emile Schrijver (Leiden and Boston: Brill, 2022), Chapter 1.

makers of books, patrons, and readership; the emergence of publishers; and decisions to be made concerning production and publication. These factors underwent tremendous changes during the fifteenth and sixteenth centuries owing to the spread of printing and the rise of Humanism in Europe. Particular focus is put on the physical evidence of books, both handwritten and printed, and what it can tell us about a book's production and its reception.

The fifteenth century saw not only the invention of the printing press and the emergence of Humanism, but also significant changes in the history of Jewish culture marked by persecutions, legal restrictions, and several expulsions, which led to migrations in numerous directions. New communities were created, new patterns of cultural exchange and entanglements developed, and Jewish cultures were given to constant processes of reorientation. All these circumstances had far-reaching effects on the earliest Jewish printing presses, the Jewish book trade, and the history of Jewish reading. The movement of Iberian Jews to Italy, the Netherlands, North Africa, and the Ottoman Empire and of Ashkenazim to Italy and to Eastern Europe resulted in the relocation not only of people but also of their books. Printing presses were opened but owing to various political and economic circumstances were often soon forced to close. Knowledge embraced in print was constantly on the move. Jewish books were not only printed in Jewish printshops but, especially in Italy, often in Christian houses. In parallel, Christian Hebraists began to develop an interest in collecting Hebrew books. Such encounters between the books and their Christian and Jewish owners and collectors were particularly instructive moments in the history of any individual copy of a book, one intricately associated with its perception, interpretation, and post-production use that suggested a change in the character and meaning of the book as an object. As the book became part of a collector's library, in conjunction with the other books in the hands of the collector, it could assume different functions beyond the ones originally intended.

The structure of this volume follows the late medieval and early modern Jewish book from its existence in manuscript form to early print culture and highlights decisions made by early printers, the uses and functions of late medieval manuscripts and prints in the early modern period, and the fate of Hebrew books in Christian collections. It begins with a series of observations about the transition from manuscript to print and the work of a Jewish scribe and illustrator who witnessed this transition during his career as a producer of manuscripts. The first section looks synchronically at the production of early modern books, some of them illustrated, in terms of the interdependence of the two media. The focus is on imaging techniques, visualization strategies, changes pertaining to the use of paratext, halakhic issues, and more. The second section centres on decisions made by editors of printed books and on the editing procedures that emerged during the early decades of the sixteenth century. Apart from considerations of marketability, the printers' primary consideration was, and is, necessarily, to facilitate the process of reading, as well, of course, as the need to make a profit. The era of early printing, finally, yielded various strategies to address readers, which is subject of the third section.

The Hebrew book did not remain unaffected by the political developments, by the complex dynamics of Jewish-Christian relationships, and by anti-Jewish measures, such as the confiscation of Hebrew books suspect of spreading anti-Christian content, the most serious of these actions having been the burnings of the Talmud in various Italian cities during the 1550s. These circumstances are addressed in the fourth section. Related, but different, were the histories of Hebrew books in Christian collections, the subject of the last section. Hebrew books reached Christian hands either because Christian Hebraists sought to purchase them or because they had been confiscated as Jewish goods during persecutions and expulsions; many Jewish books simply had to be left behind. There are individual books with visible signs of use by Christians. Perhaps more significant is the observation that occasionally entire collections of Hebrew books were transferred to Christian collections. The culture of early modern Christian Hebraists and their use of Hebrew books had a significant impact on the ways Hebrew books were handled in their new environment.

The range of methodological perspectives applied on the pages to follow is wide. Thus, media change is looked at from an art-historical angle by a systematic assessment of graphic devices employed by Joel ben Simeon, an itinerant Jewish scribe and illustrator active in the Rhineland and northern Italy between the 1440s and the 1490s. Rodica Herlo-Lukowsky argues that these devices were chosen and developed strategically with possibilities of 'mass' customization in mind and under the influence of the graphic style of printed materials. Her method is basically comparative and contextualizes the observations made in the history of manuscript and print culture at a time when the two were intensely entangled.

Joel ben Simeon was a particularly prolific producer of books, and while his work calls for consideration along the cultural- and social-historical questions pertaining to book culture, there are still some basic art-historical questions of attribution to be tackled and new attributions to be resolved. Such questions are addressed by Evelyn Cohen, who employs the stylistic method towards an assessment of Joel's artistic development and adds a new book to the long list of this scribe's work. Portugal and the Portuguese Diaspora was another arena of media change, and Débora Marques de Matos's essay looks at it from the angle of the agents involved in the production of both manuscripts and printed books and the various ways in which they echo issues of identity and puts these in tandem with material aspects of book production. She thus bridges both geographical and cultural gaps and, at the same time, connects the abstract notion of identity with the concrete idea of the material artefact. Matos's discussion takes a synchronic approach discussing the books in question not in terms of evolution from one medium to another but in parallel.

The handling of paratext beyond basic recording and description is another field that suffers from underrepresentation. Avriel Bar Levav looks at its development from manuscript colophons to printed title pages as sites of personal communication from the producer(s) of the book to the community of readers. At a point where paratext becomes an egodocument, information about origin, date, and printer's name is a manifestation of the 'printing self' and calls for analysis in terms of communication and mediality. Paratext as a tool for understanding the circumstances of a book's production is discussed by Pavel Sládek. Highlighting the coexistence of manuscripts and printed books in the sixteenth century rather than as a transition from one medium to another, Sládek compares two instances in which halakhic and astronomical treatises were printed. He reveals a complex web of personal and economic considerations that predetermined the process of publishing each work in print. His study also questions the presumption that early modern readers were aware of the distinction between the two media and that they associated them with different values. An additional set of qualities attributed to each of the media is suggested by Annett Martini, who examines early modern halakhic discussions on the possibility of printing Torah scrolls. She shows that despite the obvious practical advantages of printing, the material aspects of Torah scrolls, performances of writing, and practices of sanctification that were integral to the scrolls' ritual validity led the rabbis to exclude printed scrolls not only from ritual use but also from the nonreligious space.

Professionals in the early print period had to invest intense efforts in the development of editing strategies and procedures. Not much is known about these features and they are not always clearly defined, but it is apparent that they guided the printers and editors through their projects. There were crucial decisions to be made: which texts to choose as models for a certain edition? How to design the page layout in relation to the expected function of a book? How to define the role of images, if applicable, in the final appearance of a book? More often than not, available blocks with images were put together sometimes at random to enhance the appearance of a text, and the result was not always an image cycle with a clearly thought through visual rationale. However, often what looks like arbitrarily juxtaposed imageries can after careful analysis emerge as a complex iconographic program. With that in mind, Sarit Shalev-Eyni explores a small booklet with blessings and shows that another kind of paratext — extensive explanatory captions added to the images — imbue the visual program with layers of import. Whereas the images could have been used multiple times in different contexts (some of them were later reused), it was the captions that invested them with individual meaning.

Similarly, Lucia Raspe's essay focuses on editorial decisions made with certain audiences in mind. Hayyim Shahor printed Jacob ben Asher's *'Arba'ah turim* in 1540, at a time when no Jews were allowed to live in Augsburg and after most other German cities had expelled them. She thus considers the culture of Christian Hebraists as one of the factors together with various other circumstances in the complex political landscape of early Hebrew printing in the German Lands. Focusing on the editorial process of printed Ashkenazi responsa, finally, Tamara Morsel-Eisenberg investigates the transformation of personal collections of halakhic decisions that had circulated in manuscript into printable literary works. She analyses the technical aspects of printing responsa, the reorganization of the material, and other editorial choices, processes that ultimately made printed responsa more easily accessible to wide and varied audiences.

A central concern of the scholarship on premodern books is the observation regarding varying degrees of readability, most often approached, thus far, from the angle of layout and appearance. Scholars have often asked questions about the readability of micrography in medieval manuscripts and have argued that the complex decorative and even narrative designs of *masora figurata* suggest that they were not meant to be read. Recent approaches imply that dealing with *masora figurata* in terms of its imagery is possible only by carefully deciphering the texts used for the outline of the designs (in non-biblical books, micrography uses texts other than *Masorah*). The chapter authored by Dalia-Ruth Halperin, who is among those promoting this approach, takes this issue a step further and poses questions about how early printers dealt with the highly flexible *Masorah* while the print medium in fact tended to stabilize texts.

Whereas research into the readability of early prints has thus far focused on issues of typography and layout, Hanna Liss takes a philological path and examines the first printed edition of the Book of Psalms with David Kimhi's commentary. The philological quality, Liss argues, varies in early prints, which suggests multifarious communities of readers. The fact that the poor quality of that edition of Psalms rendered it unfit for Jewish learning suggests that it might have been designed from the outset for a Christian Hebraist readership. Federico dal Bo poses similar questions by studying a large number of editions of various texts and comparing their typography and layouts with the aid of a digital tool. The resulting observations yield several typographic categories, each with a different set of qualities relevant for different kinds of books and different circles of readership.

Among all Jewish books, the Babylonian Talmud was particularly vulnerable to non-Jewish suspicions. By the first half of the thirteenth century, it had become clear that Jews do not live by the Bible alone, but by the Oral Torah, and the Talmud was suspected of disseminating anti-Christian content to wide Jewish circles. Focusing on the observation that it was the *book* and not its makers or readers that was accused, David Stern revisits two burnings of the Talmud, the first during the early 1240s in Paris and the second that took place in various Italian cities in 1553. He compares these events by focusing on the different — medieval and early modern — circumstances not only in terms of Church politics, but also, or primarily, in terms of the material features of talmudic books. He also considers how these features effected and impacted the decisions made by the Church and the developments that eventually led to the burnings. The comparison between these burnings is also at the focus of the study of Yakov Mayer, who juxtaposes Jewish reactions to the events and highlights the role the materiality of the Talmud played in the writings of medieval and early modern rabbis. He argues that in the medieval period the Talmud was perceived as a metaphysical entity that existed independently of its physical container — the book — and that therefore the act of burning could not destroy it. In contrast, with the advance of printing, the metaphysical text came to be associated with the material book, thereby making the Talmud far more vulnerable and prone to destruction.

Christian conceptions of Jewish books often wavered between polemics and condemnation, on the one hand, and the appreciation and appropriation of Jewish literature, on the other. Christian uses of Hebrew manuscripts and printed books and Christian efforts in collecting them have attracted renewed scholarly attention in recent years, shedding further light on this dichotomy. The range of meanings Christians attributed to Jewish books found expression in textual additions, annotations, and other ways of treating a book as a material object, all of which mark the transition of the Jewish book from its native Jewish setting to the context of Christian readership. To understand the kinds of uses to which Christians put the Jewish Bible, Judith Olszowy-Schlanger examines a thirteenth-century Hebrew Psalter and the alterations introduced in the manuscript in medieval and Tudor England. The changes and additions that she observes attest to a keen interest in Hebrew philology in English monasteries and houses of learning and, at the same time, 'convert' the Jewish Psalter into a Christian one.

Reconstructing the afterlife of a group of Hebrew manuscripts of mostly biblical content that ended up in the University of Vienna in the wake of the expulsion of the Jews from Vienna in 1421, Ilona Steimann shows how Jewish books were dealt with by Christians who could not read Hebrew. She traces various modes of adaptation of Jewish books for Christian use and stresses that the lack of knowledge of Hebrew did not prevent Viennese scholars from engaging in polemics with the books as objects. Saverio Campanini turns his attention to the history of Christian reception of kabbalistic works. By scrutinizing the manuscripts of *Sefer ha-peli'ah* ('Book of the Mystery') consulted and annotated by Egidio da Viterbo, Campanini explores Christian strategies of organization, retrieval, and dynamization of received knowledge. Javier del Barco focuses on Hebrew grammar and exegesis among sixteenth-century Spanish Hebraists. He examines the peculiarities of manuscripts produced by Alfonso de Zamora and contextualizes them within political and intellectual developments of the time that impacted the field of Hebraic studies. The exploration of Jewish literature among Christians, which intensified during the printing era, required new approaches towards the structuration and systematization of the knowledge that became copiously available. The contribution of Maximilian de Molière offers a deeper insight into classification schemes and bibliographical research of Jewish literature undertaken by early modern Christian scholars.

He demonstrates that not only Jewish texts, their history, and transmission piqued scholarly interest, but also that the materiality of Jewish books was a valid bibliographic category.

Making books, holding them in one's hand, reading them, annotating them, collecting them, selling them, appropriating them, polemicizing against them, experiencing new technologies, and using old books to make new ones — all these acts and processes are put in focus in this volume from various angles: material culture, interreligious dynamics and tensions, transcultural processes, visualization strategies, editing concepts, varieties of expected and unexpected readerships, and more. What binds these studies together is the conviction that a book is much more than a lifeless container of the texts it contains, but a cultural agent of multiple dimensions.

PART ONE

Media Change

RODICA HERLO-LUKOWSKI

Changes in Bookmaking

Joel ben Simeon's Manuscripts in the Transition from Customized to Mass Production

Introduction

The fifteenth century was an era of profound change, a time of discovery and innovation. Gutenberg's invention of letterpress printing with movable type was one of the most significant developments, as it brought about far-reaching changes in many areas of life,[1] in particular, the production of books and the culture of reading, a sphere that research has explored from various aspects. One important feature of book production which has been the subject of increasing attention over the last few decades is the way the advent of printing impacted the work of scribes and book illustrators in the fifteenth century, which is the subject of the present essay. Focusing on the illustration techniques and artistic vocabulary of the Jewish scribe and illuminator Joel ben Simeon, I show how the dawn of printing influenced the way he worked. I discuss the choices he made and the methods he utilized to maximize the benefits of handwriting and make use of some of the advantages of printing, which endowed his manuscripts with characteristics that allow us to identify them as artefacts of both individual and 'mass' production.

The following study features a comparative analysis of Joel's manuscripts and selected Christian and Jewish printed works. First, I sketch out Joel's strategic choice of mass customization as a response to the ability of the printing press to produce books quickly and to reach wider audiences. Mass customization, a key competitive factor to this day, enabled Joel to offer a ready-made book that could later be tailored to the buyer, thereby expanding and diversifying his customer base. Further, I show how the graphic style of the printed materials, which soon replaced hand-painted and time-consuming miniatures, influenced Joel's drawing style and focus on tendencies towards standardization and rationalization in his visual vocabulary.

---

1 Lucien Febvre and Henri-Jean Martin, *The Coming of the Book: The Impact of Printing 1450–1800* (London: Verso, 1990), pp. 248–333; Elisabeth Eisenstein, *The Printing Press as an Agent of Change: Communications and Cultural Transformations in Early-Modern Europe*, 2 vols (Cambridge: Cambridge University Press, 1979), I, pp. 3–43. Abraham Berliner, *Ueber den Einfluss des ersten hebräischen Buchdrucks auf den Cultus und die Cultur der Juden* (Frankfurt a. M.: Kauffmann, 1896).

Rodica Herlo-Lukowski • Institute for Jewish Studies, University of Münster

Changes in Book Production

The years immediately before and after the invention of printing comprised a transitional period of intensive experimentation which resulted in such hybrid products as single-leaf woodcuts and chiro-xylographic block books.[2] However, the manuscript codex did not suddenly become obsolete. Manuscripts and printed books continued to be produced side by side for many years, and the two processes impacted one another.[3] As the designers of printed books initially tried to imitate the layout of manuscripts as closely as possible, they first illustrated them by hand. Soon, however, the laborious and time-consuming handmade miniatures were replaced by woodcuts, which were not geared to the preferences of a single patron but to the general taste of a wider public. The result was the mass production of standardized books with graphic and highly rationalized images, and all the books in an edition were identical.

The great demand for books, the changes that printing engendered in their production, and the resulting competition had an impact on manuscript makers, who began to react.[4]

Teamwork in organized workshops became increasingly common and these ateliers began to produced secular literature in a range of vernaculars[5] which were kept in stock to be sold to future customers on the free market.[6] They divided up the production process, began using paper instead of parchment, and created sketchy and lightly coloured drawings instead of fully painted miniatures in order to increase the volume of production and reduce the necessary labour and costs.[7] Like their Christian counterparts, Jewish scribes and book illustrators were confronted with the socio-economic conditions that fostered the development of letterpress printing and were well aware of the opportunities and risks involved in that burgeoning industry. However, the political situation of the Jews[8] as well as Jewish traditions

---

2 Sandra Hindman, 'Cross-Fertilization: Experiments in Mixing the Media', in *Pen to Press: Illustrated Manuscripts and Printed Books in the First Century of Printing*, ed. by Sandra Hindman and James Douglas Farquhar (College Park: University of Maryland, 1977), pp. 101–56.

3 Ursula Rautenberg, 'Medienkonkurrenz und Medienmischung', in *Die Gleichzeitigkeit von Handschrift und Buchdruck*, ed. by Gerd Dicke and Klaus Grubmüller, Wolfenbütteler Mittelalter-Studien, 16 (Wiesbaden: Harrassowitz, 2003) pp. 167–203.

4 The impact of print on the work of Christian manuscript makers has received increased attention in recent decades and has been widely discussed in the academic world. See, e.g., with its exhaustive bibliography, Lieselotte E. Saurma-Jeltsch, *Spätformen mittelalterlicher Buchherstellung. Illustrated Manuscripts from the Workshop of Diebold Lauber in Hagenau*, 2 vols (Wiesbaden: Reichert, 2001) and Christine Beier, 'Producing, Buying and Decorating Books in the Age of Gutenberg: The Role of Monasteries in Central Europe', in *Early Printed Books as Material Objects*, Proceedings of the Conference Organized by the IFLA Rare Books and Manuscripts Section, Munich, 19–21 August 2009, ed. by Bettina Wagner and Marcia Reed (Berlin: De Gruyter, 2010), pp. 65–133.

5 From the extensive literature on this subject, see *Laienlektüre und Buchmarkt im späten Mittelalter*, ed. by Thomas Kock and Rita Schlusemann, Gesellschaft, Kultur und Schrift, 5 (Frankfurt a. M.: Peter Lang, 1997); *Wort und Bild: Studien zu den Wechselbeziehungen zwischen Schrifttum und Bildkunst im Mittelalter*, ed. by Wolfgang Stammler (Berlin: Erich Schmidt, 1962).

6 The concept is rather understood as a combination of only a few stored works and production on demand Saurma-Jeltsch, I, p. 74.

7 The organization of the non-Jewish workshops and their methods of production have already been the subject of several investigations. See, e.g., Saurma-Jeltsch, I, pp. 16–154; Christine Beier, 'Missalien massenhaft: Die Bämler-Werkstatt und die Augsburger Buchmalerei im 15. Jahrhundert', *Codices Manuscripti*, 48/49 (2004), pp. 55–78; *Aus der Werkstatt Diebold Laubers*, ed. by Christoph Fasbender, Kulturtopographie des Alemannischen Raums, 3 (Berlin: De Gruyter, 2012).

8 For example, late medieval Ashkenazi Jews were not allowed to join Christian guilds or to found their own guilds. Despite these rules, it has been shown that Jewish craftsmen were occasionally employed in one way or another in Christian workshops: see, among others, Sarit Shalev-Eyni, *Jews among Christians: Hebrew Book Illumination from Lake Constance* (London

of book production and consumption[9] were unlike those of the Christians. The question of the impact of the advent of the printing press on Jewish scribes and book illustrators, which has not yet been the subject of much attention in the field of Jewish studies, should be investigated in detail.[10] My dissertation on Joel ben Simeon, of which this essay is a part, is a preliminary step in that study.

Joel ben Simeon was a Jewish scribe and illustrator who lived and worked during the period that manuscript and print were produced in parallel. For the most part, details of his life, as for most medieval craftsmen, remain hidden. Everything that research has discovered about him — his biography, his professional career, and some stages in his life — is based on studies of his oeuvre.[11] It is known that Joel came from the Rhineland and worked both north and south of the Alps from about 1449 to 1490. He has been associated with at least thirty-seven manuscripts,[12] although there is still no agreement as to whether they can all actually be attributed to him and whether he worked alone or was the head of his own workshop with apprentices in attendance. His manuscripts reveal several characteristics related to the print-engendered labour-saving techniques, some of which I introduce below, suggesting that he actually benefited from some of the advantages afforded by the new mechanical methods of image and text reproduction and made use of them in his work.

'Mass' Customization to Increase Competitiveness

The printed book was a finished product that was immediately available for purchase. In order to reach a wide audience — as opposed to a single patron — the printer ensured that its layout and decoration would appeal to a more general taste. Even though the operation of a print shop was often associated with the investment of a financier, the latter did not necessarily have a say in the design of the books.

---

and Turnhout: Harvey Miller and Brepols, 2010). For an overview of the history of Jewish guilds, see Mark Wischnitzer, 'Notes to a History of the Jewish Guilds', *Hebrew Union College Annual*, 23/2 (1950–51), pp. 245–63.

9 Malachi Beit-Arié assumes that the production of a Hebrew book in the Middle Ages was always the result of private enterprise and never a collective effort: Malachi Beit-Arié, *Hebrew Codicology: Historical and Comparative Typology of Hebrew Medieval Codices Based on the Documentation of the Extant Dated Manuscripts Using a Quantitative Approach*, Preprint internet English version 0.4 (February 2020), pp. 90–121 (p. 93), https://web.nli.org.il/sites/NLI/English/collections/manuscripts/hebrewcodicology/Documents/Hebrew-Codicology-continuously-updated-online-version-ENG.pdf [accessed in July 2020].

10 The research on the transition from manuscript to printed book has been summarized by Kogman-Appel in her recent work on the *Prague Haggadah*, Katrin Kogman-Appel, 'Designing a Passover Imagery for New Audiences: The Prague Haggadah', in *Unter Druck – Mitteleuropäische Buchmalerei im 15. Jahrhundert, Tagungsband zum internationalen Kolloquium in Wien, Österreichische Akademie der Wissenschaften, 13.1–17.1.2016*, ed. by Jeffrey F. Hamburger and Maria Theisen (Petersberg: Michael Imhof, 2018), pp. 180–94 (pp. 180–82).

11 For a summary of his vita, which has been reconstructed in several publications covering various aspects of his oeuvre, with a selected bibliography, see Katrin Kogman-Appel, 'The Illustrations of the Washington Haggadah', in *The Washington Haggadah: A Fifteenth-Century Manuscript in the Library of Congress*, with an introduction by David Stern and Katrin Kogman-Appel (Cambridge, MA: The Belknap Press of Harvard University Press; Washington, DC: The Library of Congress, 2011), pp. 52–113 (pp. 53–57).

12 They were last listed by Evelyn M. Cohen, 'Joel ben Simeon's "Missing Leaves"', in *Studies in Honor of Menahem Hayyim Schmelzer*, ed. by Shmuel Glick, Evelyn M. Cohen, and others (New York: Jewish Theological Seminary; Jerusalem: Schocken, 2019) pp. 120–24.

Moreover, an edition was generally produced without an order from a specific patron as the printer could not respond to individual customer requests. In contrast, mediaeval manuscript production had an individual character. As a professional scribe, Joel generally copied and illuminated manuscripts on behalf of a number of wealthy patrons for whom he even changed his location if necessary.[13] As commissioned works, these manuscripts were tailored to the needs and wishes of his clients and reflect such preferences as size,[14] particular text genres and rituals,[15] and individual illustration and decoration programmes. These characteristics are apparent in all of Joel's manuscripts, which can clearly be recognized as commissioned works by the colophons bearing the patrons' names.[16] Nevertheless, some of Joel's manuscripts have features that suggest his attempt to take advantage of certain benefits of printing along with those of handwriting: they were produced without commission in advance and could be customized for a particular purchaser. The main purpose of this 'mass' customization, which is still an important competitive production tool, was to minimize production costs (an advantage of standardized mass production in print) while meeting the specific requirements of customers (an advantage of customization in manuscript).

Among Joel's manuscripts that reflect mass customization is the so-called *Washington Haggadah*,[17] which he copied and illuminated during one of his (at least two) stays in the German Lands.[18] Although the colophon records Joel as the scribe and the date on which he copied the manuscript, it does not include the name of a patron.[19] Since Joel was a professional scribe and was generally eager to disclose information about his involvement or about patronage in a manuscript, it is difficult to imagine that the fact that he did not do so in this case was just a coincidence or that he simply forgot to put the patron's name in the colophon. Thus, we

---

13 His manuscripts bear traces of various places of production, such as the name of the city in the colophon or miscellaneous codicological and palaeographic references to a specific geographical and cultural area. For references that codicology and palaeography give to a specific geographical and cultural area, see Malachi Beit-Arié, *The Making of the Medieval Hebrew Book: Studies in Paleography and Codicology* (Jerusalem: Magnes Press, 1993), esp. pp. 93–109 and pp. 233–38 for Joel manuscripts; Beit-Arié, *Hebrew Cogicology*; Colette Sirat, *Hebrew Manuscripts of the Middle Ages*, ed. and trans. by Nicholas De Lange (Cambridge: Cambridge University Press, 2002).

14 The size of the parchment sheets undoubtedly determined the size of the manuscript. However, it ultimately depended on the price the client was prepared to pay for the parchment. For parchment and formats of the Hebrew Book, see e.g.: Sirat, pp. 112–19.

15 He even used the Italian semi-cursive script in the *Maraviglia Siddur* (London, British Library [BL], Add MS 26957) although he was trained in Ashkenazi script.

16 Haggadah, southern Germany (Jerusalem, Israel Museum [IM], MS 181/60, fol. 27^v); siddur, southern Germany (Parma, Biblioteca Palatina [BP], MS Parm. 3144, fol. 188^r); haggadah, southern Germany (BL, Add MS 14762, fol. 48^v); siddur, northern Italy (BL, Add MS 26957, fol. 112^r); Commentary on the Psalms, Modena (BP, MS Parm. 2841, fol. 174^r).

17 Washington, DC, Library of the Congress (LC), MS Heb. 1, https://lccn.loc.gov/2018757799 [accessed in May 2022]. See also *The Washington Haggadah: A Facsimile Edition of an Illuminated Fifteenth-Century Hebrew Manuscript at the Library of Congress Signed by Joel ben Simeon*, ed. by Myron M. Weinstein (Washington, DC: Library of Congress, 1991), and *The Washington Haggadah: Copied and Illustrated by Joel ben Simeon*, facsimile trans. by David Stern (Cambridge, MA: The Belknap Press of Harvard University Press; Washington, DC: The Library of Congress, 2011) with a selected bibliography.

18 The Ashkenazi provenance of the *Washington Haggadah* was established by Malachi Beit-Arié on the basis of codicological criteria: Malachi Beit-Arié, 'Codicological Description and Analysis of the Washington Haggadah', in *The Washington Haggadah: A Facsimile Edition of an Illuminated Fifteenth-Century Hebrew Manuscript*, pp. 103–37 (pp. 122–27).

19 LC, MS Heb. 1, fol. 34^v.

can assume, as Beit-Arié suggests,[20] that what is now known as the *Washington Haggadah* was made in advance for sale on the free market,[21] a notion that is also supported by other evidence. For example, the intended customization of the haggadah was provided for by the three blank folios in the final quire on which Joel added two supplementary blessings (*'Eruvei hatzerot* and *'Eruvei tavshilin*).[22] According to the usual arrangement of prayer books, those two blessings should have appeared at the beginning of the haggadah, so their presence at the end suggests an Ashkenazi buyer who asked for them to be added after purchasing the manuscript.[23]

Determining the additions Joel might have made to the already existing basic illustration and decoration programme once the manuscript had been sold is far more difficult than identifying the textual supplements. All we have in this case is circumstantial evidence, such as the large amount of free space around the initial words, which was intended for additional decorations but remained empty. The haggadah's initial word adornments consist of large decorated panels with gold letters, coloured backgrounds, and gold frames, as well as some small ornaments and filigree embellishments with masks and human heads.[24] Other opening words written in red and blue ink are not decorated and are surrounded by spaces of different sizes. Those with more empty space around them seem to a certain extent to be lost in it.[25] Since the opening words were decorated elsewhere,[26] we can assume that in this case, too, the space was intended to incorporate later decorations at the future customer's request. This assumption is supported by the fact that several other initial words reflect penwork decoration in a highly diluted violet ink; these look unfinished and may have been added at a later date.[27]

Although the margins of the *Washington Haggadah* feature a great deal of free space, Joel added only a limited number of marginal illustrations drawn from his basic programme, a feature that can also be found in other of his haggadot.[28] More striking is the absence of such larger of his known compositions as scenes of the Egyptian persecution and the Israelites crossing the Red Sea. As those scenes, for which Joel

---

20   This was probably the case for the *Bodmer Haggadah* (Cologny-Genève, Fondation Martin Bodmer, Cod. Bodmer 81) and the *Second New York Haggadah* (New York, Jewish Theological Seminary of America [JTS], MS Mic 8279): Beit-Arié, 'Codicological Description', p. 106. See also, Beit Arié, *The Making of the Medieval Hebrew Book*, pp. 216–49 (pp. 216–17).

21   Among the haggadot which Joel produced without commission for the open market are the Cod. Bodmer 81; JTS, MS Mic 8279 and the *Moskowitz Mahzor* (Jerusalem, The National Library of Israel [NLI], MS Heb. 4o 1384). Beit-Arié, 'Codicological Description', pp. 103–37 (p. 106) and Beit-Arié, *Hebrew Codicology*, pp. 90–122 (pp. 109–10).

22   LC, MS Heb. 1, fols 35^r–38^v. The same phenomenon occurs with the *Moskowitz Mahzor* (NLI, MS Heb. 4o 1384), were the empty leaves were filled with hymns and prayers added by Abraham Judah Camerino: See Shlomo Zucker, *The Moskowitz Mahzor of Joel Ben Simeon: Ashkenazi/Italian Scribe and Illuminator of Hebrew Manuscripts, MS. Heb. 4o1384* (Jerusalem: The Jewish National and University Library, 2005), p. 17.

23   The text of the *Washington Haggadah* generally follows the Ashkenazi rite, although it also contains some earlier features of this tradition as well as some Italian elements: David Stern, 'Washington Haggadah: The Life of a Book', in *The Washington Haggadah: Copied and Illustrated by Joel ben Simeon*, pp. 33–37).

24   On fols 2^r and 6^v are some unprofessional later additions, where it is also not clear whether Joel wrote the initial words himself: *The Washington Haggadah: A Facsimile Edition*, p. 13.

25   LC, MS Heb. 1, fol. 12^v.

26   LC, MS Heb. 1, fols 7^v and 24^r.

27   LC, MS Heb. 1, fols 15^v, 20^v and 20^r.

28   An idea posited by David Stern, 'Washington Haggadah', p. 32. For the description of the haggadah's illustration program, see Bezalel Narkiss, 'The Art of the Washington Haggadah', in *The Washington Haggadah: A Facsimile Edition*, pp. 27–103 (pp. 56–85) and Katrin Kogman-Appel, 'The Illustrations of the Washington Haggadah', in the same volume, pp. 52–113 (pp. 57–62).

further developed the iconography, do appear in his other haggadot, one would expect them to have been included here as well.[29] However, such large compositions, which in Joel's case spread over two pages, would have increased the price of the book to a significant degree. Producing an expensive book and then waiting for a customer initially required an investment that a scribe could hardly afford. Thus, the obvious conclusion is that in order to limit the cost and increase the number of potential buyers, Joel decided to omit the elaborate compositions, and to add them only on demand and price the manuscript accordingly, which was, in effect, a mass customization strategy.

Mass customization enabled Joel to reach a wider and more diverse audience. By producing the *Washington Haggadah* for sale on the open market, he was also able to attract customers who appreciated the immediate availability of printed books, as well as those who were travelling and could not wait for a manuscript to be copied. That haggadah already featured a basic set of illustrations and decorations, but because Joel was able to customize it for a specific buyer by copying additional texts and decorations on demand, he also acquired customers who valued a personalized book.

A Linear Graphic Drawing Technique to Accelerate Production

The mass reproduction of pictures actually began well before the advent of the movable type printing press. The aim was to imitate the unique works of the illustrator, only faster and more cheaply. These images, reproduced by means of woodcuts and engravings, were graphic representations with a special emphasis on contour. The woodcuts and engravings informed the style of Joel's illustrations, rendering them significantly different than those found in lavish manuscripts, which were traditionally painted with gold and opaque gouache. It seems that he preferred this graphic style from the beginning of his career and used it for illumination in all of his manuscripts, whether they were commissioned or produced for the open market.

The so-called *Maraviglia Siddur* was a commissioned manuscript for which the decoration programme was tailored to the customer's demands.[30] According to the colophon, this Italian rite siddur was written by Joel ben Simeon Feibush for Rabbi Menahem ben Samuel and his daughter, Lady Maraviglia.[31] Typical of the Ashkenazi book tradition of the Middle Ages, the manuscript features unframed marginal illustrations which, apart from the simple liturgical content, also depict the contemporary viewer and his or her world.[32] As the prayer book was also

---

29 Narkiss, 'The Art of the Washington Haggadah', p. 51; Kogman-Appel, 'The Illustrations of the Washington Haggadah', p. 69.

30 BL, Add MS 26957, https://www.bl.uk/manuscripts/FullDisplay.aspx?ref=Add_MS_26957 [accessed in May 2022]. George Margoliouth, *Catalogue of the Hebrew and Samaritan Manuscripts in the British Museum*, 4 vols (London: British Museum, 1899–1935), II (1905), p. 207, no. 615. Beit-Arié, *The Making of the Medieval Hebrew Book*, pp. 96–97; Sheila Edmunds, 'The Place of the London Haggadah in the Work of Joel ben Simeon', in *Journal of Jewish Art*, 7 (1980), pp. 25–34 (pp. 25–26). For another discussion of this work, see also Evelyn Cohen's contribution to the current volume.

31 BL, Add MS 26957, fol. 112r.

32 Kogman-Appel has dealt with the complex relationship among scribe, artist, and client in the context of books and their socio-cultural history. See, e.g., Katrin Kogman-Appel, 'The Illustrations of the Washington Haggadah', pp. 87–106; Katrin Kogman-Appel, 'The Audiences of the Late Medieval Haggadah', in *Patronage, Production, and Transmission of Texts in Medieval and Early Modern Jewish Cultures*, ed. by Esperanza Alfonso and Jonathan Decter (Turnhout: Brepols, 2014), pp. 99–143; Katrin Kogman-Appel, 'Joel ben Simeon:

clearly intended for use by the Lady Maraviglia, Joel customized the illustration programme for a woman.[33] Thus, the images in the margins show a young woman actively participating in religious rituals that are usually performed by a man. The figures are all shown in profile as busts or half or full figures, their dress reflecting the Italian fashions of the fifteenth century. Similar to the Italian portraits of Renaissance women (Figures 1.1 and 1.2),[34] the portrayals in the siddur have

Figure 1.1. *Portrait of a Young Woman*, Piero del Pollaiuolo (Florence 1441–Rome 1496), *c.* 1465. Milan, Museo Poldi Pezzoli, Ident. nr. 442.

Looking at the Margins of Society', in *Intricate Interfaith Networks in the Middle Ages: Quotidian Jewish-Christian Contacts*, ed. by Ephraim Shoham-Steiner (Turnhout: Brepols, 2016), pp. 287–315.

33 Whether Joel may also have adapted the text of the three morning blessings for a female user, as was the case in other manuscripts from Italy, cannot be said, since the siddur is incomplete and this part is missing at the beginning of the manuscript. See Evelyn M. Cohen, 'Women's Illuminated Hebrew Prayer Books in Renaissance Italy', in *Donne nella storia degli ebrei d'Italia: Atti del IX Convegno internazionale Italia Judaica, Lucca, 6–9 Giugno 2005*, ed. by Michele Luzzati and Cristina Galasso (Florence: Giuntina, 2007), pp. 305–12 and Evelyn M. Cohen, 'Can Colophons Be Trusted? Insights from Decorated Hebrew Manuscripts Produced for Women in Renaissance Italy', in *The Hebrew Book in Early Modern Italy*, ed. by Joseph R. Hacker and Adam Shear (Philadelphia: University of Pennsylvania Press, 2011), pp. 17–25 (pp. 21–22).

34 *Portrait of a Young Woman* by Piero del Pollaiuolo (Florence 1441–Rome 1496), *c.* 1465, Milan, Museo Poldi Pezzoli, Ident. nr. 442, https://museopoldipezzoli.it/dipinti/#/dettaglio/119286_Ritratto%20di%20dama [accessed in May 2022]. See *Gesichter der Renaissance: Meisterwerke italienischer Portrait-Kunst*, Berlin, Bode-Museum, 25 August–20 November 2011 (New York, The Metropolitan Museum of Art, 21 December 2011–18 March 2012), ed. by Keith Christiansen and Stefan Weppelmann (Munich: Hirmer, 2011) pp. 101–05, nr. 9, and *Portrait of a Woman and a Man in a Window Niche* by Fra Filippo Lippi (Florence *c.* 1406–Spoleto 1469), *c.* 1440–44, New York, The Metropolitan Museum of Art, Marquand Collection, Ident. 89.15.19, https://www.metmuseum.org/de/art/collection/search/436896 [accessed in May 2022]. See *Gesichter der Renaissance*, pp. 96–97, nr. 6.

Figure 1.2. *Portrait of a Woman and a Man in a Window Niche*, Fra Filippo Lippi (Florence *c.* 1406–Spoleto 1469), *c.* 1440–44. New York, The Metropolitan Museum of Art, Marquand Collection, Ident. nr. 89.15.19.

high bare foreheads, wear low-cut dresses with elaborately embroidered sleeves, and are shown with Burgundian headdresses (Figure 1.3)[35] or with braided hair entwined with jewellery (Figure 1.4).[36] Although the iconography is very close to that seen in the portraits of Italian Renaissance paintings,[37] the technique that Joel used to represent them was completely different and much closer to that of Italian engravings, which obviously had a strong influence on his drawing style. This becomes more evident when compared with selected Florentine engravings of the Fine Manner from the fifteenth century, such as the *Triumph of Chastity* of the 'Master of the Vienna Passion' (Figure 1.5)[38] and the portrait of the Ottoman Emperor Sultan Mehmet II, The Conqueror (1444–46 and 1451–81), known as *El gran Turco* (Figure 1.6).[39]

The composition with the personified Chastity in the Florentine engraving makes it clear that Joel did not really portray the Lady Maraviglia, but rather reproduced a contemporary figure of an Italian woman from the urban upper-middle class, as is also usually found in Italian paintings and engravings of the time.[40] This observation is further supported by the figure of Rabbi Akiva's half-figure depicted with an open book in his hand (Figure 1.7),[41] which shares much with the fantasy shoulder-length portrait of the Sultan (Figure 1.6). The striking resemblance between the two figures with their aquiline noses, long hair, beards, and striking headdresses[42] leaves no doubt that Joel was familiar with the Florentine engraving.[43] Both the *Maraviglia Siddur* and the cited Florentine engravings reflect a graphic style of representation, in that the line remains decisive for the design of the shapes and figures.

---

35 As, e.g., the half figure of a woman in profile with a chalice on fol. 31^r (BL, Add MS 26957).

36 Half figure of a woman in profile presenting the matza on fol. 45^r (BL, Add MS 26957).

37 The Italian portrait art of the fifteenth century, reflects the idealization efforts typical of this period, in which individual features were conformed to a certain type of portrait. See Stefan Weppelmann, 'Zum Schulterblick des Hermelins: Ähnlichkeit im Portrait der italienischen Frührenaissance', in Christiansen and Weppelmann, *Gesichter der Renaissance*, pp. 64–77 (p. 66).

38 *The Triumph of Chastity* (Vienna, Albertina Museum, Inv.-Nr. DG1935/423) of Master of the Vienna Passion, is the no. 2 of the Florentine engravings based on Petrarch's account of the successive triumphs of Love, Chastity, Death, Fame, Time, and Divinity. See Arthur M. Hind, *Early Italian Engraving: A Critical Catalogue with Complete Reproduction of all the Prints Described*, 4 vols (London: Bernard Quaritch, 1938; Nendeln: Kraus Reprint, 1970), part 1.I, A.I.19., p. 34 and II, plate 19.

39 Berlin, Staatliche Museen zu Berlin Preußischer Kulturbesitz, Kupferstichkabinett, Inv. Nr. 140–1879, https://smb.museum-digital.de/object/97142 [accessed in May 2022]. The portrait was most probably engraved in the same workshop as the *Triumph of Chastity* of the 'Master of the Vienna Passion', *c.* 1460, probably after Antonio Pollaiuolo (Florence 1431/32–Rome 1496). See Hind, part 1.I, D.I.5, p. 195, and II, plate 268, p. 195.

---

40 Portraits of this kind appear in *Maraviglia Siddur* (BL, Add MS 26957) on fols 31^r, 55^v, 74^v and 45^r. Similar depictions can be found in numerous other Florentine engravings of the Fine Manner *c.* 1460–70. See Hind.

41 Chest piece in profile of Rabbi Akiva on fol. 43^v (BL, Add MS 26957).

42 The so-called '*alla greca*' hat was an item of headwear associated with the Byzantine Emperor John VIII Palaeologos, who ruled from 1425 to 1448 and was well-known in Florence for the medal with his portrait by Pisanello. See Roberto Weiss, *Pisanello's Medallion of the Emperor John VIII Palaeologus* (London: British Museum, 1966). In the case of the Turkish emperor, it is decorated with a dragon of the typical Florentine type that also appears in the siddur on fol. 37^r and 53^v and can be found in two other manuscripts associated with Joel: Cod. Bodmer 81, fol. 5^r and Paris, Bibliothèque nationale de France, MS hébr 418, *Pisqe Rabbi Asher ben Yehiel*, fols 27^r, 272^r, 279^r and 350^r.

43 Zirlin has also pointed out his familiarity with new methods of image reproduction in her iconographic study of Joel's early works: Yael Zirlin, 'The Early Works of Joel ben Simeon, a Jewish Scribe and Artist in the Fifteenth Century' [in Hebrew] (unpublished doctoral dissertation, the Hebrew University of Jerusalem, 1995).

Figure 1.3. Half figure of a woman in profile with chalice. BL, Add MS 26957, fol. 31ʳ.

28 RODICA HERLO-LUKOWSKI

Figure 1.4. Half figure of a woman in profile presenting the matza. BL, Add MS 26957, fol. 45ʳ.

Figure 1.5. *The Triumph of Chastity*. Vienna, Albertina Museum, Inv.-Nr. DG1935/423, Master of the Vienna Passion.

Figure 1.6. *El gran Turco*. Berlin, Staatliche Museen zu Berlin Preußischer Kulturbesitz, Kupferstichkabinett, Inv. Nr. 140–1879, workshop of the Master of the Vienna Passion.

Figure 1.7. Half figure in profile of Rabbi Akiva. BL, Add MS 26957, fol. 43ᵛ.

With this graphic representation technique, which he also seemed to prefer as a scribe, Joel drew his figures very sparingly. Their clear and continuous outlines sometimes appear as 'bold delineations',[44] as in Rabbi Akiva's profile. However, if we compare the Rabbi's robe and headdress with the highly decorated robe and headdress of the Sultan in the Vienna engraving, it is striking how drastically Joel rationalized his drawing,[45] so that the image of the Rabbi appears simply as a mirror-inverted sketch of the Turkish ruler's chestpiece. Such sparse pen-and-ink drawings were very well suited to illustrating a small-format volume such as the *Maraviglia Siddur*.[46] Moreover, they could be produced more quickly and cheaply than the traditional elaborate illustrations, which would have made the codex more labour-intensive and thus more expensive.[47] The graphic representations in the siddur reflect the fact that both Joel and the commissioner were familiar with the printed materials of the surrounding gentile culture. Moreover, since the drawings would have not been made without the commissioner's consent, they also reveal his receptivity to the visual language of Italian culture and his willingness, or even desire, to identify with it, thus reflecting the degree of his acculturation and the political situation of the Jews in Italy at the time.[48]

Rationalized Images to Make Production More Efficient

The woodcut was a graphic printing technique that produced highly rationalized images, especially in its early days. The extent of the rationalization was due to the material used and the craftsmanship of the draftsmen and the form cutters.[49] As the woodblock did not allow for the carving of delicate lines, the woodcut omitted all unnecessary detail and reproduced only what was absolutely required for an understanding of the depiction.[50] Similarly rationalized illustrations are also among the characteristic features of Joel's manuscripts and point to a conscious,

---

44 Narkiss described it as characteristic of Joel's Italian style: Narkiss, 'The Art of the Washington Haggadah', p. 47.

45 For the rationalization of the drawing see the following section.

46 The rather small format (140 × 95 mm) of the siddur with a total of 113 folios (incomplete) suggests personal use. Similarly, Joel added only a few pen drawings to the haggadah text in the *Parma Siddur* (BP, MS Parm. 3144). See, Beit-Arié, *The Making of the Medieval Hebrew Book*, pp. 94–96. Prayer books were generally poorly illustrated unless they were intended for use in the synagogue as in the case of the *Leipzig Mahzor* (Leipzig, Universitätsbibliothek, MS V 1102, I–II). See, with further bibliography, Katrin Kogman-Appel, 'Der Leipziger Machsor und die jüdische Gemeinde von Worms', in *Die SchUM-Gemeinden Speyer – Worms – Mainz: Auf dem Wege zum Welterbe*, ed. by Pia Heberer and Ursula Reuter (Regensburg: Schnell und Steiner, 2013), pp. 207–20.

47 Scribes often co-operated temporarily for this purpose, as was the case with Joel for BP, Parm. 3144: Beit-Arié, *The Making of the Medieval Hebrew Book*, pp. 94–96. For cooperation in Hebrew book production in general and the halakhic regulation on shared copying, see Beit-Arié, *Hebrew Codicology*, pp. 90–121.

48 On the link between the willingness of Jews to reject or adopt the pictorial language used in their environment and the extent of their acculturation, see Katrin Kogman-Appel, 'Kulturaustausch und jüdische Kunst in der Spätantike und im Mittelater', *Cilufim* (4/2008), pp. 79-118. For the three-way relationship among patrons, artists, and viewers, see Katrin Kogman-Appel, 'Pictorial Messages in Medieval Illuminated Hebrew Books: Some Methodological Considerations', in *Jewish Manuscript Cultures: New Perspectives*, Studies in Manuscript Cultures, 13, ed. by Irina Wandrey (Berlin: De Gruyter, 2017), pp. 443–67.

49 This development is clearly visible in the woodcuts of the German artist Albrecht Dürer (1471–1528) from the turn of the century. See *Albrecht Dürer: Woodcuts and Wood Blocks*, ed. by Walter L. Strauss (New York: Abariy Books, 1979).

50 Towards the end of the century, the situation changed, due, on the one hand, to the more skilled form cutter and, on the other hand, to the copperplate, a medium which allowed more details and shaded outlines.

Figure 1.8. Moses receives the Tablets of the Law. JTS, MS 8892, fol. 139ʳ.

economically motivated decision. The figures in the *Maraviglia Siddur* (Figures 1.3, 1.4, and 1.7), for example, are more sparingly depicted than the comparative Florentine engravings (Figures 1.5 and 1.6). Joel paid little attention to the fine details of the clothing, jewellery, and headdresses, leaving lines and dots to give the pictures an appearance of fullness, which in reality was only hinted at and quickly sketched. The *Second New York Haggadah*, which, according to the colophon (fol. 59[r]), Joel copied, vocalized, and illuminated in 1454,[51] features this rationalization of the illustrations, which could hardly have been due to a lack of drawing skills. Rather, it was a print-inspired timesaving technique that was favoured by his customers, whose tastes had changed with the widespread use of mechanically reproduced images. This method is also reflected in the apparently little effort that Joel put into creating more elaborate scenes with a large number of figures. For these, he placed the more important figures in the foreground while the figures in the back rows increasingly lose their significance for the pictorial message. In the scene on the opening of *Pirqei'avot* ('Chapters of the Fathers') in the *Rothschild Mahzor* (Figure 1.8),[52] for example, where Moses receives the Tablets of the Law, Joel depicted only the headdress of the Israelites in the back row at the foot of the mountains in two or three alternating colours and sketched repeating profiles for the figures in the centre of the crowd. But in the foreground he depicted a small number of various facial shapes for men and women and different age groups, similar images to those that appear in others of his manuscripts.

The repetition of the same figures within a composition also occurs in illustrations reproduced by woodcut and engraving, as shown by the depiction of the Israelites crossing the Reed Sea in the *Prague Haggadah* (Figure 1.9)[53] — the earliest Jewish codex printed and illustrated with woodcuts that has been preserved in its entirety.[54] The repeated and undifferentiated figures in the crowd in the woodcut also testify to the minimal effort the artisan expended on

---

51 The *Second New York Haggadah* (JTS, MS 8279), https://digitalcollections.jtsa.edu/islandora/object/jts%3A235214#page/1/mode/1up [accessed in 8 May 2022] proves the high level of drawing skills that Joel had reached by that time. Kogman-Appel, 'The Illustrations of the Washington Haggadah', pp. 52–113 (p. 56).

52 Moses receives the tablets of the law, JTS, MS 8892, fol. 139[r], https://digitalcollections.jtsa.edu/islandora/object/jts%3A320007#page/1/mode/1up [accessed in 2022]. See Evelyn M. Cohen, 'The Rothschild Mahzor: Its Background and Its Art', in *The Rothschild Mahzor: Florence, 1492*, ed. by Menahem Schmelzer, Evelyn M. Cohen, and others (New York: Jewish Theological Seminary of America, 1983), pp. 41–56 (p. 50 and plate VII) and David Wachtel, 'How to Date a Rothschild', in *Studia Rosenthaliana*, 38/39 (2005/06), pp. 160–68.

53 The *Prague Haggadah* (Prague: Gershom Katz, 1526), p. 21. Several prints of this edition have been preserved. They are kept in various libraries, one of them, from which I used the images, is in Zurich, Collection René Braginsky, no. 211, p. 21[r]. https://braginskycollection.com/ajaxzoom/single.php?zoomDir=/pic/BCB/BCB_211&zoomFile=BCB_211_000a.jpg [accessed in May 2022]. For a facsimile edition, see *The Passover Haggadah of Gershom Cohen printed in Prague in the Year 5287/1527* (Tel Aviv: Sinai, 1954). See, also Abraham Yaari, *Bibliography of the Passover Haggadah from the Earliest Printed Edition to 1960* (Jerusalem: Bamberger and Wahrman, 1960), p. 1, no. 6; Yosef Hayim Yerushalmi, *Haggadah and History: A Panorama in Facsimile of Five Centuries of the Printed Haggadah from the Collections of Harvard University and the Jewish Theological Seminary of America* (Philadelphia: The Jewish Publication Society, 2005), plates 9–13. For Hebrew printing in Prague and the illustrations of the *Prague Haggadah*, see Charles Wengrov, *Haggadah and Woodcut: An Introduction to the Passover Haggadah Completed by Gershom Cohen in Prague on Sunday, 26 Teveth, 5287/December 30, 1526* (New York: Shulsinger Brothers, 1967).

54 Several early illustrated fragments of the haggadah have been preserved, although scholars still disagree as to the time and place of their creation. About this issue with further reading, see Kogman-Appel, 'Designing a Passover Imagery', p. 183. For the history of the printed Jewish book with an extensive bibliography, see Emile G. L. Schrijver, 'Jewish Book Culture Since the Invention of Printing (1469–c. 1815)', in *The Cambridge*

Figure 1.9. The Israelites crossing the Reed Sea. *Prague Haggadah*, Zurich, Collection René Braginsky, no. 211, fol. 21ʳ.

the representation of a larger composition. Yet, while the monochrome woodcut shows a somewhat neutrally dressed group of men,⁵⁵ in Joel's illustration the people figured in the foreground of the crowd include men, women, and children, all in contemporary dress. However, he put little effort in depicting the rich and complex fabric patterns and embroidery on their robes and headwear that were typical of that period in Italy. By quickly sketching lines and dots, he only produced the appearance of an abundance of shapes. Thus, despite the use of a limited colour palette, the patterns are not very different from those in the monochrome pen-and-ink drawings of Maraviglia siddur."

Joel's tendency to rationalize his drawings is also evident in the ornamentation of the opening words, where a continuous development can be observed from the large and elaborate initial word panels in one of his early works, known as the *First Nuremberg Haggadah* (Figure 1.10),⁵⁶ to the filigree pen-and-ink drawings in the *Moskowitz Mahzor*

History of Judaism, ed. by Jonathan Karp and Adam Sutcliffe (Cambridge: Cambridge University Press), pp. 291–315.

55 Kogman-Appel has already pointed out the rather general character and timeless costumes of the figures in the *Prague Haggadah*. Kogman-Appel, 'Designing a Passover Imagery', p. 186.

56 IM, MS 181/60, formerly Jerusalem Schocken Library, MS 24086, e.g., fol. 6ʳ, https://www.nli.org.il/en/discover/manuscripts/hebrew-manuscripts/viewerpage?vid=MANUSCRIPTS&docid=PNX_MANUSCRIPTS990001899320205171-1#$FL60654732 [accessed in May 2022]. See Beit-Arié, *The Making of the Medieval Hebrew Book*, p. 99 and Zirlin, 'The Early Works'.

Figure 1.10. Initial word panel with hunting scenes. IM, MS 181/60, formerly Jerusalem Schocken Library, MS 24086, fol. 6ʳ.

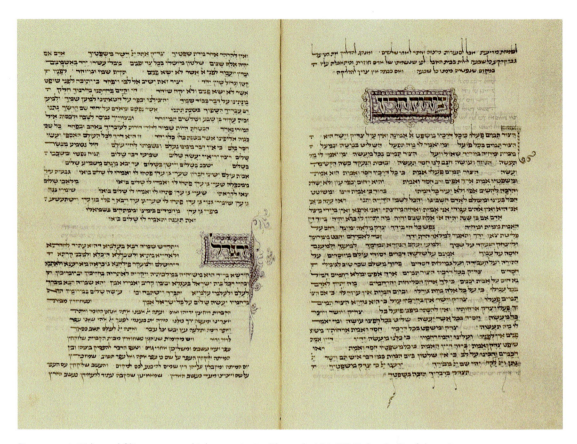

Figure 1.11. Initial word filigree pen-and-ink ornament with mask. NLI, MS Heb. 4°1384, fol. 195ʳ.

(Figure 1.11),⁵⁷ which he produced towards the end of his career. Abiding by the Ashkenazi tradition of book illumination, Joel decorated the initial panels in the *First Nuremberg Haggadah* with a variety of hunting motifs and biblical scenes in the spare-ground technique, which was very popular in the German Lands and widely used in both Jewish and Christian book illumination. After crossing the Alps in the middle of the fifteenth century, Joel began to show a strong tendency towards delicate and filigree feather ornaments. Nevertheless, he kept the elaborately decorated initial word panels in his decorative repertoire and began using them side by side with filigree penwork decoration for the initial words in the same manuscripts, mainly haggadot. Over time, he developed this filigree penwork into an easily repeatable mesh of geometric structures woven around the opening word, to which he then added other elements such as zoomorphic and astrological symbols, architectural elements, vases, and grotesque figures. Even with these additional elements, Joel's initial word decorations remained simply executed pen-and-ink drawings which could be drawn during the copying process, thus shortening the time he needed to produce a manuscript (Figure 1.12).⁵⁸

---

57 NLI, MS Heb. 4°1384, e.g., fol. 195ʳ, https://www.nli.org.il/en/discover/manuscripts/hebrew-manuscripts/viewerpage?vid=MANUSCRIPTS&docid=PNX_MANUSCRIPTS990000448660205171-1#$FL36831905 [accessed in May 2022]. See Zucker, *The Moskowitz Mahzor*.

58 For example, initial word decoration with fleuronnée and mask, *Maraviglia Siddur* (BL, Add MS 26957, fol. 39ʳ).

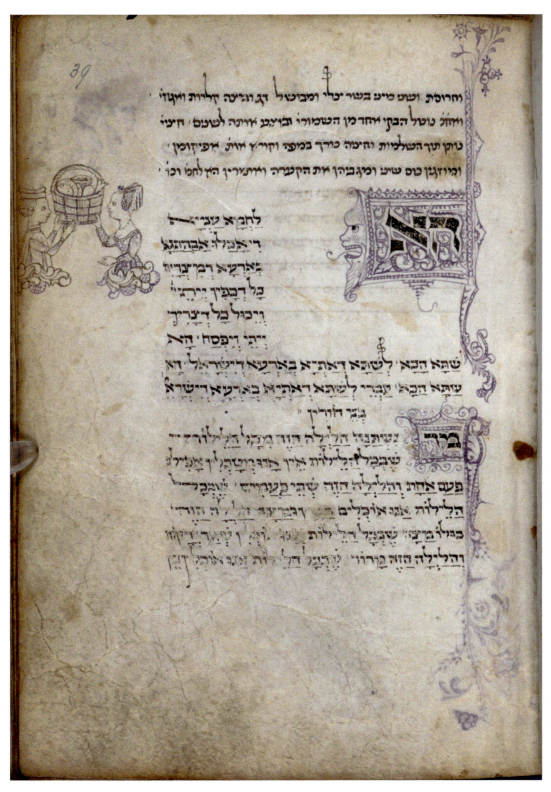

Figure 1.12. Initial word with fleuronnée decoration and mask. BL, Add MS 26957, fol. 39ʳ.

Similarly rationalized drawings and a similarly reduced use of colour as are evident in Joel's work can also be seen in the serially produced manuscripts executed in contemporary Christian workshops.[59] However, the rationalization measures were not necessarily geared towards mass production.[60] Rathe they were introduced into the work process to make production more efficient, which would lead to higher productivity; mass production would be only one of the possible results. By rationalizing his images, Joel, too, was able to reduce the amount of work, shorten his production time, and copy more manuscripts, albeit without aiming for large-scale production.

Standardization Tendencies Through Reduced and Repeated Visual Language to Increase Productivity

An essential feature of mass-produced products is standardization, which is also a way to rationalize the work process. Once transferred to a woodcut or copperplate, an image could be replicated quickly and without much effort, and, as I noted, illustrations had been reproduced in large numbers even before Gutenberg invented his printing press. For the same technical reasons, a printing press was able to publish books in large quantities, all with the same text, layout, and illustrations. The included images were all identical and could only be individualized by colouring, as occurred in the case of the monochrome Berlin copperplate *El gran Turco* (Figure 1.6) and one of its partially coloured copies in Saray Museum, Istanbul.[61] The figures created with woodcuts and engravings reflected a general taste, which made them attractive to a wider audience. As they were often devoid of attributes attributed to a particular character, they simply suggested the action described in the text instead of illustrating it, so the same image could be reproduced in different contexts in the same codex, obviating the need for an extensive illustration program. A similar limited visual language is also evident in Joel's manuscripts, as he repeated existing forms and motifs, albeit slightly altered, in the same or other manuscripts, which to a certain extent is reminiscent of the standardization inherent in printing.

Such stereotypical repetition of woodcuts appears, for example, in the *Prague Haggadah*, which is one of the most richly illustrated among the printed haggadot,[62] where the same woodcut was used for Rabbi Eliezer (fol. 15^v), Rabbi Gamaliel (fol. 18^r), and the righteous teachers

---

59 For example, 'The workshop from 1418', that of Diebold Lauber in Hagenau and of Johannes Bämler in Augsburg. See Saurma-Jeltsch, I, pp. 16–154; Beier, 'Missalien massenhaft', pp. 55–78; Sheila Edmunds, 'New Light on Johannes Bämler', in *Journal of the Printing Historical Society*, 22 (1993), pp. 29–54.

60 Michele Tomasi, 'L'art multiplié: matériaux et problèmes pour une réflexion', in *L'art multiplié. Production de masse, en série, pour le marché dans les arts entre Moyen Âge et Renaissance*, ed. by Michele Tomasi and Sabine Utz, Études lausannoises d'histoire de l'art, 11 (Rome: Viella, 2011), pp. 7–25 (p. 13).

61 See David Landau and Peter W. Parshall, *The Renaissance Print: 1470–1550* (New Haven: Yale University Press, 1994), pp. 91–97; Gülru Necipoğlu, 'Visual Cosmopolitanism and Creative Translation: Artistic Conversations with Renaissance Italy in Mehmed II's Constantinople', in *Muqarnas*, 29 (2012), pp. 1–81 (pp. 18–19).

62 It contains fifty-nine illustrative woodcuts (excluding the full-page illustration and the initials), but only thirty-six different motifs. The production of the woodcuts seemed to have been time-consuming and therefore expensive. The higher price of the woodblocks can be recognized in the resale of the older ones, which were reused despite considerable impairment of the print quality. For this reason, the Jewish printer bought the used decorative woodblock prints from his Christian colleagues, which he then had to cut and rearrange for the new layout. See, with further readings, Marvin J. Heller, *Further Studies in the Making of the Early Hebrew Book* (Leiden: Brill, 2013), pp. 3–35 (pp. 5–13).

Figure 1.13. The righteous teacher, *Prague Haggadah*. Zurich, Collection René Braginsky, no. 211, fol. 31ʳ.

(Figure 1.13).⁶³ The illustration depicts an old man in foreign-looking clothing and a conical hat, his left hand pointing to his right hand, which is stretched out with the palm opened towards the viewer. Since all the attributes are missing, and the figure's gender, age, and clothing are not necessarily representative, the image cannot be associated with a particular biblical or rabbinic character. Nevertheless, it was obviously sufficient to recall the wise rabbis of the past into the visual memory of the contemporary observer, so that it was repeated each time the text referred to one of them and separate woodcuts were no longer necessary. Similarly, the woodcuts depicting figures with wine glasses in their hands or in a posture of worship were repeated each time the text referred to prayers and blessings. The *Prague Haggadah* was printed in 1526 and is thus not a Hebrew incunabulum. However, featuring as it does, the stereotypical repetition of the same figure it reflects a printing practice, one that would continue for many years, observed in Christian printing, which began using woodcuts for illustrations in books printed with movable type much earlier than Jewish print shops.⁶⁴

Joel's monochrome and highly reduced pen-and-ink drawing of Rabbi Akiva holding a book

---

63 The righteous teacher, *The Prague Haggadah* (Prague: Gershom Katz, 1526), fol. 31ʳ.

64 However, this practice was already evident in the first dated book printed with types and woodcut-illustrated book, *Der Edelstein* by Ulrich Boner (1280–1350), which was printed by Albrecht Pfister in Bamberg in 1461. The only preserved copy of this edition is kept today in Wolfenbüttel, Herzog August Bibliothek, A: 16.1 Eth. 20 (1), http://diglib.hab.de/inkunabeln/16-1-eth-2f-1s/start.htm [accessed in May 2022].

in his hands in the *Maraviglia Siddur* (Figure 1.7) also appears in slightly altered forms in the *Parma Haggadah* as a partially coloured full-length figure of a standing man presenting the *maror* (Figure 1.14),[65] in the *Washington Haggadah* as a drawing in watercolour of a seated man lifting the second cup of wine to the left of the word *lefikhakh* ('Thus [it is our duty…]') (Figure 1.15),[66] and in the Hamburger *Moreh nevukhim* ('The Guide for the Perplexed') as a pen-and-ink drawing next to the fleuronnée decoration.[67] Similarly, the figure of the woman in one of the images of the *Maraviglia Siddur* (Figure 1.3) appears in an almost unchanged posture among the figures on a donkey's back in the eschatological scene for the *Shefokh* ('Poor [out Your wrath…]') passage on fol. 19ᵛ of the *Washington Haggadah* (Figure 1.16). Moreover, in the *London Haggadah*,[68] Joel repeated the head of the young wandering Aramean (Figure 1.17)[69] at least three times almost unchanged in the crowd of Egyptians in the scene of Pharaoh's army pursuing the Israelites (Figure 1.18)[70] and as a full-length figure in the same pose at the front of the Pharaoh's army in the same scene.

This limited visual vocabulary was due to Joel's reluctance to waste time endlessly creating new motifs and, together with the graphic style and rationalization of the drawings, it was part of a chain reaction triggered by developments in book production. The inevitable consequence of a limited visual language was a repetition of motifs, which in turn led to a certain degree of standardization. Standardization in printing reached a very high level, but Joel's illustrations were reproduced freehand and with minimal changes, so that they retained a certain degree of uniqueness despite the tendencies towards standardization. Since standardization is a means of rationalization in the production process with the goal of making work easier and faster, it is obvious that Joel's inclination towards standardization, including the reduction of his visual vocabulary, had the same effect.

---

65 BP, MS Parm. 2998, fol. 10ᵛ, https://www.nli.org.il/en/discover/manuscripts/hebrew-manuscripts/viewerpage?vid=MANUSCRIPTS&docid=PNX_MANUSCRIPTS990000914670205171-1#$FL16878042 [accessed in May 2022]. See Giuliano Tamani, *Elenco die manoscritti ebraici miniati e decorati della Palatina di Parma* (Florence: Olschki, 1967), p. 114, no. 197; *Hebrew Manuscripts in the Biblioteca Palatina in Parma: Catalogue*, ed. by Benjamin Richler and Malachi Beit-Arié (Jerusalem: Hebrew University of Jerusalem, Jewish National and University Library, 2001), p. 293, no. 1120; Beit-Arié, *The Making of the Medieval Hebrew Book*, pp. 102–07.

66 LC, MS Heb. 1, fol. 17ʳ. It should be noted that the following examples are intended as *pars pro toto* for a phenomenon that is common in Joel's work but owing to the limited scope of the paper, no further examples can be considered here.

67 Hamburg, Staats- und Universitätsbibliothek, Cod. Levy 115, fol. 155ᵛ, a manuscript whose illustrations Amirov associated with Joel, https://www.nli.org.il/en/discover/manuscripts/hebrew-manuscripts/itempage?vid=MANUSCRIPTS&docId=PNX_MANUSCRIPTS990000924330205171 [accessed in May 2022]. Amirov, Franziska, *Jüdisch-christliche Buchmalerei im Spätmittelalter* (Berlin: Deutscher Verlag für Kunstwissenschaft, 2018), pp. 193–94.

---

68 The *London Haggadah*, BL, Add MS 14762. Margoliouth, II, pp. 203–04, no. 610; *Ashkenazi Haggadah: A Hebrew Manuscript of the Mid-15th Century from the Collections of the British Library*, notes, transcript. and trans. by David Goldstein (London: Thames and Hudson, 1985) [facsimile]; Edmunds, 'The Place of the London Haggadah', pp. 25–34; Glatzer, 'The Ashkenazi and Italian Haggadot', pp. 137–69; Yael Zirlin, 'Joel Meets Johannes: A Fifteenth-century Jewish-Christian Collaboration in Manuscript Illumination', *Viator*, 26 (1995), pp. 265–82; Kogman-Appel, 'London Haggadah Re-visited', to be published in a Festschrift, 2021, https://www.bl.uk/manuscripts/FullDisplay.aspx?ref=Add_MS_14762 [accessed in May 2022].

69 BL, Add MS 14762, fol. 11ᵛ.

70 BL, Add MS 14762, fol. 14ᵛ.

Figure 1.14. Figure of a man presenting the *maror*. BP, MS Parm. 2998, fol. 10ᵛ.

42 RODICA HERLO-LUKOWSKI

Figure 1.15. Sitting man with a cup of wine in his hand. LC, MS Heb. 1, fol. 17ʳ.

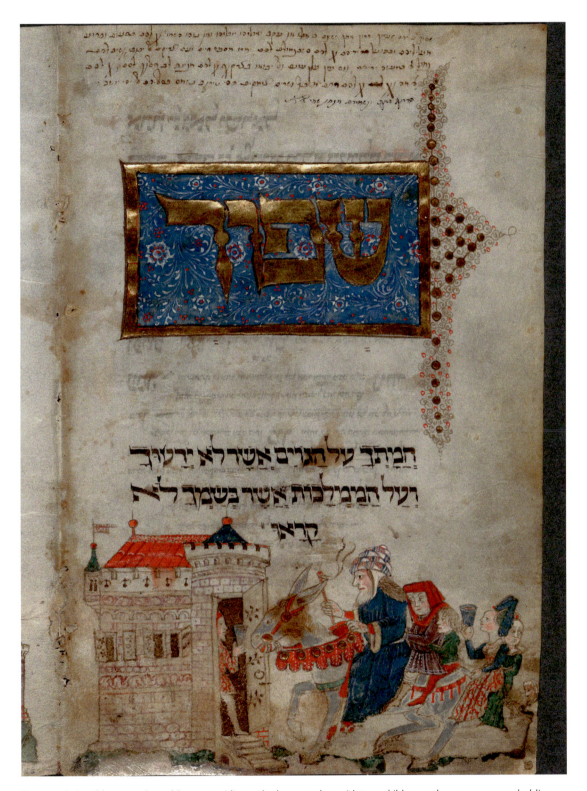

Figure 1.16. An old man and an old woman riding a donkey together with two children and a young woman holding a wine goblet. LC, MS Heb. 1, fol. 19ᵛ.

Figure 1.17. The wandering Aramean. BL, Add MS 14762, fol. 11ᵛ.

Figure 1.18. Pharaoh's army pursuing the Israelites. BL, Add MS 14762, fol. 14ᵛ.

Final Remarks: Joel's Manuscripts Reflect the New Technology-Driven Trends in Book Production

As an integral part of European book culture, Joel ben Simeon was confronted and challenged by the developments in book production engendered by print techniques. His manuscripts reveal certain characteristics that prove that he reacted to the new mechanical methods of text and image reproduction. As was typical of medieval book production, he continued to produce manuscripts commissioned by patrons, always using parchment and never resorting to paper, even though the latter was becoming increasingly available and cheaper. Although he was a traditional scribe, Joel was flexible enough to consider alternative ways of working. Stimulated by new developments in book production, trade, and consumption, apart from his commissioned works, he also produced manuscripts which were apparently intended for sale on the open market. Blank pages at the end and plenty of space around the introductory words testify to the intended option for subsequent customization. Mass customization allowed Joel to take advantage of both print and manuscript techniques and enabled him to compete with the print media by expanding his customer base. By offering a finished book, as was typical for printing, combined with the possibility of adapting it for a specific buyer, as was customary for manuscripts, he was able to add to his usual clientele of patrons others who were used to buying books quickly but appreciated the resilience of parchment and the concept of a personalized codex.

Joel's manuscripts, whether commissioned or produced for the free market, feature illustrations that differ greatly from the more elaborate and opaque colour illustrations of traditional medieval book illumination. They were decorated and illustrated in a flat and linear technique that resembled the graphic representations in woodcuts and copperplate engravings. Using this drawing technique, Joel quickly and easily created sketched pen-and-ink drawings, sometimes consisting only of doodles and often remaining colourless or only partially water coloured. Such drawings could easily be added while he copied the manuscript, reducing production time and increasing his productivity. Further, they were rationalized to show few internal details and only as much of the environment as was necessary for an understanding of the pictorial message — another timesaving method that Joel exploited to work more efficiently. Moreover, this rationalization led to replication of his illustrations. Thus, instead of wasting time creating new ones, Joel simply repeated existing illustrations, in slightly altered forms, in the same codex and in others. This resulted in a limited formal vocabulary, which is clearly evident in his manuscripts. The surprisingly little effort that Joel put into illumination is also reflected in the more elaborate compositions, where he merely created an impression of richness and diversity through sketched and repeated forms and motifs. The repetition of existing patterns inevitably led to a certain standardization of his formal visual language. However, as the patterns were hand drawn and varied slightly, the standardization was much less pronounced than in print.

All of these features in Joel ben Simeon's manuscripts are reminiscent of mechanically reproduced images, whose advantages he seemed to have recognized very early on. The new developments in book production were designed to produce a large number of books on paper within a short time and with little effort. The books and images manufactured in this way have characteristics that can be attributed to various rationalization measures within the production process. Similarly, Joel developed several methods to adapt the benefits of printing in terms of productivity, efficiency, and economy to his own work process, which he added to techniques of writing by hand.

By moving elegantly between the advantages of printing and those of the manuscript production, Joel was able to exploit the benefits both methods of book making. The mixture of handwriting and printing techniques evident in Joel' manuscripts places them somewhere between individual and mass production, so that they are telling reflections of the transition period from handwritten to printed books. In this respect, Joel ben Simeon is an excellent subject of study for researching Jewish book culture.

EVELYN M. COHEN

Joel ben Simeon in Transition*

Introduction

In art as in life, nothing stands still. As artists' experiences become more varied their style evolves, sometimes naturally and sometimes intentionally, in order to adapt to the changing tastes of the time or a new location. This is evident in the manuscripts produced by Joel ben Simeon, both as a scribe and an artist. Although twelve manuscripts contain colophons in which Joel specified that he was the scribe or the artist, or both, he still remains a somewhat enigmatic figure. Although he is undoubtedly the most studied scribe-artist of Hebrew manuscripts of the fifteenth century, aside from information provided in his colophons, verifiable details of his life and career remain elusive. In addition to his signed works, at least twenty-five manuscripts have been ascribed to him. These works may provide a greater sense of the scope of his productivity, but, as they are attributions rather than signed works, they may also add to some of the uncertainty surrounding his career. This chapter sheds light on Joel and his evolution as an artist in the hope that it will aid in further studies down the road.[1]

---

* I am indebted to the National Endowment of the Humanities and to the Renaissance Society of America – Samuel H. Kress Foundation Fellowship for supporting my research on Joel ben Simeon. This chapter is based on a lecture presented at the conference on The Jewish Book 1400–1600: From Production to Reception, held at the Westfälische Wilhelms-Universität Münster, Institute for Jewish Studies, June 24–27, 2019. My subsequent findings have been incorporated into this text. I would like to thank Samantha D. Bowser, David Kambhu, Ari G. M. Kinsberg, Havva Charm Zellner, and especially Rahel Fronda for their helpful input in the course of my preparing this chapter.

1 Several scholars have researched the career of Joel ben Simeon and provided lists of his works. Most notable are Joseph Gutmann, 'Thirteen Manuscripts in Search of an Author: Joel ben Simeon, 15th-Century Scribe-Artist', *Studies in Bibliography and Booklore*, 9 (Spring 1970), pp. 93–94 (pp. 76–95); Malachi Beit-Arié, 'Joel ben Simeon's Manuscripts: A Codicologer's View', *Journal of Jewish Art*, 3/4 (1977), pp. 25–39; Malachi Beit-Arié, 'Codicological Description and Analysis of the Washington Haggadah', in *The Washington Haggadah: A Facsimile Edition of an Illuminated Manuscript at the Library of Congress: Signed by Joel ben Simeon*, ed. by Myron M. Weinstein (Washington, DC: Library of Congress, 1990), II, pp. 105–35 (pp. 127–29); Bezalel Narkiss, 'The Art of the Washington Haggadah', in *The Washington Haggadah*, pp. 27–101 (pp. 31–40); David Stern and Katrin Kogman-Appel, *The*

Evelyn M. Cohen • Independent Scholar

Joel ben Simeon's Earliest Works

In order to trace a progression in Joel ben Simeon's work more securely, focus must be placed on his signed and dated manuscripts. It is unfortunate that the two earliest manuscripts that include colophons identifying the scribe — the *First Nuremberg Haggadah*[2] and the *First New York Haggadah*[3] — are undated and damaged, with illustrations cut off from their outer and bottom borders. Ashkenazi in appearance and rite, the style of their art seems to be less advanced than the other signed works. In the colophons of both, Joel used a scribal formula found in many medieval manuscripts that refers to a donkey ascending a ladder. In the *First Nuremberg Haggadah* the reference is to him, whereas in the *First New York Haggadah* it is to his patron[4]

The *Parma Tefillah*, the first of Joel's extant work that includes a date, is a prayer book from 1449 in which the scribe stated that he, Joel ben Simeon, known as Feibush, was from Bonn.[5] The locale where he copied the manuscript was not specified. It is unfortunate that the colophon in this prayer book, which is Ashkenazi in its rite, script, and codicological features, was altered. It was partially obliterated, and the name of a later owner replaced that of the original patron. As for the person who commissioned it, Joel stated that the patron should be protected forever, until a donkey ascends a ladder. To this he added that he, the scribe, should be unharmed forever, until a bull ascends a ladder.

Joel ben Simeon in Italy

The next dated manuscript, the *Turin Mahzor*, was copied three years later, in 1452, in Cremona.[6] In terms of its calligraphy and decoration, its appearance is still Ashkenazi. Two separate

---

Washington Haggadah, Copied and Illustrated by Joel ben Simeon (Cambridge: The Belknap Press of Harvard University Press and Washington, DC: The Library of Congress, 2011), esp. pp. 115–16; Franziska Amirov, *Jüdisch-christliche Buchmalerei im Spätmittelalter: Aschkenasische Haggadah-Handschriften aus Süddeutschland und Norditalien* (Berlin: Deutscher Verlag für Kunstwissenschaft, 2018), pp. 292–95; Evelyn M. Cohen, 'Joel ben Simeon's "Missing Leaves": Folios from the *Rothschild Haggadah*, the *Turin Mahzor*, and the *Rothschild Pentateuch*', in *Meḥevah le-Menaḥem: Studies in Honor of Menahem H. Schmelzer*, ed. by Shmuel Glick, Evelyn M. Cohen, Angelo M. Piattelli, and others, (Jerusalem: The Schocken Institute for Jewish Research, 2019), pp. 107*–31* (pp. 120*–24*); Sandra Hindman and Sharon Liberman Mintz, *I Am the Scribe: Joel ben Simeon* (New York, Paris, and Chicago: Les Enluminures, 2020), pp. 125–49.

2 Jerusalem, The Israel Museum, MS 181/060. A microfilm of the manuscript is available online at https://web.nli.org.il/sites/NLI/English/digitallibrary/pages/viewer.aspx?&presenterid=MANUSCRIPTS&docid=PNX_MANUSCRIPTS990001899320205171-1#|FL60654765 [accessed in May 2022].

3 New York, The Library of the Jewish Theological Seminary (JTS), MS 4481. The manuscript can be viewed in its entirety at https://www.nli.org.il/en/discover/manuscripts/hebrew-manuscripts/viewerpage?vid=MANUSCRIPTS&docid=PNX_MANUSCRIPTS990001084080205171-1#$FL28305916 [accessed in May 2022].

4 On the use of the expression 'until the donkey ascends a ladder', see Michael Riegler, 'Until a Donkey Ascends a Ladder: A Concluding Formula in Colophons in Hebrew Manuscripts from the Middle Ages' [in Hebrew], *Sinai*, 147 (2014), pp. 72–92, and Alexander Scheiber, 'Donkey-Ladder', in *Essays on Jewish Folklore and Comparative Literature*, ed. by Alexander Scheiber (Budapest: Akadémiai Kiadó, 1985), pp. 19–22.

5 Parma, Biblioteca Palatina, Cod. Parm. 3144, fol. 188ʳ. To view the manuscript in its entirety, see https://web.nli.org.il/sites/NLI/English/digitallibrary/pages/viewer.aspx?&presenterid=MANUSCRIPTS&docid=PNX_MANUSCRIPTS990000914320205171-1#|FL22792853 [accessed in May 2022]. See also Benjamin Richler, *Hebrew Manuscripts in the Biblioteca Palatina in Parma* (Jerusalem: The Hebrew University of Jerusalem / The Jewish National and University Library, 2001), cat. no. 1037, p. 259.

6 Turin, Biblioteca Nazionale Universitaria, MS A. III. 14.

colophons appear in this work.[7] The first originally bore the names of the patrons, Abraham ben Jacob and his wife Hannah bat R. Isaiah. In its current—damaged—state only the wife's name remains. As in the three other manuscripts mentioned above, Joel once again used the scribal formula alluding to a donkey ascending a ladder. The second colophon appears on another leaf of the *Turin Mahzor* (Figure 2.1). Here only the last part of Joel's name remains. He identified himself as Reiner, indicating that he was from a locale on the Rhine. Although his first name is now missing owing to damage, according to Abraham Berliner, who viewed the manuscript when it was intact, the name appearing on folio 474[r] was Feibusch (Feibush) Reiner.[8] Aside from Joel's calligraphy, therefore, his Ashkenazi background is clearly asserted in this manuscript produced in Italy. Again, the scribe referred to a donkey that ascends a ladder, though here Joel included an illustration of the scene, the only one known to exist in a manuscript by his hand.[9]

Created only two years later, in 1454, Joel's next known dated manuscript is the *Second New York Haggadah* (Figure 2.2).[10] In his colophon on folio 59[r] Joel again accentuated his Ashkenazi background. When stating that he was known as Feibush Ashkenazi, he included pen flourishes above the last word. He continued that he was from the city of Cologne on the Rhine. This

Figure 2.1. *Turin Mahzor*, Turin, Biblioteca Nazionale Universitaria, MS A. III.14, courtesy of the author.

colophon is of particular importance because Joel specified that he copied, vocalized, and decorated the manuscript, making it one of only three works in which he specified his role as an artist.[11] Although the name of the patron

---

7 On the rediscovery of both colophons in this manuscript, see Cohen, 'Joel ben Simeon's "Missing Leaves"', pp. 113*–18*.

8 Abraham Berliner, *Hebraeische Bibliographie*, 20 (1880), p. 129.

9 A more crudely executed donkey drawn by Joel appears in the *First New York Haggadah*, fol. 14[v], in the illustration of the Messiah riding an ass as he approaches a youth who stands at the open doorway of a house (see Figure 2.4 below).

10 JTS, MS 8279. To view the entire manuscript, see https://web.nli.org.il/sites/NLI/English/digitallibrary/pages/viewer.aspx?presenterid=MANUSCRIPTS&docid=PNX_MANUSCRIPTS990001112210205171-1#|FL29231866 [accessed in May 2022].

11 The others are the *Ashkenazi Haggadah*, London, British Library (BL), Add MS 14762, in which only some of the illustrations are by Joel, and six leaves with depictions relating to the Tabernacle, formerly JTS, Acc. No. 0822. Its current location is unknown.

52 EVELYN M. COHEN

כי לנא בילנא הסית במלי
תמים בחלב המיבזי אמר
לי לחול לביל להלי לה הבמלה

לשנה הבאה
בחשלם

אני הלבד יואל בר שמעון זל
הםבונה ויכבש אשבנזי מעיר
קלוניא על נהר ריבוס כתברתי
שרהתי רצירתי ההגדה זה וסיימתי
אותו בירחה אילול שנת ריד לפרט

Figure 2.2. *Second New York Haggadah*, Library of JTS MS 8279, fol. 59ʳ, courtesy of the Library of JTS.

and the city where Joel created the haggadah are not mentioned, and the appearance of the script is Ashkenazi, the liturgy, as well as the instructions and customs presented are those of Italy. Moreover, the style of the illustrations and decorations reflects the influence of Italian art. This is especially noticeable in the mastery of foreshortening on either side of the hanging textile on which the initial word הודו appears, on folio 50^r (Figure 2.3).

In this haggadah, Joel utilized a strikingly different iconographic program from that used for the *First New York Haggadah*, where, in accordance with the Ashkenazi tradition, numerous illustrations were placed in the margins around the text, in the outer or the bottom borders.[12] Included were scenes related to the personages and events mentioned in the text, as well as an eschatological scene of the Messiah riding a donkey and blowing a shofar that accompanies the text שפוך חמתך ('Pour out thy wrath') on folio 14^v (Figure 2.4).[13]

By the time Joel created the *Second New York Haggadah*, the next extant manuscript for which he provided a date, he had developed an original approach towards haggadah illustrations. He abandoned completely the Ashkenazi decorative program in which images were placed in the outer and bottom borders. Among the few traditional depictions is a hare chased by a hound. Rather than appearing in its typical location as a punning illustration for the mnemonic יקנה"ז,[14] its placement where the Exodus of the Israelites is discussed on folio 24^v is unusual. The next customary image, an outstretched arm, is placed traditionally, but with an inventive twist. Instead of being drawn in the outer margin as an accompaniment to the text, the words ובזרוע נטויה ('and with an outstretched arm') are penned in small letters in red on the drawing of the arm itself, placed within the text column on folio 26^r. Other than these two representations, additional depictions such as a double triskele, formed from two sets of three human legs in alternating red and blue (fol. 30^r), and an arrow piercing a heart (fol. 43^r) are unusual. Among the embellishments surrounding initial words that are unique to this haggadah are four hares sharing conjoined ears (fol. 57^v), four acrobats with their legs on one another's shoulders (fol. 58^r), a shield carried in the mouth of an eagle (fol. 58^v), and a Wildman blowing a long trumpet from which a hanging fabric contains the initial word (fol. 58^v).

It is possible that the undated *Bodmer Haggadah* served as a transitional work in which the scribe identified himself exactly as he did in the *Second New York Haggadah*, as Joel ben Simeon known as Feibush Ashkenazi from Cologne on the Rhine.[15] The *Bodmer Haggadah* contains many illustrations that are commonly found in other

---

12 Although many of the border illustrations have been cut out throughout the manuscript, it is still possible to determine what most of the images originally depicted.

13 See Joseph Gutmann, 'When Kingdom Comes: Messianic Themes in Medieval Jewish Art', *Art Journal*, 27/2 (1967–68), pp. 168–75, and 'The Messiah at the Seder: A Fifteenth-Century Motif in Jewish Art', in *Studies in Jewish History Presented to Professor Raphael Mahler on His Seventy-Fifth Birthday*, ed. by Shmuel Yeivin (Merhavia: Sifriat Poalim with the assistance of the Tel-Aviv University, 1974), pp. 29–38 (pp. 32–33, plates 4–9).

14 The acronym is a reminder of the order of the benedictions to be recited when the Seder occurs on a night when the Sabbath is ending, and additional blessings are recited in the *kiddush*. As the acronym, pronounced *yaknehaz*, sounds similar to *Jagd den Hasen*, German for hare hunt, in Ashkenazi haggadot a hunting scene sometimes accompanies this text.

15 *Bodmer Haggadah*, Cologny-Geneve, Bibliotheca Bodmeriana-Fondation Martin Bodmer, Cod. Bodmer 81. The colophon appears on fol. 34^r. The manuscript has been reproduced in a facsimile edition. See Maurice-Ruben Hayoun, *Haggadah de Pessah: la pâque juive: manuscrit du xve siècle copié et enluminé par Joël ben Siméon Feibusch Ashkénazi* ([Cologny]: Fondation Martin Bodmer, 2011). It can also be viewed online: https://www.e-codices.unifr.ch/en/searchresult/list/one/fmb/cb-0081 [accessed in May 2022].

Figure 2.3. *Second New York Haggadah*, Library of JTS MS 8279, fol. 50ʳ, courtesy of the Library of JTS.

Figure 2.4. *First New York Haggadah*, Library of JTS MS 4481, fol. 14ᵛ, courtesy of the Library of JTS.

fifteenth-century Ashkenazi haggadot. Among them is the search for leaven (fol. 1ʳ), the Seder basket (fol. 5ʳ), the pouring of the second cup (fol. 5ᵛ), the Israelites in slavery (fol. 6ʳ), the Wise Son (fol. 7ʳ), the Wicked Son, the Simple Son, and the Son Who Does Not Know How to Ask (all on fol. 7ᵛ), a wayfarer illustrating 'Go forth and learn' (fol. 8ᵛ), the infant Moses placed in the Nile, the daughter of Pharaoh dispatching her servant to retrieve him (fol. 9ʳ), a man throwing two infants into the Nile (fol. 10ʳ), Moses and the burning bush (fol. 11ʳ), and Daniel in the lion's den (fol. 28ʳ).

Three unusual decorations, however, appear in both the *Bodmer Haggadah* and the *Second New York Haggadah*. The former depicts a grid inhabited by human heads posed at different angles; their shoulders, head coverings, and the upper parts of their clothing are portrayed as well. This appears on folio 4ᵛ opposite the text of הא לחמא עניא ('This bread of affliction') on the facing page. The grid is formed of four squares across and six down. Each of the twenty-four sections contains a head that represents someone whose appearance and station in life varies notably from that of the figure adjacent to it. By contrast, the grid in the *Second New York Haggadah* on folio 15ᵛ no longer faces the initial word הא written on the facing page, but appears, instead, around the word itself (Figure 2.5). Forty squares alternate a rosette motif with a human head; twenty heads portray different types of people, while twenty flowers fill the other spaces, which have vivid red backgrounds. This arrangement creates a vibrant pattern. As the haggadah text in this passage includes an invitation to all who are hungry to come and eat and to all who are in need to come and celebrate Passover, in both manuscripts the artist took advantage of this opportunity to create a mélange of society, similar to those found in medieval model books.

The next unusual motif found in both manuscripts is an arch that surrounds elements in the text. In the *Bodmer Haggadah*, on folio 15ᵛ, the initial word לפיכך is written on a fabric that hangs from under an archway. The base of a column on either side rests on the shoulders of a crouching man. In the *Second New York Haggadah* a more complicated structure serves as an organizational device that frames a lengthy text that pertains to the laws regarding the Seder meal, from the eating of the matzah through שפוך חמתך. The architecture, now comprising two arches, appears on facing pages (fols 37ᵛ–38ʳ). Reading from right to left on folio 37ᵛ, the bases of the columns rest on the back of an elephant, the shoulders of a seated man, and the back of a lion. In contrast to what for the time were exotic animals, on the opposite page, folio 38ʳ, the columns rest on the back of an ox at the right and a horse at the left. Once again, a seated man functions as the support for the middle column. On both pages, the central column rests on the shoulders of a man who, unlike the squatting males in the *Bodmer Haggadah*, is convincingly rendered as seated on a stone pedestal. Each figure turns his torso somewhat in a pose that is more sophisticated than those in the *Bodmer Haggadah*. The architecture in the *Second New York Haggadah* is the more elaborate of the two. Whereas the *Bodmer Haggadah* has a simple architrave at the top of the structure, the *Second New York Haggadah* depicts a complex entablature that includes crenelated towers above an architrave decorated with three medallions, each with a male head.

A final example of an unusual motif appears in the use of textiles in both haggadot. In the *Bodmer Haggadah* the initial word לפיכך, written in large display script on folio 15ᵛ, is embellished with a blue fabric containing a scalloped design and a bottom border formed of tassels. The visually appealing textile is rendered as totally two dimensional. Another fabric, a curtain suspended from a wooden rod, functions as a background for the initial word שפוך on folio 18ᵛ. The textile, embellished with a repeating circular motif and a red border at the bottom, conveys a spatial dimension. This curtain, no

Figure 2.5. *Second New York Haggadah*, Library of JTS MS 8279, fol. 15ᵛ, courtesy of the Library of JTS.

longer flat, undulates. At the extreme right the artist conveyed a stronger sense of depth, as the foreshortened fabric seems to project closer to the viewer. A related motif, even more convincingly conveying a sense of depth is found in the textile that serves as a backdrop for the initial word הודו on folio 50ʳ in the *Second New York Haggadah*. Here the curtain hangs from a rod held by two hands. The pattern of the fabric is bold, with animals painted in red and black framed by circular forms. The spatial dimension is more pronounced than in the *Bodmer Haggadah*, with the edges on both sides foreshortened in a more proficient manner, providing a stronger sense of forward projection. The bottom red border undulates throughout, in contrast to the curtain in the *Bodmer Haggadah*, which although depicted as having folds, is much flatter.

The range of pigments used for the *Bodmer Haggadah* make it seem likely that it was a more expensive commission. In the *Second New York Haggadah*, Joel used a more limited palette and no gold. It is the latter, however, that displays a more advanced style.

All the elements described here lead to the conclusion that while related in terms of their innovative iconography, from a stylistic point of view it is likely that the *Second New York Haggadah* of 1454 was produced slightly later. At this point in his career Joel abandoned the traditional iconographic elements of medieval haggadot and moved on to something more artistically creative.

The *Maraviglia Tefillah*

The next manuscript by Joel ben Simeon that bears a date is the *Maraviglia Tefillah* of 1469.[16] By this time he had developed further as a specifically Italian scribe and artist. In the colophon of this prayer book, on folio 112ʳ, he began with the formulation 'כבודך ה ('Your glory to God'), which Malachi Beit-Arié has shown was used solely by Italian scribes.[17] It is noteworthy that Joel no longer made mention of his Ashkenazi background as he had beginning with the *Parma Tefillah* of 1449. Moreover, beginning with the *Maraviglia Tefillah* he ceased to refer to himself as Feibush as he had in the dated manuscripts: the *Parma Tefillah* of 1449, the *Turin Mahzor* of 1452, and the *Second New York Haggadah* of 1454, and in three undated manuscripts: the *Bodmer Haggadah*, the six leaves with depictions relating to the Tabernacle,[18] and the *London Ashkenazi Haggadah*.[19] It is not until his last dated manuscript, David Qimhi's Commentary on Psalms copied in Modena in 1485, that Joel returned to referring to himself as Ashkenazi.[20] From the manuscripts that have survived, for a period of almost twenty years he ceased to mention his Ashkenazi background.

As evidenced in the *Maraviglia Tefillah*, Joel's art underwent a change that reflected his experience in Italy. This manuscript produced for Maraviglia, the daughter of Menahem, contains several illustrations of a woman performing Jewish rituals, such as reciting *havdalah* on a cup of wine (fol. 31ʳ), raising a Seder basket along

---

16 Although in his colophon Joel provided the date of the twenty-sixth of the month of Kislev 5030, he clearly erred by 200 years and intended 5230, which is, 30 November 1469. The manuscript, housed in BL, Add. MS 26957 can be viewed online: https://www.bl.uk/manuscripts/Viewer.aspx?ref=add_ms_26957_fs001ʳ [accessed in May 2022].

17 BL, Add. MS 26957, fol. 112ʳ. Malachi Beit-Arié, *The Makings of the Medieval Hebrew Book: Studies in Palaeography and Codicology* (Jerusalem: Magnes Press, 1993), p. 107. Although the patron may have specified the desired rite for the liturgy, as well as the customs to be depicted, the formula that the scribe used for his colophon was his decision and reveals a change of approach in favour of an Italian usage.

18 Formerly JTS, Acc. No. 0822.

19 BL, Add MS 14762.

20 Cod. Parm. 2841, fol. 174ʳ.

with a young man (fol. 39ʳ), counting the *omer* (fol. 55ᵛ), and reciting a confessional prayer on the Day of Atonement (fol. 74ᵛ). Presumably the female images portray Maraviglia, who has a high, shaven forehead and wears elaborate headdresses capped off with a jewel. The dresses are decidedly Italian in their design, with low-cut necklines that reveal décolletage in accordance with the ideal of beauty in Renaissance Italy. Of the manuscripts under discussion so far, Maraviglia's prayer book exhibits the greatest adoption of the practices of an Italian scribe and artist.

A Full Repertoire of Motifs: Solomon Segal's 'Arba'ah Turim

Up to this point I have focused on Joel ben Simeon's signed manuscripts; in order to develop a greater insight into the continued evolution of Joel's art it is necessary to turn to additional dated works that have been ascribed to him.[21] A revealing example that helps trace Joel's development as an artist while he was in Italy is found in a copy of Jacob ben Asher's fourteenth-century halakhic code, the *'Arba'ah turim*. The manuscript was penned as four separate volumes which are now housed in libraries in four different countries. This recent attribution to Joel ben Simeon is based on similarities in style and iconography to other works associated with him.[22] The last three volumes bear dates, thereby revealing the artist's development over a period of time.

The first part, *'Orah hayyim* (אורח חיים), unlike the other three, does not include a colophon.[23] The one fully decorated page in this volume, folio 17ᵛ, is quite damaged. The silver putti at the bottom of the page hold up a roundel containing a family emblem divided into two areas. At the right, half of a black eagle stands against a gold ground, while at the left — highly abraded and difficult to see — half of a standing male nude holds a golden pitcher. The two are united by a towel above them, presumably a reference to the Levites' role in drying the hands of a Kohen. The emblem appears again in a smaller, even more damaged version, at the upper right. Although it lacks a colophon, it seems likely that the manuscript was produced for a Levite.

In terms of the decoration, the vases and floral designs in the margins were probably added by another artist, while the red penwork around the initial words, typical of his own scribal decorations, were mostly executed by Joel himself. Although the figures, are too abraded to enable an attribution, Luisa Mortara Ottolenghi noted the similarity between the scribal decorations in this volume and the third part, now in the Biblioteca Palatina, but did not ascribe them to a specific artist.[24]

The ornamentation in the subsequent volumes of this *'Arba'ah turim* is increasingly more elaborate and more clearly in the style of Joel ben Simeon. The opening page, folio 1ʳ, of the second part, *Yoreh de'ah* (יורה דעה) contains two decorated areas: the initial word panel at the top right,

---

21 Cohen, 'Joel ben Simeon's "Missing Leaves": Folios from the *Rothschild Haggadah*, the *Turin Mahzor*, and the *Rothschild Pentateuch*', pp. 120*–24*; and Hindman and Mintz, *Joel ben Simeon*, pp. 144–48.
22 See Cohen, 'Joel ben Simeon's "Missing Leaves"', p. 124*, and Hindman and Mintz, *Joel ben Simeon*, p. 148.

23 Milan, Biblioteca Ambrosiana, X 123 sup. For a description of this volume and a reproduction of fol. 17ᵛ, see Luisa Mortara Ottolenghi's entry in *Hebraica Ambrosiana II: Description of Decorated and Illuminated Hebrew Manuscripts in the Ambrosiana Library* (Milan: Edizioni Il Polifilo, 1972), pp. 138–39, pl. XI.
24 Ottolenghi, *Hebraica Ambrosiana*, p. 138.

surmounted by the upper part of an eagle, and a family emblem at the bottom.[25]

The decoration of the initial word and the eagle above it reflect Joel's style, as does the family escutcheon below. Most strikingly, the appearance of the truncated eagle whose head turns to its right, its tongue protruding from its open mouth, appears in other manuscripts associated with Joel. As in the volume in Milan, the family emblem in the Bodleian manuscript comprises an eagle and a nude Levite who pours water into a basin. Here, however, the arrangement of the two figures is different. Placed back to back they are united by the large crown above their heads, in addition to the towel depicted in the previous volume. The banderole above the escutcheon is inscribed יוסף הלוי יצו ('Joseph ha-Levi, may his Rock and Redeemer preserve him').

Adorning the initial word panel containing the word תניא at the top of folio 11ᵛ is a drawing in red ink of an elephant with a tower on its back. As in other works attributed to Joel ben Simeon, its tusks point upwards while the end of its trunk flares outwards like a trumpet. Beneath the panel, an animal in pursuit of a duck bites its victim's neck. The bottom border of the page contains a family emblem. Its basic components are arranged differently than they were on the opening page for rather than standing on the same level, a nude Levite pouring water into a basin sits astride the outspread wings of an eagle. The raptor, shown in its entirety, is posed in a manner that is similar to the truncated representation above the initial word seen on folio 1ʳ. The inscription, יקחהו ישאהו על אברתו ('takes them up, and bears them aloft on its pinions'), Deuteronomy 32:11, speaks of an eagle that takes its nestlings and carries them aloft on its wings. Not only is the figural style that of Joel

ben Simeon, so too are the rosettes that flank the family badge. Similar floral forms appear in the *Second New York Haggadah* of 1454, in which Joel identified himself as the artist, and in the *Rothschild Haggadah* in the National Library of Israel, MS Heb. 4° 6130, whose art is attributed to Joel.[26] The scribe wrote in the colophon on folio 222ᵛ of the Bodleian volume, *Yoreh de'ah*, that he was Eliezer ben David ha-Levi, who completed the work on Wednesday, the 5th of Sivan 5239 [= 1479]. While the name of the patron has been partially obliterated, it is possible to reconstruct that it was R. Solomon ben Yehiel Segal. As was usually the case, the name of the artist was not provided.

The first decorative element in the third part of the *Arba'ah turim*, *'Even ha-'ezer* (אבן העזר), placed above the initial word panel ornamenting the word יהי on folio 3ʳ, depicts a lion crouching next to a vase containing a topiary.[27] These motifs are commonly found in Joel's artistic vocabulary, as seen, for example, in the *Washington Haggadah*, completed in 1478, one year before this volume of the *Tur*.[28]

The initial word panel around the word לא at the top of folio 9ᵛ is ornamented in a manner commonly found in manuscripts attributed to Joel. In the family emblem at the bottom of the page, the eagle and the nude Levite stand back-

---

25 Oxford, Bodleian Library (Bod.), Can. Or. 15. See https://digital.bodleian.ox.ac.uk/objects/6d5d9a6c-864b-4a22-8f2d-10546975c186/surfaces/d2272f56-4ce6-4c95-bc1e-9d28d16beaf8/ [accessed in May 2022].

26 Jerusalem, National Library of Israel (NLI), MS Heb. 4° 6130.

27 Cod. Parm. 2236. For a brief description of this manuscript, see *Cultura ebraica in Emilia-Romagna*, ed. by Simonetta M. Bondoni and Giulio Busi (Rimini: Luisè editore, 1987), pp. 417–18. The decoration on fol. 3ʳ is reproduced in Figure 7.1:3. A detail of the colophon that displays a head emerging from a flower in the manner of Joel ben Simeon is reproduced on p. 419. To view the manuscript in its entirety, see: https://www.nli.org.il/en/discover/manuscripts/hebrew-manuscripts/viewerpage?vid=MANUSCRIPTS&docid=PNX_MANUSCRIPTS990000707790205171-1#$FL14864559 [accessed in May 2022].

28 Washington, DC, Library of Congress, MS Heb 1.

to-back as they did in the Bodleian volume, with their heads united under a crown. In this case, the red penwork forming the flat background, as well as the features of the young man with heavy-lidded eyes, are typical of Joel's style in Italy, already in evidence in many figures in the *Maraviglia Tefillah*.

Characteristic of Joel's art is the human head depicted in profile that emerges from a flower on folio 161ᵛ, beneath the colophon. As in the second part of the *Tur*, the scribe noted that he was Eliezer ben David ha-Levi. Although someone attempted to erase the name of the patron, the words Solomon ben Yehiel Segal are still legible. The scribe completed the work in Borgonuovo on Tuesday the 16th day of Av 5239, which, as in the previous volume, is 1479. Although the date and place of production for the first volume is unknown, the colophons in the second and third volumes indicate they were executed only two months apart in two different towns in northern Italy, Piacenza and Borgonuovo.

The fourth part of this *'Arba'ah turim*, *Hoshen mishpat* (חושן משפט), is housed in Cincinnati.[29] The colophon in the text column at the left on folio 392ᵛ indicates that this volume, too, was copied by Eliezer ben David ha-Levi for his patron Solomon ben Yehiel Segal, but seven years later than the previous two parts. It was completed on Thursday, the 19th of Tammuz 5246 [= 1486], in Crema. Thus, the colophons of the last three parts of this *Tur* indicate that although the scribe and patron remained the same over time, each volume was produced in a different city in northern Italy.

As seven years passed before the last part of the *'Arba'ah turim* was completed, noteworthy changes in approach towards decoration developed. As the length of this volume is more than double the previous two combined, it is not surprising that it contains significantly more ornamentation. The degree to which it is embellished, however, is surprising. Almost 150 pages are adorned with banners, castles, animals, plants, architectural motifs, and, especially, masks.

The decoration begins on the opening page of the text on folio 2ʳ (Figure 2.6). Enhancing the initial word panel is penwork of a type frequently found in works attributed to Joel. Also typical of his oeuvre is the crouching hare adorned with gold beneath the panel. Along the inner margin, penwork in red and purple includes a mask typical of those found in manuscripts associated with Joel ben Simeon. At least eighty-five pages in this volume are adorned with masks of various types: young faces, bearded men, and grotesques. Many have gaping mouths from which lines and other forms emerge. The initial word panel on folio 2ʳ is enhanced with penwork that is frequently found in works attributed to Joel.

A family emblem appearing at the bottom right of folio 19ʳ reflects a more advanced style than that of the previous volumes (Figure 2.7). Not unexpectedly, the design of the clothing has evolved; the hat worn by the Levite pouring water is in keeping with the fashion of the 1480s. So too, the imagery used for the family emblem changed. The Levite, now shown clothed, wearing a fifteenth-century doublet, is a half-length figure supported by an eagle whose head is concealed beneath the man's clothing. This unusual fusion of the two figures diverges greatly from the approach used for the family emblem in the other volumes of this manuscript.

This page includes another human form, a man seated in the outer margin facing away from the initial word panel. The panel contains the acronym Rashbag, which makes it likely that the figure depicted is Simeon ben Gamliel,

---

29 Cincinnati, Hebrew Union College, Klau Library, MS 676. I am indebted to Jordan Finkin at HUC for locating this volume, as all published references recorded the shelfmark as MS 675, which is a different copy of the *Tur*. The manuscript can be viewed at http://mss.huc.edu/ajaxzoom/single.php?zoomDir=/pic/zoom/MS_676 [accessed in May 2022].

Figure 2.6. *Hoshen mishpat*, Hebrew Union College, Klau Library, MS 676, fol. 2ʳ, courtesy of HUC.

Figure 2.7. *Hoshen mishpat*, Hebrew Union College, Klau Library, MS 676, fol. 19ʳ, courtesy of HU.

a prominent *nasi* ('president') of the Sanhedrin, whose dictum appears immediately below. The panel's vibrant red and black colour scheme and the firmly outlined animal forms that decorate it contrast starkly with this figure that is delicately drawn in purple ink. All of these elements, however, reflect Joel's style.

These four richly ornamented volumes of the *Tur* contain virtually the entire repertoire of motifs found in Joel ben Simeon's later works produced in Italy. Among the images depicted repeatedly are animals, masks of various types including young, old, and grotesque faces, and medieval castles with towers.

A manuscript that should be considered within the context of the dated *'Arba'ah turim* is an undated and unlocalized commentary by Levi ben Gershom (Gersonides) on the Pentateuch, housed in the Bodleian Library.[30] All of its ornamentation was executed in red ink. More than fifty of the pages contain initial words framed by either panels or banners, embellished with masks, as well as various animals and floral forms similar to those found in manuscripts associated with Joel ben Simeon.[31] The undulating banners that bear inscriptions in both the Gersonides commentary and the *'Arba'ah turim* also appear in two later manuscripts from Italy attributed to him: the *Moskowitz Mahzor* in the National Library of Israel[32] and the *Rothschild Mahzor*, produced in Florence in 1490 and now housed in New York in the Library of the Jewish Theological Seminary.[33] A particularly striking similarity is found in the image of a crowned eagle turning to its right, its tongue emerging from its open beak, found in both the *'Arba'ah turim* and the *Moskowitz Mahzor*.[34]

Conclusion

The four volumes of this *'Arba'ah turim* are significant in that they provide a sense of Joel ben Simeon's development as an artist while working for one specific patron over a period of at least seven years. Although the decision to include more ornamentation in the last volume may reflect the taste of the patron rather than that of the artist, as his art evolved Joel's style and artistic vocabulary began to resemble more closely

---

30 Oxford, Bodleian Library, MS Michael 361, produced in either Ashkenaz or Italy in the late fifteenth century. Whatever information is available for this manuscript is found in Adolf Neubauer, *Catalogue of the Hebrew Manuscripts in the Bodleian Library and in the College Libraries of Oxford* (Oxford: Clarendon Press, 1886), col. 48, no. 248, and Malachi Beit-Arié, *Catalogue of the Hebrew Manuscripts in the Bodleian Library: Supplement of Addenda and Corrigenda to Vol. 1 (A. Neubauer's Catalogue)*, ed. by R. A. May (Oxford and New York: Clarendon Press, 1994), col. 36, no. 248. The only published image from this manuscript, a detail from folio 52ᵛ, appears in *Jewish Treasures from Oxford Libraries*, ed. by Rebecca Abrams and César Merchán-Hamman (Oxford: Bodleian Library, University of Oxford, 2000), pp. 210–11, fig. 105.

31 Comparable images are also found in the manuscript referred to as the *Veneto Siddur-Sefer Minhagim* analysed in Hindman and Mintz, *Joel ben Simeon*, now in a private collection in Zurich.

32 NLI, MS Heb. 4° 1384. For a detailed description of this manuscript, which includes many of its illustrations, see Shlomo Zucker, *The Moskowitz Mahzor of Joel ben Simeon: Ashkenazi-Italian Scribe and Illuminator of Hebrew Manuscript MS. Heb. 4° 1384* (Jerusalem: The Jewish National and University Library, 2005). In an inscription on fol. 238ᵛ, the scribe refers to himself as Joel. The manuscript is available digitally at https://www.nli.org.il/he/manuscripts/NNL_ALEPH000044866/NLI?volumeItem=3#$FL91794047 [accessed in May 2022].

33 JTS, MS 8892. Joel ben Simeon's workshop was one of three that decorated the mahzor. For a description of the illustrations, see Evelyn M. Cohen, 'The Rothschild Mahzor: Its Background and Its Art', in *The Rothschild Mahzor: Florence 1492* (New York: The Library of the Jewish Theological Seminary of America, 1983), pp. 41–57. The manuscript can be viewed at https://digitalcollections.jtsa.edu/islandora/object/jts:320007#page/180/mode/2up [accessed in May 2022].

34 Compare, e.g., Bod., Can. Or. 15, fols 1ʳ and 11ᵛ with NLI, MS Heb. 4° 1384, fol. 110ᵛ.

the imagery he would use in later manuscripts he decorated in Italy.

Shlomo Zucker believes that the *Moskowitz Mahzor* and the *Rothschild Mahzor* were produced at about the same time.[35] When he published his study of the *Moskowitz Mahzor* in 2005, the date in the colophon of the *Rothschild Mahzor* was still misread as 1492.[36] Now that the date has been firmly established as 1490, it is likely that Zucker would assign the *Moskowitz Mahzor* to that year as well. The last volume of the *'Arba'ah turim* was completed in 1486, only four years earlier. As three volumes of the *'Arba'ah turim* are dated and localized, with the last having been completed in 1486, it is now possible to trace in a more detailed manner Joel ben Simeon's development as an artist in Italy in the last years in which he was active.

---

35 Zucker, *Moskowitz Mahzor*, p. xiv.
36 For the correct reading of the date, see David Wachtel, 'How to Date a Rothschild', *Studia Rosenthaliana*, 38–39 (2006), pp. 160–68.

DÉBORA MARQUES DE MATOS

Jewish Books from Portugal to the Early Sefardi Diaspora*

Introduction

During the later decades of the fifteenth century, Lisbon witnessed a sudden and unprecedented flourishing of Jewish manuscript illumination. Probably owing to a workshop, this proliferation of books coincided with the establishment of three Jewish printing presses, one in Faro, one in Lisbon, and one in Leiria. However, this thriving production of Jewish books in Portugal was short-lived. By the end of 1496, all Jews passing through or residing in the country were faced with expulsion or conversion. Those who stayed, undoubtedly the majority, were forcibly converted in 1497 and prevented from leaving for more than a decade; the few who escaped settled along the Mediterranean, and some returned to their former trades — including book printing. For the early years of the sixteenth century, the sphere of activity of several presses led by Iberian exiles points towards a deep attachment to a Portuguese identity. But that attachment did not last and would eventually be replaced by a newly fostered Sefardi identity in the Ottoman Empire, to some extent in Italy, and, later, by the so-called *Nação Portuguesa* ('Portuguese Nation') in various other places.

My intention in this chapter is to contribute to studies concerned with Jewish book history in the period of transition between the late fifteenth and early sixteenth centuries by surveying and contextualizing the still relatively unknown intellectual and artefactual production in Portugal and by Portuguese Jews in diasporic spaces. As this period was marked by a series of material, geographic, and epochal transitions, I have a twofold purpose: first, I demonstrate that it is increasingly hard to separate Iberian and early diasporic book production and that Portugal often played an intermediary role. Second, I relate to the fact that Portugal had already articulated most of the 'marks' of early modern Jewish cultural development, even if on an entirely different scale. We can foresee accelerated mobility, a heightened sense of communal cohesiveness, and a noticeable increase of knowledge production

---

* This chapter is based on research conducted under the project 'From Manuscript to Printing Press: The Illustrated Book in Jewish Culture (1300–1600)', led by Katrin Kogman-Appel between 2016 and 2018 at the Institute for Jewish Studies, University of Münster.

Débora Marques de Matos • Institute for Jewish Studies, University of Münster

Premodern Jewish Books, Their Makers and Readers in an Era of Media Change, ed. by Katrin Kogman-Appel and Ilona Steimann, Bibliologia, 67 Turnhout: Brepols, 2024, pp. 65–85.

in Portugal well before the crisis in rabbinical authority and the blurring of religious identities that unfolded in the Sefardi Diaspora.¹

Hence, I begin by discussing how the broader Portuguese Jewish identity in the late Middle Ages was forged from a unique socio-political reality combined with a broader Iberian experience. Further, I explore the way that identity shaped book production in Portugal on the eve of the sixteenth century and foreshadowed some of the most defining intellectual trends in the early Sefardi Diaspora.

Secondly, to determine how books from this period reflect such trends, I focus on such issues as apostasy and religious identity, as well as on the incorporation of some aspects of Portuguese aristocratic culture in Jewish intellectual production. A third section is devoted to a series of entanglements in Portugal in the transition from manuscript into print and how book materiality from this period was characterized by asynchronous transitions that would, eventually, be solidified in the Sefardi Diaspora. In the fourth and final section, I look at book production in diasporic spaces associated with Portuguese immigration. I argue that in the first half of the sixteenth century, book production was marked by the transference of a cultural repertoire and was deeply rooted in a Portuguese identity which would, eventually, give way to a broader Sefardi identity.

Three observations frame my approach. First, as artefacts, books are particularly suitable for crystallizing a 'relational field' of material, social, economic, intellectual, and emotional milieux; their itineraries are often non-linear and cumulative knowledge-making.² Second, the notion of entanglement should be understood more literally and not as the conceptual approach seen in the discourse of transcultural interactions. I argue that Portuguese Jewish identity was deeply entangled with Iberian Judaism and, at the same time, with the Portuguese social and cultural ambience. Further, the relationship between manuscript and print is complex and beyond simply continuity or rupture; materiality, means of production, markets, and so many other aspects were entangled, entwined, interwoven. Therefore, for the analysed period, rather than an Eisensteinean 'revolution', we have to discuss the broader phenomenon of asynchronous transitions.³

Jewish, Portuguese, and Iberian: Entangled Identities

In the last decade, interest in Portuguese Jewish medieval materials has moved beyond the vague 'Sefardi' and 'Spanish' categories into a re-evaluation of the historically complex and rich background of Jewish cultural production in Portugal.⁴ In the matter of book production, Jewish manuscripts have been addressed at

---

1 These are the five primary components of the early modern experience for Jews, as identified by David Ruderman, in *Early Modern Jewry: A New Cultural History* (Princeton and Oxford: Princeton University Press, 2010), p. 11.

2 The concept of artefacts as 'relational fields' is advanced by Tim Ingold, as quoted in Pamela H. Smith, *Entangled Itineraries: Materials, Practices, and Knowledge across Eurasia* (Pittsburgh, PA: University of Pittsburgh Press, 2009), pp. 5–6.

3 Despite the criticisms to her early work, Elizabeth Eisenstein reiterated her views on print as a 'sudden communications revolution' in the preface to the last edition of *The Printing Revolution in Early Modern Europe* (Cambridge: Cambridge University Press, 2005 [1983]). For a contrasting view, see Anthony Grafton, 'How Revolutionary Was the Print Revolution?', *The American Historical Review*, 107 (2002), pp. 84–86.

4 Among the most recent works on medieval Portuguese Jewry is *Portuguese Jews, New Christians, and 'New Jews'. A Tribute to Roberto Bachmann*, ed. by Claude B. Stuczynski and Bruno Feitler (Leiden and Boston: Brill, 2018). See also José Alberto

length,⁵ but discussions concerning printing are still mostly limited to surveys of Iberian Hebrew editions, even though catalogues of some of the principal Jewish incunabula collections contribute insights into these books' materiality, agents, textual contents, typographical, and artistic features.⁶

In the few studies where the relationship between manuscripts and print is addressed, the findings are somewhat contradictory. In the 1970s, Gabrielle Sed-Rajna argued that there was clear artistic connection between illuminated manuscripts and printed books from Lisbon and suggested that both types of books were produced in the same environment, possibly a workshop initially created for manuscripts.⁷ Thérèse Metzger, who analysed the same corpus of books, reaches an entirely different conclusion. She correctly demonstrated that the ornamental printing materials used in Lisbon were acquired in Híjar and refutes the idea that there was a workshop for the illumination of Jewish manuscripts. Instead, Metzger argues, but without solid evidence, that these manuscripts were the work of individual scribes and artists from other parts of the Iberian peninsula who sought refuge in Portugal.⁸

Recently, I suggested that there is enough evidence to confirm the existence of a workshop in Lisbon exclusively for manuscripts, which opened sometime before 1482 and functioned until about 1491–1492, run by local scribes and artists.⁹ Almost twenty high-end codices were copied and decorated in that atelier, including some outstanding examples of fifteenth-century Jewish book art.¹⁰ Bibles and prayer books from

---

Tavim and others, *The Jews in the Iberian Peninsula during the Middle Ages* [in Portuguese] (Coimbra: Almedina, 2018).

5   For recent studies on illuminated fifteenth-century Jewish manuscripts from Portugal, see in particular *Sefardi Book Art of the Fifteenth Century*, ed. by Luís U. Afonso and Tiago Moita (Turnhout: Brepols, 2019).

6   The majority of manuscripts mentioned throughout the essay can be consulted on Ktiv, unless indicated otherwise. See https://web.nli.org.il/sites/nlis/en/manuscript [accessed in April 2022]. I have opted to provide references to the Bibliography of the Hebrew Bible (BHB) for early printed books. See http://uli.nli.org.il/ [accessed in April 2022] For books pre-1501, I also include references to *Der Gesamtkatalog der Wiegendrucke* (GW) as it keeps an updated list of the links to the artefacts already digitized. See https://www.gesamtkatalogderwiegendrucke.de/GWEN.xhtml [accessed in April 2022]. Finally, for books post-1501, I refer mainly to Yeshayahu Vinograd's *Thesaurus of the Hebrew Book* [in Hebrew] (Jerusalem: The Institute of Computerized Bibliography, 1993). For books printed in Istanbul, see Abraham Yaari, *Hebrew Printing in Constantinople* [in Hebrew] (Jerusalem: Magnes Press, 1967).

7   Gabrielle Sed-Rajna, *Manuscrits hébreux de Lisbonne: Un atelier de copistes et d'enlumineurs au XVᵉ siècle* (Paris: Centre National de la Recherche Scientifique, 1970), pp. 11–13.

8   Thérèse Metzger, *Les manuscrits hébreux copiés et décorés à Lisbonne dans les dernières décennies du XVᵉ siècle* (Paris: Fundação Calouste Gulbenkian, Centro Cultural Portugais, 1997), pp. 11–17.

9   Débora Marques de Matos, 'Script and Decoration in Late Fifteenth-Century Portuguese Hebrew Manuscripts: A Digital Approach' (unpublished doctoral thesis, King's College London, 2019).

10 Among the examples are the *Lisbon Bible*: London, British Library (BL), MS Or. 2626–28, a three-volume Bible copied by Samuel ibn Musa in 1482 for Joseph ben Judah Alfaquim and decorated by two artists. Also, the *Paris Siddur*: Paris, Bibliothèque national de France (BnF), hébr. 592, copied by Eleazar Gagos and an anonymous collaborator in 1484 for Isaac ben Isaiah Cohen, and decorated by one of the Lisbon Bible's artists. Another example is the less known *Guenzburg Pentateuch*: Moscow, Russia State Library, MS Guenzburg 662, copied by Samuel ibn Musa for Abraham Rico-Homem. A member of the same family, Samuel Rico-Homem, was later involved in Hebrew printing in Istanbul with Astruc de Toulon, where he edited Qimhi's *Sefer ha-shorashim* in 1513. The Masorah of the Guenzburg Pentateuch was (partly) copied by Moses ibn Hayny and the volume was decorated by one of the Lisbon Bible's artists. The date is given as an acrostic and can be read as 1491 or 1496, but based on palaeographic features, Masorah, and the decorative designs, the first date seems more plausible. The manuscript's whereabouts are currently unknown.

the Lisbon workshop reflect masoretic excerpts, similar textual errors, scribal idiosyncrasies, and decoration programmes to an extent that suggests a 'proto-serialization'.[11] Owing to their technical nuances and iconographic repertoire, the artists' hands can also be identified in at least two Latin incunabula, which are decorated with borders and filigree patterns that are nearly identical to those in the Lisbon Jewish manuscripts.[12]

The Lisbon workshop catered to the Portuguese Jewish elite, and many of its patrons were well-known figures. A case in point is the Ibn Yahya family. Judah ben Gedalya ibn Yahya acquired a large-format Bible decorated exclusively in micrography.[13] His brother, Joseph ben Gedalya, commissioned several books, including the luxurious so-called *Lisbon Maimonides*.[14]

Another relative, David ben Solomon ibn Yahya, left Portugal before 1497 and took at least 400 books with him, 300 of which were sold in Italy to secure his freedom, which suggests that his library in Lisbon must have been outstanding.[15] Finally, David ben Joseph Ibn Yahya was directly involved with the Lisbon press, where he worked as an editor. One of his poems serves as an incipit for the Pentateuch of 1491.

Although none of the Lisbon workshop manuscripts carries his name, Isaac Abravanel's role in book patronage can be deduced from the size of his library, which was confiscated when he was accused of treason in 1483.[16] Abravanel was not only a prolific author in Hebrew, but his Portuguese writings have been described as a 'landmark in the cultural process of assimilation of humanism by the Jewish elite'.[17] He was among a small elite that experienced the cultural transformation fostered by the Avis dynasty first-hand. Emphasis on aristocratic education, the culture of the book, the importance placed on Graeco-Roman philosophy, history, and other

---

11 By proto-serialization I mean a type of production in series that still allows the customization of artefacts. Serialization would become predominant with print.

12 See Michele Carcano's *Collection of Sermons on Sin and Use in the Penitential Church Seasons of Advent and Lent* [in Latin], printed in 1476 in Venice by Franz Renner and Nicoló da Francoforte: Lisbon, National Library of Portugal (NL), Inc-590. Available at https://purl.pt/32639 [accessed in April 2022]. See also a Catholic Bible printed in 1479 by Nicholas Jenson in Venice: Lisbon, NL, Inc-634. Available at https://purl.pt/32308 [accessed in April 2022]. See also *Commentary of Gerardus de Sienna to the First Book of Petrus Lombardus's Book of Sentences* [in Latin]: Coimbra, University Library, MS 727. Images available at https://digitalis-dsp.uc.pt/bg3/UCBG-Ms-727/UCBG-Ms-727_item1/P3.html [accessed in April 2022].

13 Known as *Balliol Bible*, this codex in an unusually large format was copied by Samuel de Medina in 1490–91, but Judah Ibn Yahya was probably not the intended initial buyer: Oxford, Balliol College, MS 382. For images of the Balliol Bible, see: https://www.flickr.com/photos/balliolarchivist/albums/72157630851340370/ [accessed in April 2022].

14 London, BL, MS Harley 5698–99. Copied by Solomon Alzuq in 1471–72. There is no reference as to the place it was copied, but, based on the patron, it is ascribed to Lisbon. The early date, distinct programme, and palaeographic features place this magnificent work outside the scope of the Lisbon workshop.

15 This episode is mentioned by Joseph Hacker in 'Some Letters on the Expulsion of the Jews from Spain and Sicily' [in Hebrew], in *Studies in the History of the Jewish Society in the Middle Ages and in the Modern Period Presented to Professor Joseph Katz on his Seventy-fifth Birthday by his Students and Friends*, ed. by Immanuel Ethes and Joseph Salmon (Jerusalem: Magnes Press, 1980), pp. 64–95.

16 Abravanel wrote, 'And so all of my books were lost to the horror as my brothers, my people, and my neighbours became my foe. They also went up and came into my house and my *bet midrash*, and took that which was beloved to my soul, and also that which I did with [= wrote] this book was destroyed or taken captive, and I did not take it with me and have not seen it since', in *Merkevet ha-mishna*, printed in Sabbioneta in 1551 (p. 1). Also, his Hebrew books were apparently much sought, including by Christians. See *Chancellery of John II*, book 24, fol. 128 [in Portuguese] (Lisbon: Arquivo Nacional da Torre do Tombo).

17 Cédric Cohen-Skalli, 'Discovering Isaac Abravanel's Humanistic Rhetoric', *The Jewish Quarterly Review*, 97 (2007), p. 74.

humanist tendencies are some of the features that contradict the idea of 'belatedness' in Portugal and align it with the cultural transformations in Europe.[18] Furthermore, the absence of serious linguistic barriers meant access to other cultural productions, and the circulation of writings by Italian and Spanish intellectuals in Portugal is amply attested.

Abravanel may have belonged to a small social group that moved between Christian aristocratic and Jewish circles, but if economic integration is the standard by which acculturation is measured[19], then, in Portugal, we find a deeply acculturated Jewish society, but one not devoid of conflict. Recurrent complaints, especially against the upper echelons, segregated quarters, clothing impositions, and discriminatory taxes were all attempts to restrict social interactions. In 1449, the main Jewish quarter in Lisbon was sacked and burned; in Braga, in the early 1480s, a convert turned friar coerced Jews into listening to his lengthy sermons. Nevertheless, it seems as though the anti-Jewish sentiment in Portugal was locally contained and was chiefly motivated by economic considerations.[20] The daily reality was somewhere between resentment and, as Joseph Hayyun noted: there were 'gentiles [...] who love us and would not speak wicked or hateful things against us'.[21]

With such an affiliation to aristocratic culture and relative social stability, why, then, such a conspicuous lack of Jewish intellectual production and, more to the point, locally illuminated books prior to the late fifteenth century? While we cannot provide definitive answer, there are several factors to consider which also reflect the circumstances of Portuguese Jews. One such factor might have been the confiscation of books in Hebrew around 1497 to enforce conversion, but, then, given their value, it would be remarkable that no extant original works or illuminated codices from that period survived.

Another possibility, specifically with regard to luxury books, is that they were primarily acquired abroad until the Lisbon workshop opened in the early 1480s. In fact, a similar phenomenon can be perceived in luxury Christian books. As Portuguese book illumination only came to the fore in the sixteenth century, until then, high-end items such as Books of Hours and Psalters were imported from regions with renowned artistic traditions such as Flanders, France, and Italy.[22] Therefore, it is possible that the Jewish market for high-end books was also

---

18 Cultural 'belatedness' is a phenomenon sometimes associated with the Iberian Peninsula, Portugal in particular, owing to geographical periphery, but it is increasingly clear that it does not necessarily apply to the late Middle Ages/Early Modern Period. For 'belatedness' in the context of the Iberian Jewish communities, see Eleazar Gutwirth, 'Belatedness, History and Authorship: The Case of Medieval Spain', in *Iberia Judaica, La Polémica Judeo-Cristiana en Hispania*, 2 (2010), pp. 297–309.

19 Such a standard is proposed in Mark D. Meyerson, *The Muslims of Valencia in the Age of Fernando and Isabel: Between Coexistence and Crusade* (Berkeley: University of California Press, 1991), pp. 99–101.

20 Maria Tavares states that the anti-Jewish sentiment was mostly directed at the elite; for instance, and apart from a few troubadour songs that mostly targeted Jewish tax collectors, it is only in the sixteenth century that anti-Jewish literature became noteworthy. For an analysis of anti-Judaism in Portugal, see Maria José Ferro Tavares, 'Economic Growth and anti-Judaism in Medieval Portugal' [in Portuguese], in *La Península Ibérica en la era de los descubrimientos (1391–1492)*, ed. by Manuel González Jiménez and others (Andalucia: Junta de Andalucía and Consejería de Cultura, 1997), vol. 1, pp. 51–67.

21 ויש אחרים רבים מאד שהאוהבים אותנו ולא ידברו נגדנו זדונות ולא דברי שנאה: Joseph Hayyun, *Commentary on Esther* (Russian State Library, MS Guenzburg 168, fols 60ʳ–97ᵛ), fol. 89ʳ.

22 For the circulation of foreign books in Portugal, see Adelaide Miranda and Luís Ribeiro, 'Foreign Fifteenth Century Illuminated Manuscripts in Portugal: A Survey', in *O livro e as interações culturais judaico-cristãs em Portugal no final da Idade Média*, ed. by Luís Urbano Afonso and Paulo Mendes Pinto (Lisbon: Cátedra Alberto Benveniste, 2014), pp. 191–215.

external. Such a possibility is corroborated by the circulation of foreign codices in Portugal, such as, for instance, one of Ibn Gaon's Bibles;[23] also, after being acquired by Portuguese owners, several Iberian Bibles were brought into the Lisbon workshop for additional decoration.[24] However, the preference for acquiring from an external book market may not have been solely due to the lack of local production. On the contrary, the foreignness of these books added to their value; they materialized a different experience that was, nevertheless, still familiar.

Another hypothesis for the scarcity of original Portuguese illuminated books, and particularly the absence of any form of figurative art, would be a prevailing inclination towards artistic conservatism that, *in extremis*, would discourage it altogether. Indeed, in the Lisbon workshop, the conservative position is seen in the prominence of the line. Metamorphosed into filigree patterns, flourishes, and arabesques, the line governs the decoration of these manuscripts. The primary locus of artistic expression and improvisation, the ornament, had no purpose but to guide the viewer through the artefact. The lack of representational art is disguised by the *horror vacui* and the colourful abstractions of acanthus leaves, flowers, and animals, an artistic language borrowed from non-Jewish art, with the last transposed into ominous signs in the Jewish manuscripts, as in the case of the owl, so often represented in the Lisbon group.

The hypothesis of artistic conservatism in Portugal is further corroborated by contemporary examples. In New Castile, the predominant artistic language in Jewish manuscripts was also fundamentally ornamental; it also revitalized earlier traditions, for example, micrography. Moreover, as noted by David Nirenberg, the 'aesthetic anxieties' were also partly extended to Christian art during this period. Alfonso de Madrigal and New Christian Hernando de Talavera, Queen Isabella's confessors, were among those who warned against idolatry and debated how images mediate between the believer and the Divine.[25]

Hence, the lack of a tradition in book decoration in Portugal prior to the late fifteenth century underscores the way one of the vectors of the Portuguese Jewish identity was located within the Portuguese context. This is articulated with a second vector of an Iberian Sefardi identity that was fostered by the access to the external markets and the trans-territorial circulation of books, people, and ideas. Moreover, the sudden appearance of a workshop for high-end books at the end of the fifteenth century in Lisbon suggests an alignment with a transnational contemporary Jewish thought[26] and a practical response to a more profound religious sentiment among Portuguese Jewry.

Finally, the third vector to consider is the singularity of the Portuguese Jewish experience. On the one hand, the newly developed layers of colonialism and national pride in Portugal rein-

---

23 See Javier del Barco, 'Joshua Ibn Gaon's Hebrew Bibles and the Circulation of Books in the Late Medieval and Early Modern Periods', in *Patronage, Production, and Transmission of Texts in Medieval and Early Modern Jewish Cultures*, ed. by Esperanza Alfonso and Jonathan Decter (Turnhout: Brepols, 2014), pp. 267–97.

24 An example is a Bible copied and ornamented in San Felices de los Gallegos in 1472. It received an additional text and it was decorated in Lisbon by Samuel ibn Musa around or after 1482: see Copenhagen, Royal Library, Cod. Heb. 3–4.

25 David Nirenberg, *Aesthetic Theology and Its Enemies: Judaism in Christian Painting, Poetry and Politics* (Waltham, MA: Brandeis University Press, 2015), p. 41.

26 Isaac Canpanton wrote:
אין חכמת אדם מגעת אלא עד מקום שספריו מגיעין ולכן ימכור
אדם כל מה שיש לו ויקנה ספרים
('One is wise only as much as the wisdom of one's books, and therefore one should sell all that he has and buy books'), in *Darke ha-talmud* ('Ways of the Talmud') [in Hebrew], chap. 6.08. in the Venice edition of 1665.

forced the old mythological roots of Sefarad and the overall belief of Sefardi supremacy.[27] Further, for most of the fifteenth century, Portuguese Jews were spared from direct conflict, as they witnessed social turmoil in other regions and, instead, were actively engaged in the Portuguese Expansion. On the other hand, Jewish and, mainly, converso immigration after 1391 eventually affected the local populations in Portugal. The accusation on the part of local authorities that Portuguese Jews aided conversos became frequent: if some were fined, others like David ben Solomon ibn Yahya were forced to flee. A growing fear of apostasy spread. The circumstances in North Africa, where Portugal secured several strongholds, were no better. Around 1472, Abravanel went to Arzila to rescue 250 enslaved Jews. In a letter to Yehiel of Pisa, he revealed his distress and his sense of the precarious situation of Jews everywhere.[28]

Eventually, the Spanish expulsion and successive bouts of plague also had a direct impact on book production in Portugal. Around 1492, both the Lisbon workshop and the Lisbon press closed their doors. Book production was clearly also minimal in the following years as there are no extant books from 1493. Hebrew printing continued in Leiria, but none of the manuscripts copied after 1492 in Lisbon include painted decorations. Still, soon after the Spanish expulsion, life seemed to return to normal, and there was no hint of the fact that in a few years, Portugal, too, would expel its Jewish population.

Jewish Intellectual Production in Transition in Portugal

In most twentieth-century sources, the lack of foresight regarding a possible imminent expulsion from Spain and the creeping apostasy was interpreted as a reflection of the absence of rabbinic leadership among the last Iberian generation, as well as a sign of intellectual mediocrity. More recently, Marc Saperstein offered critical counterpoints to such views, arguing that leadership during that period should be evaluated in its specific historical context and not from a modern perspective. Further, contesting the notion of intellectual mediocrity, he distinguishes between oral and written productions, noting that religious influence was predominantly achieved orally, particularly through sermonizing. Finally, he contends that a leadership role should not be construed as the ability to see the future or chart new paths but rather as the capacity to strengthen the commitment to tradition, which, for Saperstein, was undoubtedly achieved by the last Iberian leaders.[29]

Saperstein is not alone in his revision. Eleazar Gutwirth also paints a brighter picture against the usual dark colours that often characterize this period;[30] Mark Meyerson goes to the extent of seeing it as a 'renaissance'.[31] Eric Lawee also

---

27 Ram ben Shalom, 'The Myths of Troy and Hercules as Reflected in the Writings of Some Jewish Exiles from Spain', in *Jews, Muslims and Christians in and around the Crown of Aragon*, ed. by Harvey J. Hames (Leiden: Brill, 2004), pp. 229–54.

28 See Isaac Abravanel's letter to Yehiel da Pisa in 1472, in Cohen-Skalli, *Letters*, pp. 101–31. See also Cedric Cohen-Skalli, 'Don Isaac Abravanel and the Capture of Arzila in August 1471: Expansion, Communal Leadership and Cultural Networks', in *Portuguese Jews, New Christians, and 'New Jews'*, ed. by Bruno Feitler and Claude B. Stuczynski (Leiden: Brill, 2018), pp. 56–72.

29 Marc Saperstein, 'The Quality of Rabbinic Leadership in the Generation of Expulsion', in *Anuario de Estudios Medievales*, 42 (2012), pp. 95–118 (pp. 102–05).

30 Eleazar Gutwirth, 'Towards Expulsion: 1391–1492', in *Spain and the Jews: The Sefardi Experience, 1492 and After*, ed. by Elie Kedourie (London: Thames and Hudson, 1992), pp. 51–73.

31 Mark Meyerson, *A Jewish Renaissance in Fifteenth-Century Spain* (Princeton: Princeton University Press, 2004). It should be noted that Meyerson builds his case

argues against the 'gloom-filled parentheses' of this period. He offers a more moderate perspective, suggesting that although the intellectual production of earlier times could not be matched, the late fifteenth century was also a defining moment for Judaism.[32] With this in mind, we can proceed to consider the works that circulated in Portugal during that period, knowing beforehand that the extant written production is a just a fraction of what was preached, written, copied, and printed. Still, it is possible to get a general idea of the predominant tendencies and, hopefully, better grasp the Portuguese Jewish intellectual production.

Apart from the scientific output, as that has been amply covered, the surviving genres suggest an active regulation of Jewish life in spiritual and behavioural terms. Solomon Alami was among the most prominent influences: 'If you ask yourself, "wherefore have these things come upon us", know that we brought this upon ourselves by our many sins'.[33] These words, penned in 1415, were written more than two decades after he arrived in Portugal. He considered that the ordeals the Iberian communities faced were a consequence of a lack of zeal for Scripture and liturgical devotion. We can appreciate the traction of Alami's words in Portugal, where the fear of apostasy only increased with the influx of Iberian émigrés, even if such fear was ascribed to the challenging of the always delicate status quo.

Alami's topoi can be discerned in literary production throughout the fifteenth century, when modes and genres such as *musar* or ethical literature,[34] biblical exegesis, and grammatical studies predominated, but *consolatio*, history, and other humanist genres are also in evidence. Two editions of Proverbs with commentaries that were printed a few years apart point towards the interest in *musar*. The first, completed in Lisbon around 1492, includes an original commentary by David ben Solomon ibn Yahya entitled *Qav ve-naqi* ('A Small but Clear Measure').[35] The other was accompanied by Menahem Meiri and Levi ben Gershom's commentaries and Targum Jonathan and was printed in Leiria.[36] The date, an acrostic, can be read as 1492 or 1497, but the latter is unlikely. Also in the *musar* category is Asher ben Yehiel's *Collection of Responsa*, known in two handwritten copies, from Faro;[37] Jonah Gerondi's *Sefer ha-yir'ah* ('Book of Piety') and *Sod ha-teshuvah* ('Secret of Repentance') were printed with Joshua ben Joseph ha-Levi's *Halikhot 'olam* ('Methodology of Mishna and Talmud')

---

around a specific location, Valencia.

32 Eric Lawee, 'Sefardic Intellectuals: Challenges and Creativity (1391–1492)', in *The Jew in Medieval Iberia, 1100–1500*, ed. by Jonathan Ray (Boston: Academic Studies Press, 2012), pp. 350–91 (pp. 351–52).

33 Solomon Alami, *Iggeret musar – Epistle of Admonition or Why Catastrophes Come*, ed. by Abraham M. Haberman (Jerusalem: Mossad Ha-Rav Kook, 1946), esp. pp. 40–49.

34 In this context, *musar* is understood as a literary mode rather than a specific genre: 'The use of the term looks back to a long history — from the Bible to the present day — and that it has thus been employed with many different connotations and in different contexts [...] *musar* manifests itself in multiple genres, multiple stylistic garbs, and multiple languages. It can offer general principles for spiritual improvement or clear instructions for everyday conduct, provide strategies for change by deliberately triggering feelings of anxiety, and serve, in the biblical sense of the word, the function of an admonisher', in Patrick Benjamin Koch, 'Mysticism, Pietism, Morality: An Introduction', *European Journal of Jewish Studies*, 14 (2020), pp. 169–76 (p. 169).

35 BHB 000304454, GW M35789. The same text was printed in the *editio princeps* of Daniel Bomberg's Rabbinic Bible of 1516–17, but not in the 1518 edition.

36 BHB 000313436; GW M35791. Sponsored by Samuel Colodro, the colophon reproduces the one in the Lisbon Bible, but the date is an acrostic.

37 One volume was copied by an anonymous scribe for Ephraim Caro in 1481 (Cambridge, University Library, MS Add. 503); the other by Manasseh ben Moses ben Benjamin for Jacob ben Nehemiah in 1489 (BnF, hébr. 420).

in Leiria,[38] the last probably during the author's lifetime.

However, it was in biblical commentaries that Portuguese Jews became prominent. Joseph Hayyun, an important figure in Lisbon, authored several such commentaries.[39] His approach to biblical exegesis can be traced to Isaac Canpanton's *iyyun* ('logic interpretation') and *pilpul* ('analytical disputation methods') for talmudic studies but also denotes humanist trends. One of the most striking aspects of Hayyun's work is that he resorted to many categories found in the Latin exordial tradition and made an unprecedented use of prologue headings and progression from topic to topic.[40]

Hayyun was the head of a yeshiva in Lisbon which was attended by several figures of the last generation of Iberian intellectuals. Nevertheless, it was not Hayyun but Abravanel who became best known as a biblical commentator.[41] The latter's voluminous works are characterized by the division of the biblical text into literary units prefaced by a series of questions and observations, a method commonly known as *accessus ad auctores*. Both Hayyun and Abravanel conveyed moderate rationalism and familiarity with Latin sources, and both adopted similar exegetical methods. However, Abravanel's scope and hermeneutic proclivities have rightfully given him a prominent place in the history of biblical exegesis, as he epitomized the transition from medieval to early modern Sefardi scholarship.

Abravanel is also known for his humanist rhetoric, seen in the consolatory style of his personal letters, including one in Portuguese.[42] The *consolatio* literary tradition would become quite popular among Portuguese New Christian authors. For Abravanel, however, the assimilation of this genre carried over into his correspondence and featured in his autobiographical introductions in biblical commentaries. According to Cédric Cohen-Skalli: 'In his introductions he entwined his own history with that of "his people" so that

---

38 BHB 139373; GW M11941. Printed between 1492 and 1496.

39 Commentaries to Song of Songs (London, BL, Or. 1004); Jeremiah (BL, Add. 27560); Esther (Guenzburg, MS 168); Psalms (with Qimhi) in an edition of Psalms and Proverbs, together with commentaries by David Qimhi and David ibn Yahya, printed in Salonica by Judah Gedalya, in 1523 (BHB 184628); and *'Avot*, printed in 1578 by the author's great great-grandson, in Istanbul (BHB 151136). As a side note, Ezra ben Solomon copied a volume for Moses ben Abraham Hayyun in 1473–74, most likely Joseph's brother (Guenzburg, MS 926) with various texts such as sermons and commentaries, including Samuel ben Moses Qimhi's commentary on Song of Songs and David Qimhi's commentary on Genesis. In addition, there is a volume copied by Joseph ben Moses ibn Hayyun, or possibly his nephew, in 1475, with Moses ibn Ezra's *Sefer ha-tarshish*, Joseph Ezobi's *Ke'erat kesef*, and Hay ben Sherira's *Sefer mishlei* (New York: Jewish Theological Seminary, MS 3167).

40 See in particular Eric Lawee, 'Introducing Scripture. The *accessus ad auctores* in Hebrew Exegetical Literature from the Thirteenth to the Fifteenth Centuries', in *With Reverence for the Word: Medieval Scriptural Exegesis in Judaism, Christianity, and Islam*, ed. by Jane Dammen McAuliffe, Barry Dov Walfish, and Joseph W. Goering (Cambridge: Cambridge University Press, 2003), pp. 157–79.

41 Commentaries to the Pentateuch, in Venice, 1579 (BHB 106706); Former Prophets, in Pesaro, 1511 (BHB 182156); Latter Prophets, in Pesaro *c*. 1520 (BHB 182156); Messianic exegetical work on Daniel, entitled *Ma'ayanei ha-yeshu'ah* ('Wellsprings of Salvation'), printed in Salonica *c*. 1526 (BHB 106695). Other works authored by Abravanel that were produced in the first half of the sixteenth century include *Nahlat 'avot* ('Inheritance of the Fathers'), printed with *Zevah pesah* ('Passover Offering') and *Rosh 'amanah* ('The Pinnacle of Faith'), a commentary on Maimonides Guide for the Perplexed in Istanbul, in 1505 (BHB 151125, 118961 and 106714). Abravanel also authored *'Ateret zeqenim* ('Crown of the Elders') and part of *Mirkevet ha-mishneh* ('The Second Chariot'), a commentary on Deuteronomy, while in Portugal. See Marvin J. Heller, *Further Studies in the Making of the Early Hebrew Book* (Leiden and Boston: Brill, 2013). See in particular p. 153, ft. 4 and p. 350.

42 The letter was published by Herman Prins Salomon in 'The Letter of Dom Isaac Abravanel to the Count of Faro' [in Portuguese], in *Cadernos de Estudos Sefarditas*, 2 (2002), pp. 135–40.

Jewish biblical commentary becomes, especially after a national disaster such as the expulsion, an essential instrument in reconstructing the leader's relationship to his community'.[43]

The interest in and writing of biblical exegesis among Portuguese Jews was only surpassed by a concern for grammar. Lexicographic works such as Nathan ben Yehiel's *Sefer he-'aruk* ('Talmudic Dictionary') and David Qimhi's *Sefer ha-shorashim* ('Book of Roots') circulated in Portugal at least from the end of the thirteenth century,[44] but there was an increase in grammatical works penned and printed by Portuguese Jews in the late fifteenth century as well. For example, David ben Solomon ibn Yahya authored *Leshon limmudim* ('Language of Learning'), a concise grammar divided into four *sha'arim* ('gates'), each subdivided into chapters,[45] and *Sheqel ha-qodesh* ('Holy Sheqel').[46]

Lisbon-born Moses ben Shem Tov ibn Habib authored *Perah shoshan* ('Flowers of the Lilies') in Naples 1484, a grammatical work influenced by Profayt Duran, which was never printed but is mentioned in later works. Ibn Habib also wrote *Marpe lashon* ('Wholesome Tongue'),[47] a didactical grammar in dialogue, which was printed with *Darke no'am* ('Ways of Delight'), a text concerned with Hebrew poetry and prosody.

Ibn Habib mentioned his Lisbon origins in the preface,[48] but both works were written in Italy in 1486. Ibn Habib eventually left Portugal for North Africa and then moved to Italy.[49] In 1488, he worked with Joseph Gunzenhauser on Abraham ibn Ezra's Commentary on the Pentateuch,[50] and two years later with Joshua Soncino on an edition of a Sefardi prayer book.[51]

This interest in Hebrew grammar links Portuguese Jews with the renewed attention to the fine details of Scripture in other parts of the Iberian Peninsula influenced by the works of Duran and Canpanton. Duran's views on the neglect of the Hebrew language and consequent Bible misinterpretations as the cause of persecution must also have served as a warning in Portugal. Hebrew was considered the 'holy language' and used for liturgical and intellectual purposes, whereas Portuguese and Castilian predominated in oral communications and daily settings. Indeed, the corpus of Portuguese in *aljamia* went beyond scientific texts and continued to grow. While more research is needed, including studies on the impact of the Portuguese language on Ladino, liturgical instructions in Portuguese prayerbooks suggest that the phenomenon of *aljamia* was common and, potentially, Judaeo-Portuguese should be revisited.

---

43 Cedric Cohen-Skalli, *Abravanel's Humanistic Rhetoric*, pp. 93–94.

44 For instance, Nathan Altasifi in Seia copied *Sefer 'arukh* in 1284–85 (Munich, Bayerische Staatsbibliothek, Cod. hebr. 142); Isaac ben Joseph Zarco copied *Sefer shorashim* in Lisbon, in 1378 (Oxford, Bodleian Library [Bod.], MS Can. Or. 67).

45 Reprinted in Istanbul *c*. 1506 together with *Sheqel* (BHB 106199). The same press edited Ibn Yahya's *Hilkhot terefot ha-sirkah* ('Laws of Adhesions in Animal Lungs'), *c*. 1515–18.

46 This work on Hebrew metre, prosody and rhetorics has been ascribed to Ibn Yahya, although opinions diverge. Apparently, Joseph Qimhi wrote a work by the same name, also on prosody.

47 BHB 106137. Printed in Istanbul *c*. 1510–14; printed also in Venice, 1546.

48 נאם משה בגו שם טוב | ספרד קירית חנה | למשפחת בני חביב | ומולדתו באשבונה | קהלה המפוארה | ובגולה לראש פינה | ובתורה ובחכמה | ובמצות מצויינה | וביחס ובעושר | ובכבוד מנוינה

('Word of Moses ben Shem Tov, who lived in the city of Sefarad, of the family of the Ben-Habib, born in Lisbon, noble community, angular stone in the Diaspora, in the Torah and in Science, and by good deeds eminent, as well as by race and wealth, and with honours endowed').

49 Ibn Habib also authored a commentary on Yedidiah Bedersi's *Behinat 'olam* ('Examination of the World') and translated medical texts entitled *She'elot u-teshuvot* ('Questions and Answers') and *Qiryat 'arba'ah* ('Town of the Four'), no longer extant.

50 BHB 106360. GW 00114.

51 BHB 306778. GW M19933.

Finally, Duran's disjuncture between external conduct and internal orientation was familiar to Portuguese Jews. Despite the fact that there was no active persecution, the duality of a well-adjusted community and inner fear of apostasy paved the way for his words in Portugal. In *Ma'aseh 'efod* ('Work of the Priestly Breastplate'), an apparently innocuous grammatical work, he 'articulated a version of a kind of converso religion: internally oriented and for the most part independent of the commandments'.[52] His vision of Jewish spirituality, defined by engagement with Scripture, challenges many aspects of late medieval Jewish thought, which saw the Talmud, philosophy, or Kabbalah as the source of that spirituality.

Material Entanglements: Markets in Transition

To some extent, Duran's views on book materiality also served as the subtext for Jewish book production in Portugal during the fifteenth century. In *Ma'aseh 'efod*, he specified three means of attaining the 'wisdom of the Torah': reading and intensive study, vocal recitation, and contemplation. For Duran, Scripture was best studied from texts in square script, which drawn carefully, can help the reader to memorize the words. He went on to recommend that one read books with script that is more 'thick and heavy' rather than 'delicate' in manuscripts that are beautifully ornamented, for 'the contemplation and study of pleasing forms, beautiful images and pictures widen and stimulate the spirit, in study halls that are pleasantly decorated'.[53]

Of course, seeing Duran's words as the single reason behind the Lisbon workshop would be simplistic, but it is also hard to ignore the fact that those manuscripts embody the somatic experience he described. For Duran, the power of Scripture was beyond meaning; to some extent, the physical presence of the object stood in place of the Divine, and in what he called *miqdash me'at* ('small sanctuary') — Scripture and a place of worship are the same.[54]

Similar to other Iberian productions, in the Lisbon handwritten Bibles, the tripartite organization — Pentateuch, Prophets, and Writings — emulates the structure of Temple and masoretic fragments were placed at the beginning of the codices to serve as a 'fence around the Law'.[55] In these books, carefully drawn script in a large module, with pronounced serifs; abundant dilation; comfortable page layouts, which contrast with the tight meshes of Castilian and Italian manuscripts; a constant number of characters per line; and aligned margins guide their contemplators, perhaps 'in order to alter their own spiritual realities — and perhaps that of the Jewish nation as a whole'.[56]

---

52 Maud Kozodoy, *The Secret Faith of Maestre Honoratu: Profayt Duran and Jewish Identity in Late Medieval Iberia* (Philadelphia: University of Pennsylvania Press, 2015), p. 177.

53 הדרך השישי שהיה העיון תמיד בספרים היפים והנאים מנוי ויופי הכתיבה והקלפים ומהודרים בזיוניהם ובכיסוייהם ושיהיו מקומות העיון רצוני בתי המדרש, in *Ma'ase 'efod*, p. 19.

54 *Ma'ase Efod*, p. 19. See also the discussion on sensory aspects of Jewish art and, particularly, Duran's views on Scripture, in Kalman P. Bland, *The Artless Jew* (Princeton, NJ: Princeton University Press, 2000), pp. 82-91.

55 Rabbi Akiva, in the Mishna, Tractate *'Avot* 3:13. For the specific use of Masorah as a 'fence', see Joseph Gutmann, 'Masorah Figurata: The Origins and Development of a Jewish Art Form', in *Sacred Images: Studies in Jewish Art from Antiquity to the Middle Ages*, ed. by Joseph Gutmann (Northampton: Variorum Reprints, 1989), pp. 49-62. See also Annette Weber, 'The Masorah is a Fence to the Torah': Monumental Letters and Micrography in Medieval Ashkenazi Bibles, *Ars Judaica*, 11 (2015). pp. 7-30.

56 Theodor Dunkelgrün, 'Tabernacles of the Text: A Brief Visual History of the Hebrew Bible', in *Impagination – Layout and Materiality of Writing and Publication: Interdisciplinary Approaches from East and West*, ed. by

At the same time, old traditions gave way to new ones in the Lisbon manuscripts. For example, we can see that the biblical text in those manuscripts was copied in a careful semi-cursive script, vocalized with ample dilation. Further, despite the acknowledged purpose of Masorah — to preserve the holy text — masoretic notes were often omitted. However, if we consider the meditative purposes of these codices, the Masorah becomes secondary. In fact, a similar phenomenon is reflected in contemporary manuscripts from south Castile, where the micrographic text of the Masorah was used to depict elaborate decorative compositions, but actually reading it is almost an impossibility.

Portuguese printed books are also interesting examples of transition in terms of page layout. For example, on the first five pages of the Pentateuch printed on vellum in Faro in 1487, the Targum Onqelos in very small type in the upper and lower margins frames the two columns of text, so that it resembles the typical layout of handwritten liturgical Pentateuchs. Apparently, there was a change of heart, and after these initial pages the Targum disappears,[57] but around that time, the same press edited and printed a small-sized edition of just the Targum.[58]

In Lisbon as well, biblical editions no longer reflected traditional manuscript layouts. In the *Lisbon Pentateuch* (1491), the biblical text is in the centre, surrounded by the Targum Onqelos in the outer margin and Rashi's commentary in the upper and lower margins; instead of masoretic treatises, a poem by David ben Joseph ibn Yahya, the editor, serves as the epigraph. The *Lisbon Pentateuch* appears in two editions, on vellum and on paper, both in two volumes. Ibn Yahya worked with Joseph Calfon and Judah Gedalya, who would later be involved in the Salonica press.[59] In the following year, the Lisbon press published an edition of Isaiah and Jeremiah with David Qimhi's commentary in the margins.[60] An edition of Proverbs, printed on an unknown date, is accompanied by David ben Solomon ibn Yahya's commentary *Qav ve-naqi*.[61]

Page layouts from Leiria closely resemble those from Lisbon. An edition of Proverbs printed there between 1492 and 1497 includes Targum Jonathan and commentaries by Menahem Meiri and Levi ben Gershom.[62] Given that the Lisbon edition was completed around 1492, the earlier date seems the more likely. The patronage of Samuel Colodro, from Lisbon, might also mean that the Leiria edition was related to the Lisbon edition of Proverbs. As I noted, Lisbon was deeply affected by the arrival of Iberian Jews and several bouts of the plague in and around 1492. In Leiria, the edition of the Former Prophets, completed in 1494, is accompanied by Targum

---

Ku-ming (Kevin) Chang, Anthony Grafton, and Glenn W. Most (Berlin and Boston: De Gruyter, 2021), pp. 47–89 (p. 81).

57 BHB 312573. GW M30631. The only extant imprint is at the British Library (C.49.c.1).
58 GW M4477610 and GW M4477620. Two leaves are kept at Bod. (MS App. Add. fol. 56), corresponding to Genesis 8:22–14:4. A badly damaged fragment of Numbers is held by the Taylor-Schechter Genizah in Cambridge (Box 12). Two leaves belonging to the former Wineman Collection were auctioned by Kestenbaum in 2004 (Lot 55). This refers to the Targum for Genesis 38:11–40:7, and Exodus 3:15–5:12. Finally, another fragment (two pages) is kept in the Michael Jeselsohn Collection (no. 7), corresponding to Exodus 7:16–9:7 and 9:8–10:17.

59 BHB 309260. GW M30638. Typographical differences suggest that the vellum was the earliest. Joseph Calfon's name appears in the colophon, and following Moses Marx, there is a reference after Genesis 49:8 to 'Leão' ('lion'), whom he identifies as Judah Gedalya, in 'A Catalogue of the Hebrew Books Printed in the Fifteenth Century now in the Library of the Hebrew Union College', *Studies in Bibliography and Booklore*, 1 (1953–54), pp. 21–47 (p. 29).
60 BHB 202667. GW M35724.
61 BHB 304454. GW M35789.
62 BHB 313436. GW M35791. The date can be read as 25 July 1492 or 30 June 1497.

Jonathan and commentaries by Qimhi and Gershonides.⁶³ From Lisbon to Leiria, juxtaposed texts gradually engulfed the biblical text, and page layouts became more complex. Clearly, in addition to contemplation, these codices were intended for study.

Most Portuguese biblical imprints include some form of adornment such as large decorative initials to signal the beginning of sections (a practice not seen in the Lisbon manuscripts),⁶⁴ at least one title panel, and full-page borders.⁶⁵ In Lisbon, Nahmanides' Commentary on the Pentateuch⁶⁶ and *Sefer Abudarham* (David Abudarham's 'Order of the Prayers') start with the same full-page border composed of delicate flourishes, floral buds, and animals, which was created with a technically well-done metal-cut device, ascribed to Alfonso Fernandez de Cordoba and first used in *Manuale Caesaraugustanum* in 1486 in or around Híjar. The frame was used only once by Eleazar Alantansi in Híjar, in the Pentateuch of 1487–1488;⁶⁷ after that, it was removed to Lisbon.

The origins of the Leiria border are harder to trace. Utilized only once in Leiria, in Jacob ben Asher's *Tur 'orah hayyim* ('Way of Life') in 1495, signs of use suggest that it was acquired second hand.⁶⁸ Stylistically, it is reminiscent of mudéjar architecture and Jewish symbolism outside of the Portuguese sphere. The animals depicted illustrate Judah ben Tema's words: 'Be bold as a leopard, be agile as an eagle, swift of foot as a stag, and strong as a lion'.⁶⁹

The high cost of typographical and ornamental materials meant that they were often acquired second-hand. The press in Lisbon was paradigmatic since materials were obtained partly in Híjar, as I discuss further on. Vellum printing, even if sporadic, further underscores the importance ascribed to biblical codices, but paper could be as costly, especially in the quantities required for an entire edition; estimates suggest that up to 50 per cent of the overall costs of production was allocated for paper alone. Press maintenance costs were also high, more than the actual setup, and type required for a single edition involved more capital than all the equipment in the print shop. The type had to be 'sturdy' enough to withstand a few thousand impressions for a book to be a profitable product.

In its early stages, then, the printing press was an expensive endeavour that continued to serve a high-end market, and the associated costs might well have accounted for the short lives of so many Iberian presses. It is possible that Eleazar Alantansi, in Híjar, had to lend or sell part of his material, including the Cordoba border, to continue to finance his press. Indeed, the Pentateuch of 1490 includes only fragments of the famous frame.⁷⁰ Similarly, the border was only used twice in Lisbon in 1489, and was removed to Istanbul shortly thereafter.

Given the cost of print, and perhaps suggested by manuscript patronage, sponsorship of printed editions was also sought and is well attested in Portugal, In order to keep their printshop afloat, in addition to Colodro's patronage of the Leiria Proverbs, the Ortas family resorted to sponsorship beyond the sphere of Jewish book culture. In 1496 they produced two editions of

---

63 BHB 313516. GW M35717.
64 For instance, the *Faro Pentateuch* begins with a large (woodcut) bet, and large decorated initials acquired in Híjar were used in Lisbon.
65 See the Leiria edition of Former Prophets.
66 BHB 150431. GW M25521. Entitled *Hidushe ha-torah* ('Commentary on the Pentateuch'). It includes Nahmanides' letter from Jerusalem to his son (*Iggeret ha-Ramban*) and 'Prayer over the Ruins of Jerusalem'.
67 BHB 312542. GW M30628.
68 BHB 302284. GW M10408. No indication of the place where it was copied, but it is typographically similar to other of Leiria's imprints.

69 הוי עז כנמר וקל כנשר ורץ כצבי וגיבור כארי in *'Avot* 5. 20.
70 BHB 312552. GW M30632.

Abraham Zacuto's *Ha-hibur ha-gadol Almanach perpetuum*: the Latin version, translated by Joseph Vizinho, which was sponsored by the Royal House and a Castilian edition intended for those not knowledgeable in Latin for export into the Spanish market.[71] In Lisbon, the relatively unknown *Qav ve-naqi* was printed when its author, David ibn Yahya, lived in that city, which also suggests that he sponsored the edition. Similarly, the inclusion of his poem in the Pentateuch may also point towards his patronage. Further, it is possible that Eliezer Toledano, whose name appears in the colophons of the Lisbon editions may have had a purely financial role. The Lisbon Nahmanides' colophon notes that it was completed in the house of the rabbis Tzorba and Eleazar on 16 July 1489. We hear no more about Rabbi Tzorba, but Rabbi Eleazar is mentioned in all the Lisbon colophons; later, Jacob ibn Habib wrote that Eleazar's surname was Toledano.

Finally, Don Samuel Gacon sponsored the edition of the Pentateuch printed in Faro, but Samuel Porteiro headed the press.[72] The Jewish community in Faro was not especially large, but it was strategically located, a commercial hub among Portugal, southern Castile, and North Africa. Faro was actually the only Portuguese press that edited talmudic treatises. The suggested number of editions vary, but at least three fragments can be ascribed to Faro, in all of which Rashi's commentary is printed in a square script, whereas other Iberian presses used a semi-cursive one.[73]

The high-end nature of the Portuguese editions is further substantiated in their typography. Several scribal practices were carried into print, which required additional effort and engendered higher costs. Malachi Beit-Arié has observed the similarity between type and script in the broader Sefardi context,[74] but the Portuguese editions are strikingly paradigmatic. If morphological aspects of script and the use of dilation mechanisms are also known from other Iberian editions, vowel points and cantillation marks were first used in Portugal.[75] A case in point is Faro. The first edition printed in that press, the 1487 Pentateuch, features vocalization marks, but the Faro marks do not reflect relevant developments in Italy, which suggests that the Faro types were cast locally.[76] Vocalization in Lisbon and, later, in Leiria was already showing improvements in

---

71 GW 115 and GW 116.
72 The identities of Gacon and Porteiro have been the subject of debate, but recently Shalom Sabar argued that Gacon was from Andalusia and fled the Inquisition to Portugal: Shalom Sabar, 'Typography, Layout and Decoration: The Printed Hebrew Book in the Iberian Peninsula and its Origins in Illuminated Manuscripts', in *Sefardic Book Art of the Fifteenth Century*, ed. by Luís U. Afonso and Tiago Moita (London and Turnhout: Harvey Miller, 2019), pp. 59–88 (p. 66).
73 These are *Masekhet gitin* ('Laws of Divorce'): GW M44828; the date, an acrostic, can be read as 1491, 1494, or 1496. See Shimon Iakerson, 'Unknown Sefardi Incunabula', in *The Late Medieval Hebrew Book in the Western Mediterranean*, ed. by Javier del Barco (Leiden: Brill, 2015), pp. 297–312. Also, *Berakhot* ('Blessings'): GW M44822 and *Shavu'ot* ('Feast of Weeks'): GW 44844.
74 Malachi Beit-Arié, 'The Relationship between Early Hebrew Printing and Handwritten Books: Attachment or Detachment', in *Library Archives and Information Studies*, ed. by Dov Schidorsky (Jerusalem: Magnes Press, 1989), pp. 1–26.
75 The first vocalized specimen is the *Faro Pentateuch*, completed on 30 June 1487. It has several limitations in terms of *dagesh* and *maqaf*, it lacks cantillation signs, and there is a 'promiscuous use of *patah, kametz, tzere*, and *segol*': Christian Ginsburg, *Introduction to the Massoretico-Critical Edition of the Hebrew Bible* (New York: Ktav, 1897), p. 819.
76 The vocalization or '*niqud* problem' was solved by Abraham ben Hayyim in Bologna in 1482. He used 'daedal' hands by Francesco Griffo da Bologna to develop vocalized Hebrew types. See the discussion in Offenberg, p. lxix.

diacritics, including the *rafe*, which was absent in Italy (and Faro).⁷⁷

The main square Lisbon type, which is not seen in the Híjar editions, strongly resembles Portuguese script and incorporates many scribal traditions apart from dilation and compression, such as detailed serifs, majuscular and minuscular characters, and a unique horseshoe diacritic.⁷⁸ The Leiria foundry was identical to the one in Lisbon, to the point of raising the question whether it borrowed the matrices from Lisbon to cast its type. The morphological resemblance to the Lisbon matrices or, more accurately, the Híjar semi-cursive type, is particularly uncanny, including a similar square variant of the *lamed* in a smaller size. The repertoire of dilated characters in Leiria was less extensive in the main square type, but it included an 'articulated *aleph*', which is not only an unusual character, but one that also appears in the manuscripts from the Lisbon workshop.⁷⁹

The presence of Híjar types in Lisbon raises a question as to the extent of the association between these presses. First, they did not operate simultaneously: the Híjar press functioned from 1485 to *c.* 1488, paused until 1490, and resumed work for its last edition that year. The Lisbon press worked in 1489, paused until 1491, and closed its doors around 1492. Of course, there could have been other editions which have not reached us, but in those we have seen there are overlaps of type and decoration materials,⁸⁰ as well as codicological practices, specifically, double-leaf signatures. Could it be that the printers and their materials moved back and forth between Híjar and Lisbon?⁸¹ If so, could this mean that Alantansi and Toledano are the same person and 'Toledano a reference to the printer's origin? If the costs associated with printing required sponsorship and also materials were constantly traded, and it is likely that mobility among printers was common. The associations among Híjar, Lisbon, and, to a lesser extent, Leiria might be examples of such mobility.

Hence, we can conclude that late fifteenth-century Portuguese books materialize a particular devotion to aesthetics, irrespective of the costs involved. In manuscripts, carefully copied texts are beautified by a colourful and delicate ornamental language; in print, such a devotion is seen in the detailed emulation of scribal practices, use of decoration, and the costly materials. To support said costs, patronage was often sought and typographical materials were acquired second- and third-hand. Moreover, the intentional replication of scribal practices in printed books as well as the interest in new page layouts in print both provide evidence of the fact that the transition from manuscript to print was an evolving process.

---

77 Of the five sets of type used in Lisbon, two were vocalized: a square type with vowel points for the central biblical text (177H) and another for the Targum (138H). The other three were from Híjar: a semi-cursive type (117H) and two square types for titles (230H and 117H), all unvocalized.

78 Still with regard to script morphology, there is a clear distinction between thick and thin strokes; as for other scribal practices, we find the use of kerning, ligatures, abbreviations, the tetragrammaton and truncation signs, and inverted *nuns*. Another prolific practice was the use of *peh* and *samekh* to indicate open and closed sections, respectively.

79 Four square types were employed in Leiria: a large one for titles (unvocalized); a medium-sized one for biblical texts, with vocalization, ligatures, compressed and dilated characters, and truncated (inverted) letters; a similar type, unvocalized, for title commentaries, and a smaller vocalized type for the Targum, also with dilated characters but lacking compression.

80 A large square type (230H) appeared in Lisbon in 1489 and in Híjar the year after; also the Cordoba frame appears only in the 1489 editions.

81 Furthermore, we cannot entirely rule out the possibility that Maimonides' *Hilkhot shehitah* ('Laws of Ritual Slaughter') was printed in Híjar, even though it is currently associated with Lisbon. Both kinds of types (230H for titles and 117H semi-cursive for the main text) were used in the two presses. The only feature that reinforces the Portuguese origin is the small size of the codex, which by itself is not enough to ascribe it to Lisbon with confidence. See BHB 313476. GW 20039.

Further Entanglements: From Portugal to the Mediterranean

In this section, I deal with book production associated with Portuguese Jews and conversos in Italy, the Ottoman Empire, and North Africa. I first note that Iberian immigration towards the eastern Mediterranean, which began before 1492, was not a mass movement, was neither immediate nor direct, and followed circuits that included North Africa and Italy. Further, Portuguese emigration has been dealt with primarily in regard to conversos, who left the country chiefly after 1536, the year that the Inquisition was officially introduced in Portugal. However, Portuguese Jews were attracted to key locations in Italy and the Ottoman Empire even before 1496, the year of the Portuguese expulsion. Immediately after that expulsion, Portuguese exiles emigrated in larger numbers, but in 1499 conversos were forbidden from leaving Portugal, an order that was not rescinded until March of 1507, in the aftermath of the Lisbon massacre of 1506.[82]

Apart from Moses ibn Habib, who worked in Italy in the late 1480s, other Portuguese exiles were actively involved in book production in Italy in the early sixteenth century. The Ibn Yahya family, whose patronage of handwritten and printed books in Portugal I discussed above, sponsored Gershom Soncino's edition of Judah ha-Levi's *Kuzari*, completed in Fano in 1506.[83] Further, David Porteiro, a relative of Samuel Porteiro (from Faro), worked with Gershom Soncino in Pesaro, serving as the editor of talmudic treatises.[84] Later, in the second half of the sixteenth century, the press in Ferrara was headed by the Portuguese conversos Yom Tob Athias (aka Alvaro de Vargas) and Abraham Usque (aka Duarte Pinhel). Among their publications was the Spanish *Ferrara Bible*[85] and Samuel Usque's *Consolaçam às Tribulaçoes de Israel* ('Consolation for the Tribulations of Israel'), both published in 1553. Their targeted market went beyond traditional Jewish circles, as they also published works by Portuguese New Christian authors such as Bernardim Ribeiro's *Menina e Moça* ('Maiden and Modest') in 1554.

The settlement of Iberian communities in the Ottoman Empire was marked by a diversity of experiences. There was no unifying Sefardi identity in the early, formative, years.[86] Language and origins were the usual loci of individual and communal identity, and we find intensely autonomous communities. In Salonica, the Portuguese exiles, as early as 1503, were organized into at least two Portuguese congregations, 'Lisbon' and 'Évora'.[87]

After an initial period of chaos, the need for a social hierarchy reasserted itself. Each community proceeded to reproduce the old social order based

---

82 Jonathan Ray, *After Expulsion: 1492 and the Making of Sefardic Jewry* (New York and London: New York University Press, 2013), p. 41.
83 BHB 000184384. The full title of the work is 'The Book of Argument and Proof in Defence of the Despised Faith'. It includes poems by Meir ben Joseph ibn Yahya of Lisbon; Joseph ibn Yahya's lineage is also noted.
84 BHB 000329271. Porteiro was also involved in the printing of *Succah* in 1515 (BHB 000328800) and *Mo'ed qatan* around 1515 (BHB 000328802).
85 The *Ferrara Bible*, in Spanish (or Ladino), was printed in 1553 in an edition dedicated to Gracia Nasi and another to the Duke of Ferrara.
86 On this subject, see Jonathan Ray, 'Creating Sefarad: Expulsion, Migration, and the Limits of Diaspora', *Journal of Levantine Studies*, 3 (2013), pp. 9–35. See also Joseph Hacker, 'The Sefardim in the Ottoman Empire in the Sixteenth Century', in *Moreshet Sefarad: The Sefardi Legacy*, ed. by Hayyim Beinart (Jerusalem: Magnes Press, 1992), pp. 109–33.
87 Joseph Garson delivered a sermon in the Évora synagogue 'on the second Sabbath following its secession from the *kahal* of Lisbon' in 1503: Minna Rozen, 'Individual and Community in the Jewish Society', in *The Jews of the Ottoman Empire*, ed. by Avigdor Levy (Princeton: Darwin Press, 1994), pp. 215–73 (p. 264, ft. 4).

on lineage and wealth. For Salonica, it is evident that social status and lineage were common motivators for marital alliances and communal organization.[88] Moreover, the increasing number of exiles led to the establishment of educational institutions. Gradually, educational and cultural facilities including communal libraries were established by wealthy families that continued to acquire manuscripts and printed works.[89] Eventually, the interest in genres beyond high culture would dominate, but in the early years of resettlement, book markets still targeted primarily a high-end Hebrew-reading clientele.

That situation was the backdrop for the first presses in Salonica. However, given the fragmentary state of so many editions, it is hard to establish the exact dates on which these presses opened. Yeshayahu Vinograd was supposedly the first to ascribe a mahzor in the Catalonian rite printed after 1500[90] and a Pentateuch, c. 1501,[91] to Salonica. If these volumes were published by Judah Gedalya, who was the first to open a press in Salonica, it is possible that he was part of one of the first waves of Portuguese immigrants in or prior to 1497. The earliest edition I consulted is a fragmentary Pentateuch with the text arranged in a single column in a vocalized square script similar to that used in Lisbon.[92] Typographically, the fragment resembles other Gedalya's editions, and Vinograd placed the imprint around 1509.

Judah Gedalya partnered with his son Moses and a daughter in his Salonica print shop. The unusual horseshoe diacritic known from Lisbon and other scribal particularities are also found in Salonica's biblical texts, which fact attests to Gedalya's involvement with both presses. Further, Gedalya marked his name in Lisbon with acrostics for both Judah Gedalya and *Leão*. Finally, his connection with Toledano is manifested in Jacob ibn Habib's introduction to *'Eyn Ya'aqov* ('Fountain of Jacob'), printed in 1516–1517.

It is reasonable to assume that the Gedalyas catered primarily to a Portuguese readership and an elitist market. Bibles, mainly on vellum, include commentaries by such Portuguese authors as David ibn Yahya for Proverbs, c. 1521, and Joseph Hayyun for Psalms, c. 1521,[93] as well as Abravanel for *Ma'ayanei ha-yeshu'ah* ('The Wellsprings of Salvation'), a commentary on Daniel, published in 1526.[94] At least one Portuguese edition was reprinted: Gerondi's *Sefer ha-yir'ah*, c. 1528.[95] They also published Portuguese-born authors such as Solomon Almoli's *Mefashar helmin* ('Dream Interpreter') in 1515[96] and Solomon Molkho's (aka Diogo Pires) *Derashot* ('Sermons') in 1529.[97]

Furthermore, there is a visual continuity between the editions by the two presses, with *targumim* and commentaries surrounding the

---

88 Joseph Hacker discusses two prominent families, the Ibn Yahya, originating in Lisbon, and Bet Ha-Levi, from Évora, in 'Continuity or Change: The Case of Two Prominent Jewish Portuguese Clans in the Ottoman Empire', in *Jewish Culture in Early Modern Europe: Essays in Honor of David B. Ruderman*, ed. by Adam Shear, Richard I. Cohen, Elchanan Reiner, and Natalie B. Dohrmann (Cincinnati: Hebrew Union College Press, 2014).

89 Menahem Schmelzer, 'Hebrew Manuscripts and Printed Books Among the Sephardim Before and After the Expulsion', in *Crisis and Creativity in the Sephardic World, 1391–1648*, ed. by Benjamin Gampel (New York: Columbia University Press, 1997), pp. 257–66.

90 BHB 330878; Vinograd, 1.

91 Vinograd, 2.

92 Vinograd, 3. As far as I know, fragments of the only known copy were previously in the Mehlman and Valmadonna Collections (twenty-eight and ten pages, respectively) and is now at the National Library of Israel in Jerusalem. There are typographical vestiges of *haftarot*.

93 BHB 184628. Vinograd, nos 28 and 30.

94 BHB 106695. Vinograd no. 36.

95 BHB: 334601. Vinograd, no. 39.

96 BHB 301059; Vinograd, no. 7. Also known as *Pitron halomot* ('Interpretation of Dreams').

97 BHB 146848; Vinograd, no. 41. Also known as *Sefer ha-mefuar* ('The Glorious Book').

biblical text; also, most of the typographical materials employed by the Gedalyas were brought from Lisbon. The two vocalized Lisbon square types were used in study Bibles,[98] but the other two Lisbon types are not found in books printed in Salonica.[99] The Híjar semi-cursive 117H was used for a Pentateuch, c. 1513,[100] *Midrash tehilim*,[101] Hagiographa with Rashi,[102] and *Mefashar helmin*, all c. 1514–1515. However, *'Eyn Ya'aqov*, 1516, was printed in a different semi-cursive script.[103] This type, which is similar to the one the Ibn Nahmias brothers employed in Istanbul, was acquired in Naples. Similarities to types also used by the Soncinos in Fano and Pesaro are considerable, so it is likely that matrices and punches were being circulated.

The next time the Híjar semi-cursive type appeared was in Fez, in Samuel Nedivot and son's *Sefer Abudarham*, 1516.[104] The edition is a faithful reproduction of the Lisbon edition, line by line, with the same diagrams but without the Cordoba border. Since the types in Fez had been used recently in Salonica, it seems reasonable to assume that the Nedivots departed from there with Gedalya's materials. The connections between Fez and Salonica are even more apparent if we consider the typographical confusion surrounding talmudic treatises ascribed to both presses and the fact that Tosafot were not included in editions from either location.[105] However, it should be noted that Astruc de Toulon published an edition of *Sefer Abudarham* in 1513 in Istanbul using the Ibn Nahmias's typographical materials. Although it does not feature the diagrams seen in the Lisbon and Fez editions, the colophon is an abridgement of the one in the Lisbon book.[106]

The overall production of Gedalya's Salonica press suggests that there were similar interests among the first generation of exiles and the Jews who remained in Portugal during the late fifteenth century, particularly the emphasis on the regulation of Jewish life. Bibles and prayer books abounded, but *musar* literature increasingly made its way into the Salonica book market.

Our final stop is in Istanbul at the David and Samuel ibn Nahmias press. The entanglements of the presses in Híjar, Lisbon, and Salonica merit some remarks, but few definite answers can be provided. It is still unclear whether the actual punches were transported to the Ottoman Empire or only the matrices. If the first was the case, the connections between Lisbon and Istanbul began immediately after the Lisbon press closed its doors. Híjar's large square type, last used in Lisbon in 1492, appeared in Istanbul's inaugural edition, *'Arba'ah turim* ('Four Rows'), completed on 13 December 1493.[107] More likely, the Ibn Nahmias brothers took decorative materials and the large type or the matrices from Híjar: the ornamental *aleph* in the *Turim* in the Híjar style is not found in the Lisbon editions and the Cordoba border does not appear in the *Turim*.

In addition to the Híjar materials, the Ibn Nahmias brothers acquired the semi-cursive type

---

98 This refers to the types used for the main text (177H) and the Targum (138H).
99 They are large square (230H) and unvocalized square (117H).
100 BHB 182159; Vinograd, no. 4. With scrolls, *haftarot*, including those for Passover, Targum Onqelos, Targum Jonathan, and Rashi's commentary. Printed on vellum.
101 BHB 146596; Vinograd, no. 5.
102 Vinograd, no. 6. Psalms, Proverbs, Job, and Daniel.
103 Vinograd, no. 8.
104 BHB 200305.
105 Marvin Heller discusses the confusion between the talmudic imprints from Salonica and Fez in *Printing the Talmud*, pp. 61–79.
106 A copy from the National Library of Israel can be consulted online: https://www.nli.org.il/he/books/NNL_ALEPH001094582/NLI [accessed in April 2022].
107 BHB 184413. Yaari, no. 1. For the discussion on the date, see Adri K. Offenberg, 'The Printing History of the Constantinople Hebrew Incunable of 1493: A Mediterranean Voyage of Discovery', *The British Library Journal*, 22 (1996), pp. 221–35.

used in the *Turim* from Joshua Soncino in Naples.[108] Following Adri Offenberg, the Soncinos prepared dilated letters for the subsequent editions, but it is possible that the Ibn Nahmias used the matrices but created their own punches.[109] Given that Gershon Soncino employed a similar semi-cursive type in Fano and Pesaro at the same time and that the Gedalyas in Salonica also used the same type after 1516, it is reasonable to assume that the matrices were in circulation. The Ibn Nahmias acquired decorative materials (a rosette and small friezes) as well as the paper they needed for their edition of the *Turim* from Italy.

For more than a decade after printing *'Arba'a turim*, the Ibn Nahmias press stopped operating. The interruption partly coincided with the war between Sultan Bayezid II and Venice, which lasted from 1496 until 1503, as very little paper was manufactured in Turkey before the eighteenth century and most of what was needed was imported from Venice. The Ibn Nahmias probably had to stop working in those years but were able to reopen in 1505. They subsequently published a Pentateuch with *haftarot*, Megillat Antiochus and Megillat Ahasuerus, Targum Onqelos, and commentaries by Rashi, Qimhi, and Ibn Ezra.[110] This edition is problematic owing to discrepancies between imprints. A fragment, now in Oxford, was printed on vellum in the Híjar semi-cursive and Lisbon square types for the text and Targum,[111] which were the types used by Judah Gedalya until 1515, and the Ibn Nahmias never worked with the Híjar semi-cursive. The Ibn Nahmias produced another edition, a copy of which is now in the Wellcome Library, using a semi-cursive type that they acquired in Naples, and the large square type is the one that appears in their 1493 edition of *'Arba'a turim*.[112] However, the types for the main text and the Targum were from Lisbon. Furthermore, the Cordoba border appears for the first time in this edition, together with the large initials used in Lisbon.[113] Thus, we cannot exclude the possibility of a close, perhaps even direct, connection between the Salonica and Istanbul presses.

Apart from the typographical entanglements, we also see an interest in Portuguese authors in Istanbul. The Ibn Nahmias published the *editio princeps* of Isaac Abravanel's *Zevah pesah* ('Passover Offering') with *Rosh 'amanah* ('The Pinnacle of Faith') and *Nahlat 'avot* ('Inheritance of the Fathers') in an edition that also features the Cordoba frame.[114] In 1506, they completed David ibn Yahya's *Leshon limmudim*, which they printed together with *Sheqel ha-qodesh*.

In 1513 Astruc de Toulon, who worked closely with the Ibn Nahmias brothers, published the second edition of *Sefer Abudarham*, which includes a colophon similar to Lisbon's *Abudarham*. Around the same year, de Toulon completed an edition of Qimhi's *Sefer ha-shorashim*, aided by Samuel Rico-Homem, whose family can be traced to Lisbon. Later, de Toulon would settle in Salonica for a short time. Thus, types, texts, and printers certainly point towards the possibility that there was a close relationship among the presses owned by Iberian exiles in Salonica, Fez, and Istanbul.

---

108 The last time the type was used in Naples by the Soncinos was for the Mishnah edition of 8 May 1492. After that, Hebrew printing in Naples came to a halt.
109 Offenberg, *The Printing History*, p. 226.
110 The Pentateuch also includes a verse from the proofreader Joseph ben Joel Vivas. Abraham ben Joseph ibn Yaish and Abraham de Paredes also worked on the edition, which was sponsored by Jeshuah ben Saadiah and Isaac Qasputah. See BHB 308832. Yaari, no. 2.
111 Bod.Vet.Or.d.Heb.3 (Heb 28).
112 For the Wellcome copy, see Nigel Allen, 'A Typographical Odyssey: The 1505 Constantinople Pentateuch', *Cambridge University Press for the Royal Asiatic Society* (1991), pp. 343–51.
113 A third imprint analysed is in the National Library of Israel (formerly Valmadonna Trust 6385), and it coincides with this one.
114 BHB 151125.

Finally, it is now possible to clarify the origins of an oblong volume with a liturgy for Yom Kippur, erroneously ascribed to Juan de Lucena.[115] Based on typographical similarities to books printed in Lisbon, specifically, the large square type for titles and what seems to be the small vocalized square type for text, it is probable that it originated in that city. The paper watermarks date from 1487,[116] and there is an inscription in Portuguese on one of the parchment folios that initially protected the book.

The oblong format is associated primarily with manuscripts from North Africa and to a lesser extent with those from the Iberian Peninsula. In Portugal, this format seems to have been popular in the fifteenth century, especially for prayer books and Psalters.[117] Also in an oblong format are two liturgies for *Tish'a b'av*, one handwritten, currently dispersed in three libraries,[118] and the other, a print fragment with *kinot*, in the Bodleian Library that can be linked to Portugal.[119] Both require more research, but textual contents of the handwritten liturgy and typographical features in the Bodleian fragment similar to those associated with the Lisbon press place them within the Portuguese sphere.

Conclusions

In the foregoing pages, I discussed the way Jewish books in Portugal and books produced by Portuguese Jews in the early years of the Sefardi Diaspora articulated the 'interconnections among intellectual creativity and the political, social, and technological conditions' that would become the pattern of the early modern Jewish cultural formation.[120] Phenomena such as mobility and enhanced contacts, communal cohesiveness, and an explosion of knowledge are particularly evident, whereas there is little that bears any witness to crises in authority or blurring of religious identities.

In Portugal, the increase in book production in the late fifteenth century took place in a specific setting, one that was marked primarily by a constant negotiation between a stable socio-political reality and the intensification of a Portuguese identity. That identity, which was anchored in deep acculturation, was created in opposition to 'others' — Iberian Jews and, especially, conversos. At the same time, the sudden local production of luxury books should be interpreted as a practical response to a renewed religious experience aligned with the broader Iberian context. The artefactual value of books, particularly Bibles, materializes that experience and further suggests that print targeted the same market. The efforts in transferring scribal practices into print, often at a cost, underscore the transitory nature of the early years of print and contradict the idea of rupture. At the same time, experiments with layout, unprecedented in handwritten Bibles, further suggest that the emphasis moved gradually from contemplation to application, that is, study, and underscore the transition process from manuscript into print.

Still not a particularly profitable business, print was primarily a labour of love. Hence,

---

115 GW M19929. The format was justified by a 'Marrano' origin of the owner, who, 'when surprised during the prayers, [would] slip it into his sleeve or pocket': in Alexander Marx, *Bibliographical Studies and Notes on Rare Books and Manuscripts in the Library of The Jewish Theological Seminary of America* (New York: Jewish Theological Seminary, 1977), p. 65.

116 The paper watermarks consist of a glove and a star extending from the middle finger, close to Briquet t 11162 (1487).

117 For the handwritten oblong prayer book for Yom Kippur, see Bod., MS Or. 5. Identified Psalters are: Parma, Biblioteca Palatina, MS Parm. 1712, copied by Samuel ibn Musa in 1476; Vatican, Biblioteca Apostolica, Vat. ebr. 463, ascribed to Ibn Musa; and Vat. ebr. 473 (Biblioteca Apostolica Vaticana), copied in 1495.

118 Lisbon, NL, MS IL. 3, London, BL, Add. 20747 and Évora, Public Library, Cod. CXXIV/2-47d, n. 3.

119 Bod.Vet.Or.e.Heb.7.

120 Ruderman, p. 11.

acquiring sponsorships and using second- and third-hand typographical materials were common practices and the same was true in the early Sefardi Diaspora. Therefore, it is hard to separate the activity of the Portuguese presses and agents from the broader Iberian and Sefardi context. Typographical materials underscore the close association between Híjar and Lisbon. Faro catered to a readership beyond the Portuguese sphere and the country's borders, and it is increasingly evident that there was also a close relationship between Lisbon and Salonica, as well as among Salonica, Fez, and Istanbul. The use of the same typographical materials in these presses and a similar interest in such authorities as Isaac Abravanel, Joseph Hayyun, and other Portuguese authors suggest an affinity between printers and readers in Salonica and Istanbul. The overlapping activity of these presses, sometimes with the same typographical materials and agency, corroborates the non-linear progression of work in the printshops.

Furthermore, in Salonica, the emphasis on Portuguese authors and the material and visual aspects of the books produced in the early Diaspora suggest an elitist attitude and an effort to reinforce a Portuguese identity among Iberian exiles. Such a position is in blatant contrast with the actions of the subsequent generations in the Ottoman Empire, which fostered a Sefardi identity and invested in non-elitist productions, a position that was aligned with the exclusivist nature of the *Nação Portuguesa* of the sixteenth and seventeenth centuries.

AVRIEL BAR-LEVAV

The Emergence of the Printing Self

Egodocuments and Micro-Egodocuments in Jewish Paratexts from Manuscript to Print*

For Elchanan Reiner

Introduction: Telling Our Story

In this chapter I attempt to establish the connection between Hebrew printed paratexts and egodocuments, a connection that scholarship has not yet clearly defined. From this comes what I suggest calling, 'the emergence of the printing self', by which I refer to a process of formulation of self-identity that was invigorated by printing. I also present what I suggest calling 'micro-egodocuments' — short stories or statements that are integrated in paratexts — and to give some examples of such texts.

Jewish manuscripts include paratexts (less often than in printed books), mainly colophons and diagrams,[1] and in some of them writers or copyists wrote about themselves as well. In the fluid history of specific manuscripts, we sometimes find layers of paratexts, from both the time of production and from subsequent years of use. However, it was with the emergence of the printed book that the personal voice found distinct places: the frontispiece, addressed to the reader, acknowledgements and dedications, printers' introductions, and colophons.[2] How can we explain this? As a unique and personal artifact, the Jewish manuscript was an object of self-expression.[3] Paradoxically, compared with

---

* Part of this chapter is based on a lecture in honour of my friend Elchanan Reiner, in Cracow, June 2014. I am grateful to Gene Matanky and Gadi Sagiv for their reading and comments.

Avriel Bar-Levav • The Open University of Israel

1 See Michael Riegler, 'Colophons of Medieval Hebrew Manuscripts as Historical Sources' [in Hebrew] (unpublished doctoral thesis, The Hebrew University of Jerusalem, 1995); Daniel Abrams, 'Kabbalistic Paratext', *Kabbalah*, 26 (2012), pp. 7–24.
2 Concerning these book sections, see Dennis Duncan and Adam Smyth, *Book Parts* (Oxford: Oxford University Press, 2019).
3 See, e.g., Bezalel Narkiss, *Hebrew Illuminated Manuscripts* (Jerusalem: Keter 1969); Katrin Kogman-Appel, *Jewish Book Art between Islam and Christianity: The Decoration of Hebrew Bibles in Medieval Spain*, trans. by Judith Davidson (Leiden: Brill, 2004). Concerning the individual nature of Hebrew manuscripts, see Malachi

the producers of printed books, the makers of manuscripts were somehow less inclined to talk about themselves, their labours, and their emotions — that is, to use a modern term I shortly elaborate on — they were less inclined to produce egodocuments. Nor were they inclined to add numerous paratexts to the volumes they produced.[4] It was the shift to the mass production of printed books, done by a group of largely anonymous individuals, instead of being the product of (usually) one copyist, for himself or for another person who commissioned the copying,[5] that prompted the makers of these new kinds of books to talk about their work and about themselves, to render themselves familiar to their potential customers, convincing them of their product's high quality, and to gain what Pollie Bromilow suggests is the authority of the book.[6] In so doing, they created a platform for presenting themselves as printers or authors — a platform that was part of 'the emergence of the printing self'.

I describe this process as having begun with members of the printing community speaking about themselves in the context of printing, in order to present their efforts regarding the book, to explain their choices, such as which manuscripts they used (e.g., for the Palestinian and Jerusalem Talmuds or the Zohar[7]), and to demonstrate the value of their product. Later on, they used these paratextual platforms to talk about themselves *qua* individuals, apart from their printing efforts, which was one of the roots of Jewish egodocuments.[8] In other words, Jewish printed paratexts, especially introductions and colophons, contain sections that are egodocuments. I suggest that we call these micro-egodocuments, as they are short personal stories that are embedded in larger texts and represent the printing self.

Egodocuments and Paratexts

Both egodocuments and paratexts existed long before these terms were coined by European scholars. 'Egodocuments' was formulated by the Dutch Jewish historian Jacques Presser

---

Beit-Arié, 'The Individual Circumstances of the Hebrew Book Production and Consumption', in *Manuscrits hebreux et arabes: Melanges en l'honneur de Colette Sirat*, ed. by Judith Olszowy-Schlanger and Nicholas de Lange (Turhout: Brepols, 2014), pp. 17–28; Malachi Beit-Arié, 'Commissioned and Owner-Produced Manuscripts in the Sephardi Zone and Italy in the Thirteenth–Fifteenth Centuries', in *The Late Medieval Hebrew Book in the Western Mediterranean: Hebrew Manuscripts and Incunabula in Context*, ed. by Javier del Barco (Leiden: Brill, 2015), pp. 13–27.

4 See, e.g., Dalia-Ruth Halperin, *Illuminating in Micrography: The Catalan Micrography Mahzor-MS Hebrew 8° 6527 in the National Library of Israel* (Leiden: Brill, 2013).

5 Sometimes several copyists executed one document, yet each had a specific part he (or in some rare cases she) worked on.

6 See the interesting volume edited by Pollie Bromilow, *Authority in European Book Culture 1400–1600* (Surrey: Ashgate 2013), and especially the introduction and the chapter by Brian Richardson, 'Manuscript, Print, Orality and the Authority of Texts in Renaissance Italy', pp. 15–29.

7 See Raphael Natan Nuta Rabbinovicz, with additions by Abraham Meir Habermann, *An Essay on the Printing of the Talmud* [in Hebrew] (Jerusalem: Mosad Ha-Rav Kook, 1952); Yakov Z. Mayer, *Editio Princeps: The 1523 Venice Edition of the Palestinian Talmud and the Beginning of Hebrew Printing* [in Hebrew] (Jerusalem: Magnes Press, 2022); Boaz Huss, *The Zohar: Reception and Impact*, trans. by Yudith Nave (Oxford: Littman Library of Jewish Civilization 2016).

8 Avriel Bar-Levav, 'When I Was Alive: Jewish Ethical Wills as Egodocuments', in *Egodocuments and History: Autobiographical Writing in its Social Context since the Middle Ages*, ed. by Rudolf Dekker (Rotterdam: Erasmus University Rotterdam and Hilversum Verloren, 2002), pp. 45–59; Joseph H. Chajes, 'Accounting for the Self: Preliminary Generic-historical Reflections on Early Modern Jewish Egodocuments', *Jewish Quarterly Review*, 95 (2005), pp. 1–15; Michael Stanislawsky, *Autobiographical Jews: Essays in Jewish Self-Fashioning* (Seattle: University of Washington Press, 2004), pp. 3–17.

and 'paratexts' by the French literary scholar Gérard Genette. I begin with paratexts. Genette introduced the term in a French book at the end of the 1980s, and an English translation appeared in the late 1990s.[9] Paratexts are writings that accompany the text and are part of the book itself, particularly the printed book, which combines the main text and paratexts on its margins; at the beginning: the frontispiece, title page, imprint; at the end: the index; above and below: the running titles, page numbers, signatures, and catchwords; and around: custodia. They have secondary divisions: paratexts are part of the book, epitexts are outside the book, for example, brochures and book reviews; and allographic paratexts, which are paratexts written by other agents and not by the author. Genette also differentiates between textual paratexts and technical paratexts — ink, paper, pagination, and more. Our late lamented friend Shlomo Berger introduced the term paratexts to Jewish studies and wrote the first relevant pioneering study,[10] culminating in his book *Producing Redemption in Amsterdam: Early Modern Yiddish Books in Paratextual Perspective*.

Let us move now to some observations about egodocuments. Egodocuments are not a genre. Rather, they conceptualize a certain aspect that appears in several genres, for example, logbooks, diaries, letters, autobiographies, confessions, and more. Further, as I suggest here, paratexts as well might contain egodocuments, or micro-egodocuments — the term I mentioned earlier. The conceptualization of egodocuments is useful because it enables us to think beyond genres. Genre-oriented scholars usually do not use the term, be they literary scholars or historians who focus on a specific genre. As for the definition of this conceptualization, it began with Jacques Presser's notion, 'historical sources in which the researcher is faced with an "I" [...] as the writing and describing subject with a continuous presence in the text'. It evolved to the more concise definition by Rudolf Dekker: 'texts in which an author writes about his or her own acts, thoughts and feelings'.[11] A main difference between the old and the new definitions is the term 'historical sources'. Presser found it necessary to emphasize this specifically, as he was refuting the claim that such documents are historically useless. After several decades of research and the astonishing ascent of egodocuments in a variety of genres and media, the historical value of egodocuments is now quite firmly established, be it in cultural history, social history, or history of mentalities. Further, there is another element in Presser's definition that is missing in Dekker's: the continuous presence of the voice that says 'I'. It may be that it was because of this demand that paratexts were previously not viewed as egodocuments, since they often tend to be short and sometimes varied in topic. Moreover, oftentimes paratexts are not fully personal but include brief personal content — which is why I suggest that they be referred to as micro-egodocuments.

As I noted above, starting in manuscripts and developing considerably in printed books, a paratext could have been the place where a written expression of the personal voice found space in the book. Moreover, in Jewish culture, early modern paratexts offered a unique area for individuals to present their own thoughts,

---

9   Gérard Genette, *Paratexts: Thresholds of Interpretation*, trans. by Jane E. Lewin (Cambridge: Cambridge University Press, 1997).
10 Shlomo Berger, 'An Invitation to Buy and Read: Paratexts of Yiddish Books in Amsterdam, 1650–1800', *Book History*, 7 (2004), pp. 31–61.
11 Rudolf Dekker, 'Introduction', in *Egodocuments and History*, p. 7; Rudolf Dekker, *Childhood, Memory and Autobiography in Holland: From the Golden Age to Romanticism* (New York: St Martin's Press, 1999), p. 7; Arian Baggerman and Rudolf Dekker, 'Jacques Presser, Egodocuments and Jewish History', in *Emotions, Imaginations, Perceptions, Egos, Characteristics: Egodocuments in Dutch Jewish History*, ed. by Dan Michman (Amsterdam: Amphora Books, 2021), pp. 15–40.

acts, and feelings, that is, to express themselves in egodocumental writing. As mentioned, this phenomenon began with people who were involved in the process of printing; initially, it involved sharing the context of the production of their book and it subsequently evolved to a place of contemplation about one's life and experiences.

Our Own Printed Paratexts

There is historical irony in the fact that the first Hebrew book to be published with the inclusion of a title page was *Sefer ha-Roqeah* (Fano, 1505, printed by Gershom Soncino),[12] by R. Eleazar of Worms of the Ashkenazi Pietists circle, which preferred not to draw attention to names of authors in their works.

A statement, which was originally written and circulated, of course, as a manuscript, by R. Judah ibn Tibbon (twelfth century), patriarch of the Tibbonite family, demonstrates the difference between manuscripts and printed books with regard to the need or willingness of their makers to write about themselves. Judah ibn Tibbon collected books and sheets of paper, and had, so he told us, a unique comprehensive private library, a rare phenomenon in an era of scattered, fragmented, and missing medieval Jewish libraries.[13] He wrote the following to his son Samuel, who was the greatest translator in the family, but with whom Judah had a complicated emotional relationship, perhaps owing to the fact that Judah was a widower and a single parent to his children: 'You have ignored all your books. You did not even want to see what they were, and their titles. Now were you to see them in the hands of others you would not even recognize them'.[14]

This is a lovely example of both the emotional attitude of the collector towards his books and the fact that every manuscript is unique and has its own special qualities. The father complains that his son ignored his books, but the subtext is a paternal complaint that his son has ignored him. Failure to recognize each book that Judah exhorted him to acquire is equivalent to not appreciating him. For the true lover of manuscripts, so we are told, each codex — having its own recognizable physical characteristics — was personally known. Apparently, Samuel was interested more in the content than in the form and his father could not understand this attitude and was disappointed by the distance that had come between him and his son.

I suggest that the uniqueness of each and every manuscript was one of the reasons that we find fewer personal paratexts of producers in Jewish manuscripts than in printed Jewish books. Indeed, many manuscripts include personal paratexts of owners — but fewer of the makers of Hebrew manuscripts. With the development of the formulaic printed book, that is, when printed books were no longer simply printed copies of manuscripts,[15] paratextual sections were

---

12 Marvin J. Heller, *The Sixteenth-Century Hebrew Book: An Abridged Thesaurus* (Leiden: Brill, 2004), p. 1; Yaakov S. Spiegel, *Pillars in the History of the Jewish Book: vol. 3: Printed Book Titles* [in Hebrew] (Jerusalem: private printing 2014).

13 On the Jewish missing library conception, see Avriel Bar-Levav, 'Libraries and the Collecting of Jewish Books', in *Encyclopedia of Jewish Book Cultures Online*, ed. by Emile Schrijver (Leiden: Brill), https://dx.doi.org/10.1163/2772-4026_EJBO_SIM_031568 [accessed in January 2022]; Avriel Bar-Levav, 'Libraries and Cultural Memory', *Henoch*, 40 (2018), pp. 95–102.

14 והתעלמת מכל ספריך. אפילו לא היית רוצה לראות מה הם ומה שמותם. כי אם היית רואה אותם ביד אחרים לא היית מכירם. See Israel Abrahams, *Hebrew Ethical Wills* (Philadelphia: Jewish Publication Society, 1927), pp. 57–58; Sarah J. Pearce, *The Andalusi Literary and Intellectual Tradition: The Role of Arabic in Judah Ibn Tibbon's Ethical Will* (Bloomington: Indiana University Press, 2017), p. 207.

15 See Moritz Steinschneider, *Vorlesungen über die Kunde hebräischer Handschriften, deren Sammlungen und Verzeichnisse* (Leipzig: Harrassowitz, 1867); Malachi Beit-Arié, *Hebrew Codicology: Historical and Comparative*

introduced and added definable characteristics to the edition of the work, such as seen in the Venetian Jerusalem Talmud and the Mantuan Zohar. Whereas manuscripts were extremely individualized and personal (according to the wishes of either the scribe or of the commissioner of the manuscript), a printed volume would be quite similar to, if not identical with, its printed siblings, that is, its other copies. The added paratexts further individuated the printed edition.

To return to Judah ibn Tibbon's note to his son Samuel, for whom all manuscripts looked alike — the son was not that careless. With the exception of exquisite, beautiful, and rare manuscripts, many of the plain textual manuscripts do indeed resemble each other — being simply paper or parchment with text. Yet they differ, of course, in form, size, colour, and shape. To recognize a manuscript when it is in the hands of another is to connect the physicality of the book to the text or texts that are contained within it.[16] When we open a book, we can of course see which text it bears. The same is true when we find a single page from a manuscript and must determine the text from which it comes. However, often when we find a single printed page, it might contain paratexts — such as a header — which makes it easier for us to discern its source.

In practice, printed books often have more traces of the personal than manuscripts, even though manuscripts are unique artefacts and printed books are mass-produced. According to the findings of Malachi Beit-Arié, only 11 per cent of Hebrew manuscripts include makers' personal inscriptions. The Jewish manuscripts in the Middle Ages were personal objects to a greater extent than Christian manuscripts, which were produced in workshops and scriptoria. About half of the Jewish manuscripts that have survived were intended for personal use, that is, copied by a person for his own needs, rather than by a scribe writing for a third party. (Here we must distinguish between an ordinary manuscript and a lavish one that is decorated and illustrated. I am referring to the ordinary kind, where the text is the main element and there are no accompanying beautiful decorations). Most of the ordinary manuscripts are anonymous. We do not know who copied them and in many cases, we also have to determine which works were copied.[17] In contrast, printed books from their inception present frontispieces, title pages, imprints, imprimaturs, and copyright pages with the names of the printer, editor, and author. In that sense, we can identify a printed book more easily than a manuscript.

The impersonalization of the printed copy, as well as the need to address new readers, some of them maybe less acquainted with traditional texts and less well versed than in the manuscript period, encouraged printers and authors to talk about themselves and their work. Such a feature might well have accounted for the difference between a successful book and a commercial failure. While people often copied Hebrew manuscripts for personal use, or by special invitation, printed books were made for different reasons. They were produced in greater numbers and the readers were only potential consumers, not yet committed to buying them. The printers had to persuade the public that their books were worth buying. At a later point, writing about one's printing labour became an opening

---

Typology of Medieval Hebrew Codices Based on the Documentation of the Extant Dated Manuscripts until 1540 Using a Quantitative Approach (Jerusalem: The Israel Academy of Sciences and Humanities), https://doi.org/10.25592/uhhfdm.9349 [accessed in January 2022].

16 On the difference between text and book see David Stern, 'Text and Book in Jewish Manuscript and Early Print Culture', in *Encyclopedia of Jewish Book Cultures Online*, https://dx.doi.org/10.1163/2772-4026_EJBO_SIM_031551 [accessed in January 2022].

17 Compare, e.g., the number of manuscripts in the *Ktiv* general catalogue of manuscripts in Hebrew characters to the SfarData codicological database, which contains only dated identified manuscripts.

to writing more about one's self. Moreover, printers were proud of their participation in this new cutting-edge technological profession and wanted to boast about it.

The following examples highlight several of the salient features of book production I described above:

1. Tractate *Berakhot* with Rashi and *Tosafot*, printed in Soncino, 1484.[18] Here we find a description of the work by its initiator, Joshua Nathan, as well as a poem he wrote as an acrostic. There is also an introduction by the editor and corrector (*magihah*)[19] providing the additional information that the initiative came from Israel Nathan, Joshua's father, and a description of his work, which also involved checking the printed version and ensuring its accuracy. Family relationships among the makers of Hebrew printed books were common, as were poems with acrostics for the names of the printer or the author at the beginning of the book.[20] Although such poems have a long tradition, in the context of printed paratexts they are part of the representation of the printing self.

2. Solomon ibn Gabirol, *Mivhar ha-peninim* ('Choice of Pearls'), Soncino, 1484.[21] Here there is an introduction by the editor, Gabriel ben Aaron Stersburk, in which he notes that the printing was done at the initiative of Solomon Nathan, and that he asked the latter to prepare copy for printing some manuscripts that he had to examine.

3. Moses Cordovero, *A Commentary on the Service of the Day of Atonement*, Venice, Giovanni di Gara, 1587.[22] The initiator was Gedaliah Cordovero, Moses' son. The frontispiece reveals that the book (40 pages, size 16°) was printed in this small measure so that it could be bound at the end of a prayer book. Gedaliah wrote that the printing began on the anniversary of his father's death (23 Tamuz), which had occurred seventeen years earlier when Gedaliah was eight years old. He mentioned his mother who helped him study and enabled him to learn with scholars and his principal teacher, Solomon Sagis.[23] This is a more developed micro-egodocument, in which the personal details included do not have direct ramifications for the printed book. Noting the day that the printing began and its sentimental value were primarily for Gedaliah himself.

Medieval poetry was often a personal genre, which might also be one of the reasons that

---

18 See Abraham Meir Habermann, 'The Printers from Soncino' [in Hebrew], in his *Studies in the History of Hebrew Printers and Books* [in Hebrew] (Jerusalem: Rubin Mass, 1978), p. 23; Shimon Iakerson, *Catalogue of the Hebrew Incunabula from the Collection of the Library of the Jewish Theological Seminary in America* (New York and Jerusalem: The Jewish Theological Seminary of America 2004), I, no. 20 (in this edition the description of the books is in both Hebrew and English).

19 See Zeev Gries, *The Hebrew Book: An Outline of its History* [in Hebrew] (Jerusalem: Bialik Institute, 2015), pp. 84–88; Yaakov Shmuel Spiegel, *Chapters in the History of the Jewish Book: Scholars and their Annotations* [in Hebrew] (Ramat Gan: Bar-Ilan University Press, 1996).

20 On printers' poems, see Michela Andreatta, 'The Poet in the Printing Shop: Leon Modena and the Paratextual Production of Authority in Early Modern Venice', in *Shirat Dvora: Essays in Honor of Professor Dvora Bregman*, ed. by Haviva Ishay (Beer Sheva: Ben-Gurion University of the Negev Press, 2019), pp. 9–29; Brad Sabin Hill, 'A Century of Hebraica at the Library of Congress', *The Jewish Quarterly Review*, 106 (Winter 2016), p. 116 note 48.

21 See Habermann, 'Soncino', p. 26; Iakerson, no. 21.

22 See Abraham Meir Habermann, *Giovanni di Gara: Printer, Venice 1564–1610* [in Hebrew], ed. by Yitzhaq Yudlov (Jerusalem: Habermann Institute for Literary Studies, 1982), p. 46; Heller, *The Sixteenth-Century Hebrew Book*, p. 749.

23 See Marvin J. Heller, 'His Hand Did Not Leave Hers until he Was Grown: Two Little Known Works from Moses Cordovero (Ramak)', in *Studies in the Making of the Early Hebrew Book* (Leiden: Brill, 2008), pp. 278–83.

many of the first printers — of the Talmud, for example, or R. Isaac Alfasi — wrote poems describing their work. I suggest that Raphael Natan Neta Rabinovitz's essay on the printing of the Talmud can also be understood as a collection of egodocuments. Similarly, Joseph Hacker's essay 'Pride and Depression: Polarity of the Spiritual and Social Experience of the Iberian Exiles in the Ottoman Empire' about the exiles from Spain, is similarly a collection of paratexts. Abraham Yaari's book *Be-Ohaley Sefer* is based on egodocumental paratexts, albeit these terms were not in use at the time.[24]

Paratexts by Others

Other places where one can speak about the printers and the authors, as well as about oneself are rabbinical approbations to books (*haskamot*). Approbations in the Italian presses, as Meir Benayahu has shown, were initially intended to preserve the printing rights of the publisher, particularly in the early stage of the press when much effort was invested in the planning of the page.[25] Yet, the approbation soon became, as in other paratexts, a place of reflection about the book, as well as the place for the printing agents to share their thoughts about their work. This was enhanced by the widespread, though not universally adopted, practice of printing the title pages and the other paratexts appearing at the beginning of the book after the rest of the book was completed rather than at the beginning of the printing process. Thus, one could acquire the approbations while printing proceeded, add necessary details in the preface, and occasionally even explain changes made in the book during printing.

Furthermore, whereas manuscripts are in many cases compilations that contain more than one work, printed books tend to have a more distinct identification, usually presenting one central text, sometimes with commentaries on the primary text. The difference in the economics of trade between manuscripts and printed books made it necessary for at least two figures to be identified: the author and the printer. Printers had to present both themselves and their work in order to persuade potential customers that their book was worth buying. Authors had to be introduced so that buyers would know what to expect and for the book to have an identity.[26] The result was the advent of 'the printing self', that is, the need of the printer and the author, as well as other agents of the trade, such as editors, translators, and typesetters, to present themselves, and in many cases describe their thoughts, emotions, and actions.

Although I stress the place of printed paratexts in the emergence of the public discourse of individuals about themselves, they were certainly not the only vector for the emergence of egodocuments. There are always many reasons for the emergence of cultural phenomena. We could think, for example, about the expulsions

---

24 See Rabbinovicz; Joseph R. Hacker, 'Pride and Depression: Polarity of the Spiritual and Social Experience of the Iberian Exiles in the Ottoman Empire' [in Hebrew], in *Culture and Society in Medieval Jewish History: Studies in Memory of Hayyim Hillel Ben Sasson* [in Hebrew], ed. by Menahem Ben Sasson, Robert Bonfil, and Joseph Hacker (Jerusalem: Merkaz Zalman Shazar, 1989), pp. 541–86; Avraham Yaari, *In the Dwellings of the Book* [in Hebrew], (Jerusalem: Rubin Mass, 1939).

25 Meir Benayahu, *Copyright, Authorization, and Imprimatur for Hebrew Books Printed in Venice* [in Hebrew] (Jerusalem: Ben Zvi Institute, 1971); Nahum Rakover, *Copyright in Jewish Sources* [in Hebrew] (Jerusalem: Jewish Legal Heritage Society, 1991). Also, Neil Netanel and David Nimmer, *From Maimonides to Microsoft: The Jewish Law of Copyright since the Birth of Print* (Oxford: Oxford University Press, 2016).

26 See Andrea Gondos, 'To Know Everything: Encyclopedias and the Organization of Kabbalistic Knowledge', *European Journal of Jewish Studies*, 16 (2022), pp. 1–27, (3–10).

from Iberia as being another facilitator of egodocuments because disaster and crisis often induce and enhance self-reflection — of theories and theologies as well as of people. Many of these self-reflections were expressed in paratexts — whether in printed books or manuscripts, such as the moving introduction of R. Judah Hayyat to his commentary on the kabbalistic work *Ma'arekhet ha-'elohut* ('The Divine Order'). This text is an example of the rich material that can be drawn from egodocuments, which frequently teach us things no other source can.[27]

'This is Me'

I conclude with two developed examples of egodocumental writings in printed paratexts. The first is from Amsterdam in 1648. In that year, Immanuel Benvenisti's printed a voluminous folio-sized edition of *Shenei luhot ha-berit* ('Two Tablets of the Covenant') by Isaiah Horowitz, former rabbi of Prague, Poznań, and Frankfurt and one of the most important Ashkenazi rabbis of the seventeenth century. At the end of the book there is an additional section, titled *Vavei ha-'amudim* ('The Hooks of the Pillars') by the author's son, R. Shabbethai Horowitz (c. 1590–1660), himself an important rabbi in Prague and Fürth. The introduction to this section is a moving egodocument in which R. Shabbethai tells the story of his intellectual development in the context of his father's journey to the Land of Israel, which the latter undertook in the year 1622. R. Isaiah, so we are informed, decided to embark on this dangerous journey, but it was too difficult for him to share this decision with his son, who was then about thirty years old. The son heard about it indirectly and his shock was great. He rushed to his father, who confirmed the rumour and was uncompromising about his proposed trip. He blessed his son and, indeed, so the son says, 'his sun sank, and my sun was rising'. After his father left, Shabbethai himself became the successful preacher in the Prague community for several years.

We can learn a great deal from this egodocument about the relationships and expression of emotion in a central rabbinic Ashkenazi family.[28] However, in 1648, it seems that the appearance in print of such an egodocument was possible only in the context of a paratext. At that time, finding a literary place to write about oneself — that is, to produce egodocumental writing — was not a foregone likelihood. In order to see the difficulty in finding a literary place to write about oneself, let us consider, for example, the printing of the mystical diary of R. Joseph Karo, one of the most central rabbinical figures in Jewish history. Karo wrote his diary during the long years of his life in the sixteenth century, but it was published only about seventy-five years after his death. He printed several editions of his famous halakhic code, *Shulhan 'arukh* (lit. 'Set Table') during his lifetime, but the mystical diary had to wait.[29] Documenting oneself is indeed a necessity for creating an egodocument but transmitting or publishing these writings is another matter altogether. The difficulty undoubtedly related to the mystical content of the work, but also to its

---

27 See Moshe Idel, *Kabbalah in Italy 1280–1510: A Survey* (New Haven: Yale University Press, 2011), pp. 213–16.

28 See Bar-Levav, 'When I Was Alive', pp. 54–57.
29 On the egodocumental aspects of Karo's *Beit Yosef*, see Tirza Kelman, 'Written with Iron and Lead Letter in Print: The Print Revolution and the Creation of the Beit Yosef' [in Hebrew], *Pe'amim: Studies in Oriental Jewry*, 148 (2016), pp. 9–26; Tirza Kelman, '"I Shall Create Halakhic Ruling… for that is the Objective": The Dimension of Halakhic Ruling in Joseph Karo's Beit Yosef' [in Hebrew] (unpublished doctoral thesis, Ben-Gurion University of the Negev, 2018. On the editing of Magid Meisharim, see Roni Weinstein, *Joseph Karo and Shaping of Modern Jewish Law: The Early Modern Ottoman and Global Settings* (London: Anthem Press, 2022), p. 161.

personal aspect. When it was finally printed, the personal aspect was diminished by the editing of the book, which followed the weekly readings of the Torah, rather than the sequence of the life cycle of the author. Karo's mystical diary, *Magid meisharim* ('Preacher of Righteousness'), was first printed in Lublin in 1646. Even then, it was not printed as it was written, that is in a diary format. It was heavily edited and organized as if it were a commentary on biblical verses, according to the order of the books of the Bible. Owing to the editing style, we have lost track of the original state of this text and can only speculate about the order in which Karo composed it.[30] Similarly, R. Hayyim Vital's *Book of Visions* was printed only in the twentieth century.[31]

I believe the reason that *Magid meisharim* was heavily edited in such a way is that in the seventeenth century egodocuments were still considered unfit to print — unless they were ethical wills or parts of paratexts. The ethical will of the Horowitz family, one of the most popular in the genre, was first printed in Prague already in 1615, and has been published in many editions since then.

Conclusion

I suggest that the difference between the fate of Karo's *Magid meisharim* and some of the printed paratexts demonstrates the unique legitimacy that was accorded to printed egodocuments as long as they were part of paratexts. This legitimacy influenced the emergence of the printing self, that is, the cultural process of constructing and claiming identity that became part of the print culture. The printing self began with the identity of printers, editors, and ancient authors and evolved into identifying contemporary authors when the work of living authors began to be printed in addition to the old classics.

The printing self evolved because of the commercial necessity of printers to identify themselves and their authors. Buyers had to understand what book they were buying, who wrote it, and who printed it. Printing the first editions of books demanded much editorial work, and the printers felt the need to present themselves, as well as the abilities that made them fit for the profession. Thus, the paratexts became a neutral and legitimate place for egodocumental writing, paving the way for modern direct egodocuments.

My last example is from a book printed in Frankfurt an der Oder in 1709 called *Semihat ha-hamim* ('Ordination of the Wise') by Naftali ha-Cohen Katz. It is a star-like poem, with thirty-two verses, with the name Naftali in the centre (Figure 4.1). As I noted, many early modern paratexts from all the places of Hebrew print (and of course, also manuscripts) include poems with acrostics for the name of the author, a model that was widespread as early as in medieval liturgical poetry. This emphasis on the name was indeed a manifestation of the printing self, celebrating his name in print. Moreover, ha-Cohen Katz also wrote a more direct egodocument — a popular ethical will.[32]

Our very own 'age of sharing', as Nicholas John has called it,[33] is the result of a long process, and printed egodocumental or micro-egodocumental paratexs are parts of its origins.

---

30 R. J. Zwi Werblowsky, *Joseph Karo: Lawyer and Mystic* (Oxford and London: Oxford University Press, 1962).

31 Hayyim Vital, *Book of Visions*, trans. and introduced by Morris M. Faierstein (New York: Paulist Press, 1999). For a fascinating collection of printed paratexts see Asher Leib Brisk, *The Words of Qoheleth* [in Hebrew], Jerusalem 1905.

32 Bar-Levav, 'When I Was Alive'; Avriel Bar-Levav, 'Ritualization of Death and Life: The Ethical Will of Rabbi Naphtali ha-Cohen Katz', in *Judaism in Practice*, ed. by Lawrence Fine (Princeton: Princeton University Press, 2001), pp. 155–67.

33 Nicholas A. John, *The Age of Sharing* (Malden, MA: Polity, 2016).

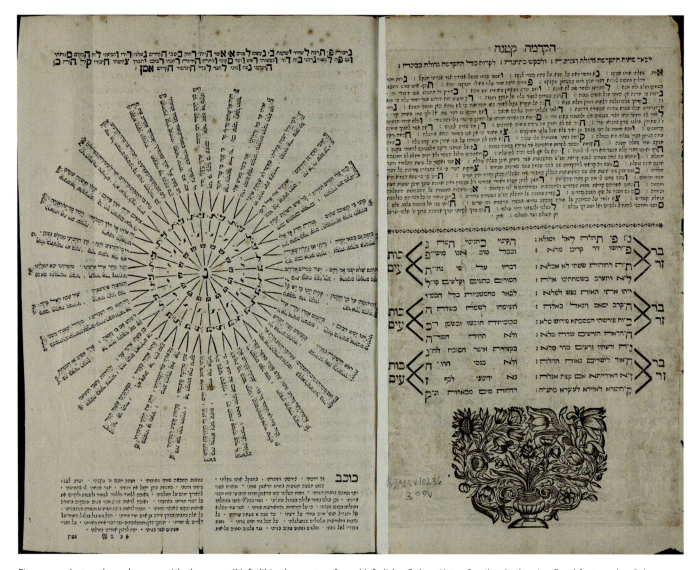

Figure 4.1. A star-shaped poem with the name 'Naftali' in the centre, from Naftali ha-Cohen Katz, *Semihat ha-hamim*, Frankfurt an der Oder, 1709.

PAVEL SLÁDEK

From Manuscript to Print and Back Again

Two Case Studies in Late Sixteenth-Century Jewish Book Culture[*]

Introduction

Over the course of the sixteenth century, the printed book became a growing presence in Jewish learned culture, and in many respects it came to represent 'the book'. Apart from texts intended for use in the synagogue (liturgy), in yeshiva studies (Talmud, halakhic codes), and at home (household rituals and family purity manuals), a wide range of other texts were published in print. Among these were books on ethics, Kabbalah, medieval Jewish philosophy, narratives, some by living authors, and also some in vernacular Jewish languages, especially Yiddish. However, the emergence of a new medium does not necessarily lead to the complete supersession of an older one. Old and new can co-exist while the functions of the older medium get modified: The CD only seemed to push the vinyl record out of use, whereas, in fact, it restricted the market for vinyl to DJs and audiophiles and turned it from a mass into a luxury product. Electronic texts are widely available in various formats in our society, but the production of printed books is still increasing, and the diverse reasons for reading determine whether we turn to an online text, a searchable pdf, or a printed work. As I show below, the sixteenth-century makers of Jewish books and the people who used them were well aware of the differences between the manuscript and print media. Earlier research has often spoken of the 'transition' from manuscript to printed book or about the 'replacement' of the manuscript by the book.[1] However, Malachi Beit-Arié pointed out as early as in 1992 that perhaps half of the surviving

---

[*] This work was supported by the European Regional Development Fund project 'Creativity and Adaptability as Conditions for the Success of Europe in an Interrelated World' (reg. no.: CZ.02.1.01/0.0/0.0/16_019/0000734) implemented at Charles University, Faculty of Arts. The Project is carried out under the ERDF Call 'Excellent Research', and its output is aimed at employees of research organizations and PhD students.

[1] Berit H. Rasmussen, *The Transition from Manuscript to Printed Book* (Oxford: Oxford University Press, 1962), p. 3. See also Sandra Hindman, 'The Transition from Manuscripts to Printed Books in the Netherlands: Illustrated Dutch Bibles', *Dutch Review of Church History*, 56/1 (1975), pp. 189–209.

Pavel Sládek • Faculty of Arts, Charles University, Prague

handwritten Hebrew books are post-medieval.[2] The co-existence of the two media in early modern Jewish culture has not been studied comprehensively. This chapter, in which I deal with two complementary case studies, presents some of the attitudes towards the two media that sixteenth-century Jews espoused and expressed and demonstrates that manuscripts and print existed side by side in a complex and by no means unidirectional relationship.

The first case study involves the peritexts of the *editio princeps* of Eliezer ben Nathan's *'Even ha-'ezer* ('The Rock of Help') (Prague 1610) by which I illustrate the journey from a manuscript to a printed book and show that this was not always a predictable process in the sixteenth century. Close attention should be paid to the circumstances surrounding the production of specific editions to reconstruct the diverse motivations of the different makers of a particular title. This case study also documents a sense of a rupture between the manuscript and printed book on the part of publishers, producers, editors, master-printers, sponsors, and other makers of Jewish books. The second case study offers a contrasting view from the perspective of a set of astronomical texts of Ashkenazi origin. These texts had such a narrow readership that they were clearly not suitable for the printing press, which as a means of mechanical reproduction was economically viable only if hundreds of copies could be sold in a relatively short time. Together, these case studies illustrate some of the modes by which the manuscript and the printed book co-existed in sixteenth-century Jewish book culture.

From Manuscript to Print: 'As Soon as Something is Published in Print for the First Time, in All Countries All Manuscripts Disappear'[3]

Ian Maclean said of the learned book in Latin:

> Why some authors managed to achieve publication and others did not is not a question that can be answered by a neat set of necessary and sufficient conditions. Beyond the variables of location, subject matter, and genre, there lies a morass of contingencies for all except the self-payer.[4]

Maclean's statement holds true for many early modern Hebrew learned texts published in print. An edition of the medieval halakhic work *'Even ha-'ezer* published in Prague in 1610 is one such case and it prompts questions about who wanted to see it printed and who were its intended recipients.[5] The author, Eliezer ben Nathan of Mainz (Raban, c. 1090–c. 1170), is known to modern scholars most notably as the author of one of the descriptions of the massacres of the First Crusade.[6] However, his narrative

---

2 Malachi Beit-Arié, *Hebrew Manuscripts of East and West: Towards a Comparative Codicology – The Panizzi Lectures* (London: British Library, 1992), p. 8.

3 I used some of the following material in a different context in Pavel Sládek, ''Even ha-ezer (Praha 1610): Několik poznámek k tištěné produkci učenecké literatury v hebrejštině', in *Paralelní existence: Rukopisy a tisky v českých zemích raného novověku*, ed. by Marta Hradilová, Andrea Jelínková and Lenka Veselá (Prague: Academia, 2020), pp. 105–36 (pp. 113–25 and 130–36).

4 Ian Maclean, *Scholarship, Commerce, Religion: The Learned Book in the Age of Confessions, 1560–1630* (Cambridge, MA: Harvard University Press, 2012), p. 93.

5 Eliezer ben Nathan, *'Even ha-'ezer – Sefer ha-Raban* (Prague: Moses ben Betzalel Katz, 1610).

6 Text and a German translation: *Hebräische Berichte über die Judenverfolgungen während des Ersten Kreuzzugs*, ed. Eva Haverkamp (Wiesbaden: Harrassowitz, 2021). English translation: *The Jews and the Crusaders: The Hebrew Chronicles of the First and Second Crusades*, trans. by Shlomo Eidelberg (Madison: University of Wisconsin Press, 1977), pp. 73–93. Eliezer ben Nathan also reflected on these events in his liturgical poetry:

seems to have had a limited circulation in the subsequent centuries,[7] and, more importantly, it is questionable whether pre-modern readers even identified him as its author.[8] Thus, there were motivations for creating a printed version of *'Even ha-'ezer* other than just Eliezer ben Nathan having been an eyewitness to the 'persecutions of the year 1096' (*gezerot TaTNU*).[9]

Eliezer ben Nathan was certainly known to sixteenth-century Jewish scholars as a halakhist, although rather indirectly. Wider awareness of his halakhic work was provided, for example, by the numerous citations of his legal opinions in Rabbi Eliezer ben Joel ha-Levi's *Ra῾vyah* (an acronym of the author's name) in Isaac ben Moses' of Vienna *'Or zarua῾*,[10] or in Isaac ben Meir of Düren's *Sha'arei Dura* ('Gates of Dura'), which was a common code of dietary laws and family ritual purity (printed seven times between 1534 and 1599).[11] Yet *'Even ha-'ezer* did not rank among the most important halakhic texts. When Moses Isserles (1530–72) enumerated the founding works 'of the *posqim* ('decisors') celebrated among Ashkenazi Jews' in the introduction to his glosses to *Shulhan 'arukh* ('Set Table'), *'Even ha-'ezer* was not on the list.[12] Not unlike other sixteenth-century Ashkenazi halakhists, Isserles knew of some of Eliezer ben Nathan's halakhic opinions, but he took them from *Sefer ha-Mordekhai* ('The Book of Mordecai'), which does appear on his list.[13] While *'Even ha-'ezer*

---

see Ephraim E. Urbach in his edition of Abraham ben Azriel's *Sefer 'arugat ha-bosem*, 4 vols (Jerusalem: Mekitzei Nirdamim, 1939–63), IV, pp. 24–39. See also Ephraim Kanarfogel, *The Intellectual History and Rabbinic Culture of Medieval Ashkenaz* (Detroit: Wayne State University Press, 2013), pp. 396–97. On Eliezer ben Nathan and his works in general, see Victor Aptowitzer, *Introductio ad Sefer Rabiah* (Jerusalem: Mekitzei Nirdamim, 1938), pp. 49–57; David Ackerman, 'The Life and Times of R. Eliezer ben Natan of Mainz (Raban)', in *Proceedings of the World Congress of Jewish Studies*, Volume 1: Rabbinic and Talmudic Literature (Jerusalem: World Union of Jewish Studies, 1993), pp. 57–64.

7 Robert Chazan, *God, Humanity, and History: The Hebrew First Crusade Narratives* (Berkeley: University of California Press, 2000), pp. 19–20. An assessment of the sixteenth-century reception of the narratives describing the suffering of the German Jews during the First Crusade remains a desideratum.

8 Haverkamp (ed.), *Hebräische Berichte*, p. 63, and the literature referred to in note 136 there. Only nineteenth-century manuscripts identify Eliezer bar Nathan as the author of the chronicle: see Haverkamp (ed.), *Hebräische Berichte*, pp. 222–23. Josef ha-Cohen knew the account of Eliezer ben Nathan and included a major part of it in his own writings but attributed it to 'Elazar ha-Levi'. See Harry Bresslau, 'Zur Kritik der Kreuzzugberichte', in *Hebräische Berichte über die Judenverfolgungen während der Kreuzzüge*, ed. by Adolf Neubauer and Moritz Stern (Berlin: Leonhard Simion, 1892), pp. xiii–xxix (pp. xvi–xvii); Josef ha-Cohen, *Chronicle of the French and Ottoman Kings* [in Hebrew], ed. by Robert Bonfil (Jerusalem: Magnes Press, 2020), vol. 1, pp. 84–97, nos 39–45. Cf. Josef ha-Cohen, *The Vale of Tears*, ed. by Robert Bonfil (Jerusalem: Magnes Press, 2020), pp. 20–29, nos 27–35 and p. 200.

9 Eliezer ben Nathan is the main protagonist in four stories, extant in MS Jerusalem, National Library of Israel, Heb. 8° 3182. As the date of origin of the collection is the subject of an unresolved debate and as there is no visible link between the stories and the Prague edition of *'Even ha-'ezer*, I will leave those stories aside.

On the stories, see Josef Bamberger, 'The King-Maker: Jewish Adaptations of Christian Legends', *Jewish Studies Quarterly*, 20/2 (2013), pp. 129–45, where other literature is discussed. Edition: *Ninety-Nine Tales: The Jerusalem Manuscript Cycle of Legends in Medieval Jewish Folklore* [in Hebrew], ed. by Eli Yassif (Tel Aviv: Haim Rubin Tel Aviv University Press, 2013), nos 8, 40, 41, 96.

10 Ackerman, 'The Life', pp. 58–59.

11 Israel M. Ta-Shma, 'Towards a Characterisation of the 13th- and 14th-Century German Rabbinic Literature' [in Hebrew], in Israel M. Ta-Shma, *Studies in Medieval Rabbinic Literature*, 4 vols (Jerusalem: Mosad Bialik, 2005), I, pp. 317–44 (p. 327). The locations in which it was printed and the span of time during which this occurred indicate a stable and global reception of *Sha'arei Dura*: Cracow 1534, Venice 1547, Constantinople 1553, Venice 1563, Lublin 1574, Basel 1599, and Lublin 1599.

12 Moses Isserles, *Hagahot*, in Joseph Karo, *Shulhan 'arukh – 'Orah hayim* (Cracow: Isaac ben Aaron Prostitz, 1570), fol. 2ᵛ.

13 The *editio princeps* of Isserles' *hagahot* does not indicate his sources. *Sefer ha-Mordekhai* is ascribed to Mordecai ben Hillel ha-Cohen (d. 1298), who was rather an editor

remained inaccessible until the Prague edition was produced in 1610,[14] *Sefer ha-Mordekhai* was printed repeatedly from 1509 on in the editions of Isaac Alfasi's compendium, and as such it became an important part of the curriculum of the sixteenth-century Ashkenazi yeshiva.[15] In what follows, I reconstruct the journey from the initial idea to the distribution and sale of the printed text.

Joseph Sofer of Poznań, who managed the production, spoke in lofty terms about the discovery of the manuscript by one Isaac ben Aaron Samuel Ashkenazi:

והנה היה מונח ספר הזה בקרן זויות, נחבא אל הכלים והיה נראה כקופה שאין לה אזנים וכשלחן בלתי רגלים בתוך גנזי ספרי הרב הגדול מהר״ר אליעזר טריוו״ש בק״ק ורנקבורט. והר״ר יצחק אשכנזי הנזכר שאב מים ממעייני הישועה בבית בני הגאון הנז׳ להשתעשע בכל יום ללמוד מתוך הספרים הנמצאים בתוך הבית. ומצא בתוכם ספר הזה שהוא אב״ן היקר, אבן בוחן היה לראש פינה, שהיה טמון וכמוס באוצרות. ואבן גדולה עליו ויצא יצחק לשוח וגלל את האבן ומצא אבן שלימה, משא ה׳ ספר הזה, טמון בתוך גנזי אוצרות הספרים, שהיה צפון כחמש מאות שנה. הוא הנקרא ראב״ן.

(This book was waiting in the corner, 'hidden among the baggage' [I Sam. 10:22] and in the library of the great Rabbi Eliezer Treves in the holy community of Frankfort it looked like a 'basket without handles' [*Canticles Rabah* 1:8] and like a table without legs. The above-mentioned Rabbi Isaac Ashkenazi drew water from the 'springs of redemption' [Isa. 12:3] in the house of the sons of the above-mentioned great Ga'on and revelled in studying every day from the books which were in the house. Thus, he found among them this book, namely, the precious stone — the *Even*, the 'keystone' (Isa. 28:16), the 'chief cornerstone' [Ps. 188:22], which was hidden and 'sealed up in the storehouses' [Deut. 32:34]. 'A large stone was on it' [Gen. 29:2] but 'Isaac went out walking' [Gen. 24:63] and he rolled away the stone and he found the stone — '*Even*, a 'complete stone' [Deut. 25:15], the 'burden of the Lord' [Jer. 23:33], hidden in the library, this book, concealed for some five hundred years. It is called *Raban*).[16]

---

of the collection, some parts of which may have been added even later. Isserles cited the opinions of Eliezer ben Nathan in *Yoreh de'ah* 55:4, 69:11, 84:4, 106:1, 129:1, *'Even ha-'ezer* 77:2, 106:2, and *Hoshen mishpat* 28:16 and 269:6. However, according to Shalom Albeck ('Introduction', in Eliezer ben Nathan, *'Even ha-'ezer*, ed. by Shalom Albeck [Warsaw: Ephraim Baumritter, 1904], pp. iii–xxvii, p. xvi), the material that was attributed to *Raban ziqni* ('my grandfather Raban') in *Sefer ha-Mordekhai* had its origin in *Sefer Ra'vyah* by Eliezer ben Nathan's grandson Eliezer ben Joel ha-Levi (d. 1225). See also Aptowitzer, *Introductio*, pp. 51–52, no. 2 and 3 on citations of Eliezer ben Nathan in the compendium of Asher ben Yehiel (Rosh) and the family connection between the two scholars.

14 It is preserved in a unique complete manuscript: MS Wolfenbüttel, Herzog August Bibliothek, MS Cod. Guelf. Aug. fol. 5.7 (this manuscript was not the model for the Prague edition). See also Alexander M. Shapiro, 'An Anti-Christian Polemic of the 12th Century' [in Hebrew], *Zion* 56/1 (1991), pp. 79–85.

15 Mordechai Breuer, *Oholei Torah (The Tents of Torah): The Yeshiva, Its Structure and History* [in Hebrew] (Jerusalem: Zalman Shazar Center, 2003), pp. 139–40 and 224. Mordecai ben Hillel ha-Cohen (attr.), *Sefer ha-Mordekhai*, in Isaac Alfasi, *Ha-hibur ha-gadol me-ha-halakhot ha-nehugot* (Constantinople: David and Samuel Nahmias, 1509). Individual parts of *Sefer ha-Mordekhai* were published in print even earlier as parts of individual tractates of the Babylonian Talmud: *Berakhot* (Soncino: Gershom Soncino, 1484), *Yom tov* (Soncino: Gershom Soncino, 1484), and *Yom tov* (Pesaro: Gershom Soncino, 1509).

16 Eliezer ben Nathan, *'Even ha-'ezer* (1610), fol. 1ᵛ, lines 16–21. On Eliezer Treves (1495–1567), see Nehemias Brüll, 'Das Geschlecht der Treves', *Jahrbücher für Jüdische Geschichte und Literatur*, 1 (1874), pp. 87–122 (pp. 105–06). On Treves' activities in printing, see

The 'discovery story' is also featured on the title page, for which the text was collated from other paratexts and put in the mouth of the master printer, Moses ben Betzalel Katz.[17] Consistent with the function of the title page, which was meant to attract the attention of prospective buyers, the 'discovery' is linked to the fact that the book had never before been published in print:

ראה זה ספר נכבד ישן וחדש. חידוש הוא אשר כבר לא היה מעולמים. ואם שעד עתה לא נדפס בדפוס, כי גם הכתב [...] מאיזה סיבות וגזירות היה טמון וגנוז וכמוס [...] כחמש מאות שנים. [...] ושאלנו ולא שמענו משום אדם שראה או ששמע מים ועד ים ממהות זה הספר.

(Look at this venerable book, ancient and new; it is a novelty which never occurred before [after Eccl. 1:10]. The reason why it has not been published in print until now is that the manuscript [...] was for some inauspicious purposes hidden, stored away, and concealed [...] for some five hundred years. [...] We asked around and we did not hear from anybody that he would have seen or heard — from one sea to another [after Exod. 23:31] — about the existence of this book).[18]

Approximately between 1570 and 1625, we find that peritexts begin to reveal a heightened awareness among Eastern and Central European Jews of the distinction between the manuscript and the printed book, one that often manifested itself as an antiquarian interest.[19] Publishers of Ashkenazi origin brought to the press for publication texts which they presented as 'discovered' after having been 'hidden', invariably highlighting the fact that the model copy they had found was handwritten and on parchment and that the book was ancient.

To be sure, 'classical' rabbinic texts were published in print from the outset and manuscripts were sought after. Bruce Nielsen wrote of Daniel Bomberg that he 'funded others' trips to the East, hoping always to acquire more ancient manuscripts in Hebrew, Arabic, Syriac, and other languages'.[20] What is novel here is that individuals, often one-time publishers, came forward and published a work which they emphatically presented as having been hidden away somewhere and then recovered from obscurity. Moreover, as I hope to show in a future study, there was a synergy between this antiquarian interest and a growing awareness of the impact of the editing process on shaping the text. The differences in the paratextual presentation found in the successive editions reveal a heightening awareness of the distinction between the manuscript and the printed book and an increasing antiquarian interest. A few examples can illustrate this phenomenon.

The second edition of *Sefer ha-roqeah* ('Perfumer') (1557), a primarily halakhic miscellany by Eleazar of Worms (d. 1238), was one of the first medieval texts to be presented to readers using a new approach. The first edition was printed by Gershom Soncino in 1505 and was presented simply as a work 'carefully edited by the expert scholar [...] Judah Pesaro'.[21] The

---

Clemens P. Sidorko, 'Eliezer Ben Naphtali Herz Treves als Pionier des jüdischen Buchdrucks in Zürich, Tiengen und Basel um 1560', *Aschkenas*, 17/2 (2010), pp. 457–72. After Eliezer Treves' death, his library was owned by his descendants.

17 See Eliezer ben Nathan, *'Even ha-'ezer* (1610), fol. 1ʳ, lines 17–18.
18 Eliezer ben Nathan, *'Even ha-'ezer* (1610), fol. 1ʳ, lines 3–8.

19 I hope to offer a fuller account of what I call here the 'antiquarian' interest in another study.
20 Bruce Nielsen, 'Daniel van Bombergen, a Bookman of Two Worlds', in *The Hebrew Book in Early Modern Italy*, ed. by Joseph R. Hacker and Adam Shear (Philadelphia: University of Pennsylvania Press, 2011), pp. 56–75 (p. 58).
21 Eleazar of Worms, *Sefer ha-roqeah* (Fano: Gershom Soncino, 1505), fol. [2ʳ].

printer of the second edition, printed in Cremona in 1557, began by criticizing the *editio princeps*:

כאשר קרה לזה הספר הנכבד, חברו [...] רבינו אליעזר מגרמייז"א, נדפס מקדם בפאנ"ו העירה, מיוחס היותו מוגה עם רב הדיוק ע"י [...] מהר"ר יהודה [...] איש פיזרו צב"י. תמיהני על פה קדוש כזה ולמה תצא כזאת מלפניו. [...] אולם המדפיסים הם אשר מעלו, אולי לא מבני ישראל המה ונתלו באילן גדול ושמשו בשרביטו של מלך. [...] והלא אין בית אשר אין שם מתחדש איזו טעות ושגיאה ולפעמים נשמט שורות שלימות.

(It happened that this celebrated book, written by [...] Rabbi Eliezer [*sic*] of Worms was printed before in the town of Fano, allegedly carefully edited by [...] Rabbi Judah of Pesaro. I was surprised by what such a holy mouth [claimed]. [...] Perhaps it was the printers who trespassed [after Lev. 26:40], who were not from the sons of Israel and they just shielded themselves with his name and used the sceptre of the king. [...] 'There was no place' [Exod. 12:30] where they did not produce a new error and mistake. Sometimes were dropped whole lines of text).[22]

In what follows, the printers wrote about their decision to prepare a new edition from a manuscript. Their words express an awareness of a distinction between a printed book and a manuscript but also a conviction that manuscripts were being side-lined by printed editions:

[...] בכל יכולתינו ומאודינו ובדקנו עד מקום שידינו מגעת להוציא יקר מזולל ולחזק את בדק הספר הזה כי רב הוא. ונשלוח ספרי' בכל מדינה זו לאמר מי בכל עם ה' החרדי' אל דברו גם

בכם ויעלה אל ידינו איזה ספר רוקח כתוב בחרט אנוש ומוגה כהלכתו שקל כסף עובר לסוחר נשקול תמורתו. יגענו ולא מצאנו תאמן זולתי אחד ישן נושן אשר במחיר יבא ברוב מוהר ומתן בלתי מוגה. ובאמת כי יצא דבר המלאכה הראשונה בדפוס, על כל הארצות כל הכתובים באים כאחד לאיבוד ואין מלמדי' מהם.

(With all our power and strength, we repaired whatever we touched, so as 'to produce what is noble out of what is worthless' [Jer. 15:19] — [to produce] a repaired [version of] this great book. We sent out letters around this whole country, saying, 'Who of all the Lord's people "who are concerned about His word" [Isa. 66:5] will provide us with a properly edited manuscript copy of the book of *Roqeah*, to him we shall "weigh for it a shekel of silver at the going merchants' rate" [after Gen. 23:16]'. We strove hard but found but one, very ancient, which was available for a price [corresponding to] a great 'bride price and a gift' [Gen. 34:12] — [and yet it] was not correctly edited. Truly, as soon as something is published in print for the first time, in all countries all the manuscripts [of that text] disappear, and people do not study from them).[23]

Another such example is the first printed edition of *Sefer ha-'agudah* ('Band', 1571), authored by Alexander Süsslin ha-Cohen of Frankfurt, a disciple of Rabbi Isaac of Düren, who served as a rabbi in Cologne, Worms, and Frankfurt. He died in the Erfurt massacre in 1349. Although sixteenth-century scholars knew about the existence of the work from citations, it seems that it was not easy to find the text. The first printed edition, produced in Cracow, was pre-

---

22 Eleazar of Worms, *Sefer ha-roqeah* (Cremona: Vicenzo Conti, 1557), fol. [2ʳ], lines 16–19.

23 Eleazar of Worms, *Sefer ha-roqeah* (1557), fol. [2ʳ], lines 27–32.

pared by Rabbi Joseph ben Mordecai Gershon Katz.²⁴ Joseph ben Mordecai was an important rabbinic scholar and a member of the Cracow rabbinic court when it was presided over by Moses Isserles, whose brother-in-law he would eventually become.²⁵ The printers acknowledged the courtesy of one Tzvi bar Manoah, known as Hirsch Qopa (קופא), who owned the only obtainable manuscript and made it available to be published in print.²⁶ The editor explained in his preface that the manuscript did not bear the author's name but that he had found it '*be-sefer yashan*' ('in an old book'). He determined the period in which the author had lived from Jacob Weil's *Responsa*, which occasionally refers to *Sefer ha-'agudah*: הגאון מהר״ר יעקב וויל כתב בתשובה ס' קס״ג וזה לשונו: אותו תיקן ספר אגודה היה לפני הגזירות והיה למדן מופלג וכו׳. (The Ga'on - aleph Jacob Weil wrote in his responsum no. 163 the following words: 'He who wrote *Sefer ha-'agudah* was before the decrees of punishment and he was a great scholar, etc.').²⁷

In the preface the editor asked rhetorically: למה הוא מונח בדור הזה בקרן זוית אין איש שם על לב ('Why in this generation is it [i.e., the book] put aside on a corner shelf, where nobody goes?').²⁸ Further, he wrote about his search for a manuscript: ודרשתי וחקרתי ולא מצאתי בכל מדינה זו מדינת פולן רק אחד וכתוב בסופו שנכתב רל״ו לפ״ק ('I sought and searched and could not find in all of the Polish land but one. At its end it is written that it was written in the year (5)236 [1475/76]').²⁹ The person who produced the edition at the Prostitz press, Samuel Boehm, also confirmed that only one copy was available for the edition.³⁰

The interest in ancient manuscripts is also attested to in the second edition of *Sefer hasidim* ('The Book of the Pious'), published in 1580 in Basel. The title page boasts that the text הועתק מספר ישן נושן מוגה ומזוקק שבעתים ('was copied from a very ancient book, edited and revised seventy times', Ps. 12:7).³¹ The editor complained about the scarcity of manuscripts and their quality in his preface: ואלו אינם מזוקקים כראוי ומוגהים כהלכה. ע״כ נתתי את נפשי בכפי על המלאכה, לתור ולבקש ולחקור אחר ספר הישר ('And these [few available manuscripts] are not properly cleaned of errors and edited according to the halakhah. Therefore, I decided to dedicate a great effort to travel, inquiry, and search for a correct book').³²

---

24 Alexander Süsslin ha-Cohen of Frankfurt, *Sefer ha-'agudah* (Cracow: Isaac ben Aaron Prostitz, 1571).

25 Asher Siev, *Rabbi Moses Isserles (Ramo): His Life, Works, and Ideas* (New York: Yeshiva University Press, 1972, in Hebrew), pp. 63–68. Some twenty years after editing *Sefer ha-'agudah*, Joseph ben Mordecai Gershon published a collection of his own responsa, to which he appended notes on *Sefer ha-Mordekhai*. In the latter, he repeatedly cited *Sefer ha-'agudah* and referred to his own edition. See Joseph ben Mordecai Gershon, *She'erit Yosef* (Cracow: Isaac ben Aaron Prostitz, 1590), second foliation, fols 7ᵛ, 8ᵛ, 10ᵛ, 11ʳ, 12ʳ, 15ᵛ, 16ʳ, 17ᵛ, 19ᵛ, 20ʳ, 21ʳ, 32ᵛ. In the context of the exegesis of the *Sefer ha-Mordekhai*, the Cracow edition of the *Sefer ha-'agudah* is referred to repeatedly also in a compilation by Barukh ben David of Gniezno, *Gedulat Mordekhai* (Hanau: s.n., 1615).

26 Süsslin, *Sefer ha-'agudah* (1571), fol. 250ʳ.

27 Süsslin, *Sefer ha-'agudah* (1571), fol. 2ʳ. The citation is taken from Jacob Weil, *She'elot u-tshuvot* (Venice: Cornelio Adelkind, 1549), no. 163, fol. 69ʳ. That collating such details was by no means commonplace can be seen from the fact that, e.g., David Gans, writing twenty years later, attributed the *Sefer ha-'agudah* to 'the students of the Rosh'. David Gans, *Tzemah David* (Prague: Solomon Kohen and Moses Kohen, 1592), I, fol. 58ᵛ.

28 Süsslin, *Sefer ha-'agudah* (1571), fol. 2ʳ.

29 Süsslin, *Sefer ha-'agudah* (1571), fol. 2ʳ.

30 Süsslin, *Sefer ha-'agudah* (1571), fol. 2ᵛ.

31 Judah he-Hasid, *Sefer hasidim* (Basel: Ambrosius Froben, 1580), fol. [1ʳ].

32 Judah he-Hasid, *Sefer hasidim* (1580), fol. [1ᵛ]. On the halakhic requirement that a book should be properly corrected (*mugah*), see Pavel Sládek, '"Before the law": Jewish Correctors of Early Printed Books', in *Printing and Misprinting: A Companion to Typos and Corrections in Renaissance Europe (1450–1650)*, ed. by Geri Della Rocca de Candal – Anthony Grafton – Paolo Sachet (Oxford: Oxford University Press, 2023), pp. 259–275.

No such interest in the source manuscript and in its antiquity can be found in the *editio princeps* (1538).³³

A more complicated situation arose when David Tevel bar Ezekiel of Cracow decided to edit the commentaries to the Song of Songs, Ruth, and Esther by Eleazar of Worms. As he explained, he edited the printed edition from a manuscript that had been copied especially for him in Worms by Samuel Zanwil ben Israel of Worms from an ancient manuscript.³⁴ In this case, the owner of the old manuscript did not want to dispose of it and so a modern manuscript copy was produced, from which the editor created the final printer's copy, enriched with his emendations.

The last example brings us back to Eliezer ben Nathan. In 1576, Yehiel bar Yedidyah Mikhl Morawczyk published a commentary on *Pirqei 'avot* ('Chapters of the Fathers'), which he compiled himself from earlier works. On the title page, he listed his sources and also mentioned שני סידורים קלף ישנים ('two ancient *siddurim* on parchment').³⁵ According to Morawczyk, Eliezer ben Nathan's comments were based on פירוש של קלף כתב ידו של מרנן ורבנן של [!] ר' אלעזר בר נתן זצ"ל שהוא ראב"ן הנמצא בפוסקים ('a commentary on parchment, a manuscript from the hand of [...] R. Eliezer bar Nathan, of blessed memory, the Raban, who is found among the decisors').³⁶ Further on in the same preface, Morawczyk was even more specific: ובא לידי פירוש ישן נושן של קלף כתב ידו של ראב"ן שנכתב בשנת תתק"ה ל"פק ('A very ancient commentary came into my hands, on parchment, written by the hand of Raban, written in the year (4)905 [1144/45]').³⁷

The publication of *'Even ha-'ezer* in 1610 was by no means the only publication of its kind and can be placed alongside a few other 'discovered' texts that were printed from 'ancient manuscripts'. This publication is nevertheless still exceptional in several ways. Unlike *Sefer hasidim*, it was not an ethical text read for individual devotional purposes. Compared to Eleazar of Worms, whose kabbalistic inclinations made him appealing to the late-sixteenth-century public, Eliezer ben Nathan avoided kabbalistic themes.³⁸ Like *Sefer ha-'agudah*, *'Even ha-'ezer* was an esteemed albeit little known halakhic text. Perhaps surprisingly, this did not necessarily entail a promise of sufficient sales, and both the master printer and the publishers were well aware of this. As in the case of most of the learned texts printed during this period, the master printer did not invest his own money but demanded external funding to cover the cost of printing. The person who sought to get the text printed, Isaac ben Aaron

---

33 Judah he-Hasid, *Sefer hasidim* (Bologna: Menahem ben Abraham of Modena and others, 1538). The editor of the Bologna edition, Abraham ben Moses ha-Cohen, celebrated the ethical qualities of the text and prided himself on having provided a table of contents to make the book searchable (fol. [1ᵛ]). In the colophon, he contrasted the general scarcity of the text with the value of its content, owing to which the buyer should excuse any possible errors in the printed edition and should not blame the printers for them (fol. [121ᵛ]).

34 Eleazar of Worms, *Yen ha-roqeah* ([Lublin]: Tzvi ben Abraham Qalonymos Jaffe, 1608), fol. [1ᵛ] (והמה בכתובים היו בעט סופר מהיר והועתק מהמכתב חרות ישן נושן על נייר חדש).

35 Yehiel ben Yedidyah Mikhl Morawczyk, *Minhah hadashah* (Cracow: Isaac ben Aaron Prostitz, 1576), fol. [1ʳ].

36 Morawczyk, *Minhah hadashah* (1576), fol. [1ᵛ].

37 Morawczyk, *Minhah hadashah* (1576), fol. [2ᵛ]. On the date, see Aptowitzer, *Introductio*, p. 56.

38 On the title page of his *Yen ha-roqeah*, Eleazar of Worms is presented as 'החכם עדיף מנביא וחוזה' ('a sage greater than a prophet and seer') and the editor employed epithets in his preface commonly used for kabbalists, such as *butzina di-nhora* ('a bright light') or *aspaklarya ha-me'irah* ('shining mirror'). See Eleazar of Worms, *Yen ha-roqeah* (1608), fol. [1ʳ⁻ᵛ]. On Eliezer ben Nathan's avoidance of mysticism in his writings, see Kanarfogel, *Intellectual History*, pp. 446–48, and Ephraim Kanarfogel, *Peering Through the Lattices: Mystical, Magical, and Pietistic Dimensions in the Tosafist Period* (Detroit: Wayne State University, 2000), pp. 161–65.

Samuel Ashkenazi, secured the funding from his father-in-law:

ושובע שמחות יחולו על ראש חמי הנעלה הקצין
והישיש והנדיב כמ"ר חיים בר שלום ז"ל, אשר הזיל
זהב מכיס וכסף בקנה שקל ובזבז הונו לכבוד קונו על
ספר הלז והתמיכני בימין צדקו.

('Let the fullness of joy' [Ps. 16:11] rest on the head of my father-in-law, the noble and senior leader, the generous master Hayyim bar Shalom, who 'squandered gold from the purse and weighed out silver' [Isa. 46:6] and generously donated his property for this book to honour his Creator. He supported me with his righteous right hand).[39]

In a similar way, the editor of *Sefer ha-'agudah* noted that he 'had to find partners to cover the expenses of the printing, because they are big'.[40] It is impossible to say if it was Isaac ben Aaron or the master printer, Moses ben Joseph Betzalel Katz, who put Joseph Sofer in charge of managing the production of the book. Joseph ben Solomon Sofer ha-Levi was the chief scribe of the *bet din* ('court of law') in Poznań and a close associate of Mordecai Jaffe. He negotiated the printing of Jaffe's works first in Venice (without success) and later in Prague.[41] Joseph Sofer arranged for *Levush malkhut* ('Royal Robe'), the halakhic part of Jaffe's multi-volume work to be printed in Prague in 1609 by the same print shop as the *'Even ha-'ezer*. All four volumes include prefaces by Joseph Sofer that detail his involvement in the production. The printing of the last volume was completed on 25 December 1609.[42] It is likely that Joseph Sofer personally supervised the printing of Jaffe's halakhic code and in that case he may also have arranged for the subsequent production of *'Even ha-'ezer*, which was completed only three months later on 25 March 1610.[43]

It is certain that Joseph Sofer was instrumental in obtaining an impressive list of signatures from renowned rabbis to attach to the approbation, which was supposed to elicit subscriptions and thus ensure quick sales and certain compensation for the expense of printing. The text of the approbation, framed by Joseph Sofer's own words, is dated 13 August 1609 in Poznań and was signed by Mordecai Jaffe, who was not only the chief rabbi of that town but also one of the most important rabbinic authorities in Poland. Among the other signatories we find other Polish rabbis (e.g., Samuel Eidels) and also the leading rabbinic authorities in Prague (Solomon Ephraim Luntschitz and Isaac ben Samson Katz, among others).[44] The central message of this letter

---

39 Eliezer ben Nathan, *'Even ha-'ezer* (1610), fol. 2ʳ, col. A, lines 27–28 and col. B, lines 1–2.

40 'יוהשתדלתי לי שותפים להוצאת הדפוס, כי רב הוא', Süsslin, *Sefer ha-'agudah* (1571), fol. 2ʳ.

41 See Pavel Sládek, 'A Sixteenth-Century Rabbi as a Published Author: The Early Editions of Rabbi Mordekhai Jaffe's *Levushim*', in *Connecting Histories: Jews and Their Others in Early Modern Europe*, ed. by Francesca Bregoli and David B. Ruderman (Philadelphia: University of Pennsylvania Press, 2019), 49–66: pp. 59–61 and pp. 238–39 notes 59–61.

42 Mordecai Jaffe, *Levush malkhut, ha-levush ha-hamishi, levush 'ir ha-Shushan* (Prague: Moses ben Joseph Betzalel Katz, 1609), fol. 206ʳ. The colophon sets the date as 'Friday, erev rosh hodesh Tevet 370'. According to Mahler, 30 Kislev of that year was Saturday, 26 December: see Eduard Mahler, *Handbuch der jüdischen Chronologie* (Leipzig: Gustav Fock, 1916), p. 580. I build on the detailed description of the Prague edition of Jaffe's *Levush malkhut* in Olga Sixtová, 'Hebrew Printing in Prague 1512–1672' (unpublished doctoral dissertation, Faculty of Arts, Charles University, 2017, in Czech), no. 141, pp. 483–87.

43 Eliezer ben Nathan, *'Even ha-'ezer* (1610), fols [1ʳ] and 154ʳ.

44 From spring 1604, Salomon Ephraim Luntschitz officially replaced the Maharal as the head of the Prague *bet din*. According to a decree issued by Emperor Rudolph II on 13 April 1604, the reason for the Maharal's resignation was ill-health related to old age. Although the Maharal formally remained the head of the yeshiva until his death on 17 September 1609, Luntschitz was clearly

was to encourage the subscribers to fulfil their promises and purchase the book:

אמרנו אנחנו להסכים על ידו וידינו והסכמותינו עמו להדפיס הספר ראב״ן לחזק ולאמץ זרועו. וכן יצא כרוז בקול חיל פה ק״ק פוזנא בכל בתי כנסיות, כמודיע לרבים: כל מי אשר ידבנו לבו יבוא על החתום לקנות הספר הנותן אמרי שפר. [...] וזריזים אשר יקדימו עצמם למצוה, יבאו על החותמת, צדקתם יעמוד לעד לקנות הספר במקח הראוי, ישמח הקונ׳ ויגל המוכר. [...] עד כה דברינו הבאים על החות.

(We decided to issue the agreement [...] to print the book *Raban*, to strengthen the arm of [the publisher]. This is why it was announced in a mighty voice here in the holy community of Poznań in all the synagogues as information for many: 'Everyone whose heart prompts him to make a donation should come and sign-up that he shall buy this book, "which gives goodly words"' [Gen. 49:21]. [...] Those who are filled with zeal and come quickly to the mitzvah and subscribe — their beneficence will last forever [after Ps. 112:3] and they will be able to buy the book for a favourable price, so that the buyer will be delighted and the seller will rejoice. [...] These are our words about the subscribers).[45]

This is one of the earliest documents attesting to the use of the subscription system to secure the sales of a book in Jewish book production (subscribers do not actually pay in advance but commit to purchasing the book when it is published).[46] More importantly, the letter reveals a surprising fact: A halakhic text with arguably little to no direct application in everyday household orthopraxy was being offered, with the support of rabbinic scholars, to people attending the synagogues in Poznań, that is, to the *patres familias* (*ba'alei batim*). In other words, *'Even ha-'ezer* is not a text that belongs to the category of practical halakhic manuals of kashrut and family ritual purity; rather, it is a work of advanced 'academic' halakhah. Yet neither yeshiva students nor scholars were the buyers that were targeted. The latter were too few in number to ensure sufficient sales and yeshiva students could not have afforded it and, more importantly, were not interested in enlarging their libraries (both in the literal and figurative sense).[47] Why, then, would a *balebos* from Poznań or Prague purchase a book that was just 'dry' halakhah?

The answer can be found in the peritextual framing of the main text. Let me quote again from the approbation letter. Here Joseph Sofer and the signatory rabbis portrayed the book as 'engraved like a holy seal [Exod. 28:36] in ancient script, the writing, which is God's writing, incised upon the tablets, copied some five hundred years ago, as can be proven from the book itself'.[48]

---

the main acting rabbinic authority in 1609, when Jaffe's works were printed in Prague and the publication of the *'Even ha-'ezer* was being prepared. Isaac ben Samson Katz was the Maharal's son-in-law, who unsuccessfully aspired to the Maharal's position in Prague.

45 Eliezer ben Nathan, *'Even ha-'ezer* (1610), fol. [1ᵛ], lines 25–30.

46 Sixtová, 'Hebrew Printing in Prague 1512–1672', pp. 175–76. Sixty years earlier, one of Marco Antonio Giustinian's workers mentioned that half of the copies of their controversial edition of Maimonides' *Mishneh Torah* were 'sold' before the printing was completed. Moses Maimonides, *Mishneh Torah* (Venice: Marco Antonio Giustinian, 1550–51), part II, fol. 2ʳ, line 41.

47 Pavel Sládek, 'Printing of Learned Literature in Hebrew, 1510–1630. Toward a New Understanding of Early Modern Jewish Practices of Reading', in *The Printed Book in Central Europe*, ed. by Elizabeth Dillenburg, Howard Paul Louthan, and Drew B. Thomas (Leiden and Boston: Brill, 2021), pp. 387–410.

48 מפותח פתוחי חות׳ קודש בכתב ישן נושן. והכתב מכתב אלקים הוא, חרות על הלוחות, מועתק זה כחמש מאות שנה, כאשר מוכח מתוך הספר זה, Eliezer ben Nathan, *'Even ha-'ezer* (1610), fol. [1ᵛ], lines 13–14.

Eliezer ben Nathan is described in the letter as ranking among the founding scholars of Ashkenazi and Northern French Jewish culture, who were regarded by late-sixteenth century Jewish scholars in East-Central Europe as the founders of their own tradition and identity.[49] Eliezer ben Nathan himself contributed to his being seen in this way. He opened his short introduction with the following words: אקרא לספר הזה אב״ן העז״ר על כי עזרני לגלות בו טעמי מנהגי ראשונים ('I call this book 'Even ha-'ezer ['The Rock of Help'] because my Rock [i.e., God] helped me to reveal in it the reasons for ancient customs').[50] Joseph Sofer poetically referred to 'Even ha-'ezer as a sefer zikaron ('A Book of Remembrance').[51] He described Eliezer ben Nathan as someone who היה חונה על דגלו מאז לתורה ולתעודה בק״ק מגנצא. משם נפוצו מעיינותיו החוצה והזריח שמש צדקתו בימו' עולם מהררי נמרים אנשי השם המאורים, הגדולים המאירים כמאורים, רש״י ור״ת ובעלי תוספות ('resided then in the holy community of Mainz, whence sprang his springs and shone the sun of his righteousness in the days of the rabbinic leopards [after Cant. 4: 8], the men of renown [Gen. 6:4], the great shining luminaries, Rashi, Rabenu Tam, and the Tosafists').[52]

This contextualization of Eliezer ben Nathan was taken even further in the so-called *Tziyunim me-hidushei dinim* ('List of Innovative Rulings'), a selective index provided by the editors. While this list navigates the reader through a selection of purportedly important halakhic decisions,

it also contains historiographical notes which reflect the editors' antiquarian interests. The editor drew attention to the parts of the text that prove its antiquity, helped to determine its date of origin, and established where Eliezer ben Nathan figures in relation to other scholars. Out of the thirty-six passages referred to in this list, in no fewer than six cases the editor pointed to a specific date, and in two places he noted the parts of the text relating to the 1096 massacres, perhaps for chronological reasons:

בסימן כו המעשה שאירע במגנצא בשנת תתקי״ב: בא אלי מורי חמי בחלום. וע״ש. [...]
בדף פ״ד עמוד ב' ואני שמעתי מפי הזקנים שלא היו נוהגין כן לפני הגזירה. ושם עמוד ג' מעשה אירע ברינשפורג שבחור מפראג היה שם. וע״ש מעניני שמחות. [...]
דף צג עמוד א' השיבו שמעון: והלא גזירה היתה ונשללו הבתים? ואיך בא השטר לידך? השיבו ראובן: מה את [!] חש? מן השמים נפל לי. וע״ש.

(Paragraph 26: In the year (4)912 [1151/52] it happened in Mainz that my teacher and father-in-law appeared to me in a dream.[53] See there. [...]
Folio 84, column B: I heard from the elders that they did not act like this before the massacre. And there, column C: A case which happened in Regensburg, a youngster from Prague was there. And see there about the issues related to the customs associated with the bereaving. [...]
Folio 93, column A: Simon answered him: 'Was not it during the massacres and were not the houses pillaged? How did the contract get to your hands?' Reuben answered: 'Why do you care? It was with the help of Heaven'. See there).[54]

---

49 Isserles, *Hagahot*, in Karo, *Shulhan 'arukh – 'Orah hayim* (1570), fol. 2ᵛ; Isserles, *Darkhei Moshe* (Fürth: Hayim Tzvi Hirsch, 1760), fol. [1ᵛ].
50 Eliezer ben Nathan, *'Even ha-'ezer* (1610), fol. [1ᵛ], line 2.
51 Eliezer ben Nathan, *'Even ha-'ezer* (1610), fol. [1ᵛ], line 12.
52 Eliezer ben Nathan, *'Even ha-'ezer* (1610), fol. [1ᵛ], lines 15–16. On the near-absence of references to pre-1096 German scholars in *'Even ha-'ezer*, see Avraham Grossman, *The Early Sages of Ashkenaz: Their Lives, Leadership and Works (900–1096)* (Jerusalem: Magnes Press, 1988, in Hebrew), p. 439.

53 Eliezer ben Nathan's father-in-law was Elyakim ben Joseph, a rabbi of Mainz. See Albeck, 'Introduction', p. viii and Aptowitzer, *Introductio*, pp. 48–49.
54 Eliezer ben Nathan, *'Even ha-'ezer* (1610), fol. [2ᵛ].

In one case, the editor added his own comment, in which he made reference to a passage in *'Even ha-'ezer* that was obviously added later. That helped him to determine when the manuscript used for the printed edition was written: בדף קם טופס גט שנת ה' אלפים ושבע ונראה מזה שבזמן זה נכתב הספר ('On fol. 140: A copy of a divorce-list probably from the year five-thousand-and-seven [i.e., 1246/47]. This shows when this manuscript was written').[55]

Five other references highlight sections that refer to North French scholars, including a passage in which Eliezer ben Nathan celebrated Rashi, the responsa sent to him by Rashbam (Rashi's grandson), and an exposition Rashbam presented before Rashi. While the editor was not familiar with Eliezer ben Nathan's account of the First Crusade, mentioned above, he was indeed interested in the event as such and in the chronological relationship some parts of *'Even ha-'ezer* have to the massacres: בסימן קיד אני אליעזר בא אלי קרובי מר יהואל ובקשני לעיין בפסק דין שלו עד בשעת הגזירה. וע״ש שהיא גזירת תתנ״ו. ('In paragraph 114: To me, Eliezer, a relative of mine, Master Yehoel, came and he requested that I study a ruling that he gave on the issue of testimony in a case that had taken place at a time of immediate external danger. [Editor's gloss:] And see there that it was the massacre of 1096').[56]

The makers of the *editio princeps* of *'Even ha-'ezer* certainly did not conceal the halakhic character of the work. Both the title page and Joseph Sofer's letter of approbation praise the book for containing 'correct rulings, laws, and decisions'.[57] They also pay tribute to the author for פיר׳ עמקי הלכות ושיטות בכל שיטות התלמוד ('explaining the deep issues of laws and their principles according to the principles the Babylonian Talmud, following the same arrangement').[58] However, time and again, the *editio princeps* was presented to potential buyers as an object of memorialization: The customs the book includes are 'ancient, from the early [scholars], all of them are true and correct'.[59] *'Even ha-'ezer* was published in print as a result of the individual initiative of a lay scholar and it was funded by his relative, also a layman. With the support of leading rabbinic authorities, it was intended for the class of pious *patres familias* and was presented to them as an object of memorialization, which resonated with a general antiquarian interest that had arisen out of the debate around the new sense of Ashkenazi identity.[60]

---

55 Eliezer ben Nathan, *'Even ha-'ezer* (1610), fol. [2ᵛ].

56 Eliezer ben Nathan, *'Even ha-'ezer* (1610), fol. [2ᵛ]. The corresponding text is on fol. 40ᵛ. Not surprisingly, linking authors or their texts to generally remembered massacres was common. For example, Jacob ben Joseph, the author of *Pisqei Mordekhai* (MS Oxford, Bodleian Library [Bodl.], Opp. 308), a compendium of *Sefer ha-Mordekhai* mentioned above, who studied with Eliezer Treves after 1552, mentioned that another master had shown him, in an old book, that Mordecai ben Hillel, the purported author of *Sefer ha-Mordekhai*, was killed in Nuremberg in the year 1349. Adolph Neubauer, *Catalogue of the Hebrew Manuscripts in the Bodleian Library* (Oxford: Clarendon Press, 1886), col. 133, no. 674.

57 'פסקים, דינים ומשפטים ישרים', Eliezer ben Nathan, *'Even ha-'ezer* (1610), fol. [1ʳ], l. 12.

58 Eliezer ben Nathan, *'Even ha-'ezer* (1610), fol. [1ʳ], lines 13–14. Although the printed edition of *'Even ha-'ezer* and of *Sefer ha-'agudah*, for that matter, are occasionally cited in subsequent halakhic works, the fact that new editions did not appear before the turn of the nineteenth century suggests that their strictly halakhic impact was limited. A partial edition of *'Even ha-'ezer* appeared in 1904 (ed. by Shalom Albeck, see above, note 9). A full edition was published by Solomon Ehrenreich (Şimleu Silvaniei: Solomon Heimlich, 1926). A modern Haredi critical edition was prepared by David Deblitzki (Benei Braq: David ben Sheraya Deblitski, 2008–12). Partial editions of *Sefer ha-'agudah* appeared in 1877 and 1899: see Hayyim B. Friedberg, *Beit Eked Sepharim*, 4 vols (Tel Aviv: Bar-Yudah, 1951–57), I, p. 16, no. 386. The only complete modern edition which is not a photostat of the *editio princeps* seems to have been edited by the Karlin rabbi Eleazar Brizel, 5 vols (Jerusalem: unknown publisher, 1966–?, NLI system no. 990012069190205171).

59 מנהגי מנהג וותיקין מקדמונים, Eliezer ben Nathan, *'Even ha-'ezer* (1610), fol. [1ʳ], lines 15–16.

60 See Joseph M. Davis, 'The Reception of "Shulhan Arukh" and the Formation of Ashkenazic Jewish Identity', *AJS Review*, 26/2 (2002), pp. 251–76.

From Print to Manuscript: 'You Will Find the Missing Sections in the Quire that I Have Written'

Even after printed books became relatively widespread, manuscripts continued to be copied for multiple reasons. Texts that were produced incrementally, with new parts being added continuously over time (such as communal ledgers and chronicles), texts produced out of a private or semi-private interest (egodocuments, family liturgies), or texts that were not supposed to be circulated among the general public (Kabbalah) were still copied by professional scribes or the texts' authors. There is yet another important category of manuscripts that originated in the era of the printed book: manuscript copies of printed books. Among the many reasons that existed for creating copies of printed books, David McKitterick, who recently pointed to this phenomenon in non-Jewish book culture, cited the 'organisational weaknesses of the early printing' resulting in the 'unavailability of texts in particular localities' as the most common one.[61]

Every student of early modern Jewish history is familiar with this phenomenon from the catalogues of Hebrew manuscripts, which often note in passing the relationship of a particular early modern manuscript to a print edition of the text. Studying Hebrew manuscripts that were copied from printed editions can teach us about Jewish reading practices in the early modern era and about the distribution of specific texts in time and space, as many early modern manuscripts can be dated and their place of origin identified (unlike the rather anonymous print copies — and even in the rare cases when those include an inscription from an owner, the information on the date and place of origin is usually inconclusive).

At this point, a few preliminary remarks on a group of Ashkenazi astronomic manuscripts and the print versions they were based on will further illustrate the relationship between the manuscript and print media.[62]

In 1546, Henricus Petrus, a printer based in Basel, printed *Tzurat ha-'aretz* ('Form of the Earth'), an astronomical work written by Abraham bar Hiyya (c. 1070–1136/45), together with *Qitzur ha-mele'khet mispar* ('Short Treatise on Arithmetic'), a mathematical work by Elijah Mizrahi. The Hebrew text of *Tzurat ha-'aretz* was accompanied by marginal explanatory glosses in Latin by Sebastian Münster and a partial Latin translation produced by Erasmus Oswald Schreckenfuchs.[63] Bar Hiyya's treatise was one of a small number of astronomical texts that constituted the curriculum for late sixteenth- and

---

61 David McKitterick, *Print, Manuscript and the Search for Order 1450–1830* (Cambridge: Cambridge University Press, 2003), p. 47.

62 This section is based on my still unpublished research of a set of manuscripts produced by and for East and Central European Jewish students of astronomy between 1550 and 1640. While the larger project aims to re-evaluate the place that the study of astronomy occupied among Ashkenazi scholars at the turn of the seventeenth century, here I use only select manuscripts to demonstrate the intricate relationship between manuscript and printed texts in the first century after the advent of the printing press. On the study of astronomy at the turn of the seventeenth century, see Y. Tzvi Langerman, 'The Astronomy of Rabbi Moses Isserles', in *Physics, Cosmology and Astronomy, 1300–1700*, ed. by Sabetai Unguru (Dordrecht – Boston: Kluwer Academic Publishers, 1991), pp. 83–98; David B. Ruderman, *Jewish Thought and Scientific Discovery in Early Modern Europe* (New Haven and London: Yale University Press, 1995); Noah Efron and Menachem Fisch, 'Astronomical Exegesis: An Early Modern Jewish Interpretation of the Heavens', *Osiris* 16 (2001). pp. 72–87; David E. Fishman, 'Rabbi Moshe Isserles and the Study of Science among Polish Rabbis', *Science in Context* 10/4 (1997), 571–588.

63 Abraham bar Hiyya (Abraham Hispano filio R. Haijae), *Tzurat ha-'aretz – Sphaera mundi* (Basel: Henricus Petrus, 1546). Moritz Steinschneider, 'Mathematik bei den Juden (1501–1550)', *Zeitschrift für Mathematik und Physik – Abhandlungen zur Geschichte der Mathematik*, 9 (1899), pp. 473–83 (p. 477); all parts of the article were re-printed together as *Mathematik bei den Juden* (Hildesheim: Georg Olms, 1964).

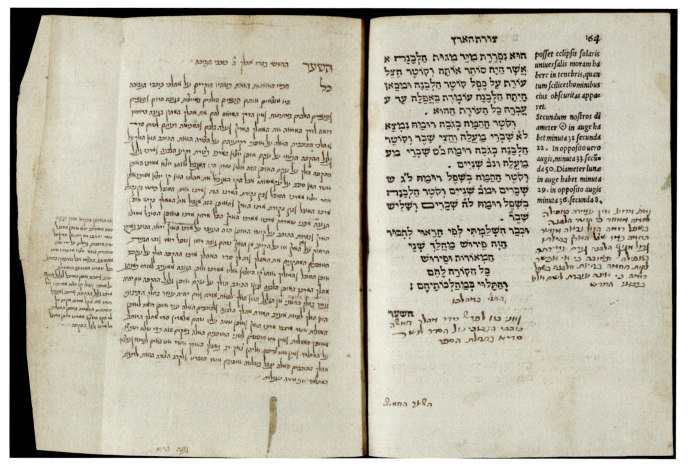

Figure 5.1. Abraham bar Hiyya, *Tzurat ha-ʾaretz*, Basel: Henricus Petrus, 1546, Oxford, Bodleian Library, Opp. 4°. 417 (2), p. 164 and the manuscript insertion.

early seventeenth-century Jewish students of astronomy. Given that the second printed edition did not appear until 1720 in Offenbach, all those students were using either the Basel edition or manuscripts.

One of the four copies of Bar Hiyya's *Tzurat ha-ʾaretz*, which are now in the Bodleian Library, has two owners' inscriptions in early modern Ashkenazi script and substantial additions to the manuscript.[64] The Jewish owners did not interfere with the Latin sections of the book, but the additions to the Hebrew portion by probably two different, careful Ashkenazi hands indicate that the copy was used intensively by at least two Jewish owners. Not only did they add extensive explanatory glosses, but one of them also pasted portions of Bar Hiyya's work that had been omitted from the Basel edition into the printed copy (Figure 5.1), which means that this scribe had access to a manuscript with a more complete version of the text. He also provided notes to help other readers navigate the text, which indicates that he also had other readers in mind: כאן חסר פתח ל״ד ופתח ל״ה ותמצאם למעלה בקונטרס שכתבתי ('Here sections 34 and 35 are

---

64 Bar Hiyya, *Tzurat ha-ʾaretz* (1546), Bodl., Opp. 4°. 417 (2); Elijah Mizrahi's *Qitzur ha-melekhet mispar* is lacking from this exemplar. The names are not completely legible: ליפמן and אפרי[ם] בכמ׳ מנחם טקנגלמן.

missing but you will find them above in the quire that I have written').⁶⁵

The same practices are documented in a copy of the Basel edition now in the Österreichische Nationalbibliothek, which shows numerous similarities to the Bodleian copy discussed above.⁶⁶ It has neat Hebrew glosses written by at least two different hands, variants on the text drawn from other manuscripts and marked with the usual abbreviation ס״א (*sefer 'aher*: 'other book'). Also in this copy one Jewish owner added some of the missing passages and glosses found in another manuscript.⁶⁷ A manuscript gloss before section 50 is word for word the same as in the Bodleian copy, so the two copies are probably related, even though neither one was copied from the other.⁶⁸ These examples attest to the simultaneous and combined use of printed and manuscript books.

There are a number of manuscript copies of *Tzurat ha-'aretz* that originated either in Eastern or Central Europe or in Italy, which the Institute of Microfilmed Hebrew Manuscripts Catalogue dates to the sixteenth and seventeenth centuries.⁶⁹

One of them is of particular interest here, namely, MS Oxford, Bodleian Library, Opp. 704,⁷⁰ which is a collection of Hebrew astronomical texts, collected and partly authored by Hayyim Lisker. It also contains a handwritten copy of Abraham bar Hiyya's treatise.⁷¹ Like so many early modern astronomical manuscripts, Lisker's handwritten copy remained unfinished — blank spaces were left for additional glosses, diagrams, and decorative incipits. Lisker collated textual variants from several manuscripts and inserted them in brackets within the main text or in the margins. As in the printed exemplars described above, Lisker added numerous glosses, some of which are identical with the manuscript additions in the Viennese copy of the Basel printed edition.

Most importantly, one of the models for Lisker's manuscript copy was the Basel edition itself. A comparison of selected portions of the text makes this clear, but it is also evident from the identical diagrams, the similar or identical page layout, and — most surprisingly — from the fact that, in several instances, Lisker copied the Latin captions for the diagrams and even a gloss in Latin by Sebastian Münster (Figures 5.2–5.7).

As I hope to show elsewhere, the use of non-Jewish sources for the study of astronomy was rather common and the early modern Ashkenazi astronomical manuscripts represent a unique

---

65 Bar Hiyya, *Tzurat ha-'aretz* (1546), Bodl., Opp. 4°. 417 (2), p. 184.
66 Bar Hiyya, *Tzurat ha-'aretz* (1546), Vienna, Österreichische Nationalbibliothek (ÖNB), call no. 68182-B.
67 Bar Hiyya, *Tzurat ha-'aretz* (1546), ÖNB, call no. 68182-B, after p. 209. The additions, filling four folios, start with two longer notes beginning with: 'This is what I found written in the margin of a manuscript of *Tzurat ha-'aretz*'. Then passages missing from the Basel edition follow, starting with: 'Then three sections 29, 34, and 35 are missing from the printed edition of *Tzurat ha-'aretz* and I found them in a manuscript'. The text is complemented with comments, obviously copied from the same manuscript.
68 The diagrams in the manuscript additions differ slightly between the two copies and based on a partial comparison. The manuscript glosses are not identical or even similar. Unfortunately, I cannot currently access the Bodleian copy to make a more detailed examination.
69 The original entries from the catalogue of Institute of Microfilmed Hebrew Manuscripts (IMHM) were merged with the central catalogue of the National Library of Israel (https://merhav.nli.org.il).
70 MS Oxford, Bodl., Opp. 704 (Neubauer 2033).
71 MS Oxford, Bodl., Opp. 704 (3), fols 36–142. Hayyim Lisker is known since Steinschneider as a student of astronomy because of MS Bodl., Opp. 704, the *terminus ad quem* (for both the manuscript and Lisker himself) is 1635/36: Moritz Steinschneider, 'Mathematik bei den Juden (1551–1840)', *Monatsschrift für Geschichte und Wissenschaft des Judentums*, 49 [13, New Series] (1905), pp. 193–204 (pp. 196–99); thirteen instalments of Steinschneider's article are interspersed in vols 49–51 (13–15) of the *MGWJ* and re-printed together as *Mathematik bei den Juden – Band II*, ed. Tony Lévy (Hildesheim: Georg Olms, 2014).

visual testimony to this fact. Another manuscript from the Bodleian Library can illustrate this point. Apart from various fragments of scientific texts, MS Oxford, Bodleian Library, Opp. 696, includes a copy of Georg Peurbach's *Theoricae novae planetarum* ('New Theories of the Planets') (1460) in a Hebrew translation.[72] Under the title *Teorika* (the Hebrew orthography varies), Peurbach's text along with a Hebrew translation of Sacrobosco's *De sphaera mundi* ('On the Sphere of the World'), called *Aspera* or *Mar'eh ha-'ofanim* in Hebrew, and a few other texts made up the standard textbooks of theoretical astronomy, mirroring the curriculum of European universities.[73] As regards the relationship between manuscript and print, the case of the Hebrew versions of Peurbach's and Sacrobosco's works in the sixteenth century is different from that of *Tzurat ha-'aretz* because no printed edition of those texts existed.[74] Yet Jewish students of astronomy seeking a new manuscript copy of the Hebrew text still resorted to the numerous Latin editions because of the diagrams. A closer look at the diagrams in MS Oxford, Bodleian Library, Opp. 696, reveals that some of them were copied from the 1542 Wittenberg edition of Peurbach's *Theoricae*, again together with Latin captions. A further comparison of these diagrams with other manuscripts from the same group shows that the same diagrams appear, for example, in MS Philadelphia, University of Pennsylvania, LJS 498, this time without the Latin captions (Figures 5.8–5.13). Again, the relationship between the two manuscripts seems to be more complicated than that of a model and a copy.

Another comparative look at the diagrams in various manuscripts in the group reveals the obstacles that these oftentimes intricate figures presented to copyists. While copying and writing manuscripts was clearly widespread in early modern Ashkenazi Jewish society, drawing complicated astronomical diagrams was not. At the same time, such diagrams were deemed essential for an understanding of an astronomical text. Moses Isserles, an avid student of astronomy, wrote about the purpose of his commentary to Peurbach's *Theorica*: כדי שכל איש משכיל היודע תחלה מעט מחכמה יוכל ללמוד ולהבין בו מעצמו כל דבריו, בפרט אם יהי׳ לו הצ[י]ורי׳ המצויירים על ספר זו הנמצאי׳ בספר הטורקי הנוצרי׳ הנמצא לרוב ביניהם ('So that every intelligent person who already knows a few of the basics of the discipline can study and understand it in its entirety on his own, especially if he has the diagrams drawn for the Christian version of this book of *Theorica*, which is widespread among them [i.e., the Christians]').[75]

The existing Hebrew manuscripts of Sacrobosco's *Sphaera* offer (in a rather consistent quality) a stable set of illustrations and diagrams, more or less identical with the sixteenth-century Latin editions, which — in consonance with

---

72 MS Oxford, Bodl., Opp. 696 (Neubauer 2258). Several Hebrew versions of the text are extant. Steinschneider identified the translation in MS Oxford, Bodl., Opp. 696 (*olim* 1665), which he dated to the beginning of the sixteenth century, as that of Ephraim Mizrahi: Moritz Steinschneider, *Die Hebraeischen Uebersetzungen des Mittelalters und die Juden als Dolmetscher* (Berlin: Kommissionsverlag des Bibliographischen Bureaus, 1893), no. 405, pp. 639–41.

73 See Robert S. Westman, *The Copernican Question: Prognostication, Skepticism, and Celestial Order* (Berkeley: University of California Press, 2011), pp. 49–55 (Peurbach), pp. 34–43 (on the *theorica/practica* distinction), pp. 40 and 166–68 (on the curriculum). On Sacrobosco in Hebrew, see Steinschneider, *Die Hebraeischen Uebersetzungen*, no. 407, pp. 642–44. See also Owen Gingerich, 'Sacrobosco as a Textbook', *Journal for the History of Astronomy*, 19 (1988), pp. 269–73.

74 Peurbach's treatise in Hebrew remains in manuscript. Sacrobosco's text was printed as part of the 1720 edition of Bar Hiyya's *Tzurat ha-'aretz* (fols 42–58). On Peurbach in Hebrew, see Y. Tzvi Langerman, 'Peurbach in the Hebrew Tradition,' *Journal for the History of Astronomy* 29/2 (1998), pp. 137–150.

75 MS Oxford, Bodl., Mich. 195 (Neubauer 1332), fol. 112ᵛ, col. B, lines 2–6.

Isserles' claim — were numerous (see Figure 5.14).⁷⁶ Before Moses Isserles, Matatiah Delacrut wrote a commentary to *Sphaera*, which is found in several extant manuscript copies. One of the first of Delacrut's glosses is accompanied by a special diagram, which means that the Jewish copyists could not resort to the Latin editions of Sacrobosco's *Sphaera* as Isserles suggested. The diagram in the MS Vienna, which is of fair quality, was pasted into the volume on a special leaf.⁷⁷ There are two copies of Delacrut's commentary in the Bodleian Library. In MS Oxford, Bodleian Library, Mich. 144, the quality of the diagram is clearly inferior to the one in MS Vienna (note that the signs of the zodiac are missing altogether).⁷⁸ In MS Oxford, Bodleian Library, Opp. 696, mentioned above, we get only a parody of the original (Figures 5.15–5.17).⁷⁹

Some of the copyists decided to delegate the illustrations and diagrams to specialists, and at times when they left empty spaces within the text, the illustrations were never added. In other cases, the producers of the manuscripts appended the diagrams after the text, sometimes with wheel charts – volvelles (Figures 5.14 and 5.18a-18d).

Students of astronomy, a science that flourished among the Ashkenazi scholars from the mid-sixteenth to the early seventeenth century, were too few in number to make printed editions with complicated diagrams economically viable. At the same time, the techniques of manuscript culture still made it possible for them to create a continuous textual tradition across several generations. In the age of print, they did not hesitate to merge the two media by producing manuscript copies from printed editions or combining printed and contemporary manuscript text in the same volume.

Conclusion

Using the two case studies detailed above, I sought to demonstrate that the relationship between printed and manuscript media in late sixteenth- and early seventeenth-century Jewish culture was multidirectional. Manuscripts did not just exist alongside printed books, each assuming a specific function, but rather the two media were involved in mutual interactions and often formed a continuum in the most material sense, for example, in the volumes that combined printed and manuscript segments.

The Jewish makers of printed books often hinted at a shift and regarded the printed medium as dominant. Many authors also gradually came to view the printed book as a more suitable and durable medium in which to establish themselves as scholars. In reality, the economy of the early modern hand press made the production of very small numbers of copies inviable, and in a small Jewish society this was an obvious handicap.

At the same time, one must keep in mind that while the average print run in the sixteenth century was between 500 and 2000 copies, there was no *a priori* reason why a much smaller number could not be printed. In other words, the absence of Jewish printed editions of Hebrew astronomical texts (and other minority genres) cannot be explained solely on the grounds that the print medium was unsuitable for small print runs. As the only obstacle was economic and not technological in nature — printing only a few

---

76 USTC lists 34 editions published before 1571, when Isserles completed his commentary. For the date, see Siev, *Rabbi Moses Isserles*, p. 177.
77 MS Wien, ÖNB, Cod. hebr. 56, fol. 6*. For the description, see Arthur Zacharias Schwartz, *Die Hebräischen Handschriften der Nationalbibliothek in Wien* (Viena, Prague, and Leipzig: Ed. Strache, 1925), no. 201, p. 236.
78 MS Oxford, Bodl., Mich. 144 (Neubauer 2027), fol. 100ʳ. Yet another execution of the same diagram, roughly corresponding in quality to MS Bodl., Mich. 144 but including the signs of zodiac, can be found in MS Bodl., Opp. 694 (Neubauer 2034), fol. 1ᵛ, which contains Sacrobosco's *Sphaera* with glosses by Manoah Hendel, who paraphrased Delacrut.
79 MS Oxford, Bodl., Opp. 696 (Neubauer 2253), fol. 12ʳ.

copies (or coming to terms with many unsold copies) would only mean higher expenses and the need to secure external funding. (We have seen that even a prestigious halakhic work such as *'Even ha-'ezer* could only be published with the help of external funding.) The existence of a fully functional manuscript culture in early modern Jewish society was not merely a residue or vestige of the pre-print era. The Jewish readership in the early modern period, probably smaller than we imagine, still favoured the intensive reading of a limited corpus of texts, rather than the fragmented and selective reading of an increasing number of texts, whereas the technology of print supported the mass production of books.[80] In Jewish culture, the production of manuscripts, including copies of texts which had already been printed, complemented the print medium and compensated for the disadvantages of the new technology for a small community of readers.

---

80 See Sládek, 'Printing of Learned Literature in Hebrew'.

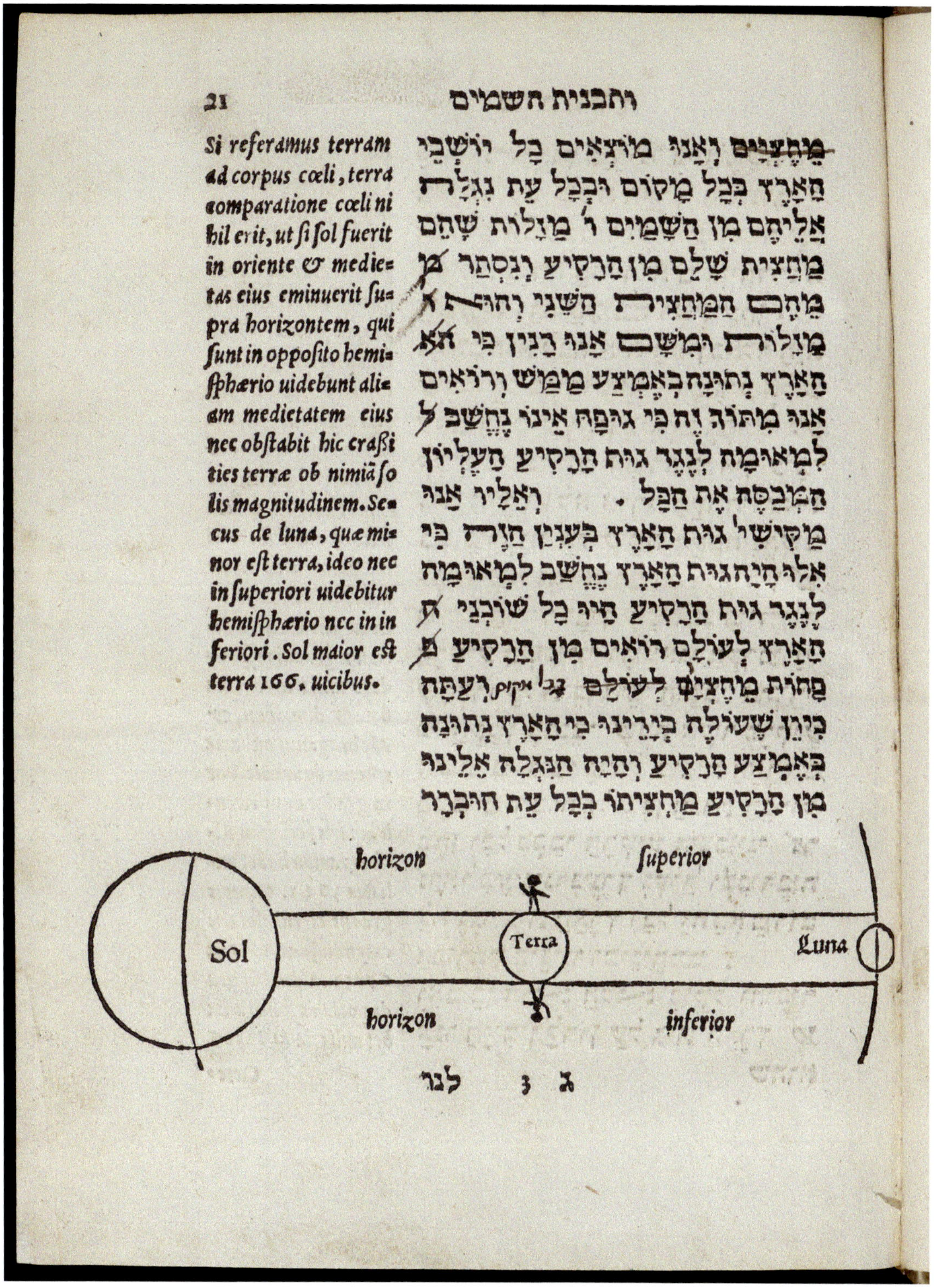

21 וְתַבְנִית הַשָּׁמַיִם

Si referamus terram ad corpus cœli, terra comparatione cœli nihil erit, ut si sol fuerit in oriente & medietas eius eminuerit supra horizontem, qui sunt in opposito hemisphærio uidebunt aliam medietatem eius nec obstabit hic crassities terræ ob nimiã solis magnitudinem. Secus de luna, quæ minor est terra, ideo nec in superiori uidebitur hemisphærio nec in inferiori. Sol maior est terra 166. uicibus.

מֶחֱצִים וְאָנוּ מוֹצְאִים כָּל יוֹשְׁבֵי הָאָרֶץ בְּכָל מָקוֹם וּבְכָל עֵת נִגְלֶה אֲלֵיהֶם מִן הַשָּׁמַיִם ו׳ מַזָּלוֹת שֶׁהֵם מַחֲצִית שָׁלֵם מִן הָרָקִיעַ וְנִסְתָּר מֵהֶם הַמַּחֲצִית הַשֵּׁנִי וְהוּא ו׳ מַזָּלוֹת וּמִשָּׁם אָנוּ דָנִין כִּי הָאָרֶץ נְתוּנָה בְּאֶמְצַע מַמָּשׁ וְרוֹאִים אָנוּ מִתּוֹךְ זֶה כִּי גּוּפָהּ אֵינוֹ נֶחְשָׁב לִמְאוּמָה לְנֶגֶד גּוּת הָרָקִיעַ הָעֶלְיוֹן הַמְּכַבֶּסֶת אֶת הַכֹּל . וְאֵלָיו אָנוּ מַקִּישׁ גּוּת הָאָרֶץ בְּעִנְיָן חַזְרָה כִּי אִלּוּ הָיְתָה גּוּת הָאָרֶץ נֶחְשָׁב לִמְאוּמָה לְנֶגֶד גּוּת הָרָקִיעַ הָיוּ כָל שׁוֹכְנֵי הָאָרֶץ לְעוֹלָם רוֹאִים מִן הָרָקִיעַ פָּחוֹת מֶחֱצָיוֹ לְעוֹלָם גַּל אִיךְ וְעֵתָּה כֵּיוָן שֶׁעוֹלָה בְּיָדֵינוּ כִּי הָאָרֶץ נְתוּנָה בְּאֶמְצַע הָרָקִיעַ וְהָיָה הַנִּגְלֶה אֵלֵינוּ מִן הָרָקִיעַ מַחֲצִיתוֹ בְּכָל עֵת חוּבַּרְנוּ

Figure 5.2. Abraham bar Hiyya, *Tzurat ha-'aretz*, Basel: Henricus Petrus, 1546, Oxford, Bodleian Library, Opp. 4°. 417 (2), p. 21.

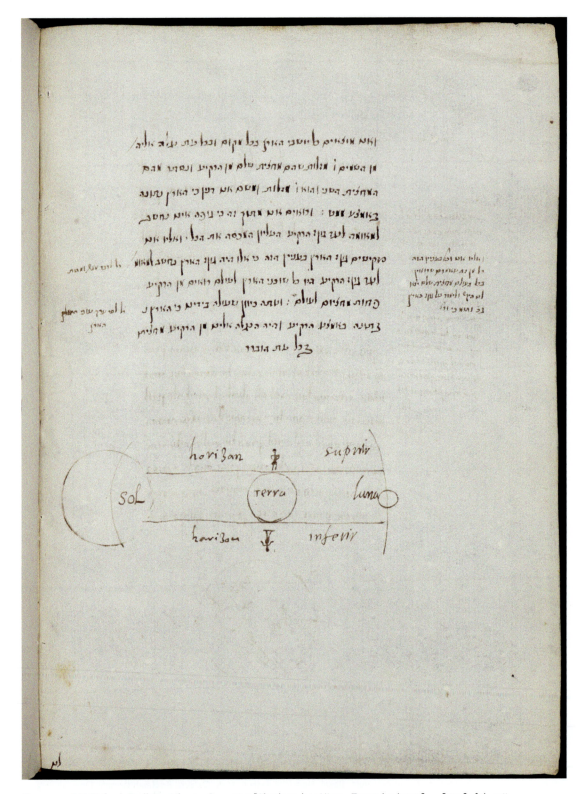

Figure 5.3. MS Oxford, Bodleian Library, Opp. 704 [Abraham bar Hiyya, *Tzurat ha-ʾaretz*] … [etc.], fol. 43ᵛ.

צורת הארץ

בְּמִזְרַח מֵאַרְצוֹת גּוֹג וּמָגוֹג וּבוּזַר
וְכָל אַרְצוֹת יְוָנִים וְרוֹמִיִּים וּר
סְטַנְטִינָא רַבָּה וּבִכְנִסוּרד בְּכָל ח
הָאֵקְלִים הַזֶּה עִם אַרְצוֹת בְּרַגְבְּנֵי
עַ‎ חַיִּם מַעֲרָב אוֹסִיָנוֹס.
הָאֵקְלִים הַשְּׁבִיעִי מַתְחִיל מִתְּחוּם
הַשִּׁשִּׁי וְהוֹלֵךְ עַד מ"ה מַעֲלוֹת וַחֲצִי
מֵאוֹפֶן הַמִּישׁוֹר צָפוֹנָה וְיוֹמוֹ הָא
חָרוּךְ י"ו שָׁעוֹת יְשָׁרוֹת וְהַקִּצּוּרָת
שָׁעוֹת וְהוּא מַתְחִיל בִּפְאַת מִזְרַח
מֵאַרְצוֹת תַּרְבִּי' וְתָאוּמִית הַנִּקְרֵאת
אַשְׁקְלַבֵּשׁ לְכָל שׁוֹכְנֵי בְּרִטַנְיָא ר

Cafdan, id eft, Chaldæ
am fed quæ in quarto
climate fuum obtinet
fitum. Affpanaia eft Hi
fpania & Peranfa ui=
detur effe prouincia
Narbonenfis, Aedom
Italia. Sextum clima
fua extremitate attin=
git Rauracos, item ter
ram Chufar quæ uide=
tur effe Scythia exte=
rior, Conftantinopo=
lim & Franciam. Sep
timũ clima tranfit per

Figure 5.4. Abraham bar Hiyya, *Tzurat ha-´aretz*, Basel: Henricus Petrus, 1546, Oxford, Bodleian Library, Opp. 4°. 417 (2), p. 42.

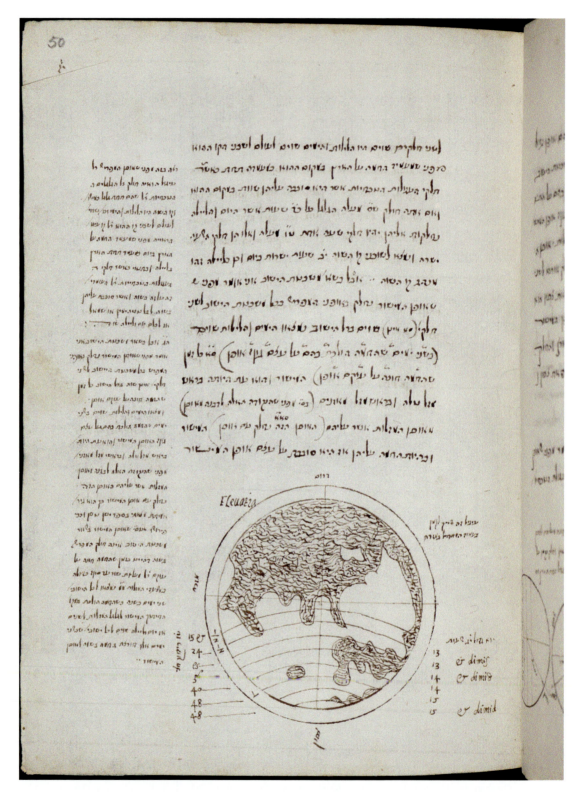

Figure 5.5. MS Oxford, Bodleian Library, Opp. 704 [Abraham bar Hiyya, *Tzurat ha-'aretz*] … [etc.], fol. 50ʳ.

צורת הארץ

רֹאשׁ נֹבַח שׁוֹכְנָיו וְאֵינָהּ נִרְאֵית לְ
לִפְאַת צָפוֹן מִגֹּבַח רֹאשָׁם כִּי אִם
לִפְאַת דָּרוֹם לְעוֹלָם וְהַצֵּל נוֹפֵל לְ
לִפְאַת צָפוֹן וְאֵינוֹ נוֹפֵל לְדָרוֹם.
וְכָל הַמַּרְחָב מַעֲמִיק בְּצָפוֹן הַחַמָּה
מַעֲמִיסָהּ לְהִתְרַחֵס מִגֹּבַח הָרֹאשׁ
לִפְאַת דָּרוֹם עַד שֶׁיַּגִּיעַ הַמַּרְחָב אֶל
סו מַעֲלוֹת בִּפְאַת צָפוֹן וּבְמַסִּים
הוּא תִּהְיֶה נְסוּרַת נֹבַח הָרֹאשׁ וְחוּץ׳
מֵאוֹפֶן הַמִּישׁוּר בְּמֶרְחָק קְטָב אוֹפֶן

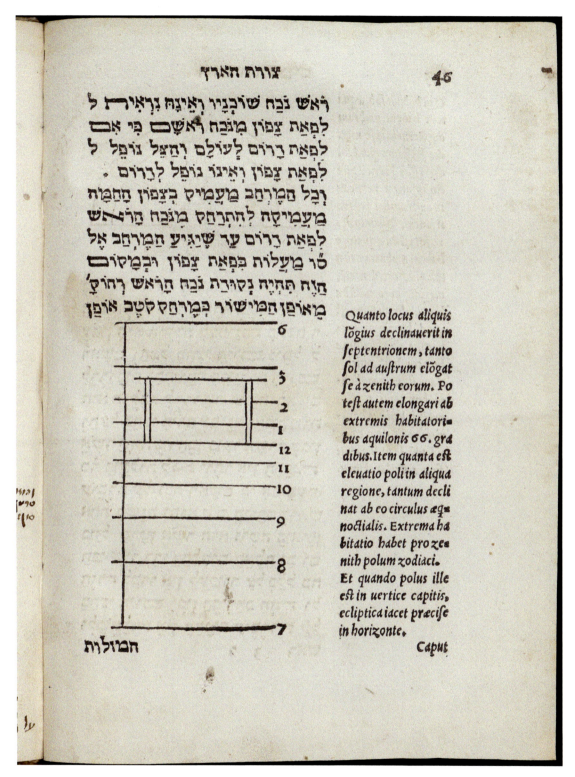

Quanto locus aliquis
lõgius declinauerit in
septentrionem, tanto
sol ad austrum elõgat
se à zenith eorum. Po
test autem elongari ab
extremis habitatori-
bus aquilonis 66. gra
dibus. Item quanta est
eleuatio poli in aliqua
regione, tantum decli
nat ab eo circulus æq=
noctialis. Extrema ha
bitatio habet pro ze=
nith polum zodiaci.
Et quando polus ille
est in uertice capitis,
ecliptica iacet præcise
in horizonte.

Caput

Figure 5.6. Abraham bar Hiyya, *Tzurat ha-ʼaretz*, Basel: Henricus Petrus, 1546, Oxford, Bodleian Library, Opp. 4°. 417 (2), p. 46.

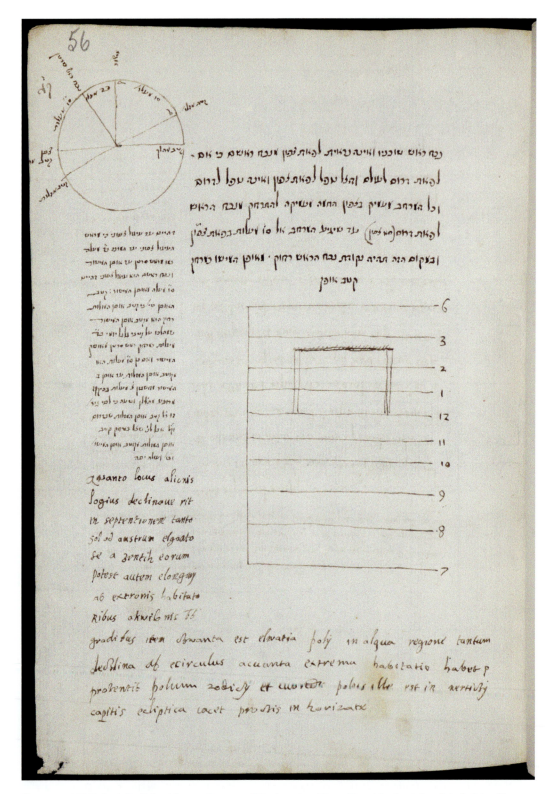

Figure 5.7. MS Oxford, Bodleian Library, Opp. 704 [Abraham bar Hiyya, *Tzurat ha-ʾaretz*] … [etc.], fol. 56ʳ.

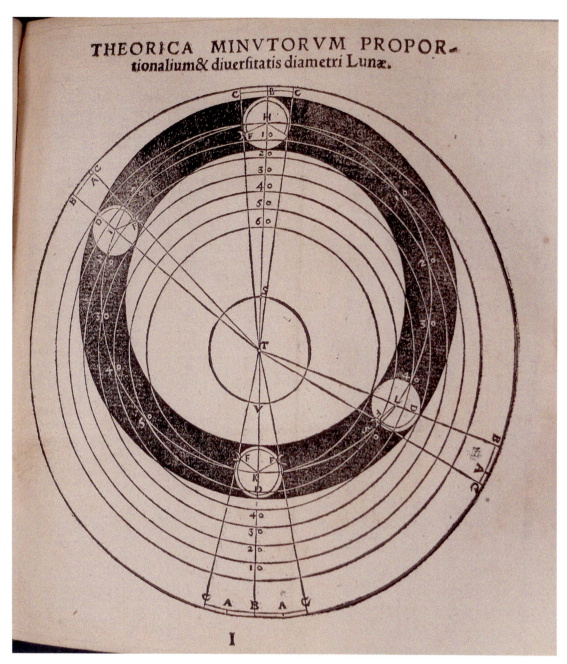

Figure 5.8. Georg Peurbach, *Theoricae novae planetarum*, Vitembergae: Joannes Luft, 1542, Prague, Library of the Royal Canonry of Premonstratensians at Strahov, AG XIII 115/b, after fol. H 8.

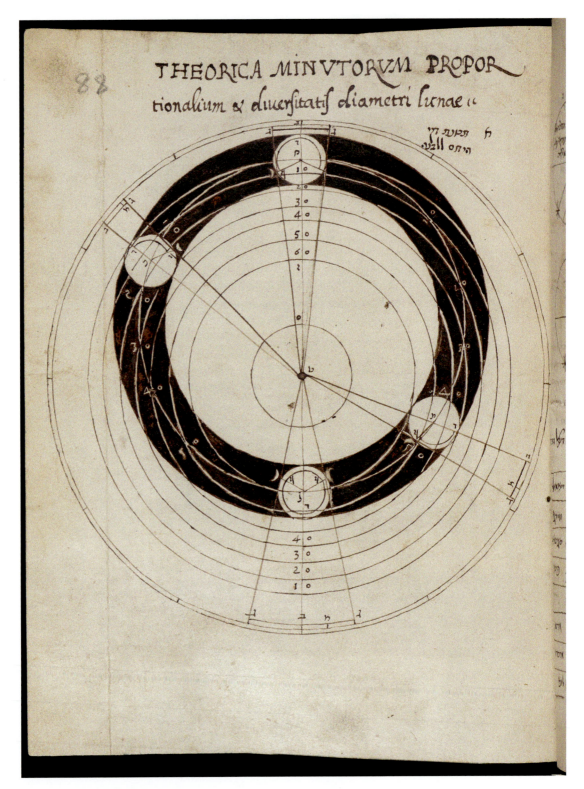

Figure 5.9. MS Oxford, Bodleian Library, Opp. 696 [Georg Peurbach, *Teoriqa*] … [etc.], fol. 88ʳ.

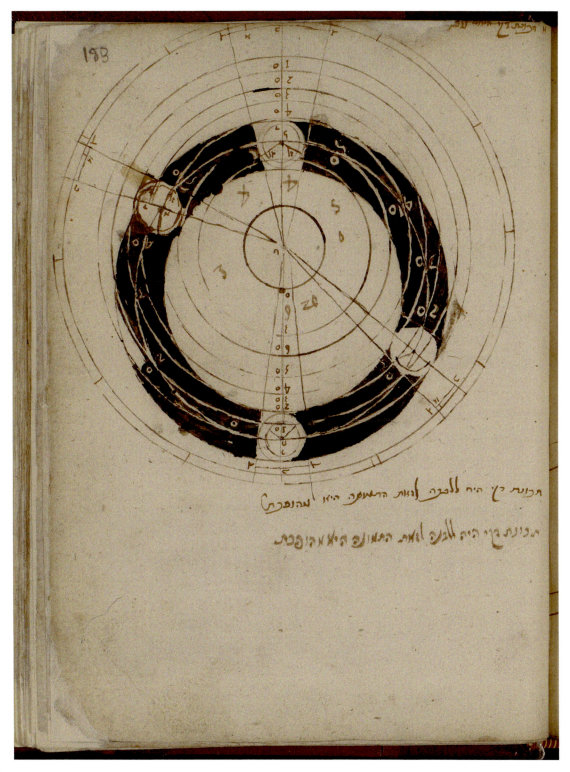

Figure 5.10. MS Philadelphia, LJS 498, [Abraham bar Hiyya, *Tsurat ha-´arets*] ... [etc.], Kislak Center for Special Collections, Rare Books and Manuscripts, University of Pennsylvania, fol. 182ᵛ.

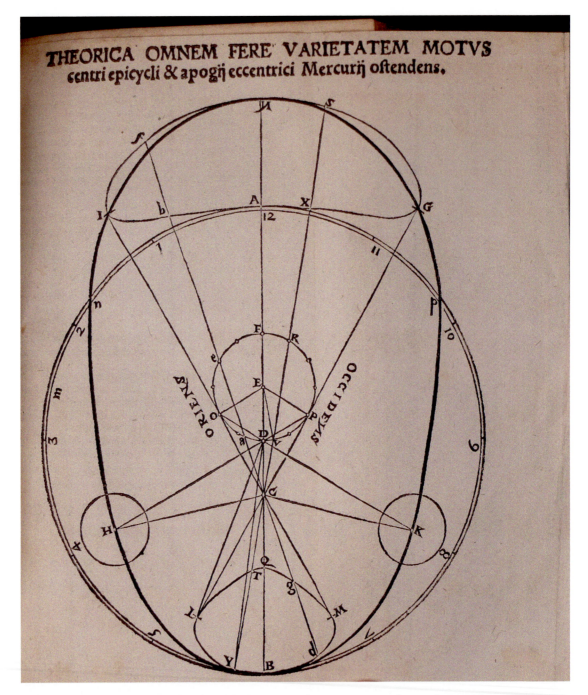

Figure 5.11. Georg Peurbach, *Theoricae novae planetarum*, Vitembergae: Joannes Luft, 1542, Prague, Library of the Royal Canonry of Premonstratensians at Strahov, AG XIII 115/b, after fol. O 2.

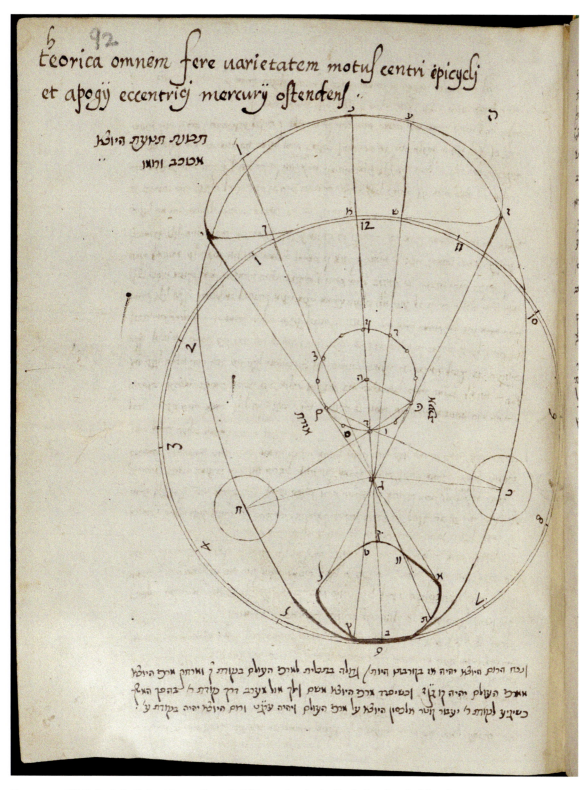

Figure 5.12. MS Oxford, Bodleian Library, Opp. 696 [Georg Peurbach, *Teoriqa*] ... [etc.], fol. 92ʳ.

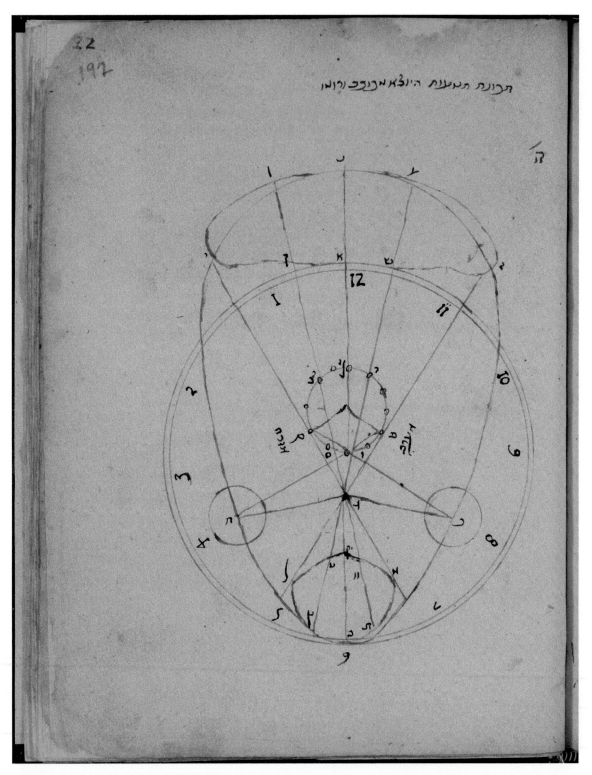

Figure 5.13. MS Philadelphia, LJS 498, [Abraham bar Hiyya, Tsurat ha-ʾarets] … [etc.], Kislak Center for Special Collections, Rare Books and Manuscripts, University of Pennsylvania, fol. 192ʳ.

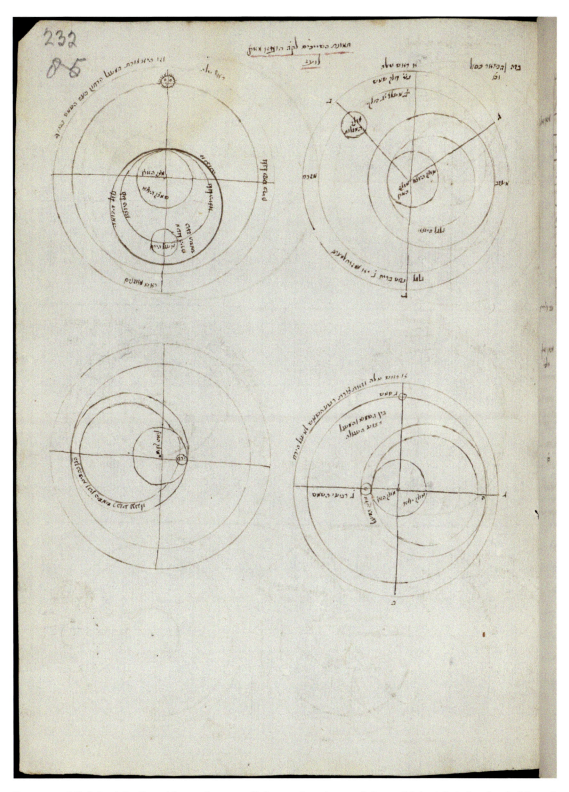

Figure 5.14. MS Oxford, Bodleian Library, Opp. 704 [Johannes Sacrobosco, *Sefer marʾeh ha-ʾofanim*] … [etc.], fol. 232ʳ.

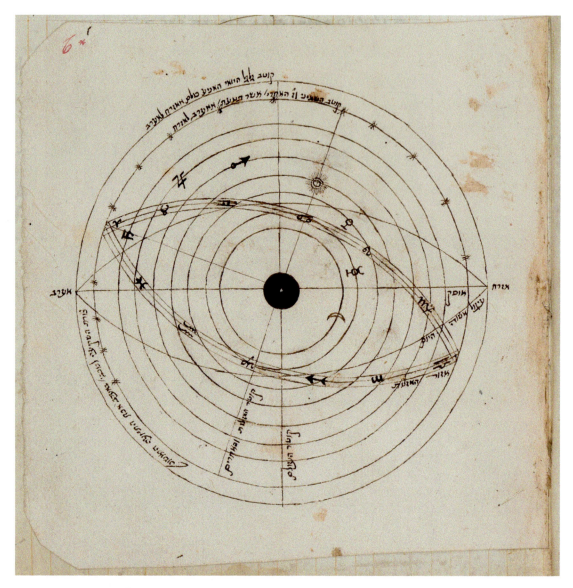

Figure 5.15. MS Vienna, *Österreichische Nationalbibliothek*, Cod. hebr. 56 [Johannes Sacrobosco, Mar´eh ha-'ofanim], fol. 6*.

Figure 5.16. MS Oxford, Bodleian Library, Mich. 144 [Johannes Sacrobosco, *Sefer mar'eh ha-'ofanim*] … [etc.], fol. 100ʳ.

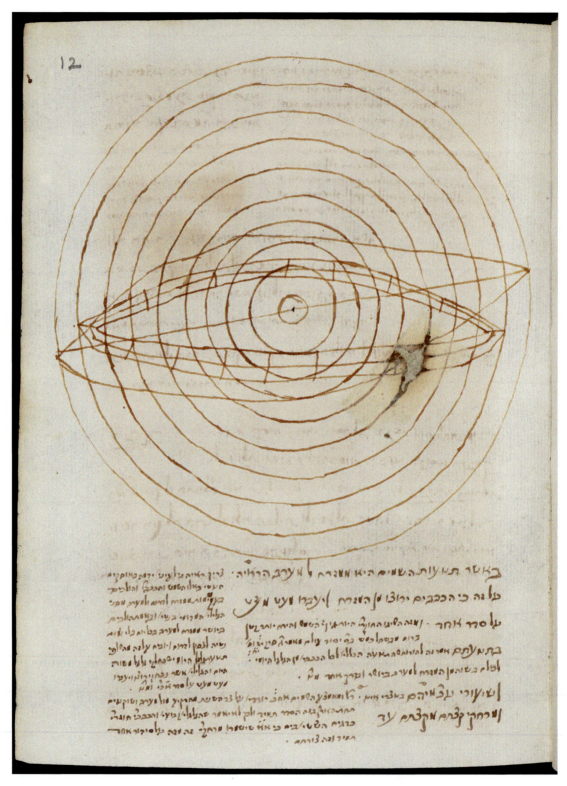

Figure 5.17. MS Oxford, Bodleian Library, Opp. 696 [Georg Peurbach, *Teoriqa*] … [etc.], fol. 12ʳ.

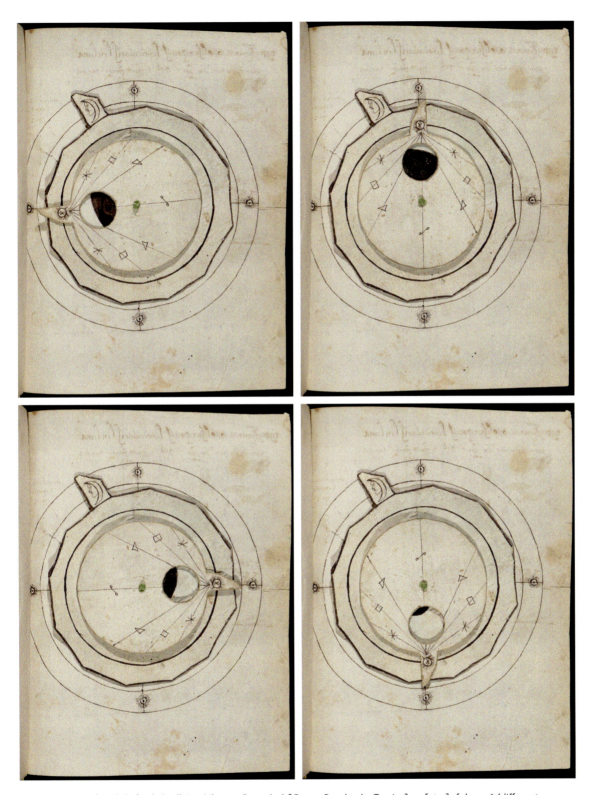

Figures 5.18a–18d. MS Oxford, Bodleian Library, Opp. 696 [Georg Peurbach, *Teoriqa*] ... [etc.], fol. 234ʳ (different positions of the wheel chart).

ANNETT MARTINI

Lishmah Qedushat Sefer Torah or the Impossibility of Printing a Kosher Torah Scroll from Rabbinic Perspectives

Introduction

I begin this chapter with a remarkable little narrative from the Babylonian Talmud, which at first glance seems to have nothing to do with the subject of the discussion:

In Tractate *Yoma*, we encounter several families that have handed down a certain expertise over the generations. Thus, the family Garmu was known all over Jerusalem for preparing excellent showbread that preserved its freshness for weeks; the house of Abtinas knew how to produce perfect incense, the smoke of which neither ascended as straight as a stick nor scattered in every direction but rose in just the right way. A certain Hygros of the tribe of Levi 'tuned his voice to a trill [...] so that his brethren, the priests, staggered backward with a sudden movement'. All of them refused to teach the secrets of their skills even when the promised reward was doubled and tripled. And so it was with Ben Kamzar, who also 'would not teach anything about [his art of] writing. It was said about him that he would take four pens between his fingers and if there was a word of four letters he would write it at once'. The Rabbanan asked all of them for their reasons for refusing to teach their skills. All the other experts found answer for their attitudes that satisfied the rabbis, but Ben Kamzar could not find one. The Talmud concludes this lesson with the words: 'Concerning [all] former ones it is said: "The memory of the righteous shall be for a blessing", with regard to Ben Kamzar and his like it is said: "But the name of the wicked shall rot"'.[1]

Despite this unpleasant prediction for Ben Kamzar and his descendants, about a millennium later the Polish halakhic authority Benjamin Aaron ben Abraham of Solnik (*c.* 1550–*c.* 1619) drew on this talmudic passage about the wondrous writing implement when he argued in favour of printing Torah scrolls. Indeed, the advantages are obvious. Copying mistakes could be avoided, *petuhot* and *setumot* ('open' and 'closed' reading portions)

---

1 Babylonian Talmud, *Yoma* 38b.

Annett Martini • Free University Berlin

would be in the right positions, the columns would be justified, and the shapes of the letters, *tagin*, and special signs, which are delineated by hundreds of halakhic rules, could be formed by printing types and always come out in the same shape. Last but not least, the mechanical production of a Torah scroll would save time and costs.

However, all these reasonable arguments for the increased accuracy possible with printing could not offset a crucial feature of a Torah scroll, which can be called the holy or even the magical dimension of all the material elements of this artefact.[2] In this chapter, I deal with the controversial halakhic discussion about what was undoubtedly the most far-reaching invention with regard to Jewish bookmaking: printing and the option for its use for producing the holy scrolls. Using a few exemplary legal positions for and against printed Torah scrolls from early modern times, I argue that there were essentially three modifications to the ancient writing rules that obtained in medieval Ashkenaz which led to the firm refusal to print in the holy realm of the STaM (acronym: *sefer torah, tefillin, mezuzot*): first, the enormous re-evaluation of the writing material as a medium of the Divine and the associated concept of ritually consecrating the parchments, letters, and particularly divine names; second, the increased perception of Christians as a potential contaminant of the sacred artefacts; and third, the concept of *kavanah*, that is, the proper intention of the scribe which as early as in medieval times found its way into the world of the *sofrei* STaM.

Arguments for Printing a Torah Scroll

Towards the end of the sixteenth century, Benjamin Aaron ben Abraham of Solnik was confronted with the question of whether printed *sefarim* would comply with the law of sanctifying the Torah scrolls in the same way as *sefarim* written by hand with a *qulmus* ('calamus'). Further, the enquirer complained that עוד שאלת על מה סומכין האידנא שכורכין ספרי׳ בכריכה וחותכין הגליונו׳ כדרך האומנין שעושין בכריכה וזורקין הגליונות לארץ ולאשפה ('Nowadays in the course of professional binding the folios of a scroll were cut and thrown on the floor into the dirt.')[3] This — he continued his complaint — would not be in accordance with the halakhah since authorities of religious law such as Moses ben Jakob from Cousy had already emphasized that once the name of God was written on a scroll, the entire scroll was holy. Thus, he

---

2   Recent studies on Torah scrolls include Judith Olszowy-Schlanger, 'An Early Palimpsest Scroll of the Book of Kings from the Cairo Genizah', *From a Sacred Source: Genizah Studies in Honour of Professor Stefan C. Reif*, ed. by Ben Outhwaite and Siam Bhayro (Leiden: Brill, 2010), pp. 237–47; Judith Olszowy-Schlanger, 'Some Palaeographical Observations on the Torah Scrolls from Medieval Crakow: Binding Fragments from the Jagellonian Library', in *Newly Discovered Hebrew Binding Fragments* (European Geniza Texts and Studies, vol. 5), ed. by Andreas Lehnardt (Leiden and Boston: Brill, 2020) pp. 228–57; Judith Olszowy-Schlanger 'The Anatomy of Non-biblical Scrolls from the Cairo Geniza', in *Jewish Manuscript Cultures: New Perspectives*, ed. by Irina Wandrey (Studies in Manuscript Cultures 13) (Berlin and Boston: De Gruyter, 2017), pp. 49–88; Mauro Perani (ed.), *The Ancient Sefer Torah of Bologna* (Leiden and Bosten 2019); Colette Sirat, 'Rouleaux de la Tora anterieurs à l'an mille', *CRAI* 5 (1994), pp. 861–87; Emma Abate and Justin Isserles (eds), 'From Cairo to Amsterdam: Hebrew Scrolls from the 11th to the 18th Centuries', *Henoch* 43/1 (2021); Jordan S. Penkower, 'A Sheet of Parchment from a 10th or 11th Century Torah Scroll: Determining its Type among Four Traditions (Oriental, Sefardi, Ashkenazi, Yemenite)', *Textus* 21 (2003), pp. 18–48; Jordan S. Penkower, 'The Ashkenazi Pentateuch Tradition as Reflected in the Erfurt Hebrew Bible Codices and Torah Scrolls', in *Erfurter Schriften zur Jüdischen Geschichte*, vol. 3: Zu Bild und Text im jüdisch-christlichen Kontext im Mittelalter, ed. by Frank Bussert, Sarah Laubenstein, and Maria Stürzebecher (Jena and Quedlinburg: Bussert & Stadeler, 2015), pp. 118–41.

3   Benjamin Aaron ben Abraham of Solnik, *Mas'at Binyamin*, responsum 99. Unless otherwise specified, quotations from rabbinic literature are based on the Online Responsa Project of the Bar Ilan University.

needed clarification regarding sanctifying the name of God in the context of printing.

In his response Benjamin first emphasized that one should not differentiate between handwritten and printed Torah scrolls because the printed scrolls reflect as much holiness as the handwritten ones. He referred to a responsum of his contemporary, the Italian rabbi and Kabbalist *Menahem* Azariah da Fano (1548–1620), who discussed the question of whether a printed *get* ('bill of divorce') was kosher or not in the light of the Talmud (Tractate *Gittin* 20). In the context of proper materials and practices for preparing a *get*, the Rabbanan differentiated between *lahqoq* (לחקק) — to engrave — and *likhtov* (לכתב) — to write and concluded that a *get* should be written. If it were engraved into a certain material the document would be considered invalid unless the letters were formed by impression and not by scraping out the material around them. *Menahem* took this view by the ancient scholars as a basis for his positive assessment of printing a *get* but with the restriction that the persons involved sign personally in ink in the empty spaces of the document left specifically for that purpose. To the objection by one of his colleagues that the printing press actually does leave an impression on the paper or parchment, so that one could indeed speak of engraving, *Menahem* Azariah replied:

ואנן בקיאינן באומנות זו ששכרנו בה פועלים הרבה ועמדנו עליהם ונתברר לנו שאין ממש בדברים הללו לא מסוגיית ההלכה ולא מעצמה של מלאכה, כי אפי' היו האותיות חקוקות בגופו של נייר ונקראות בו בלא דיו כה"ג הוי חק ירכות וכשר בגטי נשים [...] אע"ג דבס"ת תפלין ומזוזות חק ירכות נמי פסול שכל שהוא מעשה בגוף האות בעינן ביה כתיבה ולא חקיקה אבל הכא בדפוסין שלנו עקר הכתיבה היא בדיו ואין האומנין כובשין את הקלף במכבש שלהם אלא כדי שתצוייר האות בדיו היטב ולא ישאר חלק ממנה בלתי מושחה.

(We have been trained in this art [of printing] since we hired many workers who we preside over, and it became clear to us that there is no problem, neither in terms of halakhah nor in terms of the guild's power in these things. For, even if the letters are engraved on the paper and can be read from there without ink, they are חק ירכות and kosher for a *get* [...].[4] Nevertheless, with respect to the *sifrei* Torah, tefillin, and mezuzot חק ירכות are invalid since the rabbis believe that the body of a letter should be made by writing and not by engraving. However, our printing corresponds to the principle of writing with ink since the craftsmen do not impress on the parchment with their press but rather the letter will be properly drawn in ink and no part of it will be left without blackening.)[5]

Benjamin Aaron ben Abraham of Solnik essentially shared the view of *Menahem* Azariah, emphasizing that printing has nothing to do with engraving but is rather a kind of writing. The letters of the text neither protrude from nor sink into the writing material but rather are made visible by *dejo* — a black ink, which is applied on an impression and manually pressed onto the paper or the parchment. Thus, he considered that there was basically no difference between printing and writing when a *qulmus* was inked and taken to the writing material in order to form the letters.

---

4 The Talmud distinguishes two scripts: The first is a so-called חק תוכות, in which the letter's form is enclosed by the ink. Thus, in many Torah scrolls, the letter *pe* is written in such a way that the letter *beit* can be recognized in the inside as in this example: פ. The second script, which is mentioned in the quotation above, is חק ירקות, where, as is common practice, the background of the script remains white. This script was also interpreted as an embedded script. With respect to Benjamin's discussion, see also Jack S. Cohen, *The 613th Commandment: An Analysis of the Mitzvah to Write a Sefer Torah* (New York: Ktav, 1983), pp. 61–69.
5 *Menahem* Azariah da Fano, responsum 93.

The discussion could have ended at this point if it were not for another sensitive issue — the writing and sanctifying of the divine name.

The Ritual Writing of the Names of God

Several early rabbinic texts deal with the sensitive subject of copying the names of God only marginally in the context of writing a proper *get*. Thus, we learn from Tractate *Gittin* that every name of God should be written with the greatest devotion to God *lishmah* — 'for its own sake'. A Torah scroll 'in which the names of God have not been written with proper intention is worthless', and the rabbis insisted that the scribe should not receive any wage for such work.[6] The consideration that the *sofer* STaM could subsequently 'go over [these names] with a *qulmus* and so sanctify them קולמוס עליהם ליעבר] וליקדשיה] was rejected by the authorities since "such a name would not be proper".[7]

Two post-talmudic minor tractates, *Masekhet sefer torah* and *Masekhet soferim*, which have been of greatest importance for Jewish writing culture, turned towards the issue of the holy names in much greater detail. In a separate chapter, each of these tractates painstakingly differentiates between holy and non-holy names. With regard to *'Elohim, 'Adonai, YHWH, 'Ehiyeh 'Asher 'Ehiyeh*, and *Shaddai*, there is no doubt that they cannot be erased by the scribe, cut out of the writing skin, or even burned together with the entire scroll. The names *''El'* for *'Elohim* or *'YH'* for *YHWH* are also affected by this interdiction, whereas *'ShD'* for *Shaddai* or *'TzVA'* for *Tzevaot* are not counted among the holiest names of God so the stricter writing rules do not apply. The biblical prefixes and suffixes of the names of God are also more likely to be considered as part of the profane world and accordingly should be treated according to a different standard than the names themselves as they do not have their own divine potential in connection with the names of God. The letters in the names of God develop their holiness only in the context of the names, that is, it is not necessary to treat them with special care when they appear within profane words.

When deciding between sacred or profane, the historical or theological context is also decisive in some cases. Divine names in the biblical stories of Lot (Gen. 19) and the idolater Micha (Judg. 17) are not of the same sacred potency as they are elsewhere. The moral deficits of the protagonists in whose environments they occur rub off on them as it were. The two tractates also discuss the measures to be taken in the event of an accidental copying error. What should be done if the scribe has inadvertently omitted the name of God? What does he have to do if he has copied a name twice in succession? What correction rules does the scribe have to observe in such cases? There is general agreement that the Tetragrammaton YHWH must be subject to utmost diligence on the part of the scribe and the most assiduous care in terms of correction. Erasing the entire name or overwriting single letters must be avoided. Furthermore, the magical interplay of the letters of the name should not be disturbed by an unfocused scribe or the profane world. Even a king has to accept his subordinate status in view of the heavenly ruler, as is symbolized very nicely in the well-known parable of an earthly king who waits patiently for a scribe's greeting.[8]

Both of these tractates include two paragraphs that fall outside the thematic framework of the rabbinical discussion about the production of the STaM and draw attention to another subject area that was obviously not so far removed from the

---

6 Babylonian Talmud, *Gittin* 54b.
7 Babylonian Talmud, *Gittin* 54b.

8 *Masekhet soferim*, 5,6.

world of the *sofrei* STaM in antiquity. Part of a series of ancient textual witnesses that evidence a magical use of the names of God, they note that the powerful names could, as a curse, cause harm to people or if written directly on the body or on a piece of furniture, provide protection against illness, evil powers, or an adverse fate. Jewish culture adapted the belief in the magical potential of divine names from surrounding cultures and more or less openly integrated it into religious practice.⁹

The magical dimension of writing the STaM was rarely mentioned in medieval European halakhic literature. The explanations for the correct treatment of misspelled divine names, the handling of disused Torah scrolls and other texts that contain divine names, and the general distinction between profane and holy names are remarkably short in the rabbinic schools of Ashkenaz compared to the ancient guidelines. Most rabbinic authorities did not deal with the subject at all. There are many reasons for this, one of which may have been the general lack of interest in the names of God as magical signs. Scholars have repeatedly pointed out that within the Ashkenazi rabbinic circles, the names of God and the angels were used principally in the context of prayer, and to a much lesser extent, owing to their perceived supernatural powers, for talismans, amulets, and other magical objects.¹⁰ According to this understanding, the divine name unfolds its effectiveness in the acoustic sphere and not in the sensual realm of writing.

However, one element came into focus in medieval European scribal literature which played only a marginal role in early rabbinic discussions: the ritual consecration of the divine names. Whereas the influential minor talmudic tractates do not even mention the sanctification of the divine names, in medieval Christian Europe the process of sanctifying in the context of producing the STaM became a prescribed, recognizable performance, which was divided into predefined sequences on which a participant drew during a rite.¹¹ In this ritual, particular importance was assigned to a formula to be pronounced. The normal flow of the writing process was interrupted for a moment and continued in a ritualized manner according to a prescribed pattern. In his famous *Qiryat sefer* ('Book Town') *Menahem* ben Solomon Meiri (d. 1316) specified the procedure for the consecration of the divine names by concluding his remarks on the ritual consecration of parchment with the following observation:

ושיכוין בתחילת הכתיבה שיכתוב הספר לשם תורת ישראל והאזכרות לשם קדושת השם [...] דרך כלל ושיכוין בתחילת הכתיבה שיכתוב הספר לשם תורת ישראל והאזכרות לשם קדושת השם.

---

9   Cf. Joshua Trachtenberg, *Jewish Magic and Superstition: A Study in Folk Religion* (New York: Atheneum, ⁵1987); Michael D. Swartz, 'Scribal Magic and Its Rhetoric: Formal Patterns in Medieval Hebrew and Aramaic Incantation Texts from the Cairo Genizah', in *Harvard Theological Review*, 83 (1990), pp. 163–80; Michael D. Swartz, 'Book and Tradition in Hekhalot and Magical Literatures', *Journal of Jewish Thought and Philosophy*, 3 (1994), pp. 189–229; Michael D. Swartz, *Scholastic Magic: Ritual and Revelation in Early Jewish Mysticism* (Princeton: Princeton University Press, 1996); Giuseppe Veltry, 'Jewish Traditions in Greek Amulets', *Bulletin of Judaeo-Greek Studies*, 18 (1996), pp. 33–47; Giuseppe Veltry, *Magie und Halakhah: Ansätze zu einem empirischen Wissenschaftsbegriff im spätantiken und frühmittelalterlichen Judentum* (Tübingen: Mohr Siebeck, 1997); Peter Schäfer, 'Magic and Religion in Ancient Judaism', in *Envisioning Magic*, ed. by Peter Schäfer and Hans G. Kippenberg (Leiden: Brill, 1997), pp. 19–44; Giedeon Bohak, *Ancient Jewish Magic* (Cambridge: Cambridge University Press, 2008).

10 Ephraim Kanarfogel, *'Peering through the Lattice'. Mystical, Magical, and Pietistic Dimensions in the Tosafist Period* (Detroit: Wayne State University Press, 2000), p. 29.

11 See Annett Martini, 'Ritual Consecration in the Context of Writing the Holy Scrolls: Jews in Medieval Europe between Demarcation and Acculturation', *European Journal of Jewish Studies*, 11 (2017), pp. 174–202.

(Concerning writing, too, the scribe should say at the beginning of the process that he writes *leshem*. With respect to the names of God, also, he should concentrate on the uniqueness of the One. [...] Usually at the beginning of writing [the scribe] says that he intends to write a Torah scroll for the purpose of the Torah of Israel and the names of God for the purpose of the Holiness of the ineffable name.)[12]

Similarly, Asher ben Yehiel Ashkenazi (late thirteenth/early fourteenth century), who was active in Germany, southern France, and northern Spain, noted, וכן כשמתחיל לכתוב ס״ת יאמר ס״ת זה אני כותב לשם קדושת תורת משה. (At the beginning of writing a Sefer Torah one should speak [aloud]: '"I write this Sefer Torah for the purpose of [*lishmah*] the holiness of the Torah of Moses".)[13] He further emphasized that a verbal declaration before writing a sacred scroll was absolutely necessary. However, when copying the name of God, he considered it sufficient to speak the formula 'for the purpose of the holiness of the name' in thoughts. Nevertheless, Asher ben Yehiel contended that although the entire procedure of writing a scroll has to be processed *lishmah*, the writing of the holy name of God stands on a higher level of scribal art, and a scroll made without sanctifying the divine name is of no worth.[14] Aaron ben Jakob ha-Cohen (thirteenth/fourteenth century) also described a ritual consecration of the names in his principal work, *'Orḥot hayyim* ('Ways of Life'). Before starting his project, the scribe 'through his mouth' must dedicate the holy scrolls to their ritual purpose and consecrate the names of God before they are written.[15]

My last example from the rabbinic milieu is Mordekhai ben Hillel ha-Cohen (d. 1298), who also argued in favour of verbalizing a formula, the effect of which depended on the proper intention of the scribe. Thus:

ובתחילת הכתיבה בס״ת תפילין ומזוזות צריך
שיאמר בפירוש אני כותב הכל לשם תורת ישראל
והאזכרות לשם קדושה וכן בגט צריך אמירה ואין
די בכל אלו במחשבה.

(At the beginning of writing a Sefer Torah it is necessary to verbalize the formula: 'I write everything for the purpose of the Torah of Israel and in the names of God, for the purpose of the holiness'. [...] And it is not enough to do all this just in thought.)[16]

This strong emphasis on the formula was observed by the following generations with minor variations. In the most influential rabbinic work of early modern times, the *Shulḥan 'arukh* ('Set Table') (1565), Josef ben Ephraim Qaro from Toledo adopted this approach and incorporated the performative declaration at the beginning of writing the scroll, copying the divine names, and preparing the parchment for its ritual purpose. The formulae for processing the skins (עורות אלו אני מעבד לשם), writing Torah scrolls and tefillin (אני כותב לשם קדושת), and copying the names (אני כותב לשם קדושת השם) correspond to the models which apparently emerged at the end of the twelfth or the beginning of the thirteenth century in France and the German Lands. Despite minor variants they even became part of modern scribal literature in such books as *Sefer benei yonah* ('Book of Young Doves') by the Bohemian Talmudist and *sofer* STaM Jonah ben Elijah Landsofer (d. 1712), *Sefer melekhet*

---

12 *Menaḥem* ha-Meiri, *Qiryat sefer*, 1,2.

13 Asher ben Yehiel, *Halakhot qetanot*, *Hilkhot sefer torah*, sec. 4.

14 Asher ben Yehiel, *Halakhot qetanot*, *Hilkhot tefillin*, sec. 3.

15 Aaron ben Jacob ha-Cohen, *'Orhot hayyim*, *Hilkhot tefillin*, sec. 24 and 25.

16 Mordekai ben Hillel ha-Cohen, *Halakhot qetanot*, (*Menahot*) chapter *Qometz rabbah*, sec. 966.

shamayim ('Book of the Work of Heaven') by Isaac Dov ha-Levi Bamberger (d. 1879), and the *Qeset ha-sofer* ('Inkstand of the Scribe') by Solomon Ganzfried. In the last treatise, Ganzfried explained why the formula should be verbalized: 'Some say that it is necessary to bring [the formula] over the lips [...], because one cannot impact sanctity by thinking alone [אין הקדושה חלה במחשבה] but by speaking since speaking makes a greater impression [שהדיבור עושה רושם גדול]'.[17]

As discussed elsewhere in detail,[18] the German Pietists devoted a great deal of attention to the writing of the names of God in the context of copying *sefarim*. The authors of *Sefer hasidim* ('Book of the Pious') drew directly on the rabbinic material from ancient times, which was virtually ignored by medieval halakhic authorities, and instigated an unsystematic renaissance. Instead of the rabbinic advice to think or speak a formula of consecration, *Sefer hasidim* mentioned the practice of writing it down — not in the *sefer* itself but on a separate piece of paper. This salient alteration can be considered an intensification of a practice that was discussed most notably within Ashkenazi rabbinic sources in the thirteenth century. Needless to say, the written word or sentence has a much stronger impact than a spoken formula or one that is merely imagined in the mind. A piece of paper could have been at hand throughout the entire working process on the writing table or even carried by a person like an amulet. The impression of a magical connotation in this context is enhanced by the following passage from *Sefer hasidim*:

אחד היה מעתיק מן הספרים ומן הפירושים והיה קורא בפיו וכותב וכל מה שהיה כותב היה קורא בפיו תחילה שאלו לו למה אתה קורא קודם שאתה כותב[?] אמ׳ קבלתי כשאדם קורא ומוציא מפיו השדים שומעים ומברכים אותו ועוד יזכור מה שיכתוב וכתיב למען תהיה תורת יי בפיך וכתיב לזכרון.

(A [scribe] copied from books and commentaries and first read [the text] aloud and only then wrote it down. Everything he wrote, he first read aloud. Someone asked him: 'Why do you read it aloud before you write it down?' He answered: 'The tradition was handed down to me that when a person reads aloud and casts out demons he will be heard and blessed'.)[19]

This narrative explicitly affiliates the copying of scriptural texts to exorcism. Reading aloud is a traditional mnemotechnical method in Jewish education and was sometimes the performative centre of incantations. It is obvious that here the ritual designation of a certain writing for its particular purpose as found within rabbinic thought merged with popular forms of belief, namely belief in demons and exorcism. Furthermore, the scribes' obligation not to disturb the absolute perfection of the names with bad writing habits was substantiated by the Pietists with several rules. Thus, in accordance with rabbinic sources, the names of God were not to be written close to a hole in the parchment and much less be perforated. Therefore, the scribe 'should not stitch through the name but only through the blank spaces at the *gevil*'[20] when a scroll or a page

---

17   Martini, 'Ritual Consecration', p. 188.
18   See Annett Martini, 'The Ritualization of Manufacturing and Handling Holy Books by the Hasidei Ashkenaz and the Impact of the Monastic Book Culture in the Middle Ages', in *Ritual Dynamics in Jewish and Christian Contexts*, ed. by Claudia Bergmann and Benedikt Kranemann, Jewish and Christian Perspectives, 34 (Leiden: Brill 2019), pp. 56–84 (pp. 74–77).

19   *Sefer hasidim* §§733, 1763 (MS Parma, H 3280), quoted according to the Princeton University *Sefer hasidim* Database.
20   אם בספר נקרע במקום השם ובא לתפור אל יתפור במקום השם מפני שתוחב השם אלא במקום הגויל שלא נכתב שם וכן לא יכתוב אדם השם במפה מפני שהנשים צריכות לתפור ולתחוב המחט בו (*Sefer hasidim* § 697 [MS Parma, H 3280]).

of a book has to be fixed. Moreover, the words before and after a divine name should be treated with a special care:

סופר שהיה כותב את השם ותיבה שלפני תיבת השם לא האיר בטוב שצריך להעביר הקולמוס עוד עליו כדי שיהיו האותיות של תיבה שלפני השם נכרים יפה בדיו וכבר התחיל לכתוב את השם ולא כתבו כולו לא יתכן שיפסיק באותיות של שם ויאיר תיבה אחרת.

(A *sofer* who has written the name of God but the word before it is not readable should again go over it with the *qulmus* so that the letters of the word will become readable. However, if he already had begun to write the name of God and not yet completed it, he must not suspend [his work on] the letters of the name in order to mend another word.)[21]

The writing flow should correspond to the absolute perfection of God's name and, thus, must not be interrupted. *Sefer hasidim* refers to the well-known image of a scribe who does not interrupt his work, not even to respond to a king's greeting. Further, the scribe must not stand up at the sensitive moment of writing a divine name when a subordinate enters his room to ask him a question, and — even more importantly — a scribe has to neglect his own needs such as the urge to spit. With respect to ritual aspects of writing the divine names, *Sefer hasidim* presents remarkable instructions, which diverge from tradition:

כתיב ויכתבו עליו פתוחי חותם קדש לייי ויכתבו לימד שבפני רבים נכתב השם כגון [...] הראשונים עושים כשכותבין ספר התורה היו כותבין השמות בעשרה צדיקים ויש אומרים הוצרך בפני רבים לכותבו כדי להזהירו שיכתוב לשמה שאם יכתוב שלא לשמה שטעון גניזה וגם האותיות בפעם אחת כולם היו.

(It is written: '[And they made the plate of the holy crown of pure gold,] and wrote upon it a writing, like to the engravings of a signet, HOLINESS TO THE LORD [יהוה]' [Exod. 39:30]. [The employed the plural:] 'and they wrote' teaches that the name should be written in the presence of a greater number of people, meaning ten persons. [...] The Rishonim, when a Sefer Torah was written, wanted the names to be written by ten righteous [men]. There are some who say [that] it is necessary to write [the name of God] in the presence of a quorum as a reminder that it was written for the sake of [the divine name]. For if it was not written for the sake of [the name the scroll] should be stored in a genizah. This holds true for every single letter.)[22]

This paragraph is remarkable because the author (Judah he-Hasid) demanded testimony of the ritual sanctification of the divine names. A group of ten righteous men shall come together for copying the Tetragrammaton to make sure that the sanctification of the name was accomplished correctly, insisting that the presence of such righteous men guarantees the holiness of the moment when God enters the world by His ineffable name. The presence of a tsadik also signifies the mercy of God, who by the righteous ensures the continuance of the world.

We do not know whether these exceptional rituals of sanctifying the divine names in the context of copying scriptural texts really found their way into practice. The question of how much influence the Hasidei Ashkenaz movement actually had is the subject of controversial dis-

---

21 *Sefer hasidim* § 715 (MS Parma, H 3280).

22 *Sefer hasidim* § 1762 (MS Parma, H 3280).

cussion.²³ Nevertheless, *Sefer hasidim* provides us with valuable insights into a rather magical perception of how *sifrei qodesh* ('holy books') should be reproduced, although its practical instruction probably reflects the radical and reformative approach of an elitist religious group within medieval Judaism. Moreover, the Pietists were familiar with and extended the manifold early rabbinic regulations with respect to the scrolls of holy texts to non-scriptural writings 'pointedly stretching the domain of sacred writings so as to encompass inscribed texts of Oral Torah (Mishnah and Talmud)'.²⁴ Moreover, as Ephraim Kanarfogel points out, their attitude towards the holy books had a real impact on the halakhic world.²⁵

Ben Kamzar's Writing Tool as an Argument for Printing a Torah Scroll

Is it possible to follow the various rules for writing the name of God in printing without infringing its holiness? In his attempt to answer this question, Benjamin Aaron ben Abraham of Solnik found inspiration in the aforementioned story of Ben Kamzar and his special writing tool. Indeed, Rashi and the Tosafot interpreted the art of writing with four pens simultaneously as an allusion to the Tetragrammaton and the procedure of writing with the wondrous pen as a form of sanctification of God's unity. The Provençal rabbi Yehonatan ha-Cohen of Lunel (b. *c.* 1149), who was a great admirer and proponent of Maimonides' teaching, was also convinced that the writing instrument was created for copying the Tetragrammaton: שם סופר ידוע שהיה קושר ד' קולמוסין בארבע אצבעות ימינו, ובבת אחת היה כותב שם בן ד' אותיות ברגע אחד, ולא היה מקדים אות אחת לחברתה. (Ben Kamzar tied four *qulmusim* together on the four right fingers and simultaneously wrote the name of the four letters at one strike since no letter should precede those surrounding it.)²⁶

According to Yehonatan, the reason for Ben Kamzar's refusal to teach other scribes the secret of his writing instrument was that not everyone valued the divine name equally. The French scholar obviously feared improper use of the writing tool for magical practices. The story about Ben Kamzar's exceptional family tradition was also adopted by philosophers and mystics, for example, by Isaac Abravanel (1437 Lisbon–1508 Venice) and Judah Moscato (*c.* 1533–90). The latter referred to the talmudic story as a metaphor for

---

23 Isaak Bear, '"המגמה הדתית-החברתית של "ספר חסידים"' ['The Religious-Social Tendency of "Sefer Hasidim"'], *Zion* 3 (1937), pp. 1–50, 18; Gershom Scholem, *Die jüdische Mystik in ihren Hauptströmungen* (Frankfurt a. M.: Suhrkamp, 1980), pp. 104–06, 113; Joseph Dan, 'Rabbi Judah the Pious and Caesarius of Heisterbach: Common Motifs in their Stories', in *Studies in Aggadah and Folk-Literature*, ed. by Joseph Heinemann and Dov Noy (Jerusalem: Magnes Press 1971), pp. 18–27; Moritz Güdemann, *Geschichte des Erziehungswesens und der Cultur der Juden in Frankreich und Deutschland* (Vienna: Hölder 1880), I, pp. 178–98 and 281–91; Ascher Rubin, 'The Concept of Repentance among the Hasidey 'Ashkenaz', *The Journal of Jewish Studies* 16 (1965), pp. 161–76; Talya Fishman, 'The Penitential System of Hasidei Ashkenaz and the Problem of Cultural Boundaries', *The Journal of Jewish Thought and Philosophy* 8 (1999), pp. 201–29; Joseph Dan, 'Ashkenazi Hasidim, 1941–91: Was there Really a Hasidic Movement in Medieval Germany?', in *Gershom Scholem's Major Trends in Jewish Mysticism 50 Years After*, ed. by Peter Schäfer and Joseph Dan (Tübingen: J. C. B. Mohr 1993), pp. 87–102; for a more complete summary of the earlier discussions, cf. Ivan G. Marcus, *Piety and Society: The Jewish Pietists of Medieval Germany* (Leiden: Brill 1981), pp. 1–20.
24 Talya Fishman, 'The Rhineland Pietists' Sacralisation of Oral Torah', *Jewish Quarterly Review*, 96 (2006), pp. 9–16, 12.
25 Ephraim Kanarfogel, 'Peering through the Lattices', pp. 144–53. See also Kanafogel, 'Rashi's Awareness of Jewish Mystical Literature and Traditions', in *Raschi und sein Erbe*, ed. by Daniel Krochmalnik and others, Schriften der Hochschule für jüdische Studien Heidelberg, 10 (Heidelberg: Universitätsverlag Winter, 2007), pp. 23–34.
26 Yehonatan ha-Cohen of Lunel, *Commentary to Isaak ben Jakob Alfasi, Masekhet Yoma* 38a.

the fact that God and His name are not in the least changed or affected by time:

כי על כן היה ראוי לכתוב בהכאה אחד שם עצמותו ית' אשר בו אותיות היה הוה יהיה כמו שהיה עושה בן קמצר הבקי בכתיבתו בנתינת ד' קולמוסים בין אצבעותיו כמסופר ממנו פ' אמר להם הממונה. כי כן יאות להתחיל קריאתו מכל אות ממנו הואיל ונכתבו אותיותיו כלן בבת אחת ומשם הערה יוצאת על הויותו ית' בלתי מקבל רושם מן הזמן כי העתיד אצלו הוא העבר והעבר עתיד ושניהם כהוה אצלו. ועל העקר הזה גנו חז"ל את בן קמצר שלא רצה ללמד על מעשה הכתיבה.

(This is why it was fitting to write in one stroke the name of the essence of the Lord, may He be blessed, which is composed with the letters HYH HWH YHYH. Indeed, this is how Kamzar did it, who was expert in the art of writing [the Tetragrammaton] by holding in his fingers four pens at a time [...]. For in this way one can start to read His name from any letter, even though its letters have all been written down in one single stroke — which brings one to the conclusion that the Blessed One is not affected by time, the future being for Him [like] the past and the past like the future, and both of them [like] the present. And it was on the basis of this principle that our Sages of blessed memory blamed Ben Kamzar for refusing to teach this way of writing.)[27]

Thus, Ben Kamzar's mysterious writing tool became a metaphor for the absolute unity of God, who exists beyond worldly categories such as time. Accordingly, to write the name YHWH in this way is an expression of the view that this name corresponds to the essence of God and therefore requires special treatment by the scribe.

As we see from these examples, Benjamin Aaron ben Abraham of Solnik could draw on a rich pool of connotations which associate the four-part writing instrument with God's name, or even predestine it for writing the name. Thus, he praised the advantages of Kamzar's invention, arguing that a simultaneous action leaves no part of the holy name incomplete at any time, whereas during the normal copying process the holy name is not complete until it is concluded. Benjamin extended this approach by declaring that the ability of Ben Kamzar 'to write all letters of the name simultaneously' should be considered as a higher level of writing:

שיש בזה סוד וקדושה רבה יותר מבשם שנכתבו אותיותיו זה אחר זה ואם כן ה"ה נמי במלאכת הדפוס שלנו שמדפיס כל הדף בבת אחת לאו גריעותא וקדושתא קלה הוא אלא אדרבה מעלה יתירה וקדושה רבה הוא.

(For therein lies a secret and even more *qedushah* (holiness) than in a name the letters of which are written one by one. And if so, we should also think of the work of our printing [in this way] since one prints an entire page at one time and there is no devaluation or less *qedushah* but rather it is much more than that, the *qedushah* increases.)[28]

However, Benjamin added that the halakhah stipulates a sanctification of each divine name in a Sefer Torah separately since the Sages deemed it necessary that: שצריך להוציא בשפתיו בכל פעם שכותב שם שכותב לשם קדושת השם ואינו מספיק שיוציא בשפתיו פעם אחת לכמה שמות. (Each time one writes the Name it should come over his lips so that he writes *leshem qedushat ha-shem* and it

---

[27] Quoted after the translation in Judah Moscato, *Sermons: Edition and Translation* (Leiden: Brill 2011), II, pp. 47–48.

[28] Benjamin Aaron ben Abraham, responsum 99.

is not enough to bring this saying over the lips once for several names.)²⁹

But what happens if there is more than one name in a column or on a folio and how, then, can this rule be followed if a Sefer Torah is printed? The Polish scholar solved this halakhic issue by arguing that this halakhah does not apply if the divine names are in immediate succession.

אין צריך לקדש כל שם בפני עצמו ולא אמרינן שצריך לקדש כל שם ושם בפני עצמו רק בשמות שאינן סמוכין שכותב כמה תיבות בין שם לשם והוי הפסקה אבל בשכותב כמה שמות בלי הפסקה די להם בקידוש אחד ... ולפי זה בספרים הנדפסים שמדפיס כל הדף בפעם אחד ובכח אחד די בקידוש אחד לכל הדף שהרי אין כאן הפסק כלל.

(It is not necessary to sanctify each name on its own [...] only in case the names are not juxtaposed, if there are some words between name and name and [if] there is an intermission. However, when writing several names without intermission it is enough for them to sanctify them at once. [...] Therefore, [for] printed *sefarim* where every folio is printed at once and by one effort, one sanctification for each folio is enough, for behold, there is no intermission at all.)³⁰

Benjamin's sophisticated argumentation for printing Torah scrolls was based on technical conditions by which the manual press printed the folios one after the other, thus allowing one to sanctify each page separately. Thus, it seemed at least imaginable to proceed in this way. Later halakhic authorities, however, could hardly refer to this argument as, of course, the more modern printing process was automated, which did not entail any intermissions that could be used to sanctify each folio individually. However, this was not the only argument against the use of printing technology for producing a Torah scroll in the time of Benjamin Aaron ben Abraham of Solnik, as we will see in the next section.

Arguments against Printing a Torah Scroll

Despite the convincing arguments of some early modern scholars for printing a Torah scroll, the voices in favour of unconditionally adhering to handwritten production of ritual artefacts prevail to this day. One of the scholars to speak out against the new technology in this special case was the German halakhist Yair Hayyim ben Moses Samson Bachrach (d. 1702), who in his famous collection of responsa *Havvot Yair* ('Villages of Yair') raised various objections to printing scrolls which shed an interesting light on this issue. In fact, in this responsum, Rabbi Yair summarized the most important arguments for and against printing the STaM in early modern times and, at the same time, related to the crucial aspects of the European medieval approach towards producing the STaM. These were, first, the critical role of non-Jews in the context of manufacturing the STaM; second, the sanctification of the material elements of the scrolls including the divine names; and third, the proper intention of the *sofer*.

First of all, Yair considered arguments that derived from ancient sources, including the case of Ben Kamzar, 'worthless':

מפני שלא ידעו לפני שי״ן שנה מענין הדפוס אף כי ראיתי בספר כח ה' שהי' בנמצא מימים קדמונים ברזילי' מוכנים לדפוס אכן לא אותיות נפרדים רק מלות שלימות מלה מלה רצופה לכן לא היו מספיקי' לדפוס המבוקש לכן אין ראיה מאוקמת' דש״ס וע״ש בט״ז ודוק.

---

29 Benjamin Aaron ben Abraham, responsum 99.
30 Benjamin Aaron ben Abraham, responsum 99.

(For they knew nothing about printing 300 years ago. Even though I have seen in *Sefer ha-koakh* ['Book of Strength' by Isaac Luria] that in ancient times there existed metal types prepared for printing, there were no separate letters, only complete words. Each word was placed consecutively. Thus, they did not have the facilities to print everything they wanted. In this respect, the case in the Talmud cannot be counted as an argument.)[31]

With respect to the decision as to whether a printed Torah scroll is kosher or not, one should first, and most importantly, ask if the printer is a gentile since רק מצד שהמדפיס הוא גוי ולא עדיפא מכותבם גוי דק"ל יגנז ('If a gentile had written them [...] we demand that such [a Torah scroll] should be stored away').[32] Yair reminded his readers of the talmudic debate (Tractate *Gittin* 45b) about how to deal with Torah scrolls written or owned by non-Jews. The Rabbanan discussed the options of burning, storing away, or using such scrolls and came to the conclusion that in any case a scroll had to be copied according to the law. This includes not only the sanctification of the divine names by a Jew but also the consecration of the parchments in the course of their manufacture. To Yair's astonishment, however:

ותמה על הקדמונים ובט"ז שלא הרגיש בזה ואפשר דמיירי בשהמדפיסם ישראל וסתמא כך הוא על הרוב וגם בזה צל"ע דהא בעינן קידוש כל שם ושם וזולתו הס"ת פסול כבגיטין.

(The earlier authorities and Taz [David ha-Levi Segal] were not aware of this. Perhaps they were talking about Jewish printers, as this is the norm in most cases. But even such a case requires further scrutiny, for we demand a separate sanctification for each and every instance of God's name. Without that, the Torah scroll is unfit for use as [it is discussed in the Talmud] in Tractate *Gittin*.)[33]

Yair also related to the fact that the Talmud (Tractate *Gittin* 45b) actually mentions the possibility that a non-Jew could write a Torah scroll that would be proper for ritual use but noted that it was a ruling he could not understand. He vehemently rejected this option, which was in accord with the attitude that began to prevail in antiquity and culminated in medieval Europe that mandated the strict exclusion of non-Jews in the production of the STaM.

The most famous example from ancient times is doubtlessly Pirqoi ben Baboi with his famous letter to the communities of Palestine. The polemical pamphlet of that talmudic scholar from the early gaonic period includes a revealing report about the practice of making Torah scrolls in the Holy Land. Pirqoi complained that 'they took *raq* [the Arabic term for a special sort of parchment] of the non-Jews, who wrote books of idolatry on it'. The skins on which they wrote the holy scrolls, Pirqoi continued his reproach, were neither tanned nor ritually dedicated to their sacral purpose as demanded by the talmudic tradition. Owing to the absence of halakhic orientation, Jews mistakenly wrote their scrolls on the flesh side of even an unkosher animal skin and without *dejo*. Pirqoi was quite clear about the reason for this religious decay:

It was the practice of evil Edom (Rome, Byzantium) to decree religious persecution against the Land of Israel that they should not read the Torah. And they hid away all

---

[31] Yair Hayyim ben Moses Samson Bachrach, *Havvot Yair*, responsum 184.

[32] Yair Hayyim ben Moses Samson Bachrach, *Havvot Yair*, responsum 184.

[33] Yair Hayyim ben Moses Samson Bachrach, *Havvot Yair*, responsum 184.

the Torah scrolls because they would burn them. And when the Ishmaelites [Muslims] came they had no Torah scrolls and there were no scribes who knew the pertinent laws for doing this'.[34]

Rabbinic scribal literature from medieval France and the German Lands dwelt on this issue, which grew into a broad debate as the non-Jew appeared as a potential contaminating factor, endangering the purity and holiness of the scrolls owing to the intentions of an idolater. The routine reference to Maimonides, who emphasized that skins which 'were processed by a gentile are unsuitable, even if [a Jew] had directed him [...]'[35] reveals the discomfort with materials such as parchment, ink, or other parts of books produced or processed by Christians. Whereas the Tosafot dealt with this issue on a rather theoretical level, early manuals for scribes offer fascinating insights into the day-by-day challenges that confronted a professional *sofer* STaM in terms of both ritual and problematic collaboration with Christian tanners and bookmakers. The influential treatise *Barukh she-'amar* ('Blessed Is He Who Spoke') from the late thirteenth or early fourteenth century, which includes an instruction regarding the proper way to make tefillin by Abraham ben Moses of Sinsheim and a commentary by his disciple Samson ben Eliezer, is a striking example of the growing concern among European scribes about being defrauded by Christian tanners, merchants, and clerics. Authors of manuals such as that one as well as a range of responsa were not confined to complaints but discussed ways to avoid the contact with Christians or at least to supervise the manufacture of writing materials.[36]

Apart from the preparation of the parchment by non-Jews, the purchase of ink for writing the STaM from Christians was considered unacceptable because the ink could contain ingredients — such as wine or vinegar — which do not correspond to the kashrut. Thus, Abraham ben Nathan ha-Yarhi from Provence, who moved to northern Spain at the beginning of the thirteenth century, complained about the practice of many *sofrei* STaM to buy ink from non-Jews. Emphasizing an explicit reference to the corresponding halakhic discussion in Tractate *'Avodah zarah* (71a), he, as many halakhic authorities after him, insisted that the ink for holy scrolls had to be separated from 'the simple wine of the nonbelievers',[37] which played an important role in 'the course of idolism'. For this reason, it had to be ensured that any wine within the ink did not come from a charge or a barrel from which a certain amount had been already drawn for Christian Mass rituals.

In his study concerned with the rabbinic positions towards *'avodah zarah* ('foreign worship') within medieval European culture, Ephraim Kanarfogel describes these politics of distance towards their Christian neighbours and identifies them as a general tendency.[38] According to Kanarfogel, one reason for this tendency was the increasing power of the Christian clergy within society. Halakhic authorities began to distinguish between laypersons and clerics

---

34 Luis Ginzberg, 'Pirqoi ben Baboi', in *Ginze Schechter: Geniza Studies in Memory of Solomon Schechter*, ed. by Louis Ginzberg and Israel Davidson (New York: Jewish Theological Seminary of America 1928), II, pp. 561–62.

35 Moshe ben Maimon, *Mishneh torah, Hilkhot tefillin, mezuzah, sefer torah*, sec. 1:11 translated from the Hebrew by Menachem Kellner, in *The Code of Maimonides. Book Two: The Book of Love* (New Haven and London: Yale University Press 2004), p. 75.

36 Annett Martini, 'Ritual Consecration', pp. 188–90.

37 Abraham ben Nathan ha-Yarhi, *Teshuvot she'alot le-ha Rabbi Abraham ben Nathan ha-Yarhi*, ed. by Simon A. Wertheimer (Jerusalem: Ginze Yerushalayim, 1896), I, p. 107.

38 Ephraim Kanarfogel, 'The Image of Christians in Medieval Ashkenazic Rabbinic Literature', in *Jews and Christians in Thirteenth-Century France*, ed. by Elisheva Baumgarten and Judah D. Galinsky (New York: Palgrave Macmillan 2015), pp. 151–68, 154.

and to associate *'avodah zarah* solely with the latter. Thus, two parallel developments within rabbinic thought can be discerned: the removal of Christian laypersons from the inner circle of idolatry, on the one hand, and the focusing of halakhic restrictions on contact with monks, priests, and other individuals who were directly involved in ecclesiastical practice, on the other.

This demand for the exclusion of Christian clergy and monks from the realm of holy books can also be observed in the environment of the Hasidei Ashkenaz. This obsession — to put it pointedly — with Christian clergy and monks substantiates the impression that the flourishing monastic culture with its highly professional scriptoria was a pivotal trigger for the Rhineland Pietists to develop a hypersensitive consciousness of Christians, who found one of their ideal prototypes in the monkish scribe.³⁹

Eventually, Rabbi Yair pointed to an important element with respect to writing a kosher Torah scroll, which also became increasingly significant in medieval Europe and was raised as a crucial argument against printing the holy scrolls. He added the following in his responsum:

ואינו מאמין בבורא כי גם הסברא נותנת ומסכמת כי קדושת הס״ת נמשכת ע״י כתיבת איש אשר נשמת חיים באפיו חלק אלוה ממעל שע״י כוונתו וציורי תבנית אותיות קדושים וכל ישראל בחזקת כך שדבקים מצד נפשותן ב״ה אלהינו ומצד זה נמשכה הקדושה לסת״מ וספרים וכל הקדושות דברים הקדושים למטה כמ״ש קדושים תהיו והייתם קדושים.

(It also stands to reason and is agreeable that the sanctity of a Torah scroll derives from the writing of a man in whom there is a soul of life [...] by means of his inten-

tions [...] holiness is drawn down into the Torah scroll, tefillin, mezuzot, books, and [into] the sanctity of every sacred object.)⁴⁰

It is worthy of note that it was Maimonides who introduced the term '*kavanah*' — which was used by Yair — in the context of writing. The enormously influential philosopher attached great importance to the rabbinic concept of pious 'intention' or 'concentration' during a ritual act, especially in relation to prayer and the execution of the commandments and deepened this concept in his halakhic and philosophical-ethical thinking. According to Maimonides, like a praying man, a *sofer* STaM also has to break away from the profane while writing and concentrate on the holy that he encounters in Scripture, but especially in the names of God. Thus, Maimonides proposed:

הכותב ספר תורה או תפלין או מזוזה ובשעת כתיבה לא היתה לו כונה וכתב אזכרה מן האזכרות שבהן שלא לשמן פסולין. לפיכך הכותב את השם אפלו מלך ישראל שואל בשלומו לא ישיבנו. היה כותב שנים או שלשה שמות הרי זה מפסיק ביניהם ומשיב.

(A Torah scroll, tefillin, or mezuzah written without correct intention [*kavanah*], that is, such that the divine names are written without proper intention [*lishmah*], is unfit. Thus, while writing the divine name, one must not respond even if greeted by a king of Israel. But if he is writing two or three names in a row, he may interrupt himself between them and reply.)⁴¹

---

39 Annett Martini, *'Arbeit des Himmels': Jüdische Konzeptionen rituellen Schreibens in der europäischen Kultur des Mittelalters*. (Berlin and Boston: De Gruyter 2022), pp. 153–63.

40 Yair Hayyim ben Moses Samson Bachrach, *Havvot Yair*, responsum 184.

41 Moshe ben Maimon, *Mishneh torah, Hilkhot tefillin, mezuzah, sefer torah*, 1:15, translated from the Hebrew by Kellner, p. 76. See also the paragraph 1:18: '[The following rule applies when] a scribe who wrote a Torah scroll, *tefillin*, or *mezuzah* states: "I did not write the names of God with the proper intent". Once they have left his hand, his statements are not believed with regard

In this case, the term *lishmah* is replaced by *kavanah*, whereby the act of writing and the scribe himself acquire contours. The early rabbinic literature is primarily concerned with the material features of the STaM and their assignment to a complex topography of purity and holiness. Apart from the fact that a *sofer* STaM should be Jewish, male and of legal age, one learns little more than that there are regulations a scribe has to comply with regarding the material and the script. Obviously, the rabbis had little interest in a scribe's inner attitude, the requirements of character in this profession, or the psychology of copying. In any case, the sources do not provide much information about those aspects. This impression persists when corresponding passages from the Talmud and the minor tractates *Masekhet sefer torah* and *Masekhet soferim* are consulted with regard to the regulations for writing the names of God. Here, too, the holy names are to be written *lishmah* and the scribe should not be distracted — not even by the imaginary king.[42] However, it is not the internal attitude of the scribe that is under discussion, but rather the necessity of avoiding errors in copying the holy names of God. In this respect, in Maimonides' understanding, the term *kavanah* opens up a hitherto hardly noticed aspect of ritual writing, which extends the metaphysical aspects of the material to the scribe in terms of a conscious attention to the Divine while copying.

The call for proper *kavanah* on the part of the scribe gained wide approval in European Judaism — even in rabbinic circles. For the Hasidei Ashkenaz, however, the right intention in a scribe's heart became a central aspect of copying not only scrolls for ritual use but holy texts in general.[43] The Hasidei Ashkenaz were convinced that the moral, emotional, and character-based disposition of the *sofer* is mysteriously transferred to the writing utensils and the copying itself. The personality of a writer shines through modesty, moderation, self-negation, and truthfulness. He does not strive for wealth, fame, and superficial knowledge. In short, he is the ideal Hasid. Even if most of writing workshops did not have such extreme demands on the personality of their scribes, this kind of expectation of a *sofer* STaM was a good reason for rejecting the mechanical production of a Torah scroll. More modern rabbinical discussions — such as the remarks by the halakhist Yair Hayyim ben Moses Samson Bachrach — about the possibility of printing emphatically support this objection.

Conclusion

To sum up: early modern times saw a lively discussion on the possibility of printing *sifrei* Torah using the new technology of letter press as an option in the ritual realm of holy scrolls. Some authorities did not see any divergence from the rabbinic law regarding the production of a kosher scroll; others wanted to restrict the printing of *sifrei* Torah to purposes of scholarship

---

to the disqualification of the scroll. They are, however, accepted to the extent that he must forfeit his entire wage.
Why is he not believed with regard to the disqualification of the scroll? Because it is possible that he wanted to cause a loss to the purchaser or to the person who hired him, thinking that with this statement all that he would be required to forfeit would be the payment for the names of God. Accordingly, were he to say that the parchment for this Torah scroll or *tefillin* was not processed with the proper intent in mind, his statements are accepted with regard to the disqualification of the sacred articles because, [by virtue of these statements,] he forfeits his entire wage. Everyone knows that if the parchments were not processed with the proper intent, he does not deserve any payment'.

42 *Masekhet sefer torah* 5:7; *Masekhet soferim* 5:6.

43 For a detailed discussion, see Martini, 'The Ritualization of Manufacturing and Handling Holy Books by the Hasidei Ashkenaz', pp. 67–73.

and learning; but most scholars pleaded for excluding printed scrolls from profane space as well as from ritual use. Their reasoning — as I detailed above by means of several examples — was influenced primarily by discussions from the European Middle Ages. The strict exclusion of non-Jews from the entire production process, the importance attached to sanctification of the material, the act of writing, and the divine names: *lishmah qedushat sefer torah*, and, eventually, the enormous appreciation of a scribe's intention — all these characteristics of the scribal culture in mediaeval Europe served as reasons for mandating handwritten Torah scrolls. The many manuals on scribal issues, which from the sixteenth/seventeenth centuries on enormously enrich our knowledge of how kosher *sifrei* Torah, tefillin, and mezuzot should be made, conveyed this approach towards printing into the present. The Jewish attitude towards the 'work of heaven' — the work of a *sofer* STaM — is a unique phenomenon in the history of religions — an anachronistic island which still is inhabited.

PART TWO

The Craft of Editing

SARIT SHALEV-EYNI

The 1514 'Grace after Meals, Sabbath Hymns and *Qiddush*' and the Experimental Beginnings of Woodcut Illustration in Prague

Introduction

In 1514, only two years after the first known printed book appeared in Prague, four men joined together to publish a booklet containing the Grace after Meals, Sabbath hymns (*zemirot*), the *qiddush*, and other related blessings. This was the first local Hebrew printed book with woodcuts illustrating the text.[1] The colophon mentions the four collaborators, all of whom are termed 'printers' (*mehoqeqim*), a general term used in relation to the different aspects of the production process (Figure 7.1). The first one named is Gershom ben Solomon ha-Cohen, a tax collector, who was probably the principal sponsor of the project and the most ambitious member of the group;[2] thirteen years later, King Ferdinand would grant him the exclusive privilege to print Hebrew books in Bohemia.[3] The second, Meir, the son of Rabbi Jacob ha-Levi Epstein, of German origin, was also an investor.[4] The third, Hayyim Shahor, another prominent figure in the history of early printing, left the kingdom after Gershom was granted exclusivity, and pursued his career elsewhere.[5] The last of the four printers, who receives more attention in the colophon than do the others, was Meir

---

1 Prague, Jewish Museum, Sign. 64 981. *Grace after meals = Birkat hamazon*: Facsimile of the 1514 Prague edition (London: Valmadonna Trust Library, 1984); Ursula Schubert, *Jüdische Buchkunst*, Buchkunst im Wandel der Zeiten, 3.II (Graz: Akademische Druck und Verlagsanstalt. 1992), pp. 143–44.

2 Olga Sixtová, 'Jewish Printers and Presses in Prague', in *Hebrew Printing in Bohemia and Moravia*, ed. by Olga Sixtová (Prague: Academia – The Jewish Museum in Prague, 2012), pp. 33–74 (pp. 33, 38–39, 41).

3 Charles Wengrov, *Haggadah and Woodcut: An Introduction to the Passover Completed by Gershom Cohen in Prague, Sunday, 26 Teveth, 5287, December 30, 1526* (New York: Shulsinger Brothers, 1967), pp. 14, 21.

4 Sixtová, 'Jewish Printers', p. 33.

5 See the chapter by Lucia Raspe in this book.

Sarit Shalev-Eyni • The Hebrew University of Jerusalem

Figure 7.1. Colophon, Prague booklet with Grace after Meals, *zemirot*, the *qiddush*, and other related blessings, Prague, 1514; Prague, Jewish Museum, Sign. 64 981, p. 80.

ben David, 'a scribe of tefillin from Prague', who probably designed the fonts for casting;[6] his poetic professional nickname was 'Mikhtam le-David', the opening words of Psalm 16, which served as his acronym (Meir *kotev tefillin [u] mezuzot*). His dominance in the colophon suggests his involvement in the setting of the colophon on the plate, as well as the texts of the entire booklet. Meir was an experienced professional, who probably played a central role in the actual production process. Of the four, only he appears in the list of publishers of that first printed book in Prague, a siddur, which had appeared two years earlier.[7] When his partners Gershom ben Solomon and Hayyim Shahor became rivals, Meir began to work exclusively with Shahor. However, after Gershon was granted the royal monopoly and Shahor left the region, Gershon hired Meir to complete his new edition of the mahzor and proofread the settings before printing, a decision probably based on Meir's experience and excellent reputation.[8]

Although the booklet's colophon (and those of books printed at about the same time) names the people involved in the production,[9] it does not note the identity of the individual responsible for the woodcuts, nor is there any information about the designer of the decoration program, the artist who drew the scenes, or the craftsman who eventually cut the blocks.

The booklet opens with a decorative frame for the initial word of Psalm 23, the psalm that was traditionally recited either before meals or just before the Grace after Meals, as in our case. Following that are the Sabbath hymns recited at the dining table and those for the end of the Sabbath. These are followed by the *qiddush* ceremony for different holidays throughout the liturgical year, beginning with Shavuot and concluding with Sukkot and Shemini Atzeret. The *qiddush* for Pesah is not included because it is part of the haggadah, the text read at the Seder, which most households would probably have had access to, either in a separate book or as a section in their siddur. The *qiddush* for the Sabbath appears only later, towards the end of the booklet. Seven illustrations, based on four woodblocks, accompany the variations of the *qiddush* for each specific occasion. A family seated around the festive table introduces the *qiddush* for Shavuot (Figure 7.2) and again the *qiddush* for regular Sabbaths (Figure 7.3). The illustration of a man holding a magnificent wine cup opens the *qiddush* for the New Year (Figure 7.4) and the one for Sukkot and Shemini Atzeret (Figure 7.5). A hunt scene, which appears three times, is shown in two different versions. This scene introduces the *qiddush* for Shavuot, the New Year, and Sukkot/Shemini Atzeret, when these three holidays begin at the end of the Sabbath (Figures 7.6–7.8). Although the identity of the artist remains unknown, we are able to learn about many aspects of the decoration process and the integration of the visual components within the texts through a study of the final product.

At first glance, the decoration program looks rather limited, even simplistic. However, by delving into the making of the booklet, I expose

---

6 Abraham M. Habermann, *The History of the Hebrew Book* [in Hebrew] (Jerusalem: Rubin Mass, 1945), p. 64.
7 Wengrov, pp. 9–14.
8 Sixtová, 'Jewish Printers', p. 35. See the colophon for the mahzor published by Gershom ben Solomon with his sons in 1529 (Sixtová, 'Jewish Printers', pp. 108–09, no. 15 and fig. 34), only four years after the publication of a similar mahzor by Hayyim Shahor and Meir ben David. However, in order to complete his project, Gershom needed Meir's expertise. It was probably Meir who phrased the colophon praising himself: ויקרא גם למכתם, אחד מן המחוקקים הראשונים להיות בעזרו ולהגיה [...] ויקם בזריזות כאח לצרה. ('And he [Gershom ben Solomon] also called to Mikhtam, one of the first printers, to help him and proofread [the text]. [...] And he came quickly, as a fellow sufferer'). It is therefore reasonable to assume that Meir was the one who arranged the letters on the plate.
9 For the colophons of the early printed books in Prague, see Bernard Friedberg, *History of Hebrew Typography in the Following Cities in Central Europe* [in Hebrew] (Antwerp 1935), pp. 1–18.

Figure 7.2. A family around a table: *qiddush* for Shavuot, Prague booklet; Prague, Jewish Museum, Sign. 64 981, p. 53.

THE 1514 'GRACE AFTER MEALS, SABBATH HYMNS AND *QIDDUSH*' AND WOODCUT ILLUSTRATION IN PRAGUE 155

גברת בעל הבית ומשתו שובתים ומלוכה · כמרדכי היהודי ויוסתר בת יביחיל ·
והוא שותה לבד והיה תובעת כוס של ברכה · כוז'ו הוא נבל והיה עשתו עביגל ·

רוֹם חִשִּׁשִּׁי וַיְכֻלוּ חַ שָּׁמַיִם

וְהָאָרֶץ וְכָל צְבָאָם וַיְכַל אֱלֹהִים בַּיּוֹם
הַשְּׁבִיעִי מְלַאכְתּוֹ אֲשֶׁר עָשָׂה וַיִּשְׁבֹּת
בַּיּוֹם הַשְּׁבִיעִי מִכָּל מְלַאכְתּוֹ אֲשֶׁר
עָשָׂה · וַיְבָרֶךְ אֱלֹהִים אֶת יוֹם הַשְּׁבִיעִי

Figure 7.3. A family around a festive table: *qiddush* for the Sabbath eve, Prague booklet, p. 90.

Figure 7.4. A man holding a goblet: *qiddush* for New Year; Prague booklet, p. 58.

Figure 7.5. A man holding a goblet: *qiddush* for Sukkot/Shemini Atzeret; Prague booklet, p. 63.

Figure 7.6. Hare hunt, *YaKeNeHaZ*: *qiddush* for Shavuot beginning at the end of Sabbath; Prague booklet, p. 56.

Figure 7.7. Hare hunt, *YaKeNHaZ*: *qiddush* for New Year beginning at the end of the Sabbath; Prague booklet, p. 61.

Figure 7.8. Hare hunt, *YaKeNHaZ*: *qiddush* for Sukkot/Shemini Atzeret beginning at the end of the Sabbath; Prague booklet, p. 67.

its complexity and different layers, which point to a sophisticated plan by one or more of the four printers who determined the relationship between the woodcuts and the ritual texts in terms of content and actual design. It is clear that the addition of rhymed captions introducing the images at the head of each section plays a central role in this complexity by adorning the images with a sense of narrative continuity while broadening both the scope of the ritual text and the family's ritual frame in which it was practiced. As I unfold the process that produced the illustrated booklet, I analyse the woodcuts and their prefatory captions in light of the vibrant tradition of the fifteenth-century Ashkenazi illuminated manuscripts, on the one hand, and the contemporary developing market of woodcuts in the Christian world on the other.

The Booklet and the Beginning of Printing in Prague

Although the 1514 project is the earliest known example of an illustrated edition of the Grace after Meals, Sabbath hymns, and the *qiddush*, the themes depicted on the woodblocks were not new. All of them were based on the well-known fifteenth-century Ashkenazi tradition of the illuminated haggadah.[10] A close example is the

---

10 Wengrov, p. 34; Katrin Kogman-Appel, 'Designing a Passover Imagery for New Audiences: The *Prague Haggadah*', in *Unter Druck: Mitteleuropäische Buchmalerei im 15. Jahrhundert – Tagungsband*, Buchmalerei des 15. Jahrhunderts in Mitteleuropa 15, ed. by Jeffrey F. Hamburger and Maria Theisen (Petersberg: Imhof, 2018), pp. 180–94 (p. 189).

London Ashkenazi Haggadah,[11] a manuscript illuminated in Ulm or Augsburg,[12] partly by the well-known itinerant scribe Joel ben Simeon, who also fixed the decoration program, and partly by Christian artists from the workshop of Johannes Bämler in Augsburg, who overpainted some of Joel's drawings.[13] All three scenes are typical of this genre: the master of the house with the prestigious *doppelkopf* made of expensive metal (Figure 7.9), the family at table, and the hunt scene representing the mnemonic YaKeNeHaZ, which alludes to the order of the five blessings recited when a feast falls at the end of the Sabbath (Figure 7.10). As scholars have argued, to the contemporary Ashkenazi ear, the mnemonic YaKeNeHaZ sounded like 'Jag den Hasen', meaning the hunt for the hare, so the hare scene was included to remind readers of the correct order of the blessings.[14] This iconographic tradition in illuminated haggadot was introduced in association with the Pesah holiday in the years when it began at the end of the Sabbath, but since its mnemonic role was also relevant for other feasts that fall on that evening, the designers of the booklet adopted it for the other three occasions. The woodcut artist(s) would either have copied the three scenes from an illustrated haggadah that served as a model or selected them from an existing repertoire suited to the Ashkenazi visual tradition.

The unknown identity of the artist(s) who drew the illustrations and cut the woodblocks has led to various assumptions. Peter Voit has suggested identifying the artist with the so-called 'Master of the Brick Background', an anonymous Christian craftsman who worked in Prague between 1510 and 1516.[15] Katrin Kogman-Appel argues that despite the shared 'brick background' seen in one of the woodcuts, the style of the figures in the booklet is clearly different, which points to another artist,[16] to whom one may attribute some of the woodcuts in the later *Prague*

---

11 London, British Library, MS Add 14762. For a facsimile edition see David Goldstein, *The Ashkenazi Haggadah: A Hebrew Manuscript of the Mid-15th Century from the Collections of the British Library* (London: Thames and Hudson, 1985).

12 For the date, see Katrin Kogman-Appel, 'The London Haggadah Revisited', in *Medieval Ashkenaz: Papers in Honour of Alfred Haverkamp Presented at the 17th World Congress of Jewish Studies, Jerusalem 2017* (Forschungen Zur Geschichte der Juden/Abteilung A: Abhandlungen, Bd. 31), ed. by Christoph Cluse and Jörg R. Muller (Wiesbaden: Harrassowitz 2021), pp. 345–66 (351–52).

13 See Sheila Edmunds, 'The Place of the London Haggadah in the Work of Joel ben Simeon', *Journal of Jewish Art*, 7 (1980), pp. 25–34; Sheila Edmunds, 'New Light on Johannes Bämler', *Journal of the Printing Historical Society*, 22 (1993), pp. 29–53 and plates 1–2, and more recently, Kogman-Appel, 'The London Haggadah', pp. 360–62.
For the workshop of Bämler and its development, see Christine Beier, 'Missalien massenhaft. Die Bämler-Werkstatt und die Augsburger Buchmalerei im 15. Jahrhundert', *Codices Manuscripti*, 48 (2003), pp. 67–78, figures 1–42 and 49 (2004), pp. 55–72. For the Hebrew manuscripts, see especially pp. 63–66. On Joel ben Simeon, see, e.g., Malachi Beit-Arié, 'Joel ben Simeon's Manuscripts: A Codicologer's View', *Journal of Jewish Art*, 3–4 (1977), pp. 25–39, reprinted in Malachi Beit-Arié, *The Making of the Medieval Hebrew Book: Studies in Paleography and Codicology* (Jerusalem: Magnes Press, 1993), pp. 93–108; Bezalel Narkiss, 'The Art of the Washington Haggadah', in *The Washington Haggadah: A Facsimile Edition of an Illuminated Fifteenth-century Hebrew Manuscript at the Library of Congress Signed by Joel ben Simeon*, ed. by Myron M. Weinstein (Washington, DC: The Library of Congress, 1991), pp. 29–101; David Stern and Katrin Kogman-Appel, *The Washington Haggadah Copied and Illustrated by Joel ben Simeon* (Cambridge, MA: Harvard University Press, 2011).

14 See the discussion, reference to earlier bibliography, and reservation in Mendel Metzger, *La haggada enluminée: Études sur le judaïsme medieval*, 2 (Leiden: Brill, 1973), p. 100.

15 Peter Voit, 'Ornamentation of Prague Hebrew Books during the First Half of the 16th century as a Part of Bohemian Book Design', in *Hebrew Printing in Bohemia and Moravia*, pp. 123–51 (pp. 130–31).

16 Kogman-Appel, 'Designing a Passover Imagery', note 63.

Figure 7.9. A man holding a goblet: *qiddush* for Passover; London Ashkenazi Haggadah; London, British Library, MS Add 14762, fol. 2ʳ.

Figure 7.10. Hare hunt, *YaKeNHaZ*: *qiddush* for Passover beginning at the end of the Sabbath; London Ashkenazi Haggadah, fol. 4ʳ.

Haggadah (1526).¹⁷ The original intention behind the choice of the woodcuts has been a source of some dispute as well. Whereas some scholars believe that they were made or ordered especially for the booklet, others have suggested that they were initially designed for a printed haggadah in which all three would have been relevant.¹⁸ Still others pointed out the generic character of the images — a hunt scene, a banquet, a man with a goblet. Since all of these would have been suitable in diverse general contexts, one may not necessarily exclude the possibility that the preliminary drawings used for the woodcuts were originally not intended specifically for a Jewish book.¹⁹ Despite this range of possibilities, it is clear that the making of the woodcuts that illustrated the booklet should be considered in the frame of the development of printing in early sixteenth-century Prague and its German roots.

The printing project of the illustrated *Prague Bible*, which lasted from 1488 until 1505, relied on cooperation with artists in workshops in several centres in the German Lands: Augsburg, Nuremberg, and Strasbourg.²⁰ A few years later, as the demand for woodcuts increased, the dependence on those other centres decreased.

Itinerant artists, probably of German origin, settled in Prague, offering their services locally, often working for several printing houses at the same time.²¹ The woodcuts in our booklet are products of this vibrantly developing environment. It is difficult to ascertain whether the artists who made the preliminary drawings and cut the woodblocks for our booklet were Jewish or Christian.²² Nonetheless, we can say with some confidence that the designer(s) who selected the scenes, determined their details, and so perfectly matched the images with the text on each plate, both physically and thematically, was certainly Jewish, most probably one or more of the four partners. Meir ben David, 'Mikhtam le-David', who was clearly experienced in the arrangement of plates for printing, must have been among them.

Augsburg and other southern German centres were also places where the general woodcut technique practiced in Prague originated. With the invention of the printing press, single printed sheets bearing images for devotional use or for transmitting religious or social messages were available for purchase in markets. The integration of woodcut illustrations in printed books began sometime later.²³ These were full-page images

---

17 Kogman-Appel, 'Designing a Passover Imagery', pp. 189–90.

18 Wengrov, pp. 79–80, 83–84; Kogman-Appel, 'Designing a Passover Imagery', p. 190. Later on (1534), the two woodcuts of the hare's hunt served Shahor as a model for two images in a haggadah he published in Augsburg; two new very similar woodblocks were made for this purpose. See Yosef Hayim Yerushalmi, *Haggadah and History: A Panorama in Facsimile of Five Centuries of the Printed Haggadah from the Collections of Harvard University and the Jewish Theological Seminary of America* (Philadelphia: Jewish Publication Society of America, 1975), pl. 15–16. See also Kogman-Appel, 'Designing a Passover Imagery', p. 191.

19 On the originality of most of the woodblocks, see Olga Sixtová, 'The Beginning of Hebrew Typography, 1512–1569', in *Hebrew Printing in Bohemia and Moravia*, p. 87.

20 Voit, p. 124.

21 Voit, pp. 123–24.

22 Cf. the possibility that Hayyim Shahor was the craftsman who produced some of the woodcuts of the *Prague Haggadah*, Wengrov, pp. 88–106. For the different opinions regarding this assumption in the scholarly literature, see Kogman-Appel, 'Designing a Passover Imagery', note 45.

23 See Peter Schmidt, *Gedruckte Bilder in handgeschriebenen Büchern: Zum Gebrauch von Druckgraphik im 15. Jahrhundert*, Pictura et Poesis, 16 (Cologne: Böhlau, 2003); Peter Schmidt, 'The Multiple Image: The Beginnings of Printmaking between Old Theories and New Approaches', in *Origins of European Printmaking: Fifteenth-Century Woodcuts and Their Public*, ed. by Peter Parshall and Rainer Schoch (Washington, DC: National Gallery of Art, 2005), pp. 37–57; David S. Areford, 'The Image in the Viewer's Hands: The Reception of the Early Prints in Europe', *Studies in Iconography*, 24 (2003), pp. 5–43; David S. Areford, *The Viewer and the Printed Image in Late Medieval Europe* (Aldershot: Ashgate,

which were often printed several times throughout the book. The development of the method is traceable through an examination of different editions of the same work. The *Seelenwurzgarten*, a collection of exempla and anti-Jewish polemic, can serve as an example.²⁴ It was printed for the first time in 1483 in Ulm and within a year,²⁵ in 1484, a new edition based on the Ulm model was published in Augsburg.²⁶ A comparison between the two editions points to the considerable development taking place in the field at that time. Many of the full-page woodcuts prepared for the Ulm edition are repeated several times throughout the volume; their numbers and sometimes the exact selections vary both from one version to another and in different copies of the same version.²⁷ For an additional fee, a buyer could purchase a hand-coloured copy done with a limited palette of water paints;²⁸ as can be seen in our booklet, the same pallet also reached Prague. The repetition of specific woodcuts allowed the publishers to prepare just a small selection of woodblocks for one printed book. But the repetition might also have been an act of interpretation, visually stressing specific themes throughout the book. However, as time passed, this method of repetition fell out of favour. The Augsburg edition of 1484 already featured the new, more progressive, method wherein the printer replaced most of the full-page woodcuts with smaller panels inserted within the text column, each appearing only once.²⁹

Both methods, the old and the new, reached Prague, and they were combined in our booklet in an unusual way. On the one hand, the Jewish designers employed the panels inserted within the text space, which required that their plan be prepared before the text was arranged on the plate. On the other hand, they also adopted the repetition that characterized the use of the full-page woodcuts. This combination enabled them not only to employ a limited number of woodcuts, but also to use the images accompanying the text as signs: the beginning of a *qiddush* text was marked by a man holding the cup of wine in one of two versions: with the family or alone. The hunt scene indicates instances of a festival falling at the end of the Sabbath. In such an arrangement, the images were helpful to the browser searching for the required text. Moreover, the repetition was used here in an unprecedented and sophisticated way through the addition of rhymed paratexts, which are written in small letters in semi-cursive script preceding each image. These accompanying rhymes, which expanded the original limits of the rigid ritual texts, changed from one image to another, and in doing so also altered the meaning of each woodcut. The use of rhymed paratexts as captions for images was also rooted in haggadot

---

2010); *The Woodcut in Fifteenth-Century Europe*, ed. Peter Parshall (Washington, DC. National Gallery of Art and New Haven and London: Yale University Press, 2009).

24 For the *Seelenwurzgarten*, see Werner Williams-Krapp, 'Der Seelen Wurzgarten', in *Die deutsche literature des Mittelalters Verfasserlexikon*, Zweite völlig neu bearbeitete Auflage ed. by Wolfgang Stammler, Kurt Ruh, and others, 14 vols (Berlin: de Gruyter, 1978–2008), VIII, cols 1027–29.

25 The first edition appeared on July 26, 1483, in the workshop of Conrad Dinckmut; a second edition on October 4 of the same year. ISTC No. is00364000, ISTC No. is00365000. See, e.g., https://digi.ub.uni-heidelberg.de/diglit/is00365000/0028/thumbs.

26 Augsburg, 1484, in the workshop of Johan Schönspreger; ISTC No. is00366000. See, e.g., https://daten.digitale-sammlungen.de/~db/ausgaben/thumbnailseite.html?fip=193.74.98.30&id=00031616&seite=16.

27 See, e.g., https://digi.ub.uni-heidelberg.de/diglit/is00365000/0024/image; https://digi.ub.uni-heidelberg.de/diglit/is00365000/0038/image.

28 Compare the palette of colours used in the booklet's woodcuts to that of the Heidelberg copy (note 26).

---

29 Compare the examples of the Ulm edition of 1483 in note 7 to the following example of Augsburg 1484, https://daten.digitale-sammlungen.de/~db/0003/bsb00031616/images/index.html?seite=19&fip=193.74.98.30.

from around the middle of the fifteenth century.³⁰ In our case, however, as we shall now see, the method was taken a step further.

The Destiny of a Hare: A Continuous Narrative in Three Stages

The hunt scene repeats three times throughout the booklet. In the first instance, preceding the *qiddush* for Shavuot that falls at the end of the Sabbath, the panel shows a hunter blowing a horn, with three large dogs and another, small one, all chasing two hares, whose heads are already stuck in the hunter's net (Figure 7.6).³¹ In the lower part of the panel, the small dog bites the leg of one of the hares. The text introducing the woodcut refers directly to the image and relates to the biting of the hare's heel and her sufferings: צורת הציד צודה הארנבת עם כלביו | והאחד תופשו בעקביו | והיא צועקת במר נפש מנוחה הדריכוני | עון עקבי יסבוני ('The image of the hunter hunting the hare with his dogs, and one [of the dogs] catches her heel. And she screams with the bitterness of her soul: they overtook me at my resting-place [Judg. 20:43]. The iniquity of my persecutors encompasses me [Ps. 49:6; in Hebrew a pun on the word "heel"]').³²

The next hunt image appears at the beginning of the *qiddush* for the New Year that falls at the end of the Sabbath (Figure 7.7). Here again we meet the hunter with his three large dogs and a smaller one chasing the two hares in a very similar composition. At first glance, it seems to be a replica of the previous one, but with the figures going in the opposite direction. Here the designer played on the well-known phenomenon of repetition in early printed books but inserted some small crucial details, which enables the reader to see it as a continuation of the hunt scene shown on one of the previous pages and to focus on the development of the narrative: in this case, the hares have succeeded in escaping the net. The preceding paratext focuses on the failure and frustrations of the hunter: צורת הציד מקונן על אידו | כי לא יחרוך רמייה צידו | על כן שער ראשו מרט | והמה נמלטו ארץ אררט ('The image of the hunter mourning his calamity, since the slothful man shall not hunt his prey.³³ Because of that he plucked the hair of his head, and they escaped into the land of Ararat').³⁴

It is the second version that is repeated at the beginning of the *qiddush* for Sukkot and Shemini Atzeret when those holidays fall at the end of the Sabbath (Figure 7.8). Here, however, the text is different, starting again with the hunter, who is described here as a 'brutish man', but continuing with a dialogue between the survivors (the hares) and the small dog, astonished by the unexpected success of their flight:

---

30 See especially the *Second Nuremberg Haggadah*, Franconia, *c.* 1460 (London, Collection of David Sofer; formerly Schocken Institute, MS 24087) and Yahuda Haggadah, Franconia, *c.* 1460 (Jerusalem, Israel Museum, MS 180/50; Katrin Kogman-Appel, *Die zweite Nürnberger und die Jehuda Haggada: jüdische Illustratoren zwischen Tradition und Fortschritt* [Frankfurt: Peter Lang, 1999]), as well as Paris, Bibliothèque nationale de France (BnF), hébr. 1333, which will be discussed below (bibliography, note 42).

31 Schubert, pp. 143–44; Sixtová, *Prague Hebrew Topography*, pp. 93–94.

32 English translations are mine, unless otherwise indicated.

33 See Proverbs 12:27.

34 See II Kings 19:37. The same verse is used to describe the fleeing of the gazelle and the ibex from a hunter in *Meshal ha-Qadmoni* (pt. 5, lines 787–88): והציד רודף אחריהם... והדרך לנגדם ירט והמה נמלטו הרי אררט. ('But they made their escape, the road's last bend. Marked on Mt. Ararat their journey end'); Hebrew and English translation, Raphael Loewe, *Meshal Haqadmoni: Fables from the Distant Past: A Parallel Hebrew-English Text*, 2 vols (Portland, OR: Littman Library of Jewish Civilization, 2004), II, pp. 624–25. For the connection between the booklet and this book of fables, see below.

צורת הצייד איש בער | רודף הארנבת בלא יער |
על כן שער ראשו מורט מרוב צער| והמה משוררים
קדמונים אחזו שער[35] | והכלב הקטן שואלם איזה
דרך עברתם שרשתינו לא הפשטנו | והן ענין הפח
נשבר | ואנחנו נמלטנו.[36]

(The image of the hunter, a brutish man, chasing the hare with no forest. He plucked the hair of his head because of his sorrow, and they, ancient poets, were affrighted. And the small dog asks them: Which way did you take, which our net did not spread to? And they answer: the trap broke and we escaped.)

While the hunter and the dogs appear in all three versions in their own characters, the hare is imbued here with a subtle symbolic meaning. Although two hares are depicted in the woodcut, the prey appears in most of the texts in the singular form. The plural form appears only towards the end of the last paragraph, where the hares are described as 'ancient poets', possibly a reference to earlier Jewish poets, the descendants of the Levites and their song in the Temple. This departure from the literal meaning of the hunt scene may allude to the continuity of sacred song among the Jews, a concept developed in response to a Christian notion that the end of the Temple music was a divine sign of the final abandonment of the Jewish people in exile.[37] A reference to 'ancient poets' in a booklet that includes hymns composed by Ashkenazi and Sefardi poets of previous generations that were to be sung communally around the Sabbath table[38] has a special meaning, an association between the fleeing hare and the celebrants. This mention of 'ancient poets' in the caption suggests the symbolic meaning of the whole narrative. While scholars long ago assumed that the image of the hare's hunt was a symbol of the persecution of the Jews in exile,[39] here, perhaps for the first time, this symbolism is clearly apparent.

The three woodcuts appearing alternately throughout the booklet join together to form a continuous sequence. The repetition of the scene, the slight but meaningful visual alterations, and the attached captions together tell a story in three parts. This continuous narrative takes the readers far beyond not only the mnemonic vehicle but also beyond the immediate ritual context in which the booklet was used, well into both the mundane and the symbolic realms.

Within the Ritual Domain: The Woman Who Dared to Demand

The woodcuts and their explanatory texts in the Prague booklet take us inside the family ritual and expose some aspects of the religious practice at home. These are hinted at the image of the dining

---

35 A variation on Job 18:20, though the word *qadmonim* lost its original meaning.
36 The last four words are based on Psalms 124:7.
37 See the commentary of the twelfth-century rabbi Ephraim of Bonn on the *piyyut* 'God be not silent': You were exiled from your land to be under our rule [...] you were left without praise for you no longer have the song of the Temple and the musical instruments that the Levites played on [...]. Hebrew, Efraim Elimelech Urbach, *Sefer arugat ha-bosem, auctore R. Abraham b. R. Azriel*, 4 vols (Jerusalem: Mekitzei Nirdamin, 1963), IV, pp. 47–48, and Sarit Shalev-Eyni, 'The Aural-Visual Experience in the Ashkenazi Ritual Domain of the Middle-Ages', in *Resounding Images: Medieval Intersections of Art, Music and Sound*, ed. by Susan Boynton and Diane J. Reilly (Turnhout: Brepols, 2015), pp. 189–204.
38 Among the Ashkenazi poets whose hymns are included in the booklet are Simeon b. Isaac (10th c.) and Barukh b. Samuel of Mainz (c. 1200); among the Sefardi poets are Dunash ben Labrat (920/925–after 985), Judah ha-Levi (1075–1141), and Abraham ibn Ezra (1089/1092–1164/1167).
39 See Rachel Wischnitzer, *Symbole und Gestalten der jüdischen Kunst* (Berlin-Schöneberg: S. Scholem, 1935), p. 79.

family, which depicts a couple seated at a table together with two others. This image is the first one in the booklet and introduces the *qiddush* for Shavuot (Figure 7.2). The man holds a cup of wine and the woman stretches her arms out to take the cup from his hands.[40] The prefatory text reads:

צורת בעל הבית מקדש להשפיע הברכה | ובני ביתו עונים אחריו כהלכה | וזו הברכה תמיד בפיו קבועה | כשחל זמן מתן תורה להיות בשבוע.

(The image of the master of the house making the *qiddush* to increase blessings, and the members of his house answer after him ['Amen'] appropriately [literally also, according to the halakhah (religious law)], and this blessing is always on his lips, when the feast of Receiving the Law [i.e., Shavuot] falls on a weekday.)

According to this inscription the protagonist of the image is the husband, whose ritual superiority is unequivocal. He is making the *qiddush* to increase blessings; his wife is not mentioned at all. Her status is relegated to that of the anonymous 'members of the house', the passive group whose participation in the ritual is restricted to replying 'Amen'. But when the same woodcut reappears towards the end as the last image in the booklet, introducing the *qiddush* for regular Sabbaths, the introductory inscription is totally different; it relates to the woman as well and changes the meaning of the image:

צורת בעל הבית ואשתו שובתים ממלאכה | כמרדכי היהודי ואסתר בת אביחיל׳ | והוא שותה לבד והיא תובעת כוס של ברכה | כאלו הוא נבל והיא אשתו אביגיל |

(The image of the master of the house and his wife, refraining from work on the Sabbath, like Mordechai the Jew and Esther the daughter of Avihail. And he drinks alone and she demands the cup of blessing, as if he is Nabal and she is his wife Abigail.)

By stressing the tension between the dining couple, the prefatory text to the image continues a fifteenth-century tradition in haggadah manuscripts in which images were combined with titles in rhyme that broadened the gender meanings beyond the ritual frame. An example is the mid-fifteenth-century Paris manuscript 1333, in which the husband, holding the *maror* (the bitter herbs eaten at the Passover Seder), points to the woman, whose hand gesture expresses her active objection (Figure 7.11).[41] The two accuse each other of representing the bitter herb. The banderoles added by the artist enable us to hear the teasing dialogue between the two. Above the male is written: מאמר הגלוף: מרור זה קולי בהרם בזה וזה גורם ('Says the man depicted: "This *maror* [namely the woman to whom he points], I recall, causes this and that"').[42] The inscription above the woman reads: תשובת האשה: הלא חשבתיך כאחד מהם ('Replies the wife: "But I thought you are one of them"'). Although, unlike in the Prague booklet, there are no other participants around the table, in the Paris manuscript, another person

---

40 Schubert, p. 143.

41 BnF, hébr. 1333, fol. 19ᵛ; Bezalel Narkiss, 'The Art of the Washington Haggadah', p. 74; Bezalel Narkiss and Gabrielle Sed-Rajna, *Index of Jewish Art*, II.1 (1978): *The Hileq and Bileq Haggadah, Paris, BnF ms. Hébr. 1333* (Munich: K. G. Saur, 1981), nos 57–58. Adam S. Cohen, *Signs and Wonders: 100 Haggadah Masterpieces* (New Milford, CT, and Jerusalem: Toby Press, 2018), p. 52. For the manuscript, see also Justine Isserles, 'La Sortie d'Égypte à la Rédemption finale: analyse de cinq folios tirés du manuscrit Hébreu 1333 de la Bibliothèque nationale de France à Paris', *Cahiers Archéologiques*, 52 (2005–08), pp. 145–60.

42 בזה וזה גורם (causes this and that) may refer to the well-known opinion appearing in the Mishnah: 'Anyone who increases conversation with the woman causes (*gorem* in Hebrew) evil to himself' ('Avot 1, 5).

is mentioned in an additional short sentence: ויבא השלישי ויסריח בינהם ('And a third [person] comes between them and makes a fuss').⁴³ However, despite the continuation of this tradition, which originated in haggadah manuscripts, the sophistication of the caption and its scholarly character in the Prague case embellish the image with more complex implications.⁴⁴

The 'cup of blessing' mentioned in the inscription in the Prague booklet is a halakhic term referring to various rituals involving wine, in the course of which, in addition to the regular blessing on the wine, another blessing referring to the specific ritual was recited.⁴⁵ Most frequently, this occurred during the recitation of the *qiddush*, a positive time-bound commandment whose performance is determined by a precise weekly or annual time frame.⁴⁶ Although positive time-bound commandments are usually only incumbent on men, the *qiddush* is one of the exceptions, being defined as the obligation of men and women alike.⁴⁷ Nevertheless, a woman can fulfil her obligation by hearing the man recite the *qiddush*, and in practice it is the master of the house who customarily performs the ritual for his wife and all the other participants at the meal.

---

43   English translation Narkiss and Sed-Rajna, nos 57–58.
44   For broader aspects of the visual tradition of the dining couple in illuminated haggadah manuscripts and its relation to the image in the Prague booklet, see Shalev-Eyni, 'Manipulating the Cup of Blessing: Gendered Reading of Ritual Images in European-Hebrew Books', *Studies in Iconography*, 39 (2018), pp. 207–34.
45   Babylonian Talmud, *Berakhot* 51a; English translation, *Babylonian Talmud*, ed. by Isidore Epstein, 18 vols (London: Soncino Press, 1961), *Seder Zera'im, Tractate Berakoth*, trans. Maurice Simon and Isidore Epstein, p. 309. See also the Tosafot on the same source (English, https://dafyomi.co.il/berachos/tosfos/br-ts-051.htm).
46   See the Babylonian Talmud, *Pesahim* 106a; English translation, *Babylonian Talmud: Seder Mo'ed, Tractate Pesahim*, trans. by Harry Freedman, pp. 553–54.
47   Babylonian Talmud, *Berakoth* 20b; English translation, *Babylonian Talmud: Seder Zera'im, Tractate Berakoth*, trans. by Simon and Epstein, p. 122.

Figure 7.11. 'This *maror*', *Hileq and Bileq Haggadah*, Middle Rhine, c. 1450; Paris, Bibliothèque nationale de France, MS héb. 1333, fol. 19ᵛ.

Although according to the halakhah, a woman can also fulfil the obligation of a man, such a situation was commonly considered improper and, in reality, it was usually only in the absence of male adults that women recited the *qiddush* and exempted others by their recitation.⁴⁸ The

---

48   See Rahel Berkovits, 'Women's Obligation in Kiddush of Shabbat', in *Come and Learn: The Halakhic Source Guide Series* (New York: Jewish Orthodox Feminist Alliance, 2008), pp. 1–20. https://www.jewishspeakersbureau.com/speakers/rahel-berkovits.

husband raises the cup of wine in his right hand and makes the blessings aloud. The wife, as well as the other participants, usually sips from the wine, but without making the blessing. Sharing the *qiddush* wine with those sharing the meal, and especially with the wife, to whom the cup is to be given first, is an accepted practice, which is recommended, but not required. According to the strict halakhic rule, the blessing by the master of the house on the cup exempted all the other participants without their sipping from the wine.[49]

In the woodcut, the man and woman are seated side by side at the centre in equivalent positions but the cup held by the man disturbs this equality, clarifying each one's specific status in the family ritual frame: the active role of the husband as the conductor of the ceremony and the passive part of his wife as a silent participant. In light of the inscription, in this case the woman's hand gestures can be understood as a demand to share the wine, a legitimate request. The biblical reference used in the inscription emphasizes the wife's active response. Whereas in the first part describing the equal observance of the Sabbath, the couple is compared with Mordechai and Esther, both positive biblical figures, who, according to some sources, were a married couple,[50] the second part, with the woman's demand, clearly distinguishes between the two. The husband is likened to Nabal, a negative biblical figure, whose flocks David had protected and who later arrogantly rejected David's request for consideration, insulted his men, and eventually found his death through divine intervention (I Sam. 25:2–10:36); the woman, in contrast, parallels Abigail, his wife, a wise and assertive female figure, who succeeded in thwarting David's planned vengeance on her husband and saved her family, later even becoming one of David's wives (18–35).

However, the term 'demand' used in this context to describe the woman's protest suggests a dubious meaning when it is used in the context of wine. This term is related to a well-known discussion in the Babylonian Talmud on the amount of wine that a woman should be allowed to drink: כוס אחד יפה לאשה, שנים — ניוול הוא; שלשה — תובעת בפה; ארבעה — אפילו חמור תובעת בשוק ואינה מקפדת ('One cup [of wine] is becoming to a woman; two are degrading. [and if she has] three she solicits directly [lit. "she demands with the mouth"]... [if she has] four she solicits even an ass in the street and cares not [*Ketubot* 65a]').[51]

According to this talmudic statement, wine was connected to female sexuality. Drinking more than two cups of wine would likely arouse her. In this situation, the expression 'demanding with the mouth' means that the woman initiates sexual relations, either with her husband or with other men. Thus, using the talmudic term 'demand' in the context of the cup of wine in our woodcut gives it a sexual connotation as well, indicating the assertive behaviour of women in the domain of intercourse,[52] It also does so by the use of the biblical figure of Abigail. When Abigail comes to David to prevent David's attack on her husband's camp, she concludes with the words 'remember thy handmaid' (I Sam. 25:31). This led some of the Sages quoted in the Babylonian Talmud to suggest that since she foresaw the fall of Nabal, she revealed her thigh to David as if initiating

---

49 See Babylonian Talmud, *Berakhot* 51b; English translation, *Babylonian Talmud: Seder Zera'im*, trans. by Simon and Epstein, p. 310.

50 Babylonian Talmud, *Megillah* 13a; English translation, *Babylonian Talmud: Seder Mo'ed, Tractate Megillah*, trans. by Simon, p. 76.

51 Babylonian Talmud, *Ketubot* 65a; English translation, *Babylonian Talmud: Seder Nashim, Tractate Kethuboth*, trans. by Samuel Daiches and Israel W. Slotki, p. 393.

52 For other aspects of the sexual connotation of the dining table in this context, see Shalev-Eyni, 'Manipulating the Cup of Blessing', pp. 223–24.

a future offer of matrimony (*Megillah* 14a–b).⁵³ Nothing happened that night, and it was only after Nabal's death that David took her for his wife, but the first seductive move in this direction was hers when she was still married. The inscription in the woodcut supports her demand in the ritual frame and empowers her, but at the same time also marks her assertiveness with a hinted aura of dubious sexuality.

The sexual connotations and gender tensions suggested by the cup of wine, as well as the image, together with the prefatory caption, its rhymes, and formula, may all lead beyond the ritual context into the world of moral literature using rhymed prose. *Meshal ha-qadmoni* ('Proverb of the Ancient'), a work of fables composed in rhymes, was written in Hebrew by Isaac ibn Sahula of Guadalajara in 1281.⁵⁴ Sahula's original intention was to accompany the fables with images.⁵⁵ No Sefardi illustrated copy has survived, which would enable us to ascertain whether he fulfilled his original goal, but in the middle of the fifteenth century, when the work was revived in the German lands, illustrations inspired by local visual traditions became an integral part of each copy; two manuscripts, the earliest dated 1450, are extant.⁵⁶ Special titles, also written in rhyme, introduce the images; as in our booklet, each of these captions opens with the same formula 'the image of'. Just a few decades later, the Ashkenazi illustrated variant of the Castilian work also reached Italy, from where another three copies, dated by Simona Groneman to 1470–80, have survived.⁵⁷ As early as around 1491, the work with woodblock illustrations was printed in Brescia by Gershom Soncino, who a few years later, in 1497–98, published a second edition in Barco.⁵⁸ Other printed editions appeared during the latter part of the sixteenth century.⁵⁹

Of special interest for our discussion is the ironic story of the adulterous wife that appears in the centre of the second chapter of the piece, which Sahula devoted to the theme of penitence. It tells of an elderly pious man who has a beautiful young wife, but he, instead of being interested in her beauty, is preoccupied with his piety during the whole of the day. Though he believes her to be a woman of valour, she seduces a young man, with whom she fulfils her desires.⁶⁰ After her lover's first visit to her home, she turns to the preparations for her husband's return:

טבחה טבחה מסכה יינה | אף ערכה שולחנה | ויהי ככלות האיש להתפלל תפלתו כדתו | ויפן ובא אל בית מנוחתו |[...] | וימהר וישב במסבו | ויאכל וישת וייטב לבו.

(Did her cooking, broached the wine and laid the table fair for them to dine. Her husband, as his wont, devotions past to

---

53 Babylonian Talmud, *Megillah* 14a–b; English translation, *Babylonian Talmud: Seder Moed, Tractate Megillah*, trans. by Simon, 84.
54 Loewe, I, pp. xv–xxiv; Alexandra Cuffel, 'Ibn Sahula's Meshal ha-Qadmoni as Restorative Polemic', *Journal of Medieval Iberian Studies*, 3/2 (2011), pp. 165–86.
55 Simona Gronemann, *The Story of Meshal Haqadmoni and its Extant Copies in 15th Century Ashkenaz* (Wiesbaden: Harrassowitz, 2019), p. 87. For the illustrations in their German cultural context, see the thorough discussion there, chapters II and III.
56 For a thorough study of the different copies, their dating and localization, see Gronemann, pp. 20–38, 91–98.
57 For the Italian copies, see Gronemann, pp. 28–38, 94–98.
58 Gronemann, p. 99. For the identification and dating of the two first editions, see Moses Marx, 'Gershom Soncino, Contributions to the History of his Printing', *Sefer ha-Yovel, A Tribute to Alexander Marx*, ed. by David Frankel (New York: Alim, 1943), pp. i–x (pp. v–viii). According to Marx, *Mashal Haqadmoni* 'is the first Hebrew book of which one printer was able to issue two editions and that in less than ten years' (p. viii).
59 Gronemann, p. 99.
60 For the full text of the fable in English, see Loewe, I, pp. 166–93. For the illustrations in the different copies, see Sara Offenberg, 'On a Pious Man, Adulterous Wife, and the Pleasure of Preaching to Others in Yitshaq ibn Sahula's *Meshal ha-Qadmoni*', *Hispania Judaica*, 12 (2016), pp. 103–25. See also Gronemann, p. 59 and Cuffel, p. 181.

find well-earned repose came home at last [...]. Taking his seat at table, keen to start he ate and drank, and felt content at heart.)⁶¹

Encouraged by his wife's request to expound on religious matters and relying on biblical and talmudic sources, he describes the exalted qualities that a good woman should adopt in detail, giving thanks to the Lord that all these virtues are embodied in his faithful wife. The scene ends in the bedroom, alluding again to the seductive character of the wife, this time in the marital frame.⁶²

As an illustration, the different copies depict the couple at the dining table. In an Italian manuscript from the 1470s, copied by an Ashkenazi scribe, as indicated by the palaeographical characteristics,⁶³ the man is raising a cup of wine (Figure 7.12). The cup and the bottle of wine under it form the central axis of the composition. The woman, whose dress, hair style, and headwear follow the contemporary local fashion, is shown in full body. She turns her hand towards the cup, almost closing the imaginary semi-triangle created between the table and the couples' raised hands, but she does not touch the cup, which is totally controlled by the man's hand. This is not the 'cup of blessing' involved in the *qiddush* or any other ritual, but an ordinary wineglass, and yet it is the axis around which the relations between the sexes take place in the image, which appears to mark the dominance of the husband.

The caption to the image reads: צורת האיש מתענג על שולחנו | ואשתו נצבה שגל לימינו ('The image of the man revelling at his board, his wife, *shegel*, at the right hand of her lord').⁶⁴ The final phrase is based on Psalms 45:10, where *shegel* is usually interpreted as a queen: 'the *shegel* stands at your right hand'. However, *shegel* is much better known in the Bible as a common verb meaning 'to lie with', sometimes in the dubious, even clearly negative connotation of a whore (e.g., Jer. 3:2). The sexual connotation of *shegel* as a noun is also used in the Bible to define a mistress or a wife (Dan. 5:23), a meaning that reappears in the Babylonian Talmud as well.⁶⁵ Ibn Sahula most probably used the word *shegel* to allude to the sexual character of the story and the seductive and adulterous character of the woman, who would later run away with her lover.

The designer of the Prague booklet was probably acquainted with Ibn Sahula's well-known story in its Ashkenazi or Italo-Ashkenazi illustrated form. Ibn Saula's dining table as an arena for sexual tensions and female assertiveness, as well as the format, the rhymed captions, and the opening formula 'the image of' may all have served as a source of inspiration for our designer(s),⁶⁶ though there is also a fundamental difference. In the booklet, the sexual tone is subtle, unlike the adulterous context of the story, and stays within the limits of the ritual ceremony and the marital bond. Moreover, Abigail plays a double role here. In the context of 'demanding', although her legitimate request bears a hidden sexual aspect, at the same time she is a woman of valour (in sharp contradiction to Ibn Saula's treacherous woman who is pretending to be a 'woman of valour'). Abigail in the woodcut's inscription is the positive contrast to the negative

---

61 English, Loewe, I, p. 174.
62 Loewe, I, pp. 174–80.
63 Oxford, Bodleian Library (Bodl.), MS Can. Or. 59, fol. 14ᵛ. For the dating and localizing of the manuscript, see Gronemann, pp. 28–30.
64 See, e.g., the German copy in Oxford (Bodl., MS Opp. 154, fol. 11ᵛ), where is a variation which seems to be closer to the original: 'The image of the man revelling at his board and *shegel* stands at his right hand'.
65 See, e.g., *Sanhedrin* 95b. See also the debate in *Rosh ha-Shanah* 4a regarding the meaning of *shegel* in Nehemiah 2:6.
66 For the connection between the captions for the third hunt scene in the booklet and *Meshal ha-Qadmoni*, see above, note 35.

Figure 7.12. The pious man and his adulterous wife at the dining table, Isaac Ibn Sahula, *Meshal ha-Qadmoni*, Northern Italy, 1470s; Oxford, Bodleian Library, MS Can. Or. 59, fol. 14ᵛ.

figure of Nabal, to whom her husband is compared. The woodcut's caption seems to be directing its critical, somewhat ironic, arrows towards both the reluctant husband and his assertive wife, but it is the husband who is directly condemned by being compared to Nabal, the obvious negative protagonist in the biblical story.

It is perhaps not accidental that the first and last woodcuts in the booklet depict the same image of the family dining, as befits the family setting in which the booklet's texts were recited. However, the caption of the first woodcut relates to the husband alone, an expression of male dominance that receives additional emphasis in the two other images for the *qiddush*, where only a man holding a goblet is depicted. One of them, the one that introduces the *qiddush* for Rosh ha-Shana, is identified as a rabbi and may refer to a communal frame; it is possible that his isolated figure represents his special status (Figure 7.4). But the same image — of a man holding a goblet — for the *qiddush* for Sukkot and Shemini Atzeret brings us back to the family frame since the caption accompanying the man here identifies him as 'the master of the house' (Figure 7.5); the woman and the other participants are totally absent in both the image and the paratext attached to it. It is only in the last woodcut and its prefatory paratext that the woman is given a clear voice as well as it presents the couple in positions of near equality, despite the sexual and gender tensions between the two. Although this image is the last woodcut, as it introduces the *qiddush* for regular Sabbaths, which was used on a weekly basis throughout the liturgical year, and not occasionally like the other variants of the *qiddush*, one can assume that it played a central role in the reception of the booklet by its users.

Conclusion

The joint project of 1514 was an impressive achievement of the early age of Hebrew printing.

A booklet gathering the ritual texts recited and sung around the dining table on Sabbaths, holidays, and special events was an innovative format. The woodcuts illustrating the texts were designed as panels introducing the different versions of the *qiddush*, changing as they illustrated one event after another. These were inserted within the text space, a form requiring a preliminary plan. The designers left spaces for the images when setting the letters on the plate and succeeded in creating proportional gaps between the different components. The repeated images not only illustrate the texts but also serve as signs to help the user browsing the booklet to find the required version of the *qiddush*. Moreover, although the booklet was a compilation of alternative passages selected according to the liturgical calendar, by the adjustment of paratexts, changing from one image to another, the designers added another aspect to the book. Images of each sort were connected one to another while creating two continuous narrative series. These were built around two axes: the communal identity and the family frame in which the ritual texts, each of which is multi-layered, were recited.

The immediate layer of the hunt scene is the mnemonic role related to the order of the blessings to be recited. The second is a continuous story of two hares running away from an experienced hunter and his four hounds. The two hares are almost caught in the hunter's net and one is even bitten on the leg by one of the hounds, but eventually, against all odds, they succeed in escaping. Such a narrative was well rooted in the popular culture, in which the noble idea of hunting spread to other levels of society. Here, however, the addition of the introductory caption adds a third, symbolic, layer through which the participants identify themselves with all of Jewry, continuously persecuted in exile. The second narrative takes us from the communal identity into the private realm, the mixed ritual frame in which men and women celebrate together at home. Here, the various layers are constructed in a sophisticated way through the contents of the paratexts attached to a relatively simple image. These reflect gender aspects related to the ritual itself and the texts recited, but also go beyond the ritual context by referring to rabbinic sources and alluding to moral literature while dealing in an ironic manner with sexual tensions and gender issues.

Although the artisan who made the woodcuts is unknown, the design is a well-planned work by one or more of the four partners, who, using only four simple woodblocks, managed to create a sophisticated result. As educated Jews well acquainted with biblical verses, talmudic notions, Hebrew poetry, moral literature, and popular culture, they knew how to combine their literary innovations with the communicative power of the visual language and the new technique of the woodcut. The result was more than a selection of blessings and hymns for recitation at the Sabbath and holyday dining table. It embellished the rigid ritual text with a whole range of cultural contexts reflecting an Ashkenazi community at the beginning of the sixteenth century.

We do not know how popular this impressive booklet was in its time. Unfortunately, only one copy has survived. However, since the booklets would have been in constant use because they included rituals and hymns referred to on a weekly basis, year in and year out, the copies probably became worn and torn with time, and this might explain why only one copy has been found. Unlike the *Prague Haggadah* of 1526, which shaped the beginning of a long and clear tradition that expanded to include different variations and spread throughout Europe and beyond,[67] the destiny of the illustrated booklet was less direct, though its impact is evident. The genre of small units for use on certain ritual occasions flourished in succeeding generations, and the format that includes *zemirot* and the Grace after Meals is still popular today.[68] The single extant copy from 1514 is the sole evidence we have for one of the most creative and influential initiatives of the early Hebrew printing age in Prague.

---

67 Schubert, pp. 40–81.
68 See the booklets of *Sefrei berakhot* common in eighteenth-century manuscripts (Schubert, pp. 144–50). Their affinity to the Prague booklet is indirect. See also Isaac Benjacob, *Ozar ha-sepharim: Tesaurus Librorum Hebraicorum*, with revision and notes by Moritz Steinschneider (Vilnius: Romm, 1880), p. 88, no. 663 and p. 160, no. 197.

LUCIA RASPE

Hayyim Shahor and Jewish Life in Sixteenth-Century Ashkenaz*

For my mother

Introduction

In the spring of 1540, an edition of the *'Arba'ah turim* ('Four Columns') was printed in Augsburg. A core text of the halakhic curriculum and a staple of Jewish culture everywhere, the four-part compendium composed by Jacob ben Asher in the mid-fourteenth century had been among the very first Hebrew books brought to press in the 1470s and had seen several subsequent editions. By the time of the Augsburg printing, however, these earlier editions had become rare. In fact, as the printer, Hayyim ben David Shahor, wrote on the first page of text, the need for a new edition had been impressed upon him by a great number of Torah students in his area. Day in, day out they had insisted that copies of the *Tur* were hard to come by and that the book had to be reprinted.[1]

Reading these words, one cannot help wondering who it was that they were meant to refer to. Presenting a printing venture as a service to the community was a common way of appealing to potential buyers, but who were the adherents of Torah study 'in these lands' who were in such dire need of Shahor's publication? The book was printed in Augsburg, an imperial city that had expelled its Jews in 1438. Since then no Jew had been allowed to stay overnight, let alone live, in the Swabian city. In order to enter its gates during the daytime, Jews had to have a special permit, they had to pay a fee, and, from 1536 onwards, they had to have a local soldier escort

---

* The research presented in this chapter was carried out while I held fellowships at the Katz Center for Advanced Judaic Studies at the University of Pennsylvania and at the Oxford Centre for Hebrew and Jewish Studies at the University of Oxford, for which I remain grateful. Completion of the manuscript was supported by a generous grant from the Gerda Henkel Stiftung.

1 Printer's preface, *'Arba'ah turim* (Augsburg 1540), fol. 1ʳ העירוני להדפסת ספר זה רוב לומדי תורה שבאילו הגלילות באמרם אלי יום יום הנה ספרי הארבעה טורים. הם הולכים וחסרים); online at http://nbn-resolving.de/urn:nbn:de:bvb:12-bsb00090162-4.

Lucia Raspe • Salomon Ludwig Steinheim Institute for German-Jewish History, University of Duisburg-Essen

them wherever they went.² The book was printed in a country that had expelled almost all of its Jews, city by city, territory by territory, during the 'long' fifteenth century, leaving barely a handful of urban communities in place.³ Who, then, were the potential buyers for whom this and other Hebrew books printed by Hayyim Shahor in the 1530–40s were meant?

The first Jew who used movable type for the printing of Hebrew books in the German Lands, Hayyim Shahor has often been viewed as an example of the central role that cooperation with Christian Hebraist patrons, bookmen, and audiences played in early Hebrew printing within the empire.⁴ Indeed, such cooperation would appear to have been a *sine qua non* in an environment that was home to hardly any Jews at all. At the same time, early Hebrew printing was also predicated upon Jewish printers having to make a living, on the one hand, and Jewish audiences dependent on the availability of Hebrew books, on the other. In what follows, I consider what Shahor and his output may be able to teach us about Jewish life in post-expulsion Ashkenaz beyond the Hebraist connection.

An outline of our protagonist's career is easily sketched.⁵ A Bohemian Jew by origin, Hayyim ben David Shahor ('black', or Černý in Czech, Schwarz in German) had been part of a consortium that had published some of the earliest Hebrew books printed in Prague from 1514 on.⁶ When his former partner Gershom Katz secured an exclusive privilege for printing Hebrew books in Bohemia in 1527, Shahor found himself forced out of business and left Prague. In 1530, he produced the first Hebrew book printed by Jews within Germany in the Silesian town of Oels (Oleśnica near present-day Wrocław).⁷

---

2 Wolfram Baer, 'Zwischen Vertreibung und Wiederansiedlung: Die Reichsstadt Augsburg und die Juden vom 15. bis zum 18. Jahrhundert', in *Judengemeinden in Schwaben im Kontext des Alten Reiches*, ed. by Rolf Kießling, Colloquia Augustana, 2 (Berlin: Akademie-Verlag, 1995), pp. 110–27 (p. 115); cf. Markus Wenninger, 'Geleit, Geleitsrecht und Juden im Mittelalter', *Aschkenas*, 31 (2021), pp. 29–77 (pp. 73–76). Among the many such permits (*Geleitzettel*) preserved in the municipal archives of Augsburg, none dates to before 1577. I am grateful to Dr Helmut Graser (Augsburg) for this information; personal communication, January 2019.

3 For a survey, see Jörg R. Müller, 'Verfolgungen und Vertreibungen', in *Geschichte der Juden im Mittelalter zwischen Nordsee und Mittelmeer: Kommentiertes Kartenwerk*, ed. by Alfred Haverkamp, 3 vols, Forschungen zur Geschichte der Juden Abteilung A: Abhandlungen, 14 (Hannover: Hahnsche Buchhandlung, 2002), I, pp. 213–21.

4 See, e.g., Katrin Kogman-Appel, 'Designing a Passover Imagery for New Audiences: The Prague Haggadah', in *Unter Druck: Mitteleuropäische Buchmalerei im 15. Jahrhundert*, ed. by Jeffrey Hamburger and Maria Theisen, Buchmalerei des 15. Jahrhunderts in Mitteleuropa, 15 (Petersberg: Imhof, 2018), pp. 180–94 (p. 182), or Marvin J. Heller, *The Sixteenth-Century Hebrew Book: An Abridged Thesaurus*, 2 vols, Brill's Series in Jewish Studies, 33 (Leiden: Brill, 2004), I, pp. xxxiv–xxxv.

5 Fundamental studies include Moritz Steinschneider, 'Hebräische Drucke in Deutschland', *Zeitschrift für die Geschichte der Juden in Deutschland*, 1 (1887), pp. 281–87 (pp. 284–87); A[vraham] M. Habermann, 'The Printer Hayyim Shaḥor, his Son Isaac and his Son-in-Law Josef b. Yakar' (Hebrew), *Kiryat Sefer*, 31 (1956), pp. 483–500; repr. in Habermann, *Studies in the History of Hebrew Printers and Books* (Hebrew; Jerusalem: Mass, 1978), pp. 103–30; Olga Sixtová, 'Jewish Printers and Printing Presses in Prague 1512–1670 (1672)', in *Hebrew Printing in Bohemia and Moravia*, ed. by Olga Sixtová (Prague: Academia, 2012), pp. 32–73 (pp. 36–38).

6 Habermann, 'Hayyim Shaḥor', pp. 483–84 and 486–90, nos 1–6; Olga Sixtová, 'The Beginnings of Prague Hebrew Typography 1512–1569', in Sixtová, *Hebrew Printing*, pp. 74–121 (pp. 101–06, nos 3–10).

7 Habermann, 'Hayyim Shaḥor', pp. 484 and 490–91, no. 7. See Markus Brann, 'Geschichte der Juden in Schlesien', pt 5: 'Vom Beginn der habsburgischen Herrschaft bis zum Ende des sechzehnten Jahrhunderts', in *Jahres-Bericht des Jüdisch-Theologischen Seminars Fraenckel'scher Stiftung* (1910), pp. 151–201 (pp. 167–68). Contemporary Christian reports about a thunderstorm which effectively ended Hebrew printing in Oels, which are sometimes taken to refer to Shahor's activity, in fact relate to that of Samuel Helicz in 1535; Stephen G.

Beginning in *c.* 1531, Shahor's activity appears to have been centred in Augsburg for some ten or twelve years.[8] However, he also travelled to Italy at least twice during this period, as we shall see, and he may have been involved in Hebrew printing elsewhere within Germany. Following the Augsburg phase of his career and joined by his son and his son-in-law, Shahor printed two more works in Ichenhausen, a market town in Swabia, in 1544–45, and another two in Heddernheim, some five kilometres north of Frankfurt am Main, in 1546.[9] Finally, in 1547, the family business moved to Lublin, where Shahor must have died soon after and his successors continued printing Hebrew books for another century and a half.[10]

Hebrew Printing in a City without Jews

The Augsburg chapter in Shahor's life, the longest period he spent in any one place after Prague and undoubtedly the most fruitful in his career, is also the phase we know the most about. The extensive work that has been done on this important printing centre in Reformation Germany, which has integrated the available evidence on Hebrew printing into its narrative, contextualizes Shahor's work in the local scene in a way that is exceptional in the extant scholarship on early Hebrew printing within Germany.[11] It is unfortunate that these findings do not seem to have garnered the attention they deserve,[12] for they offer rich insights into the workings of Hebrew printing in a city without Jews.

Two letters written by two members of the local elite on 21 January 1535 are especially noteworthy for the light they shed on the circumstances of Shahor's activity in Augsburg.[13] Both were occasioned by the attempt of one Sebastian

---

Burnett, 'German Jewish Printing in the Reformation Era (1530–1633)', in *Jews, Judaism, and the Reformation in Sixteenth-Century Germany*, ed. by Dean Phillip Bell and Stephen G. Burnett, Studies in Central European Histories, 37 (Leiden: Brill, 2006), pp. 503–27 (p. 507 and note 17).

8 Habermann, 'Hayyim Shaḥor', pp. 484–85 and 491–95, nos 8–16.

9 Habermann, 'Hayyim Shaḥor', pp. 485 and 496–98, nos 17–18 and 19–20.

10 B[ernhard] Friedberg, *History of Hebrew Typography in Poland*, 2nd Ed. (Hebrew; Tel Aviv: Baruch Friedberg, 1950), pp. 45–47; Habermann, 'Hayyim Shaḥor', pp. 485 and 499–500, nos 22–27; Heller, I, p. xli; Magdalena Bendowska and Jan Doktór, *The Amsterdam of Polish Jews: Old Hebrew Printed Works from the Collections of the Jewish Historical Institute, Warsaw*, trans. by Marek Czepiec (Warsaw: The Emanuel Ringelblum Jewish Historical Institute, 2016), pp. 23–25.

11 See Hans-Jörg Künast, *'Getruckt zu Augspurg': Buchdruck und Buchhandel in Augsburg zwischen 1468 und 1555*, Studia Augustana, 8 (Tübingen: Niemeyer, 1997); Hans-Jörg Künast, 'Hebräisch-jüdischer Buchdruck in Schwaben in der ersten Hälfte des 16. Jahrhunderts', in *Landjudentum im deutschen Südwesten während der Frühen Neuzeit*, ed. by Rolf Kießling and Sabine Ullmann, Colloquia Augustana, 10 (Berlin: Akademie-Verlag, 1999), pp. 277–303. Künast's conclusions have also found entry into the standard work on sixteenth- and seventeenth-century printing within Germany; Christoph Reske, *Die Buchdrucker des 16. und 17. Jahrhunderts im deutschen Sprachgebiet*, 2nd Ed., Beiträge zum Buch- und Bibliothekswesen, 51 (Wiesbaden: Harrassowitz, 2015), pp. 39–40.

12 See esp. Künast's discussion, in 'Hebräisch-jüdischer Buchdruck', pp. 281–82, of 'August Wind', a spurious printer first introduced into the discussion by B[ernhard] Friedberg, *History of Hebrew Typography [...] in Central Europe* (Hebrew; Antwerp: Jacobowitz, 1935), pp. 29–30, and apparently based on a misinterpretation of *Aug[usta] Vind[elicorum]*, the Latin name of Augsburg as given in Moritz Steinschneider, *Catalogus librorum Hebraeorum in Bibliotheca Bodleiana* (Berlin: Friedlaender, 1852–60), cols 3047–48, no. 9245. The same printer has since been resurrected in a number of works.

13 The original documents appear to have been lost. Copies preserved in the Veesenmeyer collection of the municipal archives in Ulm were edited in Julius Endriß, *Sebastian Francks Ulmer Kämpfe: Ein Vortrag mit Anlagen* (Ulm: Höhn, 1935), pp. 36–39, nos 3–4. Their relevance to the history of Hebrew printing in Augsburg was first recognized by Paul Geissler, 'Neues vom hebräischen

Franck (1499–1542), a somewhat controversial Protestant author, to open a printing press in nearby Ulm. Wealthy Augsburg patrician Jörg Regel (1466–1547/8), like Franck originally from Donauwörth and a long-time supporter, took the lead. Addressing his missive to the burgomasters of Ulm, Regel set out the many advantages that Franck's project had to offer. Not least among them, Regel wrote, was that admitting Franck would gain Ulm the opportunity to engage the services of a certain Jew now in Augsburg, who owned — and was able to use — a set of Hebrew fonts and had offered to join Franck and print Hebrew books for him, which might prove a highly profitable venture and help Franck make a living.[14] That Jew, he added, was a good man and completely devoted to his printing; he had stayed with Bonifaz for weeks at a time over the past two or three years and had never bothered anyone.[15]

The man referred to as Bonifaz concurred. At Regel's behest, Bonifatius Wolfhart (1485/90–1543), a Zwinglian preacher influential in Augsburg at the time,[16] likewise recommended that Ulm seize the opportunity to have Franck print in all manner of languages. He, too, thought that as far as Hebrew was concerned, securing the help of a Jew who had printed at Silvan's shop in Augsburg for the past three years might be an added boon. Although Wolfhart, like Regel, did not mention Shahor by name, he confirmed that he had himself hosted the same Jew for long stretches of time and could vouch for his character. The man had better Hebrew fonts than could be found anywhere else in Germany; for Wolfhart's sake, he was ready to put them at Franck's disposal, provided he could himself print the Bible and other Hebrew works in his employment, which would benefit Franck as well.[17]

Silvan, the man whose printing shop Shahor had been using in Augsburg, was Silvan Otmar, one of Reformation Augsburg's most productive printers. Situated in the quarter near the former monastery of St Ursula that had the greatest density of printers, bookbinders, and booksellers

---

Frühdruck in Augsburg', *Gutenberg-Jahrbuch*, 42 (1967), pp. 118–21. See also Künast, 'Hebräisch-jüdischer Buchdruck', pp. 281–87.

14 Endriß, pp. 36–37 ('ein Jud ist hie, der hat hebräisch Buchstaben und kann selbst setzen, der wollt hebräisch bei ihm [= Franck] drucken, dieselben Bücher sind von Stund an bar Geld, da hoffte er in einem Jahr etlich 100 Gulden über alle Kosten zu gewinnen außerhalb der teutschen Bücher zu drucken, das auch ein guten Nutz tragen wurde; damit so käm der gut, fromm und gelehrt Mann [= Franck] auf grün Zweig und wäre ihm geholfen, daß er (so Gott will) forthin nimmer dürft am Hungertuch nähen'). See Endriß, esp. pp. 15–16; cf. Künast, 'Hebräisch-jüdischer Buchdruck', p. 283, and Yvonne Dellsperger, 'Sebastian Franck und der Buchdruck', *Buchkultur im Mittelalter: Schrift – Bild – Kommunikation*, ed. by Michael Stolz and Adrian Mettauer (Berlin: De Gruyter, 2005), pp. 243–59.

15 Endriß, p. 37 ('Dieser Jud ist ein fromm Mensch, jedermann ungeärgert von ihm, wartet allein dem Drucken aus, ist in zwei oder drei Jahren oft und viel hie gewesen bei dem Bonifaz viel Wochen lang').

16 Heinz-Peter Mielke, 'Wolfhart, Bonifatius', in *Biographisch-Bibliographisches Kirchenlexikon*, ed. by Friedrich Wilhelm Bautz and Traugott Bautz, 41 vols (Nordhausen: Bautz, 1975–2020), XXIX (2008), col. 1575. For background, see Michele Zelinsky Hanson, *Religious Identity in an Early Reformation Community: Augsburg, 1517 to 1555*, Studies in Central European Histories, 45 (Leiden: Brill, 2009), pp. 12–19.

17 Endriß, p. 38 ('Denn er willens ein solche Druckerei anzurichten, die einer löblichen Stadt Ulm nit allein nützlich, sondern auch ehrlich sein würde, so er bei euch allerlei gute Bücher in den Sprachen durch den Druck an Tag brächte. Dazu ihm gar dienstlich wäre, vornehmlich die hebräisch Sprach belangend, ein Jud, der jetzt bei drei Jahren hie beim Silvan gedruckt [...]. Ich hab ihn selbst lange Zeit bei mir gehabt [...]. Dieser ist ein feiner Künstler und die hebräisch Sprach zu drucken fast geschickt, hat auch Schriften dazu besser, weder man's jetzt in teutschen Landen finden mag, welcher mir zu Gefallen dem Seb. Francken seine Schriften wollt zustellen mit dem Geding, daß er bei ihm in Knechtsweis arbeiten, die Bibel samt andern Büchern in hebräischer Sprach drucken möchte, davon nit ein kleiner Nutz dem Francken würde zustehn').

in Augsburg at the time, the Otmar printing house had been founded by Silvan's father, Johann, in 1502. It turned out more than 500 editions between 1515 and 1539; Silvan's son Valentin took over in 1540 and ran the shop until his own death in 1563.[18] It was thus in the very heart of the printing business in one of the chief centres of Central European book production that Shahor did his printing during the Augsburg phase of his career, and it was apparently in his patron Bonifatius Wolfhart's own dwellings within the former Carmelite Convent of St Anna, where Luther had lodged in 1518, that he stayed when he was in the city.[19]

Shahor's plans to collaborate with Sebastian Franck in Ulm may indeed have come to fruition.[20] Supported by two men from Augsburg's religious and lay elites, Franck succeeded in obtaining the burgomasters' permission and opened his shop in Ulm in the fall of 1535; however, the enterprise folded only four years later when Franck was expelled from the city for his nonconformist views.[21] Although no Hebrew book with an Ulm imprint has been preserved, it appears that at least one was printed. This is indicated by an expert opinion in Latin that the same Bonifatius Wolfhart wrote for the humanist politician and bibliophile Konrad Peutinger (1465–1547), also of Augsburg. Peutinger, who owned one of the largest private libraries of his time, had somehow obtained a Hebrew book and needed help in deciding whether to keep it or not, as he could not read it. Wolfhart, who could, reassured him: The book, although printed by a certain Jew named Hayyim 'partly in Augsburg, partly in Ulm', was a perfectly harmless piece of Jewish liturgy; it certainly merited inclusion in his library.[22]

Wolfhart, in other words, appears to have been aware that some of Shahor's own printing was being done in Ulm, presumably using Franck's press. According to his description, the volume contained prayers that were recited on specific holidays and new moons in the course of the Jewish year. The volume in question may thus have been one of the several editions of the Ashkenazi siddur that Shahor produced during the Augsburg phase of his career, which contained both daily prayers and basic liturgies for Rosh Hodesh and the festivals. Most of these have only reached us in defective copies lacking title pages or colophons, so they are difficult to date.[23]

---

18 Künast, 'Getruckt zu Augspurg', pp. 101–02, 132; Künast, 'Hebräisch-jüdischer Buchdruck', p. 284.
19 [Karl] Wolfart, 'Beiträge zur Augsburger Reformationsgeschichte. III. Caspar Schwenkfeld und Bonifacius Wolfhart', *Beiträge zur Bayerischen Kirchengeschichte*, 8 (1902), pp. 97–114, 145–61 (p. 102); Künast, 'Hebräisch-jüdischer Buchdruck', p. 283.
20 *Pace* Geissler, p. 119, Künast, 'Hebräisch-jüdischer Buchdruck', p. 284, and Reske, pp. 1016–17.
21 Geissler, p. 119; Reske, p. 1017; Dellsperger, pp. 248–49.

22 Wolfhart's undated missive is cited from an eighteenth-century edition in *Konrad Peutingers Briefwechsel*, ed. by Erich König, Humanistenbriefe (Munich: Beck, 1923), pp. 473–74, no. 288 ('Liber Hebraeus, quem heri ad me misisti, a Chaim (si quisquam alius) vero Israelita partim Ulmae, partim hic excusus est nec certum authorem praefert. Videtur enim non ab uno aliquo, sed pluribus idque diversis temporibus consarcinatus. Continent autem orationes Iudaeorum plane pias et innocuas, ut puta ex Scripturis desumptas, quas singulis festis et neomeniis adeoque per totum anni curriculum orare solent. Quare librum hunc haud indignum esse duxerim, quo bibliotheca tua optimis alioqui omnium tum linguarum tum professionum auctoribus instructa exornetur'). My reading of this text differs from that given in Künast, 'Hebräisch-jüdischer Buchdruck', p. 286, note 32, according to which Wolfhart wrote the letter in his capacity as the censor of Hebrew books printed in Augsburg, which would have been highly exceptional in Germany before 1553; Burnett, p. 518.
23 See Steinschneider, *Catalogus*, col. 306, no. 2072; Habermann, 'Hayyim Shaḥor', p. 491, no. 8, and p. 495, no. 16; Mosche N. Rosenfeld, *Der jüdische Buchdruck in Augsburg in der ersten Hälfte des 16. Jahrhunderts / Jewish Printing in Augsburg during the First Half of the 16th Century* (London: n.p., 1985), pp. 32–33, nos 37–38, and p. 38, no. 48. The copy extant at Universitätsbibliothek Basel (https://doi.org/10.3931/e-rara-80967), whose colophon has been preserved, would seem to date from January 1532. A copy made up of two parts dated to December 1532 and June 1532, respectively, was recently

The copy that had come into Peutinger's hands must have been printed sometime between 1535 and 1539. While his correspondence does not indicate whether he did or did not keep the book, the volume is not mentioned in the extant autograph catalogues of Peutinger's collection.[24]

Book Art between Jews and Christians

It is not surprising that Shahor's collaboration with Christian bookmen has left traces in his books — certainly in their outward appearance. Originally, of course, Shahor was from Prague. Although the assumption that he himself was responsible for the creation of some of the artwork in early imprints from that city no longer seems tenable,[25] he had been socialized into the multifaceted art of bookmaking in the Bohemian capital and was keenly aware that the aesthetic appeal of a book might have an impact on its sales.

Shahor's original connection to Prague book art is most evident in the woodcut border featuring Adam and Eve, as well as Judith and Samson, that was used for the first text page of the liturgical Pentateuch (*humash*) printed at Ichenhausen in 1544–45 (Figure 8.1).[26] A less refined mirror copy of the border that had framed the text of *Shefokh hamatkha* ('Pour out Thy Wrath') in the famous *Prague Haggadah* of 1526 (Figure 8.2),[27] it would seem to have been created by an artist who had that book in front of him. After it was used for the *Ichenhausen Pentateuch*, the same woodcut modelled on the one in the *Prague Haggadah* reappeared in an edition of penitential prayers (*selihot*) printed in Heddernheim in 1546 (Figure 8.3);[28] it was subsequently reused by Kalonymos Yafe, the husband of Shahor's granddaughter, in Lublin as late as 1602.[29] By that time, the wooden block had suffered significant damage; worn out after almost six decades of use, it cannot have lasted much longer.

It is tempting to speculate that Shahor may originally have commissioned the woodcut copied from Prague for a haggadah of his own,[30] but no folio haggadah printed by Shahor has been preserved. The smaller haggadah that we do have, printed in Augsburg in 1534, indeed features a number of woodcuts reminiscent of earlier Prague editions.[31] At the same time, it is typical of the Augsburg phase in Shahor's career in that its title

---

sold at auction; https://www.kestenbaum.net/auction/lot/auction-69/069-147. For evidence of two Augsburg editions dated to 1535 and 1538, see Zipporah Baruchson, 'In Search of the Lost Books of the 15th–16th Centuries' (Hebrew), *Alei Sefer*, 16 (1989/90), pp. 37–58 (p. 55, nos 193–94).

24 See Hans-Jörg Künast and Helmut Zäh, *Die Bibliothek Konrad Peutingers: Edition der historischen Kataloge und Rekonstruktion der Bestände*, 2 vols, Studia Augustana, 11 and 14 (Tübingen: Niemeyer, 2003–2005).

25 As originally suggested by Aron Freimann, 'Zur Geschichte der jüdischen Buchillustration bis 1540', *Zeitschrift für hebräische Bibliographie* 21 (1918), pp. 25–32 (p. 31). See Sixtová, 'Jewish Printers', p. 38; Petr Voit, 'Ornamentation of Prague Hebrew Books during the First Half of the 16th Century as a Part of Bohemian Book Design', in Sixtová, *Hebrew Printing*, pp. 122–51 (pp. 146–47); Kogman-Appel, p. 193, note 45, and the literature cited there.

26 Steinschneider, *Catalogus*, col. 21, no. 107; Habermann, 'Hayyim Shaḥor', p. 497, no. 18.

27 For a discussion of the original image and its possible implications, see Richard I. Cohen, *Jewish Icons: Art and Society in Modern Europe* (Berkeley: University of California Press, 1998), p. 93.

28 Steinschneider, *Catalogus*, cols 431–32, no. 2835; Habermann, 'Hayyim Shaḥor', p. 498, no. 20.

29 http://sammlungen.ub.uni-frankfurt.de/urn:nbn:de:hebis:30:1-157745. See also Steinschneider, *Catalogus*, col. 27, no. 144; Sixtová, 'Jewish Printers', p. 37, pl. 5.

30 As suggested by Sixtová, 'Jewish Printers', p. 37.

31 Habermann, 'Hayyim Shaḥor', p. 491, no. 10, and p. 493, pl. 2. See Cecil Roth, 'The Illustrated Haggadah', *Studies in Bibliography and Booklore* 7 (1965), pp. 37–56 (p. 40); Yosef Hayim Yerushalmi, *Haggadah and History: A Panorama in Facsimile of 5 Centuries of the Printed Haggadah from the Collections of Harvard University*

Figure 8.1. *Ḥumash*, Ichenhausen, 1544 (The Bodleian Libraries, University of Oxford, Opp. fol. 47, fol. 2ʳ).

Figure 8.2. Haggadah, Prague, 1526 (Frankfurt am Main, Universitätsbibliothek Johann Christian Senckenberg, Ausst. 246, fol. 25ʳ).

Figure 8.3. *Seliḥot*, Heddernheim, 1546 (The Bodleian Libraries, University of Oxford, Opp. fol. 1247, fol. 1ᵛ).

page displays a woodcut originally created for Silvan Otmar, the local printer whose press he was using. Unlike the mirror-image version of the border copied from the *Prague Haggadah*, these woodcuts do not recur in Shahor's post-Augsburg work, hence may have been rented from Otmar. The border used for the title page of the haggadah produced in Augsburg had been designed by Daniel Hopfer (*c.* 1470–1536) in 1517; it had last been used by Otmar for Caspar Turnauer's history of the Jews in biblical times in 1528.³² An

even more elaborate woodcut by the same artist frames the first page of text of Shahor's *Seliḥot* (Augsburg 1536).³³ Again created some twenty years before it was first recycled in a Hebrew book (Figures 8.4, 8.5), Hopfer's design was probably beginning to fall out of fashion.³⁴ Nevertheless,

---

and the Jewish Theological Seminary of America, 2ⁿᵈ Ed. (Philadelphia: Jewish Publication Society, 1976), pl. 14–17; Kogman-Appel, pp. 188–89, 190–91.

32 See *Hollstein's German Engravings, Etchings and Woodcuts ca. 1400–1700*, ed. by Friedrich Hollstein and others (Amsterdam: van Gendt, 1954–), XV: Elias Holl to Hieronymus Hopfer (1986), pp. 168–69, no. 150; cf. Rosenfeld, *Augsburg*, pp. 34–35, no. 42, and p. 53, pl. XX;

Künast, 'Hebräisch-jüdischer Buchdruck', p. 285, note 29. For evidence that Shahor had similarly reused materials originally created for Christian publishers in both Prague and Oels, see Sixtová, 'Beginnings', p. 88; Voit, p. 123.

33 As noted by Freimann, pp. 31–32. See Steinschneider, *Catalogus*, col. 431, no. 2834; Habermann, 'Hayyim Shaḥor', p. 492, no. 13; Alfred Forbes Johnson, *German Renaissance Title-Borders* (Oxford: Oxford University Press, 1929), no. 18; Hollstein, XV, pp. 173–74, no. 153.

34 Compare the well-known woodcut designed by Hans Holbein the Younger, which was more than eighty years old when it was reused on the title pages of Basel imprints in both Hebrew and Yiddish in *c.* 1600; Joseph Prijs, *Die Basler hebräischen Drucke (1492–1866)*, ed. by Bernhard Prijs (Olten and Freiburg i. Br.: Urs Graf,

Figure 8.4. *Sassenspegel*, Augsburg, 1516 (Munich, Bayerische Staatsbibliothek, 2 J.germ. 105 x, fol. 1ʳ).

Figure 8.5. *Seliḥot*, Augsburg, 1536 (Jerusalem, National Library of Israel, R 2° 61 A 1511, fol. 2ᵛ).

Figure 8.6. *Ḥumash* in Yiddish, Augsburg, 1544 (Munich, Bayerische Staatsbibliothek, Res/2 A.hebr. 9#Beibd.1, fol. 119ʳ).

the same block was later reused once more as a title page introducing the Five Scrolls (*megillot*) in the Yiddish Pentateuch printed at Augsburg in 1544 (Figure 8.6).

The woodcut border framing the first page of text of the Augsburg *Tur*, finally, has become somewhat notorious in the history of Hebrew printing for its explicitly Christian imagery.[35] Featuring a visual representation of God on the sixth day of creation complete with a cruciform halo, the woodcut had originally been created by Jörg Breu the Elder (d. 1537) for an early edition of Luther's translation of the Old Testament.[36] By 1527, it had passed into Silvan Otmar's stock (Figure 8.7). Shahor's use of the same border for his edition of the *Tur* (Figure 8.8) remains difficult to explain.

The Question of Audience

If, as we have seen, Hayyim Shahor did much of his printing under the patronage of a Christian Hebraist and in close cooperation with a Christian printing house, were his imprints also intended for Christian readers? Several of his colleagues then engaged in printing Hebrew books in

---

1964), pp. 50–51 and 245; Hollstein, XIV: Ambrosius Holbein to Hans Holbein the Younger (1988), pp. 152–56, no. 10.

35 Steinschneider, *Catalogus*, cols 1183–84, no. 5500/7; Habermann, 'Hayyim Shaḥor', pp. 492–95, no. 14. See A[vraham] M. Haberman[n], *Title Pages of Hebrew Books* (Hebrew; Safed: Museum of Printing Art, 1969), pp. 21–22, pl. 6–7; Sixtová, 'Jewish Printers', p. 36, note 22.

36 Jutta Breyl, 'Beobachtungen zur Geschichte des Augsburger Titelblattes vom 15. bis zum Ausgang des 18. Jahrhunderts', in *Augsburger Buchdruck und Verlagswesen: Von den Anfängen bis zur Gegenwart*, ed. by Helmut Gier and Johannes Janota (Wiesbaden: Harrassowitz, 1997), pp. 243–89 (pp. 265–66); Hollstein, IV: Beischlag – Brosamer (1957), p. 158, no. 2.

Germany have been noted for targeting — more or less explicitly — both Jewish and Christian audiences. This is true of the Protestant Hebraist Paulus Fagius (1504–49), who employed the great Elijah Levita in his short-lived print shop in Isny in 1540–41, where he produced both Hebrew and bilingual Hebrew-Latin, as well as Yiddish imprints.[37] Fagius's pioneering edition of the liturgical Pentateuch in Yiddish, published in Constance in 1544 after Levita had left,[38] appeared in two versions which differed only in their title pages and prefaces. One, intended for Jews, had a title page in Yiddish and Hebrew and a preface in Yiddish, whereas the other featured both a title page and a preface in German.[39] Much the same can be said for the Yiddish *humash* published in Augsburg only a few months later and brought to press by Paulus Aemilius, a convert to Roman Catholicism who appears to have taken Shahor's place in Augsburg after Wolfhart had passed away in 1543.[40]

There is little indication that Shahor followed a similar strategy — at least not within any single one of his imprints. Comparing the four different editions of the liturgical Pentateuch in whose printing Shahor (or his immediate family) was involved — Prague 1514–18,[41] Oels 1530,[42] Ichenhausen 1544–45, and Lublin 1556–57[43] — we find that Shahor was quick to adopt the Christian chapter divisions first introduced into the printed Hebrew Bible in Daniel Bomberg's Venice edition of 1517.[44] Its appearance in his edition of the Pentateuch published in Oels may perhaps be interpreted as a concession to his then patron, Duke Charles I of Münsterberg, whose coat-of-arms appears on the title page;[45] indeed, the copy today in the Bodleian Library includes extensive annotation in Latin. By contrast, when he printed the Pentateuch in Ichenhausen fifteen years later, Shahor reverted to a text that did not have chapter divisions. The Ichenhausen Humash also lacked Rashi's commentary, present in both the Prague and the later Lublin edition. Altogether more modest, it would clearly seem to have been designed for a — perhaps somewhat less elite — Jewish audience.

---

37 Richard Raubenheimer, *Paul Fagius aus Rheinzabern: Sein Leben und Wirken als Reformator und Gelehrter* (Grünstadt/Pfalz: Verein für Pfälzische Kirchengeschichte, 1957), esp. pp. 23–50; Gérard E. Weil, *Élie Lévita: Humaniste et Massorète (1469–1549)*, Studia Post-Biblica, 7 (Leiden: Brill, 1963), esp. pp. 133–51.

38 Steinschneider, *Catalogus*, cols 177–78, no. 1187.

39 Max Weinreich, *Shtaplen: fir etyudn tsu der yidisher shprakhvisnshaft un literaturgeshikhte* (Berlin: Wostok, 1923), pp. 97–102; Morris M. Faierstein, 'Paulus Fagius and the First Published Yiddish Translation of the *Humash*, Constance, 1544', *Judaica: Beiträge zum Verstehen des Judentums*, 73 (2017), pp. 1–35; Morris M. Faierstein, 'The Yiddish *Humash* in the Sixteenth Century', in *The Way of the Book: A Tribute to Zeev Gries*, ed. by Avriel Bar-Levav et al. (Hebrew; Jerusalem: Carmel, 2021), pp. 243–58 (pp. 247–52).

40 The precise circumstances remain open to speculation. See the sources published in Joseph Perles, *Beiträge zur Geschichte der hebräischen und aramäischen Studien* (Munich: Ackermann, 1884), pp. 166–77, and Hans Striedl, 'Paulus Aemilius an J. A. Widmanstetter: Briefe von 1543/44 und 1549', in *Ars iocundissima: Festschrift für Kurt Dorfmüller zum 60. Geburtstag*, ed. by Horst Leuchtmann and Robert Münster (Tutzing: Schneider, 1984), pp. 333–45, and cf. Habermann, 'Hayyim Shahor', pp. 484–85; Geissler, pp. 120–21; Künast, 'Hebräisch-jüdischer Buchdruck', pp. 287–89. For the two versions of the Augsburg *humash*, see Morris M. Faierstein, 'Paulus Aemilius, Convert to Catholicism and Printer of Yiddish Books in Sixteenth Century Augsburg', *Judaica: Beiträge zum Verstehen des Judentums*, 71 (2015), pp. 349–65; Faierstein, 'The Yiddish *Humash*', pp. 252–55.

41 Steinschneider, *Catalogus*, cols 7–8, no. 31; Habermann, 'Hayyim Shahor', pp. 486–88, no. 3; Sixtová, 'Beginnings', pp. 101–02, no. 4.

42 Steinschneider, *Catalogus*, cols 13–14, no. 63; Habermann, 'Hayyim Shahor', pp. 490–91, no. 7.

43 Steinschneider, *Catalogus*, col. 27, no. 144; Habermann, 'Hayyim Shahor', p. 500, no. 27.

44 David Stern, *The Jewish Bible: A Material History*, The Samuel and Althea Stroum Lectures in Jewish Studies (Seattle and London: University of Washington Press, 2017), p. 145.

45 Brann, pp. 167–68 and frontispiece. For the conjecture that Shahor's family may have hailed from Silesia, see Sixtová, 'Jewish Printers', p. 36.

Where, then, was that audience to be found? Ichenhausen was a small place at the time. Regarding the question of why Shahor moved his activity there of all places when he left Augsburg some time before 1544, scholars have simply taken for granted that it was home to a Jewish community.[46] In fact, it was not. Moreover, there was never another printer, Jew or Christian, in Ichenhausen.[47] A single Jewish resident is mentioned there in 1541, but it was not until the 1560s that the number of Jewish households rose to about a dozen, a level sufficient for the emergence of communal institutions.[48] In the mid-1540s, Ichenhausen — like Augsburg — had little to offer in the way of a local Jewish audience.

It seems likely, therefore, that Shahor's ambitions went beyond the strictly local.[49] One possibility is that his production was meant to cater to Ashkenazi Jews south of the Alps. Northern Italy had attracted growing numbers of Jews emigrating from Germany since the end of the fourteenth century, thus preceding the emergence of the new centre of Ashkenazi culture in Poland-Lithuania by a generation or two. The Ashkenazim in the many small Jewish settlements that had sprung up since in the Friuli, in Veneto, and in Lombardy cultivated their own 'Ashkenaziness' in a very intense way.[50] This found expression, not least, in their continued adherence to the Western Ashkenazi rite of synagogue liturgy. Shahor was clearly aware of that fact. According to a manuscript note on the final leaf of a parchment copy of the festival prayerbook (mahzor) printed in Augsburg in 1536 and today among the holdings of the British Library, he personally sold the volume to one Shimshon bar Yaacov haKohen in Mantua in the summer of 1536.[51] We may assume that he sold more than that one copy. After all, the Western Ashkenazi mahzor had not been reprinted since the edition published in Pesaro (or Rimini?) in c. 1515/21.[52] The early editions printed in Prague had followed the local rite, which reflected the Eastern Ashkenazi form of Jewish liturgy; they were of limited use in Italy and the western parts of Germany.[53] Thus, there is a distinct possibility that Shahor's decision to reprint the Western Ashkenazi mahzor alongside his editions of the Western Ashkenazi siddur was made with an eye to the Italian market.

The same considerations may have guided Shahor's choices regarding the third major format of Ashkenazi liturgical imprints, that of penitential prayers. This was a field that had retained more local variety than the simple

---

46 Künast, 'Hebräisch-jüdischer Buchdruck', p. 280.

47 Reske, p. 419.

48 *Juden auf dem Lande: Beispiel Ichenhausen*, ed. by Haus der Bayerischen Geschichte, Veröffentlichungen zur bayerischen Geschichte und Kultur, 22 (Munich: Haus der Bayerischen Geschichte, 1991), pp. 18–19, 52–54; Stefan Rohrbacher, 'Die Anfänge der jüdischen Gemeinde zu Ichenhausen im 16. Jahrhundert', in *Ichenhausen: Von den Anfängen bis zur Gegenwart*, ed. by Georg Kreuzer, 2 vols (Ichenhausen: n.p., 2007), I, pp. 29–34.

49 As noted by Künast, 'Hebräisch-jüdischer Buchdruck', pp. 285–86, 289–91.

50 See Lucia Raspe, 'Portable Homeland: The German-Jewish Diaspora in Italy and Its Impact on Ashkenazic Book Culture, 1400–1600', in *Early Modern Ethnic and Religious Communities in Exile*, ed. by Yosef Kaplan (Newcastle upon Tyne: Cambridge Scholars Publishing, 2017), pp. 26–43, and the literature cited there.

51 Steinschneider, *Catalogus*, col. 369, no. 2448; Habermann, 'Hayyim Shaḥor', p. 492, no. 12. See the London copy, fol. 256ʳ קניין כספי קני' מן כמ"ר חיים שחור פה מנטואה בעד עשרה ריינש היו' יו' יח אב רצ"ו שמשון ב"ר יעקב הכהן יצ"ו. A facsimile of the note can be found in Rosenfeld, *Augsburg*, p. 8, and cf. ibid., pp. 15 and 36, nos 44–44b.

52 Steinschneider, *Catalogus*, col. 367, no. 2444.

53 For the distinction between East and West in Ashkenazi liturgy, see Daniel Goldschmidt's introduction to his edition of the High Holiday prayer book according to the various Ashkenazi rites, *Mahzor layamim hanora'im lefi minhagei benei Ashkenaz lekhol 'anfeihem*, 2 vols (Jerusalem: Koren, 1970), I, pp. 13–14, or Ruth Langer's revision of Goldschmidt's 1971 article, 'Liturgy', in *Encyclopaedia Judaica*, 2nd ed., Ruth Langer's 2007 revision, XIII, pp. 131–39 (p. 134).

distinction between East and West manifested in the printed prayerbooks for daily and festival use. In all, thirteen different *selihot* rites — eight of the Western, five of the Eastern Ashkenazi variety — were brought to print between the late fifteenth and the mid-nineteenth century.[54] Yet the two editions printed in Augsburg in 1536 and in Heddernheim ten years later were not geared towards local usage. Rather, they followed the relatively recent rite of Ashkenazi émigrés living in Italy, which had seen its first edition in Piove di Sacco near Venice in *c.* 1475, one of the earliest Hebrew books ever printed.[55]

Shahor's reliance on the Italo-Ashkenazi *selihot* rite for the first editions of penitential prayers printed in Germany may seem counterintuitive, and it has caused no little confusion among scholars.[56] It seems that these editions, too, were intended to be marketed in Italy. Again, the *selihot* according to the rite customary among Ashkenazim south of the Alps had not been reprinted since the days of Gershom Soncino.[57] Steinschneider notes that while the Augsburg edition is not found either in the collection built by David Oppenheim (1664–1736), today at the Bodleian Library, or among the printed books formerly owned by Heimann Joseph Michael of Hamburg (1792–1846) and today at the British Library, he had personally seen three copies in Padua.[58] Similarly, liturgical imprints from Augsburg can be found in quite a few of the *c.* 400 book lists submitted to the Inquisition by members of the Jewish community of Mantua in 1595.[59] Shahor's Mahzor left the press on the 2 May 1536, his *Selihot* on 23 June of the same year. A mere six weeks later, on 5 August, Shahor himself was selling books in Mantua. Not only was his journey apparently undertaken in order to market his output south of the Alps but the editions themselves had been planned accordingly. In short, it would seem that Ashkenazi Jews living in Italy played a key role in Shahor's marketing strategy.

---

54 They are listed in Goldschmidt, *Mahzor*, II, p. 13, or, at greater length, in the introduction to his editions of the two rites that remain in use among Ashkenazi Jews in Israel today, those following the Polish and the Lithuanian traditions. I have used *Seder haselihot keminhag Lita* (Jerusalem: Mossad Harav Kook, 1965), pp. 6–8.

55 Steinschneider, *Catalogus*, col. 430, no. 2829. See Lucia Raspe, 'The Migration of German Jews into Italy and the Emergence of Local Rites of *Selihot* Recitation', in *The Jews of Europe around 1400: Disruption, Crisis, and Resilience*, ed. by Lukas Clemens and Christoph Cluse, Forschungen zur Geschichte der Juden Abteilung A: Abhandlungen, 27 (Wiesbaden: Harrassowitz, 2018), pp. 173–93; Lucia Raspe, 'Tradition, Migration, and the Impact of Print: Local Rites of *Selihot* Recitation in Early Modern Ashkenaz', *Jewish Quarterly Review*, 113 (2023), pp. 83–104.

56 Indeed, the Augsburg *Selihot* has mistakenly been referred to as the *editio princeps* of the penitential prayers according to the rite of Frankfurt am Main, which came to dominate Western Ashkenazi usage from the seventeenth century onwards; Goldschmidt, *Seder haselihot keminhag Lita*, p. 7, no. 1. Rosenfeld, *Augsburg*, p. 37, no. 45, is similarly erroneous.

57 See Steinschneider, *Catalogus*, cols 430–31, no. 2830 (Barco 1496); col. 431, no. 2831 (Fano *c.* 1505).

58 Steinschneider, 'Hebräische Drucke', p. 284. For the two 'German' collections, see Gregor Pelger, *Wissenschaft des Judentums und englische Bibliotheken. Zur Geschichte historischer Philologie im 19. Jahrhundert*, Minima judaica, 8 (Berlin: Metropol, 2010), pp. 106–21, 121–44; for a recent study of Oppenheim's, Joshua Teplitsky, *Prince of the Press: How One Collector Built History's Most Enduring and Remarkable Jewish Library* (New Haven: Yale University Press, 2019).

59 For a study of these lists, see Shifra Baruchson, *Books and Readers: The Reading Interests of Italian Jews at the Close of the Renaissance* (Hebrew; Ramat-Gan: Bar-Ilan University Press, 1993), or the condensed French version, Shifra Baruchson-Arbib, *La culture livresque des juifs d'Italie à la fin de la Renaissance*, trans. by Gabriel Roth, rev. by Patrick Guez (Paris: CNRS, 2001); cf. above, n. 23.

Hebrew Books in Post-Expulsion Germany

Nevertheless, that is only part of the answer. In fact, like several of his contemporaries engaged in Hebrew printing, Shahor may well have attempted to address more than one audience at the same time. The Augsburg *Selihot* edition is of key importance here, for it has preserved clear indications that this was the case; it therefore merits closer examination.

As any edition of penitential prayers, the volume printed in Augsburg in 1536 contains the text of the liturgical poems recited during the fall season of repentance, beginning during the week before the New Year and culminating on the Day of Atonement, and on the other fast days over the course of the Jewish year. The selection included in Shahor's edition — 181 poetic pieces in all — follows the earlier editions of the rite customary among Ashkenazi émigrés living in Italy piece by piece, occasion after occasion. However, the edition also includes twenty-one additional poems, which appear at the very end.[60] Although like many of the Hebrew books printed at the time, the volume does not have a title page, the colophon located at the seam between the two parts of the book indicates that the larger part just finished offers the *selihot* 'as printed in Italy'; it adds that what follows is a number of pieces 'which they recite in the land of Ashkenaz'.[61]

'In the land of Ashkenaz', when used in opposition to Italy, was apparently meant to refer to the historical area of Jewish settlement within Germany itself, but it is not very specific. In the fifteenth century, before the wave of expulsions upset the geography of Ashkenazi liturgy, most Jewish communities in the *regnum teutonicum* — certainly those in the larger urban centres — presumably followed a *selihot* rite of their own.[62] What rite, then, were the twenty-one pieces included in the appendix of the Augsburg edition meant to represent? At first sight, they do not seem to follow any particular order. Upon closer inspection, however, it turns out that the selection of these additional pieces was by no means haphazard. In fact, it closely parallels a *selihot* rite which has been preserved in two manuscripts.

The first of these two, today at the National and University Library in Strasbourg, is a handbook of liturgical customs (*minhagim*) in Yiddish copied in Ulm for a man named Zalman Augsburg in the final quarter of the fifteenth century,[63] whose text includes specifications regarding the penitential prayers recited on the various Jewish fast days.[64] The same manuscript also includes a list, added at the very end, of the *selihot* customary on each day of the week before Rosh Hashanah, on the Days of Awe between Rosh Hashanah and Yom Kippur, and during the three major services on Yom Kippur itself. That list is headed 'the Order of Ulm and of Augsburg'.[65]

The second manuscript, a hefty folio volume on vellum now housed in Munich, contains the full text of a complete set of *selihot*, beginning with the week before Rosh Hashanah and including

---

60 *Selihot* (Augsburg 1536), fols 106ᵛ–117ᵛ, nos 182–201; online at https://www.nli.org.il/he/books/NNL_ALEPH001167500/NLI" read "https://rosetta.nli.org.il/delivery/DeliveryManagerServlet?dps_pid=IE34251085.

61 *Selihot* (Augsburg 1536), fol. 106ʳ (נשלמו הסליחות כמו שהייו נדפסים בארץ לועז | ומכאן ואילך הם סליחות האומרים בארץ אשכנז [!]).

62 Goldschmidt, *Seder haselihot keminhag Lita*, p. 6; Jonah Fraenkel and Avraham Fraenkel, 'Prayer and Piyyut in the Mahzor Nuremberg' (Hebrew; 2008), online at https://web.nli.org.il/sites/nlis/he/manuscript/Documents/fraenkel_j_a.pdf, pp. 97–98.

63 MS Strasbourg, Bibliothèque nationale et universitaire 4.099 (https://web.nli.org.il/sites/NLI/English/digitallibrary/pages/viewer.aspx?&presentorid=MANUSCRIPTS&docid=PNX_MANUSCRIPTS990001926390205171-1#|FL61213990). See Lucia Raspe, '*Minhagim* Books in Yiddish: A Tentative Taxonomy', in *Rabbinical Literature in Yiddish and Judezmo*, ed. by David M. Bunis, Katja Šmid, and Chava Turniansky (forthcoming).

64 MS Strasbourg 4.099, fols 20ʳ, 32ʳ–33ʳ, 99ᵛ–100ʳ, 104ᵛ.

65 MS Strasbourg 4.099, fols 122ʳ–123ʳ (סדר מאולים ומאוישפורג).

Figure 8.7. *Wormser Propheten*, Augsburg, 1527 (Staatsbibliothek zu Berlin – Preußischer Kulturbesitz, 4" Bv 1007, fol. 1ʳ).

Figure 8.8. *'Arba'a turim*, Augsburg, 1540 (Augsburg, Staats- und Stadtbibliothek, 2 Jud 8, fol. 7ʳ).

selections for all relevant occasions throughout the year; it would seem to date from the early fifteenth century.[66] Although this second manuscript has neither a title nor a colophon that might tell us when and where it originated, the inclusion of a five-piece liturgy meant to commemorate the death of one Avraham the Proselyte, a man from Augsburg martyred in 1264,[67] has led scholars to conclude that it reflects the *selihot* rite of that city and was written for the use of the cantor in the local synagogue.[68] As the Jewish community of Augsburg was expelled in 1438, the implication is that the manuscript was written prior to that date.

A comparison between these two manuscripts and the appendix of Shahor's Augsburg *Selihot* reveals that every single one of the twenty-one penitential prayers added to his edition is part of the rite recorded in the two codices. Moreover, their order in the printed appendix exactly

---

66 MS Munich, Bayerische Staatsbibliothek Cod. hebr. 67 (http://nbn-resolving.de/urn:nbn:de:bvb:12-bsb00103787-0). See Moritz Steinschneider, *Die hebräischen Handschriften der K. Hof- und Staatsbibliothek in München*, 2nd ed. (Munich: Palm, 1895), pp. 45–46.

67 MS Munich 67, fol. 185ᵛ (אלו הסליחות אומרים על הקדוש ר' אברהם גר צדק שנשר' באוגשפורק כ"ב' בכסליו על יחו' הש'); a later hand added the year (שנת חמשת אלפים חמש ועשרים). For background, see Zvi Avneri, 'Sinzig', in *Germania Judaica*, II: *Von 1238 bis zur Mitte des 14.*

Jahrhunderts, ed. Zvi Avneri (Tübingen: Mohr Siebeck, 1968), pp. 766–68 (p. 766), and the recent discussion in Paola Tartakoff, 'Martyrdom, Conversion, and Shared Cultural Repertoires in Late Medieval Europe', *Jewish Quarterly Review*, 109 (2019), pp. 500–33.

68 Steinschneider, *München*, p. 46 (citing Leopold Zunz).

matches the sequence in which they appear in the manuscripts. It would seem, therefore, that when Shahor printed the Augsburg *Selihot* in 1536, he followed the Italo-Ashkenazi editions for the bulk of the volume. At the same time, he also had the text of the penitential prayers according to another rite at his disposal, from which he added the pieces that were not part of the Italo-Ashkenazi rite in order to make the volume applicable to that second rite and thus increase his edition's appeal to a wider circle of potential buyers. And that second source apparently followed the prayer rite (*minhag*) of late medieval Augsburg itself as documented in the two manuscripts.

Again, there was no Jewish community in Augsburg in the 1530s. Shahor was able to do his printing at a time when no Jews were allowed to live in the city. However, Augsburg had served as the centre of a network of smaller places of Jewish settlement at least since the first half of the fourteenth century.[69] Jews living in these more rural locations, referred to as *yishuvim* or *havurot* and sometimes made up of no more than one or two families, relied on the Augsburg community for basic religious services. They joined prayer services in its synagogue on the major festivals, buried their dead in its cemetery, and were subject to the authority of its rabbinic court. The specific selection of the *selihot* included in the appendix of the 1536 edition suggests that an awareness of the prayer rite that had been customary in Augsburg had survived the expulsion from the city itself among Jews resident in the region and that they continued to uphold its traditions. It was precisely this group that the supplement in Shahor's edition was meant to address.

Zalman Augsburg, the man who commissioned the Yiddish *minhagim* manuscript based on the usage 'of Ulm and of Augsburg', is a good example. Originally from Augsburg, as his name would seem to indicate, or at least resident in Augsburg at a certain point in time, he must have left the city at the time of the expulsion, in 1440 at the latest. When the manuscript was written for him in *c.* 1480, he was still living in Ulm but about to move to Leipheim, a much smaller place on the Danube. Although closer to Ulm, Leipheim had been part of the Jewish hinterland of Augsburg since the mid-fourteenth century. More Jews were to follow when Ulm, too, expelled its Jews in 1499.[70]

The evidence preserved in the pages of the Augsburg *Selihot*, then, offers a rare glimpse of the transition from the medieval Jewish regions (*medinot*) centred on the old urban communities to the *Landesjudenschaften* that were to characterize rural Jewish life in the German Lands in the early modern period. From the second half of the seventeenth century on, these federations of individual Jews resident in a given territory became instruments of absolutist rule.[71] In the

---

69 For Jewish regions such as this, oriented towards a central urban community and in many cases roughly analogous to the respective Christian bishoprics, see Christoph Cluse, 'Zu den räumlichen Organisationsformen von Juden im christlichen Umfeld', in *Zwischen Maas und Rhein: Beziehungen, Begegnungen und Konflikte in einem europäischen Kernraum von der Spätantike bis zum 19. Jahrhundert. Versuch einer Bilanz*, ed. by Franz Irsigler, Trierer Historische Forschungen, 61 (Trier: Kliomedia, 2006), pp. 285–96; for Augsburg specifically, see Rainer Barzen, 'Regionalorganisation jüdischer Gemeinden im Reich in der ersten Hälfte des 14. Jahrhunderts: Eine vergleichende Untersuchung auf der Grundlage der Ortslisten des Deutzer und des Nürnberger Memorbuches zur Pestverfolgung', in Haverkamp, *Geschichte der Juden*, I, pp. 293–366 (pp. 329–30), and III, map F 4.

70 Raspe, '*Minhagim* Books in Yiddish'; cf. Christian Scholl, *Die Judengemeinde der Reichsstadt Ulm im späten Mittelalter: Innerjüdische Verhältnisse und christlich-jüdische Beziehungen in süddeutschen Zusammenhängen*, Forschungen zur Geschichte der Juden Abteilung A: Abhandlungen, 23 (Hannover: Hahnsche Buchhandlung, 2012), pp. 159–60, 344–58, 362–64.

71 Daniel J. Cohen (ed.), *Die Landjudenschaften in Deutschland als Organe jüdischer Selbstverwaltung von der frühen Neuzeit bis ins 19. Jahrhundert: Eine*

early sixteenth, what Hebrew sources call 'the land of Swabia' was a loose association of Jews dispersed across the area between the Lech and the Danube then under the rule of the Habsburg margrave of Burgau — a kind of Augsburg Diaspora united by a shared past, a shared orientation towards an urban centre since lost, and a shared preference for its erstwhile liturgy (Map 8.1).[72] It is thus not accidental that there is a record of a chief rabbi serving the *medinat Schwaben*, whose authority paralleled that of the earlier rabbinic court of Augsburg, as early as 1525.[73] And it is certainly not accidental that Shahor printed books in Augsburg, of all places, that were meant to serve the needs of the Jews living in precisely that region.

It has been suggested that Shahor's activity in both Augsburg and Ichenhausen may have been supported financially by Burgau Jews.[74] In fact, it would seem that the *Landesrabbiner* himself was involved — a man named Isaac Segal, resident in Günzburg since the 1530s, hence also referred to

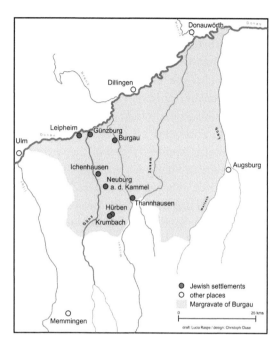

Map 8.1. Places of Jewish Settlement in the Margravate of Burgau in the Sixteenth Century.

as Ayzik Günzburg, but originally from Mantua.[75] To the best of our knowledge, Shahor travelled to Italy at least twice during the Augsburg phase of his career. His first visit, in the summer of 1536, was undertaken to market his output among Ashkenazi Jews south of the Alps. On a second trip in 1542–43, meant to explore the possibility of opening a printing house in Ferrara, Shahor was joined by the man who was to replace him in Augsburg soon after: the convert Paulus Aemilius. Aemilius's patron was the diplomat Johann Albrecht Widmanstetter, one of the most accomplished Christian Hebraists of the day and the owner of a collection which was to form one of the nuclei of the Hebraica held in the present-day

---

Quellensammlung, 3 vols, Fontes ad res Judaicas spectantes (Jerusalem and Göttingen: Israel Academy of Sciences and Humanities and Akademie der Wissenschaften zu Göttingen, 1996–2001). See Stefan Rohrbacher, 'Die jüdischen Gemeinden in den *Medinot Aschkenas* zwischen Spätmittelalter und Dreißigjährigem Krieg', in *Jüdische Gemeinden und ihr christlicher Kontext in kulturräumlich vergleichender Betrachtung von der Spätantike bis zum 18. Jahrhundert*, ed. by Christoph Cluse, Alfred Haverkamp, and Israel J. Yuval, Forschungen zur Geschichte der Juden Abteilung A: Abhandlungen, 13 (Hannover: Hahnsche Buchhandlung, 2003), pp. 451–63.

72 Stefan Rohrbacher, 'Medinat Schwaben: Jüdisches Leben in einer süddeutschen Landschaft in der Frühneuzeit', in Kießling and Ullmann, *Landjudentum*, pp. 80–109.

73 Cohen, *Landjudenschaften*, III, pp. 1453–54, no. 36:1; Reinhard H. Seitz, 'Günzburg', in *Germania Judaica*, III: 1350–1519, ed. by Arye Maimon, Mordechai Breuer, and Yacov Guggenheim (Tübingen: Mohr Siebeck, 1987–2003), pp. 478–82 (p. 480).

74 Burnett, p. 523.

75 Rohrbacher, 'Medinat Schwaben', pp. 95–99; Cohen, *Landjudenschaften*, III, pp. 1455–57, no. 36:3 (pp. 1456–57, note 6). See also Eric Zimmer, *Aspects of the German Rabbinate in the Sixteenth Century*, 'Kuntresim' Texts and Studies, 62 (Jerusalem: Dinur Center, 1984), p. 24, note 49, and p. 48.

Bavarian State Library in Munich.[76] When the Ferrara project fell through and the two men fell out, Widmanstetter supported Aemilius against Shahor and sent a letter — drafted in German, then written in Hebrew — to the chief rabbi of Swabia, asking him to help Aemilius and force Shahor to reimburse his expenses.[77] After all, Widmanstetter reminded the rabbi, the agreement between the two had been made in Günzburg's own presence. Scholars have concluded that the rabbi himself had initiated the project.

What may have moved Günzburg to send Shahor and Aemilius on their joint journey? It bears recalling that by 1541, both Daniel Bomberg's press in Venice and the one in Bologna had ceased printing.[78] Fagius's attempt to fill that void — recorded in Levita's preface to the bilingual edition of his *Sefer hatishby* (Isny 1541) — had been short-lived. Günzburg and Shahor may have seen an opening here. Why the rabbi thought that having the Jewish printer partner with a convert was a good idea remains an open question. Aemilius, to be sure, had spent significant time in Italy, his patron was exceptionally well-connected there, and his assistance may have been expected to prove useful in negotiating the necessary privileges.

Whether Ayzik Segal really intended to have Shahor and Aemilius print the Babylonian Talmud from the famous manuscript then in the possession of a Jewish family in Günzburg and today in the Bavarian State Library,[79] can hardly be ascertained. What seems clear, though, is that his involvement in the matter was very much in line with what we see reflected in Shahor's earlier publications. The chief rabbi of Swabia must have had an interest in seeing his clientele in the isolated Jewish settlements scattered across the margravate provided with books — be they cheap prayerbooks or more ambitious volumes intended for an emerging market of Jewish householders.[80] Augsburg was ideally located for that. Nevertheless, Burgau Jews probably did not furnish enough buyers to sustain Shahor's business over time; hence his attempt to secure an additional foothold in Italy.

It was when the prospect of establishing a print shop in Ferrara fell through and Wolfhart's death closed Augsburg off to Shahor, and to Jewish printing in the city at large, that Ichenhausen entered the picture. A mere ten kilometres south of Günzburg and recently come under the sole authority of a local nobleman who appears to have seen the granting of privileges to Jews as a convenient way of displaying his sovereignty and raising his income at the same time,[81] Ichenhausen must have seemed a natural choice. We have

---

76 See Hans Striedl, 'Geschichte der Hebraica-Sammlung der Bayerischen Staatsbibliothek', in *Orientalisches aus Münchener Bibliotheken und Sammlungen*, ed. by Herbert Franke (Wiesbaden: Steiner, 1957), pp. 1–37 (pp. 2–10), and the contribution by Maximilian de Molière in the present volume.

77 MS Munich, Bayerische Staatsbibliothek Oefeleana 249, nos 5 (in German) and 16 (in Hebrew), published in Perles, pp. 171–77, no. IV, and Striedl, 'Paulus Aemilius', pp. 341–42 and 356, no. VII; see also Steinschneider, 'Hebräische Drucke', p. 285, and Rohrbacher, 'Medinat Schwaben', pp. 96–98. Widmanstetter's two drafts are dated 27 March 1543; the first mentions that Aemilius had spent eight months on the project, indicating that the two men must have set out in the summer of 1542 at the latest.

78 For Bomberg, see Striedl, 'Paulus Aemilius', p. 345, note 47; cf. Künast, 'Hebräisch-jüdischer Buchdruck', p. 290. For a recent look at Hebrew printing in Bologna, see Joseph A. Skloot, 'Printing, Hebrew Book Culture and Sefer Ḥasidim' (unpublished doctoral thesis, Columbia University, 2017), pp. 19–58.

79 As suggested by Perles, p. 172. The earliest evidence that links the manuscript to the Ulma Günzburg family in fact dates to 1588. See MS Munich, Bayerische Staatsbibliothek Cod. hebr. 95 (http://nbn-resolving.de/urn:nbn:de:bvb:12-bsb00003409-3), fol. 156ᵛ; cf. Raphael Rabbinovicz, *Variae Lectionis in Mischnam et in Talmud Babylonicum* (Hebrew; Munich: Rösl, 1867), pp. 34–35.

80 As argued by Elchanan Reiner for the Augsburg *Tur* in a presentation given at the Münster conference and unfortunately not included in this volume.

81 Rohrbacher, 'Ichenhausen', p. 29.

no way of knowing why the arrangement did not last. It is noteworthy, though, that Shahor's next location, Heddernheim near Frankfurt am Main, the last before he left Germany for Lublin, reflects a similar endeavour to serve a Jewish population settled nearby.[82] Yet the Heddernheim episode was also short-lived for reasons unknown. It was not until the 1590s that Jews resident in Swabia made another attempt to establish a print shop, and it was not before the early seventeenth century that Jews from Frankfurt found an opportunity to print their own books in nearby Hanau.[83]

Ultimately, then, the story of the first Jew to have printed Hebrew books in Germany is a story of failure. Compared to Prague, to northern Italy, and to the emerging new centre in Poland, what had remained of Jewish life in the German Lands looked bleak — too bleak, apparently, to provide even one family of Jewish printers with a living over time. Nevertheless, the evidence of Shahor's career — the circumstances of his activity, his repertoire, and the various textual and material aspects of his imprints — would seem to offer unique insights into Jewish life in sixteenth-century Ashkenaz. On the one hand, we get a sense of what the loss of almost all of the old urban centres must have meant for the Jews left behind in what had been their peripheries. On the other, the traditions of the old Jewish 'lands' proved remarkably resilient. When the *selihot* rite of what was then referred to as the lands of Swabia and Switzerland was first printed as a stand-alone edition some two hundred years later, in Wilhermsdorf in 1737,[84] the selection included was again very similar to what is documented for late medieval Augsburg. That again testifies to an unexpected continuity of Ashkenazi culture across the great divide of the late medieval expulsions, and it underscores the — perhaps similarly unexpected — potential of liturgical editions to shed light upon Jewish life in post-expulsion Germany, a dark age in Jewish history in more than one respect.

---

82 See esp. Shahor's edition of the supercommentary to Bahya ben Asher's commentary on the Pentateuch (Heddernheim 1546) by Naphtali Hirts Treves, cantor of the Frankfurt community, whose son Eliezer served as its rabbi at the time; Steinschneider, *Catalogus*, col. 2029, no. 6620/1; Habermann, 'Hayyim Shahor', pp. 497–98, no. 19. On Eliezer ben Naphtali and his later activity in Hebrew printing, see N[ehemias] Brüll, 'Das Geschlecht der Treves', *Jahrbuch für Jüdische Geschichte und Literatur*, 1 (1874), pp. 87–122 (pp. 105–06); Zimmer, pp. 41–43; Clemens P. Sidorko, 'Eliezer Ben Naftali Herz Treves als Pionier des jüdischen Buchdrucks in Zürich, Tiengen und Basel um 1560', *Aschkenas*, 17 (2007), pp. 457–72. A Jewish resident of Heddernheim is first mentioned in 1579; Dietrich Andernacht, *Regesten zur Geschichte der Juden in der Reichsstadt Frankfurt am Main von 1520–1616*, 2 vols, Forschungen zur Geschichte der Juden Abteilung B: Quellen, 2 (Hannover: Hahnsche Buchhandlung, 2007), I, pp. 250–51, no. 1211.

83 Burnett, pp. 510, 514–17.

84 *Selihot* (Wilhermsdorf 1737), title page (סליחות כמנהג מדינות שוואבן ושווייץ). See Moshe N. Rosenfeld, *Jewish Printing in Wilhermsdorf: A Concise Bibliography of Hebrew and Yiddish Publications Printed in Wilhermsdorf between 1670 and 1739* (London: n.p., 1995), p. 192, no. 181; Goldschmidt, *Seder haselihot keminhag Lita*, p. 7, no. 5.

TAMARA MORSEL-EISENBERG

Of Roots and Signs

Printing Ashkenazi Responsa in Sixteenth-Century Venice

Introduction

The Antwerp-born Christian printer Daniel Bomberg operated his press in Venice between 1515 and 1548. He employed editors, typesetters, and correctors — many of them Jews — who were familiar with the texts being printed. Rabbi Hiyah Meir ben David (d. *c.* 1531) was one of those experts.[1] Apart from overseeing the printing of some of the most important canonical works of halakhah, including the Babylonian Talmud, Rabbi Hiyah was also charged with editing the first two books of responsa, or *ShUT* (short for *she'elot u-teshuvot*, or 'questions and answers') from fifteenth-century Ashkenazi rabbis ever to be printed. In 1519, Bomberg's press produced the responsa of both Rabbi Joseph Colon, *ShUT Maharyq* (Maharyq being an acronym of the author's name) and Rabbi Israel Isserlein, *Terumat ha-deshen* ('Removing of the Ashes'). In the present chapter, I consider those two works and compare their manuscript versions to their first appearance in print. I ask what these works can tell us about the cultural transition from manuscript to print and its significance for organization, readership, Ashkenazi legal culture, and generally for Jewish law. I adopt Rabbi Hiyah's perspective as the printshop editor who contributed to the transformation of these books, homing in on the technical aspects, the decisions, and the ensuing consequences — intended and unintended — that contributed to the dynamics of this transformation.

Responsa, or answers to questions about concrete issues of Jewish religious law, prove particularly illuminating for an understanding of print and its transformational impact. The premise of the genre is to present questions culled mostly from actual situations that were brought before a rabbi, rather than to offer a scholarly treatise or commentary. As such, this material reflects the

---

[1] His dates are uncertain, but he is first mentioned with a blessing for the dead in 1531. See Yacov Boksenboim, 'Introduction', in *ShUT R. Azriel Dienna*, [in Hebrew], ed. by Yacov Boksenboim (Tel-Aviv: Tel-Aviv University Press, 1977–79), pp. 22–23 note 66, where the excerpt is cited. This letter is part of Budapest, Hungarian Academy of Sciences Library, MS Kaufmann, 150. There are several responsa by Rabbi Hiyah Meir printed in *ShUT Binyamin Ze'ev* (§15, §38, §298, and §391). On Rabbi Hiyah Meir, see Refael Natan and Neta Rabinovitz, 'Article on the Printing of the Talmud' [in Hebrew] in *Dikdukei sofrim* (Munich: Huber, 1877), pp. 33–34 note 41. See also Avraham Haberman, *The Printer Daniel Bomberg and his Press* [in Hebrew] (Safed: Museum for the Art of Printing, 1978), p. 16.

Tamara Morsel-Eisenberg • New York University

variety and multiplicity of real life, making for a multifarious collection typically lacking in unity. Moreover, the writings that make up responsa collections were often assembled throughout the author's lifetime. This piecemeal collection of texts likewise contributes to the heterogeneity of the genre. It is precisely this heterogeneous tendency that makes the genre of responsa a useful case study for the way books are forged out of fragmented textual material.

The relevance of responsa for Jewish law is richly complicated. Responsa are, in the first instance, documents engendered by daily life and produced by a rabbi in the course of his rabbinic activity. They are written not as scholarly literature for posterity but as scholarship and legal decision-making in action, created to solve a concrete problem. Both the original letter composed by the rabbi and the scribal copy usually sent to the recipient are the material documents regarding this problem-solving action. Whether the document was intended for publication beyond that moment is another question. Before print offered a means of textual reproduction, the transition from personal temporal document to a text published for posterity was gradual, often hardly distinguishable from the writing and copying that was part of the creation and dissemination of the responsum-document in its initial stage. However, in the age of print publishing a work required a set of decisions and actions that were sharply different from the circumstances that generated the text in the first place.[2] This sharp distinction set a higher threshold between personal correspondence and published book, between temporal document and literary contribution. Print thus brings the two lives of a responsum into sharp relief.

This contrast not only persists throughout the trajectory of the responsum's text and its publication but goes to the heart of the legal function of these texts. The place of responsa in the larger world of the Jewish authoritative legal canon is not always clear.[3] On the one hand, the responsum's origin in specific cases rather than theoretical discussions renders these materials more authoritative and more reflective of real rabbinic decisions. On the other hand, their very specificity can be a liability as to their authority: the decision can always be attributed to some particular aspect of the concrete situation and thus limit its wider applicability. In this sense, the printing of these works of responsa allows us to ask: When and how does particular information become authoritative knowledge? When does a case become a precedent, and what qualities make for a 'good' case, be it the specificity and concreteness or, conversely, its generality and universality? Such questions animate many fields of knowledge that utilize cases, such as law, but also medicine and sciences.[4]

---

2 On the transmission of responsa in the manuscript era, see Yaakov Shmuel Spiegel, *Chapters in the History of the Jewish Book* [in Hebrew], 2 vols (Ramat-Gan: Bar Ilan University Press, 2005), II: *Writing and Transmission*, pp. 229–304. On responsa in the age of print, see Shmuel Glick, *The New Handbook of Responsa: A Bibliographic Anthology for Responsa Literature from the Beginning of Print to the Year 2000* [In Hebrew], 4 vols (Ramat Gan: Bar Ilan Law Library Press, 2006), pp. 1–101.

3 See Spiegel, *Chapters*, II, 275–304; Yitzhak Ze'ev Kahana, 'The Halakhic Decision and the Responsum', in *Studies in Responsa Literature* [in Hebrew] (Jerusalem: Mossad haRav Kook, 1973), pp. 97–107; Menahem Elon, *Jewish Law: History, Sources, Principles*, trans. by Bernard Auerbach and Melvin J. Sykes (Philadelphia: Jewish Publication Society, 1994), III, p. 1454; Berachyahu Lifshitz, 'The Legal Status of Responsa Literature' [in Hebrew], *Shenaton ha-Mishpat ha-Ivri*, 9–10 (1982–83), pp. 265–300.

4 John Forrester, 'If p, Then What? Thinking in Cases', *History of the Human Sciences*, 9 (1996), pp. 1–25. Reprinted in John Forrester, *Thinking in Cases* (Cambridge: Polity, 2017); Lauren Kassel, 'Cases', in *Information: A Historical Companion*, ed. by Ann Blair, Paul Duguid, Anja-Silvia Going, and Anthony Grafton (Princeton: Princeton University Press, 2021), pp. 358–65; Gianna Pomata, 'Observation Rising:

These two related contrasts — personal communication versus public work and concrete case versus general law — become especially poignant when it comes to the Ashkenazi halakhic tradition. Until the sixteenth century, the religious scholarship of Ashkenaz was especially personal and fluid. It favoured local difference over general unifying law. Its transmission relied on oral teachings and rabbi-to-student instruction. In its mode of writing, it expressed itself in personal notes and glosses. Many of its hallmark legal texts, especially in the fourteenth and fifteenth centuries, were assembled in fluid compilations that varied by location, personal trajectory, and individual exposure, and the practices for circulating these texts relied heavily on individuals copying sections of material into their personal collections.[5] Characteristics such as local difference, fluidity, and oral transmission are in many ways opposed to print, which is appropriate for a large, general audience and enhances textual stability. As such, the transition of this particular legal culture into the age of print makes for an especially good opportunity to gauge the ways in which print technology challenged this scholarly and religious universe and this culture's reaction to the challenge.

Evocative as the idea of historical change *ex machina* may be, the idea that print transformed culture on its own is, of course, an oversimplification.[6] Cultures involve not only the texts themselves and the machines that reproduce them, but also the people writing, (re)producing, and reading those texts. For that reason, I employ the perspective of one of the agents involved in this change. Since the objective of this study is the sixteenth-century transformation around print, I focus not on the authors of these works of responsa in the fifteenth century, but rather on the figure who brought them to print in the sixteenth: Rabbi Hiyah Meir ben David. By taking Rabbi Hiyah's perspective, I look at the role of such editors in actively transforming and shaping the culture of reading.

Birth of an Epistemic Genre, 1500–1650', in *Histories of Scientific Observation*, ed. by Lorraine Daston and Elizabeth Lunbeck (Chicago: Chicago University Press, 2011), pp. 45–81.

5 Elchanan Reiner, 'The Ashkenazi Élite at the Beginning of the Modern Era: Manuscript versus Printed Book', *Polin*, 10 (1997), 85–98 (p. 91). For other such descriptions, see Yedidya Dinari, *The Sages of Ashkenaz in the Late Middle Ages: Their Ways and Their Writings in Halakhah* [in Hebrew] (Jerusalem: Mosad Bialik, 1984), pp. 93–99; Israel Ta-Shma, *Ancient Ashkenazic Custom*, [in Hebrew] (Jerusalem: Magnes Press, 1992), pp. 16–17; 22; 26 note 29; Israel Ta-Shma, *The Literature of Talmudic Interpretation* [in Hebrew], (Jerusalem: Magnes Press, 2000), p. 75; Israel Ta-Shma, *Halakhah, Custom and Transmission in Ashkenaz, 1100–1350* [in Hebrew] (Jerusalem: Magnes Press, 1996), p. 61 note 11; Eric Zimmer, *The Fiery Embers of the Scholars* [in Hebrew], (Be'er Sheva: Ben Gurion University Press, 1999), p. 256; Shlomo Zalman Havlin, 'Rabbi Yeḥiel Ashkenazi and His Responsa: An Ashkenazic Sage in the Lands of Islam', *Shalem*, 7 (2002), 71–132), pp. 75–76.

6 For a discussion about the perils of overstating the impact of print, see Anthony Grafton, Adrian Johns, and Elizabeth Eisenstein, 'AHR Forum: How Revolutionary Was the Print Revolution?', *American Historical Review*, 107 (2002), 84–86 (p. 84); Michael Johnston and Michael Van Dussen, 'Introduction: Manuscripts and Cultural History', in *The Medieval Manuscript Book: Cultural Approaches*, ed. by Michael Johnston and Michael Van Dussen (Cambridge: Cambridge University Press, 2015), pp. 1–16. Continuities between manuscript and print have been noted regarding typology, aesthetics, and codicology. See, for instance, David McKitterick, *Print, Manuscript and the Search for Order 1450–1830* (Cambridge and New York: Cambridge University Press, 2003); Konrad Haebler, *The Study of Incunabula* (New York: Grolier Club, 1933). See also Joseph A. Dane, *The Myth of Print Culture: Essays on Evidence, Textuality, and Bibliographical Method* (Toronto: University of Toronto Press, 2003), pp. 10–32. For reflections on continuities between print and manuscript in Hebrew texts, see, for instance, Malachi Beit-Arié, 'The Connection between Early Hebrew Print and Manuscripts' [in Hebrew], in *Essays and Studies in Librarianship Presented to Curt David Wormann on his Seventy-fifth Birthday*, ed. by Curt David Wormann, Mordekhai Nadav, and Jacob Rothschild (Jerusalem: Magnes Press, 1975), pp. 27–39.

As we will see in the following pages, the printed *ShUT Maharyq* and *Terumat ha-deshen* mark a profound change in scholarly culture, including habits and practices, in the learned textual corpus, and even in notions of religious legal authority. These halakhic texts had previously been circulating in manuscript in fluidly varying shapes and forms. Through a combination of pre-existing factors and a series of publishing decisions and editorial choices, they were now being published in print as standardized, complete works ordered by general categories rather than personal miscellanies. Their contents were presented as treating universal principles rather than idiosyncratic details. Legal documents became scholarly texts; responsa collections became published books; and cases became authoritative precedents — changes that resulted from the technological possibilities seized upon by editors and printers.

Rabbi Hiyah Meir ben David

Rabbi Hiyah Meir ben David's origins are unknown, though there is reason to believe that he was from Greece.[7] He first appears in the historical record as a student in the Ashkenazi circle of Rabbi Judah Mintz in Padua. In his chronology, Rabbi Elijah Capsali (c. 1483–1555) noted that Rabbi Mintz's yeshiva was the most prominent such institution in Italy.[8] Capsali memorably described the *pilpul* section of the Talmud classes, in which only the head of the yeshiva held a book and all the others gave verbal complex casuistic arguments intended to sharpen the mind.[9] Rabbi Hiyah, whose name is featured in Capsali's list of those yeshiva's students, likely participated in these sessions.[10] Rabbi Bendit Axelrad, who taught in the yeshiva in Venice, singled Rabbi Hiyah out for his *pilpulistic* talents. He once claimed that he had ordained only a handful of rabbis in his entire career, among them Rabbi Hiyah. שאם חס ושלו' תשתכח תורה מישראל ('If, God forbid, Torah were to be forgotten from the Jewish people'), Rabbi Axelrad wrote about Rabbi Hiyah, מהדר ליה בפילפוליה ('he could restore it with his *pilpul*').[11] Capsali described Rabbi Hiyah as חריף ומחודד והיה תם וישר ויר"א א-לוהים וסר מרע ('sharp and clever, complete and straight, God-fearing and avoidant of evil').[12] The much younger Rabbi Benjamin Ze'ev of Arta (in Greece), arguably the first rabbi to see his responsa printed as a stand-alone work in his

---

7 Meir Benayahu, *Prolegomenon to Sefer Benyamin Ze'ev* [in Hebrew] (Jerusalem: Yad HaRav Nissim, 1989), p. 39.

8 Elijah Capsali, *Seder Eliyahu Zuta* [in Hebrew], ed. by Meir Benayahu, 4 vols (Jerusalem: Machon Ben Zvi, 1975–83), II (1977), p. 248; See also Roberto Bonfil, *Rabbis and Jewish Communities in Renaissance Italy*, trans. by Jonathan Chipman (Oxford: Littman Library, 1990; repr. 2004, 3rd ed.), p. 18.

9 Often translated as 'casuistry', although Bonfil's translation of this passage has it as 'discussion', *pilpul* is a highly sophisticated form of inquiry and reasoning that went through various forms throughout the history of Talmud study. See also, Bonfil, *Rabbis and Jewish Communities*, p. 22. On *pilpul* in Ashkenaz, see Hayyim Zalman Dimitrovsky, 'By Way of Pilpul' [in Hebrew], in *Salo Wittmayer Baron Jubilee Volume*, ed. by Saul Lieberman (Jerusalem: American Academy for Jewish Research, 1975), pp. 110–81; M. Breuer, 'The Rise of *Hillukim* and Pilpul in the Ashkenazic Yeshivot' [in Hebrew], in *Memorial Volume for Rabbi Y. Y. Weinberg* (Jerusalem: Feldheim, 1970), pp. 241–55; Elchanan Reiner, 'Transformations in the Polish and Ashkenazic *Yeshivot* during the Sixteenth and Seventeenth Centuries and the Dispute over Pilpul' [in Hebrew], in *According to the Custom of Ashkenaz and Poland: Studies in Honor of Chone Shmeruk*, ed. by Israel Bartal, Hava Turniansky, and Ezra Mendelsohn (Jerusalem: Machon Zalman Shazar Press, 1993), pp. 48–50; Shalem Yahalom, 'The Pilpul Method of Talmudic Study: Earliest Evidence' [in Hebrew], *Tarbiz*, 84/4 (2017), pp. 543–74.

10 Capsali, *Seder Eliyahu Zuta*, II, 248; See Bonfil, *Rabbis and Jewish Communities*, p. 18.

11 *Pesakim*, ed. by Hiyah Meir ben David (Venice, 1519), p. 3a.

12 Capsali, *Seder Eliyahu Zuta*, II, p. 248.

lifetime (Venice, 1539), often relied on Rabbi Hiyah's support during the many controversies in which he was engaged. He once described Rabbi Hiyah as: כלי קטן ומוחזק ככלי גדול ('a small vessel held in regard like a great vessel'), leading some historians to wonder whether the well-respected Rabbi Hiyah was of especially short stature.[13]

As Roberto Bonfil has clarified, rabbis in Italy, were neither officially appointed nor communally financed. Rabbi Mintz, whose yeshiva was apparently supported by a community stipend, was an exception to the rule. Rather than being run by a general community leadership with collective dues, Italian Jewish communities were structured around individual Jews, usually bankers, who had the capital and power to make themselves useful to local rulers. In exchange for these services, rulers would extend privileges to those Jews and their retinue, around which a small community would form. Rabbis would often serve as private tutors to those powerful Jewish families and would defend them in any halakhic disputes that arose in the context of their ventures. Historians compared this relationship to the Humanist patronage that typified other Renaissance communities.[14] The lack of community support required many rabbis to supplement their incomes by engaging in other occupations.

One such occupation was to work in printing presses as editors and correctors. Sometimes, rabbis would become publishing entrepreneurs, investing in books that they would bring to print at an existing press.[15] Rabbi Hiyah took on such employment as an editor and corrector. In addition to running the Venice yeshiva alongside Rabbi Axelrad, he assisted in the printing some of the most important works at Bomberg's press, including the first edition of the Babylonian Talmud. He later moved (or returned) to Greece, where he served as a rabbi. At one point, the communities of Patros issued an ordinance against men and women dancing together. Correspondence concerning this community ordinance mentions Rabbi Hiyah as an important figure in one of the local communities at the time.[16] He died sometime before 1531, leaving only a few written responsa behind.[17]

Rabbi Hiyah appears to have been a very keen editor. Bomberg printed a work titled *ShUT ha-Ramban* ('The Responsa of Nahmanides'), which in fact was a collection of responsa from Rabbi Solomon ben Aderet, not, as the title implied, from Nahmanides. As the book's editor, Rabbi Hiyah was aware of this misattribution and managed to deftly recognize the questionable authorship without harming the work's worth in the eyes of potential buyers: וכל איש מדע יקבל האמת ממי שאמרו ('Every man of knowledge will accept the truth from whomever said it'), he wrote on the title page, ואם כי אינם מתשובות הרמב"ן ('even if they are not the responsa of Nahmanides').[18] This statement shows Rabbi Hiyah in his role as an editor at a for-profit printing press, carefully balancing accuracy with marketability.

Rabbi Hiyah took his editorial work very seriously, even as he recognized that most readers did not. At the conclusion of a collection of apocryphal talmudic tractates, printed in 1524–26, he added an apology for any errors before noting

---

13 Rabbi Benjamin Ze'ev of Arta, *ShuT Benyamin Ze'ev* (Venice, 1539), §71; and see Benayahu, *Prolegomenon*, p. 41.
14 Bonfil, *Rabbis and Jewish Communities*, pp. 100–86, 198.
15 See Bonfil, *Rabbis and Jewish Communities*, pp. 190–91; Bernard Cooperman, 'Organizing Knowledge for the Jewish Market: An Editor/Printer in 16th Century Rome', in *Perspectives on the Hebraic Book: The Myron M.

Weinstein Memorial Lectures at the Library of Congress, ed. by Peggy K. Pearlstein (Washington, DC: Library of Congress, 2012), pp. 79–129.
16 Benayahu, *Prolegomenon*, p. 42.
17 See above, footnote 1.
18 In that case, however, Rabbi Hiyah explained that he was reluctant to interfere too much in terms of editing, as he had only this one manuscript.

in his own defence: כל מצפצף ישים יד לפה בחקור אחרי טבע הדפוס ואז ידום ('May any complainer first place his hand before his mouth and inquire into the nature of print and then he will be silent').[19] *Terumat ha-deshen* includes a similar statement by Rabbi Hiyah: והיודע מלאכת הדפוס ואיכותו יראה בעין שכל היותו מדוייק ומתוקן ככל האפשר אלה הם דברי בן דוד חיא מאיר המדפיס במצוות ובבית דניאל [...] פה וויני״ציה ('And he who knows the labour of print and its characteristics will see with his mind's eye that this is as precise and correct as possible. These are the words of ben David, Hiyah Meir, printing on the command and in the home of Daniel [...] in Venice').[20]

Owing in large part to their appearance in print, *ShUT Maharyq* and *Terumat ha-deshen* became known far and wide. In a responsum from 1565, Rabbi Yehiel Ashkenazi of Jerusalem wrote of *ShUT* Maharyq: של המהרי״ק] ולא אביא לשונותיו [יען כי תשובות מהרי״ק מצויות בבית כל בר בי רב זיל קרי בי׳ וכו' ('I will not quote the exact language here because the responsa of our master, Rabbi Colon, are to be found in the home of every learned person; go read it there').[21] Thus, in less than half a century after the book was first printed, it had become so widely circulated that a scholar in Jerusalem expressed with confidence that 'it can be found in the home of every learned person'. As he was referring to a printed version whose text in all the various copies was practically identical, he no longer saw any need to quote his source verbatim or to paraphrase the gist of the opinion, as earlier scholars would have done. Instead, he simply instructed the addressee to 'go read it there'. *Terumat ha-deshen* was the only recent Ashkenazi work that Rabbi Joseph Qaro included frequently in his *Beit Yosef* ('House of Joseph', a gloss on a fourteenth-century halakhic code), an inclusion that historians have connected to the fact that the work existed in print.[22]

'How Great Were the Deeds of Hiyah?'

The first book of fifteenth-century Ashkenazi responsa to be printed was Rabbi Joseph Colon's collected responsa (*c.* 1418–83) *ShUT Maharyq*. Its colophon announces: והיתה השלמת הספר יום ד' כ״ב אדר רעט על ידי האחים מזרע ישראל בני ברוך

---

19 Tractate *Sofrim* is one of the seven so-called 'small tractates', or 'external tractates' of the Talmud. It was printed by Bomberg in Venice in 1524–26 together with *'Avot* and two other 'external tractates' (*Semahot, Kallah*).

20 *Terumat ha-deshen*, apology:
ואני שפל המצב עמוס התלאות קטן שבתלמידים חיא מאיר בכהר״ר דוד זלה״ה שמתי עיני על המלאכה לעשותה כהוגן ולהסיר מכשול וטעיות כפי האפשרי כאשר תשיג קוצר שכלי ומעוט השגתי ואם באולי ימצא בו איזה שגיאות סהדי במרומים כי לא במרד ולא במעל.
('And I, the lowly of stature [*matzav*] and full of hardships, the smallest among the students, Hiyah Meir son of [...] Rabbi David [...] have set my eyes on the labour to do it properly and to remove any stumbling block and mistake according to my ability, as my slow mind and limited understanding can grasp and if perhaps there might be found in it some errors, my witnesses are in heaven that it was not done on purpose to mislead').

21 Published in Simcha Assaf, 'From the Archives of the Jerusalem Library', in *Minḥa le-David: Jubilee Volume for David Yellin* (Jerusalem: Rubin Mass, 1935), pp. 233–35. See also Jeffrey Woolf, 'The Life and Responsa of Rabbi Joseph Colon b. Salomon Trabotto (Maharik)' (unpublished PhD dissertation, University of Michigan, 1991), p. 249. Concerning Rabbi Yehiel Ashkenazi, see Eliezer Rivlin, 'A Book of the History of the Sages of Jerusalem' [in Hebrew] (Jerusalem: Salomon Press, 1927–30), p. 108.

22 Tirza Kelman, '"I Shall Create Halakhic Ruling… for That Is the Objective": The Dimension of Halakhic Ruling In Joseph Karo's Beit Yosef' (unpublished PhD dissertation, Ben Gurion University, 2018); Tirza Kelman, 'The Use of Ashkenazi Legal Decisors in the Book Beit Yosef: The Laws of Menstrual Impurity and Ritual Bathing as a Case Study' [in Hebrew] (unpublished MA thesis, Ben Gurion University, 2012).

אדי״ל קינ״ד במצות ובבי' אדוננו דניאל בומבירגא מאננווי״רשה ('The completion of the book was on Wednesday, the 22nd of Adar 5279 [1519], by the brothers from the seed of Israel, the sons of Barukh Adelkind, under the command and in the house of our master, Daniel Bomberg of Antwerp').[23] The brothers Adelkind, who had their start at Bomberg's press, would go on to print books on their own, but this is the first time they are mentioned in print. We know the name only of the brother who converted to Christianity and changed his name from Israel to Cornelio. He hints at his conversion in the opening of a work he printed in 1546: ישראל שמי וקורנליו היה זכרי ('Israel was my name and Cornelio is how I am remembered').[24] Perhaps the reference in the *ShUT Maharyq* colophon to being 'from the seed of Israel' denotes both Cornelio's Jewish origins and his original name. The title page of *ShUT Maharyq* announces:

ונדפסו ונחקקו ע״י המרומם ומפואר בפי כל המחזיק ידי עושי המלאכה במאודיו. הלא שמו נודע בשערים דניאל בומברגי מאנווי״שה והיתה תחלת מלאכה המפואר' הזאת בשנת רע״ט לפ״ק בקריה רבת' ועליזה וויניזי״יה אשר תחת ממשלת השררה יר״ה.

(And they [the responsa] have been printed and engraved by the elevated and praised by all, who, with his possessions, strengthens the hands of those who do the labour. His name is known in the gates, Daniel Bombergi of Anversa, and the beginning of this grand labour was in the year 1519 in the great and cheerful city of Venice, which is under the rule of the lord, may his honour be elevated).[25]

Rabbi Hiyah, who prepared *ShUT Maharyq* for print, likewise laboured 'under the command and in the house of' Bomberg. In the colophon of *ShUT Maharyq*, the Adelkinds praised Rabbi Hiyah's editorial and correctorial work: וכמה גדולי' מעשי חיא ('how great were the deeds of Hiyah'), they exclaimed, continuing: כאשר המופת יוכיח כי בכל מקו' אשר ידו הגיעה שמה בדק ולא השאיר אחריו חסרות ויעה הגהותיו כל מחסה כזב ושקר ('as the evidence will prove, for everywhere his hand could reach he checked and did not leave behind him anything lacking, and his glosses removed any shelter for falsehood and lies').[26] They advertised Rabbi Hiyah's editorial skills, likening him to a master silversmith and skilled gardener who purified the material:

ותשלם כל המלאכה מזוקקת שבעתי' צרופה כבמצרף כסף. סוקל מאבן הטעויות ומעמקי מצולת השבושים מושלל מכל סיג נברר מכל פסולת זורה כבמזרחת הוגה ע״י ה״ה רוחב שכלו כרחב ים הגאון מהר״ר חיא מאיר בכהר״ר דוד זצ״ל אשר כלה קוצי' מן הכרם ועדר ונכש השדה בלי יעלה עוד קמשוני' וחרולים.

---

23 Rabbi Joseph Colon, *ShUT Maharyq* (Venice, 1519), colophon.

24 Concerning them, see Avraham Me'ir Haberman, *The Hebrew Book and its Development* (Jerusalem: Rubin Mass, 1968), p. 113; and Haberman, *The Printer Cornelio Adelkind and His Son Daniel* (Jerusalem: Rubin Mass, 1980), pp. 10–15; Hayim Friedberg, *The History of Hebrew Printing in the Lands of Italy… Since its Beginnings* [in Hebrew] (Tel Aviv: Bar-Yuda, 1956, 2nd Ed.), p. 60 note 1.

25 Colon, *ShUT Maharyq*, title-page.
The text opens as follows:
ברוך אדון המציאות אשר לא השבית לנו היום מורה צדק מפקח עיני עורות מוליך האנשים בדרך סלולה בבקיעותיו ובפלפוליו. ה״ה הגאון מהר״ר יוסף קלון זצ״ל מ״ע אשר זכה הרבים בתשובותיו והאיר עיני ישראל בחדושיו.

('Blessed is the Lord of existence who has not withheld from us today a just teacher who opens our [blind] eyes, leads the people on paved paths with his capacity for analysis and sharpness. He is the gaon our master Rabbi Joseph Colon of blessed memory, may he rest in Eden. Who bestowed merit upon the masses with his responsa. And enlightened the eyes of Israel with his novellae').

26 Colon, 'colophon'.

(And the work was completed, distilled seven times, purified as in a smithy of silver. He removed from it the evil/stones ['aven/'even] of mistakes and the depths of errors, cleared of all slag, separated from all waste with shovel and fan edited by the rabbi, the wise [...] the breadth of his intellect is like the breadth of the sea, the sage Hiyah Meir son of his honour, Rabbi David of blessed memory, who removed the thorns from the vineyard).[27]

Print publication posed certain challenges for Christian and Jewish editors alike. The brothers apologized for any errors but stressed that certain mistakes are almost inevitable when printing, such as typesetters confusing letters that look similar. These have nothing to do with the editor, they insisted, but should be blamed on others: ובאולי השמיטו המדפיסי' הפועלי' או האומני' איזה אות או החליפו רי"ש בדל"ת או איפכא בזה אין להאשימו וירצה מלפני האל יתברך פעלו וצדקתו תעמוד לעד ('And if perhaps the labouring printers or craftsmen left out a letter, or if they exchanged a letter *resh* for a letter *dalet*, or vice versa, he should not be blamed for that').[28] A more substantial challenge when printing old texts, whether for Jewish editors like Rabbi Hiyah or Humanist printers like Aldus Manutius, was the problem of finding reliable and legible manuscripts from which to create the printed books.[29] The manuscript state of some works was worse than others, which sometimes made their jobs very difficult.

Rabbi Hiyah concluded *ShUT Maharyq* with a short blessing and a prayer that he might merit printing many more books. Indeed, he would print his next book very soon. Barely two months after *ShUT Maharyq* was published, *Terumat ha-deshen*, an older work of fifteenth-century Ashkenazi responsa, left Bomberg's press.[30] The work's colophon concluded with a prayer that places it in the context of a larger project to print more writings that had been circulating in manuscript:

ונתפלל לאל יתברך ויתרומם שמו לעד ולנצח נצחים. כי כאשר זכינו להשלמת זה הספר הנכבד רוב התועלת הרשו' בכתב אמת כן נזכה להדפיס עוד כהנה וכהנה. וימלא עצת ורצון הנעלה אדונינו דניאל בומביר"גי אשר נדבה רוחו ונתן ה' בלבבו. להכנס במלאכת שמים. להדפיס כל החדושים ימצאו בנפוצת ישראל בעזרת הש"י ובישועתו.

(Just as we have merited the completion of this respectable and very useful book [...] so, too, shall we merit to print many, many more like this. And may He fulfil the idea and will of our esteemed master Daniel Bombirgi, whose spirit, which God placed in his heart, moved him [Lev. 35:21], to enter the labour of heaven. To print all the novellae to be found in the disseminations [*nefotzat*] of Israel with the help of God and his salvation).[31]

Beyond its obvious reference to the dispersed Jewish communities, the word *nefotzat* ('disseminations') may perhaps also hint at the state of the manuscripts themselves. The responsa — spread across different manuscript collections — had to be assembled and organized before they could be

---

27 Colon, 'colophon'.
28 Colon, 'colophon'.
29 Martin Lowry, *The World of Aldus Manutius: Business and Scholarship in Renaissance Venice* (Ithaca, NY: Cornell University Press, 1979).
30 There are striking similarities between the language used in the title page of *Terumat ha-deshen* and that of *ShUT Maharyq*. Rabbi Hiyah used identical formulations in some cases. This is not surprising, as he was probably working on both at the same time. At the time that this colophon was being written, *Iyar* of 1519, the next work to be printed in this project, *Terumat ha-deshen*, was essentially ready, as the latter was finished in *Adar* of the same year.
31 Rabbi Israel Isserlein, *Terumat ha-deshen* (Venice, 1519), colophon.

printed. Depending on the states of the various manuscripts, this was not always a simple task.

In the colophon of *ShUT Maharyq*, after the Adelkind brothers absolved Rabbi Hiyah of blame for small mistakes, they deflected more substantial errors by lamenting the dearth of good manuscripts:

ואם באולי ימצא טעות מה אין ראוי להאשימו. ולא עליו תלונתיכם. כי ההעתקה אשר ממנה נדפס היתה משובשת בתכלית ולא היו בנמצא ספרי' מוגהים כראוי ומוכרח למלאכה זו. אכן ממנו לא נחסר לתקן ככל מה שאפשר. גם בלילה שינה בעיניו לא ראה מרוב טרדת ועמל היה לו בו. ע"כ ראוי לדונו לכף זכות וכל אחד יתקן המעוו' אם ימצא. הגם כי ברור לנו כי לא ימצא כי אם מעט מזער.

(And if perhaps there can be found some mistake, it is not proper to blame him. And your complaint should not be on him. For the copy from which it was printed was entirely defective, and there were no properly edited books in existence, as would be needed for this labour. Indeed, he has not withheld anything from himself in correcting it as much as possible. Also at night his eyes did not see sleep due to his hard work and labour. Therefore, he should be judged favourably, and everyone can correct any mistakes that are found, although it is obvious to us that these are only few).[32]

Indeed, as the brothers Adelkind mentioned, very few manuscripts were available for Rabbi Colon's responsa. In the case of *Terumat ha-deshen*, the situation was significantly better but the challenges persisted. How had these materials that eventually became *ShUT Maharyq* and *Terumat ha-deshen* been transmitted until Rabbi Hiyah began to assemble them? What kinds of manuscripts could he have consulted, and how much did they differ from the printed works? In what state did Rabbi Hiyah, who would be continuing their traditional transmission by the new means of print, encounter them? Or, to rephrase the Adelkind brothers' exclamation as a question: 'How great *were* the deeds of Hiyah?'

Traditional Transmission

Rabbi Joseph Colon, author of the responsa in *ShUT Maharyq*, spent most of his life in northern Italy,[33] where he taught, adjudicated, and wrote responsa. His origins, however, lay in Chambery, France. His southward move to Italy was representative of fifteenth-century Ashkenaz.[34] The fate of his writings was also quite typical for Ashkenazi texts of this kind. Though he died not long before printing commenced, Rabbi Colon's writings had not been circulating in any unified and clearly defined collection. Some of his responsa circulated in manuscript alongside other halakhic material from his school, such as testimonies from his students concerning their rabbi's conduct in ritual and halakhic matters.[35]

---

32 Colon, 'colophon'.

33 On Rabbi Colon's life and times, family, works, and method, as well as on the origin of the name 'Colon', which is derived from 'columbo' ('dove'), see Woolf, 'The Life and Responsa'.

34 On Ashkenazim in Italy, see Bonfil, *Rabbis and Jewish Communities*; Moshe Shulvass, 'Ashkenazic Jewry in Italy', *Yivo Annual of Jewish Social Science*, 7 (1952), pp. 110–31. For a more recent work, see Lucia Raspe, 'The Migration of German Jews into Italy and its Impact upon the Legacy of Medieval Ashkenaz', in *The Jews of Europe Around 1400: Disruption, Crisis, and Resilience*, ed. by Lukas Clemens and Christoph Cluse (Wiesbaden: Harrassowitz, 2018), pp. 173–94.

35 See Woolf, 'The Life and Responsa', pp. 239–40. One example is the manuscript *Rashei perakim me-halakhot ve-dinim* ('Outline of Laws and Rules') by David Modena, a student of Rabbi Colon, a compilation of teachings, testimonies, behaviours, interpretations, etc., which he wrote as a student. This manuscript collection was evidently copied several times.

Still others of his responsa appear among the writings of contemporaries, students, and correspondents, such as Rabbi Israel Bruna and Rabbi Judah Mintz, themselves authors of responsa that would eventually be printed. Some of his individual responsa were copied alongside other material in untitled manuscript miscellanies and in larger collections.[36] As Rabbi Hiyah himself admitted, many responsa did not make it into his hands, and remained only in manuscript. Some of those were forever lost; others were eventually printed much, much later.

Centuries after Rabbi Hiyah's death, in 1984, some fifty of Rabbi Colon's, responsa culled from six different previously unprinted manuscripts, were published under the title *ShUT Maharyq ha-hadashim* ('New Responsa of Maharyq').[37] The manuscripts consulted for this new edition provide a further glimpse into the ways in which Rabbi Colon's responsa had been circulating when Rabbi Hiyah was searching for manuscripts from which to print *ShUT Maharyq*. One of the six manuscript collections from which the 'new' responsa were printed contained 127 responsa, of which thirty-eight do not overlap with the previously printed ones.[38] There are signs that this latter collection was some sort of verified and approved manuscript copy because most of the responsa include a signature from the scribe who copied it, testifying that it was copied letter by letter from Rabbi Colon's own writing, and sometimes two witnesses added their names to attest to this fact.[39]

If some of these manuscript collections, such as the official-looking one, included mostly responsa, others were filled with a variety of disparate halakhic material.[40] Even those manuscripts that were clearly based on Rabbi Colon's responsa copied these in very different forms from the responsa as we know them. One manuscript known as the *mafteah* ('key'), for instance, lists short descriptions for 311 responsa by Rabbi Colon, including some of those printed in Bomberg's edition. The list, dated within forty years of Rabbi Colon's death, clearly circulated in manuscript, as its multiple manuscript copies attest.[41] It opens with a declaration: אלו הם סימני שאלות ותשובות ממהר״ר יוסף קולון טרבוט זלה״ה עם הפסק בקצור בלתי ראיותיו הנוראות ('These are the *simanim* [signs/sections] of the questions and responses from our rabbi, the Rabbi Joseph Colon Tarbot, may his memory be a blessing,

---

36 For instance, a manuscript miscellany in the Florence, Biblioteca Medicea Laurenziana (BML), MS Plut. 88.47, contains one responsum by Rabbi Colon about divorce issues, alongside similar later material from other rabbis.

37 *ShUT ha-Maharyq ha-hadashim*, ed. by Eliahu Dov Pines (Jerusalem: Machon Yerushalaim, 1984). See Woolf, 'The Life and Responsa', pp. 244–46, and 245 note 36, concerning individual responsa or groups of responsa mainly from Maharyq found in 'various manuscripts containing halakhic miscellany', such as Paris, Bibliothèque Nationale de France, MS A10H, (publ. Pines *Hadashim*, no. 41), Parma, Biblioteca Palatina, Cod. Parm. 1334/3 (13031), fols 315–18; and *Seder ha-get*, Oxford, Bodleian Library, MS Mich. Add. 59, fols 174ʳ–174ᵛ; root #39.

38 MS Parma 3469, (Formerly, S. G. Stern collection, no. 2).

39 The witnesses in question are Moshe, son of Rabbi Gershom, sometimes together with Moshe, son of Rabbi Meshullam, and other times with Shlomo, son of Rabbi Gershom. There are also several remarks from the scribe, such as כאן חסר ('here it is missing'), and לא מצאתי יותר ('I did not find more').
See Pines, 'Introduction', pp. 5, 26. Notably, the responsa that do overlap with the printed collection are all from the latter part of the book (root 77 and on), so perhaps the latter part of the printed book was taken from one larger manuscript collection to which others also had access.

40 See Pines, 'Introduction', p. 5.

41 See Pines, 'Introduction', p. 5. Two of these lists are still extant in manuscript (London, British Library, MS Add. 27129 and Cambridge, University Library [Camb.], MS Add. 648). The former was signed by an 'Eliezer' in 1517.

with the decision in short, without his awesome proofs').[42] The listed responsa are concisely summarized, providing only legal conclusions without any of the halakhic argumentation that make up the content of responsa.

A large body of halakhic writings copied from, based on, or summarizing Rabbi Colon's responsa thus circulated not in any standard unified collection but in many different forms and contexts, both before and after the printed work. Nor had Rabbi Colon's responsa been copied in any complete or systematic fashion by his students. Perhaps Rabbi Colon had, at some point, begun creating such a full definite collection of his own responsa and those verified copies with their official signatures were what remained. Whatever its intended purpose, that collection was never completed and was certainly not widely copied or disseminated in this form. Only after his death, once plans for printing Rabbi Colon's responsa emerged in Venice, did Rabbi Hiyah start seeking out material for the projected book.

Rabbi Hiyah likely prepared the manuscripts for *Terumat ha-deshen* and Rabbi Colon's responsa at the same time, as the two works were printed mere months apart. Rabbi Colon died close to the geographical area and chronological period of his printed work but the same cannot be said about the author of the second work of fifteenth-century Ashkenazi responsa that Rabbi Hiyah had printed that year. The author of *Terumat ha-deshen*, Rabbi Israel ben Petahya Isserlein (c. 1390–1460, Wiener Neustadt), was one of the last and greatest rabbis of the Ashkenazi tradition as it existed in its original geographical environs. Prior to printing, Rabbi Isserlein's teachings circulated in several forms. Apart from the collection titled *Terumat ha-deshen* printed by Bomberg, we know of two other substantial collections of his responsa that were eventually printed. An anonymous student of Rabbi Isserlein's compiled one collection, *Pesaqim u-ketavim* ('Rulings and Writings'). Where it overlaps with responsa in *Terumat ha-deshen*, *Pesaqim u-ketavim* represents the earlier form of this material and *Terumat ha-deshen* a more polished version. Bomberg printed *Pesaqim u-ketavim* and *Terumat ha-deshen* at the same time. The other extant collection from the school of Rabbi Isserlein is *Leqet yosher* ('Righteous Gleanings'). Collected by Reb Joseph (Yoizel) ben Moses Ostreicher (1463–75),[43] *Leqet yosher* is centred mainly on customs and habits, but also includes responsa and other halakhic material.[44] Rabbi Yoizel, the collector-copier of this collection, often intruded by means of glosses and comments, inserting himself into the writings (including questions that he himself had asked Rabbi Isserlein).[45] The collection also

---

42 Camb., MS Add. 648; See Pines, 'Introduction', p. 4.

43 See Moritz Steinschneider in the catalogue of *Die hebräischen Handschriften der K. Hof- und Staatsbibliothek in München* (Munich, 1895, 2nd Ed.), p. 29, for a description of what is possibly an autograph of this collection. On Yoizel Ostreicher, see his introduction in *Leqet yosher* as well as the foreword in *Leqet yosher, Orah hayim*, ed. by Yoel Katan and Amihai Kineret (Jerusalem: Machon Yerushalaim, 2010), pp. 18–22 (Future page references to this work refer to this edition unless otherwise specified).

44 *Leqet yosher* contains a mixture of copied material (such as responsa) and Rabbi Yoizel's own notes, many of them observations. He emphasizes that he learned these while eating at his master's table and even sleeping in his bedroom. When Rabbi Bruna visited Rabbi Isserlein, he declined to lead the grace after the meal, in order to watch Rabbi Isserlein do it and perhaps learn something new (see *Leqet yosher*, pp. 65–66). These examples demonstrate the close connection between copying of halakhic material and learning from one's rabbi — not only from his writings but from all of his deeds — internalizing this knowledge and subsequently transmitting it. Copying responsa was but one way of doing so. We also see the social and moral weight associated with copying, to the degree that others tell Rabbi Yoizel that not sharing his copies after Rabbi Isserlein's death constitutes a grave sin.

45 He also often mentions the sources from which he copied, whereas *Pesaqim u-ketavim*'s anonymous author almost never does.

includes a few sermons and *hanhagot* ('customs') of a rabbi other than Rabbi Isserlein.[46] It was first printed only in 1903.[47]

No complete extant manuscripts of *Terumat ha-deshen* exactly match the printed book, but several are very similar to the printed work in their contents and formulation. Edward Fram has described three manuscripts containing the same responsa as those included in *Terumat ha-deshen*:[48] one is incomplete and the other two feature the same 354 responsa as the printed work. One of these manuscript collections includes a deed of sale dated 1511, following the 281st entry, which is interrupted.[49] The location of this deed of sale three-quarters of the way into the work means that at least the first part of the collection dates from before Bomberg printed *Terumat ha-deshen*. After the deed of sale, question §281 was completed, along with the remaining 74 entries.[50] The document's various hands attest to the collection having been copied by three different scribes. The collection also includes a table of contents, also penned by multiple scribes.[51] The texts of these responsa collections are largely consistent with their printed versions, but the order in which the responsa appear in those manuscript collections differs from the printed work.[52] In the case of *ShUT Maharyq*, Rabbi Hiyah had to deal with a rather small number of responsa that he had to track down, 'north and south, and front and back'. In the case of *Terumat ha-deshen*, he had a fuller inventory. In both cases, the responsa were also copied in other collections, in different orders, and with other material.

Before turning to Rabbi Hiyah's specific editorial work, we ought to consider a perhaps even more important preliminary intervention: the decision of what to print. When it came to printing the fifteenth-century works from the German Lands, these two collections were the first chosen. Who decided that these were works worth printing?

Both Rabbi Colon and Rabbi Isserlein were pivotal figures in the transmission of Ashkenazi knowledge. Geographically, temporally, and intellectually, Rabbi Colon linked the older period of the late Middle Ages with the newer one of the early modern period.[53] Born in the Ashkenaz of the fifteenth century, north of the Alps, he himself made the transition to the Ashkenazi

---

46 About Rabbi Solomon Shapira (b. Speyer–d. Breslau 1453), see Israel Yuval, *Sages in Their Generation: The Spiritual Leadership of German Jewry at the End of the Middle Ages* [in Hebrew] (Jerusalem: Magnes Press, 1989), pp. 245–56.

47 *Leqet yosher*, ed. by Yacov Freiman (Berlin: Itzkovich Press, 1903–04).

48 Yedidya Dinari, *The Sages of Ashkenaz*. Dinari seems to think that *Trumat ha-deshen* was printed more or less directly from a manuscript that resembled the printed work. In any event, he does not delve deeply into the nature of the work's form prior to print. See Edward (Yehezkel) Fram, 'On the Order of the Responsa in the Printed Edition of *Terumat ha-Deshen*' [in Hebrew], *Ale sefer*, 20 (2008), pp. 81–96; and Pinchas Roth, 'The Missing Entry in the Book *Terumat ha-deshen*', *Ale Sefer*, 21 (2010), pp. 179–81. I thank Pinchas Roth for his helpful comments and clarifications.

49 New York, Jewish Theological Seminary (JTS), MS 7148 R1419.

50 Fram assumes that the remaining responsa were copied on the basis of the printed book. See Fram, 'On the Order of the Responsa', p. 82.

51 The third manuscript that Fram describes contains a very small selection — only thirteen responsa — from *Terumat ha-deshen*: Biblioteca Medicea Laurenziana, MS Plut. I 8/6.

52 The absence of such a manuscript does not necessarily mean that it did not exist. They may very well have lost track of the manuscript copy used by the printer as soon as the work was printed and it was no longer needed. (Manuscripts that were not brought to a printer were more likely to be preserved). See, for instance, the fate of manuscripts used to print books at Bomberg's press: Haberman, *Daniel Bombirgi*, p. 21.

53 These periods are sometimes called, respectively, the *rishonim* ('first ones') and *aharonim* ('last ones'). On this periodization in Ashkenaz, see Israel I. Yuval, 'Rishonim and Aharonim, *Antiqui et Moderni*: Periodization and Self-Awareness in Ashkenaz', *Zion*, 57/4 (1992), pp. 369–94.

communities in northern Italy that would flourish in the sixteenth. He died towards the turn of the century, probably in its last decade or two.⁵⁴ Some historians suggest, without evidence, that Rabbi Hiyah had studied with Rabbi Colon.⁵⁵ Even if this was not the case, it is certainly true that Rabbi Colon brought the teachings from fifteenth-century Ashkenaz to Rabbi Hiyah and his contemporaries.

If Rabbi Colon was the connecting link between Ashkenaz in its original environs and its presence in sixteenth-century Italy, Rabbi Isserlein before him was regarded as the capstone of the last Ashkenazi generations of the previous century, 'the last of the *aharonim*' (latter authorities), as Rabbi Yoel Sirkis, a seventeenth-century rabbi, described him.⁵⁶ As the last great rabbi of Ashkenaz when these communities were still living in their original territories, in the eyes of subsequent generations Rabbi Isserlein represented the Ashkenazi past before its geographical dispersion and served as the repository of its knowledge. Writing in Eastern Europe two centuries later, Rabbi Sirkis remarked: אנו במדינתינו שבכל ההוראות אנו שותין מימי הרב ר' איסרלין ז"ל ('We, in our lands, in all our teachings drink from the wellsprings of the rabbi, Rabbi Isserlein of blessed memory').⁵⁷

The decision to print works by Rabbis Colon and Isserlein no doubt reflects their key positions in the Ashkenazi chain of transmission. But the story of printing these works bears more nuanced consideration.

The Art of Selection

One aspect of editing is the art of selection. The responsa in *ShUT Maharyq* and *Terumat ha-deshen* certainly appear to have been carefully selected. Unlike the responsa in the Ashkenazi manuscript compilations and in works of responsa that would be printed later in this period, the works arranged by Rabbi Hiyah contain only responsa, and only the responsa of Rabbis Colon and Isserlein themselves.⁵⁸ The entries in the printed *ShUT Maharyq* are consistently signed, mostly with the words נאם הצעיר יוסף קולון במהר"ר שלמה זלה"ה, | ושלום מאתי הצעיר יוסף קולון במהר"ר שלמה זלה"ה. ('from me, Joseph Colon, son of our master Rabbi Solomon'), or with some other conclusion, such as וכ"נ לענ"ד ('and so it

---

54 It is not known when Colon died, and his grave in Pavia was destroyed. See Woolf, 'The Life and Responsa', p. 7. David Gans in *Tzemah David* provides 1480 as a date of death, but admits that he does not have any certainty. In his *Geschichte der Juden*, Heinrich Graetz conjectured that Colon was born in the 1420s. He delineated 1460–80 as the period of Colon's flourishing, but not 1480 specifically as his date of death: Heinrich Graetz, *Geschichte den Juden von der ältesten Zeiten bis auf die Gegenwart aus den Quellen neu bearbeitet* (Lepzig: O. Leiner, 1870; 3ʳᵈ Ed. 1890), VIII, p. 153; See also A. Ch. Freiman, 'Emissaries and Pilgrims: 15ᵗʰ-Century Documents from Candia' [in Hebrew], *Historical Society of Israel*, 2/1 (1936), pp. 185–207 (pp. 190–91).

55 Meir Benayahu and Moshe Assis, 'On the Question of Who Edited the Yerushalmi Printed in Venice' [in Hebrew], p. 30 note 36 [forthcoming].

56 Rabbi Sirkis is also known as BaH, an acronym of his work *Bayit hadash* ('New Home'), a gloss on *Shulhan 'arukh*. The quote is from *ShUT haBaH* in a responsum to Rabbi Avraham of Brisk: *ShUT ha-BaH ha-hadashot*, §66. The citation continues: שהי' מבני אשכנז, ובתראי דבתראי הוא ('who was from the sons of Ashkenaz, and the last of the latter sages').

57 Another seventeenth-century Polish rabbi offered a similar characterization of Rabbi Isserlein: וידוע כי בעל ת"ה [תרומת הדשן] היה גדול שבאחרונים ומימיו אנו שותים. ('And it is known that our Master Rabbi Israel of blessed memory, the author of *Terumat ha-deshen*, he is the greatest of the *ahronim* and it is from his wellsprings that we drink'). Rabbi Moshe Lima (1604–58, Poland) in his gloss on *Shulhan 'arukh*: (*Helqat mehoqeq*, *'Even ha-'ezer*, §17:21).

58 It does include two responsa mistakenly attributed to him (although such a mistake does not, of course, counter the book's intention of including only the author's writings): root #74 is from *Or Zarua*, not from Rabbi Colon, and root #163 is from Rabbi Yacov Weil. See Spiegel, *Chapters*, II, p. 246.

seems, in my humble opinion').⁵⁹ In the case of *Terumat ha-deshen*, too, the responsa are concise and self-contained. Each responsum has its own numbered section; each question is preceded by the word 'question' in larger type; and each response is preceded by the word 'response' in larger type. Almost every response opens with the same formula ויראה ('and it seems'), or יראה לי ('it seems to me'), and many conclude with the same formula, כך יראה לי לעניות דעתי ('so it appears to me, in my humble opinion').⁶⁰

Organizational markers like the headings שאלה ('question') or תשובה ('response'), as well as the author's signature after each response were sometimes added by scribes or print editors, and might not necessarily be found in the original manuscript copies.⁶¹ Still, the consistent conclusions in these two collections are telling and the consistent and clear division of the responsa is remarkable. In typical Ashkenazi collections, individual responsa were not always distinguished from one another, nor were all the responsa in a collection authored by one person. This made it almost impossible to always add a distinct opening and the same signature for every responsum even if an editor had wanted to do so. Responsa are often parts of longer letters that deal with a series of unrelated issues, which is how they appear in some manuscript collections. In other responsa collections, material is only partially copied or is merged with different pieces, and several responsa frequently appear under a single section number.

In *Terumat ha-deshen*, personal names of questioners and subjects are replaced with generic, anonymous names. Contemporary rabbis are often referred to as 'one of the great scholars'. Comparison of those responsa to equivalents as they appear in the two other collections of Rabbi Isserlein's writings, *Pesaqim u-ketavim* and *Leqet yosher*, where the names are specified, shows that the full names were present in earlier iterations of the correspondence. Thus, it is clear that the names were removed in preparing *Terumat ha-deshen*.⁶² All of these changes have the combined effect of transforming *Terumat ha-deshen* from a haphazard,

---

59 Colon, *ShUT Maharyq*, passim. On signatures in medieval responsa, see Haym Soloveitchik, *Responsa as a Historical Source* [in Hebrew] (Jerusalem: Machon Zalman Shazar Press, 1990). Soloveitchik considers that the presence of an opening greeting or a signature points to minimal tampering with the question by copyists, as the opening greeting and concluding signature would have been the first things to remove. See Ephraim E. Urbach, 'The Responsa of Rosh in Manuscripts and in Print', *Shenaton ha-mishpat ha-ivri*, 2 (1975), pp. 1–153, which contains a detailed description of the responsa of Rabbi Asher ben Yehiel, which were taken apart and rearranged by a student. Urbach considered responsa from manuscript collections and attempts to reconstruct the original responsa with appropriate salutations before they were taken apart and rearranged.

60 This also holds true for the JTS manuscript collections, except that שאלה ('question') and תשובה ('response') are sometimes replaced by just the first letters (ש and ת, in larger script), and the concluding formula is usually written as an acronym כיי״ל לענ״ד [rather than כך יראה לי לעניות דעתי].

61 See Spiegel, *Chapters*, II, p. 249 note 100. For such an example in the case of Rabbi Isserlein's writings, see Rabbi Yoizel Ostreicher's introduction in *Leqet yosher*, note 81 below, where Rabbi Yoizel explains that he will write 'thus said Israel' at the end of every responsum: ובשאלה ראשונה אכתוב ההתחלה מן הכתב, ובשאלה אחרונה אכתוב סיום הכתב בלשון נאום ישראל, ואם יהיה לי יותר אזי אכתוב יותר.

('And in the responsum's beginning I will write the beginning of what is written [the letter?], and in the responsum's end I will write the ending of what is written [the letter?], with the formulation 'ne'um Israel' ['thus said Israel'], and if I have any more, then I shall write more').

62 For example, specifically regarding the omission of the name: §204 in the printed edition reads, וראיתי בתשובת אחד מן הגדולים שכתב בשם רבו אחד מן הגדולים, דכל מה שהוא בחבית[...].
('And I saw in the responsum of *one of the great ones* who wrote in the name of his rabbi, one of the great ones, that everything which is in the barrel...').
By contrast, in *Leqet yosher, Yoreh De'ah, hilkhot yayin nesekh*, §12 (Jerusalem: Machon Yerushalaim, 2010), p. 19, this statement is cited in the name of השר ('the

personal compilation into a structured, edited, and accessible book. These elements certainly make the work appear more comprehensively edited; it is even possible that many of these editorial interventions were already part of the work's manuscript transmission.⁶³

---

prince') a reference to Rabbi Shalom, author of *Minhagei Maharil*, אמר מורי, כתב המהרי"ל בשם השר שבחבית קרי הפסד מרובה ('My teacher said, our master Rabbi Moellin wrote in the name of the prince that in a barrel it is considered a great loss'). This replacing of names can be observed in the manuscript versions of *Terumat ha-deshen* as well as in the printed version. (Compare the same responsum in JTS R1419, for instance, [the equivalent of §204 in the printed work is §319 in this manuscript], where it is written the same way as in the printed edition, as אחד הגדולים 'one of the great ones'). For a theory related to the choice of generic names versus real names in citing rabbinic authorities in *Terumat ha-deshen*, see Naftali Ya'akov ha-Cohen, 'Repository of the Great Sages, Leaders of Jacob' (Bnei-Braq: s.n., 1968), 6, p. 50. ועוד בספרים הפוסקים זה דרכו שבכ"מ שמביא סברת ותשובות מאחד מהגדולים שהיו משנות קו"ף ולמעלה (אחרי שנות הגזירות קח וקט) באשכנז ואוסטרייך מביא רק בשם אחד מהגדולים בלי הזכרת שם [...] ורק סברות גדולות שהיו קודם שנת קו"ף כמו סברת תלמידי מהר"ם מרוטנבורג ותלמידיהם [...] מביאם בשמם [...] וכל זה בספר הפסקים אבל בכתבים ותשובות שם כותב הכל משמם המיוחד בשם אומרו. ('Moreover, in the books of the adjudicators, this is his method, wherever he cites an opinion or responsum from one of the great ones that lived in the year 1340 and on [after the persecutions of 1348–49], in the German Lands and Austria, he simply cites it in the name of "one of the great ones" without mentioning the name... and only important opinions before 1340, such as the students of R. Meir of Rothenburg and their students... those he cites by name... and all this in his book of adjudication, but in his writings and responsa, there he writes everything in its specific name, citing it in name of who said it').

63 As for why *Terumat ha-deshen* was, indeed, such a complete, organized collection even in its manuscript state, Ta-Shma attributes this to the influence of Rabbi Ya'aqov, the son of Rabbi Asher ben Yechiel (the thirteenth-century halakhist known as Rosh), who left Ashkenaz for Spain. Once in Spain, his son organized his father's responsa according to principles, by dividing, editing, and rearranging, and creating a table of contents. '... from then on', Ta-Shma writes,

Terumat ha-deshen is a paradigmatic example of an Ashkenazi responsa collection from the fifteenth century, but it is also the work from that milieu that is most often accused of inauthenticity. הלא נודע ('It is well known'), an important commentator on the *Shulhan 'arukh* ('Set, or Ordered, Table'), wrote, שהשאלות שבתרומת הדשן עשה מהרא"י בעל התשובות עצמו ולא ששאלוהו אחרים כמו בפסקיו וכתביו ('that the questions in *Terumat ha-deshen* were created by Rabbi Isserlein, the author of the responsa himself, and not that others asked them of him').⁶⁴ Historian Israel Ta-Shma went so far as to call the responsa 'fictive'.⁶⁵ The reason the work is considered both a prototypical Ashkenazi book of responsa and inauthentic is its exceptional degree of organization.

Terumat ha-deshen makes an immediate impression of being thoroughly edited, very complete, and unprecedentedly well-organized — so much so, that a tradition developed in Ashkenaz in the sixteenth and especially in the seventeenth century that the questions in *Terumat ha-deshen* were invented by the author rather than culled from actual cases.⁶⁶ In his introduction

---

'the situation changed', and Ashkenazi authorities, too, began to organize their responsa collections in this more Sephardi style. The example Ta-Shma provides for this change caused by Rabbi Ya'aqov ben Asher is *Terumat ha-deshen*: Israel Ta-Shma, *Collection of Studies: Inquiries into the Rabbinic Literature of the Middle Ages* [in Hebrew] (Jerusalem: Mosad Bialik, 2004), p. 121.

64 Rabbi Shabbetai Kohen, *Siftei Cohen* on *Yoreh de'ah*, §196:20.

65 Ta-Shma, *Collection of Studies*, p. 121.

66 For additional instances of this tradition, see Rabbi David ha-Levi Segal's gloss, *Turei zahav* on *Yoreh de'ah*, §328:2: וידוע הוא דרכו של תרומת הדשן שהוא עצמו סידר השאלות ('And it is well known that the method of *Terumat ha-Deshen* was that he himself made his questions'). For more examples and a discussion of the halakhic import of such an assertion, see Dinari, *The Sages of Ashkenaz*, p. 303 note 223. Dinari attempts to verify whether the responsa were truly invented or authentic (mainly by comparing which responsa in *Trumat ha-deshen* appear in a less edited form in *Pesaqim*

to the most recent edition of *Terumat ha-deshen*, the editor wrote:

בהשוואה לשאר ספרי השו״ת של חכמי אשכנז בתקופתו של רבינו — כמו שאלות ותשובות מהרי״ל מהר״י וייל מהר״י ברונא — יש יחוד בולט לספר תרומת הדשן, שונה הוא במהותו ובצורתו משאר ספרי התשובות של החכמים בני דורו...

(In comparison to the other works of responsa of the Ashkenazi sages in the period of Rabbi [Isserlein] — such as the responsa of Maharil [Rabbi Molin], Mahari Weil [Rabbi Weil], and Mahari Bruna [Rabbi Israel Bruna] — *Terumat ha-deshen* has a uniqueness that stands out, for it is different in its essence and form from the other works of responsa by the sages of his time).[67]

This uniqueness, he explained, is expressed in the separation of question from answer, the deliberate reformulation of the question, the relative formalization and uniformity of the responsa, and other editorial and organizational characteristics.[68] Each of these qualities signals editorial interference. Thus, when these responsa are described as 'inauthentic', what is really meant is that they were edited more thoroughly than was typical for responsa from that milieu and era. If the reader expected responsa to look a certain way — more like the actual, temporal, documents, and less like a collection intended for publication — *Terumat ha-deshen* displayed the characteristics of a collection deliberately edited.

How much of *Terumat ha-deshen* existed in such an organized, edited, state before it was printed? Even its manuscripts were exceptional. Some of these features may date to the days of Rabbi Isserlein himself and were perhaps his own doing. With regard to the removal of personal names and the more generic phrasings of the responsa themselves, as well as the consistent division and conclusions of the responsa and the labelling of 'question' and 'response', the two complete preprint manuscripts mentioned earlier closely resemble the printed edition. This supports the idea that Rabbi Isserlein himself selected the contents for *Terumat ha-deshen*, decided on the number of responsa and the title, and did some of the editing.[69] The most recent edition of *Terumat ha-deshen* refers to

---

u-ketavim or *Leqet yosher*). He concludes that we cannot determine this with certainty. In any event, this tradition that *Terumat ha-deshen* was inauthentic is significant primarily because it emphasizes that *Terumat ha-deshen* indeed appeared out of place compared to other works of responsa from its time and place because it was so thoroughly edited, organized, and complete. For more on this question, see Spiegel, *Chapters*, II, p. 286.

67 Rabbi Moshe Menashe Friedman, introduction in *Terumat haDeshen*, ed. Friedman (Ḥokhmat Shlomo: Jerusalem, 2016), I, 70.

68 Friedman, 'Introduction', I, p. 70.

יחוד זה מתבטא במספר מאפיינים. לדוגמא,בשאר קבצי התשובות שבאותה תקופה לא מיוחד כל סימן מסימני הספר דווקא לנידון אחד, ולעיתים יש תשובה שנמשכת בשני סימנים או יותר, מה שאין כן בספר תרומת הדשן לעולם כל סימן וסימן מיוחד לשאלה ותשובה אחת בלבד. שינוי נוסף, בשאר קבצי התשובות של אותה תקופה בדרך כלל הסימן נפתח בדברי המשיב כששאלת השואל מובלעת בתוך התשובה,מה שאין כן בספר תרומת הדשן כל סימן נפתח בשאלה מנוסחת אחרי

תיבה פותחת: שאלה, ואחריה לאחר תיבה פותחת: תשובה, באה התשובה. שינוי נוסף,בשאר קבצי התשובות פעמים רבות בשאלה עצמה נכלל משא ומתן בצדדי השאלה בנימוקים או ראיות מן המקורות,מה שאין כן בתרומת הדשן השאלה כוללת רק את פרטי השאלה בקיצור, ובדרך כלל ללא כל משא ומתן הלכתי או אסמכתות מן המקורות בנוסח השאלה.הבדל נוסף,בשאר קבצי התשובות באותה תקופה התשובה נפתחת בפניה אל השואלים בשמם ובדברי ברכה אליהם ומסתיימת בדברי סיום,מה שאין כן בספר תרומת הדשן אין שום סממנים אישיים אלו. התשובות בתרומת הדשן הם בלא חתימת שם המשיב,והסיומת היא: הנראה לענ״ד כתבתי.

69 I checked several of these at JTS. For instance, responsum §143 in the printed edition = §201 in JTS, MS 7148 R1419 (= §242 in JTS MS 7149 R1532); the formulation is identical, omitting the personal names, etc., in comparison to the version in *Pesaqim u-ketavim*, this from the section that precedes the deed of sale in R1419. Thus, it seems that the responsa were edited in such a way prior to the printed work.

additional manuscript copies which resemble the two completed ones.⁷⁰ In other words, Rabbi Isserlein himself likely edited some form of official collection of his responsa. This not only prepared the ground for Rabbi Hiyah and made his job easier, but it also presented the work as an obvious candidate for print.

The Emergence of a Book

On the printed book's title page, Rabbi Hiyah announced the work's title and author:

ספר תרומת הדשן | חבר ויסד הגאון מהר"ר ישראל זצ"ל. אשר שמו נודע בשערים ונקרא בין האשכנזים מהר"ר איסרלן זצ"ל. אשר הניח אחריו ברכה לזכות הרבים בתשובותיו. ונדפסו ונחקקו על ידי הנעלה המחזיק ידי עושי המלאכה בממונו. הלא שמו נקרא בחוצות דניאל בומבי"רגו מאנווירשה יצ"ו

(The Book *Terumat ha-deshen*. Composed and created by [...] Rabbi Israel of blessed memory, whose name is known in the gates⁷¹ and who is called among the Ashkenazim Our Teacher Rabbi Isserlein of blessed memory).⁷²

The title page credits Rabbi Isserlein, who had 'left הניח אחריו ברכה לזכות הרבים בתשובותיו behind him a blessing, to benefit the masses with his responsa').⁷³ Rabbi Hiyah likely brought *Terumat ha-deshen* to print using a pre-existing manuscript collection that, unlike so many other manuscript responsa, had intentionally been 'left behind' by the author for posterity and already featured some of the organizational characteristics of a book. There is also evidence that *Terumat ha-deshen* was received as a *bona fide* book even before Rabbi Hiyah had it printed. Indeed, Rabbi Isserlein's contemporaries sometimes referred to his responsa as a 'book', rather than just citing knowledge in his name, implying that there was a defined collection before it was printed.⁷⁴ This brings us to yet another atypical characteristic that created the impression of *Terumat ha-deshen* as more 'book-like' than its contemporaries: its title.

In the colophon to *Terumat ha-deshen*, Rabbi Hiyah thanks the Lord for aiding him in finishing the printing of זה החבור הנאה הנודע בישראל

---

70 Friedman compares the responsa in *Terumat ha-deshen* parallel to or overlapping with material in *Pesaqim u-ketavim* and *Leqet yosher*, as well as some responsa from other sources. (Yedidyah Dinari carried out a similar though less complete comparison for many of these in his work, see above). The question of the authenticity of the responsa also led Friedman to closely examine seven manuscript collections of *Terumat ha-deshen*. Of these, three contain all the responsa printed in the Venice 1519 edition. (Friedman counts one of these full collections, made up of two scribal hands at two points in time as two separate manuscripts); two are partial; and another is lost. All but one, which is in private hands, are microfilmed and available at the National Library of Israel, and were known to the earlier scholars who worked on *Terumat haDeshen* before Friedman. The manuscripts all appear to belong to the same manuscript tradition, either copied from the same source or copies thereof (except for one which may have been partially copied from the printed *Terumat haDeshen* at a later point). The order of the responsa in those copies, as Friedman points out, differs from the printed work, but — order aside — they are all rather similar to one another in textual formulation and order.

71 Proverbs 31:23. Perhaps this is also a reference to Rabbi Isserlein's glosses on Rabbi Itzhaq of Düren's *Sha'arei Dura*. Rabbi Isserlein's glosses had become commonplace among the layers of glosses in this work.
72 Isserlein, *Terumat ha-deshen*, title page.
73 Isserlein, *Terumat ha-deshen*, title page, the line continues:
ונדפסו ונחקקו על ידי הנעלה המחזיק ידי עושי המלאכה בממונו הלא שמו נקרא בחוצות דניאל בומבי"רגו מאנווירשה יצ"ו.
('And they were printed and etched by the elevated, he who supports the hands of the laborers with his money, his name is known far and wide, Daniel Bomberg of Antwerp').
74 Dinari assembled several early references to a work or book by Rabbi Isserlein. For examples, see Dinari, *The Sages of Ashkenaz*, p. 303.

וביהודה שמו תרומת הדשן ('this beautiful work, known among the people of Israel and Judaea, its name is *Terumat ha-deshen*').[75] It appears that the work had been known by that name long before Rabbi Hiyah's labours began. In contrast, most Ashkenazi works of responsa lacked a real title, neither in their manuscript circulation nor when they were printed. They were simply named 'the Responsa of', followed by the author's name. Furthermore, we often find the same rabbi's collection referred to using alternate terms for responsa, some of which are not exactly in the same category. They are sometimes referred to simply as *liqutei* ('the gleanings of') Rabbi so-and-so, or as *yalqut* (a noun indicating compilations), *nimuqei* ('remarks of'), *yesod* ('foundation'), *matbe'a* ('coinage'), *seder* ('order'), *quntres* ('quire/booklet'), *gilyonot* ('booklets'), *pesaqim* ('rulings'), or *qovetz* ('booklet').[76] These fluid titles reflect the books' fluid contents and genres, and their varied authors. In printing *ShUT Maharyq*, Rabbi Hiyah did not give it a fanciful title; he simply followed the convention for naming such works, but *Terumat ha-deshen* already had a title.

In his colophon, Rabbi Hiyah explained the name *Terumat ha-* deshen: שבח והודיה לאדון המציאות אשר אמץ זרועותינו והגיענו להשלמת זה החבור הנאה הנודע בישראל וביהודה שמו תרומת הדשן. כי מספר תשובותיו דש"ן ('Praise and thanks be to the Master of Existence, who strengthened our arms and helped us arrive at the completion of this beautiful work known to [the People of] Israel and Judaea, its name is *Terumat ha-deshen* because its responsa number 354').[77] *Terumat ha-deshen*'s title is linked to the work's contents in an inherent and stable manner. The consciously chosen number of responsa in the collection is yet another atypical characteristic for collections of Ashkenazi responsa in the manuscript age, which tended to circulate in arbitrary and usually uneven collections, varying from copy to copy. In contrast, *Terumat ha-deshen* contains exactly 354 responsa, a number that corresponds numerically to the letters in the word *deshen*; hence the title of the book. This points to the stable transmission of a closed-ended work of set content, rather than the flexible, open-ended transmission practices of manuscript collections in which various textual materials from different sources, genres, and authors would be copied in different combinations and orders by individual scribes. In the printed book itself, the only references to the title are in the colophon and on the title page, not within the text itself, which creates the impression that the title was a late addition. But *Terumat ha-deshen*'s atypical title was probably determined long before Rabbi Hiyah edited the work, as is indicated by two earlier allusions to the work.

---

75 Rabbi Israel Isserlein, 'colophon'.

76 See Simcha Emanuel, *Fragments of the Tablets: Lost Books of the Tosafists* [in Hebrew] (Jerusalem: Magnes Press, 2006), p. 250. On Rabbi Eliezer ben Yoel ha-Levi's interchangeable use of *kuntresim* and responsa, see Avigdor Aptowitzer, *Introduction to Rabbi Eliezer ben Yoel ha-Levi* [in Hebrew] (Jerusalem: Meqitze nirdamim, 1984), p. 85. Salo Baron translates the word *kuntres* as 'a *quntres* (handbook, probably derived from the Latin *commentarius*)'. See Salo W. Baron, *A Social and Religious History of the Jews*, 18 vols (New York: Columbia University Press, 1958, 2nd Ed.), VI: *Laws, Homilies, and the Bible*, p. 49. Baron is referring to Rashi's own accumulation of written texts, which his students (the Tosafists) referred to as Rashi's *kuntres*. On the term *kuntres*, see also Malachi Beit-Arié, *Hebrew Codicology: Historical and Comparative Typology of Medieval Hebrew Codices Based on the Documentation of the Extant Dated Manuscripts until 1540 Using a Quantitative Approach*, ed. by Zofia Lasman (Jerusalem and Hamburg: The Israel Academy of Sciences and Humanities Press, 2021), pp. 249–52 https://www.fdr.uni-hamburg.de/record/9349#.YgfJAerMI2w [accessed in February 2022].

77 Rabbi Israel Isserlein, 'colophon'. Emphasis in the original, to highlight that 'Israel' is also the author's first name.

We cannot be entirely sure that the title and its relation to the contents were Rabbi Isserlein's own doing, but it certainly took hold during his lifetime. Preprint sources rarely mention the work's title or the number of responsa contained within., but there are some that do reveal knowledge of the book's title. In a responsum to another rabbi, Rabbi Israel Bruna (c. 1400–80) tantalizingly referred to Rabbi Isserlein's contributions by using the word *terumot* ('contributions/offerings') reminiscent of the book's title. Moreover, at the beginning of *Leqet yosher*, the compilation of Rabbi Isserlein's material assembled by Rabbi Yoizel, the collector lists labels that he used to designate the various types of source material:

וכל היכא שכתבתי בסתם, דרש או מעשה, או פ״א או הורה,[או תשובה], כתבתי בחייו כמו שאמר או כמו שראיתי [...] אבל היכא שכבתבי וזכרוני, או מצאתי, או העתקתי, כתבתי לאחר מותו. וכל היכא שכתבתי תשובה היא התשובה שכתוב בספר שעשה הגאון ז״ל [...]

(Where I wrote simply, 'he said', or 'an occurrence', or 'one time', or 'he taught', [or 'a response'], it was written in his lifetime as he said or as I observed [...]. But where I write 'and I remember', or 'I found', or 'I copied', I wrote after his death. And where I wrote 'responsa', it is the responsum as it is written *in the book* [emphasis mine] that the *ga'on* of blessed memory made).[78]

This list offers a glimpse of the evolution of *Terumat ha-deshen* into a coherent collection of specific responsa, and later a book with a title — all long before Rabbi Hiyah printed the work. Rabbi Yoizel's reference to 'the book' that Rabbi Isserlein 'made' indicates the existence of a consciously selected collection of written responsa. Rabbi Yoizel's explanation of the label 'responsa', makes it clear that even when he was already copying some of his rabbi's writings, he was, at first, unaware of it as a responsa collection. His knowledge of the title and number of entries came even later:

וכל היכא שכתבתי תשובה היא התשובה שכתוב בספר שעשה הגאון ז״ל (שקרא תרומת דשן משום שיש בו שנ״ד תשובות כמו הילוך לבנה שהוא שנ״ד ימים), וכל היכא שכתבתי כתב בספרו ולא כתבתי בלשון תשובה הוא משום שלא ידעתי באותו זמן שכתבתי אותו דין שהיה [אותו דין] כבר כתוב בספרו עד לאח״כ שנגלה הספר שלו, אז כתבתי כתוב בספרו.

(And there where I wrote 'responsa', it is the responsum as it is written in the book that the sage of blessed memory made [that was called *Terumat ha-deshen* because it contained 354 responsa like the lunar cycle which is 354 days] and everywhere I wrote 'he wrote in his book', and I did not mention the term 'responsum', it is because I did not know at the time that I wrote that law that it was already written in his book until afterwards, when his book was revealed, then I wrote 'it says in his book').[79]

---

78 Ostreicher, 'Introduction'.

79 Ostreicher, 'Introduction'. It continues:

כל היכא שכתבתי כתב, פי שהשיב הגאון ז״ל בכתב לחכמי ישראל והיכא דאפשר אכתוב שמותם אי״ה ובשאלה ראשונה אכתוב ההתחלה מן הכתב, ובשאלה אחרונה אכתוב סיום הכתב בלשון נאום ישראל, ואם יהיה לי יותר אזי אכתוב יותר.

('Wherever I have written "he wrote", it means that the Gaon of blessed memory responded to this in writing to the sages of Israel, and wherever possible I will write their names, God willing, and in the responsum's beginning I will write the beginning of what is written [the letter?], and in the responsum's end I will write the ending of what is written [the letter?], with the formulation "*ne'um* Israel" ["thus said Israel"], and if I have any more, then I shall write more').

Rabbi Yoizel thus had access to his rabbi's writings before he knew about the collection of responsa that would become the famous book. He continued to edit *Leqet yosher* throughout his life, and he seems to have adapted his labelling of the sources he had copied at later points as well, sometimes in the margins, if the nature of those sources had changed in the meantime. At one point, when Rabbi Yoizel had been copying material, his rabbi's 'book' was not yet 'revealed'. He apparently became aware of its existence only later and, subsequently, added 'it says in his book' to the entries in his manuscript of *Leqet yosher* that corresponded to responsa in the book that was eventually titled *Terumat ha-deshen*. Rabbi Yoizel labelled the responsa as 'responsa' only after finding them in the book, rather than labelling them as such because they were, in fact, responses to halakhic questions. As designated here by the brackets, which also appear in the first printed edition of *Leqet yosher*, the words in the introduction referring explicitly to the title and the 354 responsa appear in different ink and were added at a later date, most likely by Rabbi Yoizel himself. Even when the work was known as 'a book', then, the title likely came later.[80] Rabbi Yoizel died before *Terumat ha-deshen* was printed, so if he was the one who added the title to his list, which is likely, then it was not Rabbi Hiyah's doing.[81]

We can thus trace the gradual emergence of *Terumat ha-deshen* as a book out of Rabbi Isserlein's manuscript collection in stages: (1) students copy material from their rabbi's papers; (2) a known collection is acknowledged as a 'book'; and (3) the title is added, sealing the distinct number of entries together with the explanation that connects the title to the number of entries and days of the year. As their completion cannot be dated, the two extant manuscript collections that feature the exact number of responsa in *Terumat ha-deshen* are inconclusive as to the moment when that number — and the title — was set.[82] But clearly the title had already

---

80 The use of 354 as corresponding to the lunar cycle has precedent in other books, but it might simply be a convention that someone followed in adding it to the manuscript later. Rabbi Yomtov Lipman Mühlhausen gives a similar explanation for the number of entries in his collection (see Dinari, *The Sages of Ashkenaz*, p. 302 note 218).

81 Regarding the brackets in the first printed edition of *Leqet yosher* (Berlin, 1903): It is not stated there why this line appears in brackets. Relying on a 1494 manuscript, Freiman had reason to believe that this line was a later addition to the original manuscript of *Leqet yosher*. Isserlein and his book are not referred to anywhere by means of the title *Terumat ha-deshen* in the rest of the introduction or in works that appeared before 1519, when

Terumat ha-deshen was printed. In regard to the brackets in Freiman's book, the editor of the *Machon Yerushalaim* edition noted that Freiman had bracketed those elements even though they were added in the margins or between the lines by Rabbi Yoizel himself. The *Machon Yerushalaim* editors distinguished between remarks that were added by the author after *Terumat ha-deshen* was printed as opposed to markings that could have been the author's corrections at any point in time: Ostreicher, *Leqet yosher*, pp. 26–27.
Steinschneider in *Die hebräischen Handschriften*, p. 225, noted that the manuscript of *Leqet yosher* was indeed corrected and emended often ('Die Einleitung des Herausg. L. Venetianer bedarf vielfacher Berichtigung'). On p. 227, he mentioned ink from different times in the margins ('am Rande von frischerer Tinte').
As Rabbi Yoizel died in 1475, if he added the remark concerning the title, that would mean the book already had this name before it was printed. The manuscript of *Leqet yosher* does contain many later marginalia such as כתוב בספרו (see Steinschneider, *Die hebräischen Handschriften*, p. 226). Pinchas Roth, who worked with an early manuscript of *Leqet yosher*, told me that the comments in brackets were added in the autograph manuscript by Rabbi Yoizel himself.

82 The fact that two of the extant manuscript collections contain the requisite number of sections and a reference to the title indicates that this number and the title likely preceded the printed work. But the only part of these manuscripts that can be reliably dated to before the printed work is the first part of one manuscript, up to §281. The reference to the exact number of 354 responsa, by contrast, is found only at the end of that collection, which could have been completed after 1519, adding all

been set by the time Rabbi Hiyah explained it in the colophon.

If Rabbi Hiyah took the title and the number of responsa in *Terumat ha-deshen* as givens, the same cannot be said of *ShUT Maharyq*. He acknowledged that the number of entries in the printed *ShUT Maharyq* was entirely arbitrary, subject to whatever he could recover. Nevertheless, as a final editorial flourish, and by means of some mathematical and linguistic gymnastics, he attempted to connect the numerical value of the number of sections (which he called roots) and subsections to a scriptural passage: ומניין מספר השרשים קצ״ה וסעיפיהם רצ״ג. וסימן השרשים עם הענפים פת״ח דבריו יאיר מבין פתאים) 'the count of the number of roots is one hundred and ninety-five, and its subsections, two hundred and ninety-three. And the sign for the roots with the subsections is "The entrance (*petah* = 488) of Your words gives light; it gives understanding to the simple" [Ps. 119:130]').[83] In creating a book where there was none, Rabbi Hiyah nowhere pretends that the number of responsa is anything but subject to the vagaries of what he could track down, yet he presented the collection as somehow having an overarching coherence and clear definition.

The strange reputation of *Terumat ha-deshen* as both the exemplary Ashkenazi work of responsa and a work of questionable authenticity highlights a dynamic that is too often ignored: the elements of what makes a book a 'real book' are inherently the opposite to what makes texts 'authentic'. A book is associated with editorial intervention and conscious planning and publication, the very qualities authentic documents lack. The difference between a responsum as a document that resulted from a rabbi's reaction to an actual need and the responsum as a legal precedent, a scholarly enterprise meant for posterity, is in the level of editorial intervention. In the case of *Terumat ha-deshen*, the manuscripts already reflected this editorial touch when Rabbi Hiyah started his work. In the case of Rabbi Colon's responsa, Rabbi Hiyah himself provided this touch.

The expectation that a book displays certain characteristics — uniformity, consistency of form, selection, clear delineation of the materials,

---

the responsa that appeared in the printed book but were missing in the manuscript: At the end of JTS MS 7148 R1419:

תם ונשלם שבח לאל בורא עולם ית' ויתעלה וסימניו שנ״ד וסימנך דש״ן על כן נקרא תרומת הדשן.

('concluded and completed, praise to the Lord, Creator of the universe, may he be blessed and elevated, and its signs (entries) are 354 and its sign is [the word] "*deshen*" [ashes, formed by the letters ש נ ד, which, together equal 354], therefore the book is called *Terumat ha-deshen*'). The second manuscript collection ends with the words, 'This book was founded by the gaon, Our Teacher, Rabbi Isserl'.

JTS MS 7149 R1532 ends with:

סיימתי ספ' נקר' תרומת הדשן תהלה לאל נותן | יזכור כל מנחותיך ועולותיך ישן | [ידשן]

('I completed the book called *Terumat ha-Deshen* praise the Lord who gives, may he receive the tokens of all your offerings and accept the fat of your burnt-offering') [Ps. 20:4].

See also Fram, *On the Order of the Responsa*, p. 81 note 3. As Fram mentions, whereas the first 280 sections definitely date from before 1511, the next 74 were added later and according to the printed edition. See Fram, *On the Order of the Responsa*, p. 82:

מילא את החסר על סדר התשובות במהדורה המודפסת או כתב יד שהמהדורה המודפסת מבוססת עליו ושלא הגיע לידינו.

('Filled in what was missing in the order of the responsa in the printed edition or the manuscript on which the printed edition was based, which we do not have'). There is also a censor's signature at the end of JTS MS 7148 R1419 dated 1598 (Domenico Irosolimitano).

83 Colon, *ShUT Maharyq*, end of *simanim*. It continues:

וברור וידוע כי יש עוד מתשובותיו בנמצאות. אכן צפון ותימן בקשנו אחריהם ולא השגנום: וקדם ואחור רדפנו להגיע ולא עלתה בידינו. ואשר נמצאו תחת ידינו נדפסו בעזרת הש״י ובישועתו.

('And it is clear and known that more repsonsa from him are extant. Indeed, we have searched for them North and South and have not found them, front and back we have chased to attain them, and we have failed. And those that we have in our possession have been printed with the help and salvation of the Lord').

unification, and a title — predates print. These notions were not created by print, which is why we can already see them at work in the fifteenth century. But print can be said to have solidified and enhanced elements such as unification, clear delineation, and consistency. This, in turn, influenced expectations of what books should look like and the choice of which books were good candidates for the printing press: *Terumat ha-deshen* presented as a book, which is perhaps why publishing it made sense to a sixteenth-century printer.

But Rabbi Hiyah did not simply print manuscripts of these responsa as he found them as haphazard collections of surviving documents copied by those in the author's circle. He introduced organization, a crucial editorial element.

Arranging Books

Rabbi Hiyah added significant new organizational elements to both *ShUT Maharyq* and *Terumat ha-deshen*, especially in terms of aids to navigate the work. The first type of such an aid, the table of contents, can be found as early as in manuscript works of halakhah. However, its use as a tool for orienting oneself in a work is limited, as it requires one to read the entire list to know where any particular item can be found. Historians of medieval books have called the table of contents 'the simplest of finding devices'.[84] As such simple finding devices require some prior familiarization with the work before contents can be located, they serve primarily to provide a concise overview of the whole work.

By contrast, the second type of navigational aid, an index, significantly improves the search process. With an index, basic familiarity with halakhah suffices for gaining entry into the work. Further, the inclusion of an index that uses halakhic topics as its scheme reflects the self-contained and homogeneous nature of a printed work. In the typical Ashkenazi manuscript collection, responsa could be found alongside a plethora of other genres. However, *Terumat ha Deshen* includes only those texts that can be part of one continuous table of contents; all the material can be ordered within one continuous organizational scheme. The possibility of searching the work by means of a topically organized navigational aid signals accessibility to a wider scholarly public as it does not require prior acquaintance with the contents as they are arranged within a particular compilation.

Nowhere in *Terumat ha-deshen* is Rabbi Hiyah's intervention clearer than in the order of the responsa and the creation of the table of contents. As I noted earlier, the order of responsa in the printed *Terumat ha-deshen* does not resemble any of the preprint manuscript collections as the responsa circulated in manuscript in various haphazard orders, combinations, and forms. In the printed *Terumat ha-deshen*, Rabbi Hiyah ordered the contents topically, under a series of subject headings, starting with the laws of the *Shema* prayer, proceeding through the laws of prayers in general, blessings, festivals, and so on, and ending with the laws of testimony. The various subject headings are also grouped together under broader halakhic topics.

Moreover, the printed work is preceded by a table of contents, called 'signs' (*simanei Terumat ha-deshen*) that reflects the work's internal organization. The list provides a short description of every responsum, with headings and subheadings for the different halakhic topics. Since Rabbi Hiyah ordered the responsa by topic, the table of contents simultaneously serves as a topical index. No other work of responsa from Ashkenaz was organized in such a manner.

For *ShUT Maharyq*, Rabbi Hiyah likewise ordered entries and created a navigational aid.

---

84 Mary A. Rouse and Richard H. Rouse, *Authentic Witnesses: Approaches to Medieval Texts and Manuscripts* (Notre Dame, IN: Notre Dame University Press, 1991), p. 198.

He divided the different segments of responsa into what he called *shorashim* (roots),[85] and listed the *shorashim* in order of their appearance. He introduced the table of contents as follows:

יען כי אלו תשובות שאלות ארוכי׳ מארץ מדה ורחבם מני ים. ובכל תשובה ותשובה על הרוב נכלל בהם עניינים מועלים זולת המכוון מאותה התשובה. לכן עוררתי רעיוני ושנסתי את מתני. אני שפל המצב הקטן שבתלמידים חיא מאיר בכה״ר דוד זצ״ל. וירדתי לסוף עומק דעת כל תשובה ותשובה. כפי קוצר השגתי ומעוט שכלי ועשיתי מכל תשובה שורש אחד אשר עיקר תוכן התשובה בנויה עליו. וסעיפים המסתעפים ממנה ודינים אחרים אשר לא מעניין השאלה. העליתי על ספר בתכלית הקצור. יועילו מאד להוגים ומעייני׳ בספר זה. ויושגו מבוקשם זולת יגיע ועמל. והש״י יצילני משגיאות ויורני נפלאות תורתיו אכי״ר.

('Seeing as these responses to questions, 'their measure is longer than the earth and wider than the sea' [Job 11:9]. And in every responsum there are usually included useful issues apart from the one intended in the response originally. Therefore, I have awakened my inquisition and girded my loins. I, the lowly and the smallest among the students, Hiyah Meir son of his honour the rabbi David of blessed and pious memory. And I have inquired into the bottom of the depth of every single response, as much as my limited understanding and little mind permit, and I have made from every response one root on which the main part of the response is built. And the subsections that extend from it and the other laws that are not directly related to the question, I have placed in the book in the most succinct manner. It will be very useful for those perusing and examining this book. And they will find what they want without hard work and labour. And the Lord, may He be blessed, will save me from errors and show me the wonders of his Torah, Amen, so may be His will).[86]

Despite Rabbi Hiyah's decision to create these roots, he did not apply any consistent effort to the specific order in which these different roots were organized. On one hand, related or similar questions are often clustered together — for instance, a succession of roots all related to ritual slaughter[87] or a certain cluster addressed only textual problems from medieval sources.[88] On the other hand, similar topics that could easily have fit within those groups recur outside of the clusters.[89] Rabbi Hiyah's remarkable editorial intervention in this case was not evident in the reordering of the sequence of the responsa or even placing only his list of the roots in an intuitive sequence to create an index, as he had done for *Terumat ha-deshen*. Nevertheless, he elevated a collection of letters written to answer contingent issues to general roots, principles of halakhah.

Rabbi Hiyah's focus on organization points to the possibilities — and limitations — of print versus manuscript transmission. Manuscript collections allowed for a personal selection of specific responsa to be copied in whatever form and order was desirable. The printed order, in contrast, implies an expectation that this set group of responsa would be transmitted in a stable order, without the possibility of adapting or personalizing their selection and arrangement. Moreover, by presenting responsa as general roots, Rabbi Hiyah emphasized

---

85 See Woolf, 'The Life and Responsa', p. 247.
86 Colon, *ShUT Maharyq*, introduction to table of contents, no pagination.
87 Colon, *ShUT Maharyq*, table of contents, roots #33–40.
88 Colon, *ShUT Maharyq*, table of contents, roots #59–62.
89 Colon, *ShUT Maharyq*, root #96, for instance, is also an explanation of a problem from one of the medieval sources discussed in roots #59–62; it could easily have been added there, but, instead, appears separately.

their importance as general legal principles of interest to all halakhic scholars to come, rather than as personal historical documents about specific occurrences. Thus, the most significant changes in the transmission of Ashkenazi halakhah resulted not from print alone, but from the editing of agents like Rabbi Hiyah who understood the new potential of print and actively selected and adapted works to accord with this potential. The following examples, one from *ShUT Maharyq* and the other from *Terumat ha-deshen*, make this clear.

Of Roots

The nature of Rabbi Hiyah's intervention in creating the list of roots in *ShUT Maharyq* can be illustrated most strongly by comparing them to an alternative list that also summarizes responsa by Rabbi Colon: the aforementioned *mafteah*. At first blush, this may seem very similar to the list of roots. The *mafteah*'s short summaries, like those of the roots, also include clusters of related topics. The *mafteah*, too, lacks consistent organization; topics reappear independently from the clusters where they would belong. But a closer look reveals deep differences. Apart from a few entries that show up in the same sequence in both lists, mainly because they were originally sections of the same question or very closely related,[90] there are few similarities between the order of Rabbi Hiyah's table of contents and that of the *mafteah*.

Not all the responsa in Rabbi Hiyah's edition are represented in the *mafteah*, but many of its entries do deal with the same laws as those in *ShUT Maharyq*, making it possible to compare them.[91] We would expect the summaries of these laws in the *mafteah* to resemble the corresponding entries in Rabbi Hiyah's table of contents, or his list of roots, since both summarize Rabbi Colon's responsa. But a comparison of the two shows subtle yet consistent differences that go straight to the heart of how Rabbi Hiyah's roots differed.

To illustrate this difference, consider the responsum under root 13 in the printed work. It concerns a husband who had forfeited his right to any of his wife's possessions but comes to regret it after she receives an inheritance. The letter's greeting and signature were retained, but the names of the couple involved were replaced by the generic names of the biblical couple Jacob and Rachel. The *mafteah* offers a brief summary of the case ('Concerning Jacob who wrote a document to Rachel his wife') followed by a summary of the decision: שטר הירושה הוא שטר חוב והוי בכלל נכסיה ומהם נסתלק לגמרי ('the will of her inheritance is a document of debt and this is included in her possessions, from which he completely forfeited his rights').[92]

Rabbi Hiyah's table of contents, by contrast, formulates the response in more general prescriptive terms: הכותב שטר סילוק בשעת החופה מסולק ג"כ משטר ירוש' שעשה האב לבתו בשעת חופה ('He who writes a document of forfeiture at the time of the marriage also forfeits his rights to the will of her inheritance that the father made for his daughter at the time of marriage'). On the next line of the table of contents (under the same root number), Rabbi Hiyah added a further — and even more general — conclusion: האומר נכסי לפלוני גם השטרות בכלל ('He who says "my

---

90 For example, the equivalents of Colon, *ShUT Maharyq*, roots #113a and 113b in the table of contents also follow one another in the *mafteah*.

91 Many conclusions in the *mafteah* have no equivalent in the printed responsa, but many others do. The number of conclusions, 311, versus the number of roots, 195, in the printed responsa should not be too misleading, as often more than one conclusion is derived from one 'root'.

92 See *mafteah*, Colon, *Maharyq hadashim*, p. 310 note 223 (§128).

possessions go to so-and-so", this also includes all documents').[93]

Such differences in formulation run consistently throughout both documents. All the *mafteah* entries use a succinct, specific paraphrase that focuses on the final decision, whereas all the roots in the table of contents distil and generalize, focusing on the broader laws in play. This accentuates the difference in purpose between the *mafteah* and Rabbi Hiyah's list of roots. The purpose of the table of roots was to extract and highlight the more general laws discussed within the book; thus, its most common formulation is *u-vo yevo'ar* ('and herein will be elucidated'). The *mafteah*, in contrast, was designed to provide a paraphrase of Rabbi Colon's ruling in a certain situation; its most common opening statement is *be'inyan* or *'al dvar* ('concerning'), followed by a short description of the specific case and the decision. The *mafteah* summarizes Rabbi Colon's decisions and was meant to be a stand-alone list, and it is similar to a list of *psaqim*, or 'halakhic rulings'. Lists of *psaqim*, found in many Ashkenazi manuscript collections, note the decisions made by an authority without explaining the reasoning. Rabbi Hiyah's table of contents, by contrast, was designed to be used together with the book to serve as search tool and highlight the general relevance of the collection and the wide range of halakhic topics to which it contributes.

This difference in purpose accounts for many of the discrepancies between the two lists. When a number of different laws concerning very different topics are addressed in one responsum, they appear as different subsections of the same 'root' in Rabbi Hiyah's table of contents. This is consistent with their use as navigational aids. For the *mafteah*, it was irrelevant whether different decisions had once been part of the same responsum. The only relevant concern was whether the decisions were Rabbi Colon's final rulings. Thus, in the *mafteah*, if rulings about disparate topics followed from one responsum, the respective records of these different rulings were often no longer adjacent to one another. They were separated and placed near other entries that dealt with similar topics. In this way, the manuscript *mafteah* was more organized than the printed table of contents, as it had a different purpose. In that sense, superior organization is not an inherent essence solely of the printed work, but is a quality that can pertain equally to manuscripts. Organization follows the intended purpose of a work. In printed books, which have to be easy to search for a wider group of potential readers previously unfamiliar with the work, it can be achieved by rearranging the contents. But it can also be attained in a list such as the roots.

These lists were not merely summaries of a larger text; the way in which they summarized would transform the text into a product in line with its intended goal. The *mafteah*, a traditional list of *pesaqim* that circulated in manuscript, was meant to be used independently as a record of a rabbi's decisions. Thus, it transformed Rabbi Colon's responsa into a record of his rulings. Rabbi Hiyah's list, by contrast, served as an accompaniment to the printed work, both as a practical navigational aid and as a way of emphasizing the general legal applications of the collection of the rabbi's halakhic writings. It thereby transformed an archive of correspondence into a series of important halakhic principles. But the creation of the roots goes deeper than a mere navigational aid. The table of contents, comprising the first pages of the printed book, effectively highlight the relevance of responsa for general halakhic study, presenting them to a potential buyer as

---

93 See Colon, *Maharyq hadashim*, pp. 261–329 for list of *simanim*.

סימן קכח — על דבר יעקב שכתב שטר סלוק לרחל אשתו ... שטר הירושה הוא שטר חוב והוי בכלל נכסיה ומהם נסתלק לגמרי

Colon, *ShUT Maharyq*, table of contents, #128: Concerning Jacob who wrote a document of forfeit to Rachel his wife... the will is a document of debt and is included in her overall assets, and from those he withdrew completely.

general roots rather than as a random collection of an authority's specific decisions.

Rabbi Hiyah's primary intervention was to present these responsa as roots by distilling the halakhic principles of the laws derived directly from each responsum as well as the more tangential laws that emerged in the responsum process.[94] This intervention takes a random collection of specific responsa which started out as halakhic correspondence and continued to be circulated in a variety of manuscript forms and contexts and highlights its its potential for more general uses. What had been a collection of individual cases became a series of roots, precedents for something larger. If the status of the manuscript responsa was unclear — whether they were the documentary remnants of temporal matters or precedents meant for posterity — printing them sealed their fate. Similarly unresolved was and is the question of authority initiated by such responsa: are responsa sources for future adjudication? Or does their contingent past (their emergence out of an actual situation with its own specificities) render them less preferable than texts written explicitly as general legal interpretations? By formulating Rabbi Colon's responsa as roots on the title page, Rabbi Hiyah took a stance on the matter. He seems to have thought that the best way to present this collection of responsa was to downplay their role as solutions to one-time occurrences and to emphasize instead their importance as legal principles.

---

94 It may be interesting to consider the use of roots in legal decisions of sixteenth-century rabbis in Italy, such as Rabbi Yehiel Nissim da Pisa (*c.* 1493–before 1572). In some of their halakhic writings, roots are used in a scholastic manner to set out the basic truths of a halakhic problem before arriving at a solution using logical deduction based on those roots. See Reuven (Robert) Bonfil, *The Rabbinate in Italy during the Renaissance* [in Hebrew] (Jerusalem: Magnes Press, 1979), pp. 162–63. Perhaps the decision to call the table of contents roots is a way of implying that these responsa can be used as a basis for further halakhic/scholastic reasoning.

Of Signs

Even for a collection as edited, complete, and easily adaptable to print as *Terumat ha-deshen*, the transition from manuscript collection to printed book required some considerable work. As the variety of extant manuscript collections indicates, the responsa had circulated in many forms apart from this 'official' collection before they appeared in print. The printed *Terumat ha-deshen* was the product of extensive reorganization to shape it into a work that showcased its most attractive possibilities of print.

In this section, I use one example to track how material from multiple responsa made it into manuscript collections of Rabbi Isserlein's writings and eventually appeared in one place within Rabbi Hiyah's newly organized *Terumat ha-deshen* and its navigation aid. Next, I compare *Terumat ha-deshen* to another collection of Rabbi Isserlein's responsa known as *Pesaqim u-ketavim*, which, as I noted, was published at the same time. Together, these two inquiries yield insight into R. Hiyah's organizational enterprise and its limitations.

Rabbi Isserlein devoted several responsa to the topic of firstborn cattle, which had been consecrated for the *kohanim* ('the priestly caste'). In the days of the Temple, a firstborn animal would be sacrificed, and the priest would keep some of its flesh. But what should be done with these animals in post-Temple times? Several legal solutions existed, but there were cases where these solutions were overlooked, resulting in consecrated firstlings. Many Jewish communities, especially in Ashkenaz, tended to err on the side of caution and gave these animals to a Jew of priestly descent. On the one hand, these descendants of priests could not sacrifice the animal, but, on the other, they were not permitted to derive any material benefit from these consecrated beasts. As a result, these priestly 'gifts' turned out to be burdens.

Among the many fifteenth-century authorities who tried to resolve this impasse, Rabbi Isserlein was the most innovative. He launched an inquiry to prove that cows never lactated before giving birth — without exception. If he could establish this fact, he could declare any animal born to a lactating mother as definitely not a firstling. Rabbi Isserlein initiated oral and written inquiries, asking if anyone had ever encountered a lactating cow that had never calved. After assembling the data, he developed a legal structure that would allow him to dismiss any calves of lactating cows from firstling status. Finally, he ended up retracting his argument somewhat because he realized that Rabbi Meir of Rothenburg, an earlier authority, would have opposed it. These stages of Rabbi Isserlein's research and scholarship appear in different forms across his writings.

The responsum on firstling calves was printed as entry number 271 in Bomberg's *Terumat ha-deshen*, easily retrievable in Rabbi Hiyah's table of contents as the fifth and final entry under the subtitle דיני פדיון הבן ופדיון בכור ('laws of redeeming the son and redeeming firstborns'). This section is to be found among דיני מילה ('the laws of circumcision'), which give way to דיני פדיון הבן ('the redeeming of the firstborn son'), דיני הקדש וחרמות ונדרים ותקנות ('the laws of consecration and vows and ordinances'), and other related issues, which connect nicely to the topic of sanctified firstling cattle. These three subtitles, each containing a reference to a handful of entries, can be easily surveyed as they are all in the same column, and the responsum in question can be located without too much effort. But how did these responsa get there?

In *Leqet yosher*, too, we find material that echoes the responsa in *Terumat ha-deshen*, but in far rougher form. Responsum 271 in *Terumat ha-deshen* addresses the permissibility of keeping a calf born to a lactating cow with an uncertain birth history. In the concise, clean, halakhic responsum, Rabbi Isserlein declared that such cows rarely lactate before giving birth, so the calf can be presumed not to be a firstling. He explained that he arrived at this information through inquiries. *Leqet yosher*, by contrast, features a similar responsum, but it also includes some of those inquiry efforts. For instance, Rabbi Isserlein's request to a colleague is included:

במטותא מינך תדרוש ותבקש לדרוש בכל גבולך מיהודאים וארמאים אם ימצא שום איש או אשה שראו מימיהם שום פרה שהיתה חולבת קודם שילדה מעולם, ומה שתעלה בידך הודיעני עי״מ

(I beg of you, inquire, and ask [others] to inquire in your whole territory from Jews and non-Jews [lit. Aramaeans] if there can be found any man or woman who ever saw in their lifetimes any cow that was producing milk before ever having given birth, and inform me about that which you find out by means of a letter).[95]

The correspondence represents the raw research material that was, at some point, copied into a collection that became *Leqet yosher*.

Some of the same material was worked into *Terumat ha-deshen* and copied in that manuscript, but in a different form and order. Many remnants of the original correspondence had already been removed, streamlined, or generalized into a standardized responsum: the personal tone of the request is gone. Moreover, Rabbi Isserlein's final hesitation and partial retraction of the

---

95 This is Rabbi Isserlein's responsum to the responsum of Rabbi Moses Mintz, *ShUT Maharam Mintz* §34. Rabbi Isserlein's response is collected both in *Pesaqim u-ketavim* §167 and in *Leqet yosher*, quoting here from *Leqet yosher*, p. 131. These compilations included, among other material, copies from their master's correspondence. *Terumat ha-deshen* does not include the remark requesting that Rabbi Mintz confer with others. We do, however, find frequent mention of Rabbi Isserlein's own inquiries, both in *Terumat ha-deshen* and elsewhere, which is in line with the work's style removing personal epistolary elements.

legal conclusion is most clearly only in *Terumat ha-deshen*. There, the responsum is formulated as a general one and included in manuscript collections that many in Rabbi Isserlein's time already thought of as a 'book', perhaps already one of 354 entries. Finally, Rabbi Hiyah used manuscript collections such as these, edited, corrected, and rearranged them, and added the table of contents. Once printed, the responsum about the firstling calf could be found in its proper, easy-to-locate, spot.

How did Rabbi Hiyah create the topical order of *Terumat ha-deshen*? The topics and their order roughly resemble the order of the subjects as they appear in Rabbi Jacob ben Asher's (Cologne, c. 1269–Toledo, c. 1343) *'Arba'ah turim* ('Four columns'), first printed in Pieve di Sacco in 1475. Still, there are some differences.[96] *'Arba'ah turim* is a comprehensive collection of practical halakhah while whereas *Terumat ha-deshen*, as a collection of responsa, is by comparison much more fragmentary. Not all the sections that are featured in *'Arba'ah turim* are represented in *Terumat ha-deshen*.[97]

Fram has traced the way Rabbi Hiyah transformed the jumbled manuscript collection into an intuitively structured printed work, complete with navigation aids. Rabbi Hiyah organized the responsa by going through the order of the manuscript collection and beginning a new topic whenever necessary, placing subsequent responsa under existing topics as he encountered them. Thus, the first responsum in the manuscript,[98] one regarding the *Shema* prayer, became the first item in the first topic with its own subject heading; the first responsum in the manuscript regarding laws of blessings became the first item under that subject heading; and so on.[99] Having divided the responsa into subject headings, Rabbi Hiyah placed these headings in succession based on thematic association. It is not completely identical to the order of any other work because he did not follow the exact order of any particular work. Instead, he created his own order from scratch.[100] When he went through the manuscript collection of *Terumat ha-deshen* and arrived at a responsum about circumcision, he began a new subsection, to which he added responsa about related issues, such as redeeming firstborn babies, which led to laws about redeeming firstling cattle. In his table of contents, these laws also appear in succession.

Rabbi Hiyah greatly contributed to *Terumat ha-deshen*'s emergence as a book, but he did not print only this beautifully edited and organized collection. Along with *Terumat ha-deshen*, he also prepared *Pesaqim u-ketavim* for print. If the responsa in *Terumat ha-deshen* were carefully edited to appear clean and general, the material in *Pesaqim u-ketavim* was decidedly not. For instance, question §143 in *Terumat ha-deshen*, regarding a formulation in the prayer for Rosh ha-Shana, has a parallel in *Pesaqim u-ketavim*. In the latter, the questioner suggested his own theory about the correct prayer and exclaimed: 'and the whole form of the prayer before and after this I

---

96 See Avraham Haberman, 'The Labour of Print in Its Beginnings', in *Tractate on Authors and Literature* [in Hebrew] (Jerusalem: Rubin Mass, 1976), p. 277. *'Arba'ah turim* is a compilation of halakhic summaries, organized into four main books (prayer and holidays; dietary laws; family law; and damages and financial law), each organized internally according to smaller subtopics.

97 For example, the very first subject heading in *Terumat ha-deshen* relates to the *Shema* prayer, whereas the *Tur* begins with the laws of waking in the morning, ritual handwashing, dressing, etc., and arrives at the *Shema* prayer about sixty subjects later. Noting that the order in *Terumat ha-deshen* does not perfectly correspond to that of the *'Arba'ah turim*, Dinari conjectured that the order is a combination of *'Arba'ah turim* and the order of Maimonides' halakhic code *Mishne torah*. Fram, however, has shown the order of responsa in *Terumat ha-deshen* to be an original creation by Rabbi Hiyah.

98 JTS MS 7148 R1419.
99 Fram, *On the Order of the Responsa*, appendix 3.
100 Fram, *On the Order of the Responsa*, p. 84.

desire to know' וכל הנוסח מקודם ועד אחריו חפץ אני לדעת. The equivalent entry in *Terumat ha-deshen* is devoid of both the questioner's suggestion and his exclamation. A similar difference is also evident in the answer: in *Pesaqim u-ketavim*, Rabbi Isserlein mentioned a relevant personal experience, having heard a relative recite the prayer in a particular way, a point that was not included in *Terumat ha-deshen*. Such changes had the combined effect of converting *Terumat ha-deshen* from a haphazard, personal compilation into a more structured, edited, and accessible book, which allowed Rabbi Hiyah to organize the work in ways that collections such as *Pesaqim u-ketavim* seemed to resist. The latter collection was also furnished with a table of contents, but since Rabbi Hiyah did not rearrange the entries, it does nothing more than summarize the contents of the work itself.

Taken together, *Terumat ha-deshen* and *Pesaqim u-ketavim* show two sides of the same coin: the printed work results not merely from print technology, but from a combination of the pre-existing material and editorial intervention. The two works were printed in the same year and are frequently found bound together. Buyers, who often decided about binding, saw the two as complementary works. However, some copies are not so bound. The two works have separate title pages, and *Terumat ha-deshen* concludes with its own colophon emphasizing the work's *hashlamah* ('completion') no fewer than three times, thus pointing to the independent nature of the two works.[101]

In Conrad Gessner's subject index for classifying books, *Pandectarum sive Partitionum universalium* ('Pandect, or General Classification', Zurich, 1548), a section on Hebrew grammar is followed by a catalogue of Bomberg's books for sale in Venice.[102] In that list, '*Pesacim uchtauim, id est iudicia & epistolae*' ('that is, judgments and letters') is listed for sale for 1 lire (among the cheapest works on that page). *Terumat ha-deshen* is not mentioned (possibly because it was sold out), the individual listing implying that they were probably sold as separate works.[103] Perhaps this implies that Rabbi Hiyah's decision

---

101 Moreover, the signatures at the bottom of the leaves, which serve to direct the printers as to the order of the pages, are separate. In addition, the *reshimat simanim* ('index') of *Terumat ha-deshen* has its own signatures for the quires, implying that the index, too, may have been printed as a separate piece. *Terumat ha-deshen* ends with signature לא, and *Pesaqim u-ketavim* starts anew, from א, thus also indicating that they were printed as stand-alone works. In addition, the index of *Terumat ha-deshen* has its own signatures for the quires and appears in different places in the copies I have seen. (In the National Library of Israel copy, it appears after the title page before *Terumat ha-deshen* proper; in Gottesman's private copy, it appears after the work.) This is in contrast to the table of contents of *Pesaqim u-ketavim*, which seems to be part of the work itself, as the signatures continue from *Pesaqim u-ketavim* itself to the table of contents at the end. It is, perhaps, also significant that Gottesman's copy of *Terumat ha-deshen* is censored throughout, whereas *Pesaqim u-ketavim* is not, perhaps indicating that they were not originally bound together. I thank the Gottesman family for allowing me to examine their copy and Theodor Dunkelgrün for checking the Antwerp and Cambridge copies for me.
102 Gessner, *Pandectarum sive Partitionum universalium* (Zurich, 1548): 'Sequuntur libri aliquot hebraici Venetijs uenales, pretio quo singuli uenduntur adscripto monetae Venetae per libras & per solidos'. ('Here follow some Hebrew books for sale in Venice, with their individual prices in Venetian currency, in pounds and solidos').
103 Spelling as in the original. I thank Theodor Dunkelgrün for his help in examining this issue. See also Theodor Dunkelgrün, 'The Hebrew Library of a Renaissance Humanist: Andreas Masius and the Bibliography to his "Iosuae Imperatoris Historia" (1574), with a Latin Edition and an Annotated English Translation', in *Studia Rosenthaliana*, 42/43 (2010–11): pp. 197–252 (esp. p. 226 note 66). See also Aron Freiman, 'Daniel Bomberg's Buchverzeichnis', in *Zeitschrift für Hebräische Bibliographie*, 10 (1906), pp. 38–42. Steinschneider's catalogue of the Bodleian lists the two separately and adds 'cura Chijja Meir b. David' for *Trumat ha-deshen* ('Oblatio cineris'), but not for *Pesaqim u-ketavim* ('Decisiones et curia'). See Moritz Steinschneider, *Catalogus Librorum Hebraeorum in Bibliotheca Bodleiana* (Berlin: Friedländer, 1852–60), I, columns 1165–66.

to invest in rearranging *Terumat ha-deshen* was sound. Nevertheless, in 1519, the same Rabbi Hiyah who had so carefully organized *Terumat ha-deshen* and created the table of contents that doubled as an index, also printed the haphazard and incomplete *Pesaqim u-ketavim*.

In the conventional view, this transitional period has been imagined as an intermediary stage in a necessary progression from manuscript to print, a time in which increasingly more works were printed and the world of messy, personal, time-bound writings surely but steadily gave way to an ordered universe of generalized halakhic collections. As we have seen, however, the transition was meandering and anything but steady. While it changed almost everything about the way texts were transmitted, profoundly upsetting earlier assumptions, the new meanings accorded to these changes would then, as before, be driven by a combination of the cultural, the social, and the technological.

Conclusion: From Case to Precedent

These first two printings of Ashkenazi responsa, *Terumat ha-deshen* and *ShUT Maharyq*, signalled broader changes in the halakhic cultural landscape. Such works of responsa had always been copied in the personal context of a scholar's building his own manuscript collection or having it prepared especially for him. Now, those two works were being printed by a team, including Rabbi Hiyah, for use by a larger, anonymous audience. In the shift from manuscript to print, the newfound stability of the text invited further generalization and streamlining. Selecting what would make it into print (even the simple act of searching and collecting) pushed alternative manuscripts that had been circulating aside.

The editorial efforts required of Rabbi Hiyah in order to transform these manuscripts into printable works attest to the extent of the changes in question. Title pages, colophons, navigational aids, and other paratexts became standard. The navigational aids created by Rabbi Hiyah illustrate this: these aids were more efficient when they supplemented a stable text, and they were also more necessary when the collection would be read by a new audience rather than individuals already familiar with the documents. At the same time, however, lists such as the *mafteah* were still being written, and even Rabbi Hiyah himself printed *Pesaqim u-ketavim*, the disordered counterpart of *Terumat ha-deshen*, without too much intervention.

At this early point in the history of printing responsa, Rabbi Hiyah had already realized that print both enables and demands improved organization, even as the conventions for doing so were not yet obvious. In the case of *Terumat ha-deshen*, he emphasized the general nature of the work in the formulation of the questions, the set number of entries related to the title, and the degree of editing. He might very well have found that some of these elements were already present in the manuscripts before him. Recognizing this potential, he rearranged the order of the contents to make the succession of responsa easier to search and added a table of contents that doubled as an index. In the case of *ShUT Maharyq*, Rabbi Hiyah related the number of entries in the work to a verse, thus presenting the collection as a non-arbitrary selection. He created generalized roots without rethinking their arrangement, as he had in *Terumat ha-deshen*. No particular kind or degree of intervention had become standard.

Those two works bring to the fore some of the most striking possibilities that print had newly introduced. Rabbi Hiyah's rearrangement of the entries in *Terumat ha-deshen* according to halakhic topics illustrates a preoccupation with heuristic access for an anonymous potential readership. Whereas manuscript books often assumed a personal familiarity with the written material, the newly printed work was designed for an audience that was geographically widespread and unknown to the book's producers. Accordingly, a printed work has to be easy to navigate even for someone who is looking at the material for the very first time. The creation of the roots in *ShUT Maharyq* exemplifies the presentation these responsa as relevant to anyone interested in general legal principles, rather than the documentary remnants of rabbinic writings about very specific cases from the past.

Some considered the strength of responsa to be founded upon the origins of these texts in real cases. For such readers, a book's orderly appearance would only have weakened the work's stance. Others, however, preferred the work precisely because it gave the impression of being removed from the actual cases, painting an abstracted and generalized picture rather than reflecting a messy reality. As I noted, *Terumat ha-deshen* was the only Ashkenazi work from that period that Rabbi Joseph Qaro chose to include in his code. The Sephardi sage was partial to *Terumat ha-deshen* precisely because of its organized form. Noting a contradiction between *Terumat ha-deshen* and *Pesaqim u-ketavim*, he concluded: ולענין הלכה נראה דיש לסמוך על מה שכתב בספר תה״ד יותר מעל מה שכתב בכתביו דמה שאדם כותב בספר יותר מדקדק בו ממה שכותב בכתביו ('Halakhically, we should rely on what he wrote in the book *Terumat ha-deshen* more than on his writings [*ketavim*], because people are more meticulous about that which they write in a book than about that which they write in their writings').[104] The great codifier of sixteenth-century halakhah unambiguously preferred *Terumat ha-deshen*.

Rabbi Hiyah's editorial interventions in both of these works of responsa printed in Venice in 1519 represent an immense shift in halakhic culture for Ashkenaz. Traditionally, halakhic authority in Ashkenaz was firmly grounded in local custom, oral instruction, and (often personal and ad-hoc) rabbinic decisions. Manuscript traditions were likewise local, personal, disorganized, and fluid. This was especially so in regard to responsa, which were less general, less universal, and less organized than any other halakhic genre. The change also represents a shift to a different form of law, which would soon culminate in the printing of *Shulhan 'arukh* in the 1560s, a code that would come to include both Ashkenazi and Sephardi halakhah. Nothing represents the first stirrings of this change better than these responsa going from personal manuscript collections to rearranged books designed for anonymous readers and from individual cases to general roots.

Yet these first decades of the sixteenth century did not give rise to a simple transitional progression to a preordained result. Standards and expectations for printed works were slowly taking shape as more and more works came off the presses. *Terumat ha-deshen* was accompanied by *Pesaqim u-ketavim*, and the roots in *ShUT Maharyq* were not reordered. The next edition of *ShUT Maharyq* was printed in Cremona almost four decades later, in 1557. Its editors rearranged the original table of contents to correspond to the organization of Maimonides' code, the *Mishneh torah* ('Repetition of the Torah'), thereby transforming the table of contents into an index and saving the reader the trouble of poring through every single line of the table of contents.[105] Rabbi Hiyah's innovations — creating his own order for *Terumat ha-deshen* and inventing the roots for *ShUT Maharyq* — shows that these possibilities were still in the making; indeed, they were being made by printers and editors such as Rabbi Hiyah.

---

104 Qaro, *Beit Yosef, Orah hayim*, §263:16.

105 Jeffrey Woolf relates this to the centrality of Maimonides' code as the main text for halakhic study in Italy at the time: 'It is safe to conclude that the Cremona printers assumed that their potential customers turned first to Maimonides when studying Halacha, and then searched for responsa related on the question before them' (Woolf, 'The Life and Responsa', p. 118).

PART THREE

Reading

DALIA-RUTH HALPERIN

The Masorete and His Readers

A Relationship Obscured Now Rediscovered

Introduction

This chapter deals with the art of micrography, the unique Jewish scribal art that forms masoretic notes in Hebrew Bible manuscripts into visual elements. For a long time, researchers neglected the study of micrography, also known as *masora figurata*, as it was thought to be simply decorative. However, in recent decades, as scholars realized that one should actually read the forming text, micrography returned to focus in both Masorah studies and art history. This renewed scholarly interest has revealed significant and meaningful ties between the forming text and the images it shapes which attest to complex visual manipulations for exegetic purposes on the part of the Masoretes.

These new understandings led me to inquire as to the when and why scholars lost the thread, or rather the keys, that allowed them to understand the secret contents of this art. My approach deals with these questions through a survey of cultural history and the changing concepts in regard to masoretic studies that are associated with developments of the Hebrew book.

Borrowing from the idea of the *impresa* — a device that combines image and a text — alongside current readings of *ductus* as a way by which a viewer is led to engage within the art, I argue that micrography should be understood along similar lines. Understanding it as a visual riddle engaging the reader reconnects it to its historical context and place within Jewish thought and offers us new keys for learning and understanding the interrelationships of scribes and their implied readers.

Micrography / *Masora figurata*

The art of forming masoretic lists into decorative designs is a singular scribal Jewish art.[1] This art is known by two names: *masora figurata*, because its forming text is the Masorah, and *micrography*, owing to the miniscule script that creates these

---

1 On *masora figurata*, its art, and forming text, see Dalia-Ruth Halperin, 'Micrography of Hebrew Script and Art', in *Encyclopedia of Hebrew Language and Linguistics* (Leiden: Brill, 2013), pp. 636–41; Dalia-Ruth Halperin, 'Micrography' in *Encyclopedia of the Bible and Its Reception*, ed. by Constance M. Furey and others (Berlin and Boston: De Gruyter, 2020), XVIII; Judith Olszowy-Schlanger, 'The Hebrew Bible' in *The New Cambridge History of the Bible. Volume 2, From 600 to 1450*, ed. by Richard Marsden and E. Ann Matter (Cambridge: Cambridge University Press, 2012), pp. 29–31.

Dalia-Ruth Halperin • Talpiot College of Education, Holon, Israel

decorations. As I deal here with Bible manuscripts, I generally use the term *masora figurata*.

The Masorah, which was constructed to safeguard the biblical text from changes, is lexical. It includes vocalization, accentuation, cantillation, verse counts, notations of singular words, and the precise spelling of words (plene or defective orthography) and their proper pronunciation, as well as the number of times each word, with its specific spelling and accentuation, occurs in the Bible and its loci.

The Masoretic Text in any given Masoretic Bible manuscript incorporates the *masora qetanah/parva* ('small'), which is notated between the text columns and counts various words on the page, and the *masora gedolah/magna* ('great'), which is usually penned in the top and bottom margins of the page. The *masora magna* is the referral system to the *masora parva*. A good example can be seen on fol. 43ᵛ of NLI, MS Heb. 4°790, known as *Damascus Keter*, from Burgos/Toledo, 1260 (Figure 10.1, 10.1a).² Folio 43ᵛ begins with a text segment from Exodus 19:6 '[and ye shall be unto Me] a kingdom of priests, and a holy nation'. The first word of the second line in the top-right column of text וגוי ('and nation') is marked with a small circle above it. This functions as a sign that the word's appearance within Scripture is counted in the *masora parva*. The *dalet* in the right margin indicates that this word occurs four times within Scripture with this particular punctuation and cantillation. The first line of the *masora magna*, at the top of the page, includes the reference וגוי ד׳ וסימנהון ('and [holy] nation number four and their sign [loci of where the phrase is found]'). The masoretic lists in this manuscript are sometimes also shaped into various decorative shapes as, for instance,

on fol. 310ʳ, where they form an elaborate carpet page.³

Owing to its lexical nature, until recently, scholars generally considered the decorations formed by this text as simply adornments and on occasion even ascribed them to the Masorete's need to alleviate boredom while copying.⁴ Although some studies pointed to a connection between the *masora figurata* and the main text that it adorns, researchers tended to view these instances as rare phenomena in late medieval manuscripts and insisted that the texts employed to create the decorations were not meant to be read.⁵ The late Stanley Ferber even went so far as to claim that the search for meaningful connections among the decorative forms, their creating texts, and the texts they adorn was specious.⁶ Owing to this widespread conviction, *masora figurata* was never examined thoroughly and the relationship between the forming micrographic text and the

---

2 Katrin Kogman-Appel convincingly argues that the manuscript should be attributed to Toledo and not as commonly attributed to Burgos. See Katrin Kogman-Appel, *Jewish Book Art Between Islam and Christianity* (Leiden: Brill, 2004), 65–67.

3 The manuscript can be viewed on the Internet via KTIV, System no.: 000042438 https://web.nli.org.il/sites/nlis/en/manuscript [accessed in March 2022].

4 On the Masorah and masoretic list, see Aron Dotan, 'Masora's Contribution to Biblical Studies: Revival of an Ancient Tool', in *Vetus Testament Supplement*, 133 (2010), pp. 57–69 (p. 58); Israel Yeivin, *The Biblical Masorah* (Jerusalem: Academy of the Hebrew Language, 2003), pp. 60–92, 114; Yosef Ofer, *The Babylonian Masora of the Pentateuch: Its Principles and Methods* (Jerusalem: Academy of the Hebrew Language, 2001), pp. 36–38, 99–300, 111–13; David Stern, *The Jewish Bible: A Material History* (Seattle and London: University of Washington Press, 2017), pp. 68–86. On the attitudes towards this art form, see George Margoliouth, 'Hebrew Illuminated Manuscripts', *Jewish Quarterly Review*, 20 (1908), pp. 118–66 (p. 131); Jordan S. Penkower, 'The Development of the Masoretic Bible', in *The Jewish Study Bible*, ed. by Adelle Berlin and Marc Zvi Brettler, 2nd ed. [revised and expanded] (New York: Oxford University Press, 2014), pp. 2077–84 (p. 2162).

5 Gabrielle Sed-Rajna, *The Hebraic Bible* (Fribourg: Office du Livre, 1987), p. 135 and fig. 161.

6 Stanley Ferber, 'Micrography: A Jewish Art Form', *Journal of Jewish Art*, 3/4 (1977), pp. 12–24.

Figure 10.1. National Library of Israel, MS Heb 4°790, fol. 43ᵛ known as *Damascus Keter*, Toledo, 1260.

Figure 10.1a. National Library of Israel, MS Heb 4°790, fol. 43ᵛ, detail.

image it created was generally not considered in any depth.

In recent years, following Rachel Milstein's work on the *masora figurata* in Hebrew manuscripts from the Middle East and Northern Africa, which demonstrated that there was indeed a close connection between the micrography-creating texts and the decorations they formed,[7] a methodological change was suggested in regard to *masora figurata* and Masoretic Text in general. The assumption that took hold was that as masoretic notation and its manipulation into decoration was part of the scribal art tradition and as the raw material for this art is text, proper research methodology requires reading the micrographic text in its entirety. Owing to this new approach, scholars have recently been able to offer an answer to the question of why micrographers penned the Masoretic Text as visual shapes, which makes it so much more difficult to decipher.[8]

This new understanding of the role of *masora figurata* actually began with the change in the conception of marginal decorations in Gothic manuscripts. Contrary to their former classification as drollery, scholars have demonstrated that the images convey reciprocal relationships with the main text.[9] Further, it became clear that they functioned as visual aids to enhance and sharpen understanding of the adjacent text while simultaneously serving as mnemonic tools.[10]

Masorah figurata has been re-evaluated in this light in recent years and research has revealed similar features in regard to micrography decoration.[11]

The synergic associations between a forming text and the image it creates are more easily demonstrated in non-biblical manuscripts because the forming text is not created out of Masorah. A notable example is the *Catalan Micrography Mahzor* (Jerusalem, National Library of Israel [NLI], MS Heb. 8°6527).[12] The texts that form the micrography are primarily from Psalms and a tight connection can be demonstrated between the clusters of psalms chosen for the full-page

---

7 Rachel Milstein, 'Hebrew Book Illumination in the Fatamid Era', in *L'Egypte Fatamide son art et son histoire*, ed. by Marianne Barrucand (Paris: Presses de l'Université de Paris-Sorbonne, 1999), pp. 429–40.

8 Dalia-Ruth Halperin, *Illuminating in Micrography: The Catalan Micrography Mahzor MS Heb 8°6527 in the National Library of Israel* (Leiden: Brill, 2013), pp. 18–21.

9 Lillian Randall, *Images in the Margins of Gothic Manuscripts* (Berkley and Los Angeles: University of California Press, 1966); Michael Camile, *Image on the Edge: The Margins of Medieval Art* (Cambridge, UK, and London: Harvard University Press, 1992).

10 Mary Carruthers, *The Book of Memory: A Study of Memory in Medieval Culture*, (Cambridge: Cambridge University Press, 1990), pp. 221–30, 242–58; Stern, *The Jewish Bible*, pp. 80–82.

11 Éllodie Attia, *The Masorah of Elijah ha-Naqdan* (Berlin: De Gruyter, 2015); Hana Liss, *Corpus Masoreticum: The Inculturation of the Masorah into Jewish Law and Lore from the 11th to the 13th Centuries: Digital Acquisition of a Forgotten Domain of Knowledge*. Long-term project: 12 years (2018–29). German Research Foundation; Hanna Liss, 'Introduction: Editorial State of the Art of the Masoretic Corpus and Research Desiderata', in *Philology and Aesthetics: Figurative Masorah in Western European Manuscripts*, ed. by Hana Liss and Kay Petzold (Frankfurt a. Main: Peter Lang, 2021), pp. 5–25 (pp. 8–9, 16–17); Hanna Liss, 'Masorah as Counter-Crusade? The Use of Masoretic List Material in MS London, British Library Or. 2091', in *Philology and Aesthetics: Figurative Masorah in Western European Manuscripts*, ed. by Hana Liss and Kay Petzold (Frankfurt a. Main: Peter Lang, 2021), pp. 45–82; Halperin, *Illuminating in Micrography*; Milstein, 'Hebrew Book Illumination'; Sara Offenberg, *Up in Arms: Images of Knights and the Divine Chariot in Esoteric Ashkenazi Manuscripts of the Middle Ages* (Los Angeles: Cherub Press, 2019); Suzy Sitbon, 'L'espace, les formes dessinées par la letter, le texte dans les bibles hébraique espagnols de XIIIe siècle', in *Jewish Studies at the Turn of the Twentieth Century*, ed. by Judit Targarona Borrás and Angel Sáenz-Badillos (Leiden: Brill, 1999), II, pp. 163–68; Susan Lynn Schmidt, *The Carpet Illuminations of Codex Leningrad, National Library of Russia Ms. Evr. I B 19a* (unpublished PhD thesis, the University of the Holy Land, Ann Arbor MI, 2019); ProQuest Dissertation Repository # 27827878. On its relation to surrounding book culture, see Stern, *The Jewish Bible*, pp. 83–98, 105–16.

12 https://web.nli.org.il/sites/NLI/English/collections/treasures/shapell_manuscripts/pray/catalon/Pages/default.aspx [accessed in April 2020].

micrography and the images they form.[13] Loose ties between the micrographic and the main texts can also be seen in the *Rylands Haggadah*, dated between 1330 and 1350 (Manchester, John Rylands University Library, MS heb. 6), where the micrographic text was taken from the Rif's (Rabbi Isaac ben Jacob Alfasi, 1013–1103) commentary on the Babylonian Talmud, Tractate *Pesahim*. Here, the micrographic text that forms the decorative carpet bands in the margins relates only to the haggadah text and has no reciprocal ties to the images it forms.[14] The same features can also be seen in Bible manuscripts, where reading the micrography illuminates the manipulation of the Masoretic Texts to convey complex polemic and eschatological messages as well as reveal theosophical and esoteric concepts.[15]

An instance of the manipulation of the Masoretic Text can be seen in a Bible, now in the Vatican, Biblioteca apostolica (BAV), Cod. Urb. ebr. 1, dated to 1294 in the German Lands, where there is a singular figurative panel depicting a mounted falconer in a hunt scene on fol. 817ʳ. The main text on the page features the closing verses of Ecclesiastics (Figure 10.2), but the *masora magna* does not refer to the *masora parva* on the page. Rather, it was taken from the grammatical referral of Section 10 in *'Okhla ve-'okhla*,[16] which has nothing to do with the main text (Figure 10.3, line α).[17] Isaac beRabbi Simeon ha-Levi, the second Masorete who worked on this manuscript, skipped twelve Masorah pair counts and then continued his penning with the words 'The sceptre shall not depart from Judah, nor the ruler's staff from between'.[18] These words, which begin Genesis 49:10, are associated with a known eschatological commentary, which, as I have suggested elsewhere, was the basis for the

---

13   Other forming texts in the mahzor are a segment from the RIF's *Hilkhot Alfasi* on Babylonian Talmud, Tractate *Rosh ha-Shanah*, a segment from II Samuel 22–23:9, and two segments from a *baqashah* composed by the Rashba (Rabbi Solomon ibn Adret, Barcelona c. 1235–c. 1310). On this aspect in the *Catalan Micrography Mahzor*, see Halperin, *Illuminating in Micrography*, chap. 6.

14   *The Rylands Haggadah: A Medieval Sephardi Masterpiece in Facsimile – An Illuminated Passover Compendium from Mid-Fourteenth-Century Catalonia in the Collections of the John Rylands University Library of Manchester*, Introduction, Notes on the Illuminations, Transcription and English Translation by Raphael Loewe (New York: Abrams, 1988) See also https://openn.library.upenn.edu/Data/0021/html/HebrewMss6.html [accessed in April 2020].

15   Hanna Liss, 'Masorah as Counter-Crusade? The Use of Masoretic List Material in MS London, British Library Or. 2091', in *Philology and Aesthetics* (Frankfurt a. Main: Peter Lang, 2020), pp. 45–86; Halperin, *Illuminating in Micrography*, chap. 6; Dalia-Ruth Halperin, 'The Three Riders: The Apocalypse in the Figured Micrography of BL Add. 21160', *Journal of Jewish Studies*, 69 (2018), pp. 340–73; Dalia-Ruth Halperin, 'Micrography Mounted Falconers: An Exegetic Text and Image' in *Philology and Aesthetics* (Frankfurt a. Main: Peter Lang: 2020), pp. 59–101; Sara Offenberg, 'A Jewish Knight in Shining Armor: Messianic Narrative and Imagination', in *Ashkenazic Illuminated Manuscripts: University of Toronto Journal of Jewish Thought*, 4 (2014), pp. 1–14; Sara Offenberg, 'Jacob the Knight in Ezekiel's Chariot:

Imagined Identity in a Micrography Decoration of an Ashkenazic Bible', *AJS Review*, 40.1 (2016), pp. 1–16; Offenberg, *Up in Arms*, pp. 85–109; Sara Offenberg, 'Illustrated Secret' Esoteric Traditions in the Micrography Decoration of Erfurt Bible 2 (SBB MS Or. fol. 1212)', in *Philology and Aesthetics* (Frankfurt a. Main: Peter Lang: 2021), pp. 105–26; Sitbon, 'L'espace'.

16   An anonymous masoretic compilation estimated to be from the tenth century, takes its title from the first two words of the opening passage: 'eating' (1 Sam. 1:9) and 'and eat' (Gen. 27:19). The compilation contains biblical word lists arranged according to various similarities of grammatical features.

17   א״ב מן חד וחד חד א׳ וחד לא׳ דלוג ול דכותה׳ וסימניהון ('Alphabetical [list of words that] occur once with and once without a *lamed* prefixed to it'); see Paris, Bibliothèque nationale de France, MS Héb. 148, fol. 14ᵛ; Solomon Frensdorff, *Das Buch Okhla we'Okhla* (Hannover: Hahn'sche Buchhandlung, 1864), p. 18.

18   The Masorete used the first six words of the full verse לא יסור שבט מיהודה ומחוקק מבין. The full verse reads: לֹא-יָסוּר שֵׁבֶט מִיהוּדָה, וּמְחֹקֵק מִבֵּין רַגְלָיו, עַד כִּי-יָבֹא שִׁילֹה, וְלוֹ יִקְּהַת עַמִּים ('The sceptre shall not depart from Judah, nor the ruler's staff from between his feet, as long as men come to Shiloh; and unto him shall the obedience of the peoples be').

Figure 10.2. Vatican, Biblioteca apostolica, Cod. Urb. ebr. 1, fol. 817ʳ.

THE MASORETE AND HIS READERS 233

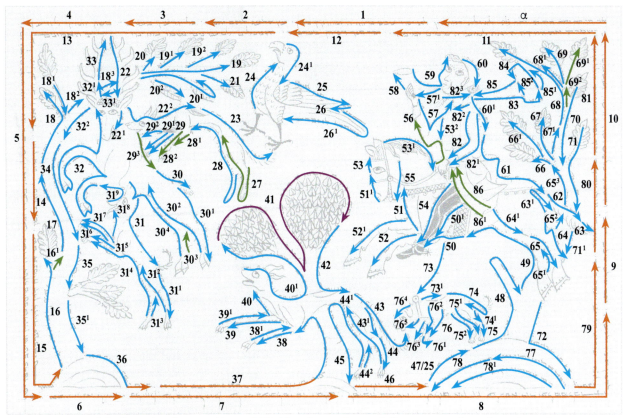

Color Separation: **Orange** – Frames; **Light blue** – Image; **Green** – Indicates a repeated use of a previous reference; **Purple** – A verse not found within the *Okhla we'Okhla* lists

Figure 10.3. Text flow of *masora figurata* on Vatican, Biblioteca apostolica, Urb. ebr. 1, fol. 817ʳ.

Masorete's choice and indicates a meaningful act of editing related to the image and the final verse in Ecclesiastes.[19]

---

19 Onqelos on Genesis 49:10 is a translation that deviates from his usual plain linguistic translation: לָא יֶעְדֵּי עָבֵיד שׁוּלְטָן מִדְּבֵית יְהוּדָה וְסָפְרָא מִבְּנֵי בְנוֹהִי עַד עָלְמָא עַד דְּיֵיתֵי מְשִׁיחָא דְּדִילֵיהּ הִיא מַלְכוּתָא וְלֵיהּ יִשְׁתַּמְעוּן עַמְמַיָּא. ('Kings shall not cease, nor rulers, from the house of Jehuda, nor sapherim [scribes DRH] teaching the law from his seed, till the time that the King the Messiah, shall come, the youngest of his sons; and on account of him shall the peoples flow together. How beauteous is the King, the Messiah who will arise from the house of Jehuda! He hath girded his loins, and descended, and arrayed the battle against his adversaries, slaying kings with their rulers; neither is there any king

A careful reading of the masoretic list choices while taking account of the iconography of the image they form elucidates the synergic ties between the forming text and the image as well as between the final message about obeying God's edicts as described in the last verses of Ecclesiastes. As BAV, Cod. Urb. ebr. 1 is dated to 1294 in

---

or ruler who shall stand before him'): see John W. Etheridge, *The Targums of Onkelos and Jonathan Ben Uziel on the Pentateuch with Fragments of the Jerusalem Targum from the Chaldee* (London: Longman and Roberts, 1862): http://targum.info/targumic-texts/pentateuchal-targumim/ [accessed in March 2020]. On this decoration, see Halperin, 'Micrography Mounted Falconers'.

the German Lands, it is very likely that it was primarily the approaching time of the redemption according to the Tosafist's calculations, which were based on Daniel 12:11–12. According to those calculations, which were based not on the end of the Jewish millennium in the year 1240, as was common in Ashkenaz, but rather on the renewal of Temple worship, the Messiah son of Joseph, who was to begin the process of redemption was to come in 1352 or 1358.[20] It is possible that it was this date, but a few decades away from the time that Isaac beRabbi Simeon ha-Levi penned this image, that prompted the creation of this messianic rider and the choice of forming text, which calls for repentance. The encapsulated message might very well have been designed to engage readers in a visual and textual deciphering regarding the projected imminent redemption of Israel.[21]

Manuscripts from the Iberian Peninsula reflect ties between the Masoretic Text and the image it forms, albeit at times without any strong correlation with the main text. One example in which we observe this feature is a fourteenth-century Bible, now in Jerusalem (NLI, MS Heb. 8°2221), known as the *Abrahm of Butera Bible* (fol. 162ʳ, Figure 10.4). The *masora magna* two referrals begin at the top of the page with the words נחש הנחשת ב ('the serpent of brass') (Num. 21:9; II Kings 18:4). The micrography text is figured into a snake — a direct correlation with the forming and the main texts. However, the two snakes on the outer margins do not relate to the Masoretic Text and the image it forms; rather they are just pictorial echoes of the subject of the main text on the page and the large serpentine figure on the top.[22]

Such a loose tie between the micrographic text and the image it shapes and the main text penned on the page can also be seen in a Bible, now in Paris (Bibliothèque nationale de France, MS héb. 20), a work by Joshua ibn Gaon, dated to 1300 in Tudela, in which there are several instances of associations between the *masora figurata* texts and the images they create. For example, the dragon on fol. 13ʳ is not related to the micrography text, whereas the image at the bottom of fol. 170ʳ bears a direct relationship to its forming text (Figure 10.5). However, the latter image was not formed by Masoretic Text but from verses taken from the main text.[23]

If such synergic ties can be shown to exist in *masora figurata*, why did researchers up to the end of the twentieth century contend that there is no connection between the decoration and the

---

20 The Tosafists were a rabbinic school that began with Rashi's grandchildren in France in the twelfth century and stretched to the German Lands. The Tosafists composed critical and explanatory glosses to the Talmud. For their commentary, see Gellis, *Sefer tosafot ha-shalem*. On their redemption concepts, see Ephraim Kanarfogel, 'Ashkenazic Messianic Calculations from Rashi and His Generation through the Tosafist Period', in *Rashi: The Man and His Work II: Rashi's Sources and His Influence*, ed. by Avraham Grossman and Sara Japhet (Jerusalem: Merkaz Zalman Shazar, 2008), II, pp. 381–401; David Berger, 'Three Typological Themes in Early Jewish Messianism: Messiah Son of Joseph, Rabbinic Calculations, and the Figure of Armilus' in *AJS Review*, 10/2 (1985), pp. 141–64 (pp. 151–52, 162–63).

21 On esoteric concepts in Ashkenazi *masora figurata*, see also Dalia-Ruth Halperin, 'The Three Riders: The Apocalypse in the Figured Micrography of BL Add. 21160', *Journal for Jewish Studies*, 69/2 (2018), 340–73; Liss, 'Masorah as Counter-Crusade'; Offenberg, *Up in Arms*; Offenberg, 'Illustrated Secret'.

22 The assortment of masoretic list words are ותקצר ('became impatient'), רב ('many').

23 In a Bible manuscript produced in Italy at the end of the fourteenth century by a Sefardi immigrant, *masora figurata* relating to the text can be found side by side with texts from psalms, verses from the main biblical text, and proverbs of wisdom and ethics: see Shlomo Zucker, *Exhibition of Torah Scrolls and Tanach Books belonging to the Syrian Community*, ed. by Rafi Weiser and Rivka Plesser, Beit HaNasi (14 November 2000) [in Hebrew] (Jerusalem: n.p., 2000), pp. 9–10.

Figure 10.4. National Library of Israel, Heb. 8°2221, fol. 162 known as *Abrahm of Butera Bible*.

Figure 10.5. Paris, BnF, hébr. 20, fols 13ʳ and 170ʳ, Tudela 1300.

adorned text in most micrography?²⁴ One obvious reason might well have been the miniscule size of the script, which was a serious impediment to reading the micrography in its entirety. These decorations are formed in letters that are never larger than a few millimetres high, and in some of the works from the Iberian Peninsula they are even smaller, measuring no more than one millimetre. It is often nearly impossible to read this tiny writing directly from the manuscript without considerable magnification. The difficulty is further exacerbated by the inevitable wear and tear over the years, which has caused the ink to fade. The technical means at our disposal today, including high-resolution digital scanning of the manuscript and graphical computer programming, which allows us to enlarge the script without significant distortion, sharpen the images, heighten

---

24 Although some of the creating texts were partially read or sampled in connection with various studies of individual decorations, to date most scholars have not yet read the micrographic texts. See Leila Avrin 'The Mocatta Haggadah and Other Works by the Master of the Catalan Mahzor', in *Hebrew Studies – Papers presented at a Colloquium on Resources for Hebraica in Europe, held at the School of Oriental and African Studies*, University of London, 11–13 September 1989/11–13 Elul 5749, ed. by D. Rowland Smith and P. S. Salinger (London: 1991), pp. 139–48; Milstein, 'Hebrew Book Illumination'; *The Rylands Haggadah*, pp. 22–20. For the concept that no ties exist, see Olszowy-Schlanger, 'The Hebrew Bible', p. 39; Penkower, 'The Development of the Masoretic Bible', p. 2162.

the contrast, reverse the colours of the writing and the parchment background, and repeatedly rotate the image for ease of reading, facilitate the research. Moreover, although the sheer extent of the text makes deciphering it a laborious process, today's various literary databases provide tools for rapid retrieval of relevant texts.

Physical impediments aside, other reasons for not believing that this art form created from script, that is, a scribal art, features any links among the forming Masoretic Texts, the images they create, and the main texts that they adorn were the variations among masoretic lists in the various Masoretic Bible manuscripts and some evidence of copying errors.[25] However, we must note that although the Masoretic Text was never codified and no two Masoretic Bibles have identical lists of Masorah, these variants are true of only a few plene pairs.[26] Thus, these copying errors may not necessarily indicate a lack of care on the part of the copyist or an absence of inherent synergic meaning between the Masoretic Texts and the images they form. These faults could have been due to known scribal copying errors that appear in the writing flow which are a result of visual and/or memory snares owing to the technical difficulty involved in dealing with such complex and copious texts. Among such snares are 'skips between similars', which include homoeoteleutons, homoearctons, and 'ashgaras.[27] Some of the above may well have been cogent reasons for scholars to have negated the notion that *masora figurata* reflects such intertextual and synergic ties between its texts and images, but it is clear that the loss of the keys for the understanding of micrography came about with the advent of printing.

Masorah in the Early Print Era

The introduction of printing in the West had a revolutionary impact on book production: it increased standardization, fixation, and the preservation of texts and brought about a tremendous surge in circulation.[28] With the founding of the renowned Soncino Press in the Duchy of Milan, Italy became a major centre for Jewish printing and the production of incunabula.[29] In

---

25 David Stern, 'The Rabbinic Bible in its Sixteenth Century Context', in *The Hebrew Book in Early Modern Italy*, ed. by Adam Shear and Joseph Hacker (Philadelphia: University of Pennsylvania Press, 2011), pp. 76–108 (p. 81).

26 As far as spelling (*ketiv*) is concerned, the biblical wording is in full agreement with the Masorah annotations. However, there are differences among those lists in connection with punctuation and cantillation: Stern, 'The Rabbinic Bible', 108.

27 Malachi Beit-Arié, 'Publication and Reproduction of Literary Texts in Medieval Jewish Civilization: Jewish Scribability and Its Impact on the Texts Transmitted', in *Transmitting Jewish Traditions: Orality, Textuality and Cultural Diffusion*, ed. by Yaakov Elman and Israel Gershoni (New Haven and London: Yale University Press, 2000), pp. 231–34; Halperin, *Illuminating in Micrography*, pp. 128–29; Leighton D. Reynolds and Nigel G. Wilson, *Scribes and Scholars*, 3rd Ed. (Oxford: Oxford University Press, 1991), pp. 222–23, 226; Martin West, *Textual Criticism and Editorial Technique* (Stuttgart: Teubner, 1973), pp. 20–21; Avishai Yorav, 'Serial Norms for the Comparison of Textual Versions: First Steps toward a Philological-Phylogenetic-Mechanized Method' [in Hebrew], *Da'at* — a site for Jewish and Liberal Arts Studies, Gush Ezion: Herzog College, http://www.daat.ac.il/daat/toshba/mechkar/norma-2.htm http://www.daat.ac.il/daat/toshba/mechkar/norma1-2.htm, sections 2a–b. On the word '*ashgara* ('fluency, routine'), see also the definition in the Even-Shoshan *Dictionary of Hebrew Language*, 12th Ed. (Jerusalem: Qiryat Sefer, 1965).

28 Stern, 'The Rabbinic Bible', pp. 137–38.

29 The Soncino family arrived in northern Italy, apparently from Speyer, in the middle of the fourteenth century. Israel ben Samuel (the father of Joshua Moses and the grandfather of Gershon) set up a Hebrew printing press in Soncino in 1483 and published his first work, the Tractate *Berakhot*, in 1484. In the years between 1521 and 1526, the press moved to several different cities, including Soncino, Casal Maggiore, Naples, Brescia,

the early sixteenth century, the hub of Hebrew book printing shifted to Venice when Daniel Bomberg, a Christian who arrived from Antwerp in 1515, launched a Hebrew press with his partner, an apostate Jew known only by the Christian name Felix Pratensis. Their publications played a significant role in turning Venice into the most important centre of Jewish printing until the eighteenth century.[30]

The first edition of the *Rabbinic Bible*, undoubtedly one of their principal publications, was published in 1517 (hereafter RB 1517) with Pratensis as the editor. As noted by Jordan Penkower, this was the first genuine print edition of the Hebrew Bible,[31] as well as the first complete edition to contain an Aramaic Targum and a medieval Jewish commentary on every book of the Bible.[32] Only eight years later, Jacob ben Hayyim ben Isaac ibn Adonijah (c. 1470–c. 1538), a kabbalist, Talmudist, and Masorah scholar, who was a proofreader and editor at the Bomberg Hebrew press, convinced Bomberg to create a second edition that would incorporate the Masorah because of its importance as a way of maintaining the correct biblical text and correcting the mistakes he found in the first RB edition. Another point proffered for this new edition was the idea that the Masorah was thought to harbour kabbalistic secrets. Bomberg was also interested in these issues, as he saw them appealing to his Christian Hebraist readership as well as to his own personal interest in Christian Kabbalah. Thus this new edition included the *masora parva* and *masora magna* on each page of text. Ben Hayyim incorporated the *masora magna* annotations for which he could not find room on those pages along with the extensive Masorah list found at the end of Sefardi Bible manuscripts in an alphabetical concordance at the end of the last volume, creating a list that became known as the *masora finalis*.[33]

Ben Hayyim's detailed introduction, which was also the first printed treatise on Masorah, and the edited Masorah corpus led to this edition becoming an authoritative text in the Jewish world and its Masoretic Text became 'canonical' in all later editions.[34] The second Bomberg edition of the *Rabbinic Bible* printed in 1524–1525 (hereafter RB 1525), which was edited based on Sefardi manuscripts, was thought to represent the accurate Aleppo Codex of the Ben Asher tradition and Sefardi Bible text study, an approach that was generally based on philological and grammatical considerations.[35] The impetus for editing and adding the Masorah text to RB 1525

Barco, Fano, and Pesaro and Rimini: see https://www.jewishencyclopedia.com/articles/13914-soncino [accessed in April 2020].

30 Emile Schrijver, 'Jewish Book Culture Since the Invention of Printing (1469–c. 1815)', in *The Cambridge History of Judaism*, ed. by Jonathan Karp and Adam Sutcliffe (Cambridge: Cambridge University Press, 2017), pp. 295–96. Emile Schrijver, 'The Hebraic Book', in *A Companion to the History of the Book*, ed. by Simon Eliot and Jonathan Rose (Oxford: Blackwell Companions to Literature and Culture, 2007), pp. 156–57.

31 Stern, 'The Rabbinic Bible', pp. 78–81; Stern, *The Jewish Bible*, pp. 142–47; Jordan S. Penkower, 'Jacob ben Hayyim and the Rise of Biblia Rabbanica' [in Hebrew] (unpublished PhD thesis, the Hebrew University of Jerusalem 1982).

32 On the contents of the RB 1517, see Stern, 'The Rabbinic Bible', pp. 81–83 note 24; Stern, *The Jewish Bible*, pp. 142–47.

33 Jordan S. Penkower, entry: Ben Asher, Aaron Ben Moses, in *Dictionary of Biblical Interpretation*, ed. by John H. Hayes (Nashville: Abingdon Press, 1999), II, pp. 361–63 and entry for Ben Hayyim; Stern, 'The Rabbinic Bible', pp. 81, 83–88; Stern *The Jewish Bible*, pp. 150–51.

34 Stern, *The Jewish Bible*, p. 150.

35 Penkower, entry: Ben Asher, I, pp. 118–19, II, pp. 362–63; Penkower, 'The Development of the Masoretic Bible', p. 2162; Stern, 'The Rabbinic Bible', p. 83; Stern, *The Jewish Bible*, pp. 91, 150; Nahum M. Sarna, 'Hebrew and Bible Studies in Medieval Spain', in *The Sephardi Heritage*, ed. by Richard D. Barnett (London: Vallentine and Mitchell, 1971), I, pp. 338, 345; 'Jacob ben Ḥayyim ben Isaac ibn Adonijah' in *Encyclopaedia Judaica*: https://www.encyclopedia.com [accessed in March 2020].

was its importance for preserving the biblical text, punctuation, and vocalization. However, Ben Hayyim noted in his introduction to RB 1525 that the Sages, apart from holding that Masorah had a Sinaic origin, also regarded it as a means of conveying exegetic and kabbalistic content that could be utilized for homilies.[36] There are several known medieval homilies based on Masorah, such as Rabbi Jacob ben Asher's (Ba'al Haturim 1269–1340) short commentary on the Torah.[37] Ben Hayyim's assertion regarding the importance of masoretic material as a way to preserve the correct biblical text as well as its potential for commentarial homiletic content renewed the use of masoretic lists as a source for synagogue homilies.[38]

Another point that Ben Hayyim referred to in his introduction to RB 1525 concerned his claim that the masoretic notes had been compromised because they were in ורובם היו כתובים בקשרים וציורים, עד שלא היה באפשרות להבין מהן שום דבר, כי כוונת הסופר היתה ליפות כתיבתו ולא להבין ולעיין בה ('contracted form and with ornaments, so much so that they cannot be deciphered, as the desire of the Masorete was only to embellish his writing and not examine or understand the sense [of the masoretic notes]').[39]

His contention fostered the scholarly assumptions I noted above that relegated the role of *masora figurata* to simple embellishment. Moreover, his inclusion of Sefardi medieval rabbinic commentators such as Abraham ibn Ezra (1089/1092 Tudela–1164/1167 Calahorra) and David Qimhi (RaDaq; Narbonne, 1160–1235) alongside Rashi's (Rabbi Solomon Yitzhaqi: Troyes, 1040–1105) commentary on the Torah promoted comparative exegetic reading of the Bible for Jewish audiences but also further stressed the grammatical and philological approach to Masorah for Christian Hebraists.[40]

The Sefardi philological and grammarian interest in masoretic material was further enhanced by the work of Elijah Levita (*c.* 1469–1558). Born in the Germany Lands, Levita immigrated to northern Italy, where he worked within a Christian milieu that afforded him the opportunity to bring new ideas on the Masorah to Jewish scholarship. In his book *Massoret ha-Massoret* ('The Tradition of the Masorah'; Venice, 1538), a critical analysis of biblical transmission and masoretic scholarship, he contradicted Ben Hayyim and ascribed the Masorah to human authorship, thereby stripping it of the Sinaic origin and mystical meaning attributed to it by the Tannaitic Sages. As noted by Deena Aranoff, 'Levita's emphasis upon the historical qualities of language and his classification of texts into historical periods locates him squarely within the humanist philological discussion of his day'.[41] Levita also edited the Masorah in the third edition of the *Rabbinic Bible*, which was printed in 1548–1567, further correcting its text.[42] Along with his assertion that the Masorah was a product of human authorship, his ideas were instrumental in the development of early modern Bible scholarship. A formative voice in the earliest

---

36 Yeivin, *The Biblical Masorah*, pp. 182–85.

37 In the introduction to his commentary on the Torah, Ben Hayyim wrote: מעט פרפראות וגימטריות וטעמי המסורות, להמשיך הלב ('containing some anecdotes and assignation of numeric values to Hebrew letters and masoretic reasoning to attract the heart'). I would like to thank Jordan Penkower for this reference.

38 Stern, 'The Rabbinic Bible', pp. 83, 106.

39 The Hebrew is found on p. 79 in Christian D. Ginsburg, ed., *Jacob ben Chajim ibn Adoniah's Introduction to the Hebrew Bible* (London: Longmans, Green and Dyer, 1867), pp. 78–79; available on-line: https://archive.org/stream/MassorahMassorethMassoretic/05.IntroducRabbinicBible.HebEng.JacobBenChajimIbnAdon.Ginsburg.1867.#page/n12/mode/2up [accessed in March 2020].

40 Stern, *The Jewish Bible*, pp. 153–55.

41 Deena Aranoff, 'Elijah Levita: A Jewish Hebraist', *Jewish History*, 23 (2009), pp. 17–40 (pp. 19–23, 28, 30).

42 Aranoff, 'Elijah Levita', p. 22 notes 37–38.

stages of critical Bible studies, his writings were part of the foundation for things to come.⁴³

RB 1525 not only codified the Masoretic Text for the very first time, but also eventually became *textus receptus*. As the Masorah was printed in straight lines, as noted by Hanna Liss, 'The artistic depictions of the Masorah faded out of focus'.⁴⁴ Along with the change brought about in Bible and Masorah study by both Christian and Jewish Hebraists focusing on the philological grammatical aspect of Masorah, the exegetic and encapsulated messages formed by *masora figurata* through the synergic relationship between forming Masoretic Text and the image it shaped were obscured. These were lost, forgotten, or waived as null until recent methodology demanded reading masoretic notations in their entirety even for *masora figurata*, a demand that led scholars to begin to rediscover and elucidate these ties.⁴⁵

The fact that no two Masoretic Bible manuscripts are identical suggests that the application of Masorah to each manuscript page, that is, the choice of which word to annotate in the *masora parva* and then to add its references in the *masora magna* may have been a very personal matter for a Masorete. If so, this might indicate that masoretic notation allowed for a creative component in the Masorete's choice of texts for forming *masora figurata*. Contrary to Levita's contention in his introduction to the 1538 *Massoret ha-Massoret* that, ובהם חסרון לא יוכל להמנות | כי הסופרים הזידו | ועל המסורת לא הקפידו | רק עיקר חשיבתם | ליפות את כתיבתם ('the scribes have perverted them [the masoretic notations], as they did not care

---

43 Aranoff, 'Elijah Levita', p. 31.
44 Liss, 'Introduction', p. 8.
45 Ben Hayyim's notes on the kabbalistic features of Masorah are dispersed throughout the *masora parva* and one *masora magna* annotation of the biblical text. These, as noted by Jordan Penkower, who was the first to read the complete RB 1525 Masoretic Text, were overlooked by later researchers owing to their lack of knowledge regarding this aspect. Penkower, 'Jacob ben Hayyim', chap. 2; Liss, 'Introduction', pp. 11–17.

for the Masorah, but only thought to ornament their writing',⁴⁶ these choices might well have been due to the Masoretes wish to manipulate the Masoretic Text into scholarly exegetic ties and encapsulated messages.

Masorah figurata as an '*Impresa*'?

The *impresa*, which first appeared in the fourteenth century, combines an image and a text (usually a motto), became popular among European nobility for heraldic emblems. It was likely favoured because although it featured the same elements required for a coat of arms, it was a less rigid visual form than a conventional coat of arms and allowed for more individualized representation.⁴⁷ Considering the features of the

---

46 Levita, *Massoret ha-massoret* with *Sefer tuv ta'am* (Basel: n.p., 1539), Introduction II, pp. 3a–b; available on-line: https://upload.wikimedia.org/wikipedia/commons/1/15/Masoret-Bahur-1539-HB20911.pdf [accessed in March 2020]; Christian D. Ginsburg, *The Massoreth Ha-Massoreth of Elias Levita: Being an Exposition of the Massoretic Notes on the Hebrew Bible, or the Ancient Critical Apparatus of the Old Testament in Hebrew, with an English Translation, and Critical and Explanatory Notes* (London: Longmans, 1867), p. 94; available on-line https://archive.org/stream/MassorahMassorethMassoretic/00.MassorethHM.EliasLevita.HebEng.Ginsburg.1867.#page/n217/mode/2up [accessed in March 2020].

47 For the set of six rules for creating an *impresa* that were noted by Paolo Giovio in his *Dialogo dell'imprese*, published in 1559: see Ursula Whitcher (aka Ursula Georges), 'Symbols and Mottoes: The Renaissance Impresa'; http://yarntheory.net/ursulageorges/imprese/imprese.html [accessed in March 2020]. See also François Velde, 'Imprese', 2000: https://www.heraldica.org/topics/imprese.htm [accessed in March 2020]. For example, see image 3 in Alciato's *Book of Emblems*, printed in Rome in 1531. The motto 'One ought never to procrastinate', which was the family's motto appears on a ribbon over the hooves of an elk, an image that alludes to being both strong and swift: https://www.mun.ca/alciato/e003.html [accessed in March 2020].

impresa as a way in which to regard micrography may shed light on *masora figurata* manipulation of text and image and the Masoretes' intentions for towards these text and image readerships. If we explore the notion that the *impresa*, as an emblem that manifested a link between 'image and motto', which was designed to incorporate an encrypted message between them that should not be completely obscured and at the same time should evince sheer beauty, we might recognize a similarity to *masora figurata* and understand this art as a visual riddle. These multivalent images formed by text encourage the reader/viewer to engage in study while appreciating their sheer beauty. Such an understanding places micrography within its context in Jewish thought and offers us new ways to learn and understand the interrelationships between scribes and their readers.

The Rhetoric of *Masorah figurata*

As I noted above, *masora figurata* is part of the scribal art tradition and as the raw material for this art is text, contemporary methodology demands a precise reading of the micrography. Such a reading sharpens and deepens the understanding of the characteristics of the scribe's writing and the system he used to fashion the flow of words that created the decoration and illuminates the correlation between the import of the forming text and the image it shapes.

Current research indeed suggests that Masoretes manipulated the Masoretic Text and used it as an exegetic space creating textual and visual loci that reveal much about the relationship between the Masoretes and their readers.[48] As scholars have begun to demonstrate in recent years, these visual polemics were intended for an audience that was aware of the theological content of the Christian models on which the images were based. It was also assumed that these readers were able to grasp the inverted meaning of the iconography created by the Jewish artists and understand that these altered models were created to strengthen the stance of Judaism.[49] Decoding the writing flow and the sequences that form the *masora figurata* reveal the tight connections between the images and their forming texts. These analyses have afforded a holistic understanding of the overall meaning of the decorations as they illuminate the interrelationship between text and image. Moreover, they have also revealed the tremendous scope of the Masoretes' erudition and their place within the artistic community of their time, as their efforts illuminate their knowledge of commentarial material and their familiarity with available artistic models. This knowledge allowed them to manipulate texts to meet their needs and ends. Careful reading of the forming text may yield the multivalent interpretations that the Masoretes expected their readership to understand. This inscribed path can be referred to as a rhetoric utilized to

---

48 Dotan, 'Masora's Contribution', pp. 57–69.

49 Michael Batterman, 'Bread of Affliction, Emblem of Power: The Passover Matzah in Haggadah Manuscripts from Christian Spain', in *Imaging the Self, Imaging the Other*, ed. by Eva Frojmovic (Leiden: Brill, 2002), pp. 58–59, 87; David Lasker, *Philosophical Polemics against Christianity in the Middle Ages* (New York: Littman Library, 1977), p. 163; Hanne Trautner-Kormann, *Shield and Sword: Jewish Polemics against Christianity and Christians in France and Spain from 1100–1500* (Tübingen: Mohr Siebeck, 1993), p. 2. That the fight over images was prominent and unavoidable, see Kalman Bland, *The Artless Jew: Medieval and Modern Affirmations and Denials of the Visual* (Princeton: Princeton University Press, 2000 [Paperback 2001]), pp. 143–44. See also Halperin, 'The Three Riders'; Halperin, 'Micrography Mounted Falconers'; Liss, 'Masorah as Counter-Crusade'; Offenberg, *Up in Arms*; Offenberg, 'Illustrated Secret'.

guide readers through the complex design of word and image.⁵⁰

Such ties between Masorete and reader have been illuminated by Rachel Sarfati in regard to a fifteenth-century Yemenite Taj (Pentateuch that marks the pericopes) now in a private collection. The manuscript includes a depiction of a labyrinth with the words: 'the shape of Jericho walls' followed by an instruction for the reader to follow the drawn map: הקורא כמהלך ('the reader shall be as a traveller') inscribed in its centre.⁵¹ This titulus corresponds to Carruthers's suggestion that, 'Ductus is the way by which a work leads someone through itself: the quality in a work's formal patterns which engages an audience and then sets the viewer [...] in motion within its structure'.⁵²

Consider again the example in BAV, Cod. Urb. ebr. 1, folio 817ʳ (Figure 10.2) with the singular figurative panel of a mounted falconer in a hunt scene at the end of the Book of Ecclesiastics. In that depiction, the image was formed using referrals from the grammatical Section 10 in *'Okhla ve-'okhla* that have no textual connection with the main text on the page. We can understand that the opening lines of this text were purposefully penned to facilitate following and comprehending the association between the forming text and the image. This suggests that the Masorete, Isaac beRabbi Simeon ha-Levi, expected his readers to be capable of deciphering the *masora figurata* along with the internal links between the image and the forming text. By indicating the masoretic list he was using, he guided the reader to the locus of the list where he was to begin his reading. Following this list, the reader would notice that he skipped twelve Masorah pair counts and only then continued his penning with the words, 'The sceptre shall not depart from Judah, nor the ruler's staff from between'.

As I noted above, these words, which begin Genesis 49:10, are associated with a known eschatological commentary. This would render the image as an *impresa*, so to speak, which links the main text and the image, slowly taking the reader through masoretic referrals carefully chosen to lead to an understanding of repentance and the ensuing redemption.⁵³ Thus, the encapsulated message can be understood as having been designed to engage readers in visual and textual deciphering regarding the coming redemption of Israel.⁵⁴

Another well-known *masora figurata* formed into a meticulously edited image of Masoretic Text rhetoric utilizing the concept of ductus can be found in the *Jonah Pentateuch*, c. 1300 (London, British Library, MS Add 21160),⁵⁵ where we see four human figures. The well-known image of the prophet Jonah on fol. 292ʳ (Figure 10.6), which gave this manuscript its name, and three mounted riders, which are seen in the lower *masora magna*.

The first rider we encounter, which appears on fol. 181ᵛ (Figure 10.7), is a mounted falconer holding a bird, who also has a dog lagging behind, its head bent submissively. Next in the sequence is the mounted rider on fol. 192ᵛ, identified by a titulus as *yoseph* (Joseph; Figure 10.8). Both

---

50 For the consideration of rhetoric in illumination, see Mary Carruthers, 'The Concept of Ductus, or Journeying Through a Work of Art', in *Rhetoric Beyond Words: Delight and Persuasion in the Arts of the Middle Ages*, ed. by Mary Carruthers (Cambridge: Cambridge University Press, 2010), pp. 190–213; Lucy Freeman Sandler, 'Rhetorical Strategies in the Pictorial Imagery of Fourteenth-Century Manuscripts: The Case of the Bohun Psalters', in *Rhetoric Beyond Words: Delight and Persuasion in the Arts of the Middle Ages*, pp. 96–123 (pp. 96–99).

51 See Rachel Sarfati, *Painting a Pilgrimage – A 14th-Century Hebrew Scroll Unveiled* (Jerusalem: Israel Museum and Ben Zvi Institute, 2020), item 20.

52 Carruthers, 'The Concept of Ductus', p. 190.

53 Halperin, 'Micrography Mounted Falconers'.

54 Halperin, 'Micrography Mounted Falconers'. On esoteric concepts in Ashkenazi *masora figurata*, see also Halperin, 'The Three Riders'; Liss, 'Masorah as Counter-Crusade'; Offenberg, *Up in Arms*; Offenberg, 'Illustrated Secret'.

55 For online digitized images, see: https://www.bl.uk/he/collection-items/yonah-pentateuch-add-ms-21160 [accessed in March 2020].

Figure 10.6. London, British Library, MS Add 21160, fol. 292ʳ, The prophet Jonah in the mouth of the Leviathan.

Figure 10.7. London, British Library, MS Add 21160, fol. 181ᵛ, mounted falconer.

Figure 10.8. London, British Library, MS Add 21160, fol. 192ᵛ, Joseph mounted.

Figure 10.9. London, British Library, MS Add 21160, fol. 201ᵛ, jousting knight.

of these riders face profile right and thus ride out of the page space. The last mounted figure on fol. 201^v (Figure 10.9) is a jousting knight, who is depicted profile left attacking a city. Depicted thus in a left profile, unlike the first two mounted figures, he is riding into the inner margin of the book.

Carruthers suggests that 'the concept of ductus' should be understood as the study of designed rhetorical images in which the artist leads the viewer through the work of art. Thus, the artist should also be considered something of a cartographer.[56] If we apply this notion to *masora figurata*, we can gain further insight into the intention that guided Isaac the vocalizer, the Masorete of the *Jonah Pentateuch*, in his manipulations of text and image. If we consider that he was leading us to an understanding of each image and its forming text and then planned for us to follow the riders' images only to stop at the well-recognized figure of Jonah in the fish's mouth, which features the seemingly unnecessary titulus *yonah* only so that we would question its need. We might then realize that it was actually a 'halt' sign that was meant to send us back to reconsider the three mounted riders together.

The seeming need for identification of the mounted rider on fol. 192^v as Joseph seems clear, as Rashbam (Rabbi Samuel ben Meir, Troyes, c. 1085–c. 1158) was the only commentator that interpreted Joseph as a viceroy on horseback rather than riding in a chariot.[57] Considering that the tituli used for Joseph and Jonah allows a new directed reading of this rider as a reference to Jonah son of Amitai — the Messiah scion of Joseph, a combined exegesis of the two names found in the rabbinic literature which would explain the use of these two tituli as readers would have deciphered 'the clue'.[58] Elsewhere, I have argued that the falconer's figure can be read as the Messiah scion of David.[59] As the first two riders are imaged in profile riding to the right so that leafing through the manuscript shows them riding 'out' of the page, the image that remains in the reader's mind has them facing the jousting knight, who is riding 'into' the margin as he faces profile left. Thus, we must consider whether this last rider, rather than being another Jewish messianic figure as are the previous two, represents a foe. Reading the forming text of the *masora magna* reveals that the knight's helmet and most of the shield are penned with Lamentations 4:12: 'that foe or adversary could enter the gates of Jerusalem'.[60] Reading the micrography texts discloses the meticulously planned design of the penning of all three images in which Isaac expanded the *masora magna* referrals from their usual three or four words to incorporate nearly complete verses in important visual loci. He

---

56 Carruthers, 'The Concept of Ductus', pp. 191–92, 196.
57 *Sefer tosafot ha-shalem: Commentary on the Bible*, ed. by Ya'aqov Gellis (Jerusalem: Mif'al Tosafot ha-Shalem, 1982), IV, pp. 139–40; Martin Lockshin, *Rabbi Samuel Ben Meir's Commentary on Genesis: An Annotated Translation* (New York: E. Mellen, 1989), pp. 290–91.

58 The son of the widow of Zarephath of Sidon (I Kings 17) was identified either with Jonah ben Amitai as in *Midrash Tehillim* 26:7, p. 110b, and *Pirqe de Rabbi Eliezer* 33, or as the Messiah ben Joseph as in *Tanna debei Eliyahu Rabbah* 18, dated to the ninth century. This latter commentary also appears in the Tosafot writings on *Baba Metzi'a*, 114b, which fits with the time and place of the manuscript. I am deeply grateful to Jordan Penkower for illuminating and clarifying these midrashic issues, which were not cited as clearly in Halperin, 'The Three Riders', 358 note 60. For expanded commentary on Jonah, see Jordan Penkower and Menahem Ben-Yashar, *The Bible in Rabbinic Interpretation: Jonah* (Ramat Gan: Bar Ilan University Press, 2021), *derasha* 63, note 10; also *derasha* 39, note 31.
59 On this image and its reflection of that commentary, see Halperin, 'The Three Riders', pp. 350–52.
60 The verse forming the bottom line of the *masora magna* that leads to the castle, which the knight faces, is formed by the final hemistich of Habakkuk 2:3: 'For it will surely come, without delay', which clearly refers to a messianic time. This allows the reader to understand the citadel to be a representation of Jerusalem. See Halperin, 'The Three Riders', pp. 382–63.

manipulated these verses not only to allow him to form a complex image but to impress his intended commentarial reference on his readers.[61] This indeed fosters Carruthers's suggestion that the artist used ductus to lead the reader/viewer through the formal patterns of the *masora figurata*.[62]

Moreover, in view of the Masorete's use of both of these tituli, we should consider that the two exegeses, which were known during the Middle Ages, might well have also been known in a combined form.[63] Thus these *masora figurata* not only suggest that there might once have been relevant material that is no longer extant, but they also reveal the broad scope of the Masorete's knowledge. Moreover, they disclose a story of redemption that unfolds in the images of the three riders, which he carefully fashioned through his choice of lexical words.[64] These textual manipulations clearly attest to his acquaintanceship with rabbinic literature. Further, they also reveal a familiarity with commentary not thought to have been known in the German Lands at the time, in particular the writings of the Rashbam, which apparently were not quoted extensively after the thirteenth century.[65] All the above indicates that the *masora figurata* was most probably intended for an audience that was aware of the forming content as well as of the artistic models used and was able to grasp the meaning of the layered iconography.[66] This contention is based on the concept of 'the implied reader', the addressee to whom the work was directed, who must have had similar 'linguistic codes, ideological norms, and aesthetic ideas that must be taken into account if the work is to be understood. In this function, the implied reader is the bearer of the codes and norms presumed in the readership'.[67] Such an understanding illuminates what knowledge was at hand on the part of the patrons and the extent of their erudition.

This complex editing of text, image, and forming texts in the *Jonah Pentateuch* clearly reflects Isaac's fervent hopes for redemption and the reinstatement of Israel. Considering the period in which the *Jonah Pentateuch* was probably produced and its ties into the Rashbam commentary noted above, Tosafist redemption dates should be considered here as well. These dates, based on Daniel 12:11–12, respectively, only a few decades and a century away from the time that Isaac penned his images, gives us cause to conclude that these approaching dates might

---

61 On the figure of Joseph where this manipulation is most noticeable, see See Halperin, 'The Three Riders', pp. 346–51.
62 Carruthers, 'The Concept of Ductus', p. 190.
63 The combination of these two readings is found in the Zohar, pericope of *Va-yaqhel*, 197b, where Jonah is identified as the son of the widow of Zarephath of Sidon and was called the 'son of Amitai' in reference to the similarity between his persona and that of Elijah spreading the True Word. On Jonah as the Messiah ben Joseph, see Yehuda Liebes, 'Jonah as the Messiah ben Joseph', *Jerusalem Studies in Jewish Thought*, III, 1/2 (1983/1984): pp. 269–72. On this reading of the tituli, see Halperin, 'The Three Riders', pp. 358–60.
64 For the full consideration of the exegesis present in the image and forming texts of these three micrography riders and their flow charts, see Halperin, 'The Three Riders', pp. 340–73.
65 Martin Lockshin, *Rabbi Samuel Ben Meir's Commentary on the Pentateuch* [in Hebrew] (Jerusalem: Horev, 2009), pp. 3–4. See also Hana Liss, *Creating Fictional Worlds: Peshaṭ — Exegesis and Narrativity in RaShBam's Commentary on the Torah*, Studies in European Jewish History and Culture, 25 (Leiden: Brill, 2011), p. 9 [EBSCO electronic resource; accessed in March 2017]. Sara Japhet notes the possibility that Rashbam travelled throughout northern France as well as to London and perhaps Worms: Sara Japhet and Robert B. Salters, *The Commentary of Samuel Ben Meir, RaShBam, on Qohelet* (Jerusalem: World Union of Jewish Studies, 1985), p. 12.
66 Freeman Sandler, 'Rhetorical Strategies', 97.
67 Wolf Schmid, 'Implied Reader', in *The Living Handbook of Narratology*, ed. by Peter Hühn and others (Berlin: de Gruyter 2009), hosted and maintained by Hamburg University, http://www.lhn.uni-hamburg.de/article/implied-reader [accessed in April 2020].

have been among the reasons that he created these messianic riders.[68]

Conclusions

In 'Between the Textual and the Visual', Zeev Elitzur noted that, 'The "object-ness" of a book tends to be overshadowed by the information encoded in the written signs enclosed in the book'.[69] I suggest that we apply this towards a possible explanation of why the idea that *masora figurata* harboured significant content as a main goal unto itself rather than serving simply to alleviate copying boredom was ignored. In all likelihood, the onset of printing and specifically the printing of RB 1525, which ushered in the codification of the masoretic content, was the main reason that this occurred. Along with later humanist interests that infiltrated the study of Masorah, Ben Hayyim's introduction on the importance of Masorah as exegetic material was ignored and overlooked. The focus on philology that ensued implied that the content of the micrography was obscured and the keys to understanding this purposeful manipulation of Masoretic Text as a visual riddle was lost. I suggest that we should consider whether these boundaries between the textual aspect — the reading of the Masoretic Text — and its visual aspect — its *figurata* — 'looked at' qualities were possibly overshadowed owing to the grammarian philological considerations of Masorah study.

Should we not consider that *masora figurata* continued Tannaitic exegeses over plene and defective spellings, which Elitzur notes is a 'crossing back and forth between the textual and the visual aspects'.[70] This could indicate that the iconic and the semantic dimensions of *masora figurata* were an attempt to engender simultaneous considerations that offered a synergic message greater than the sum of its parts. These complex manipulations, which reflect the intricacy and subtlety of the scholarship and the knowledge of both the Masoretes and their readers, are now being brought back from the oblivion to which they were consigned by the printing of RB 1525. Current research is reopening a window through which we can re-evaluate this singular Jewish art.

---

68 On the Tosafists and their redemption concepts, see above note 19.

69 Zeev Elitzur, 'Between the Textual and the Visual: Borderlines of Late Antique Book Iconicity', *Postscripts*, 6 (2010), pp. 83–99 (p. 84).

70 Elitzur, 'Between the Textual and the Visual', pp. 89–97.

HANNA LISS

Early Hebrew Printing and the Quality of Reading

A Praxeological Study*

Introduction

A praxeological investigation into the production of Hebrew Bibles (with or without commentaries) in the liminal phase of Hebrew book printing — that is, between 1469 and 1525 — is especially fascinating in light of the numerous Hebrew Bible manuscripts produced in the Ashkenazi and Sefardi cultural realms between the eleventh and fourteenth centuries. Such an investigation should consider the change in the material used for producing print Bibles (from parchment to paper), the greater possible variability in both the content and the amount of text, in the layout, and in the quire binding. It should also explore the differences and/or change in the respective producers and those who acquired the work: Jewish scribes who wrote the biblical text, the Targum, and the Masorah in manuscript gradually made way for both Jewish and Christian printers, typesetters, and proofreaders. The Hebrew Bible was used not only in the *bet midrash* (the Jewish classroom) and in the synagogue but also found its way into the private study rooms of Christian Hebraists. The question is, principally, which Bible editions reached the various interested parties, and in which form? What are their differences with respect to the amount of text and hypertext (Masorah, Targum), their layouts, their formats, and the composition of the quires? Is it possible to link specific printed and handwritten textual witnesses to specific religious agent groups?

Scholars have already discussed certain matters concerned with early print, that is, books from the second half of the fifteenth century through the first half of the sixteenth. Among these are the so-called printing revolution,[1] the

---

* I thank the members of the *Collaborative Research Center 933* and the fellows of the *Maimonides Centre for Advanced Studies* (Universität Hamburg) for having discussed various topics related to these questions with me. Some of the issues mentioned here will also be dealt with in the paper by Federico dal Bo (see in this volume p. ###), who joined the CRC 933 in 2019 and is currently working specifically on the question of the praxeological relevance of layouts in various genres in the sixteenth and seventeenth centuries (Bible and Talmud prints and Kabbalah literatures).

1 *Printing Evolution and Society 1450–1500: Fifty Years that Changed Europe*, ed. by Cristina Dondi (Venice: Edizioni Ca'Foscari – Digital Publishing, 2020); Elizabeth L. Eisenstein, *The Printing Revolution in Early Modern Europe*, 2nd Ed. (Cambridge and New York: Cambridge

Hanna Liss • Hochschule für Jüdische Studien Heidelberg

role of the printing press at the beginning of the Reformation in Germany,[2] the influence of humanist tradition on the Jews,[3] the beginning of Christian Hebraism in Germany and Italy,[4] and the various print shops in Bologna, Faro, Mantua, Naples, Rome, and Soncino.[5] However, particularly in regard to the first incunabula of Hebrew Bibles/Pentateuchs and/or printed Bible editions with or without commentary, modern scholars, at best, mention these early printed editions, but they almost completely refrain from analysing and qualifying them in detail and/or posing some of the questions noted above.[6] Usually, they go straight to the description of the so-called 'Rabbinic Bibles', Bomberg (1517) and Bomberg (1525).[7] At most, palaeographical and codicological issues, that is, the respective mode or type of printing (square letters or

---

University Press, 1998); Uwe Neddermeyer, 'Wann begann das Buchzeitalter', in *Zeitschrift für Historische Forschung*, 20 (1993), pp. 205–16; Elchanan Reiner, 'The Ashkenazi Élite at the Beginning of the Modern Era: Manuscript versus Printed Book', in *Jews in Early Modern Poland*, ed. by Gershon D. Hundert (London and Portland: Littman Library of Jewish Civilization, 1997), pp. 85–98.

2 See recently Thomas Kaufmann, *Die Mitte der Reformation: Eine Studie zu Buchdruck und Publizistik im deutschen Sprachgebiet, zu ihren Akteuren und deren Strategien, Inszenierungs- und Ausdrucksformen* (Tübingen: Mohr Siebeck, 2019); see the extensive bibliography on the early printings of the main protagonists of the Reformation in Kaufmann, pp. 1–3.

3 Bernard D. Cooperman, *Jewish Thought in the Sixteenth Century* (Cambridge, MA: Harvard University Center for Jewish Studies, 1983); Aaron W. Hughes, 'Translation and the Invention of Renaissance Jewish Culture: The Case of Judah Messer Leon and Judah Abravanel', in *The Hebrew Bible in Fifteenth-Century Spain*, ed. by Jonathan P. Decter and Arturo Prats (Leiden and Boston: Brill, 2012), pp. 245–66; Arthur Michael Lesley, 'Jewish Adaptation of Humanist Concepts in Fifteenth- and Sixteenth-Century Italy', in *Essential Papers on Jewish Culture in Renaissance and Baroque Italy*, ed. by David B. Ruderman (New York: New York University Press, 1992), pp. 45–62; Gianfranco Miletto, *Glauben und Wissen im Zeitalter der Reformation: Der salomonische Tempel bei Abraham ben David Portaleone (1542–1612)* (Berlin: De Gruyter, 2004).

4 *Gottes Sprache in der philologischen Werkstatt. Hebraistik vom 15. bis zum 19. Jahrhundert*, ed. by Giuseppe Veltri and Gerold Necker (Leiden and Boston: Brill, 2004); Thomas Willi, 'Christliche Hebraistik aus jüdischen Quellen: Beobachtungen zu den Anfängen einer christlichen Hebraistik', in *Gottes Sprache der philologischen Werkstatt Hebraistik vom 15. bis zum 19. Jahrhundert*, pp. 25–48.

5 David Amram, *The Makers of Hebrew Books in Italy* (Philadelphia: J. H. Greenstone, 1909; repr. London: Holland Press, 1963); *The Hebrew Book in Early Modern Italy*, ed. by Joseph R. Hacker and Adam Shear (Philadelphia: University of Pennsylvania Press, 2011);

Adriaan K. Offenberg, *Hebrew Incunabula in Public Collections: A First International Census* (Nieuwkooop: Graaf, 1990).

6 Marco Bertagna, 'Not Wanderers but Faithful Companions: A Brief Overview on the Hebrew Incunabula Held in Italian Libraries', in *Printing Evolution and Society 1450–1500: Fifty Years that Changed Europe*, pp. 299–319; Adrian Schenker, 'From the First Printed Hebrew, Greek and Latin Bibles to the First Polyglot Bible, the Complutensian Polyglot: 1477–1517', in *Hebrew Bible / Old Testament: The History of Its Interpretation*, ed. by Magne Sæbø (Göttingen: Vandenhoeck & Ruprecht, 2008), II (From the Renaissance to the Enlightenment), pp. 276–91 [includes an extensive bibliography]; Shimon Iakerson, 'Early Hebrew Printing in Sepharad (ca. 1475–1497?)', in *Biblias de Sefarad: Bibles of Sepharad*, ed. by Esperanza Alfonso and others (Madrid: Biblioteca Nacional de España, 2012), pp. 125–47; David Stern, *Jewish Literary Cultures* (University Park. PA: Penn State University Press, 2019), II (The Medieval and Early Modern Periods), esp. pp. 112–46; Stern, *The Jewish Bible: A Material History* (Seattle: University of Washington Press, 2017), pp. 137–57; Stern, 'The Rabbinic Bible in Its Sixteenth-Century Context', in *The Hebrew Book in Early Modern Italy*, ed. by Joseph R. Hacker and Adam Shear (Philadelphia: University of Pennsylvania Press, 2011), pp. 76–108.

7 Jordan S. Penkower, 'Bomberg's First Bible Edition and the Beginning of his Printing Press', *Qiryat Sefer*, 53 (1983), pp. 586–604; Penkower, 'Jacob Ben Hayyim and the Rise of the Biblia Rabbinica' (unpublished doctoral thesis, the Hebrew University of Jerusalem, 1982); Penkower, *Masora and Text Criticism in the Early Modern Mediterranean: Moses Ibn Zabara and Menahem de Lonzano* (Jerusalem: Magnes Press, 2014); Penkower, 'The Chapter Divisions in the 1525 Rabbinic Bible', *Vetus Testamentum* 48 (1998), pp. 350–74.

semi-cursive mode), the material (parchment or paper), and the composition of quires have been discussed and related to their geocultural background.[8] However, as early as in 1779, the German Orientalist Oluf Gerhard Tychsen[9] and later Christian D. Ginsburg in 1897[10] published various articles on these early printings. They offered detailed descriptions as to their text-critical value, their spelling peculiarities, the question of the integration of the Masorah, the recension of the respective exegetical commentary at hand, and the colophons to be found in these books.[11]

It is clear, though, that Tychsen and Ginsburg did not concern themselves with such praxeological issues as detailed in the queries noted above.

In what follows, I start with some praxeological considerations on confessional reading boundaries and afterwards discuss one of the earliest printed editions [*Psalms with Qimhi* (1477)] in more detail. I focus on the question of what it reveals in regard to its targeted readers and their needs and expectations, that is, who would have read this text, who could have read it, and what might this edition have been designed to achieve. I also take a look at the metatext and evaluate the glosses and the colophon with regard to these questions. As the colophons in particular bear information about the printer and his typesetter(s) as well as about all the other individuals involved in the printing process, I take a closer look at the diversity of knowledge and skills within the Jewish communities and the self-perceptions of those who shaped this important era in Jewish intellectual history.

Reading Boundaries for Manuscripts and Early Printings

A Bible is always read within a denominational frame. This becomes quite obvious when looking at manuscripts: Hebrew manuscripts (with a very few exceptions) are 'Jewish' in that they were produced by Jews for Jews,[12] many Arabic and Greek manuscripts might have been used by

---

8 See, e.g., Malachi Beit-Arié, 'The Relationship between Early Hebrew Printing and Handwritten Books: Attachment or Detachment', in *Library Archives and Information Studies*, ed. by Dov Schidorsky (Jerusalem: Magnes Press, 1989), pp. 1–26; Beit-Arié, *The Makings of the Medieval Hebrew Book: Studies in Palaeography and Codicology* (Jerusalem: Magnes Press, 1993), esp. pp. 251–77.

9 Oluf Gerhard Tychsen (1734–1815) was a typical eighteenth-century German Lutheran scholar. He was an orientalist, a Hebrew scholar, and one of the founding fathers of Islamic numismatics. From 1778 he taught at the University of Rostock and worked as the librarian of the university's library. Tychsen studied at the universities in Jena and Halle, but he also attended the Altona synagogue and learned with Jonathan Eybeschütz, who from 1750 onwards was the elected rabbi of the communities in Altona, Hamburg, and Wandsbek. Tychsen embarked upon rabbinic studies for reasons of his missionary work towards the conversion of Jews, but his philological skills were extraordinary and his scientific work merits scholarly attention even today.

10 Christian D. Ginsburg (1831–1914) was born Jewish and converted to Christianity in 1846. Like Tychsen, he was very actively engaged in missionary work.

11 See, e.g., Oluf Gerhard Tychsen, 'Beschreibung der ersten jüdischen Psalmen-Ausgabe vom J. 1477 / Die erste jüdische Ausgabe der Psalmen Davids vom J. 1477 Beschrieben und mit der Hoogtischen verglichen', in *Repertorium für Biblische und Morgenländische Litteratur*, 5 (1779), pp. 134–58; Tychsen, 'Kritische Beschreibung des Bononischen Pentateuch's vom J. 1482 / Kritische Beschreibung des Bononischen Pentateuchus', in *Repertorium für Biblische und Morgenländische Litteratur*, 6 (1780), pp. 65–103; Christian D. Ginsburg, *Introduction to the Massoretico-Critical Edition of the Hebrew Bible* (London: Trinitarian Bible Society, 1897), esp. pp. 779–976.

12 However, as early as in the twelveth and thirteenth centuries, Christian exegetes consulted Hebrew/Hebrew-Latin manuscripts, as can be seen by the inventory list of the library of the St Victor monastery, which includes a Hebrew-Latin psalter, see Matthias M. Tischler, *Die Bibel in Saint-Victor zu Paris: Das Buch der Bücher als Gradmesser für wissenschaftliche, soziale und*

various parties (Jewish, Christian, and Muslim),[13] and Latin Bible manuscripts were always written for and read by Christian scholars. The nature of manuscripts is very much determined by the geocultural area in which they were produced. The Oriental and Sefardi manuscripts that originated in Islamic countries differ from their Ashkenazi equivalents in regard to the recension of the biblical text, the layout, and the metatextual elements.[14] Likewise, the sequence of the Later Prophets and the Writings differs between the Oriental and the Ashkenazi Bibles.[15] In Ashkenaz, where Bible manuscripts were often confiscated, Jews tried to preserve extra-biblical material (e.g., Masoretic lists or exegetical hints) by integrating it into a Bible codex, knowing that no Christian scholar could decipher this material.[16]

This situation in connection with the denominational reading boundaries changed with the beginning of the print era. The 'effects of prints [...] changed the very nature of the Jewishness of the Jewish book'.[17] However, it was not an abrupt transition: the first incunabula of the Hebrew Bible and halakhic texts, as well as commentary literature, appeared alongside the handwritten tradition between the second half and the end of the fifteenth century (initially in Italy and on the Iberian Peninsula).[18]

At the beginning of the typographical age, we can observe a differentiated juxtaposition and coexistence of the biblical text (as hypotext) and its various commentaries (as hypertexts): Bible commentaries, Aramaic Targum, and Masoretic notations (*petuha/setuma; ketiv/qere; puncta extraordinaria; scriptio plene/defectiva; memoria technica; liturgica*). A comparison between the handwritten manuscripts and the early printings shows fundamental differences in the mutual

---

ordensgeschichtliche Umbrüche im europäischen Hoch- und Spätmittelalter (Münster, Westfalen: Aschendorff, 2014), esp. pp. 107–08.

13 See, e.g., Ronny Vollandt, *Arabic Versions of the Pentateuch: A Comparative Study of Jewish, Christian, and Muslim Sources* (Leiden and Boston: Brill, 2015).

14 See Hanna Liss and Kay Joe Petzold, 'Die Erforschung der westeuropäischen Bibeltexttradition als Aufgabe der Jüdischen Studien', in *Judaistik im Wandel. Ein halbes Jahrhundert Forschung und Lehre über das Judentum in Deutschland*, ed. by Andreas Lehnardt (Berlin: De Gruyter, 2017), pp. 189–210, esp. pp. 203–06 (https://doi.org/10.1515/9783110523478-016 [accessed in March 2022]); Hanna Liss, 'A Pentateuch to Read in? The Secrets of the Regensburg Pentateuch', in *Jewish Manuscript Cultures: New Perspectives*, ed. by Irina Wandrey (Berlin and Boston: De Gruyter, 2017), pp. 89–128 (https://doi.org/10.1515/9783110546422-005 [accessed in March 2022]).

15 Likewise, Latin Bibles show a great variety of different orders in the biblical books. It was only from the twelfth century on that a Latin 'canon' for the order of the books was gradually established (see Tischler, esp. pp. 51–53, 95–99).

16 See, e.g., Hanna Liss, 'Aschkenasische Bibelcodices als Träger exegetischer und theologischer Geheimnisse', in *700 Jahre jüdische Präsenz in Tirol: Geschichte der Fragmente, Fragmente der Geschichte*, ed. by Ursula Schattner-Rieser and Josef M. Oesch (Innsbruck: Innsbruck University Press, 2018), pp. 203–23.

---

17 Stern, 'The Rabbinic Bible in Its Sixteenth-Century Context', p. 77.

18 See, e.g., *Thesaurus Typographiae Hebraicae Seaculi XV: Hebrew Printing in the Fifteenth Century*, ed. by Aron Freimann and Alexander Marx (facsimile reproduction of the 1924–31 edition; Jerusalem: Universitas Bookseller, 1968); Freimann, *Ueber hebräische Inkunabeln. Vortrag geh. in der bibliothekar. Sektion d. 46. Versamml. deutscher Philologen* (Leipzig: Harrassowitz, 1902); Freimann, *Die Familie Soncino* (Berlin: Holten, 1925); Freimann, 'Die hebräischen Inkunabeln der Druckereien in Spanien und Portugal', Sonderabdruck Gutenberg Festschrift (Mainz: n. p., 1925), pp. 203–06; Ginsburg, pp. 779–976; Shimon Iakerson, *Catalogue of Hebrew Incunabula from the Collection of the Library of the Jewish Theological Seminary of America*, 2 vols (New York and Jerusalem: The Jewish Theological Seminary of America, 2004–05); Iakerson, 'Early Hebrew Printing in Sepharad (ca. 1475–1497?)', in *Biblias de Sefarad: Bibles of Sepharad*, ed. by Esperanza Alfonso and others (Madrid: Biblioteca Nacional de España, 2012), pp. 125–47; Herbert C. Zafren, 'Bible Editions, Bible Study, and the Early History of Hebrew Printing', *Eretz-Israel: Archaeological, Historical and Geographical Studies*, 16 (1982), pp. *240–*251.

reception of Ashkenazi and Sefardi (Northern Italy) and Sefardi-Tiberian text traditions (Iberia), and in general reflects an increasing loss of Ashkenazi text and Masorah traditions. Above all, this decline bears praxeologically relevant results with regard to the affordance of the artefacts in their liturgical and/or scientific use. Sefardi printings often did not reflect liturgical peculiarities and reading practices: one can find chapter details of the biblical books, but no indication of the *parashiyot* or the (special) *shabbatot*. The binding of the partial editions determined whether the *megillot* (the books of Ruth, Song of Songs, Ecclesiastes, Lamentations, and Esther) were attached to the book of the Pentateuch closest to that particular festival in the liturgical cycle.[19] Jewish readers wanted the *megillot* for liturgical reading on relevant holidays in the context of the Torah, that is, bound after the Pentateuch.[20] Christian Hebraists, who were mostly interested in the Hebrew language and text criticism, read the *megillot* as part of the Writings.

As for the layout, the early printings show that books form the basis of group-specific educational canons and, thus, the basis for the rational exploration of [one's own] culture. In 1521, the first Pratensis edition (1517)[21] underwent a 'Jewish remake' through the elimination of the papal dedication to Leo X and integration of the masoretic notes. The first incunabula were based on the Ashkenazi text and layout traditions, whereas the printings of the late fifteenth and early sixteenth centuries [Pratensis (1517 and 1521); Bomberg (1525)] were produced in a Christian press whose Jewish employees were among the group of Jewish scholars expelled from Spain in 1492. These printers and typesetters knew only the Oriental textual traditions and printed them. The humanist ideal that guided the Christian printers can also be seen in the commentaries that were added to the editions of these Bibles or were printed separately. Apart from Rashi, all of these printed commentaries originated in Spanish exegetical schools, including those of Ibn Ezra, David Qimhi (Provence), and Levi ben Gershon (Ralbag; Languedoc). They were not only well known by the Jews who had been expelled from Spain, but also represented a commentary tradition that precisely matched the needs of the Christian Hebraists. They were deeply rooted in the philological and rationalist tradition of science and in that replaced the Franco-German exegetical and Tosafist schools, that is, the commentary of Rashi and its respective supercommentaries by, for example, Rashbam, R. Joseph Qara, R. Joseph Bekhor Shor, Yom Tov of Joigny, R. Judah he-Hasid, Hezekiah ben Manoah (Hizquni), Isaiah di Trani, and/or Judah ben El'azar (Minhat Yehuda).[22] Christian Hebraists found the grammatical-linguistic

---

19 See, e.g., the *editio princeps* of Tanakh [Soncino] 1488 (4 vols); likewise, in Bomberg's second quarto edition 1521 the *megillot* were not bound within the Writings but after the Pentateuch; cf. Kay Joe Petzold, *Masora und Exegese. Untersuchungen zur Masora und Bibeltextüberlieferung im Kommentar des R. Schlomo ben Yitzchaq (Raschi)* (Berlin and Boston: De Gryuter, 2019), esp. pp. 54–73: https://www.degruyter.com/view/title/543379 (accessed in March 2022).

20 See also the quarto edition printed by Gershom Soncino in Pesaro in two volumes: Pentateuch, Megillot and Former Prophets (12 April 1511); Latter Prophets and Writings (24 January 1517); the divine names were printed as אלדים and ידוה; cf. Petzold, *Masora und Exegese*, pp. 68–69.

21 The first Bomberg edition, published in Venice in 1517, was most notably an edition by the convert Felipe de Prato (Felix Pratensis, 1460–1559), an Augustinian friar from Prato (Florence), who converted in 1506. He taught (among others) Cardinal Egidio de Viterbo and was an editor in Daniel Bomberg's printing house.

22 See in particular Eric Lawee, 'Biblical Scholarship in Late Medieval Ashkenaz: The Turn to Rashi Supercommentary', *Hebrew Union College Annual*, 86 (2015), pp. 265–303.

as well as the philosophical commentaries far easier to read than those from the medieval Western European Tosafist schools, as most of them lacked the knowledge to understand the latter. The difficulties were grounded not only in the Tosafist exegetical discourse but also in the fact that the Ashkenazi commentary tradition did not always accord with the Oriental-Sefardi Bible text tradition(s).[23]

Thus, the development of printing, which at the beginning of the sixteenth century was dominated by Christian presses, led to a gradual decline in the Western European Ashkenazi tradition of text and learning culture. This waning involved the loss of the tradition of oral learning from a teacher using *individual excerpts* based on an enormous *plurality of handwritten* text recensions. As Elchanan Reiner noted:

> Tosafot Medieval Ashkenazi tradition almost died out; very little survived of the old literary canon and the medieval Halakhic traditions. Hebrew printing and, especially, the commercial printing presses of Venice in the first half of the sixteenth century, brought about a momentous drive of canonization in Jewish culture in general and Ashkenazi culture in particular: the printing of the Bible and its commentaries, the printing of the Talmud and its commentaries, of Midrashim and medieval Halakhic literature — all these entirely transformed Ashkenazi Jewry's attitude to its past.[24]

The printing of the Bible and the Talmud as well as a limited selection of Bible commentaries created a new Hebrew canon and thrust a whole range of Hebrew-Aramaic (and even vernacular) text traditions aside. *Masorah figurata* was never printed, so its exegetical and theological value was not appreciated from the printing era on. Likewise, the Hebrew-French glossaries mostly from the thirteenth century that encompass *in toto* some 105,000 *le'azim* were printed only in the twentieth century,[25] although they are exceptional witnesses to a Jewish French (Bible) reading culture in Western Europe that developed precisely at the time that the *Bible française du 13ᵉ siècle* (*Bible de Paris*) was written.[26] An important part of the Franco-Ashkenazi knowledge culture simply perished and was never revived.

The Christian printing presses created a new Hebrew canon as a kind of a collection of 'Judaica Classics', and although it was used

---

23 See Ginsburg, p. 818.
24 Elchanan Reiner, 'The Attitude of Ashkenazi Society to the New Science in the Sixteenth Century', *Science in Context*, 10 (1997), pp. 589–603 (p. 599, see also p. 601: 'Ashkenazi's real war, therefore, was directed against the new library taking shape before his very eyes, the new library that was visibly destroying the traditional literary canon […] 'new' was not the New Science but the New Library').

25 The number of 105,000 *le'azim* adds up to *c.* 21,000 lemmata, i.e., *c.* 25 per cent of the entire Old French thesaurus; for editions, see, e.g., *Les gloses françaises dans les Commentaires talmudiques de Raschi*, ed. by David S. Blondheim, I: *Texte des Gloses* (Paris: Champion, 1929); II: *Etudes lexicographiques* (Baltimore: John Hopkins University Press, 1937); *Glossaire biblique hébreu-français, 1 q. XIII s., champenois, ms. Bâle A III 39*, ed. by Menahem Banitt, Corpus Glossariorum Biblicorum Hebraico-Gallicorum Medii Aevi, 2 vols (Jerusalem: Israel Academy of Sciences and Humanities, 1972); Banitt, *Le Glossaire de Leipzig*, Corpus Glossariorum Biblicorum Hebraico-Gallicorum Medii Aevi, 4 vols (Jerusalem: Israel Academy of Sciences and Humanities, 1995–2005), esp. IV (Introduction); *Les gloses françaises du glossaire biblique B.N. hébr. 301. Édition critique partielle et étude linguistique*, ed. by Marc Kiwitt (Heidelberg: Universitätsverlag Winter, 2013).
26 See, e.g., Marc Kiwitt, 'Les glossaires bibliques hébraïco-français et le transfert du savoir profane', in *Transfert des savoirs au Moyen Âge – Wissenstransfer im Mittelalter. Actes de l'Atelier franco-allemand, Heidelberg, 15–18 janvier 2008*, ed. by Stephen Dörr and Raymund Wilhelm (Heidelberg: Universitätsverlag Winter, 2008), pp. 65–80.

by the Jews, it was increasingly shaped for the Christian Hebraists, who used the texts both to learn Hebrew (Ibn Ezra, Qimhi) and to acquire philosophical knowledge (Ibn Ezra, Ralbag). This 'print canonization' led to a monopoly on authoring. The fact that the Sefardi employees as well as the converts in the printing works entered into an unholy 'mesalliance' with their Christian employers is a particularly bitter side of history.

In 1525, following the quarto edition printed by the convert Cornelius ben Baruch Adelkind[27] (Venice 1521) and the Soncino edition (Pesaro 1511/17), Daniel Bomberg printed an edition of the *Miqra'ot gedolot* with Jacob ben Hayyim ibn Adonijah. It included the *masora parva* and *magna* as well as the *masora finalis*, Targum, commentaries by Rashi and Ibn Ezra on the Pentateuch, by Rashi, Qimhi, Ralbag, and Ibn Ezra on the Prophets and the Writings (though not all of them in every biblical book).[28] The introductions to the Prophets by Qimhi and Ralbag as well as Ibn Ezra's introduction to the Writings were added.[29] With these Bomberg editions, the Hebrew Bible developed into a Christian source that was then further shaped according to the needs of Protestant theologians. Many Christian Hebraists and Reformers, including such figures as Mikael Agricola, Bernhard Ziegler, and Martin Luther, used the third quarto edition of Bomberg (1525) as a concise version of the Hebrew Bible. Johann Buxtorf the Elder revised the third Bomberg edition in 1547, which was printed by Adelkind, by adding Oriental readings and with his *Biblia sacra hebraica & chaldaica* (Basel, 1620) created a *Miqra'ot gedolot* edition that eventually became the *textus receptus* for Christian Hebraists. In 1626, Yedidyah Solomon Norzi (Goder Peretz) prepared another 'Jewish' Bible edition which sought to qualify the diversifications and inconsistencies between the print editions and Torah scrolls, but it was only printed more than 100 years later (1742) by Rafael Hayyim Basile in Mantua under the title *Minhat Shay*.

Against this background, it is obvious that from the early eighteenth century at the latest, Protestant Bible studies distinguished between an 'authentic' consonantal text of the Bible and the (post-biblical) 'Jewish' vocalization and Masorah tradition.[30] This approach, which still shapes Protestant scholarship, goes along with the preference for the Palestinian-Tiberian text type, although it had never been decisive for the Western European Bible commentary and halakhic tradition.[31] The Hebrew printing press laid the foundation for a scholarly understanding of the Hebrew Bible that was shaped not only by the context of the Christian ideal of education, but also by the exclusion of specifically Ashkenazi and exegetically motivated readings.

---

27 On Adelkind as well as on the converts in Bomberg's print shop, see Hanoch Yalon, 'Two Notes on Cornelio Adelkind' [in Hebrew], *Qiryat Sefer*, 6 (1929), pp. 145–46.

28 For further details, see in particular Penkower, *Jacob Ben Hayyim and the Rise of the Biblia Rabbinica*; Penkower, 'Bomberg's First Bible Edition'; Penkower, 'The Chapter Divisions in the 1525 Rabbinic Bible'; Petzold, *Masora und Exegese*, pp. 65–73.

29 Petzold, *Masora und Exegese*, pp. 73–77.

30 See Johann David Michaelis, *Deutsche Übersetzung des Alten Testaments, mit Anmerkungen für Ungelehrte: Der erste Theil welcher das Buch Hiobs enthält* (2. verb. u. verm. Ausg. Göttingen and Gotha, 1773), I, XXIX: 'Die Puncte, dadurch im Hebräischen die Vocales und sonst noch allerley die Erklärung bestimmendes ausgedrückt wird, sind nicht von den heiligen Schriftstellern selbst, sondern erst von Juden, die etliche hundert Jahr nach Christi Geburt lebten [...]'.

31 On this topic, see in particular Liss and Petzold, 'Die Erforschung der westeuropäischen Bibeltexttradition', esp. pp. 192–97.

The Philological Quality of the Print Edition

The *editio princeps* of the Book of Psalms with the commentary of R. David Qimhi,[32] printed on paper on 29 August 1477, was described in detail by Tychsen[33] and Ginsburg.[34] The place of printing is not mentioned explicitly but was typographically reconstructed. Since the semi-cursive Italian type used for the Qimhi commentary is the same as that in the 1482 edition of the Bologna Pentateuch, Tychsen, Ginsburg, Freimann, and Heller all assumed that it was printed in Bologna.[35] The semi-cursive script resembles the contemporary hands of the second half of the fifteenth century.[36] The page numbers are not printed but are written by hand,[37] probably by a/the first(?) reader, who also added biblical verses as well as the numbering of the psalms (though only sporadic) and *ketiv/qere* remarks as glosses in the margins.[38] This layout — Bible verses alternating with the commentary — is found in handwritten (Hebrew) Bible manuscripts in Ashkenaz only for Bibles with the Targum,[39] not for the *Glossae*, that is, Bibles with exegetical commentary(ies). There is no explicit numbering of the psalms, but the beginning and end of the respective five *sefarim* — the division of the Book of Psalms into five books — is marked.[40] The text starts with Psalm 1:1.[41] With the exception of the first pages that feature the biblical text in Psalms 1:6–4:3; 5: and 12–13[42] with 'some rude

---

32 The printed edition I had access to (photographs) is Cambridge, University Library (henceforth UL), Inc. 3.B.74.A.2 (see also below Figure 11.1) and the Valmadonna Trust Fund Library (Faksimile of A 52 R 1035) see https://www.nli.org.il/he/books/NNL_ALEPH002009528/NLI [accessed in March 2022]. This last copy of the edition is neither censored nor were any glosses added in the margins. The main difference between these copies is that in the colophon's epigraph the copy Cambridge, UL, Inc. 3.B.74.A.2 mentions an additional (family?) name (?) (ונריה) among persons who executed the printing, whereas this name is missing (and indeed it seems that it was not printed, not just simply erased!) in the Faksimile of A 52 R 1035 (see in below esp. note 67).

33 Tychsen, 'Beschreibung der ersten jüdischen Psalmen-Ausgabe', pp. 134–58; Ginsburg, pp. 780–94; see also Petzold, *Masora und Exegese*, pp. 56 f. The edition is also listed in Zafren's list on the early printings as no. 7 without any further details (see Zafren, pp. *242–*245).

34 Tychsen, 'Beschreibung der ersten jüdischen Psalmen-Ausgabe', pp. 134–58; Ginsburg, pp. 780–94; see also Petzold, *Masora und Exegese*, pp. 56–57. The edition is also listed in Zafren's list on the early printings as no. 7 without any further details.

35 Cf. Marvin J. Heller, *The Sixteenth Century Hebrew Book: An Abridged Thesaurus* (Leiden and Boston: Brill, 2004), I, pp. xxiv–xxv; Freimann, 'Ueber hebräische Inkunabeln', p. 6; Ginsburg, p. 781; Tychsen, 'Beschreibung der ersten jüdischen Psalmen-Ausgabe', pp. 141–42. Zafren, p. 242* assumes only Italy and does not specify any other printing place.

36 Beit-Arié, 'The Relationship between Early Hebrew Printing and Handwritten Books', pp. 7–8.

37 The numbering is not entirely correct; it runs from leaves 2–152 in the upper left corner of the recto leaf (leaf 1 with Psalm 1. 1–5 torn out, leaf 87 counted twice); in this paper I refer to this numbering. On leaf 110^r (left corner lower margin) a second foliation starts and runs from 20–62 (leaf 30 counted twice). Beit-Arié, 'The Relationship between Early Hebrew Printing and Handwritten Books', p. 23, seems to refer to a different copy of this 1477 edition.

38 See as an example Cambridge, UL, Inc. 3.B.74.A.2, leaf 10^v: Psalm 10. 5 is missing. The typesetter took Psalm 10. 4a and followed it with 10. 6. The gloss is cut on the right side, but one can see that the reader added Psalm 10. 5; see also leaves 11^r; 12^r; 23^r; 25^r; 48^v; 49^r a. fr.

39 Cf. Élodie Attia, 'Targum Layouts in Ashkenazi Manuscripts: Preliminary Methodological Observations', in *A Jewish Targum in a Christian World*, ed. by Alberdina Houtman, Eveline van Staalduine-Sulman, and Hans-Martin Kirn (Leiden and Boston: Brill, 2014), pp. 99–122.

40 Book 2 starts leaf 46^v; book 3: leaf 77^r; Book 4: leaf 97^v; Book 5: leaf 117^v.

41 In Cambridge, UL, Inc. 3.B.74.A.2, the first leaf is missing (torn out?).

42 Cambridge, UL, Inc. 3.B.74.A.2, leaves 2^r–4^r; leaf 6^r.

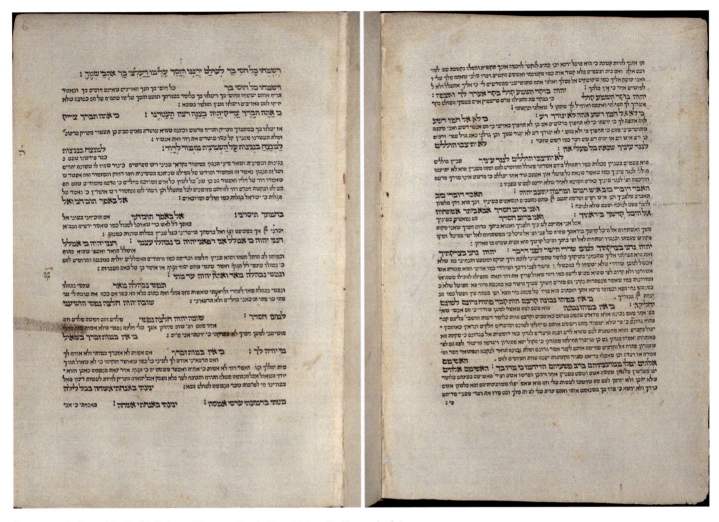

Figure 11.1. Psalms with Qimhi. Bologna(?), 1477. Cambridge, University library, leaf 6r.

vowel-points',[43] the text, which is printed in an Ashkenazi square type, is unvocalized. There are no enlarged initials, and the text lacks accents or any other diacritical signs such as *dagesh* points or *maqqafim*; only the *sof pasuq* was integrated, though not throughout. The biblical text reflects many omissions. Ginsburg counts more than 154 omissions of entire verses, half-verses, or single words,[44] in particular the words/phrases that Qimhi did not explain. Usually, the Tetragrammaton in the biblical text is written in full, but unvocalized. The commentary has a Tetragrammaton substitute but sometimes the Tetragrammaton is vocalized in a very strange

---

43 David Sandler Berkowitz, *In Remembrance of Creation: Evolution of Art and Scholarship in the Medieval and Renaissance Bible* (Waltham, MA: Brandeis University Press, 1968), p. 72, no. 122.

44 Ginsburg, pp. 789–90; see above Tychsen, 'Beschreibung der ersten jüdischen Psalmen-Ausgabe', p. 138.

way:⁴⁵ יְהֹוָה — יְהֹוָה — יוֹהֹה and sometimes the letters *vav* and *he* are turned upside down⁴⁶ or are even missing.⁴⁷ The biblical text features many *matres lectiones* (ו for *shuruq* and *holam*; י for *hiriq*, *tzere*, and *segol*),⁴⁸ but in many cases these letters are missing in a defective spelling, although the Hebrew requires them.

There are many errors in the printed text that do not seem to have been the result simply of the lack of letters; rather the indications are that the typesetter was simply not well trained in the Hebrew language and textual world of the Psalms: יארו instead of יֹאמְרוּ (Ps. 35:25), תגלה instead of תָּגֵלְנָה (Ps. 51:10), שמש instead of שְׁמַע (Ps. 66:19), מרמזר instead of מִזְמוֹר (Ps. 67:1), בארז instead of בָּאָרֶץ (Ps. 67:5), על instead of אֶל (Ps. 85:9), לעשותו instead of לַעֲצָתוֹ (Ps. 106:13), העמים instead of הָאֻמִּים (Ps. 117:1), טהרתי instead of בָחַרְתִּי (Ps. 119:30), to list but a few.⁴⁹ The exchange of '*ayin* and '*alef* and *zayin* and *tzade* as well as the writing of a noun instead of a verb and vice versa (Ps. 66:19 and 106;13) suggest that this printed biblical text was produced by someone who not only lacked the philological skills of a medieval scribe, but also did not take care to ensure that the printed edition was thoroughly proofread. In some cases, the layout of the biblical text suggests that the printer did not understand which parts of the verses belong together. For example, in Psalm 19:8–9,⁵⁰ he connected the last word of verse 19:8, פתי ('the simple'), with the first words of 19:9, 'פקודי ה ('the precepts of the Lord'). That this printer's lack of education and care was not unusual is clear from Elia Levita's complaint that his book *Mahalakh shevile ha-da'at* ('Course of the Paths of Knowledge') went to press without his approval and authorization.⁵¹

Regarding the (missing!) Masorah, several observations merit attention. Very often, the *qere* instead of the *ketiv*⁵² with its appropriate *masora parva* note was printed.⁵³ As an example, take Psalm 5:9:⁵⁴ the printed text reads הישר instead of הושר. The typesetter/printer probably did not understand the *ketiv/qere* case at hand, and as a corollary, part of the Qimhi commentary is corrupted. Let us compare the edition in *Mikra'ot gedolot ha-keter* with our text at hand (excerpts):

---

45 Psalm 1. 6, leaf 2ʳ.
46 See, e.g., Psalm 89. 53, leaf 97ᵛ.
47 See, e.g., Psalm 119. 1, leaf 127ʳ (bottom) reads בתורת יהיה instead of בתורת יהוה. Sometimes the Tetragrammaton is missing, but the text reflects a lacuna (Psalm 20. 10, 26. 8, a. fr.), sometimes even this lacuna is missing (Psalm 26. 12); however, in all these cases, the sentence is corrupt.
48 Also compare the extensive list in Ginsburg, pp. 784–89.
49 Further examples in Tychsen, Beschreibung der ersten jüdischen Psalmen-Ausgabe vom J. 1477, pp. 143–58; Ginsburg, pp. 788–89.
50 Cambridge, UL, Inc. 3.B.74.A.2, leaf 20ʳ.
51 'But this, indeed, makes me feel uncomfortable, because I know that there are quite a few mistakes in this (book), partly on the part of the printers, partly on my own account. This is because it is now more than 30 years ago since I shaped the comment, and I was not as good at grammar then as I am now' (ובאמת צר לי על ככה כי ידעתי כי יש בו טעותים לא מעט קצתם מצד הדופסים קצתם מצדי כי זה יותר משלשים שנה שחרתיו ולא היה כחו אז בדקדוק ככחי עתה); all translations are mine unless otherwise stated). The text is edited in Moritz Peritz, 'Ein Brief Elijah Levita's an Sebastian Münster, nach der von letzterem 1531 besorgten Ausgabe desselben auf's Neue herausgegeben und mit einer deutschen Uebersetzung und Anmerkungen versehen', *Monatsschrift für Geschichte und Wissenschaft des Judenthums*, 38 (N.F. 2), H. 6 (1894), pp. 252–67; see also, e.g., Deena Aranoff, 'Elijah Levita. A Jewish Hebraist', *Jewish History*, 23 (2009), pp. 17–40.
52 Qere ve-la ketiv ('read although not written') and ketiv ve-la qere ('written but not read').
53 For the comprehensive list, see Ginsburg, pp. 790–91.
54 Cambridge, UL, Inc. 3.B.74.A.2, leaf 5ᵛ.

Mikra'ot gedolot ha-keter	Edition Italy 1477
הישר — בא בתנועות היו״ד פ״א הפועל, שלא כמנהג נחי הפ״א; וכמהו 'היצא אתך' (בר׳ ח , יז). והכתוב הוא בוא״ו, על מנהג נחי הפ״א. ובא בפתח עי״ן הפעל, כמו 'הנחת יי׳ גבוריך' (יואל ד , יא)	הישר בא בהנעת היוד פא הפועל פא כ כמנהגו נחי הפא וכמוהו היצא אתך והכתוב הוא בויו על מנהג נחי הפ וסן בפתח עין הפעל כמו הנ ינחת יי׳ גבוריך

(In) הישר 'make plain', the *yod* of the first radical is pronounced, and it is not like those cases in which the first radical is silent. And likewise (in the verse) היצא אתך ('bring out with you'; Gen. 8:17); however, it is written with (the letter) *vav*, as in those cases in which the first radical is silent, and (likewise in those cases) in which the second radical is vocalized with a *patah*.

In Psalm 5:9, the written form (*ketiv*) הוֹשַׁר is to be read (*qere*) הַיְשַׁר. This is a good example of what happens when the text does not include masoretic metatext such as *masora parva*, *masora magna*, and/or *ketiv*/*qere* notes. Qimhi explained the *ketiv*/*qere*,[55] but this explanation is quite sophisticated, and since both the biblical text and the commentary are printed without vowels, I would not expect one to read the *qere* הַיְשַׁר *ad loc* correctly. This is even less probable as the commentary contains quite a few errors and, obviously, the typesetter did not take note of the fact that the biblical text and the commentary do not match.

In Psalm 6:4, the biblical text reads only the *ketiv*: ואת (the *qere* being: ואתה), but there a later reader noted and left a handwritten masoretic note: תה קר. One last example offered here shows that in particular in regard to the *ketiv*/*qere*, the biblical text and the commentary do not match, and the printer did not relate to that. In Psalm 9:13,[56] the biblical עניים is the *ketiv* (the *qere* being: עֲנָוִים), and Qimhi offered an exegetical explanation for this *ketiv*/*qere*: 'It is written with a *yod* [עניים ("the poor")], and is read [as if written] with a *vav* as ענוים ("meek"), for the meek are for the most part the poor and helpless',[57] but this explanation does not make sense in this rendering of Psalm 9:13, where only the *qere* is printed.[58] We can only speculate as to whether the absence of the Masorah in this early printing was actually the result of an anti-rabbinic attitude.[59] In Ashkenaz, the Masorah was an instrument for preserving the exegetical and theological polyphony of the text in recensions of the Bible; in the edition at hand, the biblical text in its *qere*-form and the Qimhi commentary (explaining the Hebrew) might have been meant to serve, all the more, as a standardization of that text.

Up to this point, one must admit that this print does not reflect any of the features that characterize the efforts of later Hebrew printing as it developed, for example, the Soncino print shop produced a book with an error-free text based on text-critical comparisons of the manuscripts.[60]

---

55 Qimhi refers to Genesis 8:17 and Joel 4:11; compare also Isaiah 45:2.

56 Cambridge, UL, Inc. 3.B.74.A.2, leaf 9ᵛ.

57 כתוב ביו״ד וקרי בוא״ו: עניים, כי העניים והחלושים ענוים ברוב (Qimhi on Psalm 9. 13).

58 Ginsburg, pp. 790–91, lists the *ketiv*/*qere* cases only with regard to the biblical text, but not in relation to the commentary.

59 It is well known that as early as in Italian manuscripts from the thirteenth century on we find a constant disregard for the Masorah: see, e.g., MS Vatican, Biblioteca Apostolica, Vat. Ross. 554 (1286; https://digi.vatlib.it/view/MSS_Ross.554 [accessed in August 2021]; see Benjamin Richler, *Hebrew Manuscripts in the Vatican Library: Catalogue* (Vatican City: Biblioteca Apostolica Vaticano, 2008), p. 592. According to Stern, those Bibles focusing on the source text without any other 'mediator' such as the Targum, the Masorah, or commentaries 'reflect the larger Humanist culture in Italy at the time' (Stern, *Jewish Literary Cultures*, p. 106).

60 See also Amnon Raz-Krakotzkin, *The Censor, the Editor, and the Text: The Catholic Church and the Shaping of the Jewish Canon in the Sixteenth Century* (Philadelphia: University of Pennsylvania Press, 2007), esp. pp. 96–119.

The text under discussion here was not typeset carefully.

Given the many errors in this edition, the value of such a book is further questioned when one takes a closer look at the layout of the text. After every verse/half-verse, the biblical text — bold and square-cut — is followed by the Qimhi commentary in Rabbinic cursive. According to David Stern (following Malachi Beit-Arié), the semi-cursive mode that dominated the print layout was 'regarded by medieval scribes and owners of books as more beautiful and elegant than the various square modes'.[61] I suggest rather that the dominance of semi-cursive characters in manuscripts as well as in the early printings is a feature of private copies of the Bible/Bible with commentary. Observe, for example, the manuscript Paris, Bibliothèque nationale de France, Cod. hebr. 27.[62] It is written in semi-cursive characters, the biblical text is only eclectically vocalized and provided with accents,[63] and it is heavily glossed. The (later) glosses reflect a range of different kinds of comments including masoretic notes, Targum, and excerpts from commentary. From those features one can assume that in a similar fashion, the early printings in Rabbinic cursive were not meant to be used in synagogues, but rather were intended for use in private homes. Support for this notion can be found in the fact that most of the text of this edition of *Psalms with Qimhi* (1477) lacks such aids for reading and/or pronunciation as vowels and/or accents.

Finally, the layout of our book is confusing. There is no indication of where one psalm ends and a new one begins, nor do the gaps in the text (which might have been introduced to suggest the *petuhot* and *setumot* in the Bible manuscripts) seem to reflect any particular system. Any reader accustomed to the manuscript culture would have rubbed his/her eyes and wondered what to do with such a book, and why one should read the psalms from such a poor and faulty edition. Herbert C. Zafren's question is still pertinent today insofar as it has not yet been properly answered:

> The historical question that soon occurred to me was 'What factors may have led to the choice of what printers printed at any given time and place?' And another question, a methodological one, presented itself: 'Might the artifactual data, that is, the books themselves, suggest possible answers?'[64]

One of these possible answers may be found in the layout of this early printing. A closer look reveals that the main text on almost every page is the Qimhi commentary since it is much longer than the biblical verses, and biblical text and commentary alternate. This layout hints at a shift in regard to the hierarchy of the sources, the book's primary source now being the Qimhi commentary, accompanied by the biblical text, which in some cases seems to be downgraded to biblical catchwords. Qimhi's commentary provides the reader with a solid explanation of the Hebrew language found in the psalms and a basic introduction into *peshat* exegesis accompanied by a careful selection of rabbinic teachings. Unlike later print editions that seek to have the biblical text match exactly with the commentary in order to ensure easy checking and comparing of the two,[65] this edition focuses primarily on Qimhi's

---

61 Stern, *Jewish Literary Cultures*, p. 107.
62 https://gallica.bnf.fr/ark:/12148/btv1b90027737/f45.item.r=Hébreu.langEN [accessed in August 2021].
63 On some pages only the *atnah* and/or *zaqef* is given; it seems that the manuscript was never completed.
64 Zafren, p. *240.
65 Some printings organize their text in two columns, e.g., *Latter Prophets with Qimhi* (Soncino, 1486) and *Psalms with Qimhi* (Naples, 1487); some present two text blocks arranged vertically, e.g., *Former Prophets with Qimhi* (Soncino, 1485); some show the biblical text block in the middle of the page with the Targum and commentary

commentary. This is underscored by the fact that the book opens with Qimḥi's introduction to the Book of Psalms, nicely set with a blank space after אמר דוד and a kind of *setuma* in the second row. The last sentence of Qimḥi's introduction is printed in an additional text row, and this sentence is typeset in the same font as the biblical text: ועתה אחל לפרש כפי אשר תשיג ידי בעזרת המלמד לאדם דעת ('And now I will begin to interpret as I shall be able by the help of Him who teaches man knowledge'). Before we think about what kind of reader we have to imagine, let us first take a look at the colophon and ask what information it offers.

The Printer and His Targeted Readers

Similar to manuscripts, many of the early printings contain colophons. *Psalms with Qimḥi* (1477) features a colophon on the last page:

בעת תושלמת מלאכת הספרים אשר בדפוסי האותיות נקבעו לסדרים באותה מלאכה ימצאו שלש מאות ספרים המהדרים מן המהדרים תהילים עם פירוש הקמחי לעיני רואיהם יבהיקו כספירים על כן לנאזר בגבורה נפארנו ברננה וקול זמרה ובשיר כל משוררים כן יזכנו להגות בהם אנחנו וכל בני עמינו לעדי עד ולדור דורים ללמוד וללמד לשמור ולעשות ולקיים את כל הכתוב בהם יזכנו יוצר כל יוצרו. ויהי נועם יי אלהי עלי. ומעשה ידינו כוננה עלינו ויברכינו. יאר פניו אתנו במלאכת ידינו כי יצליחנו בכל משלח ידינו מראשיתנו ועד אחריתנו בעשרים יום בחודש אלול בשנת רלז נגמרה פעולתינו. צור מעוזינו יחיש גואלינו במהרה בימינו המעתירים ככה בהם עושי המלאכה מייישטר יוסף ונריה חיים מרדכי וחזקיה מונטרו סליק סליק סליק.

(At the time, when the techniques of [printing] books were first acquired, that enabled the printing of [moveable] letters set in rows — 300 copies of this book were produced — the most ever diligent [copies of] the [book of] Psalms with the commentary of the Qimḥi, shining brilliantly like sapphires to all who behold them. Therefore, let us extol Him *who is girded with might* [Ps. 65:7] with *shouts of joy* [Ps. 100:2] *and melodious song* [Ps. 98:5] of all the singers. May He now grant us to recite from them — we and all the children of our people forever and ever, and from generation to generation, to learn and to teach, to keep [it], to do [it], and to fulfil all that is written herein. May the Creator of all created beings grant [this] to us.
May the favour of the Lord, our God, be upon us; let the work of our hands prosper [Ps. 90:17]. *May God be gracious unto us and bless us; may He show us favour* [Ps. 67:2] in the skill of our hands. He has granted us success in all our undertakings from the beginning until the end. On the twentieth day of the month of Elul, in the year [5]237 [i.e., Friday, 29 August 1477] our work was finished. May the rock of our strength hasten our redeemer speedily in our days. Thus, pray those who do this [kind of] work: Maestro Yosef Venria(?) / Ḥayyim Mordekhai and Ḥizqia / Monṭero. Finis. Finis. Finis.)[66]

The colophon tells us that *Psalms with Qimḥi* (1477) was finished on 20 Elul (5)237, that is, 29 August 1477 by 'Meister' (מיישטר ['master/ maestro']) Joseph and two of his colleagues

---

surrounding it on three sides, e.g., *Pentateuch with Targum and Rashi* (Bologna, 1482); for bibliographical details of these print editions, see Zafren, p. *243. For the various layouts, see Gerhard Powitz, 'Textus cum commento', in *Codices manuscripti* 5 (1979), pp. 80–89, esp. p. 82.

66 *Psalms with Qimḥi* (1477), leaf 152ᵛ, edited in Ginsburg, p. 781; see also Tychsen, 'Beschreibung der ersten jüdischen Psalmen-Ausgabe', pp. 83–84.

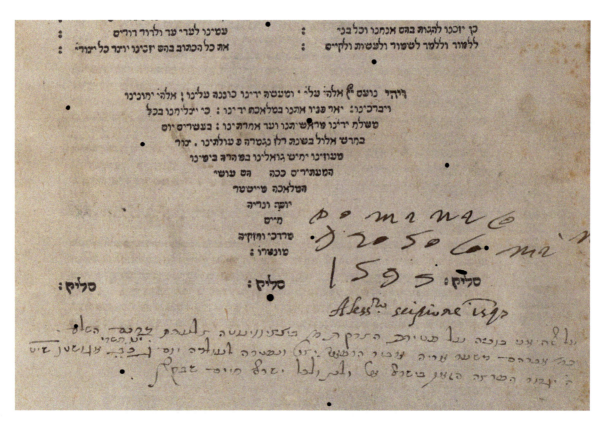

Figure 11.2. Psalms with Qimhi. Bologna(?), 1477. Cambridge, University library, leaf 152v.

(Hayyim Mordekhai and Hizqia Montero; Figure 11.2).⁶⁷ The title 'Meister' (German for 'master craftsman') marks the Ashkenazi origins of Maestro Joseph. From the fact that in many places the text displays a peculiar spelling with *holam* (*vav* in plene scripture) instead of *qamatz*,⁶⁸ Tychsen inferred that the typesetter followed a Polish pronunciation of the Hebrew.⁶⁹

The book itself belies the colophon's complimentary assessment in almost every respect. Our study so far indicates that the philological quality of the biblical text and the commentary as well as the

---

67 Freimann, 'Ueber hebräische Inkunabeln', p. 6, does not mention the name 'Neria' at all (see the copy Faksimile A 52 R 1035; see above note 33); Ginsburg, p. 781, translated as 'Master Joseph and Neriah, Chayim Mordecai and Ezekiel of Ventura'; Tychsen, 'Beschreibung der ersten jüdischen Psalmen-Ausgabe', p. 140, explains נריה as Joseph's dynasty/family name as 'van Reh / Venria', and introduces in addition to Joseph 'Chajim Mardochai' and 'Hiskia Montro oder Monetro, Monteru, oder noch anders' as co-workers (ibid, p. 141; likewise Schenker, p. 277); Petzold, *Masora und Exegese*, p. 56, translated as 'Yoseph, Neria Chajim, Mordechai und Ḥiskia aus Ventura' (see above Berkowitz, p. 72, which reads 'Joseph, Neriah, Chayyim Mordecai, and Hezekiah de Venturo'), but to the best of my knowledge we do not know of a place called Ventura/Venturo, and the dot on the *Waw* of the word מונטרו is a possible indication of a name. Since the text reads יוסף ונריה

instead of נריה יוסף, one has to either assume a second person or decide for reading it as a transliteration of a foreign name as Tychsen proposed. I decided for the latter, but this reconstruction remains uncertain.
68 Psalm 71. 20 צָרוֹת is written as צורות; Psalm 84. 7 הבוכה instead of הַבָּכָא; Psalm 90. 11 וכיראותך instead of וּכְיִרְאָתְךָ.
69 Tychsen, 'Beschreibung der ersten jüdischen Psalmen-Ausgabe', pp. 138–39.

layout do not reflect 'the most ever diligent [copies of] the [Book of] Psalms with the commentary of the Qimhi', but the poor quality of the philology fits perfectly with the special emphasis on skill and business. Colophons in medieval manuscripts do not generally include a request for the divine blessing for prosperity and for the success of the business. They rather were intended to provide the reader with basic information in regard to the manuscript's production — the scribe, the patron, the place, and the date.[70] The more learned a scribe was, the more he would highlight his philological, artistic, and intellectual abilities. Sometimes, even praxeological information can be deduced from a colophon: In MS Vatican, Biblioteca Apostolica, Vat. ebr. 14, written in 1239 in Rouen by Elijah ben Berekhyah ha-Naqdan for a certain, though unknown, R. Asher, Elijah introduced himself among others as 'I, the scribe, the *naqdan* [punctuator] and the *masran* [masorete],... the *qara* [Bible teacher], the *hadran* [the one who runs a *heder*]), and the *pashtan* [exegete]'.[71] From that we learn that Asher's manuscript was meant to serve as a book for basic Jewish study. Clearly, Elijah's colophon refers less to the patron who commissioned the manuscript and more to its intended functions within a Jewish educational setting.

Today a manuscript colophon provides a historian with information in connection with purchase and production practices, but its most important feature is its explicit reference to individual and private circumstances, and, usually, this information was meant to be kept private as well.[72] A colophon in a printed book at the beginning of the printing era did not differ substantially from manuscript colophons, but it served a completely different function: it offered an entire reading community (in our case 300 readers) basic information in regard to the production process, the costs, and the number of books in the edition. Thus, it was not by chance that Meister Joseph highlighted his professional success. Although his business was less emphasized than his skills, it is already quite clear what that would lead to, namely the printing industry's financial gains. This becomes even clearer when we compare it with the colophon of the Bologna edition *Pentateuch with Rashi and Targum* (Bologna, 1482) that appeared only five years later.[73] In this edition, the colophon elucidates in detail that printing was not only a philological endeavour but all the more a technical and costly task. The proofreader, Joseph Hayyim, offered abundant information not only in regard to his own claims, but also in connection with the printing process as such:

אני יוסף חיים בהר׳ אהרן זלה׳ה שטרשבורג צרפתי
ראיתי המלאכה הנכבדת אשר החלו לעשות חומש

---

70 On further information to be found in the colophons such as scribal formulae or blessings, see in particular the description in Malachi Beit-Arié, *Hebrew Codicology: Historical and Comparative Typology of Hebrew Medieval Codices Based on the Documentation of the Extant Dated Manuscripts in Quantitative Approach* (Jerusalem and Hamburg 2021: The Israel Academy of Sciences and Humanities Press; DOI English-Version https://doi.org/10.25592/uhhfdm.9349 [accessed in March 2022]), pp. 123–215; see also Evelyn M. Cohen, 'Can Colophons Be Trusted? Insights from Decorated Hebrew Manuscripts Produced for Women in Renaissance Italy', in *The Hebrew Book in Early Modern Italy*, ed. by Joseph R. Hacker and Adam Shear (Philadelphia: University of Pennsylvania Press, 2011), pp. 17–25.

71 The entire text is quoted in Élodie Attia, *The Masorah of Elijah ha-Naqdan: An Edition of Ashkenazi Micrographical Notes (Ms. Vat. Ebr. 14, Book of Exodus)*, Materiale Textkulturen, 11 (Berlin: De Gruyter, 2015), p. 127.

72 Cf. Malachi Beit-Arié, 'Commissioned and Owner-Produced Manuscripts in the Sephardi Zone and Italy in the Thirteenth–Fifteenth Centuries', in *The Late Medieval Hebrew Book in the Western Mediterranean: Hebrew Manuscripts and Incunabula in Context*, ed. by Javier del Barco (Leiden and Boston: Brill, 2015), pp. 15–27, esp. pp. 16–18. According to Bet-Arié (p. 17), the *Worms Mahzor* represents an exceptional case because it was not produced for personal use.

73 I had access to the Cambridge edition, UL, Inc. 2.B.10.16., leaf 219ᵛ; see also Zafren, p. *243.

ותרגום ופירוש רשׂיּ בכרך אחד ובחנתי כי מאת ה׳
היתה זאת נפלאת היא ונתתי את לבי להגיה הפירוש
מרשׂיּ ולהחזיר העטרה לישנה כפי האפשר וזאת
היתה משמרתי … ותשלם כל המלאכה מלאכת
עבודת הקדש חומש ותרגום ופירוש רשׂיּ בכרך
אחד מדוקדקים במאד בכל הצריך להם והעיר ה׳
את רוח המפואר משכיל ונבון האלוף כמר יוסף
קרוויטה יצ״ו בכמר׳ אברהם זלה״ה להכין את כל
העבודה לעשות אותה בכספו וזהבו הכין כל כליה
והשכיר אומנים ופועלי הבקיאיּ וזריזים במלאכת
הדפוס חכם חרש יבקש לו וגם יודעי ספר להגיה
החומש גם במלא וחסר וקרייןׂ ולא כתיבן וכתיבן
ולא קריין בנקודו וטעמיו והתרגוֹ כהלכתו וגם
פירוֹ רשׂיּ להעמידו על ממכונו ותלו. ויבחר לו איש
בקי במלאכת אומן יקרא אין כמוהו בכל הארצות
במלאכת הדפוס בכתב אשורי ובלשׂוֹ עבר שמו נודע
בשערים מישׂטרה אברהם יצ״ו בכמר׳ חיים זלה״ה מן
הצבועים מארץ פיסרו ונשלמה המלאכה התמימה
ביום שׁשׁי בחמשה ימים לירח א׳ אדר הראשון שנת
חמשת אלפים ומאתים וארבעים ושתים לבריאת
עולם פה בולונייא. כל הקונה מאלו הספרים טוב
טוב יאמר הקונה וההוגה בהם יראה זרע יאריך ימים
וחפץ ה׳ בידו יצלח וחיים ושלום על ישראל אמן.

(I, Yosef Ḥayyim Strasbourg, a Frenchman, son of Rabbi Aharon, May His Memory Be Blessed for the Life in the World to come, saw this honourable work that they had undertaken to produce, that is, the Pentateuch, the Targum, and the commentary of Rashi[74] in one volume, and I found out that this honourable [work] was from the Lord, and I have tried diligently to correct Rashi's commentary [in a way that] restores its former glory insofar as possible, and this was my task. […] Thus, the entire work was finished, the sacred work, the Pentateuch, the Targum, and the commentary of Rashi in one volume, very carefully [corrected] in any respect, and the Lord raised up the noble, discerning, and wise, the first in his field, Maestro Yosef Qarweṭa [Caravita], son of the honoured teacher Avraham, May His Memory Be Blessed for the Life in the World to come, to prepare the entire work and to execute it at his own expense, to prepare all the implements [needed], to hire craftsmen and experts, proficient and nimble in the printing work. He sought out a wise artisan as well as proofreaders to correct the Pentateuch in regard to the *plene* and *defective* [writing], the *qere ve-la ketiv* ['read although not written'] and *ketiv ve-la qere* ['written but not read'] spellings in connection with their vocalization and their accentuation; the Targum according to its [grammatical?] rules; and, similarly, restore the Rashi commentary to its original standard.

He also chose for himself the proficient expert in this business, [the one who] is called the unrivalled best across all national borders in the art of typography as well as in the [Hebrew] square script and in the Hebrew language, the well-known Maestro Avraham, son of the honoured teacher Hayyim, May His Memory Be Blessed for the Life in the World to come, from the dyers of Pesaro ['dei Tintori of Pesaro'[75]]. This excellent [printing] work was completed on the sixth day [Friday] on the fifth of the month *Adar Rishon* [Adar I] in the year 5242 [counted from the] creation of the world, in this city of Bologna. Anyone who buys one of these books will be called for good, and whoever thinks deeply with them will be blessed with offspring, extend his days and fulfil the will of the Eternal, everything will

---

74 Note the acronym רשׂיּ.

75 On this term see the discussion in Tychsen, 'Kritische Beschreibung des Bononischen Pentateuchs', pp. 86–87.

work out for him, and he will bring life and peace upon Israel. Amen.)⁷⁶

Without going into the philological quality of this print edition in more detail,⁷⁷ this mission statement by Joseph Hayyim clearly describes a sophisticated division of labour, since he himself was responsible for the philological quality of the text, whereas the printing press belonged to Maestro Joseph ben Abraham Qarweta (Caravita) who — at his own expense and risk — acquired the necessary tools and craftsmen and hired Abraham ben Hayyim *dei Tintori* of Pesaro (מן הצבועים מארץ פיסרו) for the typesetting. Blessings are promised first and foremost to those, 'who buy one of these books'. In describing all the financial and technical efforts that went into this printed book edition, the colophon addresses especially the rich and extravagant Jewish and Christian purchasers of books (perhaps knowing that far more Christian scholars than fellow Jews were there to be inspired).

Hence, we can observe a general shift that I characterize as a 'shift of spatial and social areas', which was another important feature of the so-called Jewish Renaissance, especially in Italy. The Jews of Italy became involved in Italian society in the fields of science, technology, medicine, and art in an unprecedented way.⁷⁸ On the one hand, they tried to keep up with society, whereas on the other they sought to actively define and help shape that new society. In order to reach this goal, they left their limited 'Jewish' space, which can be characterized as a large, though still 'private' sphere, and moved into the non-Jewish environment, the public space. The Jews went 'outside' as doctors, financiers, printers, and booksellers; they engaged in their activities in this non-Jewish public space; and their professions and occupations — corresponding to the those in the non-Jewish world — had to be adapted to that space. Modern scientific and technological knowledge as well as educational achievements, which at least some elements of the Jewish population did not want to neglect, now had to be redefined within the discourses of Jewish learning and living, and technical achievements were declared a genuine part of religion.

Thus, the sheltered space was opened, and this was also true of the printing industry. At the latest, from the time when the first print editions were produced and had to be sold and distributed, the Jewish printers entered the public space and began to target potential customers not only in their own fellow group but also in the non-Jewish environment, that is, the Christian Hebraists. Given the facts that Bibles and Bible commentaries (in particular Rashi, Levi ben Gershon, and David Qimhi) make up a large part of the extant incunabula⁷⁹ and that it is hardly possible to trace in detail to whom the books

---

76 Cambridge, UL, Inc. 2.B.10.16., leaf 219ᵛ and the Bologna Pentateuch, 1482 from the *Judaica & Rosenbachiana Collection* (https://rosenbach.org/collection-highlight/the-bologna-pentateuch-1482/; digital access https://archive.org/details/Hamishah_Humshe_Torah [no foliation; accessed in March 2022]); slightly differently edited in Ginsburg, *Introduction*, pp. 795–96; see also Tychsen, 'Kritische Beschreibung des Bononischen Pentateuchs', pp. 83–84.

77 Compare the description in Tychsen, 'Kritische Beschreibung des Bononischen Pentateuchs', esp. pp. 91–103, and Ginsburg, pp. 794–802.

78 Compare, e.g., the Jewish doctor and polymath Judah ben Yehiel Rofe Messer Leon (*c.* 1420–*c.* 1497), who is often regarded as *the* Jewish Renaissance personality; cf. Hughes, 'Translation and the Invention of Renaissance Jewish Culture'; Hanna Liss, '"Schrift ohne Tradition?" – Einige Aspekte zum Verständnis der Bibel im jüdischen Italien des 15. und 16. Jahrhunderts', in *An der Schwelle zur Moderne: Juden in der Renaissance*, ed. by Giuseppe Veltri and Annette Winkelmann (Leiden and Boston: Brill, 2003), pp. 51–77, esp. pp. 56–63.

79 Bertagna, pp. 302–03 lists 231 incunabula in thirteen Italian libraries of which more than 50 per cent are Bible/Bible-commentary editions.

belonged,[80] so the question of ownership in many cases remains unanswered, it appears that circulation of even the early printed editions was not limited to the Jewish community.

In regard to *Psalms with Qimhi* (1477), it is, indeed, not easy to imagine this kind of book for 'the children of our people to learn and to teach' from: What should have been taught and learned? What was there to be kept and fulfilled? On the one hand, we can hardly assume that reading and learning psalms was the goal that was to be achieved by using this printed book. On the other hand, the commentary might well have been used by less educated Jews to acquire a basic knowledge of Hebrew, that is, Jews who in former times would not have had the opportunity to learn from books (*quntresim*; manuscripts) but had to study with a Bible master. We have no detailed information regarding the prices of these early Hebrew printings but it is reasonable to assume that this edition was perhaps less costly than a handwritten manuscript.[81] Therefore, it might have been general economic optimism that led to the development of the printing industry, as providing Christians with Hebrew books turned out to be a profitable business,[82] even though the early printings did not meet the philological quality standards that were the norm in the manuscript cultures.

Thus, it is quite likely that our edition of *Psalms with Qimhi* (1477) was produced as an early response to the 'emergence of Christian Hebraism with its emerging interest in classical Jewish texts'.[83] However, modern scholarship often seems too romantic in describing the 'intellectual exchanges between Jewish and Christian humanists'[84] in the Italian printing presses too positively as kind of a Golden Age of Jewish-Christian relations. Even though the Jews worked in the printing presses, they remained outcasts as long as they chose to remain Jewish. The 'adoption of Jewish literature along with the rejection of the Jewish position'[85] might have led, at least in the beginning of the printing era, to an attitude among the Jews that had them gladly leaving the printing products to the Christians, as long as it meant that they were given unrestricted access to the Hebrew manuscripts. It would, indeed, take a special talent to turn the text written in a(ny) manuscript into a printed text of such a low philological quality as is the case in this edition of the *Psalms with Qimhi* (1477).[86]

There is yet another argument fostering the notion that the early printings should, more than

---

80 See Bertagna, pp. 304–05: 'In the incunabula I checked, Christian owners seldom appear before the seventeenth century. However, Jewish owners are not usually present in the last phases of their history. Based on this observation, we can maintain that Hebrew incunabula circulated among Jews in the earliest centuries of their existence and, after that, for reasons that are still unclear (perhaps because the exacerbation of censorship on Hebrew books made circumstances more difficult for Jewish collectors), there is a prevalence of Christian owners'.

81 On the book prices and the decrease in prices during the 1480s and 1490s, see esp. Cristina Dondi, 'From the Corpus Iuris to "psalterioli da puti", on Parchment, Bound, Gilt… The Price of Any Book Sold in Venice 1484–1488', in *Printing Evolution and Society 1450–1500: Fifty Years that Changed Europe*, pp. 577–99, esp. p. 578.

82 On the numbers and titles of Hebrew prints found in Christian book collections, see in particular Stephen G. Burnett, *Christian Hebraism in the Reformation Era*

(1500–1660) (Leiden: Brill, 2012), esp. pp. 160–67 (my thanks to Ilona Steimann who drew my attention to this chapter).

83 Stern, *Jewish Literary Cultures*, p. 109.
84 Stern, *Jewish Literary Cultures*, p. 109.
85 See in particular Raz-Krakotzkin, p. 100.
86 Schenker, p. 284, notes that 'the quality of the texts used depends on the manuscripts the printers had at their disposal. These were not outstanding masoretic manuscripts'. I suggest that Schenker's evaluation of the manuscripts is guided by the high value that Christian Bible scholars placed on the Oriental manuscript tradition (vs. the Ashkenazi tradition), similar to that of Ginsburg, who qualifies the manuscripts against a *textus receptus*. However, the many mistakes in the edition at hand were not due to the use of an Ashkenazi manuscript.

hitherto, have been interpreted as a (Jewish) product for the Christian world. A handwritten Hebrew manuscript was usually executed by one or several scribes, punctuators, and/or masoretes, who even added *masora figurata* illustrations to the pages. All of those tasks required the highest level of erudition and training. Even among the Jews there were no longer many individuals who had the appropriate scribal skills. Moreover, it was difficult for Christians to catch up with this scribal culture, but their need to access the Hebrew texts, at the latest from the beginning of the confrontation between Catholics and Protestants, became more and more urgent.[87] As a corollary, the printing industry, which initiated a division of labour, generated a higher demand for people involved in book production, including Jewish craftsmen who had never written a manuscript and typesetters who had reading knowledge but lacked good philological skills. They all benefited from this Christian need.[88] *Psalms with Qimhi* (1477) notes several individuals involved in the 'skills of [printing] books'. Even though well-educated men on the Christian side such as Johannes Reuchlin (1455–1522) acquired Hebrew books (manuscripts as well as early printings) in order to improve their understanding of *hebraica veritas* (and would, thus, have been disappointed by such a poorly executed edition),[89] for book sellers and book collectors, many of whom were not even able to read Hebrew,[90] an edition such as *Qimhi with Psalms* (1477) would not have done any harm.

Therefore, the early printings should not be regarded simply as 'printing exercises' in general. It might have been that they were meant as part of an upcoming Jewish *business* (later on in Christian printing houses) in the public space that was not necessarily meant to replace the handwritten manuscript culture for erudite Jewish men. It was only in the first quarter of the sixteenth century that the Jewish community realized and had to accept that, step-by-step, the Christians had taken over the Hebrew Bible for their own purposes *and* that its own manuscript culture was irretrievably lost. At that point, the erudite and well-educated had to react and thus took part in this leap towards the future. The prints of the first and second Rabbinic Bible (1517, 1523) are the best representatives of this complex evolution in text and design that reflects the attempts to return Bible study to the Jewish community.

---

87 On the peculiar role that Elia Levita played in the circulation of the writings of Qimhi among Christian scholars, see Ludwig Geiger, *Das Studium der hebräischen Sprache in Deutschland vom Ende des XV. bis zur Mitte des XVI. Jahrhunderts* (Breslau: Schletter'sche Buchhandlung, 1870); Emma Abate, 'Elias Levita the Lexicographer and the Legacy of *Sefer ha-Shorashim*', *Sefarad*, 76 (2016), pp. 289–311.

88 See above Neddermeyer, p. 215: 'Das grundsätzliche Problem muß somit anders formuliert werden: Leitete erst eine technologische Revolution das Buchzeitalter ein oder ermöglichte die gestiegene Nachfrage nach Büchern die Einführung einer neuen Technik bzw. erzwang sie gleichsam?'.

89 Cf., e.g., Reimund Leicht, 'Johannes Reuchlin's Collection of Hebrew Books: Its Afterlife and Influence', in *Jewish Manuscript Cultures: New Perspectives*, ed. by Irina Wandrey (Berlin and Boston: Brill, 2016), pp. 227–42; on Pfefferkorn's confiscation of Hebrew books, see David H. Price, *Johannes Reuchlin and the Campaign to Destroy Jewish Books* (Oxford: Oxford University Press, 2011).

90 On the book collector Hartmann Schedel (1440–1514) from Nuremberg who owned eight Hebrew codices without knowing any Hebrew, see Ilona Steimann, 'The Preservation of Hebrew Books by Christians in the Pre-Reformation German Milieu', in *Jewish Manuscript Cultures: New Perspectives*, ed. by Irina Wandrey (Berlin and Boston: Brill, 2016), pp. 203–26, (pp. 204–06).

Figure 11.3 Psalms with Qimhi. Bologna(?), 1477. Cambridge, University library, leaf 3r.

The Censored Book

Finally, our copy of the *Psalms with Qimhi* (1477) clearly shows one of the book's ultimate destinations on a Christian bookshelf, as it reflects various signs of censoring.[91] The censor was the well-known Domenico Irosolimitana (also known under the names Gerosolimitano[92] and Hierosolymitano;[93] 1555–1621), an apostate and convert[94] (born in 1555 and baptized in 1593), who censored the book in 1595 and signed on the last page (fol. 152ᵛ; Figure 11.2),[95] but who

Figure 11.4. Parma, Biblioteca Palatina, Cod. Parm. 1872, leaf 6ᵛ. Parma, Biblioteca Palatina.

can also be easily identified by the censored sections of the book.

Take, for example, the censored section in Psalm 2:12 (נַשְּׁקוּ־בַ֡ר פֶּן־יֶאֱנַ֤ף; Figure 11.3). The lines erased are the same as in two Parma manuscripts of the Qimhi commentary — Parma, Biblioteca Palatina, Cod. Parm. 1872 (thirteenth century; fol. 6ᵛ [signature fol. 289ᵛ][96] [Figure 11.4]) and

---

91 Cambridge, UL, Inc. 3.B.74.A.2, leaves 3ʳ–3ᵛ (Ps. 2:12); 7ʳ (Ps. 7:8); 20ʳ (Ps. 19. 8); 20ᵛ (Ps. 19. 10); 25ʳ (Ps. 22. 23); 50ᵛ (Ps. 45. 18); 72ᵛ (Ps. 69:10); 76ᵛ–77ʳ (Ps. 72:20); 79ᵛ (Ps. 74:12); 87ᵛ (Ps. 80:14); 93ᵛ (Ps. 87:7); 122ʳ (Ps. 110:7); 135ᵛ (Ps. 120:5); 138ʳ (Ps. 127:5); 138ᵛ (Ps. 129:7); 143ᵛ (Ps. 137:6); 145ᵛ (Ps. 139:21) — most of these polemical passages were integrated in the so-called התשובות הרד״ק לנוצרים, translated and explained in Bernard H. Mehlman and Daniel F. Polish, 'The Response to the Christian Exegesis of Psalms in the Teshuvot la-Nozrim of Rabbi David Qimhi', in *Jewish Civilization: Essays and Studies: Judaism and Christianity*, ed. by Ronald A. Brauner (Philadelphia: Reconstructionist Rabbinical College Press, 1985), III, pp. 181–208, (184–94).

92 Cf. Raz-Krakotzkin, esp. pp. 84–94, 120–74; see above William Popper, *The Censorship of Hebrew Books* (New York: Knickerbocker Press, 1899; repr. New York: Ktav, 1969), esp. pp. 50–89.

93 Cf. Judith Thomanek, *Zeugnisse christlicher Zensur des frühen hebräischen Buchdrucks im Greifswalder Gustav Dalman-Institut* (Leipzig: Evangelische Verlagsanstalt, 2017), pp. 236–38.

94 See in particular Gila Prebor, 'From Jerusalem to Venice: The Life of Domenico Yerushalmi, His Writings and His Work as a Censor' [in Hebrew], *Pe'amim: Studies in Oriental Jewry*, 111/12 (2007), pp. 215–42.

95 Bertagna, p. 315, mentions Irosolimitana as having also censored the edition *Writings with Qimhi* (Naples 1487) (see esp. Figure 15 showing Irosolimitana's signature); Tychsen, 'Beschreibung der ersten jüdischen Psalmen-Ausgabe', p. 139, had a copy of the 1477 edition at hand in which the name of the censor was illegible owing to faded ink. The 1477 edition from the Valmadonna Trust Fund Library (Faksimile von A 52 R 1035): see https://www.nli.org.il/he/books/NNL_ALEPH002009528/NLI [accessed in March 2022] was not censored at all.

96 https://t1p.de/e5xl [accessed in March 2022]. The second person censoring this manuscript was Giovanni Domenico Carretto, 1618 (leaf 289ʳ). I thank my doctoral candidate Johannes Müller, who is currently working on his thesis on Qimhi's commentary on Psalms, for sharing his research on the censored manuscripts with

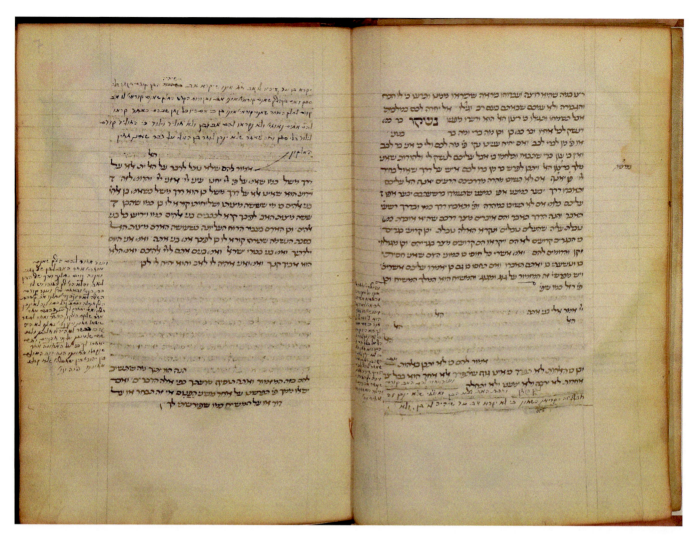

Figure 11.5. Parma, Biblioteca Palatina, Cod. Parm. 2881, leaves 6ᵛ–7ʳ.

Cod. Parm. 2881 (fourteenth century; censored in 1597; fol. 6ᵛ–7ʳ [signature fol. 160ʳ];[97] Figure 11.5) — that were also censored by Irosolimitana.

me; for Domenico's censoring, see in particular Gila Prebor, *'Sepher Ha-Ziquq' by Domenico Yerushalmi* [in Hebrew] (Jerusalem: Magnes Press, 2008); Prebor, '"Sefer HaZiquq" as a Source for Hebrew Bibliography' [in Hebrew], *Alei Sefer: Studies in Bibliography and in the History of the Printed and the Digital Hebrew Book*, 23 (2013), pp. 63–80.

[97] https://t1p.de/m1yq [accessed in March 2022]. The second person censoring this manuscript was, again, Giovanni Domenico Carretto, 1617 (leaf 160ᵛ).

Likewise, our copy of *Psalms with Qimhi* (Naples, 1487) shows strong blackening of the same verse(s). Thus, one can see that almost 120 years after this book had been printed, the printed copies were still treated as if they were manuscripts. It seems quite odd to censor a printed book, since the censor was dealing with only one copy of the book, not with the print model that represented the entire edition. Clearly, censorship of printed books became much more powerful when the censors eventually intervened in the printing process in order to have *all the copies* of a book printed in accordance with the theological ideology that guided the rules of censoring.[98] However, it would take another forty years until Felipe de Prato (Felix Pratensis), in the course of the preparation of the first Bomberg edition (1517) removed the polemical and anti-Christian sections from the Qimhi commentary and had them printed as an independent treatise entitled התשובות שעשה רד״ק לנוצרים ('The Responses that RaDaQ Prepared against the Christians'). This treatise was later reintegrated into the printed edition of Psalms produced by Paulus Fagius (Isny, 1541),[99] but not in every copy of the Fagius edition.[100] In any case, the treatise had been well known and popular among Christian scholars.

In his *Sefer ha-Ziquq*, that is, the *index expurgatorius*, a handbook for censors,[101] which discussed the general rules for censorship, Irosolimitana also listed almost 500 titles, meticulously labelling the paragraphs to be erased or deleted. As far as the early printings are concerned, we find twenty-four entries for *Psalms with Qimhi* (Naples, 1487)[102] and six entries for *Psalms with Qimhi* (Mantua, undated). Our copy of *Psalms with Qimhi* (Naples, 1487) does not reflect censorship in all twenty-four places where the *Sefer ha-Ziquq* required erasures or strikethroughs,[103] but we do not have access to a Mantua edition of the book.[104] If this model could be shown to refer to our edition, Italy, 1477, for which the city of printing remains uncertain, we would have to admit that our copy of the book shows many more erasures than *Sefer ha-Ziquq* prescribed.[105] Clearly, these findings explain why *Sefer ha-Ziquq* was written: a printed book that was widely known and printed in various copies represented a serious danger for the Christian faith, far more dangerous than a single manuscript, so censorship became an integral part of the printing process.

The censoring entries hint at the fact that during the sixteenth century in particular, Christian readers had turned to the printed Hebrew sources. Psalms as well as the Former Prophets, the Book of Job, and Proverbs have always had more importance for Christians than for Jews. It is not by chance that between 1469 and 1495, out of the twenty-three dated/printed Bibles/Bible parts[106]

---

98 The edict of censorship issued in 1486 by the archbishop of Mainz Berthold von Henneberg indicates that printed books were censored after the printing process.
99 See also Raz-Krakotzkin, p. 247; Heller, I, p. xxxvi.
100 Siegmund Jakob Baumgarten, *Nachrichten von merkwürdigen Büchern*, vols 7–8 (Halle: Gebauer, 1755), p. 386 mentioned Fagius's edition with this appendix entitled אלו הן התשובות שעשה רדק לנוצרים על קצת המזמורים וגם ההקשים שחבר עליהם ובתחלה במזמור שני למה רגשו, stating that Wolf had searched in vain for these *teshuvot* in his copy of the Isny edition ('Von diesem Anhange der gegenwärtigen Ausgabe… schreibt Wolf… *in hac autem* [editione anni 1542] *frustra quaesiui obiectiones illas Kimchi*; welches daher rüret, daß gedachter Anhang nicht allen Exemplaren beigefüget zu seyn scheinet'). It seems, therefore, that this appendix was not printed in every copy of Fagius's print from 1541. On this issue, see also Heller, I, p. 259.
101 See in particular the introduction into the edition by Prebor, 'Sepher Ha-Ziquq', pp. 7–25.
102 Cambridge, UL, 140 A 87a IX b2 5074; see also Zafren, pp. 243* and 247*, no. 19.
103 The *Sefer ha-Ziquq* (Prebor, 'Sepher Ha-Ziquq', pp. 98–99) requires erasure for the Naples print 1487 for Psalm 2 (see, e.g., מזמור ב׳ בסופו והתועים מפרשים אותו (עד סוף המזמור ימחה, for 7, 19, 21, 22, 45, 50, 69, 72, 80, 81, 86, 87, 110, 119, 122, 124, 127, 129, and 137. In the copy of the *Psalms with Qimhi* (Naples, 1487): Cambridge, UL, 140 A 87a IX b2 5074 [photograph]), erasures for Psalm 2 [והנוצרים instead of והתועים]; Psalms 19: 22, 45, 87, and 110 are visible (page numbers could not be made out owing to the fact that the paper is torn, so that most pages lack a page number). There might have been censor entries on some other pages, but the ink has already faded.
104 Likewise, Prebor, 'Sepher Ha-Ziquq', p. 125, admits to not having found a Mantua edition of the Psalms with the Qimhi commentary.
105 The *Sefer ha-Ziquq* (Prebor, 'Sepher Ha-Ziquq', p. 125) requires erasure for the Mantua(?) print 1477 for Psalms 50, 75, 80, 86, 95, 97, 124, and 129 (perhaps parts missing here).
106 Zafren. pp. 247*–248*, lists four or five full Bibles, nine editions of the Pentateuch, one edition of the Latter Prophets See also Freimann, 'Ueber hebräische Inkunabeln'.

and nineteen dated Bible/commentary editions, seven editions of the Psalms/Psalms-Job-Proverbs (without commentary), as well as two editions of Psalms with Qimhi, four editions of (Former and Latter) Prophets with Qimhi, as well as four editions of the Writings with Qimhi, Immanuel of Rome, Gersonides, or Ibn Yahya have survived.[107] Among the commentary editions that feature the text of the commentary, we find mainly works of medieval philosophers such as Nahmanides, Gersonides, and Qimhi.[108]

The censoring of the edition we have on hand as well as of the later editions with (mainly philological and philosophical) commentaries was done after the foundation of the Congregation of the Index in 1572.[109] That commission for the censorship of Hebrew literature, which functioned from 1572 to 1583, focused particularly on Bible commentaries, that is, on the genre that teaches one how to read and understand the biblical text: The books discussed by the Index were Bible commentaries, including those of Rashi, Radaq (R. David Qimhi), Ralbag (Gersonides; R. Levi ben Gershon), Itzhak Abrabanel, Nachmanides, Menachem Recanati, and Ovadia Sforno. These books were of great interest among Hebraist scholars; this teaches us that the central aim of the council was to approve the literature for the use of a Christian readership.[110]

This means that by the end of the sixteenth century at the latest, Qimhi's commentary (among others) not only went beyond a Jewish readership, but for some time remained in the Christian, foreign, realm. It was only from the late nineteenth century on that Qimhi and his commentaries regained some importance among the representatives of the *Wissenschaft des Judentums*.[111]

---

107 Zafren, pp. 247*–248*, lists among the dated text/commentary editions six editions of the Pentateuch with Rashi.
108 Zafren, pp. 247*–248*.
109 See in particular Raz-Krakotzkin, pp. 77–94 (pp. 81–84).
110 Raz-Krakotzkin, p. 82.
111 Jacob Tauber, *Standpunkt und Leistung des R. David Kimchi als Grammatiker* (Breslau: Selbstverlag des Verfassers, 1867); Abraham Geiger, 'Toldot ha-Radaq', *Otzar Nehmad*, 2 (1857), pp. 157–73.

FEDERICO DAL BO

Hegemonies of Reading

*Layout, Materiality, and Authorship in Early Hebrew Prints**

Introduction: Layout and Materiality of the Hebrew Book

In this chapter, I discuss an unusual feature of early Hebrew books — their layout or *mise-en-page* — from the perspective of material history. This brief study is based primarily on David Stern's views on the Jewish Bible as a material object, be it a scroll, a codex, or a printed book.[1]

Basically, material history, a relatively new branch of historiography, is the study of objects and the narratives that are implicitly 'archived' in them. This includes exploring the physical environment in which a culture was embedded and offers a sort of counter history to the 'big narratives' that usually focus on the history of ideas and symbols rather than on things, utility, and empirical facts. This does not mean that one should dismiss proper historical research for merely analysing artefacts but rather that one should acknowledge that, despite any Romantic or post-Romantic tropes, culture structures behaviour, taste, and design. Any and all of these factors also contribute towards an appreciation of social utility and mediate human relationships, since people are eager to symbolize — in Cassirer's notion of the symbolic — their status through display and consumption. In this respect, books represent a conspicuous example of this connection between culture and object: a book obviously is a means of circulating knowledge, but it is also a status symbol.

In his seminal text *The Jewish Bible: A Material History*, Stern follows the development of these forms from the Hellenistic era to the present, focusing mainly on the medieval and early modern eras. Although a vast amount of scholarship has explored a new perception of the Bible as a material object, Stern sheds new light on the 'history of the book' from a generally neglected dimension of Jewish culture: the development of the layouts of Hebrew Bibles from antiquity to modernity, from Torah scroll to codex to print. One of Stern's principal concerns in his research on the Bible as a 'concrete object' is the layout of the text. He suggests that the question of layout shows that there are not only 'material' limitations to the writing supports — texture, dimensions,

---

* I would like to thank Prof. Katrin Kogman-Appel and Dr Ilona Steimann for their careful reading and suggestions, as well as editor Evelyn Grossberg for her corrections.

1 For a brief summary of these topics, see Richard Grassby, 'Material Culture and Cultural History', *Journal of Interdisciplinary History* 35/4 (2005), pp. 591–603. Cf. *The Oxford Handbook of Material Culture Studies*, ed. by Dan Hicks and Mary C. Beaudry (Oxford: Oxford University Press, 2010).

Federico Dal Bo • University of Modena and Reggio Emilia

durability, and design — but also hermeneutical expectations at work that are not always manifest.

The Materiality of Early Hebrew Prints

In this chapter I briefly explore the history of early Hebrew prints from the end of the fifteenth through the sixteenth century from a specific perspective: the evolution of the page arrangement — the *mise-en-page* or layout. I deal especially with fourteen early Hebrew editions that include Scripture and Qimhi's commentary thereon and discuss the relationship between materiality, forms, and paratextual elements. The French literary theorist Gérard Genette examined these paratextual elements in his influential *Paratexts: Thresholds of Interpretation* (1987). He maintained that these subdivisions and dependencies are integral components of a text — which is conceived of in a minimalist way as the sheer existence of a written document.[2]

Many scholars have already studied the rise of Hebrew prints, their circulation, and their impact on Jewish literacy and Jewish-Christian relationships in detail. As I noted above, David Stern contends that 'the layout of the biblical text at Qumran also anticipates its presentation in later Rabbinic Torah scrolls' since 'words are separated by spaces'.[3] He also emphasizes that 'the page layout of the Masoretic codex as we know it (as represented in the Aleppo Codex, for example), and as it continued to be copied throughout the Middle Ages, was the creation of the Tiberian school'.[4] Stern pays particular attention to the print revolution in the Renaissance, when printing of Scripture culminated in Daniel Bomberg's second *Rabbinic Bible* in 1524–1525 and its extraordinary layout:

> It not only invited but almost demanded comparative exegetical study and thereby made study of the Bible with multiple interpretations virtually normative for Jews. In doing this, the Rabbinic Bible page format restored to Jewish biblical exegesis a certain midrash-like spirit: a motivating desire to use Bible study to discover the text's richness and multiplicity, its capacity to sustain different, sometimes conflicting meanings, rather than the single universal sense that had been the object of medieval *peshat* interpretation.[5]

It is also worth noting Marvin J. Heller's seminal studies in the history of early modern Hebrew prints.[6] His work offers an impressive insight into the circumstances of early Hebrew prints, the economic and cultural tensions that they eventually evoked, and Christians' increasing curiosity about the Jewish world. The importance of some books — such as the first print of the Talmud, the print of the first *Rabbinic Bible*, the print of the second *Rabbinic Bible*, and the first prints of the Zohar — can hardly be underestimated when it comes to shedding light on quality, influence, and scientific collaboration between Jews and Christians. The Jewish participation in printing was a true cultural event for both Jews and Christians, one which symbolically

---

2   See: Richard Macksey, 'Foreword: Pausing on the Threshold', in Gérard Genette, *Paratexts: Thresholds of Interpretation* (Cambridge: Cambridge University Press, 1997), pp. xi–xxii.
3   David Stern, *The Jewish Bible: A Material History* (Seattle and London: University of Washington Press, 2007), p. 25.
4   Stern, *The Jewish Bible*, p. 74.
5   Stern, *The Jewish Bible*, p. 154.
6   Marvin Heller, *The Sixteenth Century Hebrew Book: An Abridged Thesaurus*, 2 vols (Leiden: Brill: 2004); Marvin Heller, *Studies in the Making of the Early Hebrew Book* (Leiden: Brill: 2007); Marvin Heller, *Further Studies in the Making of the Early Hebrew Book* (Leiden: Brill: 2013).

ended the cultural and theological juxtaposition that was predominant during the Middle Ages. Renaissance scholars still encountered great differences between Judaism and Christianity, but this did not preclude their working together in the printing of Hebrew books, which spread Jewish culture in Europe and the Near East.

From the printing of basic Hebrew texts in the late fifteenth century by Jewish editors and printers, such as those produced by the Soncino family, by the early sixteenth Hebrew book culture had evolved into publishing a wide range of books printed in a Jewish-Christian milieu. This evolution strongly impacted a book's texts, its paratextual features, its commentaries, and its potential audience. In effect, owing to the influence of Italian Renaissance humanism, its understanding of the classics, and its love for grammar and rhetoric, early Hebrew prints passed from being a 'Jewish' product designed for Jewish readers to being a 'Jewish-Christian' one for both Jews and Christians. The prints of the first (1517), but especially of the second *Rabbinic Bible* (1523) are the best representatives of this complex evolution in text and design.[7] The first Hebrew incunabula, most of them produced by the Jewish Soncino family, reflect several basic characteristics: the main text is printed with none or only basic paratextual features and the typographic style tends to imitate Hebrew manuscripts in both font and layout.[8] This suggests that the first incunabula were meant to resemble the aesthetic patterns that had been established for more than a millennium, which would have addressed only Jewish or Christian readers who were familiar with Hebrew manuscripts. The font may imitate Hebrew handwritten letters, just as contemporaneous prints from Greek and Latin classics usually follow a manuscript format. The layout is frequently simple if not minimalistic, even in the case of biblical commentaries that conflate both the biblical text and commentary on the same page. As a result, the experience of reading is difficult, especially with books that have large volumes of text, such as Bibles and Talmud tractates.

In this chapter I examine the different types of early Hebrew prints from the fifteenth to the end of the sixteenth century based on my ongoing field research, my earlier studies, and my attempts to identify a general typology.[9] I address the

---

7 For the significance of the first and the second edition of the *Rabbinic* Bible respectively by Felice da Prato (Felix Pratensis) and Jacob ben Hayyim ibn Adonijah, see Jordan S. Penkower, 'Jacob ben Hayyim and the Rise of the Biblia Rabbinica' (unpublished PhD thesis, Hebrew University of Jerusalem, 1982) [in Hebrew]. See also Eyal Poleg, *A Material History of the Bible* (Oxford: Oxford University Press, 2020).

8 The term *incunabula* — from *incunabulum*, 'cradle' — usually designates early prints before the sixteenth century, as a conventional cut-off date in scholarship. Some 28,500 editions survive today in several copies around the world. These editions are fully recorded by the *Incunabula Short Title Catalogue* (accessible online: https://data.cerl.org/istc/) and typographically described in the *Gesamtkatalog der Wiegendrucke* (accessible online: http://www.gesamtkatalogderwiegendrucke.de/). See also Penkower, 'Jacob ben Hayyim'; Jordan S. Penkower, 'Rabbinic Bible', in *Dictionary of Biblical Interpretation*, vol. 2 (Nashville: Abington Press, 1999), cols 361b–364a; Benjamin Williams, 'The 1525 Rabbinic Bible and How to Read It: A Study of the Annotated Copy in the John Rylands Library', *Bulletin of the John Rylands Library*, 92/1 (2016), pp. 53–72.

9 Thus far, I have examined the findings at the Cambridge University Library and associated College at the British Library in London. Yet further exploration of early Hebrew prints according to the research plan at the SFB 933 'Material Text Cultures' (University of Heidelberg) (www.materiale-textkulturen.de) was regrettably suspended at the time of the COVID-19 pandemic in early 2020 to 2021. I made a few updates in 2022 by visiting Italian libraries in Bologna, Ferrara, Modena, Piacenza, Parma, and Venice and in the first half of 2023 by visiting Italian libraries in Milan, Florence, and Rome. Field research has also been implemented with the following visual and bibliographical resources: *Austellung Hebräischer Druckwerke* (Frankfurt: Knauer, 1902); *Hebräische Inkunabeln, 1475–1496 mit 33 Faksimiles,*

question of authorship vis-à-vis the evolution of layout with a focus on the transformation from a full-page commentary to a complex design that allows for the display of the main text together with the relevant commentaries on the same page, which offers a panoptic view of both text and tradition. This kind of layout questions the humanistic notion of 'authorship'; it complicates it and associates it with the no less intriguing question of 'administering' it.[10] The commentator has no authoritative privilege over the commented text; rather, the commentary is a complementary component that is published just 'beside' it. Authorship seems rather to pertain to the editor who selects the commentators, decides how to arrange the layout, and establishes an implicit 'discipline' of reading. In his seminal work *Discipline and Punish*, Foucault famously stated that disciplinary power — differently from absolutist and juridical power — does not involve the brute fact of the domination but rather 'the multiple forms of domination that can be exercised in society'.[11] In this respect, a layout also imposes a form of reading by which the reader has to abide. This kind of design reflects an inherent hermeneutics: the main text — either the Bible

---

Katalog 151 von Ludwig Rosenthal's Antiquariat, (Leipzig: Publisher Unknown, 1912); Aron Freimann, *Thesaurus typographiae hebraicae saeculi XV* (Berlin: Marx & Co, 1924); Aron Freimann, *Die hebräischen Inkunabeln der Druckereien in Spanien und Portugal* (Mainz: Gutenberg-Festschrift, 1925); David Fränkel, *Hebräische Inkunabeln 1475–1494* (Vienna: Druck der Offizin Haag, 1931); Aron Freimann, *Die hebräischen Drucke in Rom im 16 Jahrhundert* (Berlin: Sonderdruck, 1937); Abraham Rosenthal, 'Daniel Bomberg and His Talmud Editions', in *Gli Ebrei a Venezia*, ed. by Gaetano Cozzi (Milan: Edizioni Comunità, 1987), pp. 375–416; Abraham Rosenthal, *The Talmud Editions of Daniel Bomberg* (Leiden: Brill, 1999), accessible online: https://brill.com/flyer/title/16278; Giuliano Tamani, 'La tipografia ebraica a Brescia e a Barco nel sec XV', in *I primordi della stampa a Brescia. 1472–1511*, ed. by Ennio Sandal (Padova: Editrice Anteriore, 1986), pp. 61–80; Clemens P. Sidorko, 'Eliezer Ben Naphtali Herz Treves als Pionier des jüdischen Buchdrucks in Zürich, Tiengen und Basel um 1560', *Aschkenas*, 17/2 (2011), pp. 457–72; David Faleck, 'The Revival of Mishnah Study in the Early Modern Period' in *CUREJ* (2008), accessible online: http://repository.upenn.edu/curej/85; *Treasures of the Valmadonna Trust Library. A Catalogue of 15th-Century Books and Five Centuries of Deluxe Hebrew Printing*, ed. by David Sclar (London and New York: Valmadonna Trust Library, 2011); Chiara Faiolo, 'Libro, diaspora e ri-costruzioni identitarie: Per una storia della tipografia sefardita portoghese nell'Italia del Cinquecento' (unpublished PhD thesis, University of Bologna, 2010); Stephen Lubell, 'Sixteenth-Century Hebrew Typography: A Typographical and Historical Analysis Based on the Guillaume I Le Bé Documents in the Bibliothèque nationale de France', 2 vols (unpublished MA thesis, University of London, 2013); Martin J. Heller, 'Unicums, Fragments, and Other Hebrew Book Rarities', *Judaica Librarianship*, 18 (2014), pp. 130–53; Simon Iakerson, 'Early Hebrew Printing in Sepharad (ca. 1475–1497?)', in *From Letter to Type: Essays on the History of the Medieval Hebrew Book* (St. Petersburg: Contrast, 2016), pp. 225–40; Chiara Camarda, 'Tracing the Hebrew Book Collection of the Venice Ghetto' (unpublished PhD dissertation, University of Venice, 2016); Chiara Carmada, *Ha-Sefarim shel Geto. I libri del Ghetto: Catalogo dei libri ebraici della Comunità Ebraica di Venezia (secc. XVI–XX)* (Venice: Il Prato, 2016); Menachem Katz, 'Catalog of the Early Talmud Bavli Printings on the "Hachi Garsinan" Website' (unpublished paper), p. 201, accessible online: https://www.academia.edu/34887582/Catalog_of_the_Early_Talmud_Bavli_Printings_on_the_Hachi_Garsinan_Website; Heller,

---

The Sixteenth Century Hebrew Book; Alexander Gordin, 'Hebrew Incunabula in the National Library of Israel as a Source for Early Modern Book History in Europe and Beyond', in *Printing Revolution 1450–1500: Fifty Years that Changed Europe*, ed. by Cristina Dondi (Venice: Edizioni Ca' Foscari, 2020), pp. 321–40.

10 For the connection between 'authority' (*Herrschaft*) and 'administration' (*Verwaltung*) in book production, I refer here to Abigail S. Armstrong – Rodney Ast – Enno Giele – Julia Lougovaya – Hannah Mieger – Jörg Peltzer – Joachim Friedrich Quack – Chun Fung Tong – Sarina Tschachtli – Banban Wang, "Kapitel 6: Politische Herrschaft und Verwaltung" in *Theorie und Systematik materialer Textkulturen: Abschlussband des SFB 933*, edited by Nikolaus Dietrich – Ludger Lieb – Nele Schneidereit (Berlin-Boston: De Gruyter, 2023), pp. 257–314.

11 For an application of Foucault's notion of discipline to philology, see Karl Palonen, 'A "Discipline of Reading,"' *Redescriptions: Political Thought, Conceptual History and Feminist Theory*, 6 (2002), pp. 179–83.

or the Talmud — constitutes the 'centre' and the commentaries only a kind of secondary text.

A Short History of Layout in Early Hebrew Books

Fifteenth-century Hebrew prints were primarily a product for a Jewish public in Italy that was culturally diverse: northern Italy was more influenced by the Ashkenazi world, whereas southern Italy was impacted by Sefardi immigrants who gradually left Spain in 1492.[12] After the Gothic War in 535–554, which crushed the Ostrogothic Kingdom in Italy, and the following Lombard invasion in 568, early medieval Italy had no sovereign State authority but was deeply fragmented and the target of French, Spanish, and German political appetites. This political composite map made the polarization between north and south highly dramatic. Owing to the *Guerre d'Italia* for the foreign domination over Italy from the late 1400s to the mid-1500s, its political and economic circumstances were dire. Nevertheless, Hebrew printing found Italy its most important home for most of the sixteenth century with the rise of Venice as a cultural and economic power.

From the beginning of the sixteenth century, the basic layout in incunabula began to evolve into more complex arrangements that included more paratextual features — title, author's name, chapters, and so on — a process that reached its peak with the publication of the first *Rabbinic Bible* (1517) and especially the second *Rabbinic Bible* (1523) in Venice, both by the Christian printer Daniel Bomberg (1483–1549). Unlike the almost basic fifteenth-century Hebrew prints, those from the sixteenth century show amazing technical progress in both layout and printing. The books offer a remarkably better reading experience, paratextual features are fairly common, and the layout changes from basic to complex. The first *Rabbinic Bible* features the biblical text together with Rashi and the Targum but its layout is still relatively simple compared to the second *Rabbinic Bible*, which encapsulates the biblical text within several paratextual items: an Aramaic translation (generally the Targum Onqelos), commentaries by both Rashi and Ibn Ezra on the Torah, and the Masorah — the latter edited by the Jewish-Christian scholar Jacob ben Hayyim ibn Adonijah. With respect of these remarkable innovations, the sixteenth-century Hebrew prints represent the first important step from a basic format that reproduced all the typical features of a Hebrew manuscript to an actual 'hypertext' that offered the reader the opportunity to access several different texts at the same time. The impact of these typographical innovations on the quality of reading was a strong one: the sixteenth-century Hebrew prints are much closer to a modern book.

By the end of the fourteenth century there was a cultural diversity among Jews in Italy. Italian Jews were joined by migrants from Iberia, France, and the German Lands.[13] In addition to these major cultural differences, there were also Jews from the Balkans, who introduced aspects

---

12 Ariel Toaff, 'Gli insediamenti ashkenaziti nell'Italia settentrionale', in *Gli ebrei in Italia*, ed. by Corrado Vivanti, 2 vols (Turin: Einaudi, 1996), I, pp. 155–71. Cf. Albertazzi Villa, *Un processo contro gli ebrei nella Milano del 1488* (Bologna: Cappelli, 1988), pp. 22–23. On the adaptation of the Ashkenazi *yeshivah* to the Italian customs and the complex relationship between the *italiani* and the *tedeschi*, see: David Malkiel, 'Renaissance in the Graveyard: The Hebrew Tombstones of Padua and Ashkenazic Acculturation in Sixteenth-Century Italy', *AJS Review*, 37 (2013), pp. 333–70. Cf. Moses A. Shulvass, 'The Jewish Population in Renaissance Italy', *Jewish Social Studies* 13.1 (1951), pp. 3–24.

13 On this, see: Renata Segre, 'Sephardic Settlements in Sixteenth-Century Italy. A Historical and Geographical Survey', *Mediterranean Historical Review*, 6 (1991), pp. 112–37.

of 'Byzantine Judaism'.¹⁴ Early Hebrew printing in Italy reflected this mosaic of Jewish cultures in both the selection of commentaries and the page layout as well as in publishing prayer books in different rites. In regard to the biblical commentators, both fifteenth- and sixteenth-century Hebrew books featured commentators from both the Iberian Jewish and the Ashkenazi worlds. Many early Hebrew prints in Italy include a range of biblical commentators from Iberia such as Ibn Ezra, from southern France, such as David Qimhi from Narbonne, and from the French-Ashkenazi world, such as Rashi from Troyes.

The layout of early Italian Hebrew prints also seems to reflect an influence from Ashkenazi book culture. The first *Rabbinic Bible* (1517) and the second *Rabbinic Bible* (1523), for example, both feature the Ashkenazi custom of copying both the biblical text and some commentary in the margins, a practice that was well received by both Jewish and Christian printers of Hebrew Bibles and progressively introduced into the market. However, the Italian printers often combined different fonts in their Bible layouts and were able to produce books that accommodated the varied demands of local Jewry. The fact that they had both Sefardi and Ashkenazi potential customers precluded opting for a single, universal model for a Hebrew Bible: both Sefardi and Ashkenazi authors were published eclectically together. This editorial choice impacted both the fonts and the general layout of the page. When published together with Ashkenazi authors, typographically generic — or culturally neutral — font types replaced those imitating Sefardi cursive script, which probably would appeal only to Sefardi readers. The predominant layout featured these commentaries together and 'normalized' them so that they appeared to be equally important and authoritative. This was true, for instance, of Ibn Ezra's 'Sefardi' and Rashi's 'Ashkenazi' commentary on Scripture, which were typically printed together in sixteenth-century Hebrew books from Italy. The cultural, political, and economic prominence of Venice until the mid-sixteenth century largely contributed to the circulation of its Hebrew prints, which progressively became models for future publications. Every Rabbinic Bible and Talmud would be arranged according to the respective printings from David Bomberg's publishing house. In particular, the Bomberg edition of the Talmud was so influential that its pagination was used for all future prints.

Yet the prevalence of these 'Venetian' products cannot be explained solely by the dominant position of Venice until the middle of the fifteenth century. We assume that early Hebrew prints from Italy also departed from the more rigid requirements of both the Sefardi and the Ashkenazi worlds. True, Iberian scholars read Rashi and Ashkenazi scholars read some of the Iberian commentators and Ibn Ezra wrote while he travelled throughout in Europe. Yet the synoptical publication of these commentaries all together implied something more than simply making them available to every reader. It also argued for their equal authority and importance. In particular, the choice to publish Ibn Ezra together with Rashi implied a specific understanding of their commentaries against the background of Italian humanism, a movement that emphasized the importance of grammar and philology together with the study of hermeneutics, and this presupposition influenced the printing of Hebrew books. Regardless of whether Ibn Ezra was considered a 'grammarian', according to the precepts of Italian humanism, his commentary

---

14 For an insight until the Middle Ages, see: Alexander Panayotov, 'Jews and Jewish Communities in the Balkans and the Aegean until the Twelfth Century', in *The Jewish-Greek in Antiquity and the Byzantine Empire*, ed. by James K. Aitken and James Carleton Paget (Cambridge, Cambridge University Press, 2014), pp. 54–76. Cf. Kenneth M. Setton, 'The Byzantine Background to the Italian Renaissance', *Proceedings of the American Philosophical Society*, 100.1 (1956), pp. 1–76.

complemented the one by Rashi, who was, at times, more accepting of narratives. While juxtaposing various commentaries, Italian printers of Hebrew books offered an innovative model that both Jews and Christians would have found acceptable: a Hebrew book modelled on the expectations of Italian humanism. In fact, early Hebrew prints in Italy mostly conformed to that approach, which considered both grammar and rhetoric important for a proper understanding of the text.

In early modern Italy, the trend toward publishing juxtaposed commentaries followed the humanistic model wherein Greek and Latin classics were printed together with a range of grammatical, philosophical, and exegetical tools that would provide the reader with a basic understanding of the text. This similarity is especially evident in the second *Rabbinic Bible* (1523), which epitomizes the use of an 'Italian humanistic model' for printing a Hebrew Bible. Indeed, a typical page in that book displays a line from the Hebrew Bible together with several grammatical and exegetical tools: a 'grammatical' commentary on Scripture by the Iberian exegete Ibn Ezra, a 'local' commentary on Scripture by the French-Ashkenazi commentator Rashi, a 'literal' Aramaic translation of the Bible (Targum Onqelos), and a philological apparatus in three versions (*masora parva*, *masora magna*, and *masora finalis*), edited by the Sefardi-Italian Ibn Adonijah.

A look at these typical traits of early Hebrew prints in Italy suggests that most of the books' success was due to their eclectic nature, which conflated the Italian, Sefardi, and Ashkenazi realms into a product that would be accepted by both Jews and Christians as they were produced by a Christian printer with the guidance of Jewish editors. In many respects, Italy was a 'cultural laboratory'. On the one hand, there is little doubt that Italian Jews — or Jews living and/or working in Italy — were culturally and economically dependent on the surrounding Christian world. On the other hand, this potentially negative situation did not prevent Italian Jews from enjoying a degree of intellectual freedom. However, such freedom was only granted when political circumstances were favourable owing to the mediation of powerful Christian agents. When political circumstances changed, so did the degree of that freedom. The burning of the Talmud in 1553 following the litigation on copyright about the printing of a commented edition of Maimonides' *Mishneh Torah* is an indication of the precarious nature of this intellectual freedom and the overwhelming dominance of the Christian authorities.[15]

A Case Study: Some Early Prints of Qimhi's Commentary on Scripture

As there is no way that I can explore the entire history of the Hebrew book from the fifteenth to the end of the sixteenth century in the present chapter, I limit myself to a case study that especially reflects the socio-cultural transformations that were engendered with the invention of print: the early Hebrew prints of Rabbi David Qimhi's (Radaq) commentaries on Psalms and Prophets.

In a chapter in the present volume, Hanna Liss examines in detail the *editio princeps* of the Book of Psalms with R. Qimhi's commentary, which was published in 1477, probably in Bologna. She observes several philological, textual, and

---

15 For instance, I cannot explore here how the Talmud in 1553 had an impact the layout, texts, and paratexts on the double prints of the Zohar in Northern Italy — in Cremona and Mantua — a few years later. These prints also showed how Italian Humanism deeply influenced the reception of the Kabbalah by both Jewish and Christian audience. See: Daniel Abrams, 'The Invention of the Zohar as a Book' in *Kabbalistic Manuscripts and Textual Theory: Methodologies of Textual Scholarship and Editorial Practice in the Study of Jewish Mysticism*, ed. by Daniel Abrams (Los Angeles: Cherub Press, 2010), pp. 224–438.

typographical errors. Reading is made difficult by the inconsistent arrangement between the biblical text and its commentary, by the incomplete quotations from the psalms within the commentary, and the variants according to the Masorah that are reported poorly in the commentary. In view of all of these issues, she suggests that this early Hebrew print might have had some didactic use among non-Jews but could not have served the scholarly interests of a Jewish clientele.[16] I assess fourteen editions that include Scripture and Qimhi's commentary thereon, excluding the third edition of Daniel Bomberg's *Rabbinic Bible*, which is very similar to the second one, and thus is not particularly relevant in the present context. For clarity's sake, I list them in chronological order below with a short description of their typographical and paratextual features.

#1 **Psalms with Qimhi's Commentary (Bologna, 1477)**: This is the first Hebrew print of Qimhi's commentary on Psalms. The book exhibits only a basic layout: biblical text and commentary are seamlessly merged in a single column, which, owing to the absence of paratextual features, makes the experience of reading difficult.[17]

#2 **Latter Prophets with Qimhi's Commentary (Guadalajara, 1481)**: This book is similar to the previous one and has only a basic layout. There are no paratextual features.[18]

#3 **Former Prophets with Qimhi's Commentary (Soncino, 1485)**: This print features two different layouts for Qimhi's commentary: the biblical text typically appears in a small box on the top of the page, with the commentary in a considerably longer L-shaped column or the biblical text and commentary appear in two columns of similar size, occasionally with a supplementary column nested within the commentary (fol. 6a). This print has poor paratextual features, which makes the reading quite challenging: unvocalized biblical text, occasional arrowed text for ornamental purposes, and the occasional use of catchwords.[19] For a more comprehensive codicological description, see the next entry.

#4 **Latter Prophets with Qimhi's Commentary (Soncino, 1485)**: A companion volume to the previous one, this print is slightly more consistent in using one kind of layout that has the biblical text and the commentary in two columns of similar size. It also has some poor paratextual features, such as the use of arrowed text and occasional catchwords. The general setting of the book is typographically consistent, but the opening of each Prophet is not. Each book of the Major Prophets is separated by two or three blank pages, whereas the Minor Prophets are printed continuously, with no plates, usually with a quarter of a page between them. Further, Isaiah has no title or special letter; Jeremiah has a bigger black initial as a title; Ezekiel begins on the top of the page from the left margin with an enlarged initial word (in white); Hosea begins in the middle of the page with an enlarged initial. The rest of the prophets appear continuously with no page separation, some of them starting on the top of the page, generally with the title printed in a regular square script. There is no title

---

16 See Hanna Liss, 'Early Hebrew Printings and the Quality of Reading', in the present volume.

17 I have examined this print at the Cambridge University Library (Inc.3.B.74.A2). For a full codicological description, see https://idiscover.lib.cam.ac.uk/permalink/f/iojq9k/44CAM_ALMA21484405780003606 [accessed in May 2022].

18 I have examined this print at the British Library (C.49.d.9). For a full codicological description, see https://data.cerl.org/mei/02124958 [accessed in May 2022].

19 I have accessed several copies of this print at the Cambridge University Library (BSS.140.A86 and Inc.3.B.54.1) and at the Trinity College Library (VI.15.4). For a full codicological description, see https://data.cerl.org/istc/ib00525760 [accessed in May 2022].

between Jonah and Micha. The first word in Nahum is vocalized by hand incorrectly as מָשָׂא rather as (מַשָּׂא); there is no title for Habakkuk, yet Zephaniah has a title in the larger script; Haggai has no printed title, so the title was written later by hand; Malachiah has no title.[20]

#5 Psalms with Qimhi (Naples, 1487): This print reflects a coherent layout: the biblical text and the commentary appear in two columns of different sizes; the main text is typically in a small box on the top of the page, while the commentary is set in a considerably longer L-shaped column. This print also has only few paratextual features: the commentary occasionally uses the third or fourth word of the psalm — typically לדוד, למנצח, or מזמור — as a catchword, features blank spaces for emphasis, and has an irregular number of lines.[21]

#6 Isaiah and Jeremiah with Qimhi (Lisbon, 1492): This print exhibits a coherent layout: biblical text and commentary appear in two columns of similar size; the main text is set in a column that is almost as long as the C-shaped one with the commentary. The biblical text is partially vocalized by hand and the commentary is printed in Sefardi cursive script — that is, in an imitation of Sefardi handwriting. The print has some paratextual features in accord with Genette's broader understanding of them: the use of square letters for catchwords; while no page numbers are indicated, chapters and verses are frequently noted at the bottom of the page, but without plates, and there is the occasional use of arrowed text (fols 75, 242).[22]

#7 Former Four Prophets with Targum, Radaq, and Ralbag (Leiria, 1494): This print reflects an idiosyncratic layout that was used only one other time and by the same Iberian publishing house: the biblical text appears in the central column together with a first commentary, while a second and a third commentary are set in two specular C-shaped columns on the left and right sides. Further, the biblical text is in either one or two columns; is vocalized by print, usually in the centre of the page; and exhibits a consistent typographical choice: Ralbag's commentary is always in the left margin, while Radaq is in the right margin — both are printed in Sefardi cursive script, are unvocalized, and have poor paratextual features: there are no page numbers and the title usually appears on the top of the page.[23]

#8 Latter Four Prophets with Qimhi (Pesaro, 1516): This print exhibits a coherent layout with the biblical text generally on the right and the commentary on the left. Yet the biblical text occasionally appears in two columns (Jeremiah) and is occasionally in the left margin (Jonah and others). The print has poor paratextual features: commentary is printed in fifteenth-century Sefardi semi-cursive — later known as 'Rashi script' — unvocalized, with catchwords in a square script; there are no big decorative plates for each book, but a small plate that is used for the first word; pages are not numbered; a title usually appears on the

---

20 See the previous footnote.
21 I have examined two copies of this print at the Cambridge University Library (BSS.140.A87 and Inc.3.B.11.14). For a full codicological description, see https://data.cerl.org/istc/ib00525870 [accessed in May 2022].
22 I have examined copies of this print at the Cambridge University Library (Inc.3.M.2.1) and at the Trinity College Library (VI.15.4). For a full codicological description, see https://data.cerl.org/istc/ib00525820 [accessed in May 2022].
23 I have examined this fragmentary copy from the Cairo Geniza at the Cambridge University Library (T–S Misc 33.1).

top of the page with some catchwords on the bottom.[24]

#9 Prophets with Targum, Rashi, and Qimhi from Daniel Bomberg's *Rabbinic Bible* (Venice, 1517) (first edition): This print exhibits a coherent layout: the biblical text and a first commentary are in two columns of similar size, while a second commentary is set in a text box at the bottom of the page. It also has some important paratextual features: the biblical text is vocalized, printed in a square script, with a clear indication of open and closed verses, and the Masorah is always on the inner margin of the page. Targum Onqelos is printed in a smaller square script, with commentary at the bottom of the page in a cursive script, usually without a title, unvocalized; some catchwords in cursive are at the bottom; there are no page numbers, and the title of the *parashah* is on the top but with no indication for chapters. Other paratextual features include a bigger plate at the beginning of Genesis and smaller plates at the beginning of each biblical book; occasional use of arrowed text embellishes a biblical book's last page. The print is typographically coherent: when a biblical text lacks a Targum, a supplementary commentary is published in its place, without any alteration in the chosen layout. Occasionally, a specific commentary is introduced with a short preface and published in an appendix. This edition comprises three volumes: the Pentateuch with some Prophets (vol. 1), Prophets (vol. 3), and Writings (vol. 3). In the context of the present chapter, it is relevant that this edition of the Prophets includes a Targum together with Rashi and Qimhi.[25]

#10 Psalms with Qimhi and Hayon (Salonica, 1522): This print — which has only survived in a largely incomplete copy — has a coherent layout: the biblical text, which appears in the central column, is flanked by two commentaries in two specular C-shaped columns on either side. It has poor paratextual features: the biblical text is vocalized but does not show open and closed verses; the title is on the top with the number of the psalm.[26]

#11 Prophets with Rashi, Qimhi, and Ralbag from Daniel Bomberg's *Rabbinic Bible* (Venice, 1524–1525) (second edition): This book is formally part of Bomberg's second *Rabbinic Bible* and reflects that typical layout, which was also used for several other canonical editions. It includes the biblical text, a Targum, the *masora parva* and *masora magna*, and two or more commentaries. The layout, which is very complex, comprises several elements: two central columns for the biblical text and the Targum, two text boxes above and below them for the *masora parva* and *masora magna*, and two specular C-shaped columns on the left and the right for two commentaries, occasionally extended to include three commentaries on the biblical text without any alteration in the typological frame. This specific layout, as David Stern has pointed out, resulted from a subtle negotiation with Felice da Prato's previous *Rabbinic Bible* and the traditional format. (Ibn Adoniyahu's edition returned to the traditional format — a strategic decision obviously intended to make the book seem familiar to its readers — albeit more complex than nearly any of its predecessors, with five distinct units on the page.[27])

---

24 I have examined this print at the Cambridge University Library (S816.a.51.5).

25 I have examined this print at the Christ's College Library in Cambridge (B.2.1-2).

26 I have examined this print at the Cambridge University Library (S816.b.52.2).

27 Stern, *The Jewish Bible*, p. 147.

Yet the case of the books of Prophets in the *Rabbinic Bible* is an unusual one as these texts are arranged a slightly different layout: the biblical text and the Targum appear in two columns of similar size, while a first commentary is in a bigger C-shaped column and a second one is either in a text box at the bottom of the page or in a narrower column on the opposite side. It also has some important paratextual features: the biblical text is vocalized with open and closed verses, there are paratextual indexes, each commentary is cited by name throughout the entire edition, and the *masora parva* and *masora magna* are to be found on each page. In the context of the present chapter, it is relevant to note that this edition of the Prophets includes a Targum (printed together with the biblical text) and three commentaries together in the same typographical frame — a specular C-shaped form: Rashi, Qimhi, and Ralbag.[28]

#12 Joel and Malachi with Qimhi (Basle, 1530): This print exhibits a coherent basic layout that is particularly suitable for a miniature format: the biblical text and commentary are seamlessly merged in a single column. It has poor paratextual features but the biblical text is vocalized. As noted in the Latin preface to the text, this print was essentially intended for Christian readers who wanted to acquire some familiarity with Jewish commentary on Scripture.[29]

#13 Psalms with Qimhi (Isny, 1541): This print reflects a coherent layout: the biblical text and commentary appear together in a single column but are separated typographically, so they are clearly distinguishable from one another. It has some paratextual features: the biblical text is vocalized and printed in square print, while the commentary, also vocalized, is in cursive script with catchwords in a square script; there are references to Scripture printed in margin, with page numbers in Hebrew, numeration for each psalm, and occasionally arrowed text for ornamental purposes at the end of a page.[30]

#14 Psalms with Qimhi (Cremona, 1561): This small print exhibits a basic layout suitable for its small format in two columns. The biblical text is set in square letters, is vocalized, and is set in a text box that is always adjacent to the outer margin; the commentary is in cursive script with catchwords in square letters, and it accounts for the main part of the page. There are only basic paratextual features: page numbers are printed in Hebrew and there is an index of psalms at the beginning of the book.[31]

Jewish Studies and Digital Humanities: A Methodological Premise

A relatively new field of study, the relationship between digital humanities and materiality is currently a matter of some debate. On the one hand, the widespread use of digital editions is a 'smoothing over of' text — and its materiality — for the sake of the machine. A digital text obviously requires reducing a manuscript's text — and its physical and paratextual features — to digital characters in binary code. This digitalization is obviously required for rendering a manuscript

---

28 I have examined this print at the Cambridge University Library (S816.a.52.1-4).

29 I have examined this print at the Cambridge University Library (S816.d.53.1).

30 I have accessed three copies of this print at the Cambridge University Library (S816.b.54.10), at the St. John's College in Cambridge (T.4.18), and at the Emmanuel College Library (302.4.77).

31 I have examined this print at the Cambridge University Library (S816.e.56.1).

into a portable format but also creates a tension 'between the surface orderliness of scholarly resources and the stubborn irregularity of textual materials'.³²

For instance, one can appreciate the issues involved in transforming paratexts into a search interface in digital editions: page numbers, tables of contents, page headings, and so on are transformed into 'navigationals' that allow one to 'browse' in the text. Accordingly, the ability to search the texts by means of software is one of the first and most promising capabilities of digital editions. This search feature shows that these digital materials still await in-depth analysis. For now, it can be said that these digital materials potentially will allow one to escape traditional, sequential reading. Furthermore, search interfaces are significantly more performative than traditional 'concordances', which typically identify all occurrences of a particular term, and also allow for more complex searches in a text. It is considerably more challenging to foresee the kind of transformation that the technological transition will bring in regard to the Bible. On the one hand, digital technology has a virtually limitless potential for gathering and providing the reader or user with access to previously scattered or unavailable sources relevant to the Bible. A website such as Sefaria: A Living Library of Jewish Texts Online (https://www.sefaria.org/), which publishes classical Jewish texts in Hebrew and English translations, posts the Bible, rabbinic midrash, and nearly every medieval commentary, as well as forums for readers' comments and modern interpretations,

appears destined to displace the Rabbinic Bible as the established venue for Bible study. Prominent educational websites such as Sefaria provide an unparalleled level of interactive engagement with the text and with a community of readers and students transcend every imaginable border and boundary. In fact, rather than in the text itself, the study of the Bible and religious literature is expected to undergo significant changes as a result of the new technology.

A method that the Italian studies scholar Franco Moretti calls 'distance reading' offers new ways to view literature, especially for massive corpora that are impossible for a single scholar to fully comprehend.³³ Researchers can zoom out from a body of data using computational tools to uncover specific types of linkages and patterns more clearly. Despite strong criticism from some academics, distance reading is becoming more and more popular as a supplement to more conventional methods of reading literature. Moreover, it is easier to understand distant reading as a component of a larger intellectual movement that is also changing the social sciences. The component of this common narrative that has received the most attention is the increase in the general availability of data, facilitated by the Internet and digital libraries. In this respect Ted Underwood has recently emphasized difficulties in approaching the study of literary texts on a large scale:

> [W]hat really matter, I think, are not new tools but three general principles. First, a negative principle: there's simply a lot we don't know about literary history [...]. Second, the theoretical foundation for macroscopic research isn't something we have to invent from scratch [...]. The third thing that matters, of course, is getting at the texts

---

32 Alan Galey, 'The Human Presence in Digital Artefacts', in *Text and Genre in Reconstruction: Effects of Digitalization on Ideas, Behaviours, Products, and Institutions*, ed. by Willard McCarty (Cambridge: Open Book Publishers, 2010), p. 93. I am following here: Michael L. Satlow and Michael Sperling, 'The Rabbinic Citation Network', *AJS Review: The Journal of the Association for Jewish Studies*, 46.2 (2022), pp. 291–319.

33 Franco Moretti, *Distant Reading* (London: Verso, 2013).

themselves, on a scale that can generate new perspectives.³⁴

However, the notion of distant reading itself suggests that this would also be a new reading modality. Some may understand this term as implying that this undertaking is still part of literary studies and represents merely another phase in our discussion of the proper methods for interpreting literature. But this is certainly not true on the large scale of the works analysed. In Moretti's distant reading we do not read texts but look at their most conspicuous aspect — their geographical and topographical dissemination. In similar terms, I have not attempted to read these early Hebrew prints but rather have only looked at their layouts.

In the present context, I have to note a very recent application of distant reading to the study of rabbinic literature. Michael Satlow and Michael Sperling have recently developed an experimental database for the study of citations in the Babylonian Talmud, which they call 'The Rabbinic Network'.³⁵ They apply quantitative methods of social network analysis to some portions of the Babylonian Talmud by means of the open-source network analysis and visualization software package Gephi.³⁶ They have established a chain of quotations by 630 rabbis that can be further analysed according to distribution, size, and density. For instance,

the study of this Rabbinic Network after the ranking of rabbis who cite them shows that the famous Rav, the third-century Amoraite Abba Arikha, has been cited by 137 users, while the no less prominent Rabbi Yochanan ben Zakkai has only been cited by eighty-five colleagues but was the most active in that he cited thirty-four his own colleagues, whereas Rav is not included in this classification.³⁷ The raw results from these data suggest that Yochanan ben Zakkai was distinguished as both an active and passive partner in the Rabbinic Network, as he was frequently cited but also cited his colleagues. This kind of analysis has allowed Satlow and Sperling to assess rabbis' positions in the Rabbinic Network and their ability to develop connections among their students, even those in Babylonia. For instance, an analysis of this database has shown that there is a strong correlation between rabbis with high degree scores and high centrality scores: despite their differences in citing and being cited, both Rav and Rabbi Yochanan ben Zakkai show the same ranking if ordered by 'betweenness centrality scores': they, respectively, scored 24,709 and 25,813 points.³⁸ These kinds of algorithms for exploring the database allow for the examination of the Rabbinic Network by a number of criteria: investigating a community, assessing the role of migration between Babylon and the Land of Israel, and/or the role of single individuals in the process of redaction. In a larger perspective, the use of this database may help us understand the dynamics of the networks established by the Rabbis if not their influence in redacting other rabbinic documents, and eventually assisting

---

34 Ted Underwood, 'Distant Reading and Recent Intellectual History', in *Debates in the Digital Humanities*, ed. by Matthiew K. Gold and Lauren F. Klein (Minneapolis, University of Minnesota Press, 2016). pp. 531–32.

35 The project is housed at http://www.rabbiniccitations.jewishstudies.digitalscholarship.brown.edu/blog/. At that site are also links to the code and datasets. Cf. Satlow and Sperling, 'The Rabbinic Citation Network'.

36 The open-source network analysis and visualization software package Gephi can be accessed here: https://gephi.org/.

37 Satlow and Sperling, 'The Rabbinic Citation Network', pp. 304–05, Table 2 and Table 3.

38 Satlow and Sperling, 'The Rabbinic Citation Network', p. 309, Table 4.

in identifying significant discrepancies among different texts.³⁹

Analysing Early Hebrew Prints with a Graph Database

My exploration of early Hebrew prints by means of a Graph database which is currently under development starts from very similar premises. I utilize a semantic graph database to collect and visualize the textual, codicological, and bibliographical data emerging from my research, and am examining those prints on a larger scale than the one treated in the present chapter. I look especially at early Hebrew prints from the three main Jewish canons — Scripture, Talmud, and the Zohar — that have been published with at least one commentary.⁴⁰

The database is being written in Cypher Query Language and managed with the second generation Neo4J graph database system, the open-source network analysis, and the aforementioned visualization software package Gephi.⁴¹ Graph databases offer an invaluable advantage over ordinary — 'tabular' — ones. Data are recorded and collected in charts but are displayed as graphs. As a consequence, the connections discrete pieces of information — each 'record' — is unbounded and can extend to any length or in any direction. Data in a graph database are usually arranged as a network graph that consists of two basic units: a node and an edge.

Each node represents a discrete entity — in the present case, an early Hebrew print — and each node represents at least one or more connections between two or more entities. As a result, graphs are visually represented by a series of nodes that are mutually connected by multiple relationships with each other. The arrangement of each node is not static but can be modified in real-time or customized by simply dragging the graph into the desired position. The most obvious application of graph databases is natural sciences, linguistics, and social sciences, but they have recently been used in the humanities — and specifically in Jewish studies — which is strongly supported by the ongoing trans-disciplinary project 'Material Text Cultures'.⁴²

My database, which is still being developed, will allow for the examination of early Hebrew prints published from the late fifteenth century to the end of the sixteenth. Together with linear information in the form of a tag, each record represents one early Hebrew edition — with possible multiple copies — and includes at least the following entries: (1) author(s); (2) kind of commentary (literal, legal, narrative, or kabbalistic); (3) printer(s); (4) editor(s); (5) Jewish culture (Sefardi, Ashkenazi, or Italian); (6) place of print; (7) date of print; (8) layout typology. Each of these parameters is mandatory for inclusion in the database, which allows for representing the typological distribution of early Hebrew prints from early print up to 1600, in Italy, North Africa, and the Near East (for an example, see the appendix).

The graphic representation of this entry looks like a series of notes connected by strings (Figure 1). As it is evident from this small section, the

---

39 Satlow and Sperling, 'The Rabbinic Citation Network', p. 318.
40 The notion of canon — as a collection of sacred books that are believed to be old and genuine — was eventually applied to the masterpiece of the Kabbalah, the Zohar, only during the Renaissance, under the influence of Italian Humanism as analyzed in detail by Daniel Abrams. See: Abrams, 'The Invention of the Zohar as a Book'.
41 The Neo4J Desktop can be accessed here: https://neo4j.com.
42 I have specifically used Sublime Text (Version 4143) for writing the database in Cypher Query Language and Neo4J Desktop (Version 1.5.6) and Gephi (Version 0.10) for representing the database. See also the online database for demotic and Greek sources: http://www.dime-online.de [accessed in May 2022].

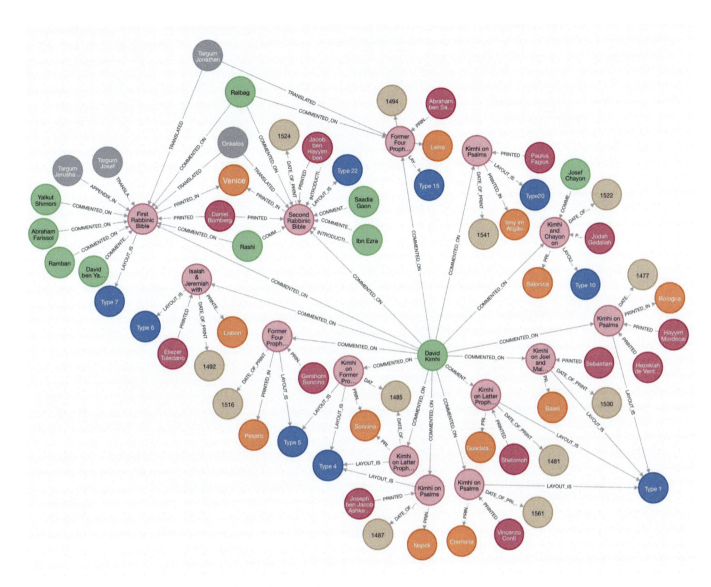

Figure 12.1: An example of the visualization of several incunabula.

database also represents several self-explanatory relationships between nodes and allows for multiple entries. More specifically, the database currently includes 122 early Hebrew prints — with sixty commentators, twenty-one editors, and fifty-six printers — distributed over ten countries and thirty-two cities. In the present case, only a portion of this larger database has been represented in the attached figure, a section that includes the surviving copies of the aforementioned fourteen early Hebrew prints of Qimhi's commentary on Scripture (Figure 2). For clarity's sake, especially considering the static nature of a picture, I have selected only a few relationships from the database and emphasized the most relevant in the context of the present chapter — title, commentator, editor, date of print, place of print, and layout typology. This network can also be represented with Gephi in a variety of formats (Figure 3).

Figure 12.2: *Psalms with Qimhi and Hayon*. Salonica, 1522 Cambridge, University Library, leaves 6a-7a..

Once finished, this database will be particularly useful for representing the evolution of layout in early Hebrew prints and the correlations among patrons, editors, publishers, and scholars. If implemented with further data on censors, it could also help to explore Christian influence in the printing process.

The Invention of Print and the Organization of Culture

As is well known, the market for Hebrew books as both commodities and cultural artefacts had its centre in early modern Italy.[43] At first,

---

43 Fernand Braudel, *Civilization and capitalism*, 3 vols (London-New York: Collins & Son and Harper & Row, 1981), I, pp. 399–401; Brian Richardson, *Print Culture in Renaissance Italy: The Editor and the Vernacular Text, 1470–1600* (Cambridge: Cambridge University Press,

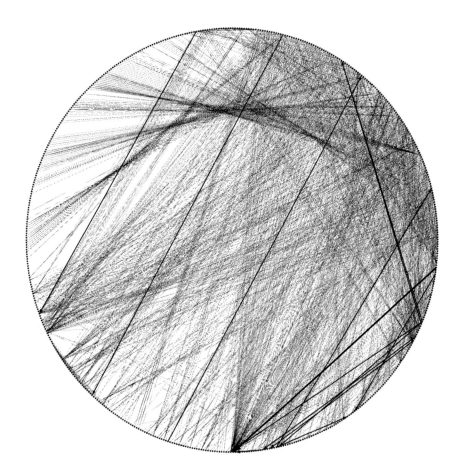

Figure 12.3: A Graph Representation of all nodes of the database with the Open-Source Network analysis and visualization software package Gephi.

Hebrew books were printed in Italy by a few Jewish 'itinerant printers' — such as those from the prominent Soncino family, However, the trade was then dominated for several decades by several central publishing houses in Venice, which were usually headed by Christians who typically engaged Jewish scholars for both the editing the works to be published and arranging for the actual printing of their Hebrew books. Some of these Jewish scholars and printers

---

1994); Angela Nuovo, *Il commercio librario nell'Italia del Rinascimento* (Milano: Angeli, 1998); Brian Richardson, *Printing, Writers and Readers in Renaissance Italy* (Cambridge: Cambridge University Press, 1999).

eventually converted to Christianity out of either personal faith or social opportunism. The case of the editors hired by the Christian printer Daniel Bomberg (1483–1549) is probably the most famous one. The remarkable beauty of his prints and the exceptional stature of his best-known Jewish collaborators — the scholars and converts Felice da Prato, (aka Felix Pratensis; d. 1539) and Jacob ben Hayyim ibn Adonijah (1470–1538?) — presented an almost unreachable model for accuracy and quality.

While the scholarship concerned with early Hebrew printing is rich and seems to be exhaustive, it has failed thus far to deal with the evolution of layout. Scholars have treated the question of layout mostly from a strictly historical, philological, or documentary point of view.[44] Some have emphasized the continuity between medieval manuscripts and early prints with the clear intention of putting the alleged novelty of printing into perspective. Others have studied the philological improvements in the study of Scripture owing to prints of reliable and comprehensive Masorah — the critical notes on Scripture and its variants.[45] Yet others have studied the evolution of typography and provided several interesting descriptions of early Hebrew prints, approaching the evolution of layout from an aesthetic point of view and focusing on details such as engravings, symbols, and typographical marks. However, proponents of each of these perspectives — as far as they are fundamental to an understanding of the historical dimension of early Hebrew prints — have usually been concerned with investigating the 'empirical nature' of these texts. True, previous scholarship has investigated typographical characteristics but has usually failed to treat them in their own 'materiality' and the impact they had on the experience of reading. A notable exception perhaps is Colette Sirat, who has emphasized that several material practices — the regulation of scribal custom, arranging a visual layout of the text, and correcting Scripture — were an integral part of the process of canonization that included the progressive sacralization of the material text, its ritual study in place of sacrifices, and its visual character.[46]

In the present chapter, I proceed on the assumption that Hebrew prints also had an impact on an epistemological level. Print did not simply increase access to books and make them easier to read but it revolutionized the experience of reading itself. The layout also impacted the epistemic organization of a book, dictated its proportions, and imposed an implicit hermeneutics of reading, which subtly identified the *central* and the *marginal* elements in a book in both an actual and a metaphorical sense. The evolution of print also introduced *typography* as a variable for the organization of a book, its main core, and its paratexts. The arrangement of complex pages in medieval manuscripts, which was hardly systematic, depended on several variables: the scribe's proficiency, his ability to access commentaries, the quality of the materials (e.g., parchment or paper, ink), the time at his

---

44   See for instance: Margaret McFadden Smith, 'Medieval Roots of the Renaissance Printed Book. An Essay in Design History', in *Forms of the "Medieval" in the "Renaissance". A Multidisciplinary Exploration of a Cultural Continuum*, ed. by George Hugo Tucker (Charlottesville: Rookwood Press, 2000), pp. 143–53; Margaret McFadden Smith, 'From Manuscript to Print. Early Design Changes', *Archiv für Gechichte des Buchwesens*, 59 (2005), pp. 1–10; Margaret McFadden Smith, 'The Design Relationship between the Manuscript and the Incunable' in *A Millennium of the Book. Production, Design, and Illustration in Manuscript and Print. 900–1900*, ed. by Robin Myers (Oxford: Oxford Polytechnic Press, 1994), pp. 23–43; Theodor Dunkelgrün, 'Tabernacles of Text: A Brief Visual History of the Hebrew Bible' in *Impagination – Layout and Materiality of Writing and Publication*, ed. by Ku-ming (Kevin) Chang, Anthony Grafton, and Glenn Warren Most (Berlin: De Gruyter, 2021), pp. 47–92.

45   See: *The Masorah of Biblia Hebraica Stuttgartensia. Introduction and Annotated Glossary*, ed. by Page H. Kelly, Daniel S. Mynatt, and Timothy G. Crawford (Grand Rapids-Cambridge: Eerdmans Publishing Company, 1998). For a philological and 'material' treatment of the Masorah, see especially: Hanna Liss and Kay Joe Petzold, 'Art. Masorah, Masoretes: I.B. Judaism: Medieval Ashkenaz; II. Visual Arts' in: *Encyclopedia of the Bible and its Reception*, vol. 17, ed. by Christine Helmer (Berlin-Boston: De Gruyter, 2019), cols 1274–1280, accessible online: http://doi.org/10.1515/ebr.masorahmasoretes. See also the online resource: http://bima.corpusmasoreticum.de/ [accessed in May 2022]. Cf. Élodie Attia, *The Masorah of Elijah ha-Naqdan. An Edition of Ashkenazic Micrographical Notes* (Berlin: De Gruyter, 2015).

46   Colette Sirat, *Hebrew Manuscripts of the Middle Ages* (Cambridge: Cambridge University Press, 2008), pp. 19–26.

disposal for copying a manuscript, and so on. In short, there was the *potential* ability to produce a complex page in a handwritten manuscript, but its actuation depended on the circumstances of writing. It was only with the invention of print that complex layouts could be arranged more easily and organized through specific procedures. In David Stern's words:

> [T]hese range from the increased standardization, fixation, and preservation of texts to the exponential increase in their diffusion and circulation; the reorganization of knowledge that took place as a result of that diffusion and enlarged readership; and the disruption of social, religious, and intellectual hierarchies produced by the demystification of textual mastery and the new forms of access to knowledge that now became available to anyone able to acquire a printed book.[47]

Thus, the invention of print made it possible to produce books in quantity as well as to establish editorial standards that would be followed by publishers, printers, and editors. The systematization of printing also required adherence to — in formal and/or informal ways — a typographical standard, which meant that several established models were used, conformed to, or adapted to circumstances by every publishing house. This was, in principle, what had been true for centuries in copying manuscripts. Yet the advantages of typography were obvious: it was easier and faster to produce a standardized version of the same book, and specific formats could easily become typical for a series, a genre, or even a publishing house. With regard to the incunabula period, Cristina Dondi observes:

> Numbers matter, because it is in these staggering numbers that we are confronted with the reality of a printing revolution. Just relying on the data, we have, if we multiply 28,500 editions by a very conservative 500 copies, we come to over 14 million copies circulating by 1500.[48]

In any event, the invention of print highlighted the arrangement of several typographical models that could be modified according to need. Scriptural source and commentary emerged as a textual complex, with the commentary usually set in the margins of the page. This disposition impacted the experience of a reader, who would subtly be directed as to the way to approach Scripture. A biblical text was typically accompanied by one or more commentaries, so could no longer be treated as an 'autonomous' text that a reader could freely access, so to say, *sine glossa*, 'without glosses'. The textual complex of a scriptural text and its commentary did not simply emerge as a constellation of texts but also dictated its hermeneutics of reading. Dependencies were created between the biblical text and its commentary or commentaries, as well as the commentaries on commentaries (supercommentaries).

I treat the history of layout as an opportunity to explore the evolution of Jewish hermeneutics by observing the material change of a page. One cannot emphasize enough that the well-known Hebrew term *daf* — conventionally used to designate a Talmud 'page' — actually means 'text', a term borrowed from the Akkadian *ṭuppu*, which was taken from the Sumerian word *dub*, meaning an inscribed 'tablet' of clay.[49] In his brilliant investigation of the history of the Hebrew Bible, Theodor Dunkelgrün suggests

---

47 David Stern, 'The Rabbinic Bible in Its Sixteenth-Century Press', in *The Hebrew Book in Early Modern Italy*, ed. by Joseph R. Hacker and Adam Shear (Philadelphia: University of Pennsylvania Press, 2011), p. 76.

48 Cristina Dondi, 'The 15cBOOKTRADE Project and the Study of Incunabula as Historical Sources', in *Printing R-Evolution and Society*, p. 3.

49 I am following here: Dunkelgrün, 'Tabernacles of Text', p. 55.

that this 'material' origin of the term somehow resonates in the ancient arrangement of Scripture in columns (*sirtut*), which 'are visual vestiges of rectangular clay or wooden tablets'.[50] The same arrangement in a new material — from tablet to parchment or paper — also allowed for a crucial transformation of a text: the use of blank margins to preclude inadvertently touching the Holy Scripture and so becoming ritually impure.[51] Blank spaces, originally intended as a scribal precaution, turned into a hermeneutical device for segmenting Scripture into minor and major unities: 'scribal manipulation of blank spaces within the columns constitutes one of the most ancient forms of biblical exegesis'.[52]

In the present context, it is interesting to see how the notion of 'page' crosses several material boundaries — passing from an inscribed 'tablet' of clay to 'parchment' and eventually to 'paper', including the 'immateriality' of an Internet webpage. Viewed from this perspective, the Jewish notion of 'page' seems to be progressively detached from the dimension of 'materiality' and 'dematerialized' into the increasingly more abstract notion of 'text'. My perspective is largely based on the premises posited at the Collaborative Research Centre 933 'Material Text Cultures' based at the University of Heidelberg.[53] This trans-disciplinary research group assumes that manuscripts, texts, and prints exhibit a particular 'materiality' that fully belongs to the 'ideal' form of a book. However, the actual dimension of a book — as it is representative of a 'material text culture' — embodies an inescapable reality that is, in principle, irreducible to the ideal form of text and also impacts the experience of reading. The invention of printing should not be thought of as a simple technological innovation — I am tempted to say 'an *update*' — of traditional manuscript culture but rather a revolution in the thousand-year-old history of writing. Printing was instrumental in perfecting the experience of reading, organizing its epistemological premises, and, as the next section shows, inducing a specific cultural hegemony.

Cultural Hegemony and the Art of Print

It is probably a truism to claim that print played a central role in disseminating culture, increasing literacy, and helping readership in the early modern period. There is no doubt that typography progressively evolved from its clumsy beginnings and that printers gradually stopped trying to reproduce texts based on manuscript culture. Technological progress and increasing competence allowed for the production of books of great complexity and accuracy.

These new books fascinated readers and helped to disseminate culture much more pervasively than before. Printing was a relatively expensive enterprise but facilitated the production of more

---

50 Dunkelgrün, 'Tabernacles of Text', p. 57.

51 The famous rabbinic statement that 'Holy Writings make hands impure' (כִּתְבֵי הַקֹּדֶשׁ מְטַמְּאִין אֶת הַיָּדַיִם) (mYad 4:6) is based on a statement from the Mishnaic tractate *Yadayim* ('Two hands') that prescribes not to touch vehicles of sanctity like the Ark, the Pentateuch as a 'biblical book' (*sefer*) or a specific 'roll' (*megillah*) from other portions of Scripture (mYad 3:5). On the theological-political subtext emerging from these assumptions, see for instance: Joseph M. Baumgarten, 'The Pharisaic-Sadducean Controversies about Purity and the Qumran Text', *Journal of Jewish Studies*, 31 (1980), pp. 157–70. Further prescriptions on text columns and margin, are to be found in the non-canonical Talmud tractate *Soferim*. On this latter tractate, see the classic of German Jewish scholarship: Joel Müller, *Masseket Soferim, der Talmudische Traktat der Schreiber: eine Einleitung in das Studium der Althebräischen Graphik, der Masora, und der Altjüdischen Liturgie* (Lipsia: Akademie der Wissenschaft im Wien, 1878).

52 Dunkelgrün, 'Tabernacles of Text', p. 59.

53 Please visit: https://www.materiale-textkulturen.de [accessed in May 2022].

copies of the same work in a much shorter period of time. In particular, the art of print was not simply faster than copying manuscript by hand but also allowed for setting, if not imposing, a series of cultural and typographical standards. This fact hardly escaped the attention of political powers, which were increasingly attentive to the technological evolution of print and its potentialities. For instance, most of the Italian publishing houses in the early modern period had to abide by the specific political requirement that they be headed by Christians, regardless of the kinds of books that they produced. This resulted in establishing publishing houses — such as Bomberg's famous one in Venice — that were formally headed by a Christian but required the irreplaceable help of Jews and Jewish converts. Such requirements enabled Christian authorities to protect their central cultural role in Renaissance Italian society and even penetrate other cultures — such as Judaism.

With respect to medieval customs, the Renaissance saw a softer approach to the question of religious and cultural dominance without necessarily introducing tolerance towards other cultural, ethnic, and religious minorities. On the contrary, other cultures and religions would only be tolerated and could even be published if they would not infringe Christian privilege. Nevertheless, the art of printing would never be a neutral field for enjoying intellectual freedom. It rather allowed for establishing a 'discipline of reading' that dictated specific conditions according to which both Christian and Jewish culture could be disseminated. This implied that every printed book was still potentially subject to emendation, censorship, or to being brutally repressed by the dominating authorities. For instance, the fantastic enterprise of printing the whole Babylonian Talmud in many editions during the late Quattrocento and early Cinquecento ended dramatically with the burning in 1553 in Italy, as the uncontrollable consequence of petty litigation between two Christian Venetian publishers over the right to publish a code of Jewish Law — Maimonides' prominent *Mishneh Torah* ('The Repetition of the Torah'). As is well known, Alvise Bragadin accused Marcantonio Giustiniani of sealing Rabbi Meir ben Isaac Katzenellenbogen's comments on Maimonides' *Mishneh Torah*. The litigation eventually involved the higher institutions from both the Republic of Venice and the Papal States, and resulted in an international case. The Church focused on the text that *Mishneh Torah* was based on — the Talmud — and eventually decided for its burning.[54]

The decision to ban the Talmud in Italy and have it burned was probably the most vivid example of the potential conflict among intellectual freedom, entrepreneurship, and political power. In a word, printing was also a question of hegemony — here intended as the complex balance between power and ethics.[55] Persuasion and consent are indeed the articulation of force through culture. In this respect, cultural production is not alien to power but, on the contrary, is instrumental in exerting force by softer means to infiltrate society. One should pay attention, for instance, to Gramsci's reference to Machiavelli's 'book' as being a part of his political realism: 'One cannot expect an individual

---

54 On the litigation between Bragadin and Giustiniani, see: Heller, *Furhter Studies*, pp. 287–88; Heller, *The Sixteenth Century Hebrew Book*, pp. 361–62; Marvin J. Heller, *Printing the Talmud: A History of the Earliest Printed Editions of the Talmud* (Brooklyn: Im Hasefer, 1992), pp. 217–40; Heller, 'Sibling Rivalry', reprinted in Heller, *Further Studies*, pp. 305–28; Avraham Yaari, 'Burning the Talmud in Italy', in *Studies in Hebrew Booklore*, ed. by Alexander Marx (Jerusalem: Mossad Rav Kook, 1958), pp. 198–234 [in Hebrew]. The two rival editions are described here: Yaakov S. Spiegel, *Chapters in the History of the Jewish Book. Scholars and their Annotations* (Ramat-Gan: Bar Ilan University Press, 1996), 548–60 [In Hebrew]; and David Stern's contribution to this volume.

55 In the present context I cannot examine the notion of hegemony as it is treated in Marxian philosophers like the Italian scholar and politician Antonio Gramsci (1891–1937) and the French theorist Michael Foucault (1926–1984).

or a book to change reality but only to interpret it and to indicate a line of action'.[56] This citation is particularly relevant and telling in the present context. Gramsci admitted that 'theorizing' on politics is not the same thing as 'doing' politics and yet he acknowledged that the writing, publishing, and distributing of specific books is an important step in establishing cultural hegemony.

The history of early Hebrew prints not only illustrates the intellectual history of the Renaissance from the specific perspectives of Judaism and Christianity but also offers the opportunity to examine the struggle for cultural hegemony that took place at the time. The art of print opens a window onto the period's complex dynamics between Jews and Christians: Jewish scholars were hired by Christian printers to publish basic books for Jewish culture. This initiative eventually resulted in establishing the typographic models for the three canons of Judaism: Scripture, Talmud, and the Zohar. In the present chapter, I have tried to show that this relationship between Jewish scholars and Christian printers was fundamentally ambiguous. Jewish scholars were not formally requested to convert to Christianity and were allowed extraordinary intellectual freedom when printing the most influential texts for the Jewish world. Consider, for instance, the first and second *Rabbinic Bible*, the Talmud, and — much later and under quite different circumstances — the Zohar. But there was a subtle process of control in regard to Hebrew books. They could be accepted for publication, occasionally censored after printing, and more or less tolerated until a specific, often unexpressed limit. When it was thought that this limit was reached, the consequences could be dire, as in the cases of the burning and banning of the Talmud in Italy in 1553 or the heavily censored print of the Talmud in Basel in 1578.

Entrepreneurship in publishing and the book trade during the Renaissance was not neutral in the context of contemporary politics. On the contrary, politicians were rather subtly involved in allowing as well supervising the production of Jewish culture in Christian Europe. The circumstances that allowed, say, prominent printers such as Bomberg to monopolize the trade in Hebrew book were not unique. Rather they reflected the implicit requirement to abide by the cultural hegemony imposed by the Catholic Church. This did not immediately imply that specific books were disqualified from market competition but rather, more subtly, that their existence 'ought to' conform to the general, often implicit cultural politics of the time. This was also the ontological imperative that Gramsci believed to be the foundation of politics. In this respect, the rise, flourishing, and decline of many Italian publishing houses as well as their progressive centralization in specific locations during the Renaissance shows how the art of print had become a true laboratory for cultural politics. Gramsci's notion of hegemony allows for the inclusion of cultural production in the construction of an ideology, not intended here solely in negative terms but also in theological-political terms: a means of exercising power, involving the masses, and educating them. The art of print was fundamental in establishing cultural hegemony.

Yet technological progress in printing and financial means to support a publishing house could not replace literacy and competence in Jewish literature. Thus, it was obvious that Jewish scholars would be hired to supervise the complex process of composing, correcting, and arranging a page according to a specific layout. This situation created a new equilibrium between Jews and Christians, editors and printers, a change that was not formally required but was perhaps welcomed. This new balance suggests that control over the cultural production of Hebrew books was exerted

---

56 Antonio Gramsci, *Prison Notebooks*, 3 vols (New York: Columbia University Press, 2007), I, p. 283 (translation modified).

in more complex ways. This 'integration' did not call for trans-cultural tolerance but permitted some intellectual freedom — under specific and limited circumstances. It would have allowed for integrating the Hebrew culture into the Christian one, as it emerges from the theological subtext hidden in the Introductions to the first and second *Rabbinic Bible*. Prominent scholars such as Felice da Prato and Ibn Adonijah discreetly converted to Christianity only after delivering an impeccable edition of the Hebrew Bible and its philological apparatus.

The print of Hebrew books interested not only Jews but also Christian Hebraists, who were concerned with interpreting Scripture. Yet this desire for knowledge was not 'revolutionary'. On the contrary, the deep purpose of disseminating Hebrew culture was fundamentally conservative: it tended to *preserve* the medieval theological-political dimensions of Jewish-Christian relationships but did not exert overtly aggressive cultural politics. Control could be exercised by more refined means. In this respect, Gramsci's notion of cultural hegemony shows that the art of print was a fundamental component in establishing a Christian cultural dominance in the Renaissance while 'disciplining' — with norms, rules, and censorship — the printing, production, and distribution of Hebrew books in a predominantly Christian society. The culture was not free of political interference but, as I noted, rather tolerated until a specific, often unexpressed limit. Thus, a monopoly on power was assured in both supervising and repressing culture. Censorship of printed copies was particularly telling in this respect. From a practical point of view, censoring a printed copy was ineffective. Indeed, it had no impact on the distribution of other uncensored copies. However, from a hegemonic point of view, censorship of printed copies was a sheer manifestation of public authority. It showed once more that the State could supervise cultural production.

Ambiguity over intellectual freedom in the book trade was instrumental in establishing a cultural hegemony through controlling the organization of culture and exercising permanent consent: given limits could provisionally be bent but not be broken. Layout played a particular role by showing the boundaries by which one should abide when reading the Holy Scriptures.

Conclusions

In this chapter, I demonstrated the potential of studying the history of early Hebrew prints from a relatively unexplored point of view: the evolution of layout. Despite the limited nature of this case study, the analysis of the layouts in the first printing of Qimhi's commentary on the Scripture (1477) undertaken with the help of a digital tool allows me to draw some significant conclusions.

Firstly, a clear preference for simple typographic types emerges. These layout types are easy to arrange, and thus relatively inexpensive. Not surprisingly, then, they account for most of the Hebrew editions considered here. Secondly, it becomes clear that alternative layouts were underutilized for a variety of reasons. On the one hand, they reflect experimental arrangements; on the other hand, there is a particularly prestigious but probably expensive layout that is usually associated with large-scale publishing enterprises, such as seen in the first and second editions of the *Rabbinic Bible* (Venice, 1517 and 1523, respectively). Consequently, only similar editions justified its use.

A case apart, however, is the evidence of another relatively inexpensive layout but it turns out that it was used only once for a single biblical printing during the entire period that I have examined so far. If this provisional result is confirmed, I shall conclude that this type — albeit inexpensive and quite readable — was then used almost exclusively for printing talmudic and law books. As a consequence, this kind of layout probably became, in time, a 'trademark' for juridical texts, so it is unlikely that it was used for other kinds of works.

These concluding remarks suggest that a typological and comparative examination of layout can offer a fairly innovative perspective on the history of early Hebrew printing and possibly the opportunity for asking further questions concerning the history of print technology, readability, and economics.

Appendix

The first incunabula examined here — #1 *Psalms with Qimhi's Commentary* (Bologna, 1477) — is encoded for being represented by the Neo4J software as follows:

CREATE (Bible1477:Bible {title: 'Qimhi on Psalms', printed:1477, tagline: 'Qimhi Commentary on Psalms'})
CREATE
(Qimhi)-[:COMMENTED_ON]->(Bible1477),
(Literal)<-[:COMMENTARY_IS]-(Qimhi),
(Sephardi)<-[:ETHNICITY_IS]-(Qimhi),
(HayyimMordekhai)-[:PRINTED]->(Bible1477),
(HezekiahVenturo)-[:PRINTED]->(Bible1477),
(Bologna)<-[:PRINTED_IN]-(Bible1477),
(Bible1477)-[:DATE_OF_PRINT]->(py1477),
(Bologna)-[:COUNTRY_IS]->(Italy),
(Italian)<-[:ETHNICITY_IS]-(Bible1477),
(Bible1477)-[:LAYOUT_IS]->(Type1)

Part Four

Confiscation and Destruction

DAVID STERN

Burning the Talmud

*Before and After Print**

Introduction

The transition of the Jewish book from manuscript to print culture has already generated a considerable body of scholarship. In this chapter, I add a modest contribution by investigating a dimension of the transition that has received less attention — how its material form and mode of circulation could change the very perception of the book and its character. The book I focus on is the Babylonian Talmud and the case study is its public burnings in the medieval and early modern periods. Whenever and wherever it occurred, the burning of the Talmud was a signal event with obvious historical, sociological, and religious dimensions, but for the history of the Jewish book, it offers a special opportunity for understanding the symbolic meaning a book can hold as a text and as a physical artefact — indeed, the different symbolic meanings it could hold for Jews, on the one hand, and for Christians, on the other. By exploring the ways in which that symbolism changed, before and after print, we may come to understand better the role technology played in changing cultural values and thereby in shaping a book's meaning.

The Babylonian Talmud was burned for the first time in Europe in Paris in 1241 (following a 'trial' of the Talmud held in 1239), but this was only the beginning of a series of burnings of the Talmud and attacks on other Jewish books that continued for the next three hundred years.[1] To name the most infamous other instances: In 1244, the Talmud was again burned in Paris, and possibly in 1248 or 1249. In 1255, it was burned in Béziers. In 1269, 1283, and 1299, Jewish books seem to have been sequestered under royal sponsorship, possibly with the assistance of Inquisitors. In 1310, three wagon loads of

---

* This essay has profited from the comments and suggestions of many colleagues and readers. In addition to the editors of this volume, I especially want to thank Kenneth Stow, Piero Capelli, Adam Shear, and Susanne Klingenstein for reading final drafts of this text, and Susanne Klingenstein for invaluable help in editing the manuscript.
1 For the dating of the Talmud's burning in 1241, see Paul L. Rose, 'When Was the Talmud Burnt at Paris? A Critical Examination of the Christian and Jewish Sources and a New Dating, June 1241', *Journal of Jewish Studies*, 62 (2011), pp. 324–39. The other incidents and dates in the list are based on Kenneth R. Stow, *Alienated Minority: The Jews of Medieval Latin Europe* (Cambridge: Harvard University Press, 1992), pp. 254–59; Marvin J. Heller, *Printing the Talmud: A History of the Earliest Printed Editions of the Talmud* (Brooklyn: Im Ha-Sefer, 1992), pp. 201–15; and the considerable earlier scholarship cited in both books.

David Stern • Harvard University

Figure 13.1. Nedarim-Nazir (end of Nedarim, beginning of Nazir), Iberia, 14th–15th c., Moscow, Russian State Library (formerly Lenin Library), Baron David Günzburg Collection 1134.

Jewish books were burned in Paris, and in the same year Bernard Gui began his inquisitorial work in the south of France, which included the confiscation of Jewish books. In November 1319, Bernard burned two wagons filled with volumes of the Talmud. In 1321, the Talmud was burned in Pamiers, and later in the year, in Paris. According to Jewish reports, there were attacks on Rabbinic works by Inquisitors in Paris and in the south of France in 1310 and 1319. In 1321 or 1322, the Talmud was again burned, either near Avignon or in Rome (by King Robert of Naples and Sicily on behalf of Pope John XXII in Avignon), and in 1415, Benedict XIII ordered the Talmud confiscated. In the early sixteenth century, in Germany, the former Jew, Johannes Pfefferkorn, tried unsuccessfully to have the Talmud burned. Finally, on the Jewish New Year in 1553, every copy of the Talmud that the Inquisition had been able to find in Italy was burned in the Campo de' Fiori in Rome. Within a month, copies of the Talmud and other Hebrew books were burned in Bologna, Ravenna, Mantua, Ferrara, Cremona, and elsewhere in Italy, and near the end of October, in the Piazza San Marco in Venice, where the burning was even more extravagant. Still more burnings followed for the remainder of the century.

We have substantial literary records and documentation for these events, but little in the way of material or visual evidence. The possible exception is a single Talmud codex of the tractates *Nedarim* and *Nazir* (Figure 13.1), written in Sefardi script, probably in the fourteenth or fifteenth century, that bears the marks of an *'ud mutzal mi-'eish*, 'a brand snatched from a fire' (Zech. 3:2). We have no idea what fire this Talmud was snatched from, but if there exists anywhere a survivor of a medieval or early modern Talmud burning, it would probably look like this codex.

These public burnings of the Talmud were not the first instances of violence directed against books in Western culture.[2] At least according to legend, if not fact, Protagoras's *On the Gods* was burned in the agora in ancient Athens.[3] In 181 BCE, sacred texts attributed to Numa Pompilius, Rome's semi-legendary second king, were publicly burned after being deemed opposed to what had then become established religion.[4] In 12 BCE, Augustus's first act as *pontifex maximus* was to burn publicly more than two thousand magical and divinatory writings. In the early fourth century of the common era, there was a rash of burnings of Christian texts by the Roman authorities, probably owing to the Empire's recognition of the centrality of books to the upstart but growing religious faith. As the Empire itself became Christianized, however, and as Roman emperors increasingly saw themselves as defenders of the Church, they reversed themselves and began deploying book burning as a weapon *against* every text expressing beliefs they deemed threatening to Rome and to Christianity. As such, books were treated like heretics and heresies, a trend that intensified in the course of the Middle Ages. In 1121 Peter Abelard was forced to burn his *Theologia* with his own hands, a typical strategy used against heretics and their books. Nor was book-burning a Christian prerogative alone. In 1232, in Montpellier, anti-rationalist opponents of Maimonides, the great al-Andalusian Jewish legalist and philosopher, are said to have handed over his works to Dominicans, who burned them as heretical books (although some recent scholars have doubted whether the burnings actually took place).[5]

In all of these events, as Daniel Sarefield has argued, the point of book-burning was not simply to destroy the book.[6] It was also a quasi-ritualized act of cleansing the pollution from society. This duality persisted in the Middle Ages in the symbolic dimension of book-burning. In Alexander Murray's formulation, it was an '"efficacious sign" — a sign which did something, and in so doing showed what had to be done'.[7] A book-burning was intended to demonstrate publicly that a work was to be condemned, not simply to be destroyed; indeed, as Thomas Werner

---

2 So far as I know there does not exist a definitive history of book-burning in Western culture although there are many excellent studies of the phenomenon in classical antiquity and in the modern period, especially in the twentieth century. For now, see Haig Bosmajian, *Burning Books* (Jefferson, NC: McFarland, 2006). Despite its subtitle, Richard Ovenden's *Burning the Books: A History of the Deliberate Destruction of Knowledge* (Cambridge: Harvard University Press, 2020) deals with the deliberate destruction of books only after the late sixteenth century. For the medieval period (up until 1520), see Thomas Werner, *Den Irrtum liquidieren: Bücherverbrennungen im Mittelalter* (Göttingen: Vandenhoeck and Ruprecht, 2007), a monumental study of more than 200 book-burnings, although he deals only briefly (pp. 30–33) with the Talmud burning of 1241 and the early burning of Maimonides' works in Montpellier. For a very helpful English summary of Werner's complicated argument, see Alexander Murray, 'The Burning of Heretical Books', in *The Making of European Culture: Medieval and Modern Perspectives*, ed. by Andrew P. Roach and James R. Simpson (Oxford: Routledge, 2016), pp. 77–88.

3 Bosmajian, pp. 33–39.

4 For the ancient Roman and early Christian book-burnings, see Daniel Sarefield, 'The Symbolics of Book Burning: The Establishment of a Christian Ritual of Persecution', in *The Early Christian Book*, ed. by William E. Klingshirn and Linda Safran (Washington, DC: Catholic University of America Press, 2007), pp. 159–73.

5 See Jeremy Cohen, *The Friars and the Jews: The Evolution of Medieval Anti-Semitism* (Ithaca: Cornell University Press, 1982), pp. 52–60, and notes for complete bibliography.

6 Sarefield, pp. 159–60.

7 Murray, p. 80.

demonstrates, *copies*, rather than originals, were typically burned; the originals were preserved as records in order to help identify other copies, or other heresies.[8] Even the procedure of burning itself had a symbolic dimension because it was seen as a uniquely thorough kind of destruction with a singularly impressive visual impact that was not true of other modes of destroying an object.

Even so, the burning of the Talmud in Paris in 1241 differed qualitatively from earlier book-burnings. In the first case, it was exclusively *the book*, not its authors or adherents or students, which was judged and destroyed. Indeed, the so-called 'trial' of the Talmud in 1239, which preceded its burning in 1241, may have been the first time in Western culture that a book was tried and condemned. But what does it mean to judge a book rather than its author(s) or students? As we have seen, book-burning itself had a symbolic dimension but then, so did the Talmud, which was not simply a literary document, neither for Jews nor for Christians. As we shall see, the Talmud was a highly charged symbol in its own right, and its symbolism emerged prominently in the course of being burned. In this chapter, I concentrate on two Talmud-burnings, Paris 1241 and Rome 1553, as I henceforth call the cases. Both events have been studied and analysed separately and extensively for their place in Jewish and European social, religious, and intellectual history, as well as for Jewish-Christian polemic and relations. My discussion of the two leans heavily on this important earlier scholarship. However, Paris 1241 and Rome 1553 have rarely been studied together, or from a comparative perspective, and to the best of my knowledge, never from the vantage point of book history. Between the times of the two burnings, the technology of print and its culture developed and evolved in Europe with dramatic consequences. The complete Talmud was printed in four separate editions in the first half of the sixteenth century:[9] Venice: Bomberg, 1519–1523; Venice: Bomberg, 1526–1538;[10] Venice: Giustiniani, 1546–1551; Venice: Bomberg, 1548–1549. This fact alone raises several questions: Did printing change the Talmud or the way it was perceived? Did print have an impact on the burning of the Talmud in 1553? Did it make that event different from its predecessor in 1241, and if so, how? I begin by summing up what we know about each burning separately, including the symbolic meanings it held for contemporary Jews and Christians, and then reflect upon the differences between the two occurrences, and how the advent of print may have played a role in making that difference.

Paris 1241: The Talmud as Heretic, the Talmud as Martyr

There is extensive documentation in Latin and Hebrew for the trial and the burning of the Talmud in 1241 as well as for the events that followed them, and both the trial and the burning as well as those subsequent events have been analysed in depth by scholars over the last century.[11] The

---

8 Werner, pp. 350–54; Murray, p. 81.

9 Heller, pp. 135–93, 400–01; Raphael N. N. Rabbinowicz, *History of the Printing of the Talmud* [in Hebrew], ed. by Abraham M. Habermann (Jerusalem: Mossad Ha-Rav Kook, 1965), pp. 35–55.

10 Heller, pp. 167–70; Rabbinowicz, *History*, pp. 43–47, believes that the edition was completed in 1531 although he admits there is no certainty about this.

11 For an overview of the primary sources, see Robert Chazan, 'Trial, Condemnation, and Censorship: The Talmud in Medieval Europe: Historical Essay', in *The Trial of the Talmud: Paris, 1240*, ed. by John Friedman and others (Toronto: Pontifical Institute of Mediaeval Studies, 2017), pp. 16–21. The full Latin dossier containing the correspondence of Gregory IX, Innocent III, and Odo of Chateauroux; Donin's *De Articulis litterarum Papae*; and the Latin 'confessions' of Rabbis Vivo (Yehiel) and Judah, are all included in Paris, Bibliothèque nationale de France (BnF), lat. 16558. The Latin text of Donin's accusations is now available in a critical edition: Piero Capelli, '*De Articulis litterarum*

narrative that has emerged from the scholarly consensus shows how the Talmud came to stand in not only for the Jews but for the very idea of Judaism itself.

In 1236, Nicholas Donin, a dissident Jew from La Rochelle, brought a series of accusations against the Talmud before Pope Gregory IX and requested that the Pope consign to the fire all copies of the Talmud found in Christendom.[12] What led to Donin's accusations is unclear.[13] As both the Hebrew and the Latin documentation testify, Donin had received an excellent rabbinic education and was familiar with talmudic literature. The Hebrew text of the trial states that around 1225 Donin was excommunicated by Rabbi Yehiel of Paris — the lead spokesperson

---

Papae: A Critical Edition', in *The Talmud in Dispute during the High Middle Ages*, ed. by Alexander Fidora and Görge K. Hasselhoff (Bellaterra: Servei de Publicacions de la Universitat Autònoma de Barcelona, 2019), pp. 29–57. In addition, Ulisse *Cecini* and Óscar de la Cruz *Palma* ('Beyond the Thirty-Five Articles: Nicholas Donin's Latin Anthology of the Talmud [With a Critical Edition])', in *The Talmud in Dispute* (pp. 59–99) have published a critical edition of a small anthology of talmudic passages found in MS BnF, lat. 16558, which they call 'The Latin Talmud Anthology' and from which they claim Donin selected his supporting talmudic passages in *De articulis*. The question as to who and how many persons translated the talmudic passages in either the original articles or in 'The Latin Anthology', has been the subject of considerable scholarship, but Alexander Fidora and Ulisse Cicini ('Nicholas Donin's Thirty-Five Articles against the Talmud: A Case of Collaborative Translation in Jewish-Christian Polemic', in *Ex Oriente Lux: Translating Words, Scripts, and Styles in Medieval Mediterranean Society*, ed. by Charles Burnett and Pedro Mantas-España [Córdoba: Córdoba University Press (UCO Press), 2016], pp. 187–99) establish that it was a collaborative project in which Donin himself translated from the original into French, and another translator turned the French into Latin; see as well Capelli, '*De articulis*', p. 29 note 1. Capelli revises the view of Cecini and Palma in their introduction to the critical edition of 'The Latin Anthology', p. 67, where they argue for separate Latin translators for the two translations with Donin as the first. In any case, it is worth noting that 'The Latin Anthology' and the far more extensive *Extractiones de Talmud*, about which I say more later, are the two earliest Latin translations of the Talmud. The Jewish side of the trial is documented mainly in a Hebrew text called *Vikuah Rabbeinu Yehiel* ('The Disputation of Our Rabbi Yehiel'), which exists in three separate versions: see Judah Galinsky, 'The Different Hebrew Versions of the "Talmud Trial" of 1240 in Paris', in *New Perspectives on Jewish-Christian Relations*, ed. by Elisheva Carlebach and Jacob J. Schacter (Leiden: Brill, 2012), pp. 109–40. Although the text has not yet been critically edited, there is now an excellent scholarly translation of the lengthiest version, along with the papal correspondence, Donin's *De Articulis* including the supporting talmudic texts, and the 'confessions' of the rabbis in *The Trial of the Talmud*. All my citations and quotations are to those translations. For the history of the trial and the 1241 burning, the most detailed study remains Chenmelech Merchavia, *The Church versus Talmudic and Midrashic Literature [500–1248]* [in Hebrew] (Jerusalem: Mosad Bialik, 1970), pp. 248–363. My summary in the following pages is largely based upon Chazan, 'Trial'; Cohen, *The Friars and the Jews*, pp. 60–76; Jeremy Cohen, *Living Letters of the Law: Ideas of the Jew in Medieval Christianity* (Berkeley: University of California Press, 1999), pp. 317–63; and the articles by Capelli cited earlier in this note as well as Piero Capelli, 'Nicolas Donin, The Talmud Trial of 1240, and the Struggle Between Church and State in Medieval Europe', in *Entangled Histories: Knowledge, Authority, and Jewish Culture in the Thirteenth Century*, ed. by Elisheva Baumgarten and others (Philadelphia: University of Pennsylvania Press, 2016), pp. 159–78; Piero Capelli, 'Jewish Converts in Jewish-Christian Intellectual Polemics in the Middle Ages', in *Intricate Interfaith Networks in the Middle Ages: Quotidian Jewish-Christian Contacts*, ed. by Ephraim Shoham-Steiner (Turnhout: Brepols, 2016), pp. 33–83. All the relevant past scholarship is cited in these sources.

12 *The Trial of the Talmud*, p. 102, and compare Gregory's *Letter 4*, 95, where he also states that the Talmud codices that are confiscated are to be burned. As Chazan ('Trial', p. 19) notes, it is significant that the outcome of the trial — the Talmud's 'guilt' — was already pre-determined at the outset.

13 The actual biographical information about Donin is relatively scarce, but the scholarship is now quite substantial. The best recent study is Capelli, 'Nicolas Donin'. For earlier sources, see Solomon Grayzel, *The Church and the Jews in the XIIIth Century* (1933; revised Ed. New York: Hermon Press, 1966), Appendix A: Nicolas Donin, pp. 339–40; and Capelli, 'Jewish Converts', pp. 47–49. See Cohen, *The Friars and the Jews*, p. 6 note 19 for a fairly exhaustive listing of earlier bibliography.

for the Jewish community in the trial — because he denied the validity of the Oral Torah and 'believes only in that written in the Torah of Moses, without any interpretation'.[14] Yehiel was the leader of the Tosafist movement in northern France at the time, and it is possible that Donin had been R. Yehiel's student, in which case the former may have wished to seek personal revenge for his humiliation.[15] Some eleven years after his excommunication, Donin converted to Christianity, and shortly thereafter, he brought his accusations to the Pope.[16] Whatever his precise motivation, Donin was a formidable adversary who knew his Talmud well.[17]

---

14 *The Trial of the Talmud*, pp. 129–30.
15 Thus, Capelli, 'Nicholas Donin', esp. pp. 174–78. A number of scholars have also noted Donin's rationalist tendencies (on the basis of his repeated accusations of the Talmud's irrationality) and have connected him to the Maimonidean controversy in Montpelier in 1232: see Cohen, *The Friars and the Jews*, p. 61; and Piero Capelli, 'Jewish Converts in Jewish-Christian Intellectual Polemics in the Middle Ages', in *Intricate Interfaith Networks in the Middle Ages: Quotidian Jewish-Christian Contacts*, ed. by Ephraim Shoham-Steiner (Turnhout: Brepols, 2016), pp. 47–49. A number of scholars in the first half of the twentieth century attempted to identify Donin as a Karaite: see Grayzel, and esp. Judah M. Rosenthal, 'The Talmud on Trial: The Disputation at Paris in the Year 1240', *Jewish Quarterly Review*, 47 (1956–57): pp. 58–76, 145–69; but for a definitive refutation, see Daniel Lasker, 'Karaism and the Jewish-Christian Debate', in *Frank Talmage Memorial Volume*, ed. by Barry Walfish (Haifa: Haifa University Press, 1993), pp. 326–28. The intra-Jewish dimension of the event's origins may also be reflected in the intensity of the debate between Donin and Yehiel (*The Trial of the Talmud*, pp. 129–30) over the dating of the Talmud's antiquity; who else except Jews would argue so fiercely over the Talmud's dating? On this debate, see Piero Capelli, 'Dating the Talmud in the Middle Ages', in *Let the Wise Listen and Add to Their Learning (Prov. 1:5): Festschrift for Günter Stemberger on the Occasion of His 75th Birthday*, ed. by Constanza Cordoni and Gerhard Langer (Berlin: De Gruyter, 2016), pp. 605–18. Talya Fishman's assertion (in *Becoming the People of the Talmud: Oral Torah as Written Transmission in Medieval Jewish Cultures* [Philadelphia: University of Pennsylvania Press, 2011], p. 174) that the burning of the Talmud could have first occurred only in the thirteenth century because the text of the Talmud had not been truly fixed in written form until then is difficult to accept for a number of reasons, the main one being that if it were correct, Donin would certainly have said so and not acknowledged that the Talmud was four hundred years old. Fishman is certainly correct, however, in suggesting that the Talmudo-centrism of the Tosafists, along with their intensive scrutiny of its text, may have led to the direction that his rebelliousness ultimately took. The emphatic Talmudo-centrism of Ashkenazi Jewry in the twelfth century was first stressed by Israel Ta-Shema, *Early Franco-German Ritual* [in Hebrew] (Jerusalem: Magnes, 1992), pp. 245–46. It is also worth remembering that until the tenth century, the Jewish presence in Christian Europe was itself negligible, and significant Jewish communities only began to appear in the eleventh century, at which point they became a felt presence in Christian society.
16 The first to note the date of Donin's conversion was Shlomo Simonsohn, *The Apostolic See and the Jews: History* (Toledo: Pontifical Institute of Medieval Studies, 1991), p. 279, a significant fact because, as Capelli observes in 'Jewish Converts', pp. 44–45, it means that Donin was essentially a man without a community — neither Jewish nor Christian — for eleven years, a remarkable state of figurative 'homelessness' in the Middle Ages that may go a long way in explaining his later behaviour. See as well Capelli's penetrating remarks in 'Jewish Converts', pp. 43–49 and the conclusion comparing Donin to other contemporaneous converts in 'Jewish Converts', pp. 71–79.
17 As Chazan remarks ('Trial', p. 40), it is noteworthy that the Jewish sources never impugn Donin's knowledge of Talmud. The sole Jewish source to acknowledge Donin's learnedness is recorded in a testimony about the Second Disputation in Paris in 1269 (preserved in Moscow, Russian State Library, MS Günzberg 1390, fol. 102b), in which the otherwise unknown Rabbi Abraham ben Samuel of Rouen, compared Pablo Christiani to Donin by saying that קטונו של המין הראשון עב׳ ממתני זה ולא היה נחשב לפניו כקליפת השום כי כל ימיו לא ידע דבר לאמתו ('the little finger of the earlier apostate [Donin] was thicker than the loins of this one [Christiani], who by comparison is not even worth a garlic-skin, since his whole life he never really knew what to say'). The Hebrew text was first published by Joseph Shatzmiller in *La deuxième controverse de Paris: Un chapiter dans la polémique entre chrétiens et juifs au Moyen Age* (Paris and Louvian: Peeters, 1994), 45; cited and translated in Capelli, 'Nicolas Donin', pp. 170. The Latin text of

In 1239, some two years after receiving Donin's accusations, Pope Gregory IX issued a series of letters ordering the rulers and prelates of France, England, Aragon, Navarre, Castile, Leon, and Portugal to impound the Talmud and other Jewish writings on the first Sabbath of Lent in 1240, and to submit these books to ecclesiastical authorities for inspection and examination. Gregory's order was ignored by everyone to whom he had written *except* Louis IX of France, who, probably on account of the powerful mendicant establishment surrounding the French monarchy, acceded to the Pope's demand. In the spring of 1240, in a surprise raid on synagogues on a Sabbath morning, every Talmud tractate that could be found was seized. Louis IX then ordered leading French rabbis, including R. Yehiel of Paris, to his court in Paris to defend the Talmud against Donin's charges before an audience presided over by the Queen Mother, Blanche of Castille.[18] There was also an inquisitorial-like panel, which was neither a formal judicial trial nor an actual inquisitorial process.[19]

Despite the efforts of Yehiel and his colleagues, the judges eventually found the Talmud guilty of all thirty-five of Donin's charges. In June 1241, on the sixth day of the Jewish month of Tammuz, twenty cartloads of Talmud codices and other Jewish books including Alfasi's *Sefer ha-Halakhot*, Rashi's commentaries, and prayerbooks were burned in the Place de Grève in Paris. According to an account written about sixty years after the burning, these cartloads contained some 1200 volumes, but this number may be something of a rhetorical exaggeration and the actual number may have been in the hundreds.[20]

The full significance of this series of events — for both Jews and Christians — can be appreciated only within its historical context. Until the twelfth century, Christian knowledge of post-biblical Judaism, let alone Rabbinic literature, was very scant,[21] and until the tenth

---

the Prologue to the Accusations (Paris, BnF, lat. 16558, fol. 211b) describes Donin, rather hyperbolically, *asin hebreo plurimum eruditum secundum testimonium Iudeorum ita ut in natura et gramatica sermonis ebraici vix sibi similem inveniret* (in English: 'a man very learned in Hebrew even according to the testimony of the Jews, so much so that one could scarcely find anyone like him in the nature and grammar of the Hebrew language', as translated in *The Trial of the Talmud*, p. 102). The Latin text was first published by Isadore Loeb, 'La controverse de 1240 sur le Talmud', *Revue des études juives*, 2 (1881), p. 252.

18 Four rabbis were actually called — R. Yehiel, R. Judah ben David of Melun, Rabbi Samuel ben Solomon of Faisal, and Rabbi Moses ben Jacob of Coucy. The Latin 'confessions' contain those of Yehiel (Vivo) and Judah. In the *Vikuah*, only R. Yehiel speaks.

19 This panel was led by Odo (Eudes) of Chateauroux, the Chancellor of the University of Paris, and William of Auvergne, the bishop of Paris. For a full discussion of the idiosyncrasies of the judicial proceeding, see Yosef Schwartz, 'Authority, Control, and Conflict in Thirteenth-Century Paris: Contextualizing the Talmud Trial', in *Jews and Christians in Thirteenth-Century France*, ed. by Elisheva Baumgarten and Judah Galinsky (New York: Palgrave McMillan, 2015), pp. 93–110, who builds upon earlier work by, among others, William C. Jordan, 'Marian Devotion and the Talmud Trial of 1240', *Ideology and Royal Power in Medieval France* (Aldershot and Burlington: Ashgate Variorum, 2001), pp. 76–91.

20 The account cited is the letter of Hillel ben Samuel of Verona to Isaac Ha-Rofei, written around 1300, published in *Kovetz teshuvot ha-Rambam*, ed. by Avraham Likhtenberg (Leipzig: Shnoys, 1859), Part III, fols 13c–15a; the number is cited on fol. 14a. As pointed out by Colette Sirat, 'Les Manuscrits du Talmud en France du Nordau XIIIe siècle', in *Le brûlement du Talmud à Paris: 1242–1244*, ed. by Gilbert Dahan and others (Paris: Cerf, 1999), pp. 120–39, a typo in an essay on the burning of the Talmud by Moritz Steinschneider, in his *Jewish Literature* (1857; later reprinted in his article in the *Allgemeine Encyclopaedie der Wissenschaften und Künste*) misrecorded the number as 12,000, which is then what was repeated and reprinted in much subsequent scholarship. Sirat herself (p. 125) thinks that even 1200 is a rhetorical embellishment; based on her own surveys of the Talmud manuscripts she has been able to identify, she suggests that the number of Talmud codices burned may at most have been in the hundreds.

21 Scholarly literature on the history of Christian anti-Jewish polemic, which constitutes the context for anti-talmudic polemic, is vast. For the latter, which is our concern, the best detailed treatment up until

century, that knowledge was largely limited to the Old Testament and to New Testament accounts of Jesus's dealings with Pharisees. Early medieval Christian polemic was closely based on early patristic polemic, which accused Jews of their enslavement to the letter of the law, their blindness and inability to understand the spiritual meaning of Scripture, and their obstinate rejection of Christ. Even learned Christians had virtually no knowledge of anything related to the post-biblical development of classical Judaism, which is to say everything represented by Rabbinic talmudic tradition, let alone Judaism as practiced by Jews of their time. Beginning in the twelfth century, however, small numbers of Jews, some of them highly educated, began to convert to Christianity. Not surprisingly, it was one of these converts who was the first Christian writer to refer to a work that can be recognized as the Talmud, although he never called it by that name.[22] Petrus Alfonsi, formerly Moses the Sefardi of Aragon (1062–1140), used the Talmud to prove not only that Jews were incapable of understanding the Bible in any way other than its carnal sense, but also that their own teachings, such as the Talmud's anthropomorphic portrayals of God, were ridiculous, against common sense, and contrary to reason itself. His conclusion was that the Talmud made it impossible for Jews to recognize the rational truth of Christianity.[23] As we will see, these arguments would resonate with later anti-talmudic polemicists.[24] The 'Talmud' as a work is first explicitly named by Peter the Venerable (1094–1156) in a chapter devoted entirely to an attack on the book in his *Adversus Iudeorum inveteratam duritiem* ('Against the Inveterate Obtuseness of the Jews'), written in 1146. Peter intensified Petrus Alfonsi's assault on the Talmud, calling it the *portentuosa bestia* ('the monstrous beast') on account of its irrational tales that had made Jews, he said, less than human.[25] Moving beyond the charge of its irrationality, however, Peter also accused the Talmud of blaspheming Christianity and Christians.[26] Peter the Venerable was not a convert; he had no first-hand knowledge of the Rabbinic texts he cited at length. As scholars have noted, while Peter was usually very conscientious in naming his sources, he was uncharacteristically silent in the case of the Talmud, and the consensus is that he derived most of his talmudic references from Petrus Alfonsi.[27] This practice among anti-talmudic, anti-Jewish polemicists of parading one's seemingly authoritative knowledge of the

---

1240 remains Merchavia; for a summary, see Fishman, pp. 167–74. See also, Amos Funkenstein, 'Polemics, Responses, and Self-Reflection', in *Perceptions of Jewish History* (Los Angeles: University of California Press, 1993), pp. 169–72 for a brilliantly succinct treatment of the main tendencies of anti-Jewish polemic; and pp. 189–96 for the place of anti-talmudic polemic within those tendencies. My discussion is based largely on Fishman and Funkenstein as well as the sources quoted in subsequent notes.

22 See Capelli, 'Jewish Converts', pp. 34–42, and especially p. 40 where he notes that the expression Alfonsi uses, '*doctrina doctorum vestrorum*' ('the teaching of your sages') while being a perfectly adequate translation of *Talmud*, was essentially directed against Rabbinic tradition in toto, a point continued by Donin as we will see.

23 On Petrus Alfonsi, see Funkenstein, pp. 183–89.
24 Fishman, p. 171.
25 Fishman, pp. 171–72, citing Dominique Iogna-Prat, *Order and Exclusion: Cluny and Christendom Face Heresy, Judaism and Islam (1000–1150)* (Ithaca: Cornell University Press, 2002), p. 301; Robert Chazan, *From Anti-Judaism to Anti-Semitism: Ancient and Medieval Christian Constructions of Jewish History* (New York: Cambridge University Press, 2016), pp. 119–32.
26 For a superb summary, Yvonne Friedman, 'Anti-Talmudic Invective from Peter the Venerable to Nicolas Donin (1144–1244)', in *Le brûlement du Talmud*, pp. 174–83.
27 Thus Yvonne Friedman, 'Introduction', in *Petri Venerabilis, Adversus Iudeorum Inveteratam Duritiem*, ed. by Yvonne Friedman, *Corpus Christianorum: Continuatio Mediaevalis*, p. 58 (Turnhout: Brepols, 1985), pp. xiv–xx; citing Saul Lieberman, *Sheqi'in* (Jerusalem: Wahrmann, 1970), pp. 27–42.

Talmud by repeating passages without citation from earlier sources, continued through the sixteenth century. Donin was an exception to this rule because he was well educated.

Nonetheless, Donin's accusations fit neatly into this tradition of Christian anti-talmudism. His charge against the Talmud entitled *De articulis litterarum Papae* consisted of thirty-five 'articles' or charges, each of which was accompanied by corroborating passages from the Talmud or Rabbinic literature translated into Latin.[28] The articles were also accompanied by an anthology of seventy-six additional translated talmudic passages, which modern scholars call 'The Latin Anthology of the Talmud', Donin did not include in his charges.[29]

Donin's thirty-five charges fall into seven basic categories, many of which were staples of the earlier tradition of anti-talmudism including accusations that the Talmud is full of anti-Christian statements and laws, blasphemies against God, Christ, and the Church, and that its extra-biblical stories are often obscene.[30] Before Donin, however, no one had ever bundled all these charges together into a single indictment of the Talmud, nor had they ever been combined with Donin's first charge, the most damning of all — that Jews claimed falsely that the Talmud represented a second, divinely revealed law which was superior even to Scripture (namely, the Christian Old Testament). This specific charge, as nearly all scholars agree, was virtually unprecedented.[31]

This specific series of charges amounted to a full-scale indictment not only of the Talmud but of Rabbinic Judaism — that is, of the Judaism practiced by Donin's thirteenth-century contemporaries. The charges effectively accused the Jews of having abandoned the Bible for a *nova lex*, a new law, and an *alia lex*, a foreign or alien law.[32] This was a devastating accusation because it destroyed the rationale that for centuries had enabled Jews to live within Christendom. The Jews were the *capsarii*, the older slaves who carried the books of the young student, or the *scriniaria*, the book chests, of Christians, the means of preserving the Law and the Prophets for Christians. By being maintained in a state of subjection, the Jews embodied the truth of the prophecies of the Old Testament, the prophecies that foretold their punishment and servitude.

The charges that Donin levelled against the Talmud profoundly subverted this doctrine. Jews could no longer serve as witnesses to the Bible inasmuch as they had *already* forsaken the Bible for another law, a new law which, in its own words, claimed to have superseded the Bible. Furthermore, this new law, the Talmud, was a human contrivance, and by falsely representing it as divine, the Jews blasphemed against God himself. Scholars have argued as to whether this charge of blasphemy was in fact an accusation of heresy.[33] As Benjamin Z. Kedar has shown, canon

---

28 The full Latin dossier of the trial can be found in MS Paris, BnF, lat. 16558. For a description of the primary sources, see note 11 above.
29 For an edition of the anthology, see Cecini and Palma.
30 For a more detailed summary of the categories of the charges and precedents in earlier anti-talmudic discourse, see Appendix A.
31 The main case for its unprecedented appearance has been made by Cohen in his two books, *The Friars and the Jews*, particularly pp. 242–61; and *Living Letters*, pp. 317–63; cf. Chazan, 'Trial', pp. 59–63. Funkenstein, pp. 189–93,

argues that the notion that the Talmud constitutes a *nova lex* is already present in Peter the Venerable's polemic, but see his qualification on 193 note 66.
32 This accusation, implicit in the *Articulis*, is actually spelled out explicitly in Gregory IX's letter to the Archbishops of France on 9 June 1239; *The Trial of the Talmud*, pp. 93–94; see Chazan, 'Trial', pp. 44–45.
33 This point has been the crux of the debate between Cohen and Chazan; in fact, none of the early charges explicitly characterizes the Talmud as heretical although Odo, in his letter of protest to Innocent IV and reaffirmation of the indictment written (probably) in 1248 does draw an analogy between the Talmud and other heresies (*The Trial of the Talmud*, pp. 100). Cf. as well the comment of Stow, 'Fruit of Ambivalence', p. 12;

law asserted that the pope had jurisdiction over the Jews in cases in which they transgress Old Testament law or invent heresies against that law (such as the claim that the Talmud superseded the Bible); Innocent IV argued that it was on that basis that he and Gregory IX burned the Talmud.[34] As Sara Lipton, in her exemplary study of the *Bible Moralisée* has shown, Jews and heretics were regularly lumped together, visually and in the Church's imagination: both heretics and Jews rejected the authority of Scripture (or at least the Church's understanding of Scripture).[35]

Whether the crime was heresy or blasphemy, the shocking feature of the accusation was that it was directed against a book, the Talmud, not against its authors or its adherents or its students. The rubric 'Talmud' was, however, a loose term apparently including all Rabbinic literature, that is, Rashi, the midrashic collections, and the liturgical texts, mainly *piyyutim*, that were later included in the dossier and its Latin translations. By placing the Talmud at the heart of this argument, its accusers elevated the book to an unprecedented position in the history of Judaism in relation to Christianity. It was these 'books full of errors', as Odo described the Talmud in a letter to Innocent IV, that 'turn the Jews away from not only a spiritual understanding [of the Law] but even from a literal one, and towards fables and fictions'.[36] In such statements, the Talmud is virtually personified, attributed with an agency of its own.[37] The Talmud, the book, *was* the offense against Christianity. The Talmud, the book, was what prevented Jews from recognizing the truth of Christianity.

The Jewish defendants were fully cognizant of the threat Donin's accusations posed to the Talmud

---

and Schwartz, 'Authority', pp. 19–20, who connects the inclusion of inner-Jewish heresy under Christian jurisdiction to the growing development of control of intellectual discourse within the University of Paris at the same time. See as well Chazan, 'Trial', p. 29 (note 50).

34 Benjamin Z. Kedar, 'Canon Law and the Burning of the Talmud, *Bulletin of Medieval Canon Law*, 9 (1979), pp. 81–82.

35 Sara Lipton, *Images of Intolerance: The Representation of Jews and Judaism in the* Bible Moralisée (Berkeley: University of California Press, 1999), pp. 82–111 (pp. 106–10) As Piero Capelli has pointed out to me, Lipton's point builds upon the analysis of Roger Moore, *The Formation of a Persecuting Society*, 2nd ed. (New York: Oxford, 2007), pp. 26–42 and 80–88 in general, but especially pp. 88–91 on the creation of a single persecuted category for Jews and heretics.

36 '… *libri erroribus… pleni… ut non solum ab intellectu spirituali Judeos avertant, immo etiam a literrali, et ad fabulas et quedam fictitia convertant*', as cited and translated in Solomon Grayzel, *The Church and the Jews in the XIIIth Century*, rev. Ed, (New York: Hermon, 1966, 276–78; also cited in The *Trial of the Talmud*, pp. 99; for exposition, see Cohen, *Living Letters*, pp. 324. By using the plural 'books' Odo seems to be referring to the commentaries of Rashi and works of *aggadah* and other Rabbinic texts that were also seized in the synagogue raids.

37 In a fascinating discussion, Federico Dal Bo, 'Textualizing, De-Textualizing, and Re-Textualizing the Talmud: The Dimension of Text in the *Extractiones de Talmud*', in *The Talmud in Dispute*, pp. 120–21, points out that in the expanded Latin Talmud anthology *Extractiones de Talmud*, compiled after the trial, the Talmud is literally given a voice. Thus, a passage in the Talmud that literally reads, 'But doesn't the Master (*mar*) say: Moses requested that the Divine Presence not rest on the nations of the world' (B. Baba Batra 15b), is translated as *nonne dicit Dominus meus — Talmud scilicet: Rogavit Moyses quod non requiesceret Spiritus Dei super gentes saeculi* ('But doesn't my Lord — that is, the Talmud — say: Moses asked that the Spirit of God not rest on the nations of the world'). The locution, *ve-ha amar mar*, 'doesn't the Master say', is commonly used in the Talmud to introduce an anonymous tradition or statement, with the word *mar*, literally 'master' or 'lord', referring to an anonymous sage. The translation of *mar* as *dominus*, 'lord' is accurate, but by capitalizing *Dominus*, *mar* effectively becomes a name for the divinity, which is then extended to the 'personified' Talmud, who/which reports the quoted tradition. As Dal Bo notes, 'The Latin translator unequivocally maintains that this "master" is not an individual but rather a book […] the Talmud has become the main actor in the communicative act between God and the Jews. It is the Talmud *itself* that speaks to the Jews and imparts them their instructions […]'. (Dal Bo, 'Textualizing', pp. 121).

and to their observance of Judaism. R. Yehiel and his colleagues defended the Talmud's veracity as a divinely mandated text that was required in order to understand Scripture. In response to Donin's claim that the Talmud was no more than four hundred years old — and thus must be a human contrivance of the Rabbis — R. Yehiel argued that it was more than a thousand years old and that no one, 'not even the priest from Rome [namely, the Pope] who knew the entire Talmud, and many other priests, had ever found anything blameworthy' in the Talmud.[38] Both the Talmud's antiquity and the novelty of Donin's accusations against it, Yehiel argued, were proofs that showed how baseless his charges must be.[39]

The 1241 burning was not the end of the story. In 1244 Innocent I, who succeeded Gregory in the papacy in 1243, renewed Gregory's decrees against the Talmud with a command to burn any copies that had escaped destruction in 1241. Shortly afterwards, however, French Jews protested that they were unable to observe Judaism properly without being able to consult the Talmud — paradoxically, observance of Rabbinic law was never itself prohibited — and Innocent convened a second inquisitorial-like commission to re-examine the charges, again with Odo (Eudes) of Chateauroux at its head. In 1244, for a second time, the commission found the Talmud guilty of charges of blasphemy and heresy. In preparation for this second commission, a far more extensive Latin translation of 1922 talmudic passages was prepared by the Dominicans of the Monastery of St Jacques in Paris under the editorship of the Dominican (and former Jew) Thibaut de Sézanne.[40] This substantial anthology, known as *Extractiones de Talmud*, survives in some nine manuscripts. While its impact during its own period or in subsequent centuries is still not clear, it was nonetheless the major translation into Latin available to Christian readers before the early modern period.[41]

In 1247, however, in a remarkable reversal of papal policy, Innocent ordered King Louis IX to

---

38 Hebrew, following MS Moscow, National Library of Russia, Günzberg 1390, fol. 101ʳ⁻ᵛ: כי התלמוד ישן נושן מיותר מאלף שנים ועד עתה לא דבר עליו שום דבר רע ואף הגלח דרומא יודע כל התלמוד שלנו ודרש וחקר הכל וכמהו גלחים הרבה…ולא מצאו בו דפי…, as cited in Capelli, 'Dating the Talmud', p. 613, and in Galinsky, 'Different Hebrew Versions', p. 115. The other manuscript of the Paris Trial, MS Paris BnF hébr. 712, has fifteen hundred years rather than a thousand. On the significance of the dispute over the dating of the Talmud, see Capelli, 'Dating the Talmud'; *The Trial of the Talmud*, p. 129. For a full exposition of Yehiel's defence on this point, see Chazan, 'Trial', pp. 59–63.

39 To be sure, Yehiel and his colleagues responded to the other charges made by Donin (as they had to). Regarding the blasphemies against Jesus, they claimed (somewhat lamely) that the passages referred to *another* Jesus, not Jesus of Nazareth. The blasphemous anthropomorphisms about God and other 'ridiculous' and 'irrational' statements were all *aggadah*, Rabbinic 'lore' that need not be taken literally or even seriously. The purportedly anti-Christian laws and statements were directed against idolaters, not Christians.

40 *Extractiones de Talmud per ordinem sequentialem*, ed. by Ulisse Cecini and others (Turnhout: Brepols, 2018); with a volume of scholarly studies entitled *Studies in the Latin Talmud*, ed. by Ulisse Cecini and Eulàlia Vernet iPons (Bellaterra: Servei de Publicacions de la Universitat Autònoma de Barcelona, 2019).

41 For its influence, see Alexander Fidora, 'The Influence of the *Extractiones de Talmud* on Anti-Jewish Sermons from the Thirteenth and Early Fourteenth Centuries', in *The Talmud in Dispute* pp. 235–47; and Alexander Fidora, 'The Latin Talmud and Its Place in Medieval Anti-Jewish Polemic', in *Studies in the Latin Talmud*, pp. 13–21. As several essays in *Studies in the Latin Talmud* make clear, the work seems to have had little if any impact on later writers whom one would have expected to know of it, figures such as Andrew of St Victor and Nicholas de Lyra. For a list of other Latin translations, see Cohen, *The Friars and the Jews*, p. 78 note 4. It is worth emphasizing that the translations in the *Extractiones*, as many as there are, hardly constitute a representative anthology of the Talmud; no one after reading them would emerge with any idea of what the Talmud is really like. Aside from having been chosen to prove the perniciousness of the Talmud, most of the selections are very brief, some quite fragmentary, and as noted by Eulàlia Vernet i Pons and Enric Cortès in their chapters

refrain from confiscating and burning further copies of the Talmud until a new investigation could re-examine it. As Innocent wrote in his letter, he was acting in response to the claim of the Jews that they could not observe and practice their religion without the Talmud.[42] In response, Odo of Chateauroux angrily protested Innocent's reversal of Gregory IX's policy; he refuted the Jews' claim that they could not observe biblical law without the Talmud as a lie; and he reaffirmed the earlier condemnation and refused to return the Talmud codices to their Jewish owners.[43] The next year, however, in 1248, Odo himself issued a new 'judicial sentence' in which he stepped back from the radical charge that the Talmud was inherently blasphemous in claiming to be a second revelation though he continued to insist that the work was sufficiently offensive to Christians in other ways that confiscated copies should not be returned to their Jewish owners.[44]

Innocent's 1247 reversal and Odo's new judicial sentence essentially undid the charge that the Talmud's very existence was a blasphemy if not a heresy, and that it was inherently disrespectful of God. As Chazan notes, the Talmud was prohibited but, in effect, the observance of talmudic Judaism was permitted.[45] Ownership of the Talmud continued to be prohibited in France for the remainder of the thirteenth century, but by 1320 — after the expulsion of the Jews in 1306, and their readmission to France some fourteen years later — both French royalty and the Church appear to have lost interest in the Talmud, and the ban was no longer enforced. In terms of the history of the Talmud *as a book*, however, a new conceptualization of its character had been shaped. For Christians, the Talmud had become a persona, as it were — a blasphemer, a heretic.

How did the Jews of France react to the burning of the Talmud, and what meaning did this event hold for them? And what does this tell us about what the Talmud signified for Jews? While the burning of the Talmud was no doubt experienced as a traumatic catastrophe, its practical impact is more difficult to gauge. The thirteenth century has been described by Jewish historians as a period of discernible decline in intellectual life, but it is not clear that the decline had much to do with the burning of the Talmud.[46] It did not stop Jewish scholarly activity although much of the activity that took place *after* the burning of the Talmud seems to have been dedicated to collecting and editing the work of previous generations of French Jewish scholars, the Tosafists in particular. While the evidence for *Christian* censorship of talmudic texts is inconsistent, there appears to have been a fair amount of *Jewish* self-censorship.[47]

Figures 13.2 and 13.3 illustrate one such passage from Tractate *Sanhedrin* 43a–b as it appears in Codex hebr. 95 (Munich, Bayerische Staatsbibliothek), the only codex to survive from

---

in *The Talmud in Dispute*, it is not always clear why some passages were ever selected to be translated and anthologized in the first place.

42 *The Trial of the Talmud*, pp. 97–98.
43 *The Trial of the Talmud*, pp. 98–100.
44 *The Trial of the Talmud*, pp. 100–01.
45 Chazan, 'Trial', p. 83.

46 For a view of the decline in the thirteenth century, see Moritz Güdemann, *Geschichte des Erziehungswesens un der Cultur der abend-ländischen Juden während des Mittelalters* [in Hebrew] (Warsaw: Ahiasaf, 1867), I, pp. 60–62; for the contravening view, Haym Soloveitchik, 'Catastrophe and Halakhic Creativity: Ashkenaz – 1096, 1242, 1306, and 1298', *Jewish History*, 12 (1998), pp. 71–85; cf. Chazan, 'Trial', p. 87.
47 See Peter Schäfer, *Jesus in the Talmud* (Princeton: Princeton University Press, 2007), pp. 131–44. It is important to note, however, that very few manuscripts of any talmudic tractate from all of Europe (and even from the Orient and Yemen) survive. There is only a single codex from before the advent of print that contains the Talmud in its entirety (Munich, Bayerische Staatsbibliothek, Cod. hebr. 95), and an additional sixty-two codices that contain a single tractate or groups of tractates, a minuscule number if it is true that more than a thousand codices from France alone were burned in 1241, but see Sirat's caveats in note 20 above.

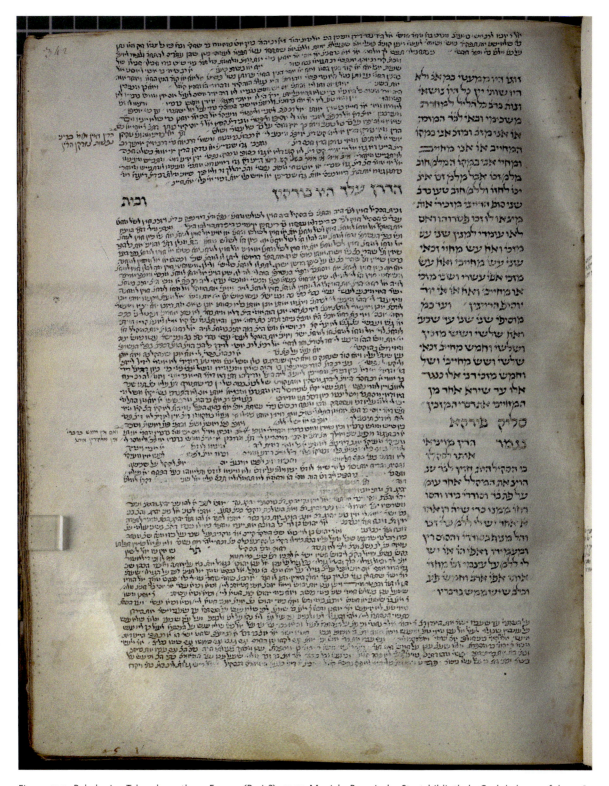

Figure 13.2. Babylonian Talmud, northern France (Paris?), 1343, Munich, Bayerische Staatsbibliothek, Cod. hebr. 95, fol. 342ʳ (Sanhedrin 43a–b).

Figure 13.3. Babylonian Talmud, northern France (Paris?), 1343, Munich, Bayerische Staatsbibliothek, Cod. hebr. 95, fol. 342ʳ (Sanhedrin 43a–b) (detail).

the period before print that includes the entire Babylonian Talmud within its covers.[48] Munich 95 was written in France in 1343, a little more than a century after Paris 1241 and about a half century before the Jews' final expulsion from France in 1394. As both the full page in Figure 13.2 and the detail from that page in Figure 13.3 show, the self-censorship in this case was virtually surgical, especially in comparison with later printed editions (down through the Vilna editions which are still reprinted today as the standard Talmud), where the entire passage about Jesus and his disciples is simply left out of the text. The following is an English translation of the passage. Bolded sections represent those words and lines that are scraped off in the manuscript.

But isn't it taught: On Passover Eve they hung **Jesus**. And a proclamation went out forty days before: **Jesus** is going out to be stoned because he practiced sorcery, incited and led the Jewish people astray. Anyone who knows of a reason to acquit him should come forward and teach it, but they did not find any reason for acquittal, and they hung him on Passover eve. Ulla said: Does this make sense to you? Was he someone whom a reason for acquittal could overturn his verdict? He was an inciter, and the Merciful One states 'Neither shall you spare, neither shall you conceal him' (Deut. 13:9). Rather, **Jesus** was different, as he had close ties with the government. **The Sages taught: Jesus the Nazarene had five disciples: Mattai, Naqai, Netzer, Buni, and Toda. They brought Mattai in to stand trial. Mattai said to the judges: Shall Mattai** be executed? But isn't it written: 'When [*Matai*] shall come **and appear before God?'** (Ps. 42:3). **They said to him: Yes, Mattai shall be executed, as it is written: 'When (***Matai***) shall die, and his name perish?'** (Ps. 41:6). **They brought Naqai in.** Naqai said: Shall Naqai be executed? But isn't it written: 'And the innocent [*naqi*] and righteous you shall not slay' (Exod. 23:7)? They said: Yes, Naqai shall be executed, as it is written: 'In secret places he kills the innocent [*naqi*]' (Ps. 10.:8). They brought Netzer in. He said: Shall Netzer be executed? But isn't it written: 'And a branch

---

48 On Munich 95, see Raphael N. N Rabbinowicz, *Sefer dikdukei soferim* (Variae Lectiones in Mischnam et in Talmud Babylonicum), 15 vols (Munich: M. H. Roesel and E. Huber, 1867–1886), I, pp. 27–35; and David Stern, *Jewish Literary Cultures II: The Medieval and Early Modern Periods* (University Park: Pennsylvania State University Press, 2019), pp. 161, 262–63 (note 25).

[*netzer*] shall grow out of his roots' (Isa. 11:1)? They said: Yes, Netzer shall be executed, as it is written: 'But you are cast out of your grave like an abhorred branch [*netzer*]' (Isa. 14:19). They brought Buni in. Buni said: Shall Buni be executed? But isn't it written: 'My firstborn son [*beni*] is Israel' (Exod. 4:22)? They said to him: Yes, Buni shall be executed, as it is written: 'Behold, I shall kill your firstborn son [*binkha*]' (Exod. 4:23). They brought Toda in. Toda said: Shall Toda be executed? But isn't it written: 'A psalm of thanksgiving [*todah*]' (Ps. 100:1)? They said: Yes, Toda shall be executed, as it is written: 'Whoever slaughters a thanks-offering [*todah*] honours Me' (Ps. 50:23).[49]

In Munich 95, only the name 'Jesus' and the very beginning of the section about the five apostles with their names (even though their names reappear in the remaining lines of the passage) were removed. In other passages, the word *goy*, 'gentile', which the Christian accusers of the Talmud argued was a reference to Christians, was frequently replaced by *'akum*, an acrostic abbreviation for practitioners of idolatry (which was not an accusation levelled against Christians). As the Munich 95 example suggests, none of these examples of self-censorship were part of a programmatic strategy.

As for the symbolic meaning that the burning of the Talmud held for contemporary Jews, the answer is much clearer. The Talmud became a martyr. The history of this figuration requires some unpacking. There are no descriptions of book (or scroll)-burnings in early Rabbinic literature, but one of the most famous legendary accounts of a rabbinic martyrdom during the Hadrianic period in the second century recounts how R. Hananiah ben Teradion was arrested by the Romans for teaching Torah publicly and executed by being wrapped in a Torah scroll and burned alive. As he died, his students asked him what he saw, and he answered, 'The parchment is burning, and the letters are flying off (Babylonian Talmud, 'Avodah zarah 18a)'. This story, along with tales of the martyrdom of nine other rabbis, became the theme of an independent narrative text called Midrash *'Eleh 'ezkerah*, which, in turn, became the subject matter of two liturgical poems. One, *Arzei Ha-Levanon Adirei Ha-Torah*, a *qinah*, a lament, is recited annually on the Fast of the Ninth of Av, which commemorates the destruction of the Jerusalem Temple, and the other, *Eleh Ezkerah*, a *selihah*, is a penitential hymn recited on Yom Kippur.[50]

This association between Torah, burned Torah scrolls, and martyrdom was inherited by Ashkenazi Jewry, who were heirs to a rich tradition of martyrological texts — chronicles,

---

49 For a transcription of the original Munich 95 passage along with the full text of the passage, see Appendix B. The full Hebrew text (and my English translation) are based on unexpurgated manuscripts of the Talmud (Florence I–II, Reuchlin 2) and incunabula up until Bomberg's *editio princeps* (Venice, 1519/1520–1523). The passage in its entirety is missing from the Vilna edition and most other printed editions of the Babylonian Talmud with the exception of the Steinsaltz Talmud, accessible through Sefaria, https://www.sefaria.org.il/Sanhedrin.43a.20?ven=William_Davidson_Edition_-_English&vhe=Wikisource_Talmud_Bavli&lang=he [accessed in November 2021].

50 Midrash *'Eleh 'ezkerah* is available in a critical synoptic edition: Gottfried Reeg, *Die Geschichte von den Zehn Märtyrern* (Tübingen: Mohr Siebeck, 1985). For an English translation and an introduction on the background, see David Stern and Mark Mirsky, *Rabbinic Fantasies: Imaginative Narratives from Classical Hebrew Literature* (New Haven: Yale University Press, 1998), pp. 143–65. The liturgical poem *'Eleh 'ezkerah* for Yom Kippur (Davidson, *Thesaurus* I 4273) can be found in Daniel Goldschmidt, *Mahzor le-Yomim Noraim II: Yom Kippur* [Jerusalem: Koren, 1970], 568–73; and *'Arzei ha-Levanon 'adirei ha-torah* for the Ninth of Av (Davidson, *Thesaurus* I 7564) in Daniel Goldschmidt, *Poems of Lament for the Ninth of Av* [in Hebrew] (Jerusalem: Mossad Ha-Rav Kook, 1968), pp. 82–85.

lists, and poems — that first took shape after the Crusader massacres in the Rhineland at the end of the eleventh century. This tradition only grew in subsequent centuries as the massacres and expulsions repeated themselves.[51] Both the chronicles and the poems record the destruction and burning of Torah scrolls among the acts of violence perpetrated by rampaging mobs.[52] These texts, the poems in particular, were composed to be recited as part of the synagogue liturgy (like the *qinah* and *selihah* about the ten martyred sages) on either the Ninth of Av or on special fast days instituted in specific communities to recall tragic events that had befallen their own inhabitants. As such, these poems always had a strong communal dimension.

The Crusades and the massacres of the Jews that attended them largely bypassed French Jewry, but with the burning of the Talmud, the Rhineland martyrological tradition came to Paris.[53] In June 1241, a young rabbinical student from Germany named Meir ben Barukh (later known as Maharam of Rothenburg after he became one of the pre-eminent sages of thirteenth-century Ashkenaz), who had come to Paris to study with R. Yehiel, appears to have watched the Talmud burn and shortly thereafter composed a remarkable lament entitled *Sha'ali serufah ba-'eish* ('Ask, O You Who Are Burned in Fire'). Meir's poem was not the only martyrology composed over the burning of the Talmud, but it is certainly the greatest. This poem has been translated and brilliantly analysed by Susan Einbinder, and I draw upon her interpretation in order to tie the poem more closely to our concerns.[54] I quote a few lines from Einbinder's translation to give a sense of the poem's grandeur.[55]

> [1]Ask, O You who are burned in fire, how your mourners fare | They who yearn to dwell in the court of your dwelling place[56] | They who gasp in the dust of the earth and who feel pain | [4]They who are stunned by the blaze of your parchment

The poem begins with an apostrophe, *Sha'ali serufah be-'eish le-shalom 'aveilayikh* (in a more literal translation: 'Ask, she who is burned in fire, after the welfare of your mourners'). This line would have been an unmistakable signal pointing its audience towards one of the models upon which Meir had based his poem — a celebrated hymn composed in the early twelfth century by the great Spanish-Hebrew poet Judah ha-Levi. The first lines of Ha-Levi's poem begin, ציון הלא תשאלי לשלום אסיריך ('O Zion, will you not ask after the

---

51 The foremost study of martyrological poetry in northern France, and one of the best books on the genre generally, is Susan Einbinder, *Beautiful Death: Jewish Poetry and Martyrdom in Medieval France* (Princeton: Princeton University Press, 2009). For an overview of the tradition and a treatment of northern French martyrological poetry, see Chaps. 1 and 2, pp. 17–69.

52 For examples of references in the Chronicles, see Solomon ben Samson's 'Chronicle of 1096' in Abraham M. Habermann, *The Decrees against the Jews in Germany and France: Memorial Accounts of Contemporary Jews during the Crusader Period and a Selection of their Liturgical Poems* [in Hebrew] (Jerusalem: Tarshish, 1945; repr. Jerusalem: Ophir, 1971), pp. 25 (Worms), 35 (Mainz), 44 (Cologne); and Ephraim of Bonn's *Book of Memory* (*Sefer zekhirah*) there, pp. 129 (Cologne), 132 (Speyer). See Einbinder, pp. 81–82, for a translation and discussion of Solomon ben Joseph's *Shemesh ve-yareah* ('O Sun and Moon'), and pp. 82–84 and notes for bibliography and discussion of still other laments over burned Torah scrolls.

53 For northern French Jewry and the Crusades, see Robert Chazan, *The Jews of Medieval Western Christendom: 1000–1500* (Cambridge: Cambridge University Press, 2006), pp. 135–39.

54 Einbinder, pp. 70–99. For the Hebrew texts of the cited passages of the poem, see Appendix C, which reproduces the poem as it appears in Daniel Goldschmidt, *Poems of Lament for the Ninth of Av* [in Hebrew], pp. 135–37.

55 Einbinder, pp. 76–77; see her text for further annotations and commentary.

56 That is, in the court of the Temple.

welfare of your captives…'). Ha-Levi originally composed his poem as a non-liturgical ode of longing for Zion, in genre a type of secular love poetry, but by Meir's time, it had been adopted in the Jewish liturgy as a martyrological lament for the destroyed homeland; indeed, the poem became so celebrated that it spun off an entire mini-genre of Zion lament poems, all of which begin by addressing Zion as a female figure.[57] These poems were recited communally as part of the synagogue service on the Ninth of Av.

The personification of *Tziyon*, Zion, at the centre of the poem would, in turn, have been familiar to every reader as based upon the figure for Mother Zion in the first chapters of the Book of Lamentations. By making the poem's narrator address the feminized personification for Zion directly, Ha-Levi invested the biblical trope with a fresh immediacy. Meir inherited, adapted, and transformed that immediacy by making the female addressed in his poem a new trope for the burned Talmud.

In his poem, Meir never explicitly identifies the *serufah ba-'eish* as the Talmud — in fact, he uses terms that invoke the features of a Torah scroll, and by refusing to name his subject as the Talmud, he implicitly plays upon the ambiguity of the word Torah as referring to both the Written and the Oral Torah (*Torah she-bikhtav* and *Torah she-be'al peh*). That ambiguity is mirrored in the fluid gendering of the poem's subject, *serufah be-'eish*, which grammatically is feminine in form, as is the Hebrew word *Torah*. The word *Talmud*, however, is masculine. Added to the grammar is the reality that the study of Talmud was always (in Meir's world) a virtually exclusively male activity. By addressing the burned Talmud as a feminine figure, Meir was both borrowing from Ha-Levi and deliberately working against literary convention, addressing a female who was *not* Zion. Further, by blurring the difference between the Oral Law and the Written Torah, Meir was simultaneously asserting the identification of the Written and Oral Torah as one, an identity that the Christian accusers of the Talmud had pointedly denied. Moreover, by figuring the Talmud as a female Zion, Meir was also evoking the Talmud not only as a book or as a divine revelation but as a virtual *Shekhinah*-like presence able to console her own mourners, 'those who yearn to dwell in the court of your dwelling place' (which is the Jerusalem Temple, albeit now in ruins). These mourners are the same Jews 'who gasp in the dust of the earth […] who feel pain […] who are stunned by the blaze of your parchment'. Indeed, the burned Talmud evokes both the destroyed Temple and the *Shekhinah* grieving over its destruction and consoling its mourners.

The poem continues several lines later: | ⁹They mourn like jackals and ostriches

And call for bitter wailing on your behalf. | How could she who was given by the flaming God be consumed by the fire | Of mortals, while the foes were not scorched by your embers? | ¹³And you, how long will you dwell in tranquillity, O dainty foe? | Have not your thorns covered my flowers? | You sit proudly to judge God's children with all | Judgment and bring them to trial. | Moreover, you decree burning for the law and regulations given in fire — | Happy the one who requites you!

Did my Rock [appear] in flame and fire to give you | Later to another fire to blaze at your helms? | ²⁷O Sinai, was this why the Lord

---

57 For the best treatment of the poem, see Raymond Scheindlin, *The Song of the Distant Dove: Judah Halevi's Pilgrimage* (New York: Oxford University Press, 2008), pp. 172–279. As Scheindlin notes, once the poem became part of the liturgy for fast days commemorating the destruction of the Temple, its meaning changed from what was partly a love poem to a martyrological lament, which is how Meir certainly understood and used it. See as well Scheindlin's remarks as to how Ha-Levi borrowed motifs from Arabic love poetry addressed to the absent beloved.

chose you, disdaining | Greater mountains to shine within your borders? | To be a sign of the Law when her glory would dwindle | And go down? Let me make an analogy: | You are like a king who wept at his son's feast-day | Foreseeing his death — so your speech foretold your end. | O Sinai, instead of your cloak, let your garment be a sack | Don the garb of widows instead of your dresses. | I will pour forth tears until like a river they reach | Unto the tombs of your most noble princes, | Moses and Aaron, on Mount Hor, and I will ask: Is there | A new Torah, that your scrolls may be burned? (ll. 1–4, 9–32)

The question in that last line — is there a new Torah? — is, as Einbinder notes, richly ambiguous in its references.[58] Does it assert the fact that the Talmud as Oral Torah is not new — not a *nova lex*, a new law that superseded Scripture, as the Christians accused the Jews of believing — but one and the same as the Written Torah? Or is it a mocking reference to the New Testament, to Christianity itself? Or does it possibly express an all but unstated anxiety on the part of its Jewish author that Christianity may, in some sense, have *really* superseded Judaism?[59]

The poem is constructed as a series of apostrophes — first to the Talmud (line 1); then to the gentile enemy ('O dainty foe') who burned the Talmud (line 13); then again to the Talmud (line 25); and finally, to Mount Sinai, the site of the giving of the Torah, both the Oral and the Written (line 27). As we have seen, Meir played against convention by addressing the Talmud as a feminine figure, but he challenged convention in other ways as well. The figure of the martyr was also by convention male (although there were in actuality many female martyrs, almost as many as there were male martyrs,

and martyrological poems about them). Yet by representing the Talmud as both martyr *and* female, Meir injected an idealized eroticism into the relationship between the Talmud and her mourners (which is to say, her students) and, as Einbinder argues, very possibly intended to invoke contemporary vernacular traditions of courtly lyrics written by Christian poets for idealized types of female figures.[60] Indeed, in some of these vernacular French poems, known as Crusader lyrics, images of sacred and secular women appear in juxtaposition, sometimes in opposition; for example, a male Crusader's longing for a beloved female he left at home is juxtaposed to his desire to serve God, and the poet finally resolves the conflict by having the male channel his carnal desire into adoration of the ultimate idealized female, the Virgin Mother. As Einbinder reminds us, at the time Meir was writing his poem, Marian devotion in northern France was at a peak; as will also be recalled, insulting the Virgin was still another of the accusations made against the Talmud. By figuring the Talmud as 'Lady Torah', Meir (so Einbinder suggests) may have been offering a Jewish polemical response to the cult of the Virgin.[61] This would be especially true if I am correct in suggesting that Meir was associating the burned Talmud with the hovering presence of the *Shekhinah*.[62] If nothing else, this poem indicates how over-determined the symbolic value of the burned Talmud had become for Jews.

---

58 Einbinder, p. 78.
59 I owe this last suggestion to Piero Cappeli.

60 See Einbinder, p. 79, for a defence of her assumption that Meir and his contemporaries could very well have been familiar with the vernacular literature of their time.
61 Einbinder, pp. 79–80. On the impact of Marian devotion on the Talmud trial, see Jordan, pp. 76–91.
62 See also Arthur Green, 'Shekhinah, the Virgin Mary, and the Song of Songs', *Association of Jewish Studies Review*, 26 (2002), pp. 1–52; although he deals with a slightly later period and mainly with kabbalistic material. Peter Schäfer, *Mirror of His Beauty: Feminine Images of God from the Bible to the Early Kabbalah* (Princeton: Princeton University Press, 2002), pp. 235–43, also

Meir's lament was not the only way in which the martyrdom of the Talmud was remembered liturgically. At some time in the aftermath of the First Crusade in 1096, a prayer known as *'Av ha-rahamim* ('Merciful Father') was composed and instituted to be recited as part of the synagogue service. Originally intended for the period between Passover and Shavuot, when the massacres occurred, *'Av ha-rahamim* begins by imploring God to remember those who gave their lives 'to sanctify His name' — the traditional Hebrew term for martyrdom — and then calls upon Him to avenge their deaths by punishing the perpetrators of the massacres. The two halves of the prayer are intrinsically related: God is beseeched to remember the martyrs *in order* that He avenge their deaths and, the prayer adds, that this act of vengeance take place 'before our eyes' (*le-'eineinu*) or, in some texts, 'in our days' (*be-ymeinu*). As Israel Yuval has pointed out, this act of vengeance was seen as an inherent part of the redemption.[63] *'Av ha-rahamim*, with its prayer for divine vengeance upon Israel's enemies, is also a prayer for immediate deliverance.

Ephraim Kanarfogel has demonstrated that linguistic expressions in *'Av ha-rahamim* indicate it was probably first composed shortly after the First Crusade.[64] On the basis of manuscripts he has studied, Kanarfogel has also shown that, in the wake of the burning of the Talmud in 1241, the phrase, *neqamat torato* ('vengeance for His Torah'), appears to have been added to the list of victims cited in the prayer.[65] To be sure, the 'Torah' referred to here could be, again, either a martyr's personal Torah scroll or the Talmud burned in 1241, but we know from other sources that the author of the passage in which this phrase first appears lived in the mid-thirteenth century in northern France, possibly was a student of R. Yehiel, and may have witnessed the burning of the Talmud, so it is most likely, as Kanarfogel suggests, that Torah refers to the Talmud. The same phrase, *neqamat torato*, appears in several other similar petitionary prayers from the same period, and in one, the reference to the burning of the Talmud is unambiguous because it states וגם התורה הקדושה הנשרפה באש כמה וכמה פעמים ('And also the holy Torah which was burned in fire several times'), as was (alas!) the Talmud.[66]

The Ashkenazi understanding of the burning of the Talmud as an act of martyrdom was far from being metaphorical.

Rome 1553: The Work of Talmud-Burning in the Age of Mechanical Reproduction

The most decisive difference between the first burning of the Talmud in Paris and the second burning in Rome 1553 was the advent of print.

The first tractate of the Babylonian Talmud to be printed, *Berakhot*, was published by Joshua Solomon Soncino in the town of Soncino, in northern Italy, in 1482. At the same time, a number

---

deals with possible Marian influence on Jewish ideas about the *Shekhinah*, albeit in the twelfth century and in Southern France.

63 Israel Jacob Yuval, *Two Nations in Your Womb: Perceptions of Jews and Christians in Late Antiquity and the Middle Ages*, transl. Barbara Harshav and Jonathan Chipman (Hebrew Ed. 2000; Berkeley, University of California Press, 2006), pp. 93–108. Note that in Meir of Rothenburg's *Sha'ali serufah be-'eish*, line 13, there is also a cry for vengeance. For another vehement prayer that God take vengeance for the burning of the Talmud, see the reconstructed original text of Tzidkiyahu of Rome's *Shibolei ha-leket* in Simcha Emanuel, 'Responses to the Burning of the Talmud in 1242' [in Hebrew], posted 21/4/19 on https://www.academia.edu/38876793/1242_התגובות_לשריפת_התלמוד_בשנת.

64 Ephraim Kanarfogel, 'On the Text and Origin of the Prayer *'Av ha-rahamim*' [in Hebrew], *Yeshurun*, 26 (2012), p. 874.
65 Kanarfogel, p. 874.
66 Kanarfogel, p. 877.

of tractates were also published by Jewish printers in both Spain and Portugal, but with the Spanish expulsion of 1492 and the forced conversion of the Jews in Portugal in 1497, Hebrew printing in Iberia came to a halt, leaving the Italians as the sole printers of the Talmud.[67] By the year 1500 some twenty-three tractates of the Talmud had been printed either by Joshua or his nephew Gershom Soncino, the foremost early Jewish printer. Gershom wanted to print an edition of the entire Babylonian Talmud but he was unable to receive permission from the ruling authorities in Venice which, by the beginning of the sixteenth century, had become the undisputed centre of printing in Europe.[68]

Sometime after 1508, Daniel Bomberg, a young Christian merchant from Antwerp with Christian Hebraist interests, settled in Venice.[69] With a former Jew, now an Augustinian monk, named Felix of Prato, Bomberg set up a press with the explicit purpose of printing Hebrew books for the very lucrative Jewish market. Shortly afterwards, Bomberg received an exclusive license from Pope Leo X and a ten-year copyright from the Venetian Senate to publish the first complete edition of the Talmud, which he then produced in the years between 1520 and 1523.

Figure 13.4 is the first page of Tractate *Berakhot*, the first tractate that Bomberg printed for his first edition of the Babylonian Talmud. Bomberg's edition literally set the Talmud in stone; virtually every subsequent Talmud edition closely followed its foliation and the layout of each of its pages, beginning and ending with the same words. Elsewhere I have traced the history of this distinctive page format, known as the glossed format, with the core text in the middle of the page flanked by commentaries on either side (Rashi on the inner side, the Tosafot on the outer).[70] The format was not invented by Bomberg. He borrowed it from the Soncinos, but even they did not invent it; it goes back to the manuscript age, and ultimately derives from the format of the Christian *Glossa Ordinaria*, which Jewish scribes adapted and Judaized, using it for different purposes in different genres of Jewish books — liturgical Pentateuchs (*humashim*), Hebrew Bibles with commentaries, Talmuds and other legal texts (such as Alfasi) with commentaries, and even prayer books.[71] Among Talmud manuscripts, however, the use of this page format is relatively rare, mainly because it is so difficult to produce by hand. In contrast, it was much easier to produce in print because printers such as Bomberg used models to guide them before they set the type for each page in the press, and then printed editions of perhaps a thousand copies. Bomberg's edition essentially served as the model book for every subsequent edition of the Talmud printed after him. As a result, it is fair to say that Bomberg not only made the glossed format the definitive talmudic page layout for all time but that he also made *his* edition's glossed format — for each page of the Talmud — the definitive format for all time.

Bomberg followed his 1520 edition with two more editions, in 1526–1539 and in 1548–1549.

---

67 Only single leaves or gatherings of these manuscripts survive; for a description of the Iberian editions with photographic facsimiles of all the surviving leaves, see Haim Z. Dimitrovsky, *S'ridei Bavli: An Historical and Bibliographical Introduction* [in Hebrew], 2 vols (New York: Jewish Theological Seminary Press, 1979); and Heller, pp. 31–49.

68 Moses Marx, 'Gershom (Hieronymus) Soncino's Wanderyears in Italy, 1492–1527: Exemplar Judaicae Vitae', *Hebrew Union College Annual*, 11 (1936), pp. 441–42, 445–56.

69 Angelo M. Piattelli, 'New Documents Concerning Bomberg's Printing of the Talmud', in *Meḥevah le-Menaḥem: Studies in Honor of Menahem H. Schmelzer*, ed. by Shmuel Glick and others (Jerusalem: Jewish Theological Seminary Press and Schocken Institute, 2019), p. 175*.

70 Stern, *Jewish Literary Cultures*, pp. 147–78.

71 Stern, *Jewish Literary Cultures*, pp. 158–60, 191–92.

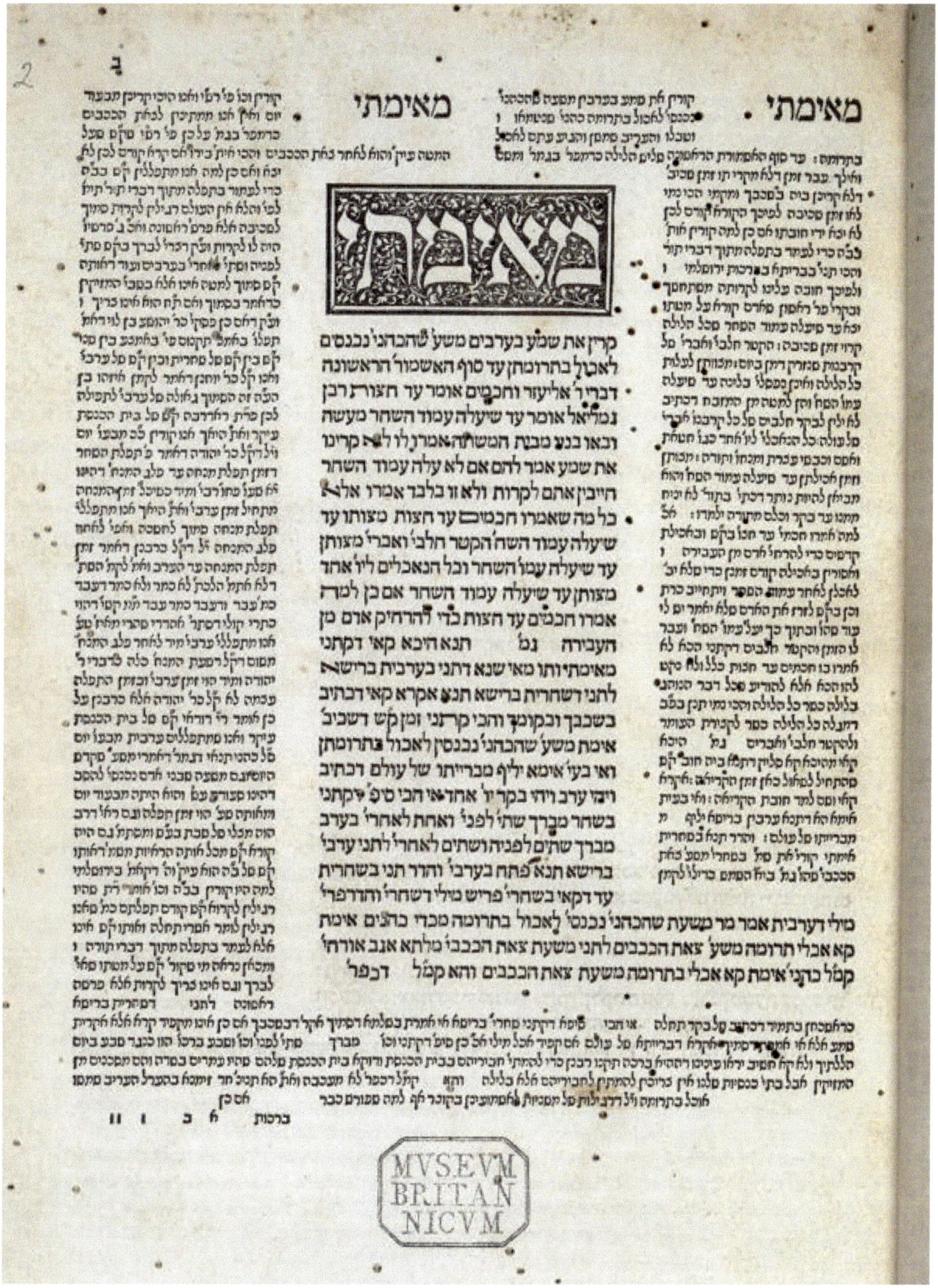

Figure 13.4. Babylonian Talmud, Berakhot fol. 2ʳ (Venice: Daniel Bomberg, 1521).

In 1545, a Venetian patrician, Marco Antonio Giustiniani, set up a new Hebrew publishing house in Venice to rival Bomberg and, between 1546 and 1551, published still another edition of the Babylonian Talmud. Tractates were generally published separately (although several tractates were typically bound together in single volumes). The print run of each tractate in these editions was probably between a thousand and fifteen hundred copies.[72] Each edition was bound into volumes that generally numbered between six and ten. If we take eight volumes as the average number of volumes per edition, and if we conservatively estimate the print runs at 1200 copies each, we can estimate that by 1553, more than 28,000 volumes of Talmudic tractates from Bomberg's press alone were circulating, mainly in Europe. (We also know that many Jews bought single volumes.) Compare that number to the 1200 volumes of Talmud collected from all of France that were burned in Paris in 1241.[73] What this all means is that there were at least twenty times as many volumes of the Talmud in circulation in 1553 as there had been 300 years earlier (and possibly even sixty times as many).[74]

I have cited these figures to suggest that in sixteenth-century Italy the Talmud was no longer the comparatively rare, peripheral presence it had been in thirteenth-century France at the time of the 1241 Paris burning. It is not, I believe, an exaggeration to say that because of its greater numbers and thus larger presence in the world, the Talmud in the sixteenth century was a qualitatively, not just quantitatively, different book than it had been in the thirteenth century. To be sure, there were also more Jews in Europe, spread out with greater density over a geographically larger area, but even so, the different status of the Talmud in the thirteenth and in the sixteenth century should not be diminished. In the former, it was a rumour among gentiles, heard of but (one assumes) rarely if ever seen. In the sixteenth century, there were almost as many volumes of the Talmud in circulation as there were Jews on Italian streets. Even if the Talmud was not read, let alone studied, by Christians (with a few exceptions), its name was known. Moreover, its name possessed an identity (nurtured by centuries of Christian condemnation) that did not depend on knowledge of the book, in the same way that

---

72 The estimated number of copies is based primarily on Tziporah Baruchson, 'Money and Culture: Financing Sources and Methods in the Hebrew Printing Shops in Cinquecento Italy', *La Bibliofilia*, 92 (1990), see p. 28 note 9 for additional bibliography; see also Heller, pp. 159, 191. Froben's censored edition of the Talmud (Basel, 1578–1581) had a print run of 1100 copies, according to an article by H. Pallman on Froben cited in Fausto Parente, 'The Index, the Holy Office, the Condemnation of the Talmud and Publication of Clement VIII's Index', in *Church, Censorship, and Culture in Early Modern Italy*, ed. by Gigliola Fragnito, trans. by Adrian Belton (Cambridge: Cambridge University Press, 2001), p. 172. For print runs of non-Jewish/non-Hebrew books in early sixteenth-century Italy, see Rudolph Hirsch, *Printing, Selling, and Reading 1450–1550*, 2nd printing (Wiesbaden: Harrassowitz, 1974), p. 61, who concludes with a quote from Friedrich Kapp (*Geschichte des deutschen Buchhandels* [Leipzig, 1886]): 'Up to the middle of the XVIth century no rule can be established for the size of editions. Available data are too incomplete'.

73 Recall, too, that Colette Sirat, on the basis of her collation of every Talmud mentioned in medieval Rabbinic literature, has questioned that number and proposed that probably no more than several hundred Talmud manuscripts were burned in France, and that there was perhaps a total of not many more in existence. See note 20 above.

74 Moshe Hagiz in his *Mishnat hakhamim* (Altona-Wandsbek: s.n., 1733), fol. 120b, no. 628, notes that, at the time of the burning, there were some 16,000 volumes of Venice editions of the Babylonian Talmud circulating in Italy 'apart from those printed in Turkey and other countries outside the Pope's jurisdiction'. Cited and discussed in Salo W. Baron, *A Social and Religious History of the Jews: Late Middle Ages and Era of European Expansion (1200–1650)*, 2nd Ed., 18 vols (New York and Philadelphia: Columbia University Press and Jewish Publication Society of America, 1952–1983), xiv: *Catholic Restoration and Wars of Religion* (1969), pp. 30–31.

the adjective 'Kafkaesque' is familiar to and used by numerous people who have never opened, let alone read, a book of Kafka's. It should come as no surprise, then, that the Talmud as a book posed a different kind of threat in the sixteenth century, even to those who knew of it only by reputation.

There was another factor at work as well. The establishment of Bomberg's press marked a decisive change in the nature of Hebrew printing itself. Before Bomberg, virtually all printing of Hebrew books was done in small print shops owned by Jews, sometimes even by itinerant Jews who carried their presses on their backs or in carts behind them and moved from town to town as their fortunes waxed and waned. From Bomberg's time on, Hebrew printing in Venice was monopolized by large publishing houses owned and managed by Christians. These Christian publishers, like Bomberg, employed Jews as editors, correctors, copyists, and typesetters, but Hebrew printing itself was no longer a Jewish industry.

The print shop, the site where these various employees worked, was also a new development of early print culture in the late fifteenth and early sixteenth centuries.[75] These print shops effectively created a new kind of social space in the history of the book. The print shop not only brought together all the different agents and actors involved in the collaborative production of a book — authors, editors, translators, typesetters, correctors, papermakers, binders, artists, and decorators. It also became a meeting-place, a point of encounter, for representatives of different religious faiths, nationalities, and social classes, all of whom supplied the various professionals involved in the production of a book.[76] The social composition of the print shop explains the full complexity of the relationships that might have emerged from these print-shop encounters. These relationships could be simultaneously productive and destructive. Their confluence created the conditions for the production of unprecedented new types of books as well as bitter rivalries and conflicts that could entangle and ensnare both the books and their producers. The print shop also produced the conditions for porous identity-formation. A number of Jews working for Christian publishers such as Bomberg had either already converted to Christianity or would do so later.

Publishing houses were major commercial enterprises that required considerable capital

---

75 For a contemporaneous picture of the early print shop, see Henri Estienne's colourful description quoted and translated in Anthony Grafton, *Bring Out Your Dead: The Past as Revelation* (Cambridge: Harvard University Press, 2001), pp. 142–43; and Grafton's analysis, pp. 141–47; for a somewhat over-vividly imagined but still quaintly charming picture of the multicultural scene in Bomberg's printing house, see David W. Amram, *The Makers of Hebrew Books in Italy: Being Chapters in the History of the Hebrew Printing Press* (Philadelphia: 1909; repr. London: Holland Press, 1963), pp. 175–77; Amnon Raz-Krakotzkin, *The Censor, the Editor, and the Text: The Catholic Church and the Shaping of the Jewish Canon in the Sixteenth Century*, trans. by Jackie Feldman (Philadelphia: University of Pennsylvania Press, 2007), pp. 101–09; and more recently, the brief but very incisive portrait in Theodor Dunkelgrün, 'The Hebrew Library of a Renaissance Humanist: Andreas Masius and the Bibliography to his *Iosuae Imperatoris Historia*' (1574), with a Latin Edition and an Annotated English Translation', *Studia Rosenthaliana*, 42/43 (2010–2011), pp. 205.

76 Worth mentioning as well is the fact that sixteenth-century Italy and Venice, in particular, was a place of refuge and haven for Jewish emigrés from Ashkenaz, Sefarad, and North Africa, and that Bomberg's print shop employed figures from all these centres including Cornelius Adelkind from Germany and Jacob ben Hayyim ibn Adonijah from Tunis. This multi-cultural makeup of Bomberg's print shop is also reflected in the unprecedented contents of some of his books, such as the *Second Rabbinic Bible*, which for the first time included both an Ashkenazi biblical commentary (Rashi) and a Sefardi one (Abraham ibn Ezra), thus bridging the two worlds.

and financial investment for the purchase of type, for printing presses, for paper, not to mention the human labour involved in printing (which was, in fact, the least expensive part of the process). As Isaiah Sonne pointed out, the history of Hebrew Venetian printing was always marked by a series of intense rivalries between publishers and especially publishing houses — first, between Gershom Soncino and Bomberg; later between Bomberg and Giustiniani; and then between Giustiniani and Alvise Bragadin, another Venetian patrician who set up a print house in 1550.[77] By 1547, Bomberg's press had declined, and his effective monopoly on Hebrew printing was taken over by Giustiniani. In that same year, in fact, Giustiniani began to publish his own edition of the Talmud, which he completed in 1551. As should be clear by now, publishing the Talmud was very lucrative. It had an audience of readers, and it should be noted that Bomberg intended that audience to include Christians, particularly Christian Hebraists. He regularly marketed his books to such Christian readers.[78] That might also have been the reason he foliated the Talmud, specifically to make it more accessible to Christians.[79] Jews had studied the unfoliated Talmud for centuries; they had other ways of identifying and remembering its sections. Only Christians needed folio pages with numbers.[80]

This complicated world that I have sketched in broad strokes was the background to the sordid tale that eventuated in the burning of the Talmud in 1553.[81]

In 1549–1550, Rabbi Meir Katznellenbogen, the head of the talmudic academy in Padua, approached Giustiniani — Bomberg's one-time rival and successor — with a proposal to publish a new edition of Maimonides' monumental code of law, the *Mishneh Torah*, with a commentary that he, Katznellenbogen, had written. Katznellenbogen's negotiations with Giustiniani broke down, however, and the rabbi took the idea to Alvise Bragadin, who was in the process of setting up his

---

77 Isaiah Sonne, 'Strolls Through a Place Where Reality and the Book — History and Bibliography — Encounter Each Other' [in Hebrew], in *Alexander Marx Jubilee Volume (On His Seventieth Year), Hebrew Section* (New York: Jewish Theological Seminary Press, 1950), pp. 216–19, 228–31.

78 Bruce Nielsen, 'Daniel van Bombergen, a Bookman of Two Worlds', in *The Hebrew Book in Early Modern Italy*, ed. by Joseph Hacker and Adam Shear (Philadelphia: University of Pennsylvania Press, 2011), pp. 68–69.

79 Nielsen, p. 72. As Nielsen notes, this attention to a Christian audience can already be seen in the fact that Bomberg added chapter divisions (based on the Latin Vulgate) to the *First Rabbinic Bible* (1517), and then chapter numbers and verse numbers to subsequent editions of the Bible. This is not to suggest that the Talmud held the same attraction or interest for Christians as did the Bible and the Kabbalah. In fact, until the seventeenth century, with the exception of a few figures such as Johannes Reuchlin, we have little evidence of Christian Hebraists seriously studying the Talmud. More on this question below.

80 Added to this is the striking observation made by Susanne Klingenstein, *Kulturgeschichte der jiddischen Literatur* (Berlin: Jüdischer Verlag and Suhrkamp Verlag, 2022), I: 1105–1597, 228–29, that Bomberg, particularly in his first edition, made the Talmud a truly *beautiful* book — indeed, one that in its workmanship and execution rivalled the editions of Manutius, as carefully typeset and printed as any book of the time. In this way, he took the Talmud, a completely defamed volume, and made it into a truly European book, one that any Catholic or Jew who loved books would want to own.

81 Surprisingly, there is less documentary evidence about the 1553 burning than about its thirteenth-century predecessor. The one contemporaneous source is Joseph ha-Cohen's '*Emeq ha-bakh'a*, pp. 81–82. All the primary sources (in '*Emeq ha-bakh'a*) are collected in Abraham Ya'ari, *The Burning of the Talmud in Italy, On the 400th Anniversary of the Decree* [in Hebrew] (Tel Aviv: Abraham Zioni, 1953); but there is nothing in English comparable to *The Trial of the Talmud*. All translations are cited from either Kenneth R. Stow, 'The Burning of the Talmud in 1553, in the Light of Sixteenth Century Catholic Attitudes Toward the Talmud', *Bibliothèque d'Humanisme et Renaissance*, 34 (1972), pp. 435–59; or from Raz-Krakotzkin. For narrative accounts of the history behind the burning, see Baron, pp. 25–32; and Heller, pp. 201–40, who also lists all previous bibliography.

own Hebrew publishing house. In 1550, Bragadin issued the edition with Katznellenbogen's commentary. Out of spite, Giustiniani responded by printing his own edition of Maimonides' work, offered it at a cheaper price, and, in an ultimate act of snarky vengeance, reprinted Katznellenbogen's commentary at the end of the volume without asking its author's permission. (To add insult to injury — literally — in the introduction to the edition, Giustiniani had its editor, Cornelio Adelkind, write a long screed denigrating Katznellenbogen's competence as a talmudic scholar.)

The two publishers went to war against each other. Bragadin appealed to one of the leading rabbis of Poland, Moses Isserles of Cracow, to issue a ruling against selling and purchasing Giustiniani's edition; this was one of the earliest instances of a copyright suit over any book.[82] Isserles ruled for Bragadin, but Giustiniani ignored the ruling, and then sent some of his employees, former Jews who had converted to Christianity, to appeal his case before Pope Julius III.[83] Shortly thereafter, Bragadin sent his own employees, also Jewish converts, to represent his side. In the course of making their cases, both groups of converts attacked the Talmud for containing blasphemous statements about Christians, Jesus, Mary, and the Church. Giustiniani's representatives most probably raised the issue of the Talmud because Bragadin had announced his intention to publish a new edition of his own which, he promised, would be superior to the one that Giustiniani published in 1551. Bragadin's converts probably responded in order to attack the deficiencies of Giustiniani's edition. In any event, the Pope responded by assigning the accusations against the Talmud to the Congregation of the Inquisition, a relatively new institution in Rome (established in 1542), which was led by Cardinal Gian Pietro Carafa, the future Pope Paul IV, a zealous pursuer of heretics, Protestants, and anything that seemed like Protestantism, and one convinced that the End of Days was imminent, which pressed upon him the urgency of converting the Jews.[84]

The Congregation reviewed the charges, condemned the Talmud for its blasphemies, and, despite opposition, recommended that it be burned. On Rosh ha-Shanah, the Jewish New Year, 9 September 1553, the Inquisition raided all the Jewish households in Rome, collected every volume of the Talmud it could find, and staged a public burning in the Campo de' Fiori.[85] Along with the Talmud, many other Hebrew books went into the fires — copies of the Mishnah, the 'Eyn Ya'aqov (an anthology of talmudic homiletical passages addressed to a larger lay audience), and other legal and non-legal texts.[86] Three days later, the Pope issued a manifesto enlarging the Inquisition's mandate to combat heresy so as to include the perfidy of the Jews and commanded every Christian prince, ruler, and Inquisitor to confiscate the Talmud and burn

---

82 For a full treatment of the legal history, see Neil W. Netanel, 'Maharam of Padua v. Giustiniani: The Sixteenth-Century Origins of the Jewish Law of Copyright', *Houston Law Review*, 44 (2007), pp. 821–70.

83 Joseph ha-Cohen, *'Emeq ha-bakh'a*, intro. and ed. by Karin Almbladh (Uppsala: Acta Universitatis Upsaliensis, 1981), p. 82, names three of the converts: Hananel da Foligno, Joseph Ha-Tsarfati (Moro; Andrea del Monte); Solomon Morano (Giovanni Battista). Morano was the grandson of Elias Levita, and the brother of Vittorio Eliano, another convert who also was involved in both the publication of Hebrew books and the burning of the Talmud in Cremona in 1559. However, Joseph ha-Cohen does not mention which of these figures worked for which of the publishers.

84 I want to thank Kenneth Stow for helping me with this characterization of Carafa's motives.

85 Thus, Joseph ha-Cohen in *'Emeq ha-bakh'a*, p. 82. As Adam Shear has pointed out to me, if one takes Ha-Cohen's words at face value, the fact that the Inquisition raided Jewish homes (*batei ha-yehudim*) in search of Talmuds in 1553, in contrast to synagogues in 1241, is a revealing indication in the changing ubiquity of the book and its ownership.

86 Ya'ari, p. 199.

it.[87] Subsequently, innumerable copies of the Talmud along with many other Hebrew books were burned in virtually every urban centre in Italy.[88] According to Moshe Hagiz (1671–c. 1750), 3328 volumes of the Talmud printed in Venice alone were burned, and to that number one must add the volumes printed in Turkey and other countries, let alone other books.[89]

Within its historical context, this sad and tawdry story was not an anomaly. As in 1241, Jewish converts to Christianity played a key role, but it should be emphasized that none of the print-shop employees in this case were Nicholas Donins, individuals acting in accord with their own agendas. Nor do any of them appear to have been particularly learned or to have used their Jewish knowledge as a weapon against their former co-religionists (aside from repeating the usual canards against the Talmud). They were all surrogates for their Christian employers in a war against a *Jewish* book that itself effectively served as a surrogate for Judaism and the threat that it was perceived to pose to Christian society. Their involvement arose out of the complex dynamics of the early modern print shop.

For all its internal logic, however, no scholar believes that the series of incidents beginning with the Maimonides edition was anything more than the proximate cause for the burning of the Talmud. A war between two greedy publishers and their factotums, no matter how nasty, does not satisfactorily explain the causes for an event so momentous as the burning of the Talmud. The traditional explanation for the Rome 1553 burning is that it was fuelled by a resurgence among Counter-Reformation Christians of the same charges of blasphemy that had been raised at the trial of the Talmud in Paris and had led to its burning in 1241.[90] More recently, historians of the early modern period and scholars of the Counter-Reformation have tended to view the Rome 1553 burning within the context of the Counter-Reformation and its war on heresy and the dangers to the Catholic faith that the Talmud and other Hebrew books posed.[91] Further, still more recently, Amnon Raz-Krakotzkin has argued for the necessity of viewing both the burning of the Talmud and the subsequent censorship of Hebrew books as part of the wider campaign waged by the Counter-Reformation to control knowledge and to ban and destroy all texts suspected of heresy or dissident belief. This campaign was made only more urgent by a threefold recognition on the part of the Catholic authorities: first, of print technology's capacity to hasten the spread of knowledge; second, of the Reformists' astonishing success in utilizing print to spread their teachings; and third, their own powerlessness to control the all too speedy diffusion of dangerous beliefs.[92] The increased

---

87 As cited in William Popper, *The Censorship of Hebrew Books* (New York: Knickerbocker Press, 1899; repr. New York: Burt Franklin, 1968), p. 32.

88 There is no exact count of the number of books burned, let alone the number of Talmuds. See Ya'ari, pp. 99–100, and 207, where he quotes a passage from an as-yet unpublished memoir by Matityahu Delacrot, who writes that in the Venice burning that followed Rome a month later, more than a thousand Talmuds, five hundred copies of Alfasi, and an innumerable number of old and new books were burned. In the same Venice burning, Judah ben Samuel Lirma lost all fifteen hundred copies of his just published commentary on 'Avot and had to rewrite the book from memory (Ya'ari, p. 208). Clearly, the Inquisitors simply threw any book written in Hebrew letters into the flames.

89 Moshe Hagiz, *Mishnat hakhamim*, fol. 120b, nos 628–29. See also Baron, pp. 30–31.

90 Rabbinovicz, *History of the Printing*, p. 59, and thus essentially Heller.

91 Paul Grendler, *The Roman Inquisition and the Venetian Press, 1540–1605* (Chicago: University of Chicago Press, 1975), pp. 63–127; Paul Grendler, 'The Destruction of Hebrew Books in Venice, 1568', *Proceedings of the American Academy for Jewish Research*, 45 (1978), pp. 103–30; Parente, pp. 163–93.

92 Raz-Krakotzkin, pp. 32–56, esp. 33–38. It should be noted that much of Raz-Krakotzkin's argument for considering the burning of the Talmud as part of the general

numbers of Talmud volumes in print and their larger (if not ubiquitous) public presence perhaps is evidence in support of this argument.

All three explanations help in understanding the various factors that led to the burning. Yet they fail to explain the essential differences between the 1241 Paris and 1553 Roman events, on the one hand, and the difference between the Talmud and the many other books that were prohibited on account of their purported heresy and condemned to the flames in the sixteenth century, on the other. Unlike its predecessor in 1241, the 1553 burning was not preceded by a trial in which the charges against the Talmud could be defended by Jews; the perfidious or blasphemous character of the Talmud was not in question in 1553. On the one hand, and somewhat surprisingly, the main charge of the 1241 trial — that the Talmud constituted a *nova lex*, a new law that by its very existence constituted a blasphemy — did not figure in 1553. On the other hand, while most books burned by the Inquisition were condemned for their heretical content — even if 'heresy' was often defined very broadly — the Talmud was never explicitly condemned as a heretical work even if it was attacked for its blasphemies.[93] Nonetheless,

the Pope and the Inquisition clearly used the Counter-Reformation campaign against heresy as an umbrella beneath which to burn the Talmud and other threatening Hebrew books.

The truly distinguishing feature of Rome 1553 was its motivation. As Kenneth Stow has convincingly argued, the key charge made against the Talmud in 1553 was that it was the main impediment to the conversion of the Jews.[94] It did not lead Jews away from the correct faith; it completely blinded them from even seeing that faith. To be sure, the conversionary motive for destroying the Talmud was not absent from Paris 1241 and its proceedings, and formed a vital part of its subtext, as it were.[95] The charges against the Talmud in Paris 1241 were that it was a *nova lex*; that it taught a Judaism essentially different from the biblical Judaism on which Christianity (using its own interpretations, to be sure) based its existence; and that this 'talmudic Judaism' that attacked Christian truth was the cause that motivated contemporaneous Jews to abandon their role as custodians (*capsarii*) of the Old Testament. These charges undermined the theological assumptions behind earlier objections to converting contemporary Jews and freed the Church, the mendicants in particular, to pursue missions of conversion (even if there was no policy to do so). Even so, by the sixteenth century, the 'conversionary model' in relation to the Talmud had come to possess a greater complexity.

In the second half of the thirteenth century, the Catalan Dominican Friar Ramon Martí added a twist to the argument for a mendicant conver-

---

campaign against heresy is based on an assertion, which he makes repeatedly, that the Talmud was believed to have 'magical powers' (through which it could enchant not only Jews but Christians). In fact, there is no evidence for this assertion, and Raz-Krakotzkin does not provide any. The Talmud was accused of many things, but magic was not one of them.

93 To be sure, not all condemned books were 'heretical' in the narrow sense of the term. Some were condemned simply because their authors were known to be Protestants; in other cases, because their authors, figures such as Erasmus, Rabelais, and Machiavelli, were deemed to be anti-papal. Although the Talmud itself was never explicitly called heretical (possibly for the same reasons it was problematic to call it heretical in 1242), its doctrines were nonetheless called "impious and inane" (*impiis et inanibus*) because they prevent Jews from knowing 'the hidden treasures of their salvation'; thus the introductory paragraph to the inquisitional order to burn all remaining Talmuds issued in May 1554', as

quoted in Kenneth R. Stow, *Catholic Thought and Papal Jewish Policy, 1555–1593* (New York: Jewish Theological Seminary Press, 1977), p. 56.

94 Stow, 'Burning', pp. 436–39; Stow, *Catholic Thought*, pp. 55–58.

95 *The Trial of the Talmud*, pp. 94 (letters 2 and 3) and 95 (letter 4) for the repeated assertion that the Talmud 'is said to be the main reason that keeps the Jews stubborn in their perfidy'.

sionary mission by claiming (in his influential polemical work *Pugio Fidei*) that the Talmud itself contained much positive testimony to the truth of Christianity (which, he argued, ancient rabbis had actually recognized but had buried in the depths of the Talmud so that later Jews would not see it) and that, if Jews could only be shown this evidence, they would willingly convert.[96] This argument for the *positive* use of the Talmud as a tool *for* conversion was one in favour of its preservation. As Stow has shown, these arguments were revived in the sixteenth century even before the burning of the Talmud, most thoroughly in the *De arcanis catholicae veritatis* of Petrus Galatinus (Colonna) (1460–1540), which borrowed much of its text from the *Pugio Fidei*.[97] Galatino's work, in turn, played a significant supporting role in Johannes Reuchlin's trial in Rome in 1516, even though it was first printed only in 1518, and by no one other than Gershom Soncino.[98] This is only another indication of the complexity of the early sixteenth-century Jewish-Christian book nexus.

In the aftermath of Rome 1553, these views persisted among opponents of the burning and eventually led to the unusual claim that there were, in effect, two Talmuds — an original 'true' Talmud, which contained evidence for the truth of Christianity, and a later 'false' Talmud added by the rabbis which concealed and obfuscated that evidence.[99] This 'preservative' view of the Talmud was no less conversionary than its 'destructive' counterpart, and it always remained exceptional. The overwhelming attitude towards the Talmud, even among those who wished to preserve and not destroy it, was resolutely hostile, but the very existence of the preservationist view testifies to the diversity of the relevant Christian approaches in the late Middle Ages and early modern period.[100] This diversity, in turn, helps to explain the repeated vacillations of the Papacy and the Inquisition *after* 1553 over the question as to whether the Talmud was to be included in the Index of Forbidden and Prohibited Books as a work to be absolutely forbidden and condemned, or whether it could be expurgated and then permitted (to Jews *and* Christians); eventually, expurgation won out over complete destruction.[101] To the great frustration of the Jews, however, for too lengthy a period, the Church went back and forth on these questions almost every other year. (All other Hebrew books could be — in fact, were required to be — expurgated but then, Jews could own and study them).

The conversionary motivation behind Rome 1553 was part of a larger initiative by the Church in the sixteenth century to encourage the Jews' conversion. That initiative included a school for new converts (*domus catechumenorumi*) established in 1542; the building of the ghetto in 1555 along with a ban on Jewish ownership of real property (both of which were prescribed in the infamous bull *Cum nimis absurdum*); and enforced attendance at weekly missionary sermons delivered by Franciscans or Dominicans. To be

---

96 On Martini, see Cohen's classic treatment in *The Friars and the Jews*, pp. 129–69; and his later refinement in *Living Letters*, pp. 342–58. In fact, Martini's argument itself was based on claims that Pablo Christiani had made in 1263: see Cohen, *The Friars and the Jews*, pp. 103–13.

97 Stow, 'Burning', pp. 443–53.

98 Galatino's *De arcanis* (*On the Hidden Elements of the Catholic Truth*) was dedicated to Reuchlin. For its role in Reuchlin's trial, see David H. Price, *Johannes Reuchlin and the Campaign to Destroy Jewish Books* (New York: Oxford University Press, 2011), pp. 182–83. There has been considerable scholarship about why Soncino published Galatino's book; for the most recent discussion, see Piattelli, pp. 172*–75*.

99 Stow, 'Burning', pp. 454–58.

100 Stow, 'Burning', p. 443.

101 For an alternative explanation of the protracted vacillations over the fate of the Talmud as the result of intra-Catholic rivalries between the Congregation of the Holy Office (the Inquisition) and the Congregation of the Index (which was tasked with drawing up the lists of forbidden books), see Parente, pp. 163–93.

sure, as Stow acknowledges, the argument for destroying the Talmud in order to eliminate it as an obstacle to the Jews' conversion was based on accepting the thirteenth-century accusations of the Talmud's blasphemy. The blasphemous contents of the Talmud, as he writes, were 'the essential fomentor of Jewish obstinancy [...]' but 'the simple elimination of blasphemy was not the purpose underlying the Inquisition's act', which was to convert the Jews.[102] To a large extent, it was a matter of emphasis, but emphasis here was everything. Neither can one discount the massive contribution that the personal zeal of such figures as Cardinal Carafa, later Pope Paul IV, added to the persecution of the Jews and the 1553 condemnation and burning.

Jews, too, recognized that conversion to Christianity was the main intention of the entire initiative: that is, to do away with them as Jews. In the sixteenth-century chronicle of Jewish sufferings, *'Emeq ha-bakh'a* ('The Valley of Tears'), Joseph ha-Cohen (1496–1575) portrayed the Jewish converts who had maligned the Talmud to Pope Julius III in the image of Haman and requoted verses from the Scroll of Esther (3:8–9), merely substituting the Talmud for the Jews whom Haman had denounced to King Ahasuerus with the purpose of doing away with them: 'There is one Talmud, scattered and dispersed among the nations, and its laws are different from all other nations, and they speak libel against our messiah, and it is not fitting for the Pope to leave them in peace'.[103] The Talmud, the book, became the Jew.

In the Scroll of Esther, of course, the Jews are miraculously saved from destruction. This was not the case with the Talmud. In their reports of the 1553 burnings, its Jewish witnesses returned repeatedly to the scene of the Talmud going up in flames, a memory they seemed unable to get out of their minds. Citing Foucault, Raz-Krakotzkin notes that these burnings were typical examples of 'the theatrical and public punishment of the Renaissance'.[104] The heightened drama, the theatricality, of these public book burnings in 1553 highlighted their symbolic dimension, but those symbolic meanings differed for the Jewish and the gentile participants in Rome 1553 just as they had in Paris 1241. In the latter, Jews had interpreted the burning of the Talmud as a martyrological tale. In contrast, the dominant metanarrative through which Rome 1553 appears to have been viewed by contemporaneous Jews was the by-then mythic destruction of the ancient Jerusalem Temple. This analogy is regularly invoked in the language used to describe the burning, in the ritual and liturgical practices enacted in its aftermath, and in the reasons sought to account for why it happened. The consistency is remarkable. One contemporary explicitly called it 'the great *hurban*' using the same term that traditionally designates the destruction of the Jerusalem Temple.[105] A Veronese rabbi, Menachem Porto (1520–1594?), who personally witnessed the burning of the Talmud in Venice, lamented; 'The [Talmud] too, the delight of our

---

102 Stow, 'Burning', p. 438.

103 ישנו תלמוד אחד מפוזר ומפורד בין היהודים, ודתיו שונות מכל עם, ועל משיחכם ידבר סרה, ולאפיפיור אין שוה להניחו. Ha-Cohen, pp. 81–82; cited also in Ya'ari, p. 17; translated in Raz-Krakotzkin, p. 48.

104 Cited in Raz-Krakotzkin, pp. 45, 219 note 54; from Michel Foucault, *Discipline and Punish: The Birth of the Prison*, trans. by Alan Sheridan (Middlesex: Penguin, 1977), pp. 32–69. I have not, however, been able to find the exact phrase in my copy of Foucault on the pages cited (which represent a full chapter) though the idea is certainly there. What Raz-Krakotzkin does *not* note is that Foucault was describing judicial criminal procedures using the scaffold and wheel (mainly in France and England), not trials of heresy in Italy or Spain. So, the analogy probably bears further investigation. As Piero Capelli has reminded me, these theatrical public displays were also typical of the Middle Ages.

105 Thus R. Abraham Menahem ben R. Jacob ha-Cohen Rofe Porto in *Minhah Belulah*, specifically in regard to the burning of the Talmud in Venice which he witnessed, cited in Ya'ari, p. 208.

eyes, in whose shadows we thought we could live among the nations, has been made into firewood'.¹⁰⁶ The phrase, 'the delight of our eyes' (*mahmad 'eyneinu*) is taken from Ezekiel 24:21, where it refers to the Jerusalem Temple (whose destruction the prophet has just prophesied); the next phrase, 'in whose shadow we thought we could live among the nations' was lifted from Lamentations 4:20, where it refers to the loss of 'the Lord's anointed one' (*mashiah 'adonai*), again in the wake of Jerusalem's destruction.

To commemorate the burning, Porto established fast days to be observed annually in the community, clearly in emulation of the Ninth of Av for, as he wrote, 'that day was as terrible as the day of the burning of the House of our God'.¹⁰⁷ Liturgical poems of lament, *qinot*, were composed for recitation as part of the synagogue service on those fast days. Five such poems are preserved, and while none of them are as powerful as Meir of Rothenburg's *Sha'ali serufah be-'eish*, the very fact of their composition attests to how completely the 1553 burning was understood in light of the Jewish tradition of catastrophe.¹⁰⁸ Revealingly, several of the *qinot* end with a prayer for the restoration of the Jerusalem Temple and the return to Zion (in contrast to the martyrological poems, which more typically end with a call for divine vengeance).

For a significant number of Jewish sages, these days also became occasions to contemplate why this catastrophic event had happened. According to the early Rabbinic sages, the Jerusalem Temple was destroyed because the Jews had forsaken the study of Torah. The most frequent answer to the cause behind Rome 1553 was that Jews had spurned the proper study of Talmud in order to devote themselves to 'gentile wisdom' primarily philosophy.¹⁰⁹ Indeed, a prominent Polish rabbi of the time, Aaron ben Gershon of Posen, specifically pinned the guilt for the burning of the Talmud in 1553 on the publication of Maimonides' classic philosophical work *The Guide to the Perplexed* in Venice two years earlier, in 1551.¹¹⁰ If Christians saw the burning of the Talmud as a way to hasten conversion to Christianity, these Jewish thinkers believed that the Talmud was handed over to the flames precisely because too many Jews had *already* left the true faith.

In classical Rabbinic historiography, the destruction of the Temple in 70 CE was a watershed moment; it was the beginning of the 'exile' of the Jews, a moment when God stopped revealing himself, even to extraordinary individuals. To what extent Rome 1553 was a comparable moment in Jewish history is difficult to say. The Talmud was never printed again in Italy (despite several attempts in cities other than Venice), but tractates if not the entire Talmud were printed in Lublin, Salonica, and Istanbul, not to mention the infamous Basel edition of 1578.¹¹¹ Because the printing of other Hebrew books was not prohibited so long as they were properly expurgated, law codes such as the Alfasi and the *'Arba'ah turim* with Qaro's *Beit Yosef*, which cited talmudic passages (often at length) as sources for their rulings, served as practical surrogates

---

106 אף זו מחמד עינינו אשר אמרנו בצלו נחיה בגויים, נתן למאכלת אש, as cited in Ya'ari, p. 216.

107 כי קשה היה היום ההוא כשריפת בית אלהינו, as cited in Ya'ari, p. 208.

108 The poems are all reprinted in Ya'ari, pp. 219–28. Three of them are composed very much on the model of classical *qinot*. One is written in *terza rima*, and one in Yiddish.

109 The phrase 'gentile wisdom' (*hakhemot nokhriyot*) is from R. Solomon Isaac Yerushalmi bar Menahem's introduction to *Pardes rimonim* (1544), cited in Ya'ari, p. 209; for additional sources blaming the burning on philosophy, see Ya'ari., pp. 216–17.

110 Ya'ari, p. 216. It is hard not to remember that in 1241 there were Jews who blamed the burning of the Talmud in Paris on those Jews who sought to burn Maimonides works in Montpellier in 1239.

111 For a full description, see Rabbinowicz, *History*, pp. 60–74. On Poland and the Ottoman Empire, Ya'ari, pp. 230–32; on aborted attempts in Italy, Ya'ari, p. 233.

for Talmud volumes.¹¹² As a result, even though there are many complaints in the literature about a lack of Talmuds in Italy for study, it is not clear how much the burnings changed Talmud study in actual practice.¹¹³

If nothing else, Rome 1553 demonstrated how vulnerable, how evanescent, the Talmud really was, despite the number of printed copies in circulation. The difference between Paris 1241 and Rome 1553 was a matter of symbolic monumentality,, the difference between martyrdom, an act of individuals, and the *hurban*, which was the destruction not only of an institution but of a symbolic structure which served as a matrix of identity. The increased number of Talmuds afforded by the technology of print, the exponential growth in the circulation of the book, and its increased *physical* presence all made, I would argue, its symbolic presence in Jewish life an even more dominant element of Jewish identity — and hence, its loss to the flames of the Church's designs differentially more traumatic for Jews than anything comparable they had experienced for centuries. In medieval Iberia, a frequent term for a Hebrew Bible codex was *miqdashyah*, 'sanctuary of the Lord', a token of the symbolic space the Bible served for Iberian Jews as a refuge from the travails of the turbulent world in which they lived.¹¹⁴ By the middle of the sixteenth century, the Talmud had replaced the Bible, and *its* destruction now became the *hurban*, which in the Jewish historical imagination of the time re-enacted the destruction of the ancient Jerusalem Temple.

In 1553, the Talmud also possessed a different symbolic meaning for the Church than it had in Paris 1241. As will be recalled, for Christians the Talmud in 1241 represented a blasphemous offense, an insult to Christ and Christianity, and a *nova lex* that impugned the authority of the Old Testament. In 1553, the explicit rationale for destroying the Talmud was that it prevented the Jews from seeing the truth of Christianity; it was the main obstacle to their conversion.

There was, however, an additional factor behind the Church's animus against the Talmud. Five days before the Talmud was burned in the Campo di Fiori, Cornelio da Montalcino, a Franciscan friar who had converted to Judaism, was burned at the stake in the same square. This may have been a coincidence, but it may also be a telling indication of an underlying anxiety on the part of Christians that drove them, days later, to burn the Talmud.¹¹⁵ Some Christians doubtless possessed genuine feelings of care for the spiritual welfare of the Jews and an overwhelming desire to see their benighted brethren enjoy the light of Christian salvation. Even so, the closeness in time between the burning of the convert to Judaism and the burning of the Talmud may point to another anxiety that may have been behind the urgency to remove the Talmud from circulation among Christians by destroying it as completely as possible.

As noted earlier, the Inquisitorial campaign against the Talmud led by Carafa and others was part of a larger initiative that included the establishment of the ghetto and the House of Converts (*domus catechumenorum*). These efforts simultaneously worked to convert Jews

---

112   Ya'ari, p. 215. Alfasi was reprinted in 1554–1555, and again, in 1558. The *Turim* was printed shortly before the 1553, and then again in 1564.

113   The one development that is sometimes cited as an unintended consequence of Rome 1553 and the difficulty of Talmud study in its aftermath is the rise of Kabbalah study in Italy, which also engendered much criticism. It is not clear how closely the burning and the increase in interest in Kabbalah were connected.

114   On *miqdashyah* Bibles and the history of the term, see David Stern, *The Jewish Bible* (Seattle: University of Washington Press, 2017), pp. 103–05.

115   The coincidence did not escape the Jews who were well aware of the auto-da-fé. It is recounted by Joseph ha-Cohen in his earlier work, *The Chronicles of the Kings of France and the Ottoman Emperors*, cited in Ya'ari, p. 204 (though he does not mention it in '*Emeq ha-bakh'a*).

and separate those not willing to convert from Christian society. Yet Christians could only convert Jews by engaging with them, and those engaging with Jews in order to convert them also ran the risk of being spiritually poisoned by the Jews and Judaism. The same ambivalence informed the place of Jews in Italian society. On the one hand, the Jews' participation in the economic sphere could be very valuable and financially remunerative; on the other hand, their activity in the public market aroused all sorts of anxieties and was often felt as damaging and dangerous, making it imperative to limit contact between Jews and Christians as much possible.[116]

Christian Hebraists interested in Jewish texts (and usually for Christological reasons!) could become embroiled in particularly fierce controversies that were also motivated by these anxieties. Less than twenty-five years before the burning of the Talmud in 1553, Pope Leo X issued his final ruling in the Reuchlin-Pfefferkorn controversy, another campaign to ban and burn post-biblical Jewish literature that has, somewhat curiously, figured less prominently in scholarship about Rome 1553 than might be expected.[117] Scholars continue to debate the question as to the real underlying problem behind the controversy. Was it the narrow issue of Rabbinic Jewish literature (along the lines of the 1241 Talmud trial) or the larger battle between humanism and scholasticism, thus anticipating the Reformation? Or was it Reuchlin's espousal of the value of Jewish knowledge (in the form of biblical philology) vs. theological orthodoxy? But whatever the case may have been, it is hard to believe that the spectre of the controversy did not linger over the 1553 proceedings, and especially the shadow of Christian Hebraism (of which Reuchlin was arguably its most important representative in the early sixteenth century).

In his extensive studies of Christian Hebraism in the sixteenth and seventeenth centuries, Stephen Burnett has pointed to 1560 as a turning point in the growth of Hebraic literacy among 'trained and capable Christian Hebraists' even if 'there were a growing number of Hebrew students' before that year.[118] Virtually all Christian Hebraist interest up until 1560 was in biblical texts or in ancillary biblical works such as grammars and dictionaries, with much less interest in Kabbalah and anti-Jewish polemic; as Burnett writes, 'few Christian Hebraists [...] had the training necessary to read Kabbalistic texts'.[119] As the Rabbis would have said, על כמה וכמה התלמוד ('All the more so the Talmud') — in other words, it was even less likely that they could read Talmud. Reuchlin is said to have admitted that he had never read the Talmud (even if the indirect evidence for this statement is not the strongest).[120]

To be sure, there were exceptions. In 1553, after the burning of the Talmud, Andreas Masius (1514–1573), arguably the foremost Christian Hebraist in the mid-sixteenth century, wrote a bitter letter of protest to Cardinal Sebastiano Pighini, one of the signatories to the decree for the burning, in which he stated, 'In fact, I have read the Talmud if not entirely then at least in large part, and I've found an infinity of unchallengeable arguments against the Jews,

---

116 Nicolas Davidson, 'The Inquisition and the Italian Jews', in *Inquisition and Society in Early Modern Europe*, ed. by Stephen Haliczer (London and Sidney: Croom Helm, 1987), pp. 26 and 22–37 more generally.

117 In fact, in the literature about Rome 1553 that I have consulted, it is rarely mentioned although it usually appears as a kind of coda in most discussions of the Reuchlin-Pfefferkorn controversy.

118 Stephen Burnett, *Christian Hebraism in the Reformation Era (1500–1660)* (Leiden and Boston: Brill, 2012), pp. 100–09.

119 Burnett, p. 105.

120 Price, p. 143; Avner Shamir, *Christian Conceptions of Jewish Books: The Pfefferkorn Affair* (Copenhagen: Museum Tusculanum Press, 2011), pp. 101–02. Shamir does not provide a source. Price's source is a statement by Pfefferkorn in the *Brantspiegel* — admittedly, not the strongest testimony.

but not a single one of any significance against Christianity'.¹²¹ Masius's own substantial library of Hebraica, including much Rabbinics, was confiscated amid the early Inquisitorial sweep, although it appears that, through his many personal and professional connections, he was finally able to retrieve the books. Indeed, the confiscation of Masius's library encapsulated the historical moment, as Theodor Dunkelgrün writes with devastating accuracy: 'The Hebrew library of a Christian humanist had become the focal point of the eclipse of Catholic attitudes towards Hebrew and Jewish scholarship and printing at the cross-roads of the Counter-Reformation, the Inquisition, and the Index. And Masius, the indispensable intermediary between Renaissance Catholic and Jewish cultures, was now caught in the web of their entanglement'.¹²²

Masius's exceptionality, however, was the proof of the rule. For most everyone else, including Christian Hebraists, the Talmud was an abstraction, known at best through a body of reported passages that had been passed down through Christian anti-talmudic tradition. In the words of Avner Shamir, the Christian conception of the Talmud was 'a conceptual projection' of their innermost fears about Jews. If they believed it was the main obstacle to Jewish conversion, that belief was not based on any actual knowledge of the Talmud. Pfefferkorn, who was in fact more interested in confiscating liturgical books so as to prevent the Jews from being able to hold services in their synagogues, was far more perceptive in understanding which Jewish books were obstacles to conversion.¹²³ In contrast, for the Church, the Talmud had become a kind of emblem for Judaism and the Jews. No more striking evidence of its emblematic nature is the telling fact that in 1564, Pius IV, reversing the earlier prohibition (of 1557) forbidding Jews to possess any Hebrew book except the Bible, now gave permission to Jews to own copies of the Talmud so long as they underwent censorship '*and the name "Talmud" was removed from the title page*' [my italics].¹²⁴ 'Talmud' was simply a name. In fact, this may be the first time in Western history that the name of the book became an emblem for the Jews.

Conclusion

The impact of print upon early modern Jewish culture was massive in many different ways. It increased the accessibility and availability of books with unparalleled speed and in unprecedented numbers; it had the effect of standardizing many texts and of doing away with texts or versions that did not make it into print, and it exposed audiences of readers to new perspectives that had previously been unavailable. At the same time, it demystified many works and types of knowledge and took them out of the hands of the intellectual elite. By doing all these things, print often disrupted social and political and religious hierarchies and created new ones to take their place.

---

121 '*quum alioqui in ea re plane caecutire, neque vestrum quisquam vel verbulum unicum in illis commentariis legisset [...] legi & ego Talmud, si non uniuersum, certe bonam partem; reperi infinita adversus Judaeos irrefragabilia testimonia, adversus Christianos ne unum quidem, quod vel nauci sit*', as cited and translated in Dunkelgrün, p. 210 note 28. Masius was probably not exaggerating about his knowledge of the Talmud. He owned a complete set of the Bomberg edition: see Dunkelgrün, p. 239 note 77; and as Dunkelgrün shows in his article, and as Masius demonstrated in the bibliography to his *History of Joshua the Commander*, edited and translated in Dunkelgrün, pp. 233–52, he was very familiar with both classical and medieval Rabbinic literature.

122 Dunkelgrün, p. 211.

123 Shamir, pp. 37–54.

124 Thus, the entry from the 1564 Index as cited in Reusch's *Die Indices Librorum Prohibitorum des A16 Jahrhunderts* (1866), quoted by Stow, 'Burning', p. 443 note 53: '*si tamen prodierint sine nomine Thalmud et sine injuriis et calumniis in religionem christianam, tolerabuntur*'.

In the case of the burning of the Talmud in Rome in 1553, however, a still darker side of the printing revolution emerged. The multiplication and diffusion of copies of the Talmud enabled by print turned the book into a weapon that was used against itself, that very same book. True, the Counter-Reformation burned many books it considered heretical, particularly those of the Reformers. But a good part of the reason for the Reformation's enormous and speedy success was its own ability to harness and exploit the new technology of print in order to spread its message. So when the Counter-Reformation burned the books of the Reformers, one can almost detect a kind of poetic justice at work. But the Talmud had done nothing to deserve burning. The vast majority of its copies had not even been printed by Jews. It was burned simply for being Jewish.

Appendix A: Donin's Charges against the Talmud

The following are the seven main categories into which Donin's accusations against the Talmud are divided in *De articulis litterarum Papae*.

(1) The Jews believe in an Oral Law contained in the Talmud which they consider more authoritative than Scripture (##1–9); (2) The Talmud conveys anti-Christian behaviour, including extensive procedures for nullifying oaths made to Christians (##10–14); (3) The Talmud teaches inane and blasphemous teachings about God (e.g., God sins; he admits to being defeated by the rabbis in controversies) (##15–25); (4) The Talmud makes blasphemous statements against Jesus (e.g., he is doomed to sit forever in hot excrement in Hell for having defied the rabbis) and against Mary (e.g., she conceived Jesus through adultery) (##26–27); (5) The Talmud commands Jews to insult and curse the Church and Christians (## 28–30); (6) The Talmud promises blessings to Jews in the world-to-come and damnation to Christians (#31–33); and (7) the Talmud contains 'evil and filthy stories' about biblical figures (e.g., Adam had sexual intercourse with all the animals in the newly created world and Eve with the serpent; Ham abused his father Noah, either castrating or sodomizing him) (##34–35).

As noted, the only truly 'original' of these categories was the first one accusing the Jews of believing in an Oral Law superior to Scripture. This category comprised the first nine articles of *De articulis*: (1) The Jews claim that God gave them the Talmud along with Scripture at Mount Sinai; (2) that it was handed down by God to Moses, and then by Moses to later generations, through word of mouth; (3) and thereby 'implanted' in the minds of Jews; (4) who continued to preserve it without committing it to writing until people known as 'scribes' and 'sages' committed it to writing in a book that exceeds in size the text of the Bible; (5) and that this book, the Talmud, contains 'silly things' that the sages believe are more valuable than the words of the Prophets; (6) that its laws are able to overturn those found in Scripture; (7) that the words of the sages and scribes are to be obeyed even if they say 'left' is 'right'; (8) that disobeying their words is a crime guilty of death; (9) and that young children are to be prohibited from studying the Bible and instead are commanded to devote themselves exclusively to the Talmud.

While these last accusations have few precedents in earlier anti-Talmudism, many of the charges constituting the first six categories were already staples of Christian polemics against Judaism by Donin's time. The charge that the writings of Rabbinic Judaism contained blasphemous teachings about God, specifically anthropomorphisms of different sorts that bordered on blasphemy (if not all of the specific passages that Donin cited) is attested since the time of Agobard of Lyon (779–840) and was repeated by both Petrus Alfonsi and Peter the Venerable (1092–1156).[125] Peter also denounced the 'evil and filthy stories' in the Talmud about biblical characters although they were not the same stories Donin cited.[126] The accusation (#2) that the Talmud teaches and encourages anti-Christian behaviour such as killing and cheating Christians is in fact undocumented before Donin but since the time of Jerome, Christians knew that the Jewish liturgy contained curses against 'heretics' (*minim*) whom Christians were convinced meant themselves, as Donin argued (#5); it is not hard to assume that rumours that Jews practiced other anti-Christian acts circulated on popular levels in Christian circles. The specific blasphemous

---

125 Friedman, 'Anti-Talmudic Invective', pp. 178–79. Karaites, of course, had long attacked Rabbinic Judaism and its literature for its many anthropomorphisms about God but it is unlikely that Donin had any first-hand knowledge of Karaite writings. See, Lasker.
126 See Friedman, 'Anti-Talmudic Invective', pp. 178–80.

statements against Jesus and Mary in the Talmud cited by Donin (#4) are, again, not documented in earlier anti-Jewish polemic, but Christians had long known about the *Toledot Yeshu* ('The Life of Jesus'), an apocryphal Jewish work dating from late antiquity with extensive scabrous and scatological stories about Jesus and Mary (including the tale of her adulterous affair and the illegitimate conception of Jesus).[127]

In sum, the last six categories of Donin's accusations were essentially familiar to Christians, probably not through the specific passages that Donin cited as evidence, but substantively or by rumour. This was not the case with the first category of charges.

---

127 On the many sides of this literature, see the essays in *Toledot Yeshu* ('The Life Story of Jesus') *Revisited: A Princeton Conference*, ed. by Peter Schäfer and others (Tübingen: Mohr Siebeck, 2011).

Appendix B: Babylonian Talmud Sanhedrin 43a-b

The following is the text of the Sanhedrin passage as found in Cod. hebr. 95, Munich, Bayerische Staatsbibliothek, fol. 342ʳ:

והתני׳ בער׳ הפס׳ תלאוהו <...> והכרוז יוצ׳ לפניו ארבעי׳ יום <...> יוד׳ ליסקל על שכישף
והסית והדיח את ישר׳ כל מי שיוד׳ לו זכו׳ יבא וילמ׳ עליו זכו׳ ולא מצאו לו זכו׳ ותלאוהו בער׳ הפסח א׳ עולא
דקרו׳ למלכו׳ <...> בר הפוכי ליה זכו׳ הוה מסי׳ הו׳ ורחמ׳ א׳ לא תחמל ולא תכס׳ עליו אל׳ שני <...> ותסבר׳
הוה ת״ר <...>
נקי <...> יהרג דכ׳ מתי אבא
יהר׳ והכת׳ ונקי וצדי׳ אל תהר׳ א״ל אין נקי יהרג דכ׳ במסתרי׳ יהרג נקי אתיו׳ לנצר א׳ להו נצר יהרג והכתי׳ ונצר
משרשיו יפר׳ אמרו לי׳ אין נצר יהרג דכ׳ ואת׳ השלכת מקבר׳ כנצ׳ נתע׳ אתיו׳ לבוני א״ל בוני יהרג והכ׳ בני
בכו׳ ישר׳ אמ׳ לי׳ אין בוני יהרג דכ׳ אנכי הורג את בנך בכור׳ אתיו לתוד׳ א׳ להו תוד׳ יהרג הכת׳ מזמר לתודה
אין דכ׳ זובח תוד׳ יכבדני

The following is the full text of the passage as it appears in other early manuscripts and the *edition princeps*. I have bolded the sections that are scraped off in Cod. hebr. 95:

והתניא בערב הפסח תלאוהו לישו והכרוז יוצא לפניו מ׳ יום ישו יוצא ליסקל על שכישף והסית והדיח את ישראל
כל מי שיודע לו זכות יבא וילמד עליו ולא מצאו לו זכות ותלאוהו בערב הפסח אמר עולא ותסברא בר הפוכי
זכות הוא מסית הוא ורחמנא אמר לא תחמול ולא תכסה עליו אלא שאני ישו דקרוב למלכות הוה ת״ר חמשה
תלמידים היו לו לישו מתאי נקאי נצר ובוני ותודה אתייוהו למתי אמר להו מתי יהרג הכתיב מתי אבוא ואראה
פני אלהים אמרו לו אין מתי יהרג דכתיב מתי ימות ואבד שמו אתייוהו לנקאי אמר להו נקאי יהרג הכתיב ונקי
וצדיק אל תהרוג אמרו לו אין נקאי יהרג דכתיב במסתרים יהרג נקי אתייוהו לנצר אמר נצר יהרג הכתיב ונצר
משרשיו יפרה אמרו לו אין נצר יהרג דכתיב ואתה השלכת מקברך כנצר נתעב אתייוהו לבוני אמר בוני
יהרג הכתיב בני בכורי ישראל אמרו לי׳ אין בוני יהרג דכתיב הנה אנכי הורג את בנך בכורך אתייוהו לתודה אמר
תודה יהרג הכתיב (תהלים ק, א) מזמור לתודה אמרו לו אין תודה יהרג דכתיב (שם נ, כג) זובח תודה יכבדני

Appendix C: Selected Hebrew Texts from *Sha'ali serufah be-'eish*

ll. 1–4

שַׁאֲלִי שְׂרוּפָה בָּאֵשׁ לִשְׁלוֹם אֲבֵלַיִךְ הַמִּתְאַוִּים שְׁכֹן בַּחֲצַר זְבֻלָיִךְ:
הַשּׁוֹאֲפִים עַל עֲפַר אֶרֶץ וְהַכּוֹאֲבִים הַמִּשְׁתּוֹמְמִים עֲלֵי מוֹקַד גְּלִילָיִךְ:

ll. 9–32

וַיִּתְאוֹנְנוּ כְּתַנִּים וּבָנוֹת יַעֲנָה וַיִּקְרָא מִסְפֵּד מַר בִּגְלָלָיִךְ:
אֵיכָה נְתוּנָה בָּאֵשׁ תֵּאָכְלָה אוֹכְלָה בָּאֵשׁ בָּשָׂר וְלֹא נִכְווּ זָרִים בְּגַחֲלָיִךְ:
עַד אָן עֲדִינָה תְּהִי שׁוֹכְנָה בְּרֹב הַשֶּׁקֶט וּפְנֵי פְרָחַי הֲלֹא כָסּוּ חֲרֻלָּיִךְ:
תֵּשֵׁב בְּרֹב גַּאֲוָה לִשְׁפּוֹט בְּנֵי אֵל בְּכָל הַמִּשְׁפָּטִים וְתָבִיא בִּפְלִילָיִךְ:
עוֹד תַּגְזוֹר לִשְׂרוֹף דָּת אֵשׁ וְחֻקִּים וְלָכֵן אַשְׁרֵי שֶׁיְּשַׁלֶּם לָךְ גְּמוּלָיִךְ:
צוּרִי בְּלַפִּיד וָאֵשׁ הֲלֹבַעֲבוּר זֶה נְתָנֵךְ כִּי בְאַחֲרִית תֵּלָהֵט אֵשׁ בְּשׁוּלָיִךְ:
סִינַי הֲלָכֵן בָּךְ בָּחַר אֱלֹהִים וּמָאַס בִּגְדוֹלִים וְזָרַח בִּגְבוּלָיִךְ:
לִהְיוֹת לְמוֹפֵת לְדָת כִּי תִתְמַעֵט וְתֵרֵד מִכְּבוֹדָהּ וְהֵן אֲמָשׁוֹל מְשָׁלָיִךְ:
מָשָׁל לְמֶלֶךְ אֲשֶׁר בָּכָה לְמִשְׁתֵּה בְנוֹ צָפָה אֲשֶׁר יִגַּע כֵּן אַתְּ בְּמִלָּלָיִךְ:
תַּחַת מְעִיל תִּתְכַּס סִינַי לְבוּשֵׁךְ בְּשַׂק תַּעֲטָה לְבוּשׁ אַלְמָנוּת תַּחֲלִיף שְׂמָלָיִךְ:
אוֹרִיד דְּמָעוֹת עֲדֵי יִהְיוּ כְנַחַל וְיַגִּיעוּ לְקִבְרוֹת שְׁנֵי שָׂרֵי אֲצִילָיִךְ:
מֹשֶׁה וְאַהֲרֹן בְּהַר הָהָר וְאֶשְׁאַל הֲיֵשׁ תּוֹרָה חֲדָשָׁה בָּכֵן נִשְׂרְפוּ גְלִילָיִךְ

YAKOV Z. MAYER

The Bookless Talmud and the Talmud Book: The Loss of Books in the Medieval and the Early Modern World

Introduction

The burnings of the Talmud provide us with a rare opportunity to look at the way medieval and early modern Jews thought about their book cultures. The Talmud was burned on two major occasions, in 1241 in Paris and in 1553 in various places in Italy — that is, once after the Fourth Lateran Council (1215) and then after the Fifth Lateran Council (1512–1517). In both cases, the Talmud was condemned to be burned, but on the first occasion, only manuscripts were involved, whereas in the latter case it was printed books that were set ablaze. A comparison of the Jewish reactions to these burnings reveals two distinctively different sets of themes in the relevant writings of the thirteenth-century medieval rabbis and their sixteenth- and seventeenth-century counterparts. These point us to a rather counter-intuitive observation: medieval Jews considered the Talmud — a book which from a modern perspective existed in an era of material scarcity — indestructible, whereas in the early modern period, the proliferation of Talmud editions made 'the book' far more susceptible to destruction in the eyes of its Jewish readers.[1]

In this brief survey, I suggest that in medieval times, the talmudic text and its material vessel, captured in a book, were considered two different things. The talmudic text, maybe in the light of its oral origin, was thought of as a metaphysical entity existing in its wholeness free from its materiality and the written book was considered merely a derivative copy thereof. Therefore, in the eyes of the medieval Jewish reader, burning copies of the Talmud could, at most, insult the Jewish people or hurt them in a political sense, but the act of burning could not destroy the talmudic text itself. By contrast, the early modern period saw the introduction of a new conceptualization of the Talmud as book. The printed text merged

---

1 For full discussion about the comparison, see Yakov Z. Mayer, *A Medieval Manuscript in the Printing Workshop: The 1523 Venice Edition of the Palestinian Talmud and Its Printer's Copy* [in Hebrew] (Jerusalem: Magnes Press, 2022). See also David Stern's chapter in this volume — Burning the Talmud before and after Print.

Yakov Z. Mayer • The Mandel Scholion Center, The Hebrew University of Jerusalem

the metaphysical text with the material object, which created the illusion that the burning of physical volumes of the Talmud also destroyed the talmudic text itself. The reactions of the early modern readers who expressed much anguish that the Talmud was gone reflect this development.

Paris 1241

In 1241, after the famous Talmud trial (1240) and following the decision of the Fourth Lateran Council, the Talmud was declared a blasphemous work and was condemned. An uncertain number of talmudic manuscripts was burned in Paris — the testimonies vary from several copies to twenty-four wagons full of books. Although the actual size of the loss is not clear, its effect on an entire generation of European Jewry was tremendous. Legendary descriptions of the historical events, poems, and testimonies were circulated among Jews in France, Germany and Italy.[2]

A short time after the dispute and the Talmud's burning to ash, Rabbi Samuel ben Solomon from Falaise, one of the scholars involved in the defence of the Talmud in Paris, was asked a legal question from someone in Düren, in the German Lands. The questioner, a certain rich man, asked Rabbi Samuel if he can force his daughter's groom to divorce her.[3]

Rabbi Samuel ben Solomon opened his responsum with the following poetic statement: אזל רוחי ותש כוחי ואור עיני אין אתי, מחמת המציק אשר גברה ידו עלינו במאד, ונפש ומחמד עינינו לקח, ואין בידינו ספר להשכיל ולהבין. שדי יקנא לעמו ויאמר לצרתינו די ('My spirit is gone, my power weakened, and the light of my eyes [= my ability to see] disappeared because of the oppressor who defeated us strongly, and took our soul and beloved one, so we do not have any book now to study and to understand. God will show his zealousness and will say "enough" to our troubles').[4]

Rabbi Samuel was mourning the burned Talmud, saying that he did not have any book to read after the catastrophe. Surprisingly, the short responsum, not more than 750 words in length — contains ten different quotations from the Babylonian Talmud, one from the Jerusalem Talmud, and a few quotes from Rashi and other medieval halakhic authorities. Clearly, for Rabbi Samuel, the lack of physical books did not mean a lack of talmudic knowledge. Only once did he say that he cannot quote a work because he does not have the book in question on hand. ואשתקד בא הדין הזה לפנינו וחייבנו האיש עפ"י האמת ונא בקשתי לכל רואי כתבי לבל יתפסוני על שגיונות כי אין לי לא לב ולא ספר, ושר ישראל יחמול על עמו ('And last year this question came in front of us, and we said the man is culpable, and I ask everyone who sees my responsum not to judge me for my second thoughts, because I have not a heart nor a book, and the master of Israel will have mercy upon his nation').[5]

---

2 See Robert Chazan, *Church, State and Jew in the Middle Ages* (New York: Behrman House, 1980); Simon Schwarzfuchs, 'Le vendredi 13 juin 1242: le jour où le Talmud fut brûlé à Paris', *Revue des études juives*, 173.3–4 (2014), pp. 439–43; Yossef Schwartz, 'Authority, Control and Conflict in Thirteenth-Century Paris: Contextualizing the Talmud Trial', in *Jews and Christians in Thirteenth Century France*, ed. by Elisheva Baumgarten and Judah D. Galinsky (New York: Palgrave Macmillan, 2015), pp. 93–110.

3 The whole story is described in Ephraim E. Urbach, *The Tosaphists: Their History, Writings and Methods* [in Hebrew] (Jerusalem: Mosad Bialik, 1954, ninth abbreviated edition 2020), pp. 529–35; *Responsa of Rabbi Meir of Rothenburg and His Colleagues*, Critical Edition Introduction and Notes by Simcha Emanuel (Jerusalem: World Union of Jewish Studies, 2012), pp. 135–36.

4 *Responsa Maharam from Rothenberg* (Prague: Moshe ben Yossef Betzalel Katz, 1608), § 250.

5 *Responsa Maharam*. See Urbach, p. 455. For some textual variations see *Responsa Maharam* (Jerusalem: World Union of Jewish Studies, 2012), p. 136 note 26.

Rabbi Samuel wrote that he had already dealt with a similar question, but did not have the heart — memory — or book — a copy of the previous responsum, so he asked those who read his new responsum and might have a copy of his previous one not to judge him by comparing the two, and instead to consider only the last responsum as valid. Physical volumes of the Talmud were certainly burnt, and contemporary accounts describe the destruction as a huge catastrophe for the whole nation. However, the only documented loss of information in this responsum is that of Rabbi Samuel's personal document, and this was not necessarily due to the burning. Unlike his personal copy of his responsa, the text of the Talmud still lived in Rabbi Samuel's memory, even though it did not exist in his hands as a material object.

Rabbi Meir of Rothenberg, known as Maharam was among the Jewish scholars present in Paris watching the flames. Born in the 1220s, probably in Worms, in the 1240s Maharam spent several years in Paris studying with both Rabbi Yehiel of Paris and Rabbi Samuel ben Solomon. Later, he returned to Germany, where he remained for the rest of his life and gained a reputation as the greatest thirteenth-century Ashkenazi halakhic authority.[6]

Maharam wrote a famous poem about the burning, which is recited every year on the Ninth of Av. In the opening lines he drew a sophisticated rhetorical image, which begins with the speaker addressing the Torah – a synonim in this context to the burned Talmud – and asking her to cry about the speaker himself, who is mourning her, the Torah. | שַׁאֲלִי שְׂרוּפָה בָאֵשׁ לִשְׁלוֹם אֲבֵלָיִךְ הַמִּתְאַוִּים שְׁכֹן בַּחֲצַר זְבֻלָיִךְ: הַשּׁוֹאֲפִים עַל-עֲפַר אֶרֶץ וְהַכּוֹאֲבִים | הַמִּשְׁתּוֹמְמִים עֲלֵי מוֹקֵד גְּוִילָיִךְ: ('O You who are burned in fire, ask how your mourners fare, They who yearn to dwell in the court of your dwelling place. They who gasp in the dust of the earth and who feel pain, They who are stunned by the blaze of your parchment').[7]

The Torah has burned to ash, and the speaker is crying for her. But she still exists as the addressee of the poem, and he is asking her to cry for him. The real loss, as is clear from these lines, is the speaker's loss, but the Torah 'itself' still exists. In his eyes, the material destruction did not harm her. According to Maharam's poem, the burning of the Talmud was a major political disaster, which he decries and mourns, a historical injustice and an immense offense to the Jewish people, but there was no destruction of the holy text itself.

It might rationally be claimed that for a great talmudic scholar as Rabbi Samuel ben Solomon or Maharam, destroying the text of the Talmud was an impossibility. The 'blindness' of Rabbi Samuel strengthens this claim, for the burning of the books would not have caused a loss of knowledge for the scholar who did not read from material books, but rather relied on his memory. But I go one step further and contend that for a medieval Jewish consumer of talmudic texts, the lack of books never meant the absence of texts, a contention that is in accord with such a medieval concept of books.

To prove my hypothesis, let us examine another example of a legal responsum from the same period that deals with the lack of talmudic

---

6 Irving Agus, *Rabbi Meir of Rothenburg: His Life and His Works as Sources for the Religious, Legal, and Social History of the Jews of Germany in the Thirteenth Century*, 2 vols (Philadelphia: Dropsie College, 1947); Urbach, pp. 521–70; Julius Wellecsz, 'Meir b. Baruch de Rothenbourg', *Revue des études juives*, 59 (1903), pp. 226–40; Ephraim Kanarfogel, 'Preservation, Creativity, and Courage: The Life and Works of R. Meir of Rothenburg', *Jewish Book Annual*, 50 (1992–1993), pp. 249–59.

7 Susan L. Einbinder, *Beautiful Death: Jewish Poetry and Martyrdom in Medieval France* (Princeton: Princeton University Press, 2002), pp. 70–99 (Chapter 3: 'Burning Jewish Books'). The poem's translation is printed on p. 76. The original Hebrew can be found in *Seder ha-qinot le-tish'a be-'av*, ed. by Daniel Goldschmidt (Jerusalem: Mossad ha-Rav Kook, 1972), pp. 135–37 (no. 42).

texts. This responsum was written by Maharam, but was not necessarily related to the burning of the Talmud.

After his return to Germany, Maharam was asked the following question: A certain Naftali wanted to move to another city but his wife refused to move with him, so he asked Maharam for permission to divorce her. Maharam wrote in response that a man may divorce a rebellious woman who does not obey her husband, as understood from a certain talmudic source from the legal composition called the Tosefta. But, he wrote, you should not follow the Tosefta since the Talmud Yerushalmi contradicts it, as noted by Avi Ha'ezri (Rabbi Eliezer ben Joel ha-Levi). However, he added: אמנם כשהייתי בצרפת ראיתי תשובה בשם רבי'[נו] תם שיישב הכל שלא תחלוק הירושלמי על התוספ'[תא] והתשובה אינה בידי וגם הירושלמי. ('Moreover, I also remember that when I was in France I saw a responsum by Rabbenu Tam explaining [= how the Yerushalmi and the Tosefta do not contradict each other], but I do not have either the Yerushalmi or Rabbenu Tam's responsum in hand'.)[8]

Maharam remembered the talmudic passage, but could not cite it from memory. He even remembered that Rabbenu Tam resolved the contradiction, but could not recall the resolution. Nonetheless, based on his vague recollection of this difference between the Yerushalmi and the Tosefta, he wrote that Naftali could not divorce his wife. His, albeit imperfect, memory was for him a source solid enough to depend on in regard to a serious halakhic question. For Maharam, the lack of books was not a lack of knowledge, but a temporary problem that might be compensated for by memory, however blurred. The exact textual knowledge did not exist in his hands in material form, yet his vague recollection sufficed as a basis for his halakhic decision.

Some short time later, a colleague from Cologne named Rabbi Eliezer ben Ephraim, who kept his own archive, copied the above-mentioned responsum of Rabbenu Tam for Maharam,[9] who was very pleased to be able to refresh his memory. He inserted a full quotation of Rabbenu Tam's responsum into a new version of his responsum and analysed it in a comprehensive fashion. He described how he had remembered it in the first place: וכבר נעשה ששלחו ממיידבור"ק לצרפת אצל מורי ה"ר שמואל ב"ר שלמה זצ"ל [...] ומורי היה חולה באותה שעה ולא היה יכול לכתוב והראה לי תשובת ר"ת וצוני להעתיקה להם וחתם עליה [...] ('And that is how it was. Someone sent [a question] from Magdeburg to France to my teacher Rabbi Samuel ben Solomon may the memory of the righteous be a blessing… and at that time my teacher was sick and he could not write, so he showed me Rabbenu Tam's responsum and ordered me to copy it for them and he signed it [with the final decision]'.)[10]

Now we understand how Maharam had gained this memory. He was the scribe who copied the responsum for his teacher when he was studying in Paris and sent it to Germany. Now, years later, he vaguely remembered Rabbenu Tam's responsum. He counted on this memory for the halakhic decision, but only when a colleague sent him the quote could he cite it fully and deal with it textually.[11] It is entirely possible that it was taken

---

8 *Responsa Maharam from Rothenberg* (Cremona: Vincenzo Conti, 1557), §36.

9 The responsum was printed in *Sefer Shaarei Teshuvot*, ed. by Moshe Aryeh Leib Bloch (Berlin: Zvi Hirsch Itzkowski, 1891), p. 188 §81.

10 *Teshuvot Maimoniot, Nashim* §28. In: *Mishne Torah*, Sh. Fraenkel edition (Jerusalem and Bnei Brak: Shabetai Fraenkel, 1975–2003).

11 The responsum was printed in the original form, without the quotation of Rabbenu Tam in *Responsa of Rabbi Meir of Rothenburg and His Colleagues* p. 867 §449. In the abbreviated form it was published in *Teshuvot Maimoniot, Nashim* §28; Rephael Nathan Rabinowitz (ed.), *Responsa Maharam bar Barukh* (Lwow: Zalman Leib Plekir, 1860) §386; M. Avitan (ed.), *Responsa Rabbi Hayyim Or Zarua*, (Jerusalem: M. Avitan, 2002), §147, and some parallels in manuscripts responsa collections.

from the same copy that Maharam himself had made and sent to Germany from France many years earlier.

Rabbi Samuel ben Solomon knew the quotes from the Talmud by heart, but he did not remember his own writing and asked the reader not to consider the old responsum if a copy of it happened to surface. It seems that in the medieval halakhic world, written materials were used as accessories and supplements to the imperfect human memory, but they were not considered as the place where the text dwells.

Medieval readers' thoughts about the Talmud split into two different realms, the metaphysical and the material. The Torah existed metaphysically and could make a temporary appearance as a material object, but it could also appear in other ways; in quotations, in memory, or as a piece of information coming from a distance. Its existence did not depend on the material object of its writing support. The metaphysical image of the Torah in the poem is in accord with the image of talmudic knowledge expressed in the above responsa, knowledge that exists in its entirety from the metaphysical point of view, but which a reader must reassemble from different incomplete and insufficient material sources. In the literary world of the medieval talmudic scholar, oral traditions and physical books were intermingled, but the knowledge of the Talmud *per se* existed, regardless of the availability of material copies.

Italy 1553

In 1553, some three hundred years after the last 'official' burning of the Talmud, The church ordered again to confiscate and burn copies of the Talmud throughout Italy. The charges were akin to those of the first burning, that is, that the Talmud was charged with being full of mistakes and heretical sayings, but the historical context was different. The invention of print had changed Christianity. In the face of the flood of relatively inexpensive printed books and the rise of the Reformation, the Catholic Church scrambled to control the spread of information and suppress heresy in new, elaborate ways. Moreover, the Talmud had also changed its face. By 1553, four printed editions of the complete Talmud as well as several separate tractates had already been on the market for several decades. These volumes were collected and burned *en masse* in Italian cities from Rome to Venice.[12]

Christians and Jews alike experienced the events as a sequel to the first episode. The tone of the elegies written about this second burning, however, was completely different, not only due to the lack of a great poet of the stature of Maharam, but also on account of fundamental changes in the relationship between readers and books. Consider, for example, the following poem by Mordecai ben Judah Blanis: וּמַה נֹּאכַל וְאֵין ... סֵדֶר זְרָעִים | תָּמִים דֵּעִים לְכָל רוֹעִים בַּתּוֹרָה | וְאֵיךְ נִשְׂמַח וְאֵין מוֹעֵד וְנָשִׁים | וּמִי יָשִׂים בְּאַפֵּנוּ קְטוֹרָה | וּמִי יֶחְכַּם וְאֵין סֵדֶר נְזִקִין | וּמִי יוֹרֶה וּמִי יָבִין סְבָרָא ... ('... What would we eat without *Seder zera'im* necessary for all these who browse in the Torah, and how would we rejoice without *Mo'ed* and *Nashim*, who will place perfume in our noses, who could be wise without *Seder neziqin*, who

---

See *Responsa Maharam and His Colleagues*, §867 note 1. For the whole correspondence, see Mayer, *Editio Princeps*, p. 215 note 9.

12 Kenneth R. Stow, 'The Burning of the Talmud in 1553, in the Light of Sixteenth-Century Catholic Attitudes toward the Talmud', *Bibliothèque d'Humanisme et Renaissance*, 34/3 (1972), pp. 435–59; Amnon Raz-Krakotzkin, *The Censor, the Editor, and the Text: The Catholic Church and the Shaping of the Jewish Canon in the Sixteenth Century*, trans. by Jackie Feldman (Philadelphia: University of Pennsylvania Press, 2007), and their references.

will judge and who will understand the right idea ...').[13]

The poet described the different parts (*sedarim*, singular: *seder*) of the Talmud and explained what each part enabled Jews to do when they still had it in their possession, activities that had become impossible without the book in hand. The ethos of destruction in this poem is very different from that expressed by Maharam. The Torah was burned, so it no longer exists: Jews can no longer live according to the Talmud; they cannot know what it says; they have forgotten everything.

Naturally, there is no surviving responsum which asserts explicitly that 'we do not have a volume of Talmud so we do not know what the law is'. After all, responsa were written in order to answer specific questions and were kept in order to be used as precedents. so responsa that testified to failure were not preserved. But other surviving sources do testify to what contemporaries thought about the Talmud after it was burned.

In 1554 in Sabbionetta, no more than a year after the burnings, Rabbi Solomon Isaac Yerushalmi (known as Zekil Ashkenazi) printed a commentary by Rabbi Shem Tov ibn Shaprut on the aggadic parts of the Talmud titled *Pardes Rimonim*. At the end of the book, he apologized that he could not correct the talmudic quotations he cited: ויען שבעוונותינו הרבים כעת הזאת לא נמצא פה באלו הגלילות ספרים כדי להגיהה ממנו הספר הזה ('Because due to our great sins no books can be found in these lands to correct this book according to them').[14]

Rabbi Avraham Provenzali, the editor of Judah ibn Tibbon's Hebrew translation of Bahya ibn Paquda's *Hovot ha-levavot* ('Duties of the Hearts'; Mantua, 1559), a book full of quotations from the Talmud, added following afterword:

מאמרי רז"ל, חוץ משל מסכת אבות, הנחנום על סדר דפי הספר הזה ולא על סדר המסכתוי'[ת], להיות התלמוד בעוונותינו הרבים בלתי נמצא אצלנו לעת עתה. ולא היה ספק בידינו לשמור סדר המוקדם והמאוחר בפ'[רק] ופרק כי הוצרכנו לרשום מקומם ממה שנשאר בזכרוננו עדיין ומדרכים אחרים בלתי סלולים.

(We indexed all of the quotations from the Talmud, except those from Tractate 'Avot, according to the pages of *this* [emphasis mine] book, and not according to the order of the Talmud, because the Talmud is not in our hands these days, owing to our many sins, and we could not remember what came first and what second concerning the order of chapters, because we had to identify them according to what was left in our memory, and by other unpaved roads.)[15]

According to Provenzali, talmudic memory existed alongside other 'unpaved roads' from which to gain talmudic knowledge, but he did not count on them. Talmudic quotations cannot be corrected and indexed without Talmud books. The talmudic text is considered something that exists solely in, and by virtue of, the physical book.

If the text dwells only in the physical book, that book becomes a desirable object and owning it has high cultural value. Sixteenth-century Jewish scholars ascribed new, unprecedented value to

---

13 Avraham Yaari, *The Burning of the Talmud in Italy* [in Hebrew] (Tel-Aviv: Abraham Zioni, 1954), pp. 47–48, reprinted in *Studies in Hebrew Booklore* (Jerusalem: Mossad ha-Rav Kook, 1958), pp. 198–234. Mordecai ben Judah Blanis lived in the second half of the sixteenth century. He is mentioned in his father's letters, printed in Yacob Boksenboim (ed.), *Letters of Jewish Teachers in Renaissance Italy (1555–1591)* (Tel Aviv: Tel Aviv University Press, 1985) (see index). For the origin of the family, see Edward Goldberg, *Jews and the Magic in Medici Florence: The Secret World of Benedetto Blanis* (Toronto: University of Toronto Press, 2011).

14 Yaari, pp. 24–25.
15 Yaari, pp. 32–33.

printed talmudic books, thus making their cultural capital higher than it had been before. The desire to own the text created substantial market forces, as reflected in the following example.

Elia of Pesaro was a student in the yeshiva of Siena in the 1540s. As his father had passed away, Elia asked his legal guardian to intervene with his brothers on his behalf to fulfil his request:

זה ימים רבים העירותי אוזן אדו'[ני] שאין אומן בלא כלים. במו פי התחננתי מול יפעתך, רוזני, תהיה לי לפה עם אחי, ישמרם צורנו ויחוננם, עד שיגולו רחמי כלם לתת לי ה"שיתא סדרי" אשר זולתו לא מצאתי ידי ורגלי בבית המדרש.

(I have been reminding your lordship for many days now that there is no craftsman without his tools. With my own mouth I begged before you, my master, that you be my mouth in front of my brothers, God bless them, until they will show their mercy to give me the six orders ['shita sidrei', the entire set of Talmud volumes] since without it I cannot find my hands or my legs in the Beit Midrash.)[16]

Elia was full of admiration for the scholarly greatness of his friends and his rabbi. He wished to take his own place in the most advanced class, known as the *pilpul ha-yeshivah*, where the students were asked to prepare their own lesson and to deliver it in front of the experienced members of the yeshiva.[17]

ואני אנה אני בא, אם אין פני הולכים ויוצאים בקרב הפלפולים הנופלים בתוך הישיבה הזאת, מלאה על גדותיה תלי תלים של הלכות, אשר מן הנמנע הוא להיות במחנם אם לא יהיה אצלי ה"שיתא סדרי" כלו

('And me, where shall I go if I cannot participate in the scholarly debates [lit. *pilpulim*] in this yeshiva, so full of knowledge [lit. *tilei tilim shel halakhot*], to which it is impossible to belong without owning the entire six orders').[18]

The existence of the entire Talmud as a private object, a personal possession belonging to a certain individual was a new phenomenon. Daniel Bomberg printed the first complete set of Talmud between 1520 and 1523 in Venice.[19] Twenty years later, it was evidently already considered a necessary tool for the study of Talmud in the eyes of Elia of Pesaro, who wrote that he would be able to join the intellectual arena of the yeshiva only if he has his own copy of the Talmud.

In contrast to the medieval instances discussed above, in the early modern period a lack of books *did* mean a lack of knowledge, and the above-mentioned scholars and printers *did* think about the loss of books as a loss of information which could not be gleaned from other sources.

This difference between medieval and early modern book cultures should not be overestimated. I have quoted the words of some of the greatest halakhic scholars of medieval Ashkenaz, Rabbi Meir from Rothenberg and his contemporaries, comparing their point of view about the absolute existence of talmudic knowledge entirely independent of the material text and the words of some representatives of the secondary elite from the sixteenth century: a forgotten poet, a miserable corrector in a printing house, and a young spoiled yeshiva student with large

---

16 Yacov Boksenboim (ed.), *Letters of the Rieti Family: Siena 1537–1567* (Tel Aviv: Tel Aviv University Press, 1987), pp. 82–83.

17 For full discussion of Elia from Pesaro and of Joseph Arli, see *Letters of the Rieti Family*, pp. 29–36. For a study of *pilpul ha-yeshivah* in its social context, see Elchanan Reiner, 'Wealth, Social Position and the Study of Torah: The Status of the Kloiz in Eastern European Jewish Society in the Early Modern Period', *Zion*, 58 (1993), pp. 287–328.

18 *Letters of the Rieti Family*, pp. 82–83.

19 See Mayer, *Editio Princeps*, pp. 34–41, and its references; Angelo Piattelli, 'New Documents Concerning Bomberg's Printing of the Talmud', in *Meḥevah le-Menaḥem: Studies in Honor of Menahem Hayyim Schmelzer*, ed. by Evelyn Cohen, Shmuel Glick, and others (Jerusalem: Schocken Institute for Jewish Research, 2019), pp. 171–99.

demands. All three of them needed a physical book to acquire the talmudic text. However, we can assume that the situation was different in connection with early modern high-profile scholars of Maharam's calibre.

In order to compare expressions of esteemed halakhic scholars in the early modern era, I suggest focusing on the exact terms in which they complained about the lack of books. This kind of complaint has been common among halakhic decision-makers throughout history, as these scholars always had to respond to specific questions within a limited time frame. But the conventional context in which scholars used this complaint changed dramatically with the transition from manuscript to print culture. In medieval responsa, as in Rabbi Meir from Rothenberg's responsum quoted above, the lack of books was mentioned as an apology to explain why the halakhic adjudicator did not quote the discussed source and instead only presented its basic argument from memory. By contrast, since the rapid spread of print in Jewish culture, the lack of books is mentioned as a reason why the adjudicator simply did not consult a certain source.

For example, Rabbi Joseph Taitazak from Salonika (1465–1546) wrote to Rabbi Joseph Qaro that he avoided the discussion of certain *mikveh* (a bath for ritual immersion) rituals as ולא היו אז בידי ספרים לעיין בענין ואיתני וגאוני עולם היו אז בעיר הזאת ולכן סמכתי על פסקם […] ('I did not have books at that specific place, and some great men were in the town back then, so I trusted their judgement […] but now, when I am back at my place, I will tell you my opinion').[20]

Another example of the same rhetorical phenomenon appears in a responsum by Rabbi Menahem Mendel Krochmal (1600–1661), who wrote that he would not express his opinion on a certain issue, since: ואין דרכי לדקדק אחר הפוסקים האחרונים כשאין חילוק ביניהם ומה גם השתא דאין ספרים שלי מצויים לפני כלל כי בהול אני עליהם והמה שמורים בכיפה מפני הדליקות שמצויים עכשיו ('My custom is not to argue against recent rulings when there is no good reason to do so. And besides, my books are not with me since I worry about them and keep them in a safe place [*shemurim ba-kipa*] because of the big fires that are so common now').[21]

These examples tell a story of cultural change. In medieval times, the talmudic text was considered to exist *a priori* and was therefore considered an indestructible entity. Physical books were thought to be partial representations of the talmudic text that enable a specific reader to read it but are not fundamental for its existence. The noted examples from the early modern period show a different attitude which attests to the deep impact of print on Jewish conceptions of the text and of law itself. It seems that print identified the talmudic text with the material object that carried it in the minds of its readers; therefore, owning that object became a necessary condition for the existence of the text, so the lack of books was considered equivalent to the text's destruction.

We tend to think that the existence of many copies of a printed book renders the text safe, even indestructible. The historical evidence presents a different, counter-intuitive, approach to the text on the part of sixteenth-century Jews. We are witnessing a change in the reader's attitude to the physical object in his hands. The sixteenth-century Jewish reader's reaction to the void left by the destruction of printed books resembled the reaction to a loss of data. This peculiar phenomenon demands an explanation, with which I conclude this brief discussion.

---

20 *Responsa 'Avqat rokhel* (Salonika: Mordekhai Nachman and David Israeliyah, 1791), §50.

21 *Responsa Tzemah tzedeq (ha-qadmon)* (Amsterdam: David Castro Artes, 1675), 61. Both rare examples noted above were written in the context of a rhetorical explanation as to the reason the responsum was delayed.

From Manuscript to Print

The reactions to the loss of texts in the medieval and early modern sources describing the loss of handwritten versus printed talmudic books have much to tell us about the meaning their readers attributed to them. Going back to the moment these books were created, I examine the meanings that their creators assigned to them. This example deals with the Jerusalem Talmud, but the situation of both Talmuds regarding the comparison between manuscript and print tradition is quite the same. Scribes commonly concluded their books with colophons, which usually included a generic apology. Rabbi Yehiel ben Yequtiel's colophon in a manuscript of the Jerusalem Talmud from 1289 (Leiden University Library, Or. 4720, Scaliger 3) offers one such example:

אני יחיאל בירבי יקותיאל בירבי בנימין הרופא נבתוי"א (=נפשו בטוב תלין וזרעו יראה ארץ), כתבתי זה הספר ירושלמי... לר' מנחם בירבי בנימין והעתקתיו מספר משובש ומוטעה הרבה עד מאד, ומה שיכולתי להבין ולהשכיל הגהתי בו כפי עניות דעתי ויודע אני שלא הגעתי לתכלית השיבושים והטעיות אשר מצאתי בהעתק ההוא ואפילו לחציים.

(I, Yehiel ben R. Yequtiel ben Rabbi Benjamin the Physician, may his soul rest peacefully and his children inherit the land, wrote this book of the Yerushalmi [...] on behalf of R. Menahem ben R. Benjamin. I copied it from a very corrupt and erroneous book. I corrected what I could understand and comprehend in my humble opinion; I know that I did not correct all the mistakes and errors that I found in that copy, nor even half of them. Therefore, one who reads this book and finds errors and mistakes therein should judge me favourably and not blame me for all of them.)[22]

The book Yehiel used as source for the Leiden manuscript is unknown, and despite several assumptions about its nature, we cannot know how damaged it was, or whether we can ascribe the scribe's evaluation to real corruption or to misjudgement of the natural language and terminology of the Jerusalem Talmud. The text that he used for comparison could not, of course, have been the printed text, not even a better manuscript. Had he possessed a better text, would he not have used it instead? The scribe imagined the source text from which he was copying as deficient in comparison to the imagined, whole, metaphysical text of the Talmud, the text that is not anchored to — indeed conceptually independent from — any physical book.

The scribe wrote that he produced 'a book', meaning a copy of the Jerusalem Talmud, and although he did his best to correct it, it was still highly corrupted. This codex copied in professional Italian Hebrew script on 674 large, beautiful parchment leaves, includes a copy of the entire Jerusalem Talmud as it is known until today.[23] To us, it is a monumental work, but in the eyes of its scribe it was but a marginal, negligible, and corrupted copy of the original text.

The fluid nature of the textual variants in the manuscript and the fact that such variants make every manuscript unique — the main characteristics of manuscripts in our eyes — are not mentioned by the scribe at all. It would not be

---

22 For full description, see Mayer, *Editio Princeps*, pp. 226-30..
23 Yaacov Sussmann, 'Before and After the Leiden Manuscript of the Talmud Yerushalmi' [in Hebrew], *Bar-Ilan Annual*, 26/27 (1995), pp. 203-20; Yaacov Sussmann, 'Introduction', in *Talmud Yerushalmi: According to Ms. Or. 4720 (Scal. 3) of the Leiden University Library, with Restorations and Corrections* [in Hebrew], ed. by Yaacov Sussmann (Jerusalem: Academy of the Hebrew Language, 2001), pp. 9-37.

too wild a guess to say that they would have been seen as characteristics of the book's corruption compared to the metaphysical Talmud.

The Leiden manuscript of the Jerusalem Talmud was transmitted from one owner to another until the beginning of the sixteenth century, when it reached the hands of the Venetian Hebrew printer Daniel Bomberg, who used it as the primary source for his printed *editio princeps* of the Jerusalem Talmud. Jacob ben Hayyim ibn Adonijah, who was the printing professional working on this edition, added the following colophon at the end of the book:

עד כאן אשכחנא מהאי תלמודא ולאינא טובא לאשלחא איגרין ואיזגדין בכל דוכתין ופרינן ולאינא ולא אשכחנא אלא איליו ד' סידרין וגליפנא יתהון בגילופין במאני אברא ופרזלא בעיונא סגין ושקלינן וטרינן בהו'[ן] טובא למיהך בארח קשוט בגירסו'[ת] הישרות עם תלת טפוסין אחרנין דוקניות דהוון קדמנא כד הווינא מגהין בהאי חיבור'[א]. וכען נצלי ונבעי רחמין מן קדם אלהא חייא עילאה דיערע קדמנא תשלום האי תלמודא ונזכה לאשלמא ליה כדקא יאות.

(This is (the four orders of the Jerusalem Talmud found in the Leiden manuscript) what we found of this Talmud. We made great efforts, sending letters and agents to all places. We ran and exerted, but found nothing but these four orders. We inscribed them using lead and iron tools and close scrutiny. We discussed them at length, following the path of truth, using good versions, along with three other precise texts that were before us when we proofread this work. We now pray and beg for mercy before the living, most high God, that He cause us to find the remainder of this Talmud and thereby complete this in a fitting fashion.)[24]

The manuscript that is now described as 'good' and 'precise' is the same as it was when the colophon was written, 234 years before it was printed. Back then, the scribe clearly noted its corrupt condition. Under what circumstances had the text suddenly 'improved'? Another manuscript among the three others Jacob ben Hayyim used for correcting the text also survived. Today in the Vatican Library (Biblioteca apostolica, cod. ebr. 133), it is not significantly different from the Leiden manuscript in terms of its textual quality (where they do differ, the Vatican manuscript differs for the worse).[25] I suggest that the difference between the colophon of the manuscript and the colophon of the print edition springs from the cultural backgrounds of their respective authors, and their different conceptualizations and cultural assumptions about the nature of the book.

The manuscript's scribe produced '*a* book', a copy of the Jerusalem Talmud. The printer, by contrast, did not testify to the production of '*a* book', the subject of his description is '*the* four orders' of the Talmud. The editor of the printed edition used the copy made by the scribe, but he was not creating another 'copy' of it in print. Instead, he was thinking about producing the Talmud "itself". The editor does not even say that he and other workers had corrected the text; he was, rather, 'following the path of truth', walking in the real textual path of the Talmud, and only being helped by the different copies. These copies, since they helped produce the talmudic text, were considered 'accurate'. With the help of the editor, the talmudic text was 'pinned' to the physical book.

The suggested point of view does not frame the whole corpus of manuscript and printed books. Neither does it define the nature of print

---

24 Mayer, Editio Princeps, ibid.

25 Yakov Z. Mayer, 'From Material History to Historical Context: The Case Study of MS Vatican Ebr. 133 of the Palestinian Talmud' [in Hebrew], *Zion* 83/3 (2018), pp. 277–321.

as a multidimensional historical phenomenon. But it *does* describe a unique historical change in the transmission of talmudic literature. The difference between Jewish reactions to medieval talmudic books and those to printed ones reflects a conceptual transformation regarding the nature of the book, a difference which is not the result of the technical development, but of the humanist intellectual and cultural processes surrounding that development. In medieval times, Jewish scholars considered the text of the Talmud and the material talmudic book as two distinct entities. The text, especially as one of religious importance, was thought to exist metaphysically as a complete whole and the material book was considered to be only an insignificant copy of it, corrupted by time and unqualified scribes. Colophons of medieval manuscripts usually testified to the corrupted condition of the copied book, of the book it was copied from, and to the scribe's inefficient efforts to fix it. In such a worldview, fire cannot destroy a piece of literature. The literary product was thought to be an abstract entity, embodied temporarily in the 'body' of a physical book. What fire could do, and did, was to hurt the people who owned the books.

But in the early modern world, after the invention of the printing press and following the humanist approach to return '*ad fontes*' ('to the sources') to the origins of the texts, a gigantic effort was made to recreate classical texts in what humanist editors believed was their full original form. Towards this end, they collected large numbers of manuscripts from which they made massive textual syntheses. Printers expressed the idea that they were not producing a corrupt or even merely imperfect copy of the text, but the text itself. They considered their new, printed books as the only place where the text could be found: in their minds, the text and its material carrier became one unified entity. This revolutionary concept of the book has affected the way we have thought of books for centuries. It created the idea that when we physically hold the material book, we also 'hold' the spirit concealed within it, and when the material is lost, the spirit is lost as well.

Part Five

Christian Collections

JUDITH OLSZOWY-SCHLANGER

A Medieval Hebrew Psalter with Latin Glosses (MS Paris, BnF hébr. 113) and Its Cambridge Connection

Introduction

Manuscript BnF hébr. 113 is one of the most unusual manuscripts held by the Bibliothèque Nationale de France in Paris (BnF). This handsome slim volume in an ornate blind-tooled brown leather binding is a multilingual manuscript: a Hebrew Psalter to which were added Latin glosses interspersed with French or rather Anglo-Norman words; there are also Greek and Runic alphabets on additional flyleaves. Although this Psalter has been mentioned and described briefly by contemporary scholars, including myself, several aspects of its origins and subsequent history still remain to be elucidated.[1] In this chapter,

1 Hermann Zotenberg, *Catalogue des manuscrits hébreux et samaritains de la Bibliothèque Impériale* (Paris: Imprimerie impériale, 1866), p. 12; Beryl Smalley, *The Study of the Bible in the Middle Ages* (Notre Dame, IN: University of Notre Dame Press, 1964), p. 348; Raphael Loewe, 'The Medieval Christian Hebraists of England: The Superscriptio Lincolniensis', *Hebrew Union College Annual*, 28 (1957), pp. 205–52; Michel Garel, *D'une main forte: Manuscrits hébreux des collections*

françaises (Paris: Seuil, Bibliothèque Nationale, 1992), pp. 90–91; Malachi Beit-Arié, *Hebrew Manuscripts of East and West: Towards a Comparative Codicology*, the Panizzi Lectures (London: British Library, 1992), p. 109; Malachi Beit-Arié, 'The Valmadonna Pentateuch and the Problem of Pre-Expulsion Anglo-Hebrew Manuscripts – MS London, Valmadonna Trust Library 1: England (?), 1189', in Malachi Beit-Arié, *The Makings of the Medieval Hebrew Book: Studies in Palaeography and Codicology* (Jerusalem: Magnes Press, 1993), 1st Ed., London, 1985; Gabrielle Sed-Rajna and Sonia Fellous, *Les Manuscrits hébreux enluminés des bibliothèques de France* (Louvain-Paris: Peeters, 1994), pp. 147–49; Gilbert Dahan, 'Deux psautiers hébraïques glosés en latin', *Revue des études juives*, 158 (1999), pp. 61–78; Judith Olszowy-Schlanger, *Les manuscrits hébreux dans l'Angleterre médiévale: étude historique et paléographique*, Collection de la Revue des études juives (Paris and Louvain: Peeters, 2003), no. 7, pp. 19–22, 181–87, and passim; David Trotter, 'Peut-on parler de judéo-anglo-normand? Textes anglo-normands en écriture hébraïque', *Médiévales*, 68 (2015), pp. 25–34 (https://doi.org/10.4000/medievales.7549); *Anglo-français: philologie et linguistique*, ed. by Oreste Floquet and Gabriele Giannini (Paris: Classiques Garnier, 2015), pp. 142–43; Sara Harris and Jane Gilbert, 'The Written Word: Literacy across Languages', in *The Cambridge Companion*

Judith Olszowy-Schlanger • Ecole Pratique des Hautes Etudes, Paris, and Oxford University

I propose to contribute to our knowledge of this manuscript and, more broadly, of the way Hebrew manuscripts were read and used by Christian scholars by considering its late medieval and early Tudor history, before it was brought to France in the sixteenth century. A hint as to the manuscript's whereabouts in the fifteenth and sixteenth centuries is provided by its binding. It has been identified as having been produced in a Cambridge workshop by Nicholas Spierinck or Segar Nicholson, but the full implication of this Cambridge connection has not yet been studied. In order to fully appreciate the relevance of the manuscript's history, I propose to briefly revisit its material and textual characteristics and also to recall the context of Christian Hebraism, which left a rich trail of annotations in the body of the Psalter.

BnF hébr. 113 is one of thirteen extant Psalters most probably produced in England between c. 1150 and the second half of the thirteenth century in which the Hebrew text is accompanied by Latin translations and/or marginal and interlinear glosses.[2] They belong to an even larger group of insular Hebrew-Latin manuscripts which feature other parts of the Bible, Rashi commentaries, a dictionary, and a grammar. These 'bilingual' manuscripts are material witnesses to the growing interest of medieval English Christians in the study of sapiential languages — Hebrew and Greek, in addition to Latin.[3] A result of the novel modes of learning and the increase in literacy brought about by the so-called 'Twelfth Century Renaissance', this interest was facilitated by close daily business interactions between English monasteries and other ecclesiastical institutions and their Jewish neighbours. Just as important,

---

to *Medieval British Manuscripts*, ed. by Orietta Da Rold and Elaine Treharne (Cambridge: Cambridge University Press, 2020), pp. 149–78.

2 Five Psalters were produced from the outset by Jewish-trained and Christian scribes working in collaboration as bilingual artefacts: London, Westminster Abbey Library, MS 2, Oxford, Corpus Christi College MS 10, Oxford, Corpus Christi College MS 11 (Psalter), Cambridge, Trinity College MS R. 8. 6, and Leiden, University Library MS Or. 4725. Psalters Oxford, Bodleian Library MS Bodl. Or. 3, Oxford, Bodleian Library MS Bodl. Or. 6; Oxford, Bodleian Library MS Bodl. Or. 621, Oxford, Bodleian Library MS Laud 174, Warminster, Longleat House MS 21 (Psalter), London, Lambeth Palace MS 435, Dublin, Trinity College MS 17 and BnF hébr. 113 were manuscripts produced for Jewish audiences and appropriated and annotated by Christian Hebraists. See Smalley, *The Study of the Bible*; Loewe, 'The Medieval Christian Hebraists of England'; Dahan, 'Deux psautiers hébraïques'; Beit-Arié, 'The Valmadonna Pentateuch'; Olszowy-Schlanger, *Les manuscrits hébreux*.

3 On Christian Hebraism and bilingual manuscripts in England, see especially Samuel Berger, *Quam notitiam linguae hebraicae habuerint Christiani medii aevi temporibus in Gallia* (Paris: Hachette, 1893); Smalley, *The Study of the Bible*; Loewe, 'The Medieval Christian Hebraists of England'; Raphael Loewe, 'Latin Superscriptio MSS on Portions of the Hebrew Bible Other than the Psalter', *Journal of Jewish Studies*, 9 (1958), pp. 63–71; Raphael Loewe, 'Jewish Scholarship in England', in *Three Centuries of Anglo-Jewish History: A Volume of Essays*, ed. by Vivian D. Lipman (Cambridge: Published for the Jewish Historical Society of England by W. Heffer, 1961), pp. 125–48; Raphael Loewe, 'Hebrew Books and "Judaica" in Mediaeval Oxford and Cambridge', in *Remember the Days: Essays on Anglo-Jewish History Presented to Cecil Roth*, ed. by John M. Shaftesley (London: the Jewish Historical Society of England), pp. 23–48; Dahan, 'Deux psautiers hébraïques'; Olszowy-Schlanger, *Les manuscrits hébreux*; Judith Olszowy-Schlanger, 'The Knowledge and Practice of Hebrew Grammar among Christian Scholars in Pre-Expulsion England: The Evidence of "Bilingual" Hebrew-Latin Manuscripts', in *Hebrew Scholarship and the Medieval World*, ed. by Nicholas De Lange (Cambridge: Cambridge University Press, 2001), pp. 107–28; Judith Olszowy-Schlanger, 'Rachi en latin: les gloses latines dans un manuscrit du commentaire de Rachi et les études hébraïques parmi des chrétiens dans l'Angleterre médiévale', in *Héritages de Rachi*, ed. by René-Samuel Sirat (Paris and Tel Aviv: Editions de l'Eclat, 2006), pp. 137–50; Judith Olszowy-Schlanger, 'Christian Hebraism in Thirteenth-Century England: The Evidence of Hebrew-Latin Manuscripts', in *Crossing Borders: Hebrew Manuscripts as a Meeting-place of Cultures*, ed. by Piet van Boxel and Sabine Arndt (Oxford: Bodleian Library, 2009), pp. 115–22.

from the mid-thirteenth century onwards, were the frequent conversions of Jewish individuals, who saw their economic status and personal security undermined by both exorbitant taxation and physical aggressions.[4]

Although it has been pointed out repeatedly that medieval Christian Hebraism was often motivated by polemical intentions regarding Jewish conversions, in fact, philological interest in Hebrew — much like the contemporary study of Greek — was also a part of the genuine scientific tradition that developed in English monasteries and schools. Although this concern was possibly never central to the Christian curriculum, the extant manuscripts show that it was rather more than a marginal erudite quirk.[5] Among the most powerful incentives for Christians to turn to the Hebrew language was its key role in accessing the original Bible, the *hebraica veritas*, and through comparison, to further the understanding of their own *scriptura sacra*, the Latin Vulgate. Aware of the corrupted state of their own manuscripts, they followed the path traced by Jerome, who urged a return to Hebrew whenever there was an inconsistency between the Greek and Latin translations of the Old Testament.[6] To enable them to fully understand Hebrew and Jewish texts, Christian Hebraists in medieval England studied with Jewish masters, acquired Jewish books, and commissioned the copying of bilingual Hebrew-Latin volumes; they also produced their own linguistic works.[7]

The Psalter BnF hébr. 113 was produced as a Jewish book but was subsequently 'converted' for Christian use. Written from right to left by a remarkable Jewish calligrapher (but one who was not a careful biblical scholar, as his text contains errors), it was most probably originally commissioned for Jewish readership and devotion. In a previous study, I suggested that the presence of unusually broad outer margins (in which parallel columns of the Latin text could be written) might be an indication that the manuscript was planned as a bilingual artefact from the outset. However, this suggestion now has to be revised: the line ruling (traced with a colourless metal point) was only done for the Hebrew text, and no such guidelines were provided for a possible abbreviated and incomplete Latin text. The large margins in question were common in medieval times, as they allowed readers to study their books 'pen in hand' and eventually to leave their glosses in the generous margins. More importantly, the margins of BnF hébr. 113 were

---

4 Robert C. Stacey, 'The Conversion of Jews to Christianity in Thirteenth-Century England', *Speculum*, 67/2 (1992), pp. 263–83.

5 Rodney Thomson, 'England and the Twelfth-century Renaissance', *Past & Present*, 101 (1983), pp. 3–21.

6 See Jerome, Epistle II, p. 249 (CVI, 2, 3): Sicut in nouo testamento, si quando apud latinos questio oritur et inter exemplaria uarietas est, recurrimus ad fontem greci sermonis quo nouum scriptum est instrumentum, ita in ueteri testamento, si quando inter grecos latinosque diuersitas est, ad hebraicam confugimus ueritatem ('As it is for the New Testament, when, among the Latins, arises a question and there is a discrepancy among exemplars, we refer to the source in Greek in which the New Testament was written; thus, for the Old Testament, if there is discrepancy among Greeks and Latins, we refer to the Hebrew truth').

7 Berger, *Quam Notitiam*; Beryl Smalley, *Hebrew Scholarship among Christians in 13th Century England as Illustrated by Some Hebrew-Latin Psalters*, Lectiones in Vetere Testamento et Rebus Iudaicis, 6 (London: Society of Old Testament Studies, 1939); Smalley, *The Study of the Bible*, pp. 342–46; Loewe, 'The Medieval Christian Hebraists of England'; Loewe, 'Latin Superscriptio MSS', pp. 63–71; Beit-Arié, *Hebrew Manuscripts of East and West*; Colette Sirat, 'Notes sur la circulation des livres entre juifs et chrétiens au Moyen Âge', in *Du copiste au collectionneur: Mélanges d'histoire des textes et des bibliothèques en l'honneur d'André Vernet*, ed. by Donatella Nebbiai-Dalla Guarda and Jean-François Genest, Bibliologia, 18 (Turnhout: Brepols, 1999), pp. 383–404; Olszowy-Schlanger, *Les manuscrits hébreux*; Judith Olszowy-Schlanger, Anne Grondeux, and others, *Dictionnaire hébreu-latin-français de la Bible hébraïque de l'Abbaye de Ramsey (XIIIe s.)* (Turnhout: Brepols, 2008).

Figure 15.1. Paris, Bibliothèque nationale de France, MS hébr. 113, fol. 3ʳ: overlap between the Hebrew psalm number (*gimel*) and the Latin translation.

Figure 15.2. Paris, Bibliothèque nationale de France, MS hébr. 113, fol. 133ʳ⁻ᵛ: the colophon.

in fact not left completely blank, as they were used for the numberings of the psalms. In some cases, the Latin verses were partly overwritten and allowed to run over these Hebrew numberings, confirming — as with the letter *gimel* to mark Psalm 3 on fol. 3ʳ — that the Latin was a later addition (Figure 15.1).

Made by Jews, then, and for Jewish use, the Psalter BnF hébr. 113 subsequently came into the possession of Christian scholars, who studied and annotated it in Latin and Anglo-Norman French. The earliest Latin hands can be dated palaeographically to the 1230s–1240s, a time of increased interest in Hebrew studies in England. Well attested throughout the second and third quarters of the century, the school of Christian Hebraism in England is thought to have been stunted by the expulsion of the Jews in 1290. However, in addition to the rich trail of Christian Hebraism from its thirteenth-century heyday, BnF hébr. 113 contains some elements which attest to its study in later periods, notably in fifteenth- and sixteenth-century learned institutions.

The Making of the MS BnF hébr. 113

The codicological and palaeographical features of BnF hébr. 113 suggest that it was made in England at the very beginning of the thirteenth century, but a more specific context regarding its production and study has still to be ascertained. The manuscript does not include any explicit mention of the time and place where it was copied, nor does it reveal the identity of the scribe. The colophon concluding the Psalter (at the foot of fol. 133ʳ and spilling over to the next page, fol. 133ᵛ) is beautifully written in calligraphic monumental script in bright vermillion consonants with brown-ink vowels on the recto and in a lapis lazuli pigment with vermillion vowels on the verso. Unfortunately, it does not provide any information of historical value but is limited to the standard scribal formula of good omen חזק ונתחזק הסופר לא יזק ('be strong and we shall be strong, may the scribe come to no harm'), a formula partly inspired by biblical quotations (Jos. 1:7: חזק ואמץ, Dan. 10:19: חזק וחזק, II Sam. 10:12: חזק ונתחזק) (Figure 15.2).[8]

A date of *c.* 1180–1190 for the Hebrew text was proposed by Michel Garel on the basis of the

---

8 Based on Joshua 1:7, whose different parts are used in scribal colophons across the Jewish world, the injunction חזק was pronounced at the end of the Bible reading in the synagogue: see *Sefer ha-manhig, Hilkhot Shabbat*, p. 182.

identification of the scribe with that of MS ex-Valmadonna 1, dated to 1182.[9] That was supported by Gilbert Dahan, who quoted Marie-Thérèse Gousset comparing the style and especially the colouring of our manuscript's decorated initial words and psalm numbering with the famous *Westminster Psalter* (BL MS Royal MS 2 A XXII), produced at the beginning of the thirteenth century.[10] A different date was suggested by Beryl Smalley followed by Raphael Loewe and Gabrielle Sed-Rajna, who independently dated BnF hébr. 113 to the middle of the thirteenth century. A detailed palaeographical analysis could not confirm that BnF hébr. 113 was copied by the scribe of MS ex-Valmadonna 1, but confirmed a date in the early thirteenth century for the Hebrew text. As indicated, the Latin translations can be dated on palaeographical grounds to the 1230s–1240s.

The manuscript features several indications of ownership. However, none is from the medieval period and all reveal an interest in this manuscript during the humanistic revival of Hebrew studies in Tudor England and in late sixteenth-century France. The manuscript belonged to Jacques-Auguste de Thou (1553–1617), president of the Parliament of Paris, humanist, lawyer, and bibliophile.[11] In 1679 his heirs sold his enormous collection of manuscripts to Jean-Baptiste Colbert (1629–1683), whose library, in turn, became part of the Bibliothèque du Roi. It has been suggested that De Thou inherited this Psalter, together with a large collection of other books, from his friend and fellow humanist, legal scholar, and philologist interested in Hebrew, Nicolas Le Fèvre (1544–1612), who was a tutor of young Louis XIII.[12] It is equally possible that the volume crossed the Channel with Le Fèvre's and De Thou's close friend, colleague, and erudite editor of antique and medieval manuscripts, Pierre Pithou (1539–1596). Of the exclusive and closely knit group of sixteenth-century Parisian humanists, Pithou was reputedly the most advanced in the study of Hebrew. He was also the one who travelled to England in May 1572 as a member of a large French aristocratic delegation led by the duke de Montmorency for Charles IX, who wanted to ratify recent political treatises as well as to arrange his marriage with Queen Elisabeth I.[13] We know that Pithou took advantage of his participation in this embassy to acquire several manuscripts in England. Pierre Pithou and his brother's love for books and passion for collecting them were thus recalled by Joseph Scaliger: 'The Pithou were on the good books' scent from as far away as a dog smells a bone and a cat a mouse'.[14] It is true that his lovingly created collection of manuscripts was damaged during the St Bartholomew's Night massacre of the Protestants (Pithou was a Calvinist) on 23–24 August 1572, but some

---

9   Beit-Arié, 'The Valmadonna Pentateuch'. Today at the Museum of the Bible, Washington, DC, https://collections.museumofthebible.org/artifacts/32220-codex-valmadonna-i?&tab=description.

10 Dahan, 'Deux psautiers', p. 64.

11 On de Thou and his library, see esp. Ingrid De Smet, *Thuanus. The Making of Jacques-Auguste de Thou (1553–1617)* (Geneva: Droz, 2006).

12 Garel, *D'une main forte*, p. 91. On Le Fèvre, see Louis Ellies Dupin, *Nouvelle bibliothèque des auteurs ecclésiastiques*, at Pierre Humbert, Amsterdam, 1711, vol. XVII, pp. 48–56; Jean-Louis Quantin, 'Un érudit gallican et politique au tournant du XVIe et du XVIIe siècle: Nicolas Le Fèvre', *Annuaire de l'Ecole Pratique des Hautes Etudes*, Section des Sciences Historiques et Philologiques, année 2008–2009 (Paris: EPHE, 2011), pp. 287–89. We know that Le Fèvre acquired some of his manuscripts from the magistrate and historian Claude Fauchet (1530–1602), as indicated by notes of possession in several extant Latin and French manuscripts in the BnF (e.g., BnF français 401).

13 Louis De Rosanbo, 'Pierre Pithou, biographie', *Revue du seizième siècle*, 15 (1928), p. 286 (pp. 279–305).

14 Quoted by Léopold Delisle, *Le cabinet des manuscrits de la Bibliothèque nationale*, vol. II (Paris, 1874), p. 8: 'MM. Pithou, sentoient les bons livres d'aussi loin que les chiens un os, ou le chat une souris'.

of his treasures escaped destruction, and he continued collecting throughout the 1570s until his death in 1596.[15] It is indeed difficult at this stage to ascertain which one of the group of French magistrates, humanists with Protestant sympathies and interest in Hebrew, all of them editors of ancient manuscripts and indefatigable bibliophiles, all competing with one another in a friendly fashion to amass ancient books, was the owner of BnF hébr. 113 before it became part of the huge library of more than 6000 volumes of Jacques-Auguste de Thou. On the upper edge of fol. 135ʳ of our manuscript, there was a note in Renaissance period Latin characters. It is possible that this note included precious information on the manuscript's provenance but it was thoroughly erased; only stubs of the letters are still discernible, and I have not yet been able to decipher what little is still visible.

Before the manuscript was removed to France, it belonged to a schoolteacher in Colchester in Essex, the home of one of the most venerable grammar schools in England; a note of ownership — 'Liber Roberti Morinaldi Colnensis ludimagistri' ('The book of Robert Morinald, elementary schoolteacher from Colchester'[16])

— appears on fol. 138ᵛ. This inscription can be palaeographically dated to the early Renaissance period. The same time frame is suggested by the term 'ludi magister' (lit. 'master of games'), inspired by classical antiquity (it designates, for instance, Cicero's master of rhetoric[17]) to identify a schoolteacher. It came into popular use in the transformed elementary grammar schools of Tudor England. For the time being, it is difficult to pinpoint the time of Robert Morinald's ownership of the book more precisely, but it is likely that it came to his possession after it was bound in Cambridge in the early decades of the sixteenth century.

The Manuscript's Composition and Contents

BnF hébr. 113 is a Hebrew Psalter that is bound together with two small quires of a somewhat different parchment type and dimensions, which constitute the front and end protective flyleaves. It is difficult to determine whether these quires were kept together with the Psalter prior to their binding. These heterogeneous leaves feature Christian Hebraist texts.

The Psalter itself is a relatively small book (19 × 12.5 cm) of 134 folios of good-quality parchment, arranged in standard quires of four bifolios.[18] It was copied and decorated by a skilled calligrapher in French-type square Hebrew script

---

15 Françoise Bibolet, 'Bibliotheca Pithoeana. Les manuscrits des Pithou: une histoire de fraternité et d'amitié', in *Du copiste au collectionneur. Mélanges d'histoire des textes et des bibliothèques en l'honneur d'André Vernet*, ed. by Donatella Nebbiai-Dalla Guarda and Jean-François Genest, Bibliologia, 18 (Turnhout: Brepols, 1999), pp. 497–521. Two manuscripts acquired in England, BnF lat. 6239 and MS Médiathèque de Troyes 1316 (incidentally, Troyes was Pitou's birthplace), are still extant: see Françoise Bibolet, 'Les Pithou et l'amour des livres', in *Les Pithou, les lettres et la paix du royaume*, ed. by Marie-Madeleine Fragonard and Pierre-Eugène Leroy (Paris: Classiques Garnier, 2003), p. 299 (pp. 295–304).

16 The identification of Colnensis with Colchester is uncertain but possible given the etymology of the town's name as derived from the river Colne, or both the town and the river as derived from Latin 'colonia', with the old medieval forms of the name being Colneceaster or Colenceaster: see Philip Crummy, *City of Victory:*

The Story of Colchester – Britain's First Roman Town (Colchester: Colchester Archaeological Trust, 1997), p. 134.

17 *Divinatio in Q. Caecilium*, XIV.47 (https://la.wikisource.org/wiki/In_Verrem/Divinatio_in_Caecilium_oratio#[XIV]).

18 For the codicology of the Psalter, see Olszowy-Schlanger, *Les manuscrits hébreux*, p. 182. The Psalter has sixteen quaternios (I–XVI) and one shorter quire made up of three bifolios at the end of the volume. The text of Psalms begins on 1ᵛ and ends on 133ᵛ, with the last folio left blank.

 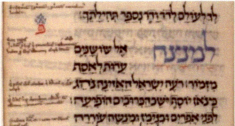

Figure 15.3. Paris, Bibliothèque nationale de France, MS hébr. 113, fols 70ʳ and 71ʳ: numbering of two psalms as 80.

in dark brown ferro-gallic ink for the consonants of the main text. The script reflects the typical 'Gothic' calligraphic elements such as fish-tail bifurcation, hairline serifs, drop-shape thickening of some verticals, flags on the ascender of the *lamed*, lozenge-shaped heads of the *gimel*, *zayin*, and *nun* and roofs on the arms of the *tet*, *ʿayin*, and *shin*. The characters are relatively large, measuring 5 × 4 mm on average. The initial words of the psalms are twice as large, and were written in carefully planned blank spaces that were left in the line to accommodate them.

The Book of Psalms in BnF hébr. 113 includes 152 psalms rather than the usual count of 150 of the Masoretic Text (MT). Psalms 1 to 77 correspond to the numbering of the MT. The long Psalm 78 (with 72 verses in MT) was divided in BnF hébr. 113: verses 1–37 were numbered as Psalm 78, and the rest of the Psalm was given number 79 and a blue initial, like the beginning of each psalm. Thus, Psalm 79 of the MT (מזמור לאסף) bears number 80 in BnF hébr. 113. It is noteworthy that the number 80 is not expressed here as usual by the letter *pe*, but by *ʿayin* and *yod* (70 + 10). However, the numbering catches up with the MT: the next psalm, Psalm 80 in MT, is numbered with the letter *pe* — 80 in our Psalter (Figure 15.3). Thus, the scribe numbered two different psalms as 80 but fabricated an alternative way of writing 80 (*ʿayin* and *yod* [70 + 10]) in order to differentiate them and to stay in line with the MT!

Psalms 81 to 117 correspond to MT, but another discrepancy occurs at Psalm 118. In BnF hébr. 113, the number 118 corresponds to MT Psalm 118 verses 1 to 4 only. The remaining verses of Psalm 118 bear number 119, whereas MT Psalm 119 is here numbered as 120. The gap widens even further at the level of Psalm 135 of the MT, which is divided in two in BnF hébr. 113. MT Psalm 135 verses 1 and 2 only are rendered as a separate psalm numbered 136, and the remaining part of the MT Psalm 135, from verse 3 onwards, was numbered 137. The discrepancy continues until the end of the Psalter, with MT Psalm 150 bearing number 152. Numbering which strays from the accepted Masoretic 150 psalms is also found in other medieval Hebrew manuscripts, reaching sometimes as many as 170 numbered divisions (e.g., MS BL Or 4227, France, *c.* 1300[19]). All of this is not indicative of any form of a Christian division of the Book of Psalms, and differs from the bilingual Hebrew-Latin Psalters which were copied to reconcile the MT and Latin Vulgate division.

That is not to say that the surrounding Christian bookmaking tradition did not have an impact on the visual aspects of BnF hébr. 113. This influence included the use of colours to mark the titles (incipits) and the numbering of the individual psalms. The psalms' initial words were written by the principal scribe in a clear space the height of two lines with the width varying according to the length of the incipit, but

---

19 It should be noted, however, that the psalm numbers in MS BL Or 4227, written in gold in the margins, were added by a later hand.

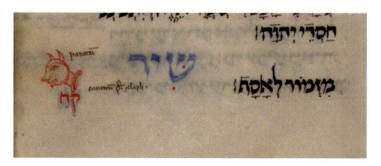

Figure 15.4. Paris, Bibliothèque nationale de France, MS hébr. 113, fol. 99ʳ: a head of a horned demon decorates the number of Psalm 108.

Figure 15.5. Paris, Bibliothèque nationale de France, MS hébr. 113, fol. 1ᵛ and Longleat House, MS 21, fol. 1ᵛ, Psalm 1.

The same blue and vermillion pigments were used for the psalms' numbering (expressed, of course, in Hebrew characters), which are located at the level of the initials in the middle of the outer margins. The numbers are decorated with pen flourishes in such motifs as zigzag lines, a four-petal flower, a crown, a dotted frame, Solomon's knot, and, in one case, on fol. 99ʳ, the number of Psalm 108 is decorated with a drawing of a horned devil's head (Figure 15.4). For Psalms 1 and 2, the colour of the number corresponds to that of the title; from Psalm 3 onwards, when the title is blue, the numbering is most often in red, and vice versa.[21] In a few cases the numbers composed of two letters are bi-coloured.[22] The penwork decorations on the numbers are often in both colours.

The alternating colours of the Initial words follow the fashion started in the Parisian ateliers that produced Latin books.[23] This colouring of the initial letters became the norm in Ashkenazi manuscripts from the thirteenth century onwards, and BnF hébr. 113 was evidently one of the earliest instances of this practice. Very similar colours for the titles of the psalms were used in the Psalter in MS Longleat House 21.[24] Datable to the same period and covered with Latin annotations by a contemporary but different hand than in BnF hébr. 113, the MS LH 21 Psalter has a similar page layout in its initial quires (Figure 15.5).

Normally reserved for the psalms' incipits, in BnF hébr. 113, colours were also used to enhance the structure of the so-called alphabetical psalm, MT Psalm 119 (here Psalm 120, fols 107ʳ–115ʳ), in

often about a half of the line. The incipits were very often placed at the beginning or the end of a line, but when they were set in the middle of a line, the line above was left blank (e.g., Psalm 7, fol. 4ᵛ).[20] These initial titles are written in alternating lapis lazuli blue and bright vermillion red consonants. The titles in blue have vowels in vermillion pigment, whereas the vermillion titles are vocalized with the same brown ink which was used for the vowels of the main text. Sometimes, the titles have a frame or are outlined in the opposite colour (e.g., Psalm 59, fol. 48ᵛ).

---

20 There are a few exceptions, e.g., Psalm 5 (fol. 3ʳ).

21 The exceptions include: fols 9ʳ–9ᵛ (Psalm 13 to Psalm 15), fol. 33ᵛ (Psalm 41), fol. 51ᵛ (Psalm 63), fol. 57ʳ (Psalms 125–26), fols 116ᵛ–117ʳ, fol. 131ᵛ (Psalm 150), and fol. 133ʳ (Psalm 152).

22 See fol. 15ʳ, Psalm 21, fol. 19ʳ, Psalm 26.

23 Gilbert and Harris, p. 157.

24 See esp. Loewe, 'Jewish Scholarship in England', p. 133; Olszowy-Schlanger, *Les manuscrits hébreux*, pp. 188–96; Olszowy-Schlanger, Grondeux, and others, *Dictionnaire hébreu-latin-français de la Bible hébraïque*.

which groups of consecutive verses begin with the same letter of the alphabet and in alphabetical order. In BnF hébr. 113, each new alphabetical group of verses begins with a coloured initial letter in alternating blue and red, with a decoration of three red dots for the beginning of each verse. The scribe made a considerable effort to accommodate each verse on a single line, spreading letters in shorter verses, and squeezing those which were too long for the line. Further, as in many Latin manuscripts, he ended each verse with a colour marking: the *sof pasuq* end-of-the-verse sign is repeated in red on every line, at some distance from the end of the verse, creating a relatively regular vertical visual reference point in the left-hand margins (Figure 15.6).

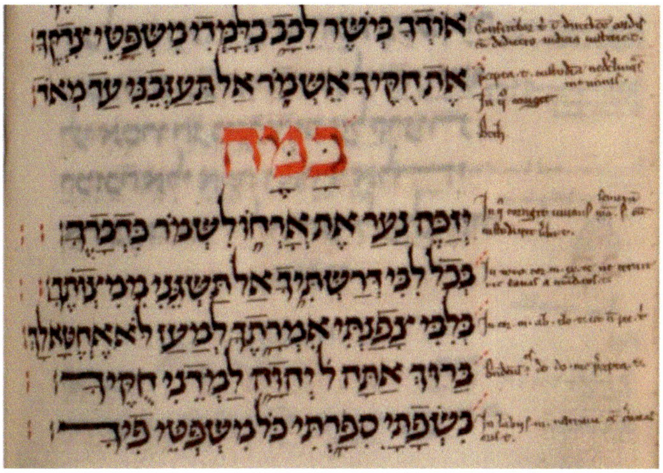

The consonantal text of the Psalter was vocalized following non-standard Tiberian tradition.[25] This Psalter is set apart from the standard Tiberian Masorah (MT) by several elements: the frequent confusion between *patah* and *qamatz* and *segol* and *tzere*, the use of *dagesh qal* in letters other than *begadkefat* at the beginning of a new word (systematically if the word begins with a *yod*) or a new syllable (not necessarily after a syllable closed by a silent *sheva*). These elements correspond to the so-called Palestinian-Tiberian or Extended Tiberian system. Particularly frequent in early manuscripts from central Italy, such as the *Codex Reuchlinianus* or the Bibles reconstructed from fragments in Nonantola and other archives, the use of this system is also apparent in some Ashkenazi manuscripts.[26] It differs from the

Figure 15.6. Paris, Bibliothèque nationale de France, MS hébr. 113, fol. 107ᵛ: marking of the initial letter and end of the verses of the alphabetical Psalm 119 (here Psalm 120).

typical simplified vocalization used by Christian scholars in medieval England, where the *qamatz* is systematically replaced by *patah* and all the *segols* by *tzere*.[27] As different from the Tiberian tradition as this vocalization is, it could have been added by a Jewish *naqdan*. It is, however, noteworthy that the ink used for the vowels differs from the consonantal text but is similar in colour to that of the corrections of the Hebrew text in slightly clumsy characters and, surprisingly, to the Latin translation (Figure 15.7). Of course, a mere change in the hue of the ink is inconclusive as to the identity of the vocalizer, but the difference is nonetheless remarkable.

---

25 For a detailed analysis, see Olszowy-Schlanger, *Les manuscrits hébreux*, pp. 132–37.

26 For the non-standard vocalization of the Codex Reuchlinianus (MS Karlsruhe, Badische Landsbibliothek, Cod. 3), see Shelomo Morag, 'The Vocalisation of Codex Reuchlinianus: Is the "Pre-Masoretic" Bible Pre-Masoretic?', *Journal of Semitic Studies*, 4 (1959), pp. 216–37. For the Italian Bibles reconstructed from fragments, see Chiara Pilocane, *Frammenti dei più antichi manoscritti biblici italiani (secc.*

XI–XII), Quaderni di 'Materia Giudaica' (Florence: Giuntina, 2004). For the non-standard vocalization in Ashkenazi liturgical manuscripts, see esp. Ilan Eldar, *The Hebrew Language Tradition in Medieval Ashkenaz* [in Hebrew], 2 vols (Jerusalem: Publications of the Hebrew University Language Traditions Project, Edah ve-Lashon, 1978).

27 Judith Olszowy-Schlanger, 'A Christian Tradition of Hebrew Vocalization in Medieval England', in *Semitic Studies in Honour of Edward Ullendorf*, ed. by Geoffrey Khan (Leiden and Boston: Brill, 2005), pp. 126–46.

Figure 15.7. Paris, Bibliothèque nationale de France, MS hébr. 113, fol. 12ʳ: ink colour of the corrections, vowels, and Latin translation.

The Trail of Christian Hebraists

Shortly after it was completed by its Hebrew scribe, the text of the Psalter was subjected to careful study and annotation in Latin and Anglo-Norman French by several Christian Hebraists. The outer margins include a Latin translation that corresponds to Jerome's latest version of the Psalter, the Hebraica, and the spaces between the lines of the Hebrew text contain some ad hoc glosses, often in vernacular French. The first Christian Hebraist, unfortunately anonymous, who took possession of the Psalter apparently had no clear plan for annotating it. He proceeded, however, in an orderly fashion, from the beginning of the book, writing his glosses as he read and studied the text. Thus, the types of notes on the initial folios 1ᵛ–4ᵛ differ from those in the rest of the volume. The translation in the margin is incomplete and an alternative translation for some words appears above the Hebrew text. From fol. 5ʳ on, the Latin translation in the margin is more complete, and from the second quire, fol. 9ʳ, it covers almost all the verses, even if in an abbreviated form. There are interlinear 'superscriptio' translations for many words on fols 2ʳ–7ʳ, but these disappear almost completely from fol. 7ᵛ on. The two graphic situations of the translations — regular lines in the margins facing the Hebrew verse and interlinear or irregular marginal additions — on the initial folios correspond, respectively, to two different Latin translations, as explained below. In the opening of Psalm 1 (fol. 1ᵛ), for example, only eight words/expressions have a Latin translation,

five in the margins and three above the relevant Hebrew words. The translations in the margins, introduced by a series of different editorial *signes de renvoi*, correspond to Jerome's Hebraica version of the Psalter. In one case, the editorial symbol refers to the wrong word: it is placed above[28] יִבּוֹל ('[shall not]wither'; Ps. 1:3, Hebraica: '*defluet*') but in the margin, it introduces the translation of the latter part of the same verse: '*et omne quod fecerit prosperabitur*' (וְכֹל אֲשֶׁר יַעֲשֶׂה יַצְלִיחַ, 'and whatever he does, he shall prosper'). Interestingly, the three translations written above the Hebrew words do not correspond to the Vulgate: בַּעֲדַת ('in the congregation'; Ps. 1:5), glossed in the margin with the translation of the Hebraica '*in congregacione*', is translated above the line as '*sinagoga*'; יוֹדֵעַ ('[the Lord] knows'; Ps. 1:6), is translated as '*sciens*' and has no Hebraica translation (which would be *novit*) in the corresponding margin; תֹּאבֵד ('shall perish'; Ps. 1:6) has also only the interlinear translation, '*disperditur*', which differs from the Vulgate ('*peribit*'). Different from both the Hebraica and the Gallicana versions, these three interlinear translations correspond to the '*superscriptio*' translation of these same words in the Psalter in MS LH 21. On the other folios of the first quire, the Hebraica translation is even sparser, except for the titles of the psalms, but there are many interlinear and marginal glosses, which are often very similar to those of the superscription in MS LH 21. As in the case of that Psalter, many translations are into French, and the marginal annotation includes Hebrew words transliterated in Latin characters. Some marginal glosses constitute short word lists, which sometimes note synonyms found in the corresponding psalm. For example, on fol. 3ᵛ, below the Hebrew text of Psalm 5, we find three synonyms for 'sin', written in a vertical column arrangement: 'b *het peccatum grande* /

---

28 When quoting the Hebrew expressions, I follow the extended Tiberian vocalization system of the manuscript.

a *Auon peccatum paruum, scilicet foruee* / c *pesa culpa*' ('b חטא, a big sin / a עוון a small sin, that is (French) 'going astray' c / פשע guilt, fault'). Some notes are basic grammatical analyses, for example, on fol. 5ᵛ, וְכֹכָבִים ('and stars') in Psalm 8:4 there is a succinct comment on the singular and plural forms: '*cocabe stella cocabim stelle*'. A conjugation of אמר ('to say') and נתן ('to give'), written by the scribe of the Hebraica translation under the colophon, with the Latin translations above the forms, shows that our thirteenth-century Hebraist learned to write in square Hebrew characters (Figure 15.2).

BnF hébr. 113 thus faithfully attests to Hebrew learning and study by thirteenth-century Christian Hebraists. Moreover, it also displays a few Hebraists' study notes written in later periods. Among these later hands are two supralinear translations from the fifteenth/sixteenth century: on fol. 5ʳ, *expoliat*, 'polish', glossing, incorrectly, יַשְׁכֵּן in Psalm 7:5 (MT Psalm 7:6); a more correct thirteenth-century note in the corresponding margin glosses this word with the Hebraica translation as '*collocet*' ('will place'), and French '*poserat*' ('[he] will lay'). On fol. 133ʳ, the same later hand added the gloss '*fortis*' ('strong'), above the first word of the colophon, חזק. As modest as they are, these two interventions show that the manuscript was studied by a Christian Hebraist some three hundred years after it was copied.

In addition to the Hebraica translation of the Psalter and the interlinear and marginal glosses on fols 1ᵛ–7ʳ, Christian Hebraists also wrote various notes on the front and back flyleaves. At the front of the book, a small quire of originally six leaves (of which one had been cut off, leaving a stub) was bound together with the Psalter. Its parchment is thin and transparent and its dimensions slightly smaller than those of the Psalter, the latter written on a soft, suede-like insular parchment. This additional quire (today flyleaves I–V) features thirteenth-century business accounts in cursive Latin script on fol. Iʳ. The parchment on which these accounts were recorded was reused for notes by Christian Hebraists. In the corner of fol. Iʳ, a later hand wrote a list of Hebrew vowels with their names in Latin characters. In *c.* 1400, the same scribe added two words in Latin in the middle of the page: '*panis, caro*' ('bread, meat'). It is difficult to ascertain whether these two isolated words allude to the Christian dogma of transubstantiation, the transformation of the Eucharist into Christ's flesh, or whether, more prosaically, the scribe was relating to the accounts on that page.

The verso of this page of accounts and the following pages of the quire include a draft of two distinct Hebrew-Latin word lists (beginning of fol. Iᵛ), both written by the same Latin hand, which differs from that of the scribe who added translations and glosses to the Psalter. The first list has Hebrew words in Hebrew characters translated into Latin, copied in the order of the Hebrew alphabet in long lines from left to right. The second list consists of Hebrew words transliterated in Latin characters. Generous spaces were left between the lines and the lines themselves are not finished, as if the copyist intended to add further items to the list progressively, whilst advancing in the reading of the Hebrew text. This specific page layout suggests that these lists may be drafts which were to be used for the elaboration of a more complete and better organized dictionary.[29] Apart from some inconsistencies, each line is devoted to a different letter of the Hebrew alphabet. The alphabetic order applies only to the first letter of the word. The Hebrew terms were not taken from one particular part of the Hebrew Bible but are, rather, common words found in the Psalter as well as in other parts

---

29 Historians of Latin lexicography have argued that alphabetical glossaries were elaborated in a very similar way, by dividing pages into alphabetical sections and copying words as they were found in a studied text. See Lloyd W. Daly, *Contributions to a History of Alphabetization in Antiquity and the Middle Ages* (Brussels: Latomus, 1967), p. 89.

Figure 15.8. Paris, Bibliothèque nationale de France, MS hébr. 113, fol. 137ᵛ: Hebrew, Greek and Runic alphabets, and a Greek and Graeco-Latin *Pater Noster*.

of the Bible. The Latin translations are written above their Hebrew equivalents.

At the back cover, the Psalter is protected by another inserted quire, originally a *ternio* (three bifolios), of thin, transparent, and slightly irregular parchment (numbered today as folios 135–38). The first folio of this small quire was cut off, which left a stub between fols 134 and 135, and the last was pasted to the back cover. Folio 137ᵛ (Figure 15.8) features three alphabets: Hebrew square letters with their names in Latin characters written above them, a Greek alphabet with similarly superscribed names of Latin letters, and the Runa with their names and their Latin equivalents. It is likely that these alphabets were written by different, albeit contemporary, scribes. The Hebrew alphabet, which imitates the ornate Gothic characters, was traced by a Christian scribe different from both the Jewish scribe of the Psalter and the Christian writer of the glossary on fols IV–V. Between the Greek and Runic alphabets, the Christian scribe wrote the *Pater Noster*, or rather *Pater Ymon*, since he wrote it in ineptly traced Greek letters. The same prayer appears again written in the Greek language but in Latin characters, below the Runa.[30] The presence of the Runa is an additional argument in favour of the insular origin of the manuscript. Although these alphabets were also copied by medieval philologists *avant la lettre* in some continental manuscripts, they represent a well-known English tradition.[31]

Thus, the Latin notes on the front and end leaves, like the palaeographical, linguistic, and historical features of the Psalter, all point towards England as their place of annotation. The difference in the quality of the parchment for the flyleaves (very thin and transparent), their sizes, and the different handwritings on them all suggest that the flyleaves were not a part of the original volume. Their texts evidently come from the same intellectual context of the Christian study of Hebrew (as well as of other exotic languages) but it is difficult to determine whether the flyleaves were together with the Psalter prior to the binding.

The Binding

Let us finally consider the binding of BnF hébr. 113, since it provides important indications on the Psalter's history. It seems that it was only with the current binding that the volume acquired its present form. It was the binder who protected the elegant Hebrew Psalter by inserting additional small quires of similar but not identical dimensions between the manuscript and its front and back covers. These small quires, produced at least partly from recycled financial accounts, feature notes left by at least three thirteenth-century and one fourteenth/fifteenth-century Christian Hebraists.

---

30 For the edition of the prayer, see Dahan, 'Deux psautiers hébraïques', p. 63.

31 For the Runic writing in medieval manuscripts, see René Derolez, *Runica Manuscripts, The English Tradition* (Bruges: Rijksuniversitet te Gent, 1954).

Figure 15.9. Paris, Bibliothèque nationale de France, MS hébr. 113, binding.

The binding itself is blind-stamped dark brown calfskin stretched over thin wooden boards (Figure 15.9). The repetitive decorative patterns were impressed on the moistened calf leather manually, using heated metal stamps and, for repetitive decorated bands, labour-saving cylindrical rolls. The surfaces of both the front and back covers display an intricate decoration. The design is enclosed in a triple fillet framed and divided into four bands vertically and horizontally. The bands are delimited by triple-filleted lines, which intersect at right angles. They create sixteen compartments, the largest central one divided into six panels on each board. The central panels are enclosed within decorated strapwork with the diaper lattice pattern created by triple fillets intersecting diagonally and creating a profusion of small lozenges each decorated in the middle with a quatrefoil motif. The central panels' rolls show the motif of the Tudor rose surmounted with a crown, with the binder's cipher beneath, a fleur-de-lys topped with a crown, and a crowned three-turreted gateway. On the front board, there is an additional tooled pomegranate motif. Originally, the binding had two clasps, which have been lost but left brass nails and an imprint of the strap on the outer edge of the tooled boards. Most importantly for our purpose, the tools imprinted the binder's personal mark. The initials 'n s', separated by a large stylized '4',

Figure 15.10. Paris, Bibliothèque nationale de France, MS hébr. 113, binding: the signature of Nicolas Spierinck.

appear once at the front and twice on the back covers, each time beneath the Tudor rose motif (Figure 15.10). As correctly identified by Michel Garel,[32] this was the monogram of the well-known Cambridge book binder Nicholas Spierinck (or Speyring) (*c.* 1470–1546).

Nicholas Spierinck arrived in Cambridge from Antwerp around 1500. He was a book binder but also a trader in books, probably attracted to the Fenlands' inner port by the growing university's demand for books. A respected member of the community of Cambridge merchants and craftsmen and a warden of St Mary's Church, in 1534 he was appointed Stationer and Printer to the University, together with two fellow Dutchmen, Garret Godfrey and Segar Nicholson.[33] The blind-tooled rolls with his signature and the aforementioned motifs (identical to BnF hébr. 113) have been found on some three hundred different books bound by Spierinck in Cambridge over the first decades of the sixteenth century, which have now reached many libraries around the world.

The Peterhouse Catalogue

The binding of BnF hébr. 113 by Nicholas Spierinck provides the first firm historical evidence of the manuscript's whereabouts, placing it in early sixteenth-century Cambridge.

In order to retrace the trail of the Psalter in Cambridge, I have undertaken a systematic search for all the Hebrew manuscripts known to have

---

32 Garel, *D'une main forte*, p. 91.
33 George J. Gray, *The Earlier Cambridge Stationers and Bookbinders* (Oxford: Oxford University Press, 1904); J. Basil Oldham, *English Blind-stamped Bindings* (Cambridge: Cambridge University Press, 1952); Liam Sims, 'An Early Cambridge Binding by Nicholas Spierink', Cambridge University Library Special Collections Blog, 3 April 2014 (https://specialcollections-blog.lib.cam.ac.uk/).

been held in Cambridge and its environs up to the time of the manuscript's binding. In fact, apart from a few early printed books belonging to John Fisher,[34] very few such manuscripts could be traced. One is a thirteenth-century Psalter borrowed in 1502 by the Provincial Master of the Franciscans, theologian Richard Brinkley (d. 1525), from Bury St Edmunds (today MS Bodleian, Laud Or. 174).[35] Another is a Hebrew-Latin Psalter, produced in Canterbury and held by King's College since its foundation in 1447 until it was taken to the Netherlands by Franciscus Raphelengius around 1564 (today MS Leiden Or. 4725).[36]

In addition, and most importantly for our purpose, two further Hebrew-Latin Psalters are listed in the medieval library catalogue of the oldest Cambridge college, Peterhouse, compiled in 1418.[37] The editors have identified entry n° 74 of this catalogue as the Psalter in MS Lambeth Palace 435. As noted by Raphael Loewe, this manuscript includes a Peterhouse ex libris (Liber Scti Petri), even if the incipit quoted in the 1418 catalogue does not correspond to the manuscript. The

Figure 15.11. Paris, Bibliothèque nationale de France, MS hébr. 113, fol. 132ᵛ: incipit '*laudent*'.

second Psalter in the catalogue, entry n° 73, has not been previously identified. The comparison of the incipits listed in the catalogue - leaves us in no doubt: Peterhouse's Psalter n° 73 is none other than our BnF hébr. 113. The catalogue entry reads as follows: '*Psalterium ebreum cum latino. Incipit in 2° fo. In ma[r]gine laudent in pe'* ('A Hebrew Psalter with Latin. Begins on the 2ⁿᵈ leaf in the margin *laudent*, in the penultimate').[38]

Indeed, this incipit *laudent* corresponds to BnF hébr. 113. It opens the Latin translation column on fol. 132ᵛ (Figure 15.11), which corresponds to יְהַלְלוּ ('they praise'), in Psalm 150:13 in our Psalter (which is MT Psalm 148:13: יְהַלְלוּ אֶת שֵׁם יְהוָה כִּי נִשְׂגָּב שְׁמוֹ לְבַדּוֹ). This is indeed the beginning of the second folio of the Psalter, when the volume is read as a Latin book, from left to right, or the penultimate folio of the volume in its Hebrew direction.

Incidentally, this mention of the incipit as found on second folio of the book confirms that in 1418, when at Peterhouse, the flyleaves with the alphabets and Hebrew glossaries had not yet been bound to the Psalter, as they were not included in the count of the pages of the volume. However, the two Hebrew translations added to the Psalter by a sixteenth-century hand appear

---

34 Peter D. Clarke and Roger Lovatt (eds), *The University and College Libraries of Cambridge*, Corpus of British Medieval Library Catalogues, 10 (London: the British Library in association with the British Academy, 2002), Peterhouse UC48, p. lxxxvii.

35 For Richard Brinkley, see Andrew G. Little, *Franciscan Papers, Lists and Documents* (Manchester: Manchester University Press, 1943), p. 140; Alfred B. Emden, *A Biographical Register of the University of Cambridge to 1500* (Cambridge: Cambridge University Press, 1903), p. 103; Robert Wakefield, *On the Three Languages [1524]*, ed. and trans. by G. Lloyd Jones (Binghamton, NY: Center for Medieval and Early Renaissance Studies, 1989), p. 35. On MS Bodleian, Laud Or. 174, see Smalley, *The Study of the Bible*, p. 342; Olszowy-Schlanger, *Les manuscrits hébreux*, pp. 266–70.

36 Gerard I. Lieftinck, 'The "Psalterium Hebraicum" from St Augustine's Canterbury Rediscovered in the Scaliger Bequest at Leiden', *Transactions of the Cambridge Bibliographical Society*, 2/2 (1955), pp. 97–104; Olszowy-Schlanger, *Les manuscrits hébreux*, pp. 205–11.

37 Clarke and Lovatt, p. 465.

38 Clarke and Lovatt, p. 465.

to confirm its study and annotation by an early Renaissance Hebraist.

Conclusions

The identification of BnF hébr. 113 with entry n° 73 of Peterhouse's medieval catalogue reveals one stage in the manuscript's history. It shows that the thirteenth-century school of Christian Hebraism which produced the Latin annotations and translation in the Psalter was not totally forgotten in the following centuries. The manuscript found its way to an important house of learning, was kept in its library and carefully catalogued some two hundred years after it was written, and someone read and annotated it in the Tudor period. It is likely that it was bound by Nicholas Spierinck when it was still in Peterhouse's possession. There are other volumes from the Peterhouse Library which were bound by the same workshop. The fact that the volume has a high-quality binding shows that it was valued. It is difficult to reconstruct the circumstances in which the book left its safe place on a shelf in a Cambridge College. It might have happened at the same time as the removal of the other Hebrew-Latin Psalter, n° 74 in the 1418 catalogue, which may be today MS 465 of Lambeth Palace Library in London. MS 465 includes notes in a sixteenth-century Latin hand, perhaps penned by Robert Wakefield, the first teacher of Hebrew in Tudor Cambridge and the first professor of Hebrew at Oxford.[39] Wakefield collected several Hebrew manuscripts from monastic and evidently also college libraries, but his private library was removed (stolen in Wakefield's words) from his house in London shortly before 1534.[40] Be that as it may, the manuscript (BnF hébr. 113 today) travelled to France in the second half of the sixteenth century to finally become part of the library of a leading Parisian humanist of his time.

---

39 Judith Olszowy-Schlanger, '"My Silent Teachers" – Hebrew Manuscripts as the Source of Robert Wakefield's Hebraism' in *Hebraism in Sixteenth-Century England: Robert and Thomas Wakefield*, ed. by James P. Carley and Charles Burnett (Toronto: Pontifical Institute of Medieval Studies, 2023).

40 On Wakefield, see esp. Wakefield, *On the Three Languages [1524]*.

ILONA STEIMANN

A Forced Journey between Two Faiths

The Hebrew Manuscripts of the University of Vienna*

Introduction

In a letter to King Matthias written in 1611, Sebastian Tengnagel (1563–1636), the chief librarian of the Vienna Hofbibliothek ('Court Library', the precursor of the Österreichische Nationalbibliothek), said that the University of Vienna owned twelve or thirteen large Hebrew manuscripts, among which were '*antiquissima Biblia Hebraica*' ('incredibly old Hebrew Bibles'). These Hebrew manuscripts were no longer in use, he continued, and were gradually being destroyed by bookworms and moths. Tengnagel asked the king to transfer these volumes to the Hofbibliothek, where they would be better preserved.[1] Despite the librarian's efforts, the Hebrew books he saw at the university only became part of the Hofbibliothek more than a hundred years later when the university libraries and the Hofbibliothek were combined in 1756.

This group of Hebrew manuscripts included the university's oldest Hebraica holdings, which had come into its possession when Jews were expelled from Vienna and its surroundings in 1421. The book-collecting activities of Christian Hebraists are a subject of growing scholarly interest,[2] but these kinds of Christian institutional collections of books in Hebrew are a much less well-known phenomenon in the history of Christian Hebraica. Although the new keepers of

---

* The research for this essay was funded by the Deutsche Forschungsgemeinschaft (DFG, German Research Foundation) in connection with Germany's Excellence Strategy – EXC 2176 'Understanding Written Artefacts: Material, Interaction and Transmission in Manuscript Cultures', project no. 390893796. It was conducted within the scope of work conducted at the Centre for the Study of Manuscript Cultures (CSMC) at the University of Hamburg, Germany.

1 Vienna, Österreichische Nationalbibliothek (ÖNB), Cod. 9737q, fol. 40ʳ; also see Arthur Z. Schwarz, *Die hebräischen Handschriften der Nationalbibliothek in Wien* (Vienna: Strache, 1925), pp. xi–xii.

2 The term 'Hebraist' usually suggests a certain degree of mastery of the Hebrew language. See Matt Goldish, *Judaism in the Theology of Sir Isaac Newton* (Dordrecht: Klewer, 1998), pp. 17–19; Aaron Katchen, *Christian Hebraists and Dutch Rabbis: Seventeenth Century Apologetics and the Study of Maimonides' Mishneh Torah* (Cambridge, MA: Harvard University Press, 1985), p. 9. Regarding fifteenth-century Christian Hebraica collections, see, e.g., Wolfgang von Abel and Reimund Leicht, *Verzeichnis der Hebraica in der Bibliothek Johannes Reuchlins* (Ostfildern: Jan Thorbecke, 2005); Bernard Walde, *Christliche Hebraisten Deutschlands am Ausgang des Mittelalters* (Münster i. W.: Aschendorff, 1916).

Ilona Steimann • Hochschule für Jüdische Studien, Heidelberg

the Hebrew books held in universities, city halls, and monasteries were rarely able to read Hebrew themselves, they attributed a range of contrary meanings to these Jewish objects and treated them accordingly. In a bid to clarify the role that Hebrew books played among Christians and the way they were used, in this essay I reconstruct the history of the Hebraica collection of the University of Vienna. I explore the way Viennese theologians selected Hebrew manuscripts for the university, what meanings they attributed to them, and how they bridged the gap between the language and content of these manuscripts and their Christian audiences. In particular, I analyse the Latin and German annotations added to those Hebrew codices as a key for coming to grips with the various ways that Christian dealt with Hebraica.

The Vienna *Gezerah* and the Confiscation of Jewish Books

As a result of the alleged Hussite-Jewish conspiracy and other Jewish 'crimes' against Christianity, Jews were expelled from Vienna and its environs in 1421. This event, which later became known as the Vienna *Gezerah* ('edict') — a term Arthur Goldmann coined on the basis of a sixteenth-century Yiddish account[3] — was the culmination of the tension that had been increasing between the Christian and Jewish communities in the region. Two years earlier in 1419 while German forces were preparing to conduct a war in Bohemia against Hussite heretics, theologians at the University of Vienna discussed the issue of the local 'enemies' of the Christian Church, that is, the Jews, who were thought to have plotted with the Hussites.[4] Whether or not there really was any Hussite-Jewish collaboration is unknown, but the alleged Jewish support of the Hussite movement could have posed a threat to the empire.[5] Coupled with the accusation that Jews had desecrated the host in the town of Enns,[6] this led to the persecution and final expulsion of the Jews from the Duchy of Austria.

In this atmosphere of growing hostility, the real reasons for the persecution were largely economic: the high cost of the anti-Hussite campaigns and the forthcoming wedding of the Duke Albrecht V of Austria, and Elisabeth, the daughter of Emperor Sigismund posed a financial challenge that the duke planned to resolve by confiscating Jewish property. An examination of related archival documents on ducal administration enabled scholars to estimate the economic impact of confiscated Jewish houses and other Jewish goods on the finances of the Duchy of Austria and to assess

---

3 Arthur Goldmann, *Das Judenbuch der Scheffstrasse zu Wien (1389–1420)* (Vienna: Wilhelm Braumüller, 1908), pp. 112–14. The most detailed treatment of the *Gezerah* appears in Samuel Krauss, *Die Wiener Geserah vom Jahre 1421* (Vienna: Wilhelm Braumüller, 1920).

4 Paul Uiblein, *Die Akten der theologischen Fakultät der Universität Wien (1396–1508)*, 2 vols (Vienna: Verband der Wissenschaftlichen Gesellschaften Österreichs, 1978), I, p. 37.

5 See Klaus Lohrmann, 'Fürsten zwischen Recht und Raub: Zu den finanziellen Aspekten von Judenvertreibungen im Mittelalter und in der frühen Neuzeit', *Österreich in Geschichte und Literatur*, 318/3 (2002), pp. 142–51 (p. 143). Several sources do actually reveal signs of interaction between Hussites and Jews. See Michael Shank, *Unless You Believe, You Shall not Understand: Logic, University, and Society in Late Medieval Vienna* (Princeton: Princeton University Press, 2016), pp. 188–89; also see Israel J. Yuval, 'Juden, Hussiten und Deutsche nach einer hebräischen Chronik', in *Juden in der christlichen Umwelt während des späten Mittelalters*, ed. by Alfred Haverkamp and Franz-Josef Ziwes (Berlin: Duncker & Humblot, 1992), pp. 59–102.

6 Goldmann, *Das Judenbuch*, pp. 132–33; Miri Rubin, *Gentile Tales: The Narrative Assault on Late Medieval Jews* (Philadelphia: University of Pennsylvania Press, 2004), pp. 116–19.

the magnitude of repayments agreed to in Jewish promissory notes.⁷

Additional income was expected from the sale of Jewish manuscripts confiscated on the same occasion. After the confiscation, the manuscripts were removed to the *Hubhaus*, which was the building used by the duke's fiscal administration and served as a transfer point for the books.⁸ In 1455, the son of Duke Albrecht V, Ladislaus 'the Posthumous' (who was king of Bohemia in 1453–1457), asked that Emperor Friedrich III return his late father's property. The items he mentioned included Jewish books in the *Hubhaus* that Albrecht V had confiscated from the Austrian Jews, which Ladislaus said were worth more than 3000 guldens.⁹ Just how many books would have cost more than 3000 guldens can be deduced from the fees recorded in two Hebrew manuscripts from the Vienna *Gezerah* that ended up at the University of Vienna; a price of 8 guldens was noted in German in each of these volumes (ÖNB, Cod. hebr. 11 and ÖNB, Cod. hebr. 15).¹⁰ Thus, the sum of money that Ladislaus mentioned suggests that that the duke kept between 300 and 400 Jewish manuscripts after the expulsion.

However, the information about the Hebraica in the *Hubhaus*, which apparently reflected the initial number of confiscated books, was outdated by 1455: Ladislaus seems to have been unaware of the fact that shortly after the confiscation, many of the books were resold to local binders for use as binder's waste or to other interested parties, among them theologians at the University of Vienna. Around a month after the expulsion, on 9 April 1421, the theologians there commissioned two professors, Nicholas of Dinkelsbühl (1366–1433) and Peter of Pulkau (*c.* 1370–1425) to acquire Hebraica for the university:

> [U]t laborarent pro aliquibus libris ebrayce lingwe saltem melioribus et magis correctis aput dominum principem et alibi iuxta consilium doctorum iuris vel alias, secundum quod ipsis melius expedire videretur pro universitate et theologica facultate.
>
> ([T]o strive before the duke and elsewhere [to obtain] some Hebrew books — at least better and more correct ones — in accordance with the advice of the doctors of law and others, according to what would seem to them best for the university and the theological faculty.)¹¹

Under these circumstances, the theologians obtained a number of Hebrew manuscripts for the University of Vienna and their own private collections, which they later bequeathed to the university. These were the same theologians who played an active part in inciting and supporting anti-Jewish propaganda and contributed considerably to the persecution of 1420–1421 by preaching against the Jews and being involved in other anti-Jewish public activities.¹² Unlike the Jews themselves, who were supposed to

---

7   The economic conditions were analysed in a paper by Petr Elbel and Wolfram Ziegler: 'Am schwarczen suntag mardert man dieselben juden, all die zaigten vill guets an under der erden… Die Wiener Gesera: eine Neubetrachtung', in *'Avigdor, Benesch, Gitl'. Juden in Böhmen, Mähren und Schlesien im Mittelalter. Samuel Steinherz zum Gedenken (1857 Güssing–1942 Theresienstadt)*, ed. by Helmut Teufel, Pavel Kocman, and others (Brünn: Essen Klartext-Verlag, 2016), pp. 201–68 (pp. 224–60).
8   Regarding the use of the *Hubhaus* as a transition point for books, see Theodor Gottlieb, *Die Ambraser Handschriften. Beitrag zur Geschichte der Wiener Hofbibliothek* (Leipzig: Spirgatis, 1900), p. 33.
9   Gottlieb, pp. 5–6; Schwarz, p. ix note 4.
10 ÖNB, Cod. hebr. 11, fol. 1ʳ ('VIII gulden') and Cod. hebr. 15, fol. 2ʳ ('VIII gulden').
11 Uiblein, I, pp. 41–42; trans. in Shank, p. 197.
12 For example, see Christopher Ocker, 'German Theologians and the Jews in the Fifteenth Century', in *Jews, Judaism and the Reformation in Sixteenth-Century Germany*, ed. by Dean P. Bell and Stephen G. Burnett (Leiden: Brill, 2006), pp. 33–65 (pp. 37–45).

disappear, some of their books were meant to be preserved, especially those with biblical content that represented the focus of Christian theological investigations at the time.

'Antiquissima Biblia Hebraica'

Among the incredibly old volumes of the Hebrew Bible that Tengnagel saw in the university library in 1611 and mentioned in his letter to King Matthias was a monumental manuscript of the Ashkenazi Masoretic Bible, now preserved in the Österreichische Nationalbibliothek, which included the Pentateuch, Prophets, and Writings (ÖNB, Cod. hebr. 4).[13] At the end of that codex, its scribe, Solomon ben Isaac ha-Levi, wrote a colophon in which he mentioned the name of his patron, Pfefferkorn ben Shemariyah, and the date of completion, 1344.[14]

In regard to the provenance of this manuscript, some information can be gathered from the owner notes. Pfefferkorn ben Shemariyah or another Jewish owner of ÖNB, Cod. hebr. 4 marked the word *shum* in Deuteronomy 17:15 ('You may indeed set over you a king whom') and interpreted it in the margin a שפירא, וורמשא, מגנצא ('Speyer, Worms, Mainz').[15] The ShUM communities, named after the sounds of the initial letters of each of those cities, formed the Rhineland league of Jewish settlements that was the centre of Ashkenazi Jewish life in the Middle Ages. The mention of the ShUM communities may indicate that the manuscript was used in that area. It is possible that ÖNB, Cod. hebr. 4 was taken from the Upper Rhine area and eventually arrived in Austria in the wake of the pogroms during the Black Death pandemic in 1348–1349 when the ShUM communities were virtually destroyed.[16] Another Jewish owner's inscription attests that the manuscript remained in Jewish hands until at least 1419 and was apparently confiscated upon the Jews' expulsion from Vienna and its environs in 1420/1421.[17]

Its first Christian owner, Heinrich Fleckel of Kitzbühel (d. 1437), a professor of jurisprudence and chancellor at the University of Vienna, must have acquired the manuscript directly from the duke.[18] Together with Nicholas of Dinkelsbühl, Fleckel attended the Council of Constance (1414–1418), which was convened primarily to end the papal schism and achieve ecclesiastical unity by condemning the Hussite movement.[19] As a personal delegate of Duke Albrecht V, Fleckel evidently had connections to

---

13 Schwarz, pp. 1–2, no. 1. Although ÖNB, Cod. hebr. 4 only includes *masorah parva* (the small Masorah) in addition to the Pentateuch, the three and four lines of ruling in the upper and lower margins suggest that the manuscript was designed to include *masorah magna* (the large Masorah) as well, although it was not actually completed.

14 ÖNB, Cod. hebr. 4, fol. 508ʳ.

15 ÖNB, Cod. hebr. 4, fol. 123ʳ.

16 Rainer J. Barzen, 'Die Schumgemeinden und ihre Rechtssatzungen. Geschichte und Wirkungsgeschichte', in *Die SchUM-Gemeinden: Speyer – Worms – Mainz: Auf dem Weg zum Welterbe*, ed. by Pis Heberer and Ursula Reuter (Regensburg: Schnell and Steiner, 2013), pp. 23–35 (pp. 32–33).

17 ÖNB, Cod. hebr. 4, fol. 1ʳ.

18 For more on Heinrich Fleckel, see *Die Matrikel der Universität Wien: Im Auftrag des Akademischen Senats herausgegeben vom Archiv der Universität Wien*, ed. by Franz Gall, Kurt Mühlberger, and others, 8 vols (Graz: Böhlau, 1956–2014), I (1956), pp. 23 and 75; Uiblein, I, p. 36.

19 Ansgar Frenken, 'Gelehrte auf dem Konzil: Fallstudien zur Bedeutung und Wirksamkeit der Universitätsangehörigen auf dem Konstanzer Konzil', in *Die Konzilien von Pisa (1409), Konstanz (1414–1418) und Basel (1431–1449): Institution und Personen*, ed. by Johannes Helmrath and Heribert Müller (Ostfildern: Jan Thorbecke, 2007), pp. 107–47 (p. 111 note 14); Dieter Girgensohn, 'Die Universität Wien und das Konstanzer Konzil', in *Das Konzil von Konstanz. Beiträge zu seiner Geschichte und Theologie*, ed. by August Franzen and Wolfgang Müller (Freiburg i. Br.: Herder, 1964), pp. 252–81 (p. 256).

Figure 16.1. Hebrew Bible, Ashkenaz, 1344. Vienna, Österreichische Nationalbibliothek, Cod. hebr. 4, fol. 1ᵛ.

the duke and so was able to obtain Hebraica. In 1431, Fleckel donated ÖNB, Cod. hebr. 4 to the Collegium Ducale ('Duke's College', 1384–1623) of the University of Vienna so that it could be used by its scholars, Paul Leubman of Melk (d. 1479), Augustine of Vienna, and Georius of Herzogenburg. The inscription on the donation reads as follows (Figure 16.1):

> Istam Bibliam donauit collegio theologorum et artistarum in Wienna venerabilis pater et dominus magister Henricus de Kitzpuhl artium et decretorum doctor etc. Tali sub conditione quod honorabiles et sanctifici magistri Paulus de Mellico, Augustinus de Wienna et Georius de Hertzenburga habeant usum eius ad vitam ipsorum 1431. Cui deus retribuat in vita aeterna.

> (The venerable Father and Lord, Master Heinrich of Kitzpuhl, Doctor of Arts and Theology, gave this Bible to the College of Theology and Arts [Collegium Ducale] in Vienna on condition that the honourable and sanctified masters Paul of Melk, Augustine of Vienna and Georius of Herzogenburg would use it their whole lives, 1431. May God reward him with eternal life.)[20]

The same hand — apparently that of a librarian who documented Fleckel's donation — stated that the volume was the property of the Collegium Ducale.[21] The Collegium was the oldest part of the University of Vienna and the heart of its Faculty of Theology.[22] Its library contained manuscripts that were used for teaching the arts and theology and was a general collection of works on the humanities, so it served as the

---

20 ÖNB, Cod. hebr. 4, fol. 1ᵛ. The same hand repeated a similar note on fol. 508ᵛ. According to this note, when Kitzbühel donated ÖNB, Cod. hebr. 4 in 1431, he was serving as *Domdekan* (head priest) in Passau Cathedral ('*patauiensis ecclesiae decanus*'); cf. Birgit Studt, *Papst Martin V. (1417–1431) und die Kirchenreform in Deutschland* (Cologne: Böhlau, 2004), p. 100 note 39.

21 ÖNB, Cod. hebr. 4, fols 234ᵛ and 399ᵛ: '*Ista Biblia est collegij ducalis in Wienna*' ('This Bible is from the Collegium Ducale in Vienna').

22 Joseph Aschbach, *Geschichte der Wiener Universität*, 3 vols (Vienna: Verlag der k.k. Universität, 1865–1888), I (1865), pp. 30–42. On the development of the university district, see Kurt Mühlberger, 'The Old University Quarter: The Medieval University', in *Sites of Knowledge: The University of Vienna and Its Buildings: A History 1365–2015*, ed. by Julia Rüdiger and Dieter Schweizer (Vienna: Böhlau, 2015), pp. 13–42 (pp. 22–41).

main library of the university.²³ As such, it was the most appropriate place to house Hebraica.

As a rule, only graduate members had access to the university's books; young students were not allowed to enter the libraries at all.²⁴ Yet Fleckel wanted to limit the group of potential users of the manuscript even further, viz. to those who could actually read Hebrew. Two of the recipients of ÖNB, Cod. hebr. 4, Paul Leubman of Melk (Mellico) and Augustine of Vienna, were converts from Judaism and had apparently been baptized as a result of the Vienna *Gezerah*.²⁵ As the registers of the Faculty of Arts show, Paul, neophyte of Melk, and Augustine, neophyte of Vienna, took Bachelor's exams at the Faculty of Arts in the winter term of 1427.²⁶ Both of them earned the status of 'licentiates' in 1429 and undertook Master's studies in 1430, which allowed them to teach at the university and to continue their studies in order to obtain a doctorate at the Faculty of Theology.²⁷ Thus, it is possible that they were given ÖNB, Cod. hebr. 4 on the occasion of their graduation as Masters of Arts in 1431.

The more successful of the two, Paul of Melk, continued to pursue an academic career after he converted. As well as occupying important positions in the Church, he served as dean of the Faculty of Arts and later as chancellor of the university.²⁸ We hear about Paul of Melk again in 1438 when he asked for help from Empress Elisabeth in a search for his aunt, a Jewess, and her child in Pressburg (Bratislava).²⁹ Paul owned numerous Latin manuscripts, most of which he bequeathed to the Collegium Ducale.³⁰

Although baptized when young, both neophytes must have had a good command of the

---

23 *Mittelalterliche Bibliothekskataloge Österreichs*, ed. by Theodor Gottlieb, Arthur Goldmann, and others, 5 vols (Vienna: Adolf Holzhausen, 1915–1971), I (1915), pp. 463–64. In addition to the library of the Collegium Ducale, each of the corporations of the University of Vienna (faculties, colleges, and *bursae*) had its own library. See Friedrich Simader, *Bücher aus der mittelalterlichen Universität Wien und ihrem Umfeld* (Vienna: Online-Datenbank, from 2007 onwards) https://webarchiv.onb.ac.at/web/20150803112700/http://www.onb.ac.at/sammlungen/hschrift/kataloge/universitaet/Bursenbibliotheken.htm [accessed in June 2021].

24 Nina Knieling, 'Libraries as Repositories of Knowledge for Teaching and Research', in *Sites of Knowledge. The University of Vienna and Its Buildings: A History 1365–2015*, ed. by Julia Rüdiger and Dieter Schweizer (Vienna: Böhlau, 2015), pp. 111–20 (p. 111).

25 ÖNB, Cod. hebr. 4, fols 1ᵛ and 508ᵛ.

26 Vienna, Archiv der Universität, Ph 7. For Paul of Melk, see fols 87ᵛ–88ʳ; published in *Acta Facultatis Artium*, ed. by Thomas Maisel, Ingrid Matschinegg, and others, 4 vols (Vienna: Archiv der Universität Wien, 2007), II, nos 5111 and 5116; For Augustinus of Vienna, see fols 87ᵛ–88ʳ (*Acta Facultatis Artium*, II, nos 5701 and 5117).

27 Archiv der Universität, Ph 7, fols 99ᵛ, 101ʳ, 103ᵛ, etc.: Paul of Melk, in *Acta Facultatis Artium*, II, nos 5643, 5690, 5791, etc.; fols 99ᵛ, 101ʳ, 109ʳ, etc.: Augustinus of Vienna, in *Acta Facultatis Artium*, II, nos 5644, 5691, 5963, etc. Georius of Herzogenburg is also mentioned in the registers of the Faculty of Arts, but it seems he was not a convert; see Archiv der Universität, Ph 7, fol. 80ʳ, etc. in *Acta Facultatis Artium*, II, no. 4952, etc. On the structure of studies at medieval universities, see, e.g., James A. Weisheipl, 'The Structure of the Arts Faculty in the Medieval University', *British Journal of Educational Studies*, 19/3 (1971), pp. 263–71.

28 Uiblein, II, pp. 252, 257, 266, and 689; also see Martha Keil, 'What Happened to the "New Christians"? The "Viennese Geserah" of 1420/21 and the Forced Baptism of the Jews', in *Jews and Christians in Medieval Europe: The Historiographical Legacy of Bernhard Blumenkranz*, ed. by Philippe Buc, Martha Keil, and others (Turnhout: Brepols, 2016), pp. 97–114 (pp. 109–11).

29 Krauss, pp. 142–43.

30 Paul of Melk bequeathed twelve manuscripts to the Collegium Ducale and one manuscript and one printed book to *Rosenburse*. Another manuscript that he copied ended up in the Benedictine abbey of Schottenstift in Vienna (Cod. 144) (Simader, *Bücher: Die Bibliothek der Rosenburse* https://webarchiv.onb.ac.at/web/20150803112710/http://www.onb.ac.at/sammlungen/hschrift/kataloge/universitaet/Rosenburse.htm [accessed in June 2021]); cf. *Mittelalterliche Bibliothekskataloge Österreichs*, I, pp. 465 and 478.

Hebrew language by then, which would have made them an important channel for Viennese theologians who wished to gain access to Jewish books. However, there is no direct evidence of their involvement in annotating ÖNB, Cod. hebr. 4 in Latin and German (which will be discussed below). While none of the Latin/German hands that added notes to this codex in the Collegium are identical to Paul of Melk's,[31] the handwritings of the other two recipients, Augustine of Vienna and Georius of Herzogenburg, are unknown, as there are no extant examples of their script for comparison. Yet even if these or other converts who had been baptized as a result of the Vienna *Gezerah* and obtained academic degrees at the University of Vienna[32] did not inscribe the manuscript personally, they must have helped (possibly orally) to render the content of the Hebrew books accessible to their Christian colleagues.

At the beginning of the sixteenth century, the humanist scholar and chancellor of the university, Georg Ratzenberger, borrowed ÖNB, Cod. hebr. 4 from the Collegium and kept it until his death in 1537. In his last will and testament, he noted '*Ain grosse Bibell mit hebreischen puechstaben auf pergamen listig geschriben*' ('A large Bible written in Hebrew letters on parchment') which should be given back to the Collegium Ducale, apparently referring to ÖNB, Cod. hebr. 4.[33] However, according to a note by Leonardus Villinus, a professor at the Faculty of Theology and a former chancellor of the university, the manuscript was only returned to the Collegium in 1558.[34]

In the second half of the seventeenth century, ÖNB, Cod. hebr. 4 was removed from the Collegium yet again when it was sold to the Augustinian Monastery of Sts Roch and Sebastian in Vienna.[35] Martin Rosnak, the biographer of Xystus Schier (1727–1772), the historian and librarian of that monastery, described ÖNB, Cod. hebr. 4 as a rare and extremely valuable manuscript of the Bible and noted that Schier obtained it from the University of Vienna's Faculty of Theology for 30 gold coins.[36] With the secularization of the monastery in 1812, ÖNB, Cod. hebr. 4 came into the possession of the Hofbibliothek.

'*Libri Collegii Ducalis*'

The earliest extant book inventory that mentions the University of Vienna's Hebrew manuscripts was compiled by Sebastian Tengnagel in 1623. Around a month before Emperor Ferdinand II's *Sanctio pragmatica* ('pragmatic sanction') came into force, which allowed the Jesuits to take over

---

31 See Paul of Melk's handwriting in ÖNB, Cod. 4867, fol. 1ʳ.

32 For details of other converts at the University of Vienna, see Keil, 'What Happened to the "New Christians"?', pp. 111–12.

33 Martin Roland, *Die Handschriften der alten Wiener Stadtbibliothek in der Österreichischen Nationalbibliothek* (Vienna: Wiener Stadt- und Landesbibliothek, 1999), p. 27 note 30.

34 ÖNB, Cod. hebr. 4, fol. 508ᵛ: '*Restitui bibliothece collegii archiducalis Leonardus Villinus theologus doctor 58 anno mense aprili*' ('Doctor of Theology Leonardus Villinus returned it to the Collegium Ducale's library in April 1558'). For more about Leonardus Villinus, see Hermann Göhler, *Das Wiener Kollegiat-, nachmals Domkapitel zu Sankt Stephan in Wien 1365–1554* (Vienna: Böhlau, 2015), p. 543.

35 ÖNB, Cod. hebr. 4, front flyleafᵛ: '*Bibliotheca Augustin. Vien in Via Regia*' ('Library of Augustinians. Vienna in Via Regia').

36 ÖNB, Cod. 7429, fol. 37ᵛ. See Ferdinand L. Miksch, 'Der Augustinerhistoriker Xystus Schier 1727–1772: Ein Beitrag zur österreichischen Gelehrtengeschichte am Beginn der Aufklärung', *Augustiniana*, 18 (1968), pp. 333–97 (p. 360 note 68). Around the same time, members of the University of Vienna also donated some Latin codices to the monastery, such as ÖNB, Cod. 2052, Cod. 2911 and Cod. 3419 (*Mittelalterliche Bibliothekskataloge Österreichs*, I, pp. 471–72).

most of the university and its libraries,[37] Tengnagel visited the university and made excerpts from its book catalogues.[38] The Hebraica appear in the first section of his inventory under the letter A and includes thirty-one titles (Appendix A: I).[39] Tengnagel listed the title of each volume (generic and often corrupted), its size (folio or quarto), and its material if it was parchment. In most cases, the manuscripts were also denoted by the abbreviation MS.[40]

A closer look at Tengnagel's inventory reveals that the Hebrew section combined at least two collections: the Hebrew manuscripts of the University of Vienna and the Hebraica that came from the collection of Bishop Johann Fabri of Vienna (1478–1541), which he bequeathed to the Collegium Trilingue ('Trilingual College' — an institution he himself had established for poor students) before his death.[41] That Tengnagel's inventory clearly embraced Fabri's collection follows from the mention of '*10 partes, fol.*'

('ten volumes, in folio') in reference to the Talmud, which appear in the catalogue of Fabri's library (twelve volumes) (Appendix A: I. 30).[42] These volumes, which are now housed at the Österreichische Nationalbibliothek, are the Bomberg *editio princeps* of the Babylonian Talmud, printed in Venice in 1520–1523.[43] Other printed editions in Tengnagel's inventory can also be traced back to Fabri's catalogue. For example, '*Biblia in 4°. No. 401*' ('Bible in quarto, no. 401') in Tengnagel's inventory obviously corresponds to '*401 Liber hebraicus*' ('401: A Hebrew book') in Fabri's catalogue (Appendix A: I. 13).[44] The same apparently holds true for Nathan ben Yehiel's lexicon on the Talmud *He-'arukh* ('Compendium') on paper (?) in quarto mentioned in both Fabri's catalogue and Tengnagel's inventory (Appendix A: I. 27).[45] However, the medieval Hebrew manuscripts in Tengnagel's inventory did not come from Fabri's library. They were the oldest Hebraica holdings of the University of Vienna, which were acquired after the Vienna *Gezerah*, and must correspond to the twelve or thirteen volumes that Tengnagel saw at the university in 1611.

When the university's books were transferred to the Hofbibliothek in 1756, the inventory of these new arrivals, which Xystus Schier copied in the same year, referred to sixteen Hebraica volumes, a number close to what Tengnagel mentioned in

---

37 On Jesuit reforms at the University of Vienna, see Tobias E. Hämmerle, 'Die Wiener Universität zur Zeit des Dreißigjährigen Krieges: Der studentische Alltag und die Universität Wien an der Wende vom 16. zum 17. Jahrhundert', *Studien zur Wiener Geschichte – Jahrbuch des Vereins für Geschichte der Stadt Wien*, 75 (2019), pp. 7–35; Rudolf Kink, *Geschichte der kaiserlichen Universität zu Wien*, 2 vols (Vienna: Gerold, 1854), I.1, pp. 308–63.

38 ÖNB, Cod. 9690, fols 219ᵛ–225ʳ; *Mittelalterliche Bibliothekskataloge Österreichs*, I, p. 471.

39 ÖNB, Cod. 9690, fols 219ʳ–219ᵛ; published in Schwarz, p. xii.

40 If the material of which the item was made goes unmentioned and the abbreviation MS does not appear in the description, then it stands to reason that the item was a printed book (Appendix A: I. 4, 13–15, 26–31).

41 Leo Helbling, *Dr Johann Fabri Generalvikar von Konstanz und Bischof von Wien 1478–1541* (Münster i. W.: Aschendorff, 1941), p. 135. For more on Fabri's book collection, see Alphons Lhotsky, 'Die Bibliothek des Bischofs von Wien Dr Johann *Fabri* (1530–1541)', in *Festschrift Karl Eder zum siebzigsten Geburtstag*, ed. by Helmut J. Mezler-Andelberg (Innsbruck: Universitätsverlag-Wagner, 1959), pp. 71–81; Friedrich Simader, 'Materialien zur Bibliothek des Wiener

Bischofs Johannes Fabri', in *Iohannes Cuspinianus, 1473–1529*, ed. by Christian Gastgeber and Elisabeth Klecker (Vienna: Praesens Verlag, 2012), pp. 268–85.

42 Fabri's catalogue: Archiv der Universität, R 44.2, fol. 2ʳ; Simader, 'Materialien', p. 280.

43 ÖNB, 20.N.2.(1–12). The Talmud was an especially valuable item in Fabri's library and was explicitly referred to in the statutes of the Collegium Trilingue as a work available for study there. See Arthur Goldmann, 'Die Universität. 1529–1740', in *Geschichte der Stadt Wien*, ed. by Anton Mayer, 6 vols (Vienna: Adolf Holzhausen; Alterthumsverein zu Wien, 1897–1918), VI (1918), pp. 1–205 (p. 162 note 3).

44 Archiv der Universität, R 44.2, fol. 17ʳ, no. 401.

45 Archiv der Universität, R 44.2, fol. 2ᵛ, no. 22.

his letter of 1611 (Appendix A: II).⁴⁶ A slightly larger number is reflected in a later inventory of the university's Hebrew books that was compiled by Johann Locher in 1775 (Appendix A: III).⁴⁷ That list mentions fourteen manuscripts, five of which are in two copies ('*in duplo*'), suggesting that there were nineteen codices in all. Locher also noted two printed items: a two-volume Pentateuch and Fabri's Talmud (Appendix A: III. 15–16).

There is not enough information in the inventories about each book, so we cannot always identify the actual manuscripts in the Österreichische Nationalbibliothek that they describe. Only two codices can be identified with certainty on the basis of Locher's list. One of them is 'Bible, Pentateuch with historical books written by Menahem the scribe, son of Eliezer' (Appendix A: III. 3), which obviously corresponds to one of the many biblical codices mentioned in Tengnagel's and Schier's inventories (Appendix B: 5). This volume is the liturgical Pentateuch copied by Menahem ben Eliezer for Simeon ben Simeon in 1302 (the aforementioned ÖNB, Cod. hebr. 11).⁴⁸ Its codicological features, such as the parchment with distinguishable sides, pricking in the inner and outer margins, ruling by plummet, and the palaeographical characteristics of its script point to its having been produced in France.⁴⁹ The manuscript may have been taken to Austria when the Jews of France were expelled in 1394.⁵⁰ A former Jewish owner, possibly one of those whose names appear on many folios of ÖNB, Cod. hebr. 11, mentioned the date 1367 in a note about the Jewish calendar.⁵¹ Shortly after ÖNB, Cod. hebr. 11 left Jewish hands, Latin annotations were added to it by its new Christian owners (to be discussed shortly).

Another manuscript that can be identified from Locher's inventory is 'Holy Bible starting from Joshua with the rest of the books and with images drawn by a reed pen, with vocalization, on parchment' (Appendix A: III. 6). This is the volume of Prophets and Writings with *masorah magna* and *masorah parva* that was copied in Franconia in 1298 (ÖNB, Cod. hebr. 16) and it obviously corresponds to one of the four manuscripts of Prophets listed in Tengnagel's and Schier's inventories (Appendix B: 9).⁵² This manuscript is decorated with micrographic floral and geometrical patterns and figurative images, a fact that Locher explicitly indicated in his inventory. In the colophon, written in the bottom margin of forty successive pages of the Psalter, its vocalizer-masorete Aberzush recounted the Rintfleisch massacres, in which thousands of Jews were killed in the southwest

---

46 ÖNB, Cod. 9520, fols 34ʳ–52ᵛ; published in Schwarz, p. xiv.
47 ÖNB, Cod. 7707, pp. 72–73, 83, 122, 128, 133, 143 and 169; published in Schwarz, pp. xiii–xiv.
48 ÖNB, Cod. hebr. 11, fol. 253ᵛ (Schwarz, pp. 12–13, no. 14).
49 Malachi Beit-Arié, *Hebrew Codicology: Historical and Comparative Typology of Hebrew Medieval Codices Based on the Documentation of the Extant Dated Manuscripts Using a Quantitative Approach* (English Internet version 0.4, February 2020), pp. 233–39, https://web.nli.org.il/sites/NLI/English/collections/manuscripts/hebrewcodicology/Documents/Hebrew-Codicology-continuously-updated-online-version-ENG.pdf [accessed in June 2021]; Edna Engel, 'Remarks on the Ashkenazic Script', in *Specimens of Mediaeval Hebrew Scripts*, ed. by Malachi Beit-Arié and Edna Engel, 3 vols (Jerusalem: The Israel Academy of Sciences and Humanities, 2002–2017), III (2017), pp. xvii–xlvi (p. xxiv).
50 Some sources show that some French Jews migrated as far as Buda. See Tamás Visi and Magdaléna Jánošíková, 'A Regional Perspective on Hebrew Fragments: The Case of Moravia', in *Books within Books: New Discoveries in Old Book Bindings*, ed. by Andreas Lehnardt and Judith Olszowy-Schlanger (Leiden: Brill, 2014), pp. 185–236 (p. 205).
51 ÖNB, Cod. hebr. 11, fol. 234ʳ. The owners' names inscribed in the manuscript are Simcha ben Samuel, Simeon ben Moses, and Abraham ben Abraham (see fols 1ʳ, 1ᵛ, 26ᵛ, 59ᵛ, 151ᵛ, 234ᵛ, 251ᵛ, and 253ʳ).
52 Schwarz, pp. 6–7, no. 5.

and central German Lands, including members of Aberzush's own family (1298).[53]

Unfortunately, we do not know who commissioned ÖNB, Cod. hebr. 16 or who owned it after the Rintfleisch persecution. The next stop that can be reconstructed in its itinerary was in Vienna. There, too, the manuscript appears in the context of anti-Jewish violence. A fire broke out in the Vienna synagogue in 1406 that lasted three days. During that time, burghers and students from the University of Vienna seized the opportunity to attack the city's Jews and plunder their houses, taking all kinds of valuable property with them.[54] According to the *Klosterneuburger Chronik* ('Chronicle of Klosterneuburg'), the total value of the looted property was more than 100,000 guldens — an enormous amount.[55] Despite the duke's order to return the looted property to its Jewish owners, only a small proportion of the valuables was eventually handed back. The property that the Christian looters plundered included Jewish manuscripts, which they intended to sell to local binders or sell back to Jews — at very high prices.[56] In 1407, ÖNB, Cod. hebr. 16 and an unidentified Torah scroll were resold to a Jew who documented the repurchase (or in his words, the 'redemption') with the following words: פדיתי ספר תורה וספר זה מן ערל בעד ג' ליטרא פחות ע"פ [שבעים פרוטות] באייר קס"ז ל[פרט] ('I redeemed a Torah scroll and this book from a Gentile for three pounds minus seventy pfennigs in Iyyar (5)167 [April 1407]').[57]

---

53 ÖNB, Cod. hebr. 16, fols 249ʳ–268ʳ; cited and trans. in Colette Sirat, *Hebrew Manuscripts of the Middle Ages* (Cambridge: Cambridge University Press, 2002), p. 225. Aberzush's colophon was also published in Christian D. Ginsburg, *Introduction to the Massoretico-Critical Edition of the Hebrew Bible* (New York: Ketav, 1966), pp. 777–78 and was discussed in Rainer J. Barzen, 'Personal Grief between Private and Public Space: A Micrographic Inscription as a Historical Source (MS Vienna Cod. hebr. 16)', in *Philology and Aesthetics: Figurative Masorah in Western European Manuscripts*, ed. by Hanna Liss (Berlin: Peter Lang, 2021), pp. 35–58. For a description of the manuscript, see Beit-Arié, pp. 188–89. For the history of Rintfleisch massacres, see Jörg R. Müller, '*Erez gezerah* – "Land of Persecution": Pogroms against the Jews in the *regnum Teutonicum* from *c.* 1280 to 1350', in *The Jews of Europe in the Middle Ages (Tenth to Fifteenth Centuries)*, Proceedings of the International Symposium held at Speyer, 20–25 October 2002, ed. by Christoph Cluse (Turnhout: Brepols, 2014), pp. 245–60 (pp. 251–54).

54 Krauss, pp. 1–8. The event was described in both Jewish and Christian chronicles: Thomas Ebendorfer, 'Chronica Austriae' in *Monumenta Germaniae Historica*, ed. by Alphons Lhotsky, Scriptores rerum Germanicarum, N.S., 13 (Berlin-Zurich: Weidmann, 1967), p. 330; Joseph ben Joshua ha-Cohen, '*Emeq ha-bak'a* (Cracow: Josef Fischer, 1895), p. 88; Hartmann J. Zeibig, 'Die kleine Klosterneuburger Chronik (1322 bis 1428)', *Archiv für Kunde österreichischer Geschichtsquellen*, 7 (1851), pp. 229–52 (pp. 238–39).

55 Zeibig, p. 238.

56 Regarding Christians' practice of reselling manuscripts to Jews at very high prices, see Israel Isserlein, *Sefer terumat ha-deshen* (Beni Braq: [n. pub.], 1971), part II (*Pesaqim u-ketavim*), p. 16, no. 69. See also Martha Keil, 'Gelehrsamkeit und Zerstörung. Hebräische Fragmente in österreichischen Handschriften und Frühdrucken', in *Fragment und Makulatur. Überlieferungsstörungen und Forschungsbedarf bei Kulturgut in Archiven und Bibliotheken*, ed. by Hanns Peter Neuheuser and Wolfgang Schmitz (Wiesbaden: Harrassowitz, 2015), pp. 209–22 (p. 216).

57 ÖNB, Cod. hebr. 16, fol. 244ᵛ. A similar inscription is found on fol. 1ʳ. Both Ginsburg (Ginsburg, p. 778 note 2) and Schwarz (Schwarz, p. 7) erroneously read the abbreviation פ"ע as ע"ע and interpreted it as שבעים עבים ('seventy *grossi*'). The second letter, obviously פ, apparently means *pruta*, which together with *litra* represents a talmudic equivalent of the Viennese currency of the time, pound and pfennig. Cf. Arnold Luschin von Ebengreuth, 'Das Münzwesen in Österreich ob und unter der Enns im ausgehenden Mittelalter', *Jahrbuch für Landeskunde von Niederösterreich*, Ser. NF, 15–16 (1916–1917), pp. 367–462 (pp. 367–75). We do not know if the Jewish repurchaser of ÖNB, Cod. hebr. 16 was one of its owners, Avigdor, Hayyim, or Asher Moses, who mentioned their names in the manuscript (ÖNB, Cod. hebr. 16, fols 1ʳ and 368ᵛ). It is also noteworthy that one of these owners, Asher Moses (fol. 368ᵛ), could be identified with Asher Moses *shamash ha-shem* — the owner of two other codices in the Collegium, ÖNB, Cod. hebr. 11 (fol. 3ʳ) and ÖNB,

ÖNB, Cod. hebr. 16 fell into the hands of Christians once again in 1421. It was apparently acquired by the theologians of the University of Vienna from the stock that Albrecht V confiscated during the Vienna *Gezerah* and had sent to the Collegium Ducale. A sixteenth-century librarian at the Collegium inscribed the volume with an ownership note: '*Iste liber spectat ad collegium ducale Vienna*' ('This book is found in the Collegium Ducale in Vienna').[58] In the Collegium, ÖNB, Cod. hebr. 16 was annotated in Latin by a fifteenth-century Christian hand.

A similar note of ownership by the Collegium appears in four additional codices of the Pentateuch,[59] which suggests that after the duke acquired these volumes, he sent them to the Collegium Ducale library. Other than this evidence, however, the Hebrew volumes do not show any material signs of the way they were preserved in the Collegium, such as holes that could indicate chaining, as can be seen in valuable non-Hebrew books from the Collegium,[60] or shelf marks labels that could point to their place in relation to non-Hebrew volumes.[61]

In addition to the Hebrew codices that can be identified on the basis of the inventories and those inscribed with the ownership notes of the Collegium, seven more manuscripts, mostly either liturgical Pentateuchs or Prophets and Writings, can be attributed to the oldest Hebraica stock of the Collegium.[62] Although these volumes bear no direct evidence of their presence there, their Hebrew texts were annotated in Latin and German in the same pattern observable in ÖNB, Cod. hebr. 4, ÖNB, Cod. hebr. 11, and ÖNB, Cod. hebr. 16. Thus, by juxtaposing later book inventories that reflect the book holdings of the university with the Hebrew manuscripts annotated in the fifteenth century in Latin and German and those that carry ownership notes from the Collegium, it is possible to single out the codices that once belonged to the Collegium and can now be found at the Österreichische Nationalbibliothek.

All in all, thirteen Hebrew manuscripts can be attributed to the oldest Hebraica holdings of the Collegium Ducale (Appendix B). These

---

Cod. hebr. 13 (fol. 1ʳ), to be discussed below. Moreover, he was also possibly the owner of another Pentateuch from *c.* 1300, today in the Vatican Library (Vatican, Biblioteca apostolica, ebr. 15, fol. 1ᵛ; see Malachi Beit-Arié and Benjamin Richler, *Hebrew Manuscripts in the Vatican Library: Catalogue* [Vatican City: Biblioteca Apostolica Vaticana, 2008], p. 11). However, these short owners' notes do not provide sufficient evidence for asserting that all these codices belonged to the same Jewish family in Vienna or its environs.

58 ÖNB, Cod. hebr. 16, fol. 368ᵛ. The inscription is written in ink and is followed by a later shelf mark of the Collegium in plummet, no. 15.

59 See ÖNB, Cod. hebr. 13, fol. 198ᵛ (Schwarz, p. 17, no. 18): '*Liber Collegii Ducalis Viennae*' ('The book of the Collegium Ducale of Vienna') in ink, followed by a later Collegium shelf mark in plummet, no. 2. ÖNB, Cod. hebr. 19, back pastedown (Schwarz, p. 11, no. 12), Cod. hebr. 25, fol. 1ʳ (Schwarz, pp. 9–10, no. 10), and Cod. hebr. 38, back pastedown (Schwarz, pp. 11–12, no. 13) all contain the same ink inscription. Next to that there are later Collegium shelf marks in plummet in Cod. hebr. 19 and Cod. hebr. 25 (nos 6 and 8, respectively).

60 Like other libraries at the university, the library of the Collegium was of a lectern type with the books chained to sloping reading desks (*libri catenati*), which served as a way of securing books and as places to read them. Take ÖNB, Cod. 1380, e.g. (the manuscript was bequeathed to the Collegium by Peter Czech of Pulkau in 1425), and Cod. 1494, both of which have two or three holes at the top of the back cover that were left by a clasp (now gone), to which a chain was once attached.

61 Cf. Simader, *Bücher: Artistenfakultät* https://webarchiv.onb.ac.at/web/20150803112655/http://www.onb.ac.at/sammlungen/hschrift/kataloge/universitaet/Artistenfakultaet.htm [accessed in June 2021].

62 ÖNB, Cod. hebr. 2 (Schwarz, pp. 66–68, no. 72); Cod. hebr. 3 (Schwarz, p. 29, no. 24); Cod. hebr. 4 (Schwarz, pp. 1–2, no. 1); Cod. hebr. 6 (Schwarz, pp. 15–16, no. 16); Cod. hebr. 14 (Schwarz, pp. 14–15, no. 15); Cod. hebr. 15 (Schwarz, pp. 4–6, no. 4); Cod. hebr. 17 (Schwarz, pp. 7–8, no. 6).

were typical late medieval codices copied in Germany, Austria (or Bohemia), and France in the thirteenth to fifteenth century. They were produced for individual patrons, were privately owned, and apparently remained in Jewish hands until the *Gezerah*, but the multiple names of the Jewish owners mentioned could not be found in other (published) sources of the time.[63] It is also evident that earlier persecutions and expulsions had a great impact on the composition of the private book collections of Austrian Jews. Such was the case for ÖNB, Cod. hebr. 16, which was not produced in Vienna, but ended up there after the Rintfleisch massacres. The persecutions in the Rhineland and France apparently set ÖNB, Cod. hebr. 4 and ÖNB, Cod. hebr. 11 in motion, and they were eventually taken to Austria.[64]

In regard to the content of the Hebrew manuscripts, when the university scholars wanted to obtain 'some Hebrew books [...] for the university and the theological faculty' from Duke Albrecht V in 1421, they were mainly interested in biblical codices. Only one of the thirteen manuscripts, a lavishly decorated talmudic compendium called *Sefer ha-Mordekhai* ('The Book of Mordechai'), copied in Ashkenaz in 1392 for Shemariyah ben Moses, is devoid of biblical content.[65] A fifteenth-century Latin hand — apparently one of its users at the Collegium — inscribed its title, 'R[abbi] Mardocheus'.[66] It is obviously this *Sefer ha-Mordekhai* that appears in Tengnagel's and Schier's inventories (Appendix B: 1).

The content of the Hebrew manuscripts was not the only reason for acquiring them for the Collegium Ducale or for the private libraries of the Viennese theologians. The theologians searched for valuable, well-preserved, and uncorrupted copies. One of the signs of the importance and integrity of the text was a manuscript's binding. At least five codices were acquired in their intact 'Jewish' bindings — wooden boards covered in brown leather and decorated in a cut-leather (*cuir-ciselé*) technique.[67] The high cost of crafting such bindings may have made the theologians assume that these volumes enjoyed a special status among Jews and that they were correctly bound and preserved in their entirety with no loss of text. Apparently, the use of the original (or nearly original) bindings as a material indicator of the completeness of the text was unavoidable, since hardly any theologian in Vienna knew Hebrew at the time of the Vienna *Gezerah* and would not have been in any position to judge the quality and condition of the Hebrew text itself.

---

63 For example, *Regesten zur Geschichte der Juden in Österreich im Mittelalter*, ed. by Eveline Brugger and Birgit Wiedl, 4 vols (Innsbruck-Vienna-Bozen: StudienVerlag, 2005–2018). Neither are they mentioned among the victims of the Vienna *Gezerah* that were entered in the *qinot* ('lament'), recited on the Ninth of Av in the neighbouring Jewish settlements. See the nineteenth-century *Pohrlitzer Memorbuch* ('memory book' dedicated to the memory of martyrs in Ashkenaz) in Heinrich Flesch, 'Das Pohrlitzer Memorbuch. Das Gedächtnis vieler "Heiligen" der Wiener Gesera von 1421', *Jahrbuch der jüdischen literarischen Gesellschaft*, 19 (1928), pp. 99–111 (pp. 99–103).

64 The same apparently holds true for ÖNB, Cod. hebr. 17, whose codicological and palaeographical features point to its French origin.

65 ÖNB, Cod. hebr. 2, fol. 241ᵛ. The manuscript includes the Austrian version of the compendium (Schwarz, pp. 66–68, no. 72).

66 ÖNB, Cod. hebr. 2, fol. 1ᵛ.

67 ÖNB, Cod. hebr. 2; Cod. hebr. 6; Cod. hebr. 13; Cod. hebr. 19; Cod. hebr. 38. The bindings of these manuscripts are discussed in Ilona Steimann, '"Beautiful Books with Beautiful Covers": The Bindings of Hebrew Manuscripts in Late Medieval Ashkenaz', *A Journal of the Schoenberg Institute for Manuscript Studies*, 7/1 (2022), pp. 76–103. The material appearance of other Hebrew manuscripts obtained by the Collegium is unknown, as they were later rebound.

Reading between the Lines: Christian Annotations

Knowledge of the Hebrew language, which was obviously a necessary prerequisite for any dealings with Hebrew manuscripts, was largely terra incognita at the University of Vienna. Driven by missionary enthusiasm, the General Council of the Church which assembled in Vienna in 1312 issued a decree that called for teaching Hebrew, Greek, Syriac, and Arabic as part of the *studium generale*. The same decree was issued again by the Council of Basel some 120 years later in 1434,[68] but in practice, it remained quite ineffective at European universities until the sixteenth century. The first official post as a Hebrew lecturer at the University of Vienna's Faculty of Arts was taken up by Anthonius Margaritha, a Jewish convert to Christianity, in 1535.[69] Prior to that appointment, there are only occasional references to teachers of Hebrew in the fifteenth century. One such case was Augustine of Buda, an otherwise unknown scholar whom the staff register of the University of Vienna referred to as a '*lector in Hebraico*' ('lecturer in Hebrew') in 1438.[70] But even if some form of instruction in Hebrew was available at the time, as a rule the Viennese theologians did not have any command of the Hebrew language.

Nonetheless, following the teachings of Nicholas of Lyra and other earlier theologians, the Viennese professors considered Hebrew essential for biblical exegesis.[71] Leading scholars at the University of Vienna, such as Heinrich of Langenstein (*c.* 1325–97) and Heinrich Totting of Oyta (*c.* 1330–97), recognized the importance of Hebrew for an understanding of the literal sense of Scripture and for refuting Jewish arguments against the Vulgate translation.[72] Regarding the latter, Langenstein wrote the following in his commentary on Genesis, which he worked on from his arrival in Vienna from Paris in 1378 until his death in 1397:

> Magnus est in ecclesia defectus eo quod non est in ea eruditio in diversis linguibus, scilicet in ebraica, greca, etc. ut alii [...] de ecclesia salubriter provisum fuit per illam[?] clementinam. Unde propter illum defectum Iudei erigunt audacius cornua sua et coram laicis et simplicibus respondendo clericis audent dicere impingendo implicite in nostras translationes se non habere sic in biblia.
>
> (It is a great deficiency in the Church that there is no instruction in various languages, namely in Hebrew, Greek, etc. [...] And because of this deficiency, the Jews boldly raise their horns; and when they answer clerics before laymen and the simple people, they dare implicitly

---

68 Robert Weiss, 'England and the Decree of the Council of Vienne on the Teaching of Greek, Arabic, Hebrew, and Syriac', *Bibliothèque d'Humanisme et Renaissance*, 14/1 (1952), pp. 1–9.

69 Wolfdieter Bihl, *Orientalistik an der Universität Wien. Forschungen zwischen Maghreb und Ost- und Südasien: Die Professoren und Dozenten* (Vienna: Böhlau, 2009), p. 10; Wilhelm A. Neumann, *Über die orientalischen Sprachstudien seit dem XIII. Jahrhunderte mit besonderer Rücksicht auf Wien: Inaugurationsrede, gehalten am 17. October 1899 im Festsaale der Universität* (Vienna: Selbstverlag der Universität, 1899), pp. 79–80.

70 *Die Matrikel der Universität Wien*, I, p. 205. The register of 1512 mentions a certain Bachler Simon Griner of Feringen who was proficient in Latin, Greek, and Hebrew. See Aschbach, II (1877), p. 63 note 3. Also see Goldmann, 'Die Universität', p. 162; Neumann, pp. 78–79.

71 See, for instance, Lesley Smith, 'Nicholas of Lyra and Old Testament Interpretation', in *Hebrew Bible / Old Testament: The History of Its Interpretation*, ed. by Magne Sæbø, 3 vols (Göttingen: Vandenhoeck & Ruprecht, 1996–2015), II (2008), pp. 49–63.

72 For an overview of their writings, see Gustav Sommerfeldt, 'Aus der Zeit der Begründung der Universität Wien', *Mitteilungen des Instituts für Österreichische Geschichtsforschung*, 30/4 (1909), pp. 291–322.

to impugn our translations, saying that [a given passage] does not read thus in their Bible.)[73]

Langenstein himself undertook the study of Hebrew outside the walls of the university. In a treatise on the Hebrew language and the mysteries of the Hebrew alphabet that he wrote in 1388, called *De ideomate ebraico* ('On Hebrew Idioms'), he noted that he had learned Hebrew from converted Jews and others in Paris and Vienna.[74] The treatise reveals that Langenstein's own knowledge of Hebrew was apparently up to the task of writing such a work, but he was an exception among Viennese theologians. It is even doubtful that that generation of Viennese scholars actually had access to Hebrew manuscripts of the Bible and had examined them personally. Rather, they tended to elaborate on the same Christian parts of the Bible that were highlighted by the Church Fathers and earlier Christian theologians.[75]

Although the next generation of theologians who studied with Langenstein and Oyta was able to consult the Hebrew Bible in the manuscripts acquired after the Vienna *Gezerah*, they continued the exegetical tradition of their teachers. The presence of this original Hebrew source material in the library of the Collegium Ducale had no obvious effect on the theological programme or on the scholars' own writings. To confirm Christian doctrinal issues, Nicholas of Dinkelsbühl, for example, mostly used typological and prefigurative evidence spotted in the biblical text by earlier Christian authors in the sermons he delivered in 1420.[76] His sermons addressed Jewish blasphemies and conversion, which became especially important after the multiple conversions that took place during the events that led to the Vienna *Gezerah*.[77] He did not mention any Jewish biblical commentaries, the Talmud, or the Midrash, nor does he seem to have used any Hebrew books in preparing his sermons.[78] Unlike earlier theologians such as Nicholas of Lyra, Dinkelsbühl, then, did not need the mediation of the Jews, their language, or their books when he studied and interpreted the Bible.

According to Christopher Ocker, the prevalence of this kind of Biblicism in fifteenth-century German-speaking intellectual circles can be linked to the persecutions of the Jews. The dwindling urban presence of Jews in the empire led to Christian neglect of Jewish biblical commentaries, which were no longer considered necessary sources for anti-Jewish polemics and missionary work. The Jewish commentaries were completely replaced by Christian commentaries that were solely concerned with the Christological meaning of Scripture.[79] The same holds true for Latin and

---

73 ÖNB, Cod. 4651, fol. 102ʳ; quot. and trans. in Shank, p. 154.
74 Erfurt, Universitätsbibliothek, Dep. Erf. CA. 4° 125, fol. 255ʳ (Wilhelm Schum, *Beschreibendes Verzeichniss der Amplonianischen Handschriften-Sammlung zu Erfurt* [Berlin: Weidmannsche Buchhandlung, 1887], pp. 384–87); published in Walde, p. 10.
75 Shank, pp. 152–54.
76 The autograph of the sermons is preserved in ÖNB, Cod. 4354, fols 9ʳ–19ʳ. See Alois Madre, *Nikolaus von Dinkelsbühl: Leben und Schriften* (Münster i. W.: Aschendorff, 1965), pp. 129–33 and 153–54. Regarding Dinkelsbühl's activities as a preacher, see Friedrich Schäffauer, 'Nikolaus von Dinkelsbühl als Prediger: ein Beitrag zur religiösen Kulturgeschichte des ausgehenden Mittelalters', *Theologische Quartalschrift*, 115/3 (1934), pp. 405–39.
77 As some of these new Christians were present at the sermons, Dinkelsbühl most likely preached in German. See Fritz P. Knapp, 'Heinrich von Langenstein Sermones Wiennenses ad Iudaeos convertendos: Die ältesten aus dem deutschen Sprachraum erhaltenen Judenbekehrungspredigten: Präsentation und Interpretation eines Neufunds', *Mitteilungen des Instituts für Österreichische Geschichtsforschung*, 109/JG (2001), pp. 105–17 (pp. 106–07); Ocker, pp. 42–43; Shank, p. 192 note 103.
78 Ocker, pp. 43–45.
79 Ocker, p. 62.

German annotations that Viennese theologians added to the Hebrew volumes, which, once again, show that the Hebrew Bible manuscripts were used to demonstrate the superiority of the Vulgate and Christianity over the Hebrew Bible and Judaism.

Although we do not know specifically which scholars annotated the Hebrew manuscripts of the Collegium, the multiplicity of Latin and German hands discernible on the manuscripts' pages suggests a kind of collective use. The best example of this is ÖNB, Cod. hebr. 4, as it was annotated by at least four Latin/German hands, possibly because this codex includes the entire Bible or because of its impressive size, which suggested its importance. The only name discernible on its pages is that of Tamasth Kunasitsth, who also wrote '1482, *Ich hoff der gnaden*' ('1482, I hope for mercy') and '*Isus Rekchs iudyorum*' ('Jesus, King of the Jews') at the beginning of the manuscript.[80] The latter inscription quotes the *titulus crucis* — a plaque inscribed in Hebrew, Greek, and Latin with the words 'Jesus of Nazareth, king of the Jews', which Pilate had ordered nailed to Christ's cross (John 19:20). Like many of his contemporaries, the author of this inscription used the *titulus* as an emblematic expression of the historical bonds among Christ, the Jews, and the Hebrew language, thereby emphasizing the relevance of this Hebrew manuscript to Christian readers.[81] It is possible that Tamasth Kunasitsth was actually Thomas Kyenast, a Prussian student of arts mentioned in the registers of the University of Vienna. He was allowed to take his baccalaureate examination (*determinatio*) in 1459.[82] However, by 1482, the year he inscribed ÖNB, Cod. hebr. 4, he must have obtained a higher academic degree and might have advanced academically at the Faculty of Theology at the University of Vienna.

Christian annotations to the Hebrew text of the manuscripts can generally be divided into three categories: structural, linguistic, and theological-interpretative adaptation of the Hebrew Bible for a Christian readership. These categories represent different aspects of the same process that was designed to clarify the text of the Hebrew Bible and bring it into line with the Latin Vulgate. The first category — structural adaptation — includes annotations that relate to the textual arrangement of the Bible. It involves running titles for the biblical books in Latin (and sometimes in German) and the division into chapters and verses in accordance

---

80 ÖNB, Cod. hebr. 4, fol. 1ʳ: read by Krafft and Deutsch as 'Tomaseh Kenasitseh' (Albrecht Krafft and Simon Deutsch, *Die handschriftlichen hebräischen Werke der K. K. Hofbibliothek zu Wien* [Vienna: Typis Caes. Reg. Aulae et Status Typographiae, 1847], p. 9) and by Schwarz as 'Damansch Kinafitsch(?)' (Schwarz, p. 2). Schwarz mentions other inscriptions that include names, which are hardly discernible today: 'Volvart To[...]us' and 'Leopoldus[...] aar[...]'.
Additionally, this folio contains general statements by its readers regarding its content. Such are, e.g., the title of the manuscript, '*Vetus testamentum iacet hic*' ('The Old Testament is found here') and more vaguely '*iudisch hurnqint [Urkunde]*' ('Jewish document'). The latter was written in code letters, an invention attributed to Duke Rudolf IV of Austria. The second part of the code inscription ('*iwd [po]?neissc?*') is illegible but apparently refers to Jews as well. For other uses of this code in medieval manuscripts, see Bernhard Bischoff, 'Übersicht über die nichtdiplomatischen Geheimschriften des Mittelalters', *Mitteilungen des Instituts für Österreichische Geschichtsforschung*, 62 (1954), pp. 120–48 (p. 133).

81 On uses of the *titulus* in the context of Christian Hebraic studies, see Ilona Steimann, *Jewish Book – Christian Book: Hebrew Manuscripts in Transition between Jews and Christians in the Context of German Humanism* (Turnhout: Brepols, 2020), pp. 175–85.

82 Archiv der Universität, Ph 8, fol. 126ᵛ; *Acta Facultatis Artium*, III, no. 13240. Also see the register of students of the University of Vienna (1456) published in Max Perlbach, *Prussia Scholastica: Die Ost- und Westpreussen auf den mittelalterlichen Universitäten* (Leipzig: Spirgatis, 1895), p. 31.

Figure 16.2. Prophets and Writings, Ashkenaz, first half of the thirteenth century. Vienna, Österreichische Nationalbibliothek, Cod. hebr. 15, fol. 21ʳ.

with the Vulgate.⁸³ Latin hands could also add subtitles for specific sections of the text, such as 'haec sunt decem praecepta' ('these are the Ten Commandments') for Exodus 20:1–17, as well as general notes about the order of the books in the Bible.⁸⁴ The titles, numeration of the chapters, and other notes on the textual structure were intended as navigational aids for readers who were not fluent in Hebrew and mark the attempt to create a bridge between the Hebrew Bible and the Vulgate.

At least two identical fifteenth-century Christian hands annotated Prophets and Writings (ÖNB, Cod. hebr. 15) and the Pentateuch (ÖNB, Cod. hebr. 11) in Latin. One hand wrote the titles of the biblical books in cursive script in the upper margins of each recto in both codices and divided the books' chapters in accordance with the Vulgate's structure. To underscore the opposite directionality of Hebrew, the hand in ÖNB, Cod. hebr. 15 often split the book titles up so that the first part of the title appeared above the right-hand column of the Hebrew text and the second one above the left-hand column on the same page.⁸⁵ In the Book of Judges (*Judicum*), for instance, *ju* was written above the right-hand column and *dicum* above the left-hand one, thereby reflecting the direction of reading in Hebrew (Figure 16.2).⁸⁶ The second hand writing in Textualis Quadrata added the titles at the beginning of the biblical books in both manuscripts. Both hands sometimes wrote the titles upside down in relation to the Hebrew text.⁸⁷ The upside-down titles suggests that two people might have been working together at the same time, one person reading the Hebrew text in the right direction and the second sitting opposite and inscribing the titles.

That ÖNB, Cod. hebr. 11 and ÖNB, Cod. hebr. 15 were used by the same Christian scholars follows from a marginal note in ÖNB, Cod. hebr. 11. Next to the title of the Song of Songs inscribed

---

83 Annotations of this kind written by different hands can be observed in ÖNB, Cod. hebr. 4; Cod. hebr. 11; Cod. hebr. 15; Cod. hebr. 16; and Cod. hebr. 17.

84 See ÖNB, Cod. hebr. 4, fol. 46ᵛ and Cod. hebr. 11, fol. 177ʳ, respectively.

85 On the right-to-left directionality of Hebrew as perceived by Christians, see Daniel Stein Kokin, 'Polemical Language: Hebrew and Latin in Medieval and Early Modern Jewish-Christian Debate', *Jewish History*, 29/1 (2015), pp. 1–38 (pp. 3–24).

86 ÖNB, Cod. hebr. 15, e.g., fol. 21ʳ.

87 The titles of the books of Samuel and Kings in Textualis Quadrata (Cod. hebr. 15, e.g. fols 40ᵛ and 49ᵛ) and in cursive on each recto are written upside down. However, the cursive titles that appear above the titles in Textualis Quadrata are written in the right direction. The direction of the titles corresponds to the Hebrew text in the subsequent biblical books.

in the manuscript as '*Cantica canticorum*', the cursive hand wrote: '*Habetur in alio volumine*' ('Found in other volume').[88] Apparently referring to ÖNB, Cod. hebr. 15, this note establishes a tangible connection between the two manuscripts.[89] Moreover, as noted above, both ÖNB, Cod. hebr. 11 and ÖNB, Cod. hebr. 15 were sold for the price of 8 guldens, and the same hand inscribed that figure in both volumes. Whether these volumes were initially obtained from the duke for a Viennese theologian's private library and were later donated to the Collegium or 8 guldens indicates the price the Collegium paid by for them is unclear.

Structural adaptation could also include a Latin list of the biblical books included in a given volume. Lists of this kind are found in ÖNB, Cod. hebr. 4 and ÖNB, Cod. hebr. 16, written by the same cursive Latin hand, thus providing evidence that the same person (a Christian) worked on both manuscripts in the Collegium's library.[90] This was the same reader who wrote the titles of the books in Latin and inserted some marginal comments in ÖNB, Cod. hebr. 16. This is, in fact, the only Latin hand that appears in the codex. By contrast, as mentioned above, at least four different hands writing in Latin and German annotated ÖNB, Cod. hebr. 4 in addition to the hand that wrote the list of biblical books.

The Hebrew text was made accessible to non-Hebrew speakers through the second category — linguistic adaptation — which involves sporadic translations of Hebrew words into Latin between the lines (*superscriptio*) and in the margins, their transliteration, and some linguistic explanations. ÖNB, Cod. hebr. 4 also includes clarification of the Hebrew alphabet; the upper line on the page that features Ruth 4:16–17, for example, was transliterated into Latin characters written above the Hebrew letters.[91] These practices were designed to explain Hebrew wording and lettering for the Christian readers at the Collegium.

Further, the translation could also reflect a theological intent. The translation of biblical verses into Latin in accordance with the Vulgate mostly appears next to the Hebrew verses that open the psalms.[92] Most frequently referred to in the New Testament, the Psalter has always been understood by Christians as predicting the coming of Christ. Through their typological, prefigurative, and Christological interpretation of the psalms, Christian theologians claimed that Hebrew Scripture anticipated the Christian era.[93] For the same reason, Christian readers of the Hebrew codices at the Collegium translated the verses from the Book of Isaiah that were routinely used in the Christian tradition for promise-fulfilment interpretations.[94] For instance, next to Isaiah 7:14, which has the words 'the young woman is with child and shall bear a son', different Latin hands translated the beginning of the verse into Latin in ÖNB, Cod. hebr. 4 and ÖNB, Cod. hebr. 15: '*Ecce virgo concipiet*'.[95] Early patristic commentators and their followers interpreted it

---

88 ÖNB, Cod. hebr. 11, fol. 155ʳ.
89 In ÖNB, Cod. hebr. 15, Song of Songs is found on fols 358ʳ–361ʳ.
90 ÖNB, Cod. hebr. 4, fol. 1ʳ and Cod. hebr. 16, fol. 368ᵛ.

91 ÖNB, Cod. hebr. 4, fol. 374ᵛ.
92 For example, ÖNB, Cod. hebr. 4, fol. 375ʳ and Cod. hebr. 16, fol. 245ᵛ.
93 For a general discussion on this subject, see Jerry E. Shepherd, 'The Book of Psalms as the Book of Christ: A Christo-Canonical Approach to the Book of Psalms' (unpublished doctoral thesis, Westminster Theological Seminary, 1995), pp. 1–34. On typology in general, see Leonhard Goppelt, *Typos: The Typological Interpretation of the Old Testament in the New*, trans. by Donald Madvig (Grand Rapids: Eerdmans, 1982) and Kenneth Woollcombe, 'The Biblical Origins and Patristic Development of Typology', in *Essays on Typology*, ed. by Geoffrey Lampe and Kenneth Woollcombe (London: SCM Press, 1957), pp. 39–75.
94 John F. A. Sawyer, *The Fifth Gospel: Isaiah in the History of Christianity* (Cambridge: Cambridge University Press, 1996), pp. 1–20.
95 ÖNB, Cod. hebr. 4, fol. 324ᵛ and Cod. hebr. 15, fol. 219ʳ.

Figure 16.3. Hebrew Bible, Ashkenaz, 1344. Vienna, Österreichische Nationalbibliothek, Cod. hebr. 4, fol. 343ᵛ.

as referring to Mary's virginal conception, which, they contended, was 'predicted' in Isaiah 11 as well.[96] Isaiah 11:10 was also translated into Latin in ÖNB, Cod. hebr. 4.[97] It refers to the tree of Jesse, which was understood as proof of Jesus's genealogical attribution to the royal line of King David, as predicted by the prophets with regard to Israel's Messiah.[98] By translating verses of a typological, prefigurative nature into Latin, then, users of the Hebraica at the Collegium mapped the textual places in the Hebrew Bible which, in their eyes, suggested a promise-fulfilment interpretation. The Latin translation of the biblical verses therefore belongs to the third category, that is, theological-interpretative adaptation, rather than to the linguistic one and attests to the reading of the Hebrew Bible through a Christological lens.

The fact that the approach of the Christian users of the Hebrew Bible codices was neither neutral nor unbiased is even more obvious in their marginal comments, which represent the principal means of theological-interpretative adaptation. Despite their scarcity, these comments specifically shed light on what the theologians meant by 'better and more correct' Hebrew books, which they attempted to obtain from the duke in 1421. The best example of this approach is found in the bottom margin of the page in ÖNB, Cod. hebr. 4 that contains an allegory about the Suffering Servant (Isa. 52:13–53:12). A Latin hand from the Collegium explained the first verse (Isa. 52:13) as follows (Figure 16.3):

> In hac columpna sinistra annexa habemus usque ad capitum 54 apertissimam propheciam de christi passione, baptizato etc. Et incipit ibi supra ecce intelliget servus meus ubi in caldeo dicitur ecce intelliget servus messias etc.
>
> (In this column attached on the left, up to Chapter 54, we have a revealed prophecy

---

96 Maarten J. J. Menken, 'The Textual Form of the Quotation from Isaiah 7:14 in Matthew 1:23', *Novum Testamentum*, 43/2 (2001), pp. 144–60. See also the marginal translation of Isaiah 9:6 ('For a child has been born for us, a son given to us'), which was commonly interpreted in a similar sense, in ÖNB, Cod. hebr. 15, fol. 220ʳ and Cod. hebr. 4, fol. 325ᵛ. The latter does not provide the Vulgate's translation of the verse, but an alternative version based on a Gregorian chant for Christmas Day, '*Puer natus est nobis*' ('A boy is born for us').

97 ÖNB, Cod. hebr. 4, fol. 326ᵛ.

98 This interpretation of Isaiah's verses was clearly manifested in multiple medieval representations of the Tree of Jesse. See Peter Bloch, *Nachwirkungen des Alten Bundes in der christlichen Kunst* (Cologne: Metzler, 1963), pp. 737–41.

about the suffering of Christ, [his] baptism, etc. On the top there, its beginning, 'See, my servant', appears in Chaldean[:] 'See, my servant Messiah', etc.)⁹⁹

Drawing on the Aramaic Targum of Jonathan ben Uzziel, which does not appear in ÖNB, Cod. hebr. 4, this Christian scribe interpreted the verse from Isaiah — 'See, my servant shall prosper; he shall be exalted and lifted up, and shall be very high' — as foretelling the suffering of Christ because the Targum explicitly identified the servant as the Messiah: 'Behold, my servant the Messiah shall prosper, He shall be exalted and extolled, and He shall be very strong'.¹⁰⁰

Using the Targum Jonathan to interpret the verse from Isaiah in a Christological sense might have been based on the tractate of the Dominican monk Petrus Nigri (1434–1483), alias Peter Schwarz, *Stern des Meschiah* ('Star of Messiah') from 1477, which apparently provides the *terminus post quem* for these kinds of annotations in ÖNB, Cod. hebr. 4. In this work, Nigri quoted the Targum Jonathan in the context of the same verse and clarified it in a similar vein.¹⁰¹ As a rule, Nigri applied prefigurative and typological arguments in *Stern des Meschiah* to demonstrate the principal dogmas of the Christian faith and the punishment faced by the Jews for their unbelief. In spite of Nigri's good command of Hebrew and his familiarity with Jewish tradition, he — like the Viennese theologians — only used Hebrew in the *Stern des Meschiah* to access biblical verses, which he understood in a typological and prefigurative sense. In several other passages, Nigri also attempted to prove the Christian truth from the Targum Onkelos to the Pentateuch and the Targum Jonathan to the Prophets.¹⁰² He wanted, in this way, to establish a 'better and more correct' version of the Hebrew Bible — one that predicted Christianity. This kind of Christian interest in Aramaic Targums emerged from the belief that the Targums were less corrupted by the Jews and transmitted the Christian truth more precisely than the Hebrew text of the Bible, especially in passages related to the Messiah.¹⁰³

The patterns of annotating the Hebrew manuscripts of the Collegium are generally paradigmatic of Christian reading of the Hebrew Bible of the time. For example, a volume of the Hebrew Prophets that belonged to the auxiliary bishop of Mainz, Siegfried Piscator (d. 1473), which he apparently acquired in the wake of the expulsion of Jews from Mainz in 1438, was annotated in a similar manner by at least two Latin hands.¹⁰⁴ Whereas the later hand often referred to Johannes Reuchlin's *Rudimenta linguae hebraicae* ('The Rudiments of the Hebrew Language') of 1506,

---

99 ÖNB, Cod. hebr. 4, fol. 343ᵛ.
100 לחדא ויתקף ויסגי יראם משיחא עבדי יצלח הא; trans. in *The Chaldee Paraphrase on the Prophet Isaiah*, trans. by Christian Pauli (London: London Society's House, 1871), p. 181.
101 Nigri, *Stern des Meschiah*, fols 139ʳ and 141ʳ (according to a copy in Munich, Bayerische Staatsbibliothek, 4 Inc.c.a. 99m).
102 See the interpretation of Isaiah 9:6–7, for instance (Nigri, fol. 33ʳ).
103 Eveline Staalduine-Sulman, *Justifying Christian Aramaism: Editions and Latin Translations of the Targums from the Complutensian to the London Polyglot Bible (1517–1657)* (Leiden: Brill, 2017), pp. 245–49. See also Stephen G. Burnett, 'The Targum in Christian Scholarship to 1800', in *A Jewish Targum in a Christian World*, ed. by Alberdina Houtman, Eveline Staalduine-Sulman, and others (Leiden: Brill, 2014), pp. 250–65 (pp. 251–53).
104 Mainz, Wissenschaftliche Stadtbibliothek (WSB), Hs I 378; Ernst Roth, Hans Striedl, and Lothar Tetzner, *Hebräische Handschriften*, 2 parts, Verzeichnis der orientalischen Handschriften, 6 (Wiesbaden: Steiner, 1965), part 2, p. 213. After Piscator's death, the Prophets passed into the hands of a former Jew, Franciscan Paul Pfeddersheim, who placed the volume in the Franciscan Convent in Mainz. For his lengthy owner inscription that elaborates on the provenance of this codex, see WSB, Hs I 378, fol. 1ʳ; published in Steimann, *Jewish Book – Christian Book*, pp. 32–33, see there also the related bibliographic references.

the earlier hand might have belonged to Piscator himself. In addition to the Latin titles of the Prophets' books and their division into chapters in accordance with the Vulgate, the Christian annotations include marginal comments to the Hebrew text. Those comments, like those of the Collegium Ducale, also emphasize the promise-fulfilment aspects of the Hebrew Prophets.[105] The earlier annotator of Piscator's Prophets used the Targum Jonathan. For instance, based on that Targum, he understood the verses from Jeremiah 23:5–6, 'The days are surely coming, says the Lord, when I will raise up for David a righteous Branch, and he shall reign as king and deal wisely, and shall execute justice. [...] And this is the name by which he will be called: "The Lord is our righteousness"', as a reference to Christ. In the margins next to these verses, he commented: '*Nota, ex hoc textu probatur christus deus esse quia nomen domini tetragrammaton pointur hic de eo secundum targum*' (A note: from this text it is approved that Christ is the God, because according to the Targum the name of God is rendered in this place as Tetragrammaton).[106] What this Christian annotator referred to was the replacement of the word *branch* with the word *Messiah* in the Targum — the replacement that allowed him to establish an identity between the Messiah, Christ, and God (the Tetragrammaton).[107] Thus, he concluded that Christ was the Messiah promised to Israel, and he is God.

The Viennese theologians, Nigri, and other fifteenth-century German scholars shared a similar position regarding the Hebrew Bible and expressed it in their sermons, in their exegetical and polemical works, and in the margins of the Hebrew manuscripts they owned. They did not use the Hebrew manuscripts to gain a deeper understanding of the Jewish tradition or to develop theological arguments of their own, but rather to look for evidence of Christological readings of the biblical verses.

Concluding Remarks

The journey of the Hebrew manuscripts discussed in this essay, moving between different geographical areas and religious traditions (Jewish and Christian), is reflected in the manuscripts' margins. The comments made in these spaces not only mirror the traumatic events of medieval Jewish life, which led to the manuscripts changing hands, but they also demonstrate that the sense of any text was in the eye of the beholder. If Jewish marginal annotations in the same manuscripts amended, explained, and interpreted the biblical text within the framework of the Jewish tradition, Christians' marginalia marked the shift to their own tradition, replacing the former apparatus of interpretation with the Christian one. By so doing, Christians also shifted the focus of a written page from the core Hebrew text to the Latin marginalia, which, in their eyes, reflected the essence of Hebrew Scripture. Although varying in their frequency and quantity, annotations made by Christian users were quite consistent in terms of their content, both in the volumes of the Collegium Ducale and in other Hebrew manuscripts owned by Christians of the time. Owing to such annotations, Christian readers were not only able to adapt the codices to their own specific needs, but could also share their attitudes and knowledge with successive readers in the library.

These attitudes towards the Hebrew biblical texts began to change with the rise of Christian Hebraism, which had spread in the German-speaking milieu by the end of the fifteenth century. Starting with Johannes Reuchlin, the Hebraists acquired Hebrew language skills and developed empirical methods of text criticism based on the

---

105 Walde, pp. 66–68.
106 WSB, Hs I 378, fol. 148ʳ.
107 Cf. John Oxlee, *The Christian Doctrines of the Trinity, and Incarnation Considered and Maintained on the Principles of Judaism*, 2 vols (London: London Society's Office, 1820), II, pp. 361–64.

Hebrew wording of the Bible and collation of its diverse manuscript copies. Although the Hebraists also looked for evidence of the 'Christian truth' in the Hebrew text of the Bible, their interest in Hebraica was much more multifaceted and they studied Jewish texts for their own sake in order to understand them from the perspective of the Jewish tradition.[108]

By the sixteenth century, as German Hebraists were gaining a better insight into Jewish texts, the Viennese theologians had lost much of their enthusiasm about the Hebraica they owned, however, and their manuscripts have very few Christian annotations from that time. By that point, the donations and bequests had dwindled away and the library of the Collegium had begun to lose its importance.[109] Thus, as Tengnagel wrote to King Matthias in 1611, the Hebrew manuscripts at the Collegium had fallen into disuse and were suffering from neglect.

---

108 For an overview, see Steimann, *Jewish Book – Christian Book*, pp. 25–52.

109 *Mittelalterliche Bibliothekskataloge Österreichs*, I, p. 470.

Appendix A: Inventories of Hebraica of the University of Vienna and the Hofbibliothek

I.
Sebastian Tengnagel, Excerpta ex Catalogo Bibliothecae Academicae Viennensis confecta 27. Septembris Anno 1623. In Litera A Libri Hebraici[110]

1. Biblia in fol. regal, membran. exemp. I.
2. Biblia in fol. memb.
3. Liber Josue usque ad Paralipomena memb.
4. *Liber Chiduschim, in 4°.
5. Biblia 4° memb.
6. Biblia una cum perusch, fol. memb.
7. Biblia scripta fol. memb.
8. Biblia MS fol. memb.
9. MS Biblia fol. reg. memb.
10. Biblia cum interpret. hebr. fol. memb.
11. Biblia MS fol. reg. membr.
12. Biblia MS fol. reg. memb.
13. *Biblia in 4°. No. 401.
14. *Biblia, fol. No. 903.
15. *Biblia fol. exemplaria duo.
16. Liber Jochiot [under *Jochiot* are dots signifying corruption] corrupt. sive Mardochaeus, fol. reg. memb.
17. Liber Arba (forte Thurim) MS fol. reg. memb.
18. Liber Hozi (forte Mose Mickotzi) fol. reg. memb. MS.
19. Liber Josue cum aliis, fol. memb. MS.
20. Liber Josue, fol. script memb. MS.
21. Liber (Notti [under *Notti* are dots signifying corruption] corrupt.) fol. reg. MS memb.
22. Liber (Chodesch corrupt.) fol. reg. MS memb.
23. Liber Therumoth fol. reg. script memb. MS.
24. Liber Josue, fol. reg. MS memb.
25. Liber Omar, corrupt. fol. reg. MS memb.
26. *Liber Chidusch, 4°.
27. *Liber Aruch seu Dictionar. Chaldaicum 4°.
28. *Lib. Maßichta Scebuoth, fol.
29. *Lib. Seder Thora, fol.
30. *Talmudis 10 partes, fol.
31. *Rabi Moses, 4°.

II.
Xystus Schier, Inventory of Manuscripts Transferred from the University of Vienna to the Hofbibliothek, 1756[111]

1. Scriptura veteris foederis hebraice punctata cum masora minori et majori fine mutila, fol. membr.
2. Josue et reliqua fine mutili, fol. membr.
3. Josue et reliqua, fol. membr.
4. Pentateuchus punctatus cum utraque masora, fol. membr.
5. Josue et reliqua cum masora, fol. membr.
6. Pentateuchus et Prophetae punctati. 4. membr.
7. Rabi Schlomojarchi commentarii in totam scripturam, fol. superregali, membr.
8. Aruch seu lexicon rabinico-talmudicum, fol. superregali, membr.
9. Compendium Talmudis, fol. membr.
10. Rabi Moisis filii Jacobi commentarius in praecepta prohibitiva, fol. superregali, membr.
11. Pars Talmudis fragmentum ex tractatu Jeschuaus(?), fol. superregali principio et fine mutilus, membr.
12. Biblia seu Lex et Prophetae[112] cum punctis, fol. membr.
13. Josue et libri sequentes, fol. membr.
14. Pars Talmudis de oblationibus, fol. superregali, membr.
15. Pentateuchus et reliqua, fol. membr.
16. Pentateuchus punctatus, fol. membr.

---

110 ÖNB, Cod. 9690, fols 219^r–219^v. Here and henceforth * denotes prints.

111 ÖNB, Cod. 9520, fols 34^r–52^v.

112 This item suggests that the manuscript includes the Pentateuch and Prophets. This, however, could be a liturgical Pentateuch with *haftarot* and other common additions.

III.
Johann Locher, Catalogus Bibliothecae Universitatis Viennensis, 1775[113]

1. Biblia cum punctis, pentateuchus et historiae[114] in membrana, hebraice M.S. f.
2. Biblia integra cum punctis in membrana in duplo, hebraice M.S. f.
3. Biblia Pentateuchus et libri historici scripti a Menachem scriba, filio Eliezer in membrana, hebraice M.S. f.
4. Biblia punctata cum notulis in membrana, hebraice M.S. 4.
5. Biblia sacra integra cum punctis in membrana, hebraice M.S. f.
6. Biblia sacra a Josue incipiens cum omnibus libris reliquis et cum figuris calamo delineatis cum punctis in membrana, hebraice M.S. f.
7. Commentarii in Biblia in membrana, hebraice M.S. f.
8. Commentarii in partes Talmudis de seminibus et de anno septimo, in membrana, in duplo, hebraice M.S. f.
9. Commentarius in biblia in membrana, hebraice M.S. f.
10. Lexicon scriptum in membrana, hebraice f.
11. Manuscriptum hebraicum f.
12. Moysis filii Jacob explicatio praeceptorum M.S. in membrana in duplo, hebraice f.
13. Pentateuchus cum punctis in membrana in duplo, hebraice M.S. f.
14. Pentateuchus et historica cum notis marginalibus rabbinorum et cum punctis in membrana in duplo, hebraice M.S. f.
15. *Idem opus [pentateuchus] cum et absque notis, volumina duo, hebraice f.
16. *Talmud babylonicum undecim voluminibus comprehensum, impressus Venetiis, hebraice f.

---

113 ÖNB, Cod. 7707, pp. 72–73, 83, 122, 128, 133, 143, and 169.
114 This is apparently a liturgical Pentateuch with *haftarot* (called by Locher '*historiae*', referring to the biblical historical books contained in the *haftarot*), as it follows from no. 3 in this inventory that could be identified as ÖNB, Cod. hebr. 11.

Appendix B: Correspondences between the Hebrew Manuscripts in the ÖNB and the Items Mentioned in the Inventories[115]

	Library shelf mark	Content	Hebraica inventories according to Appendix A (I: Tengnagel, 1623; II: Schier, 1756; III: Locher, 1775)
1	ÖNB, Cod. hebr. 2	Mordekhai ben Hillel, *Sefer ha-Mordekhai* (490 × 355 mm)	I. 16 II. 9
2	ÖNB, Cod. hebr. 3	Rashi, Commentary on the Bible (482 × 356 mm)	II. 7 III. 7, 9
3	ÖNB, Cod. hebr. 4	Bible with *masorah parva* to the Pentateuch (475 × 356 mm)	I. 1–2, 7–9, 11–12
4	ÖNB, Cod. hebr. 6	Pentateuch with Onkelos Targum, *megillot*, *haftarot*, Job, and verses from Jeremiah (455 × 315 mm)	I. 1–2, 7–9, 11–12 II. 12, 15–16 III. 1, 13
5	ÖNB, Cod. hebr. 11	Pentateuch, *haftarot*, *megillot*, and Job (404 × 315 mm)	I. 1–2, 7–9, 11–12 II. 12, 15–16 III. 3
6	ÖNB, Cod. hebr. 13	Pentateuch, *haftarot*, *megillot*, Job, and verses from Jeremiah (360 × 280 mm)	I. 1–2, 7–9, 11–12 II. 12, 15–16 III. 1, 13
7	ÖNB, Cod. hebr. 14	Pentateuch with Onkelos Targum, *megillot*, Job, verses from Jeremiah, *haftarot*; with *masorah magna* and *parva* and Rashi's commentary (338 × 265 mm)	I. 6, 10 II. 14
8	ÖNB, Cod. hebr. 15	Prophets and Writings (from Joshua to Chronicles) (323 × 270 mm)	I. 19–20, 24 II. 2
9	ÖNB, Cod. hebr. 16	Prophets and Writings (from Joshua to Chronicles), with decorative *masorah magna* and *parva* (330 × 245 mm)	I. 3 II. 5 III. 6
10	ÖNB, Cod. hebr. 17	Prophets (from Joshua to Malakhi), with *masorah parva* (323 × 250 mm)	I. 19–20, 24 II. 3, 13
11	ÖNB, Cod. hebr. 19	Pentateuch, *megillot*, and *haftarot* (305 × 214 mm)	I. 1–2, 7–9, 11–12 II. 12, 15–16 III. 1, 13
12	ÖNB, Cod. hebr. 25	Genesis, Exodus with Rashi's commentary and *masorah parva*, *haftarot* (310 × 230 mm)	I. 6, 10 II. 4
13	ÖNB, Cod. hebr. 38	Pentateuch and *megillot* with *masorah magna* and *parva*, *haftarot* (246 × 190 mm)	I. 5 II. 6

---

115 Given the too general and inaccurate character of the inventories, the references to the inventories in the left column indicate possible correspondences between the actual manuscripts in the ÖNB and the items listed in the inventories. Listing more than one corresponding inventory item, repeated next to several manuscripts, indicates that any of these inventories' items can correspond to any of these manuscripts.

SAVERIO CAMPANINI

'Ben Hacane Liber qui dicitur Pelia'

Egidio da Viterbo's Kabbalistic Excerpts

Die politische Sündflut brach über das üppige Rom herein.

Ferdinand Gregorovius

Introduction: A Book and Its Readers

The diffusion and reception of the kabbalistic commentary on the first section of the Book of Genesis known as *Sefer ha-peli'ah* ('Book of the Mystery') among Christian readers is an interesting example of a transformative passage from one specific cultural and religious environment to a completely different one. A certain geographical restlessness is inscribed even in the early stages of the history of this book, a vast pseudoepigraphic miscellany attributed to one Elqanah of Ben ha-Qanah. If one accepts the most widespread theory concerning its rather mysterious origins,[1] it travelled from the Balkans in the mid-fourteenth century to Spain. It eventually reached Italy in the fifteenth century, if not earlier, in one instance, at least, accompanying the exiles from the Iberian Peninsula. The book, with its mysterious provenance, which is after all only appropriate for a treatise bearing the word 'mystery' in its title, includes several short pieces and some complete works, such as the *Gan na'ul* ('Enclosed Garden') by Abraham Abulafia (*c.* 1291), clearly of Iberian

---

1 Israel Ta-Shma, 'When Were the Books *Ha-Qanah* and *Ha-Peli'ah* Written?' [in Hebrew], in *Studies in the History of Jewish Society in the Middle Ages and in the Modern Period Presented to Professor Jacob Katz on His Seventy-Fifth Birthday*, ed. by Immanuel Etkes and Joseph Salmon (Jerusalem: Mosad Bialik, 1980), pp. 56–63; repr. in Israel Ta-Shma, *Studies in Medieval Rabbinic Literature* [in Hebrew] (Jerusalem: Mosad Bialik, 2006), III, pp. 218–28; Moshe Idel, 'The Kabbalah in Byzantium: Preliminary Remarks' [in Hebrew], *Kabbalah*, 18 (2008): pp. 197–227; augmented and updated version: *The Kabbalah in Byzantium: Preliminary Remarks*, in *Jews in Byzantium: Dialectics of Minority and Majority Cultures*, ed. by Robert Bonfil, Oded Irshai, and others (Leiden: Brill, 2012), pp. 659–708. See also Nicholas De Lange, 'Hebrew Scholarship in Byzantium', in *Hebrew Scholarship and the Medieval World*, ed. by Nicholas De Lange (Cambridge: Cambridge University Press, 2001), pp. 23–37; Philippe Gardette, 'Prolégomènes concernant l'apport de la kabbale judéobyzantine à la Renaissance humaniste italienne: Gilles de Viterbe et le sefer ha Temunah', *Byzantinoslavica*, 1/2 (2009): pp. 291–330; Philippe Gardette, *Les juifs byzantins aux racines de l'histoire juive ottomane: Essai de réflexions spéculaires ou tentative d'habillage d'une absence de représentation* (Istanbul: Isis, 2013).

Saverio Campanini • Alma Mater Studiorum, Università di Bologna

origin. After it circulated in Italy and the Eastern Mediterranean region, it reached Eastern Europe, where it was first printed in Korets in 1784 and again, in a more correct version, in Przemysl in 1883. Moreover, the same Hasidic circles which were responsible for the first publication of *Sefer ha-peli'ah* in print, also produced the first commentary on this work, penned by Menahem Mendel of Shklow, a pupil of the Vilna Gaon (Elijah ben Solomon Zalman, d. 1797), which was published only recently.[2] In religious circles, the Book of the Mystery has been associated with a large and, from our perspective, rather heterogeneous group of literary works which also includes *Sefer ha-Qanah* (with which it has been associated and sometimes identified or confused), *Sefer ha-temunah* ('Book of the Image'), and even *Bahir* ('Book of Radiance'), which were all published together in a massive volume under the title *Torat ha-Qanah*, also available in a three-volume edition.[3]

The history of the reception of *Sefer ha-peli'ah* among Jews, which is still to be written and studied as it deserves,[4] is only one part of a more complex picture, or I should say, one side of a diptych, whose other panel relates to the history of its reception among Christians. That reception was characterized by several interesting aspects not only from a theological or ideological point of view, but also, as I try to show in some detail here, from the perspective of book history and of the organization, retrieval, and dynamization of received knowledge. Elsewhere I have traced a brief sketch of the diachronic development of the Christian readership of *Sefer ha-peli'ah* in the Renaissance, focusing on the Venetian Franciscan Francesco Zorzi (d. 1540), his pupil Arcangelo da Borgonovo (d. 1568), and the later Hebraist Blaise de Vigenère.[5] On this occasion, upon examining a few manuscripts copied at the beginning of the sixteenth century and relying on some indirect hints found in letters and other historical pieces of evidence, I give a more detailed account of the reception and the use of *Sefer ha-peli'ah* by Egidio da Viterbo (d. 1532), Cardinal, Hebraist, and Kabbalist.[6] Egidio, an Augustinian friar, became general of his order before receiving the cardinal's hat in the consistory of 1517, led the order to which Martin Luther belonged and preached reform of the Church at the Lateran Council. He was also, as we will see, a distinguished Hebraist, a fervent adept of the Christian Kabbalah, and an avid book collector.

---

2   Menahem Mendel of Sklow, *Commentaries on the Sefer ha-Peli'ah* [in Hebrew] (New York: Makhon ha-Gara', 2003).

3   *Torat ha-Qanah. Sefer ha-peli'ah* (Jerusalem: Nezer Shraga, 1997). The other volumes were produced in the same publishing house in 1998 together with a massive volume of more than 1100 pages that encompasses all four works (*Sefer ha-peli'ah, Sefer ha-Qanah, Sefer ha-temunah,* and *Sefer ha-bahir*).

4   A first attempt at a comprehensive monograph on *Sefer ha-peli'ah* and of *Sefer ha-Qanah* is Michal Kushnir-Oron, *The Sefer ha-Peli'ah and the Sefer ha-Kanah: Their Kabbalistic Principles, Social and Religious Criticism and Literary Composition* [in Hebrew] (Jerusalem: The Hebrew University, 1980). However, the main focus of this important study is not the reception of these works, but a systematic reconstruction of their kabbalistic ideology and theological standpoint.

5   Saverio Campanini, '"Elchana Hebraeorum doctor et cabalista". Le avventure di un libro e dei suoi lettori', in *Umanesimo e cultura ebraica nel Rinascimento italiano*, ed. by Stefano Baldassarri and Fabrizio Lelli (Florence: Angelo Pontecorboli editore, 2016), pp. 90–114.

6   A preliminary study concerning Egidio's attitude towards historical events such as the Sack of Rome of 1527, which he read through the looking-glass of his Kabbalistic books in Latin translation, has now appeared in Saverio Campanini, 'Dal Sacco di Roma alla fine del mondo. Profezie cabbalistiche tra le carte di Egidio da Viterbo', in *Rinascimento plurale. Ibridazioni linguistiche e socioculturali tra Quattrocento e Cinquecento*, ed. by Giulio Busi and Silvana Greco (Castiglione delle Stiviere: Fondazione Palazzo Bondoni Pastorio 2021), pp. 71–99.

The Cardinal's Book

The first mention of Egidio's interest in *Sefer ha-peli'ah* is documented in a letter he sent to his 'agent' the Augustinian friar Gabriele della Volta (d. 1537) residing in Venice on 9 January 1514:

> De libro quem scribis, sine mercede viginti aureorum exemplari non posse, qui quidem liber Bencana dicitur super primum cap., hic scribentibus volumina hebraica pro singulo quaternione Marcellos praebemus duos; idcirco curato quantum poteris detrahere, sed ut habeatur liber Bencana nullis pecuniis stetur.
>
> (Concerning the book you mentioned, called Bencana on the first chapter [of Genesis], saying that it cannot be copied for less than 20 gold ducats, here we pay the copyists 2 *marcelli* for a quire; therefore, try to get a discount as big as you can, but in order to obtain the Bencana one should not be afraid of spending.)[7]

As early as in December 1512, as general of the Augustinian order, Egidio had written to Gabriele Veneto (as Della Volta was also known) to tell him to invest a considerable sum, made up from the proceeds of alms, to purchase Hebrew books, especially Jewish commentators on the Bible.[8] However, *Sefer ha-peli'ah* was apparently not among the books that Gabriele Veneto acquired for him, as Egidio was still asking for it at the beginning of 1514.

Egidio's renewed interest in the book had most likely been triggered by information which Gabriele shared in a no longer extant letter. Apparently, that letter revealed that one of the most erudite Christian Kabbalists living in Venice, the Franciscan of the Observance Francesco Zorzi, had found a copy of the coveted treasure among the books of Damiano di Castiglia, a Jewish physician of Spanish origin, who was living and practicing medicine in Venice. It is most likely that it was his assistant, the convert Marco Raphael, who informed Zorzi about this Spanish refugee who had the book for which he had been searching.

The story of how Zorzi was able to acquire this book is fascinating but since I have already reconstructed it elsewhere,[9] it will suffice to note that he was able to convince the Council of Ten, a major governing body in Venice, to beg Damiano to lend him his copy of *Sefer ha-peli'ah* against a deposit of 500 ducats, which was indeed a very large sum of money. The book was lent, and the transaction recorded on 18 June 1512. However, after some obscure manoeuvres, Zorzi was able to acquire the volume, which he called 'Elchana', from Damiano for a negligible sum. As a matter of fact, Damiano had been accused of practicing medicine in Venice without recommending that his patients call a priest for confession while prescribing potentially lethal medicines and had

---

7 The letter, preserved in Rome, Biblioteca Angelica, MS 688, fols 49^{r–v}, was first published in David Gutiérrez, 'De antiquis Ordinis Eremitarum Sancti Augustini bibliothecis', *Analecta Augustiniana*, 23 (1953–54): pp. 164–372 (p. 172); Gérard Weil, *Elie Lévita, humaniste et massorète (1469–1549)* (Leiden: Brill, 1963), p. 80; Francis Xavier Martin, 'The Writings of Giles of Viterbo', *Augustiniana*, 29 (1979): pp. 141–93 (p. 180); Egidio da Viterbo, *Lettere familiari*, ed. by Anna Maria Voci Roth (Rome: Institutum Historicum Augustinianum, 1990), II (1507–17), p. 181; Wilhelm Schmidt-Biggemann, *Geschichte der christlichen Kabbala. 15. und 16. Jahrhundert* (Stuttgart and Bad Cannstatt: Frommann-Holzboog, 2012), p. 356; Emma Abate, 'Filologia e qabbalah. La collezione ebraica di Egidio da Viterbo alla Biblioteca Angelica di Roma', *Archivio Italiano per la Storia della Pietà*, 26 (2013): pp. 413–51 (p. 424). Abate remarks that the same letter is copied also in the MS 1001, fols 295^v–296^r of the aforementioned library.

8 Cf. Egidio, *Lettere familiari*, p. 174.
9 Campanini, 'Elchana Hebraeorum', pp. 93–100.

to pay a heavy fine. As early as in December 1513, Egidio must have heard something about the large collection of Hebrew and kabbalistic books held by the Franciscan, and he hastened to write to Gabriele Veneto: I will be most pleased if you will let me know the titles of the books that you have told me are in the possession of the friar of Saint Francis, and whether 'apud alios' ('in the possession of other [collectors]') 'alia volumina hebrea' ('other Hebrew books') can be found.[10] Gabriele Veneto's answer has not been preserved nor is it known whether Egidio was able to get a copy of *Sefer ha-peli'ah* for 20 ducats or for less (at a rate of 2 *marcelli*, i.e., 1 *lira*, for every quire of five sheets). Here we face the first of the problems confronting us in connection with Egidio's reception of this kabbalistic book: Has at least one Hebrew manuscript of *Sefer ha-peli'ah* from Egidio's library been preserved? On the occasion of a recent survey of the extant manuscripts that were once in Egidio's library, unrecognized so far, in the Biblioteca Casanatense in Rome, Margherita Palumbo observed, quite prudently, that one particular manuscript, MS 3154 of the Casanatense, causes the cataloguing librarian some striking difficulties.[11] That manuscript contains *Sefer ha-peli'ah* and there are annotations in the margins in Egidio's familiar hand. Moreover, occasionally the outer and bottom margins reflect typical features of Egidio's style of annotation: the animals,[12] his habit of adding a resumé of the main contents of a given page in Latin in the bottom margin,[13] the use of Greek for marginal glosses,[14] and the unmistakable drawing of the coat of arms he chose upon being elected cardinal, that is, the three hills, one of them (as in other instances[15]) surmounted by a cross.[16] Moreover,

---

10 I paraphrase the letter, written in a typical mixture of Latin and Italian, which can be read in the Biblioteca Angelica, MS 688, fols 48ʳ–49ʳ, and in Egidio, *Lettere familiari*, pp. 179–80. Cf. Francesco Fiorentino, 'Egidio da Viterbo e i pontaniani di Napoli', *Archivio storico delle provincie napoletane*, 9/3 (1884): pp. 430–52 (p. 445); then in Francesco Fiorentino, *Il risorgimento filosofico nel quattrocento* (Naples: Tipografia della Regia Università, 1885), p. 265; Giovanni Semprini, *I platonici italiani* (Milan: Athena, 1926), p. 104; François Secret, *Le Zôhar chez les kabbalistes chrétiens de la Renaissance* (Paris: Mouton, 1964), p. 43; Cesare Vasoli, *Profezia e ragione: Studi sulla cultura del Cinquecento e del Seicento* (Naples: Morano, 1974), p. 151; Marc Deramaix, 'La genèse du De Partu Virginis de Jacopo Sannazaro et trois églogues inédites de Gilles de Viterbe', *Mélanges de l'Ecole française de Rome. Moyen Age*, 102 (1990): pp. 173–276 (p. 233); Gulio Busi, *L'enigma dell'ebraico nel Rinascimento* (Turin: Aragno, 2007), p. 168; Francesco Zorzi, *L'armonia del mondo*, ed., trans., and comm. by Saverio Campanini (Milan: Bompiani, 2010), p. cxxi; Margherita Palumbo, 'I codici postillati di Egidio da Viterbo, dal Sant'Uffizio alla Casanatense', in *Egidio da Viterbo: Cardinale agostiniano tra Roma e l'Europa del Rinascimento*, ed. by Myriam Chiabò, Rocco Ronzani, and Angelo Maria Vitale (Rome: Centro Culturale Agostiniano – Roma nel Rinascimento, 2014), pp. 299–322 (p. 310).

11 Palumbo, p. 309.

12 Rome, Biblioteca Casanatense, MS 3154, fols 200ʳ and 383ʳ. On Egidio's habit of drawing animals and other figures in the margins, see John Whittaker, 'Greek Manuscripts from the Library of Giles of Viterbo at the Biblioteca Angelica in Rome', *Scriptorium*, 31 (1977): pp. 212–39 (pp. 214–15).

13 See, for instance, Casanatense, MS 3154, fol. 417ᵛ.

14 See, e.g., Casanatense, MS 3154, fol. 416ᵛ: Ανδρόγινος [*sic*], commenting the Hebrew אנדרוגינס in the text. The peculiar orthography or rather the wrong spelling of the Greek is not untypical of Egidio, since it is found many times, even in the manuscript in Paris, Bibliothèque nationale de France (BnF), lat. 527, fol. 468ʳ (twice in Latin: 'androginus/androginos').

15 Giuseppe Signorelli, *Il cardinale Egidio da Viterbo, agostiniano, umanista e riformatore* (Florence: Libreria Editrice Fiorentina, 1929), p. 67; Francis Xavier Martin, 'Giles of Viterbo and the Monastery of Lecceto: The Making of a Reformer', *Analecta Augustiniana*, 25 (1962): pp. 225–53; Benedict Hackett, 'A "Lost" Work of Giles of Viterbo: Critical Edition of His Treatise on Lecceto', in *Egidio da Viterbo, O.S.A. e il suo tempo: atti del V Convegno dell' Istituto Storico Agostiniano, Roma-Viterbo, 20–23 ottobre 1982* (Rome: Analecta Augustiniana, 1983), pp. 117–36; Whittaker, p. 219; Benedict Hackett, 'The Augustinian Hermitage of Lecceto', in *Augustine in Iconography: History and Legend*, ed. by Joseph C. Schnaubelt and Frederick van Fleteren (New York: Peter Lang, 1999), pp. 333–56.

16 Casanatense, MS 3154, fol. 200ʳ.

in the margin next to a polemical mention of the prophet of Islam, we see the drawing of a hand with the thumb between the forefinger and the middle finger,[17] the infamous gesture of the '*fiche*' evoked by Dante as having been made by the damned Vanni Fucci, which recurs, for example, in the autographs of Giovanni Boccaccio.[18] In this case, however, one cannot be completely sure that this particular drawing was made by Egidio since, as far as I know, there are no ascertained instances when he penned such a vulgar gesture. Even after having recognized Egidio's hand in the manuscript and knowing his scribal habits, the question of whether he owned or perused it is far from settled. As Palumbo notes, the manuscript's colophon states that this particular copy was completed in Venice by Isaac ben Moses ibn Zerah on 13 Kislev 5295, corresponding to 20 November 1534 in the Julian calendar:

אני הסופר יצחק בר הה״ר משה בן זר״ח נ״ע ועשיתי אותו הספר וסיימתי אותו | פה בויניסיאה בי״ג לחדש כסליו משנת חמשת אלפים ומאתים ותשעים וחמשה | ליצירת עולם ביום ו׳. תם ונשלם שלב״ע ת״ם בילא״ו.

(I, the scribe Isaac son of the late Moses ben Zerah, have copied this book and I completed it here in Venice on Kislev 13 of the year five thousand two hundred and ninety-five from the creation of the world, on a Friday. It is finished and complete, praise to the Lord who created the world. It is finished, blessed be the Lord forever. Amen and Amen.)[19]

Obviously, Egidio could not have possessed or read, even less glossed, a manuscript if it was written two years after his death on 12 November 1532. Although not being in any way keen about ignoring a piece of evidence such as the one provided by the colophon, I try, in the following discussion, to weigh it against the evidence provided by the clear signs that Egidio did peruse and annotate this manuscript to argue in favour of correcting the information provided by the scribe.

More Manuscripts

We are fortunate enough to have two further manuscripts copied by the same scribe in the same place, all of them containing *Sefer ha-peli'ah*. The earlier of the two is now housed in the Russian State Library of Moscow and, as its colophon states,[20] it was copied by Isaac ben Moses ibn Zerah in Venice on 25 April 1513[21] (less than one year after Damiano di Castiglia had been summoned by the Council of Ten). The manuscript does not show apparent signs of having been copied for a Christian (the place for the name of the owner, described as 'the noble and elevated', was left blank), even though we know from an inscription in the colophon, '*Domus Venetae Societatis [Iesu] cat. Inscr.*', that at a later point in time, it was in the library of the Jesuits in Venice. The Jesuits were expelled

---

17 Casanatense, MS 3154, fol. 319ʳ.
18 Marco Petoletti, 'Il Marziale autografo di Giovanni Boccaccio', *Italia Medievale e Umanistica*, 46 (2005), pp. 35–57 (p. 43).
19 Casanatense, MS 3154, fol. 442ʳ.

20 Moscow, The Russian State Library, MS Günzburg 377, fol. 380ᵛ: אני הסופר יצחק בר הה״ר משה בן ז׳ זרח נ״ע ועשיתי אותו הספר לנשא ונעלה הה״ר וסיימתי אותו בשנת חמשת אלפים ומאתים שבעי׳ ושלשה ליצירה כ״ב יום בל״ד לעומר בויניציאה. תם ('I am the scribe Isaac son of the venerable Moshe Ibn Zerah, whose soul is in Paradise, and I have made this book for the noble and elevated sir [name missing] I have completed it in the year 5273 of Creation, on the 22nd of Yiyar, the 32nd day of the "Omer, in Venice. It is complete"').
21 I deduce the date from the indications in the colophon, since the 34th day of the counting of the 'omer, a Monday, corresponds to 19 Iyyar 5273, that is 25 April 1513 according to the Julian calendar.

from the Venetian Republic twice, in 1606 and in 1773, and on both occasions their library was dispersed, so it is no wonder that one of its books could resurface among the treasures of the Guenzburg collection in the Russian Empire. It is curious to note that the name of Jesus has been carefully erased, or censored, most probably by one of the subsequent Jewish owners of the book, perhaps Jacob Raqah (d. 1891) or his son David or, before them, the well-known Hayyim Joseph David Azulay (d. 1806).

As we already know, the book was circulating in Venice, probably having come from Spain in the second decade of the sixteenth century. The same scribe completed another copy of the same work, also in Venice, on 17 Elul 5275, corresponding to 28 August 1515, which is now kept in the British Library.[22] As I argued on another occasion,[23] after having corrected the previous reading of the name of the owner of the copy, which George Margoliouth, followed by Michal Kushnir-Oron[24] and Giulio Busi,[25] read as 'Raphael',[26] into 'Daniel', I surmised that this particular copy could have been made for a Christian reader, that is, for the printer Daniel Bomberg (d. 1549), who, with the indispensable help of the convert the Augustinian friar Felice da Prato (d. 1559), was planning his major printing enterprise in the city on the lagoon. In a letter to the authorities of the Republic of Venice dated 23 April 1515, Felice da Prato claimed to have translated *Sefer ha-temunah* (*temunot*) and the *Imre shefer* ('Words of Beauty') by Abraham Abulafia from Hebrew into Latin. He also mentioned having composed a Hebrew grammar with a dictionary.[27] Egidio led Felice's order at the time, and he is known to have been active in Venice in the first decades of the sixteenth century. He had a decisive role in initiating the printing of several books of philosophy and prophecy (first and foremost Joachim of Fiore's commentary on the Apocalypse) and was particularly active in collecting kabbalistic books and promoting their translation into Latin and even into Italian. Thus, it is very unlikely that Bomberg's project could have been implemented without Egidio da Viterbo's encouragement and assistance.[28] Felice was in Venice at the time to arrange for the printing of his Latin translation of the Psalter with kabbalistic commentaries for Daniel Bomberg in Peter Lichtenstein's shop. Thus, one can assume that he had a part in obtaining a copy of the coveted *Sefer ha-peli'ah* for Bomberg and, perhaps, also the one for Egidio. According to a letter written in 1547 by Bomberg's well-known collaborator Cornelio Adelkind (d. after 1554) to Andreas Masius (d. 1573), a manuscript of *Sefer*

---

22 London, British Library, MS Harl. 5515 (George Margoliouth, *Catalogue of the Hebrew and Samaritan Manuscripts in the British Museum* [London: British Museum, 1909], III, no. 789), fol. 420ᵛ: אני הסופר יצחק בר הה"ר משה נ' זרח נ"ע ספרדי מעיר שקאביי"ה וסיימתי פה ויניסיא"ה שנת רע"ה י"ז לחדש אלול. בילא"ו. וכתבתי לאדון המשכיל ונבון מיסיר [דניאל] יצ"ו השם יחייהו ויבינהו מה שכתוב בו אמן ('I am the scribe Isaac son of the venerable Moshe Ibn Zerah the Spaniard from the town of Segovia and I have finished the copy in Venice in the year 5275 on the 17th of the month Elul, blessed the Lord forever Amen and Amen. I have written it for the learned and wise *Messer* [Daniel], may the Lord give him life. May the Lord let him live a long life and understand what this book contains, Amen').

23 Campanini, 'Elchana Hebraeorum', pp. 102–03.

24 Kushnir-Oron, p. 36.

25 Gulio Busi, 'Francesco Zorzi: A Methodical Dreamer', in *The Christian Kabbalah: Jewish Mystical Books and their Christian Interpreters*, ed. by Joseph Dan (Cambridge, MA: Harvard University Library, 1997), pp. 97–25 (p. 104).

26 Margoliouth, III, pp. 95–96 (p. 96).

27 Rinaldo Fulin, 'Documenti per servire alla storia della tipografia veneziana', *Archivio Veneto*, 12 (1882), pp. 84–212 (pp. 181–82); see also Jordan S. Penkower, 'The First Edition of the Bible Printed by Bomberg and the Beginning of His Printing Press' [in Hebrew], *Qiryat Sefer*, 58/3 (1983): pp. 586–604 (p. 597).

28 See Moshe Idel, 'Egidio da Viterbo and the Writings of Abraham Abulafia' [in Hebrew], *Italia*, 2/2–3 (1981): pp. 45–50.

ha-peli'ah figured among the books in Bomberg's library.²⁹ As it happens, the colophon in the copy supposedly made for Bomberg, which is now in the British Library, is incorrect. It seems, in fact, that the date was mistakenly written as קע״ה, which means that the manuscript would have been produced one hundred years earlier (1415), so Margoliouth was led astray and dated it to the fifteenth century.³⁰ Actually, it seems to me that the copyist himself noted the mistake and tried to erase the vertical line of the letter *qof* in order to make it look like a *resh* so as to change it to the right date ([5]275 = רע״ה).

What can be stated with confidence is that within two years, Isaac ben Moses ibn Zerah produced two copies of the same book in Venice, one of them most probably for a Christian client.

As we have seen, the first known copy of *Sefer ha-peli'ah* that surfaced in Venice, attracting the sustained curiosity of influential and powerful potential Christian readers, was the one in the hands of Damiano di Castiglia, mentioned in official documents in 1512. Before the Council of Ten, Francesco Zorzi claimed to have in his service a copyist who would be able to reproduce it quickly. The same was demonstrably true of Egidio da Viterbo and most probably of Daniel Bomberg as well, with or without the help of their common acquaintance Felice da Prato. We know from Egidio's letters to Gabriele della Volta, that Felice was helping Egidio to acquire Hebrew books and that he also worked for another Augustinian, the German Caspar Amman, in buying Hebrew books from Italian Jews.³¹

Be that as it may, according to the colophon in the third copy of *Sefer ha-peli'ah*, also made in Venice by Isaac ben Moses ibn Zerah, the manuscript was produced in 1534, two decades after the scribe penned the first two copies. But, as we have seen, the codex bears robust traces of having been used by a reader with the unmistakable hand of Egidio da Viterbo. Moreover, the manuscript was among a group of Hebrew books which certainly belonged to Egidio. Finally, in at least one other instance,

---

29 The letter, in Munich, Bayerische Staatsbibliothek (BSB), Clm 23736, was printed by Joseph Perles, *Beiträge zur Geschichte der Hebräischen und Aramäischen Studien* (Munich: Theodor Ackermann, 1884), p. 210. The relevant passage is quoted, not without adding some printing mistakes, in Robert J. Wilkinson, *Orientalism, Aramaic, and Kabbalah in the Catholic Reformation: The First Printing of the Syriac New Testament* (Leiden: Brill, 2007), p. 83. See also Bruce Nielsen, 'Daniel van Bombergen, a Bookman of Two Worlds', in *The Hebrew Book in Early Modern Italy*, ed. by Joseph Hacker and Adam Shear (Philadelphia: University of Pennsylvania Press, 2011), pp. 56–75 (p. 74); Theodor Dunkelgrün, 'The Hebrew Library of a Renaissance Humanist: Andreas Masius and the Bibliography to his *Iosuae Imperatoris Historia* (1574), with a Latin Edition and an Annotated English Translation', *Studia Rosenthaliana*, 42/43 (2010/11): pp. 197–252; Ilona Steimann, 'Jewish Scribes and Christian Patrons: The Hebraica Collection of Johann Jakob Fugger', *Renaissance Quarterly*, 70/4 (2017): pp. 1235–81.

30 Margoliouth, III, p. 95. The dating has been questioned, on purely palaeographical grounds, by the expert eye of Malachi Beit-Arié, as reported by Kishnir-Oron, p. 32. The early date proposed by Margoliouth had been already discussed by Benzion Netanyahu, 'Establishing the Dates of the Books "Ha-kane" and "Ha-Pelia"' [in Hebrew], in *Salo Wittmayer Baron Jubilee Volume*, ed. by Saul Lieberman (Jerusalem: American Academy for Jewish Research, 1975), III, pp. 247–68.

31 Two letters, one from Egidio to Caspar Amman dated 15 December 1513 and the other one from Felice da Prato to Amman, dated 4 October 1514 are preserved in a copy by the addressee, in a manuscript (MS 11) of the Hebrew Bible with Targum in the Stiftsbibliothek of Göttweig in Austria (see Arthur Z. Schwarz, *Die hebräischen Handschriften in Österreich ausserhalb der Nationalbibliothek in Wien* (Leipzig: Karl W. Hiersemann, 1931), pp. 2–4; they were published by Paul Jakob Bruns, 'Epistolae ineditae Aegidii Viterbiensis, Cardinalis, et Felicis Pratensis, Ex-Judaei', in *Annales Litterarii Helmstadienses*, ed. by Heinrich Ph. C. Henke and others (Helmstadt: M. G. Leuckart, 1782), I, pp. 193–98. See Saverio Campanini, 'Una lettera in ebraico e una in latino da Matthaeus Adriani a Caspar Amman sul nome di Gesù', *Bruniana & Campanelliana*, 24/1 (2018): pp. 25–47 (p. 45).

the copyist had shown his carelessness in noting the date of his work. Therefore, I believe, that it is not too far-fetched to assume that the scribe, although he did write 90 (תשעים), should have written 70 (שבעים), and the corrected date would correspond to 1 December 1514. I am persuaded that Gabriele della Volta or Felice da Prato or both were successful in convincing the copyist or the owner to sell this manuscript and managed to send it to Rome to its eager reader Egidio. Unfortunately, both 1 December 1514 and 20 November 1534 fell on a Friday,[32] so the mention of the day of the week in the colophon does not resolve the issue. Optimistically, one can at least still conclude that the revised date is not untenable from a chronological point of view.

A further problem arises. The Bavarian State Library in Munich has a copy of *Sefer ha-peli'ah* penned in 1554 by Hayyim ben Samuel ibn Gattegno for Johann Albrecht Widmanstetter.[33] According to a note written by the latter it was copied in Rome from a manuscript kept in Egidio da Viterbo's library. From a rather cursory examination, it would appear that the Munich manuscript was not copied from the one now at the Casanatense, since the texts of the two versions do not coincide. However, we know and as I discuss in the following pages, Egidio's library was displaced, damaged, and dispersed during the Sack of Rome in 1527. It is, thus, plausible to assume that Egidio obtained a second copy of the same kabbalistic work and that this second version was the model for ibn Gattegno's later copy. For the time being, my case in favour of a revision of the date found in the colophon will have to rest on the evidence that I have been able to collect and review so far.

Latin Translations

Additional evidence of Egidio's interest for *Sefer ha-peli'ah* can be gleaned from the fact that at around the same time he — most probably with the help of a Jewish or convert assistant — prepared a Latin translation of that book, which is now preserved at the Bibliothèque Nationale de France (BnF) in Paris (lat. 3667).[34] In a signature Egidio calls himself 'frater' and not 'Cardinalis', which led Francis X. Martin to conjecture that the translation should be dated prior to 1517.[35] Martin's argument, however, is not decisive, since in private Egidio might have neglected to mention his official title. Either way, if my supposition is correct, Egidio da Viterbo worked on the translation after he had added brief comments in the margins of his Hebrew manuscript, the one that is now at the Casanatense Library. The features of this translation, seldom if ever studied, deserve a closer look. However, before I describe its principal characteristics, I should note that another manuscript held in

---

32 Cf. Eduard Mahler, *Handbuch der jüdischen Chronologie* (Leipzig: G. Fock, 1916), pp. 576–77.

33 BSB, Cod. hebr. 96. See Moritz Steinschneider, *Die hebräischen Handschriften der K. Hof- und Staatsbibliothek in München* (Munich: Palm, 1895), pp. 60–61. On Widmanstetter, see Maximilian De Molière, 'Ex Bibliotheca Aegidiana: Das Fortleben der Bücher Kardinal Egidio da Viterbos in der hebraistischen Bibliothek Johann Albrecht Widmanstetters', in *Die Bibliothek: Denkräume und Wissensordnungen*, ed. by Andreas Speer and Lars Reuke (Berlin: De Gruyter, 2020), pp. 775–92; Maximilian De Molière, 'Johann Albrecht Widmanstetter's Recension of the "Zohar"', *Kabbalah*, 41 (2018): pp. 7–52.

34 Cf. Egidio da Viterbo, *Scechina e Libellus de litteris Hebraicis*, ed. by François Secret (Rome: Centro internazionale di studi umanistici, 1959), I, p. 17; Charles Astruc and Jacques Monfrin, *Livres latins et hébreux du Cardinal Gilles de Viterbe: Bibliothèque d'Humanisme et Renaissance*, 23 (1961), pp. 551–54 (p. 553).

35 Martin, 'The Writings of Giles of Viterbo', p. 179; see also Davide Muratore, *La biblioteca del cardinale Niccolò Ridolfi* (Alessandria: Edizioni dell'Orso, 2009), I, p. 334, as quoted in Palumbo, p. 309.

the BnF[36] includes, among many other texts, a different translation of large sections of the same work, written in Egidio's hand along with copious comments in the margins.

As it appears at a first glance, the two translations are certainly in Egidio's hand but they are far from identical. One should first clarify their relationship in order to establish, if possible, which one was penned first and how the undeniable differences between them can be explained. Furthermore, one should assess their features more precisely, whether they are to be considered veritable translations or rather excerpted notes on the contents of the Hebrew original, and, finally and most importantly, once one determines their natures, it should not be too difficult to establish their intended functions. A thorough examination of the two versions goes beyond the scope of the current paper and will hopefully be provided elsewhere. For the time being, I limit myself to an initial assessment of their relationship, of their relative chronology, and of their possible functions.

From a quick comparison of the two manuscripts, it is clear that they were not derived one from the other, which leads to the inescapable conclusion that Egidio 'translated' the same book twice. In the short history of Christian Kabbalah there is, to the best of my knowledge, only one instance in which the same person translated the same work from Hebrew into Latin twice. The Jewish convert Flavius Mithridates (d. after 1489) was on the verge of translating two kabbalistic works twice for his patron Giovanni Pico della Mirandola (d. 1494). He noticed, after having started the second translation of *Sefer shorshei ha-qabbalah* ('Book of the Kabbalistic Roots') by Joseph ibn Waqar (14th c.) that he had already rendered the same work into Latin and he added in the manuscript a gloss for Pico to the effect that since the latter already had the work before him in Latin, he would not go on with the second translation, which was evidently based on a different Hebrew manuscript source.[37] In another instance, probably owing to the fact that the original (a commentary on the Tetragrammaton by Asher ben David) is preserved in several versions of different lengths, Mithridates translated it twice from two different manuscripts.[38] In the case of Egidio da Viterbo we have, among the surviving manuscripts from his library, several examples of duplicated Latin translations of one and the same Hebrew work. As a matter of fact, the same is also true of the two Latin versions of *Sefer ha-temunah*, the above-mentioned one by Felice da Prato, now lost, which was most probably the one used by Egidio in 1517 in order to prepare his *Libellus de litteris Hebraicis* ('Booklet on the Hebrew Letters'), and a second one preserved in great disarray in MS lat. 527(1) of the BnF.[39] The latter translation was made, as I have shown

---

36 BnF, lat. 527(2), fols 478–588; cf. Egidio, *Scechina*, p. 17.

37 See Saverio Campanini, '*Liber de ordine Geneseos*: A Short Commentary on Creation Attributed to Nachmanides and Other Unknown Kabbalistic Texts in Flavius Mithridates' Latin Translation', in '*Let the Wise Listen and Add to Their Learning*' (Prov. 1:5), *Festschrift for Günter Stemberger on the Occasion of His 75th Birthday*, ed. by Constanza Cordoni and Gerhard Langer (Berlin: De Gruyter, 2016), pp. 619–43 (p. 635).

38 I have published the longer version, from the manuscript in the Vatican, Biblioteca apostolica, ebr. 190, in Saverio Campanini, '*Libellus de expositione nominis Tetragrammaton a Flavio Mithridate translatus*', in R. Asher Ben David, *His Complete Works and Studies in his Kabbalistic Thought* [in Hebrew], ed. by Daniel Abrams (Los Angeles: Cherub Press, 1996, pp. 289–98; the shorter version, from the Vatican manuscript, ebr. 191, together with a revised edition of the previous version, were published in *Four Short Kabbalistic Treatises: Asher ben David, Perush Shem ha-Meforash; Isaac ben Jacob ha-Kohen, 'Inyan Gadol; Two Commentaries on the Ten Sefirot. Flavius Mithridates' Latin Translation, The Hebrew Text, and an English Version*, ed. by Saverio Campanini (Castiglione delle Stiviere: Fondazione Palazzo Bondoni Pastorio, 2019), pp. 69–81 and 100–20.

39 Cf. Egidio, *Scechina*, pp. 16–17.

elsewhere, during the election of Clemens VII in 1523.⁴⁰

The present case of concern, *Sefer ha-peli'ah*, is easier to assess since both versions are preserved and it is not too difficult to establish a relative chronology. In BnF lat. 527(2), we find two annotations in Egidio's hand that allow us to date the manuscript with fairly great precision. Since the author of *Sefer ha-peli'ah* presented an elaborate calculation of the time at which the end of the *galut* ('exile') would come, Egidio took the occasion to comment, polemically, that the prophecy indicated in the text had not been realized. In order to understand the calculations proposed in *Sefer ha-peli'ah*, it will suffice to know that its author established a correspondence between the ten *sefirot*, the ten dimensions of the kabbalistic Godhead, and the epochs of the world, each one lasting 500 years. After the year 5000, corresponding to 1239, a new epoch began under the domination of the first *sefirah*, *Keter* ('the Crown'). According to *Sefer ha-peli'ah*, the exile should have ended in the middle year of this period, that is, in the year 5249/50 of the creation. Egidio glossed that the year 1490 CE has passed without any sign of redemption, and he noted '*nunc sunt* 5275', adding an even more precise date according to the Julian calendar: '*Julio* 1515'.⁴¹ A few pages further on, another gloss indicates that Egidio was still working on the same translation, as he wrote the correspondence between the year in which he was writing, 1516, and the Jewish year 5276.⁴² Thus the dating suggested by Martin, that is, prior to 1517, is fully confirmed by internal evidence. If my correction of the colophon holds, one can even state with some precision that Egidio started to gloss MS 3154 of the Casanatense Library, the Hebrew manuscript then at his disposal, at the end of 1514. As he worked, he saw that he needed more space and started to extract the bulk of the text on separate sheets, which are now bound in BnF, lat. 527(2). This effort lasted for several months, from 1515 to at least part of 1516, which is far from surprising if one considers the size of the work and Egidio's many other engagements even before he became a cardinal, when he was general of his order and he was charged with delicate diplomatic missions, such as his journey to the German Lands in 1516.

Given that Egidio translated and commented on *Sefer ha-peli'ah* between the end of 1514 and 1516, why would he have started anew to translate and comment on the same Hebrew work, as is attested by BnF lat. 3667? When was this second translation done, and why? As I noted earlier, comparing the two versions allows us to ascertain that the second manuscript is not a copy of the earlier one. As was Egidio's habit, both versions are subdivided into numbered paragraphs for easier retrieval, but the two numerations differ completely: BnF lat. 3667 falls into 426 paragraphs, whereas BnF lat. 527(2) is divided into 442. The dating of the later version is not as simple, as there are fewer unequivocal indices suggesting a definite point in time. What can be stated with confidence is that the second version is shorter and quite likely was done rather more quickly. A simple comparison of the *explicit* of the two versions shows a clear change of mood: the older one ends with words of hope and thankfulness:

> Laudes tibi sanctissimi יי״י, et tibi eterne eius fili sapientia patris clementiarum [...]⁴³ qui ascondisti hec sapientibus et prudentibus, et

---

40 See Saverio Campanini, *Dal Sacco di Roma alla fine del mondo*, cit.
41 BnF, lat. 527(2), fol. 407ʳ.
42 BnF, lat., 527(2), fol. 437ʳ.

43 Here a few words are separated from the rest by parentheses, signalling that the words, connected to *Sefer ha-peli'ah* (Jerusalem edition, p. 670) do not belong to the final eulogy, but were, most probably, a gloss referring to the text: '*Noac invenit gratiam* חן נח. *Amen, deus fidelis numerat el neeman amen*' ('Noah found

revelasti ea parvulis, inter quos ut hec revelans me annumerasti: ita me adducas ad lumen quod reposuisti. Amen. Finis Ben Hacane.

(Praises to you most holy Tetragrammaton, and to you eternal Son of his, wisdom of the merciful Father, 'because you have hidden these things from the wise and the intelligent and have revealed them to infants' [Matt. 11:25], and you have numbered me among the latter in revealing to me these things; so guide me to the light that you have set aside. Amen. End of the Ben Hacana.)[44]

The later version ends in a distinctively sober tone, not to say on a desperate note:

Dixit dominus delebo hominem a terra, postquam homo superior abstulit se a terra ideo, etiam homo inferior tollatur a terra, obruatur.

('The Lord said: I will destroy man from the earth: since the superior man detached himself from the earth, therefore the inferior man will be eliminated from earth, let him be ruined'.)[45]

Egidio's concern regarding the eschatological end became increasingly pressing in his last years, and we know that he was feverishly looking for signs of the coming fate as early as during the election of Pope Clemens VII in 1523, when he started a new commentary on *Sefer ha-temunah*, envisaging 1530/31 as the predicted year for the end in that kabbalistic work.

Between the Sack of Rome of 1527, a tragedy of monumental proportions, and the coronation of Charles V in Bologna in 1530, Egidio's messianic preoccupations increased visibly until, in the latter year, he was summoned by the pope to write the treatise *Scechina* (*Shekhinah* — a Hebrew term for the dwelling of the divine presence), in which he imagined that the divine presence instructed Emperor Charles V about Kabbalah and about his messianic role. As a matter of fact, Egidio had commented on the allusions to Caesar (קיסר) and the successor to the throne, or the Viceroy (פלגא), in the earlier version of the Hebrew original of *Sefer ha-peli'ah*,[46] which was copied while Maximilian I of Habsburg (d. 1519) was still ruling. He commented again in the later version,[47] where he translated the two terms of talmudic origin[48] using majuscules: CAESAR and SEMICAESAR. I contend that this latter version was penned sometime after Charles V had assumed power in Italy and suggest that Egidio read these remote allusions with an eye towards contemporary world politics.

In other words, the two versions, albeit the second a result of material loss, were determined and very much influenced by two different agendas. We recall that it is most likely that Egidio was forced to retranslate *Sefer ha-peli'ah* because he had either lost the earlier version or it was simply not available to him after the Sack of Rome. Only the latter translation reflects a particular interest in eschatology and in the role of the emperor and, possibly, of the viceroy (of Naples) in hastening redemption. This could explain why in the treatise *Scechina*, which Egidio wrote towards the end of his life, the emperor is lauded for his triumph over the Turks and Suleyman the Magnificent in Vienna in 1529. Egidio also exhorted Charles V to accept his full calling as

---

grace נח חן [the name Noah and the Hebrew word for grace, *hen*, are anagrams]. Amen, faithful God El [*Melek*] *Neeman*, is its acronym').

44 BnF, lat. 527(2), fol. 491ᵛ.
45 BnF, lat. 3667, fol. 36ʳ. The passage corresponds to *Sefer ha-peli'ah* (Jerusalem edition), p. 655.

46 BnF, lat. 527(2), fol. 494ʳ.
47 BnF, lat. 3667, fol. 20ᵛ.
48 Babylonian Talmud, *Sanhedrin* 98b.

emperor of the entire world, to bring about peace within Christianity, but at the same time not to content himself with the role of 'half-emperor', taking inspiration from the splendid model of King Solomon.⁴⁹ In the tractate *Sanhedrin* of the Babylonian Talmud, the Messiah is likened to an emperor, whereas King David is figured as a viceroy (*palga*). Therefore, Charles should aspire to the crown of the true empire, which is the *Sefirah malkut* ('Kingdom'), and not to the role of a mere viceroy, being only the emperor of this world, which, in comparison with the true Kingdom, is like a mustard seed compared to the sky.⁵⁰ This messianic perspective seems to have been the driving force that motivated Egidio to read both *Sefer ha-peli'ah* and *Sefer ha-temunah* once again in order to find clues by which to decipher the convulsions on the historical and theological scene of his world.

The practice of preparing multiple versions of the same text is attested by other books in Egidio's library, but they are usually, albeit different, copies of one and the same archetype, such as the two Hebrew-Latin dictionaries and odd translations of a monolingual dictionary. There are in fact two copies of David Qimhi's *Sefer ha-shorashim* ('The Book of the Roots'), one of which is now in the Biblioteca Angelica in Rome the other in the University Library in Saint Andrews in Scotland.⁵¹ The case of *Sefer ha-peli'ah* under discussion is different, as the two versions are not identical and were not copied one from the other. I could not find a definitive answer as to why Egidio felt the need to create two complete collections of long commented excerpts from one and the same book. Other scenarios come to mind: he could have loaned out his translation for a long period of time or he was far from his library, such as during his diplomatic missions to Spain or to the German

---

49 BnF, lat. 3363, fol. 315ᵛ. See Egidio, *Scechina*, II, p. 223: 'Qua propter sapientes David patrem cum septem, semi Caesarem, filium cum octo Caesarem appellarunt, ut cogites Carole ad veram Caesaris rationem pertinere, ut vere quis dici Caesar possit: ut non angustiis valletur, non terminis claudatur, non hostem sua obsidentem, non ampla regna tenentem, non vi, non armis, non terrore imminentem, non Pannonias vastantem, non Viennam bello petentem, urgentem, prementem, non Urbi Romae et universi imperio aspirantem patiatur. Eam ob rem David priorem vallo septenarii septum, semi Caesarem, posteriorem, qui claustra, qui portas aereas, qui vectes ferreos fregit, tam supra in aedificio, quam infra in inferis, et non partem orbis sed totum orbem cepit, Caesarem et non semi-Caesarem nuncupavere' ('For this reason the sages called David the father with seven Half-Caesar and the son with eight Caesar, so that you, Charles, might consider what belongs to the real nature of Caesar so that one can rightly be called a Caesar. He should not be encircled; he should not be enclosed within any boundaries; he should not tolerate an enemy besieging him or controlling vast realms, or threatening him with violence, an army, or with terror, or devastate the Danubian region or attempt an assault on Vienna, or aspire to conquer the City of Rome and the whole empire. For that reason, David, who was protected by the wall of the seven, was called Half-Caesar, whereas his successor, who eliminated all enclosures, demolished the brazen gates and the iron bars and did not content himself with a portion of the world, but conquered it all, was called Caesar').

50 BnF, lat. 3363, fol. 217ʳ. See Egidio, *Scechina*, I, p. 224: 'Nunc animo opus est Caesar, accedit Caesar ad Caesarem sed ad immortalem mortalis, hoc Malcut, hoc regnum, hoc imperium meum est, vides latissimum mundum, cui vester ille comparatus, multo longeque minor est, quam supremo caelo sinapis semen' ('Now, Caesar, courage is needed, now Caesar enters into the presence of Caesar, a mortal one in the presence of the Immortal, that is *Malkut*: this is my reign, this is my empire, as you can see an immense world compared to which your world is much smaller than, if compared to the outmost sphere, a seed of mustard'). See also Roland Béhar, '*In medio mihi Cæsar erit*: Charles-Quint et la poésie impériale', *e-Spania* https://doi.org/10.4000/e-spania.21140 [accessed in April 2022].

51 Saverio Campanini, '"Thou bearest not the root, but the root thee": On the Reception of the *Sefer ha-shorashim* in Latin', *Sefarad*, 76/2 (2016): pp. 313–31; see especially Giacomo Corazzol, 'Les manuscrits latins du *Sefer ha-shorashim*', in *Liber radicum, Sefer ha-shorashim*, 2019. https://shorashim.hypotheses.org/109 [accessed in April 2022].

Lands. However, the most likely explanation would be that, fearing that his books were lost when his home was pillaged during the Sack of Rome, while preparing the *Scechina*, Egidio urgently needed a Latin version of the kabbalistic prophecies of *Sefer ha-peli'ah*. This urgency would explain why the later version is shorter, less accurate, and its marginal commentaries much more laconic in comparison to the first one. Both versions are characterized, although in different ways, by the typical style of reduction, concentration, and dynamization of knowledge Egidio adopted in many of his surviving excerpts. In themselves already partial translations or extractions, the older version features a further reduction of its contents into a synthesis of the second degree in the outer margin and a third layer of annotations, reducing the contents of a page (more than one in the Hebrew original) to a couple of catchwords in the bottom margin. The third layer is absent from the later version, a possible sign of the haste with which the extraction was made in order to integrate it into the unfinished project of the *Scechina*. As a matter of fact, one finds at least one explicit mention of the '*Liber Pelia ben Hacane*' in the *Scechina*,[52] in connection with the interpretation of *tzelem* and *demut* as male and female in order to create the androgyne corresponding to the *du partzufim* ('*duae facies*' — 'two faces') on high.[53]

Contemporaries, among them Lucillo Maggi (d. 1570), also known as Filalteus, noted Egidio's desperation at the prospect of having lost his library during the Sack of Rome and his sombre thoughts about the remote possibility that the books might have been stolen for he would not have been able to raise the ransom for such a vast collection.[54] The fact that both versions survived demonstrates that his collector's fears were exaggerated, but since we do not know when or even if he was able to recover the original Latin version, it is reasonable to assume that he felt the need of commenting anew on *Sefer ha-peli'ah*. Perhaps even if he still had the previous excerpts of his *Bencana* at his disposal, he would have decided that the radically new situation engendered by the consolidation of the emperor's power in Europe had to be interpreted anew in the light of a kabbalistic book of eschatological prophecies.

Anti-Christian Thorns

One last point appears to me to merit a brief consideration: the unanimous enthusiasm of the Christian readers of *Sefer ha-peli'ah* does not seem to have been diminished by the fact that all the censorship and self-censorship notwithstanding, the book is full of quite venomous attacks against Christianity and most notably against Jesus. Nevertheless, in the early days of its reception among Christians, not a single voice was raised in public to condemn or even to criticize its aggressive or rather reactive approach. Quite to the contrary, Francesco Zorzi, who was the first to receive a copy of the book and who did so much for its circulation among Christian readers, quoted it in the most laudatory terms in all of his works, published and unpublished. In his appeal to the Council of Ten, he described *Sefer ha-peli'ah* as a book 'in quo continentur quamplurima secreta ipsorum Hebraeorum pertinentia et digna noticia Christianorum ad declarationem veritatis et confirmationem fidei nostrae Christianae' ('in which many secrets of

---

52 Cf. BnF, lat. 3363, fol. 333ʳ; Egidio, *Scechina*, vol. I, p. 264.
53 The relevant passage is found, as expected, in BnF, lat. 3667, fol. 21ʳ.

54 *Lucilli Philalthaei Libri Tres Epistolarum in adolescentia familiarium primum in lucem editi* (Pavia: Bissi, 1564), fols 40ᵛ–44ᵛ; see also Massimo Danzi, *La biblioteca del Cardinal Pietro Bembo* (Geneva: Droz, 2005), p. 15.

the Jews are contained, which the Christians should know in order to explain the truth of Christianity and to confirm our faith').[55] Upon studying Zorzi's attitude towards his sources, Giulio Busi remarked on his silence regarding the anti-Christian passages in *Sefer ha-peli'ah* and suggested that Zorzi, far from overlooking them, 'probably decided that the precious secrets in the book were more important than the occasional polemical attitude of its author'.[56]

When looking for the relevant passages in Egidio's extractions, it becomes evident that he noticed them and that he adopted different strategies to signal his awareness of these issues in the margins of the Latin summaries. At times, he limited himself to noting that Jesus was mentioned, or rather meant, in the text,[57] collecting evidence that the expression 'odo isc' (sic for אותו האיש — 'That man') was a coded reference to him.[58] The peculiar orthography, accidentally, if not caused by distraction, suggests that he could have been simply reproducing what his translator dictated or what he learned from his oral explanation.

At times it seems that Egidio downplayed the author's potentially defamatory remarks. One example is the use of the derogatory expression איש תחבולות ('trickster') in reference to Jesus, accusing him of deceiving his own followers. This expression is translated in Egidio's manuscripts once as '*vir ingenii*'[59] ('clever') and in the later version as '*astutus*'[60] ('wily'/'cunning') rather than as '*mendax*' or worse. In one case, though, a particularly venomous passage from *Sefer ha-peli'ah*, in which a complicated *gematria* is revealed in order to associate Jesus with the plague of darkness, provoked a reaction, at least in the margins: first Egidio (or his translator) seems to have misunderstood the calculations to get from the biblical expression וימש חשך of Exodus 10:21 ('a darkness that can be felt'), corresponding to the numerical value 684, to the supposed equivalent ישו הנצרי (Jesus of Nazareth), whose sum is only 671. The first mention in the text seems to suggest that the correspondence is incorrect. But upon reading the original text more carefully, Egidio noted, this time in the bottom margin, that from the larger number one should subtract 10, or rather, that one should add to the *epitheton* 'Yeshu ha-notzri' (ישו הנצרי), the letter *yod*, as the initial of '*Yimah shemo ve-zikhro*' ('May his name, and his memory be erased'). The total was still not reached, but in *Sefer ha-peli'ah* the number 3 is formed by the three letters of Jesus's name in Hebrew (*Yeshu*). Egidio translated only part of this explanation, but he added two critical notes in the margins: in the outer margin: '*Dicunt impii hostes. Et mentitur cecus hebraeus*' ('This is what the impious enemies say. The blind Jew lies') and in the bottom margin: '*Jesu nomen impii mentiuntur* | חשך ישו *mendaces Judei*' ('The name of Jesus, the impious lie | חשך ישו the Jews are liars') and again: 'וימש חשך' and under it 'ישו הנצרי *Numerant 674 sublato iod* [...] *cum literis 3, hoc tempore Romani Amalec perdituri*' ('They count 674 for ישו הנוצרי after subtracting *yod*, that is ten [...] with three letters, in that time the Romans, that is Amalek, will be destroyed').[61] As one can see, Egidio did not comment on the ultimate goal of this remark, that is to say the assumption that the end of exile will coincide with the violent end of the Roman domination, blatantly identified with the eternal biblical enemy Amalek.

Nevertheless, only one page before the one I have just commented on, in a passage that the

---

55 Campanini, 'Elchana Hebraeorum', p. 98.
56 Busi, 'A Methodical Dreamer', p. 104.
57 See, e.g., BnF, lat. 3667, fol. 6r.
58 BnF, lat. 527(2), fol. 405r.
59 BnF, lat. 527(2), fol. 405r. The passage corresponds to *Sefer ha-peli'ah* (Jerusalem edition), p. 49.
60 BnF, lat. 3667, fol. 6r.

61 BnF, lat. 527(2), fol. 468v.

author of *Sefer ha-peli'ah* copied and reproduced quite freely from Abraham Abulafia's *Gan na'ul*,[62] we find that Christians are called fools, since they use a *gematria* or rather an anagram (בצלו [*be-tzelo*] — 'in his shadow'[63] to suggest צלוב [*tzaluv*] — 'of the Crucified'). In *Sefer ha-peli'ah* we read that it is heretical to believe that and that the corpse suspended from the cross is cursed. Egidio, apparently unimpressed, did not comment on these words, but repeated the essential sentences in Latin in the outer and the bottom margins: '*sub umbra crucifixi*' ('in the shadow of the crucifix'), '*Crucis umbra, in qua desiderabam sedi*' ('The shadow of the cross, under which I wished to sit'), '*desiderat sedere in umbra crucifixi*' ('He desires to sit in the shadow of the Crucified')[64] and '*maledictus qui pendet in ligno crucis*' ('Cursed be the one who hangs from the wood of the cross'),[65] a plausible translation of the biblical expression.[66]

True Books

Thus, in the face of the meaning of these texts for Egidio and for the Christian Kabbalists of the Renaissance, who avidly sought them and repeatedly read and quoted from them with the utmost respect, we have to consider how they were received and understood. A possible solution for the blatant contradiction between the high level of expectation shared by these enthusiastic Hebraists and Christian Kabbalists and the reality of the anti-Christian exegeses and polemical arrows these books contained can be found in the classical reversal of Balaam's ineffectual curses. As Abraham Abulafia himself noted, many kabbalistic calculations of the numerical value of biblical words can be used to good or bad ends.[67] Very early in the development of Christian Kabbalah, polemical calculations were employed with their meanings reversed, especially in the glosses of Flavius Mithridates[68] and in Pablo de Heredia's *Epistula de secretis* ('Letter on the Secrets').[69] These two converts were masterful in reinterpreting anti-Christian *gematriot* to prove the opposite of what the original authors had intended. Certainly, the polemical value of these retorts is remarkable, but one is entitled to ask: If the neutralization of the polemical stings of these texts came at the cost of demonstrating their arbitrariness, what heuristic value could they behold?

Nevertheless, as we have seen, Egidio remained enthusiastic about *Sefer ha-peli'ah* both before and after having acquired it and even after having excerpted it twice. His expression of gratitude in the colophon written at the end of the first series of excerpts, a strange mixture of a quotation from the Gospels and an allusion to the kabbalistic

---

62 Cf. Abraham Abulafia, *Gan na'ul* (Jerusalem: A. Gross, 1999), p. 23.
63 Song of Songs 2:3.
64 BnF, lat. 527(2), fol. 466ᵛ.
65 BnF, lat. 527(2), fol. 467ʳ. For the Hebrew original, see *Sefer ha-peli'ah* (Jerusalem edition), p. 314.
66 Deuteronomy 21:23.
67 Cf. Gershom Scholem, *Zur Geschichte der Anfänge der christlichen Kabbala*, in *Essays Presented to Leo Baeck on the Occasion of His 80th Birthday* (London: East and West Library, 1954), pp. 158–93; revised French version: *Considérations sur l'histoire des débuts de la kabbale chrétienne*, in *Kabbalistes Chrétiens* (Paris: Albin Michel, 1979), pp. 17–46 (p. 42); Engl.: 'The Beginnings of the Christian Kabbalah', in *The Christian Kabbalah: Jewish Mystical Books and their Christian Interpreters*, ed. by Joseph Dan (Cambridge, MA.: Harvard University Library, 1997), pp. 17–51 (p. 44).
68 Flavius Mithridates, *Sermo de Passione Domini*, ed. by Chaim Wirszubski (Jerusalem, The Israel Academy of Sciences and Humanities, 1963), p. 40; Chaim Wirszubski, *Pico della Mirandola's Encounter with Jewish Mysticism* (Jerusalem: The Israel Academy of Sciences and Humanities, 1989), p. 118.
69 François Secret, 'L'Ensis Pauli de Paulus de Heredia', *Sefarad*, 26/1 (1966): pp. 79–102 (p. 101).

book *Bahir*,[70] a text also translated by or for Egidio,[71] on the light hidden by the Lord for the righteous in the world to come, shows that Egidio was still persuaded that *Sefer ha-peli'ah* was a deeply mysterious but truthful book. This was confirmed by his sober subscription in the later version: the devastation of Rome, prophesized in *Sefer ha-peli'ah* and experienced directly by Egidio in 1527, confirmed in his eyes that the eschatological end, even if belated, was approaching.[72] Beyond contradiction and dialectic tension, his encomium for the prophecies of *Sefer ha-peli'ah* clearly reveals the cardinal's enduring benevolent attitude towards his beloved kabbalistic books. According to a traditional Christian theological habit of thought, which had become an almost automatic reflex, the value of Jewish books consisted precisely in the fact that, notwithstanding or even against the intentions of their authors, they were harbingers of a deeper truth.

The history of a particular book, precious and dangerous for all its possessors, is revealed by the traces left by its readers, no less than by the marks of the passing of time. A translated, controversial book transported from a given cultural environment to a completely different one compounds all these aspects. Even before being read, it was preceded by its fame, it was translated and annotated as a prophecy, and, after traumatic events, was again meditated and excerpted in search of new meaning from an old text for a journey into the unknown future. Book history is always the history of interpretation: the vicissitudes of *Sefer ha-Peli'ah* among unintended readers are by no means exceptional.

---

70 See *Sefer ha-bahir* §147 and 160; cf. *The Book of Bahir. Flavius Mithridates' Latin Translation, the Hebrew Text and an English Version*, ed. by Saverio Campanini (Turin: Aragno, 2005), pp. 108* and 118*.
71 BnF, lat. 527(2), fols 152ʳ and 153ʳ.
72 For Egidio's attitude towards the Sack of Rome from a millenaristic perspective, see Gennaro Savarese, *Un frate neoplatonico e il Rinascimento a Roma. Studi su Egidio da Viterbo* (Rome: Roma nel Rinascimento, 2012), esp. pp. 89–107.

JAVIER DEL BARCO

Alfonso de Zamora and Hebrew Manuscripts on Grammar and Exegesis in Sixteenth-Century Spain[*]

The Study of Christian Hebraism in Sixteenth-Century Spain

In 1975, Ángel Sáenz-Badillos published an article entitled 'Tres gramáticas hebreas españolas de la primera mitad del s. XVI' ('Three Spanish Hebrew Grammars from the First Half of the Sixteenth Century') in which he posed the question of why no Spanish authors had ever been mentioned in studies of sixteenth-century Christian Hebraism:

> ¿Será posible que la España de los Reyes Católicos y de Carlos I, que produciría tantos y tan competentes especialistas en la gramática latina y griega, dejara totalmente olvidado el campo del hebreo, en el que había tenido durante siglos la preeminencia indiscutible? (Is it possible that the Spain of the Catholic Monarchs and Charles I, which would produce so many competent specialists in Latin and Greek grammar, left the field of Hebrew completely forgotten, in which it had had indisputable pre-eminence for centuries?)[1]

His answer was that there were indeed Spanish Hebraists who composed treatises on Hebrew grammar in the sixteenth century, and he described the previously little-known relevant works by three Spanish humanists from the first half of that century: Antonio de Nebrija, Martín Martínez de Cantalapiedra, and the convert Alfonso de Zamora (c. 1476–c. 1545).

---

[*] Research on this subject has been possible thanks to the collaborative research project entitled 'Legado de Sefarad III. La producción material e intelectual del judaísmo sefardí bajomedieval', which is based at the Universidad Complutense de Madrid and funded by the Plan Nacional de I+D+i (PDI2019-104219GB-I00). I would like to thank Natalio Fernández Marcos for his useful comments and suggestions on a previous draft of this chapter.

[1] Ángel Sáenz-Badillos, 'Tres gramáticas hebreas españolas de la primera mitad del siglo XVI', *Miscelánea de Estudios Árabes y Hebraicos*, Sección de hebreo, 24 (1975), 13–35 (p. 14).

Javier del Barco • Universidad Complutense de Madrid

It would seem that it is the widespread ignorance concerning Spanish Hebraism among non-Spanish scholars that accounts for the almost total absence of Spanish authors in general studies of sixteenth-century Christian Hebraism published in the twentieth century and even at the beginning of the twenty-first,[2] the exceptions being accounts of the production of the *Complutensian Polyglot Bible* and the *Antwerp Bible* or *Biblia Regia*.[3] It has only been in the last twenty years that the activities of Hebraists working in the context of Spanish humanism, such as those mentioned above, have attracted any attention.[4] These activities revolved primarily — though not exclusively — around projects such as the *Complutensian Polyglot Bible* and were sponsored by the nobility and Church elites.

The publication of the *Complutensian Polyglot Bible* at the University of Alcalá, sponsored by Cardinal Francisco Jiménez de Cisneros, is an example of the humanistic work that was done in the first two decades of the sixteenth century around the study of the original texts of the Bible — in Hebrew, Latin, and Greek.[5] For this

---

2 As noted by Jesús de Prado Plumed, 'Al lasso, fuerça: La convivencia de impresos y manuscritos en la carrera del hebraísta converso Alfonso de Zamora (d. c. 1545)', in *De la piedra al pixel: reflexiones en torno a las edades del libro*, ed. by Marina Garone Gravier, Isabel Galina, and Laurette Godinas, Colección Banquete (Mexico City: Universidad Nacional Autónoma de México, 2016), pp. 157–202 (p. 162), 'El hebraísmo cristiano ibérico e iberoamericano, tanto portugués como castellano o aragonés, ha pasado en general desapercibido para el consenso investigador centrado en los logros del hebraísmo de la Europa septentrional' (Iberian and Ibero-American Christian Hebraism, whether Portuguese, Castilian or Aragonese, has generally gone unnoticed by the research consensus focused on the achievements of Hebraism in northern Europe). This absence can be seen, e.g., in Jerome Friedman, *The Most Ancient Testimony: Sixteenth-Century Christian-Hebraica in the Age of Renaissance Nostalgia* (Athens, OH: Ohio University Press, 1983), and even in Sophie Kessler Mesguich, 'Early Christian Hebraists', in *Hebrew Bible/Old Testament: The History of Its Interpretation*, ed. by Magne Sæbø, 3 vols (Göttingen: Vandenhoeck & Ruprecht, 2008), II, pp. 254–75, who only mentions Johannes Reuchlin, Christian Hebraists in Basel (Conrad Pellican and Sebastian Münster), and the case of Elijah Levita, a Jew who taught and collaborated with several Christian Hebraists.

3 See, e.g., Basil Hall, 'The Trilingual College of San Ildefonso and the Making of the Complutensian Polyglot Bible', *Studies in Church History*, 5 (1969), pp. 114–46; Adrian Schenker, 'From the First Printed Hebrew, Greek and Latin Bibles to the First Polyglot Bible: The Complutensian Polyglot, 1477–1517', in *Hebrew Bible/Old Testament*, ed. by Sæbø, II, pp. 276–91 (pp. 286–91), and the bibliography mentioned there; Adrian Schenker, 'The Polyglot Bibles of Antwerp, Paris and London. 1568–1658', in *Hebrew Bible/Old Testament*, ed. by Sæbø, II, pp. 774–84, (pp. 775–79), and the bibliography mentioned there.

4 In addition to some Spanish scholars, such as Ángel Sáenz-Badillos, Natalio Fernández Marcos, Emilia Fernández Tejero, Jesús de Prado Plumed, and Santiago García Jalón, who have worked or are currently working on early modern Spanish Hebraism and biblical studies in the context of Spanish humanism (see bibliography), we should also mention Stephen G. Burnett, who devoted some lines to Spanish Hebraism in 'Christian Hebrew Printing in the Sixteenth Century: Printers, Humanism and the Impact of the Reformation', *Helmántica: Revista de Filología Clásica y Hebrea*, 51 (2000), pp. 13–42, and Theodor Dunkelgrün, 'The Christian Study of Judaism in Early Modern Europe', in *The Cambridge History of Judaism* (Cambridge: Cambridge University Press, 1984–2021), ed. by Jonathan Karp and Adam Sutcliffe (2017), VII: *The Early Modern World, 1500–1815*, pp. 316–48, who succeeds in incorporating Spanish Hebraism within a broader narrative about sixteenth-century Christian Hebraism in Europe.

5 Apart from the classical studies by Franz Delitzsch, *Studies on the Complutensian Polyglot* (London: Samuel Bagster and Sons, 1872), and Mariano Revilla Rico, *La políglota de Alcalá: estudio histórico-crítico* (Madrid: Imprenta Helénica, 1917), and several articles and studies on the Complutensian Polyglot texts, we should also mention the recent catalogue of the exhibition celebrating the 500th anniversary of the *Complutensian Polyglot Bible* in 2017, *V Centenario de la Biblia Políglota Complutense: la universidad del Renacimiento, el renacimiento de la Universidad*, ed. by José Luis Gonzalo Sánchez-Molero (Madrid: Universidad Complutense de Madrid, 2014). Other recent multi-author works published around the Polyglot's anniversary include

project, Cisneros brought together in Alcalá some of the sixteenth-century's most prominent theologians, humanists, and grammarians of the original languages of the Bible, including Hernán Núñez de Toledo y Guzmán, known as El Pinciano; Pedro Sánchez Ciruelo; Diego López de Zúñiga; Juan de Vergara; and the converts Pablo Núñez Coronel, Alonso de Alcalá, and Alfonso de Zamora.[6]

A small treatise on Hebrew grammar was printed in 1515 together with Volume 6 of the *Complutensian Polyglot Bible* (Figure 18.1), most or all of which has been attributed to Alfonso de Zamora.[7] Entitled *Introductiones Artis Grammaticae Hebraicae* ('Introduction to the Art of Hebrew Grammar'), this small book carries the same name as the enlarged edition that Zamora published in 1526 in Alcalá de Henares with the printer Miguel de Eguía. It was not the first treatise on Hebrew grammar printed in Latin — Johannes Reuchlin had published his *De rudimentis hebraicis* ('On the Elements of Hebrew') in 1506 — but it does show that work was being done in Alcalá not only on editing the original texts of the Bible but also on studying the grammar of the languages in which these original texts were written, including, of course, Hebrew.[8]

In fact, the converts who worked on the *Complutensian Polyglot Bible* and, in particular, Alfonso de Zamora, played crucial roles in the transmission of knowledge concerning the understanding of the Hebrew Bible and its interpretation by the Jews of Sefarad to the Christian intellectual milieu. This transmission had a significant impact on the incipient humanistic activity around the study of the original languages

---

Preparando la Biblia Políglota Complutense: los libros del saber, ed. by Elisa Ruiz García and José María de Francisco Olmos (Madrid: Universidad Complutense de Madrid, 2013); *Una Biblia a varias voces: Estudio textual de la Biblia Políglota Complutense*, ed. by Ignacio Carbajosa and Andrés García Serrano, Studia Biblica Matritensia, 2 (Madrid: Ediciones Universidad San Dámaso, 2014); and *La Biblia Políglota Complutense en su contexto*, ed. by Antonio Alvar Ezquerra (Alcalá de Henares: Publicaciones de la Universidad de Alcalá de Henares, 2016).

6 These three converts were mentioned in José Rodríguez de Castro, *Biblioteca española*, I: *Que contiene la noticia de los escritores rabinos españoles desde la época conocida de su literatura hasta el presente* (Madrid: Imprenta Real de la Gazeta, 1781), pp. 397–400. Alfonso de Zamora has received scholarly attention, mostly in Spain, ever since Neubauer first studied and described some of the manuscripts that he copied or used: See Adolf Neubauer, 'Alfonso de Zamora', *Boletín de la Real Academia de la Historia*, 27 (1895), pp. 193–213. The classic study by Federico Pérez Castro, *El manuscrito apologético de Alfonso de Zamora* (Madrid: Instituto Arias Montano, 1950), has been followed by several works focusing on different aspects of Zamora's life and work. See, e.g., Moshé Lazar, 'Alfonso de Zamora, copiste (notes pouvant servir à compléter sa biographie)', *Sefarad*, 18 (1958), pp. 314–27; Carlos Carrete Parrondo, 'Tres precisiones de Alonso de Zamora ante el tribunal de la Inquisición', *Sefarad*, 34 (1974), pp. 115–17; Carlos Alonso Fontela, 'Anotaciones de Alfonso de Zamora en un comentario a los Profetas Posteriores de Don Isaac Abravanel', *Sefarad*, 47 (1987), pp. 227–43; Carlos del Valle Rodríguez, 'Notas sobre Alfonso de Zamora', *Sefarad*, 47 (1987), pp. 173–80; Prado Plumed, '*Al lasso, fuerça*'; Jesús de Prado Plumed, 'Alone Among the Sages of Sepharad? Alfonso de Zamora and the Symbolic Capital of Converso Christian Hebraism in Spain After 1492', in *Connecting Histories: Jews and Their Others in Early Modern Europe*, ed. by Francesca Bregoli and David B. Ruderman (Philadelphia: University of Pennsylvania Press, 2019), pp. 189–96; María Antonia Muriel Sastre, 'Esbozo bio-genealógico del hebraísta judeoconverso Alfonso de Zamora', *Studia Zamorensia*, 16 (2017), pp. 119–41. In addition to these, Ahuva Ho, 'Alfonso de Zamora: His Life and Work' (unpublished PhD dissertation, Claremont Graduate University, 2016), deals comprehensively with all the manuscripts that Zamora copied and used, and argues for his Crypto-Jewish identity.

7 Sáenz-Badillos, p. 28.

8 Antonio de Nebrija (1441–1522), the author of the first work on Spanish grammar (*Gramática… sobre la lengua castellana*, 1492), also published a small treatise on Hebrew grammar at the beginning of the sixteenth century — *De litteris hebraicis* ('On the Hebrew Letters') — but the exact date of the first printing of this treatise is unknown: see Sáenz-Badillos, pp. 15–17.

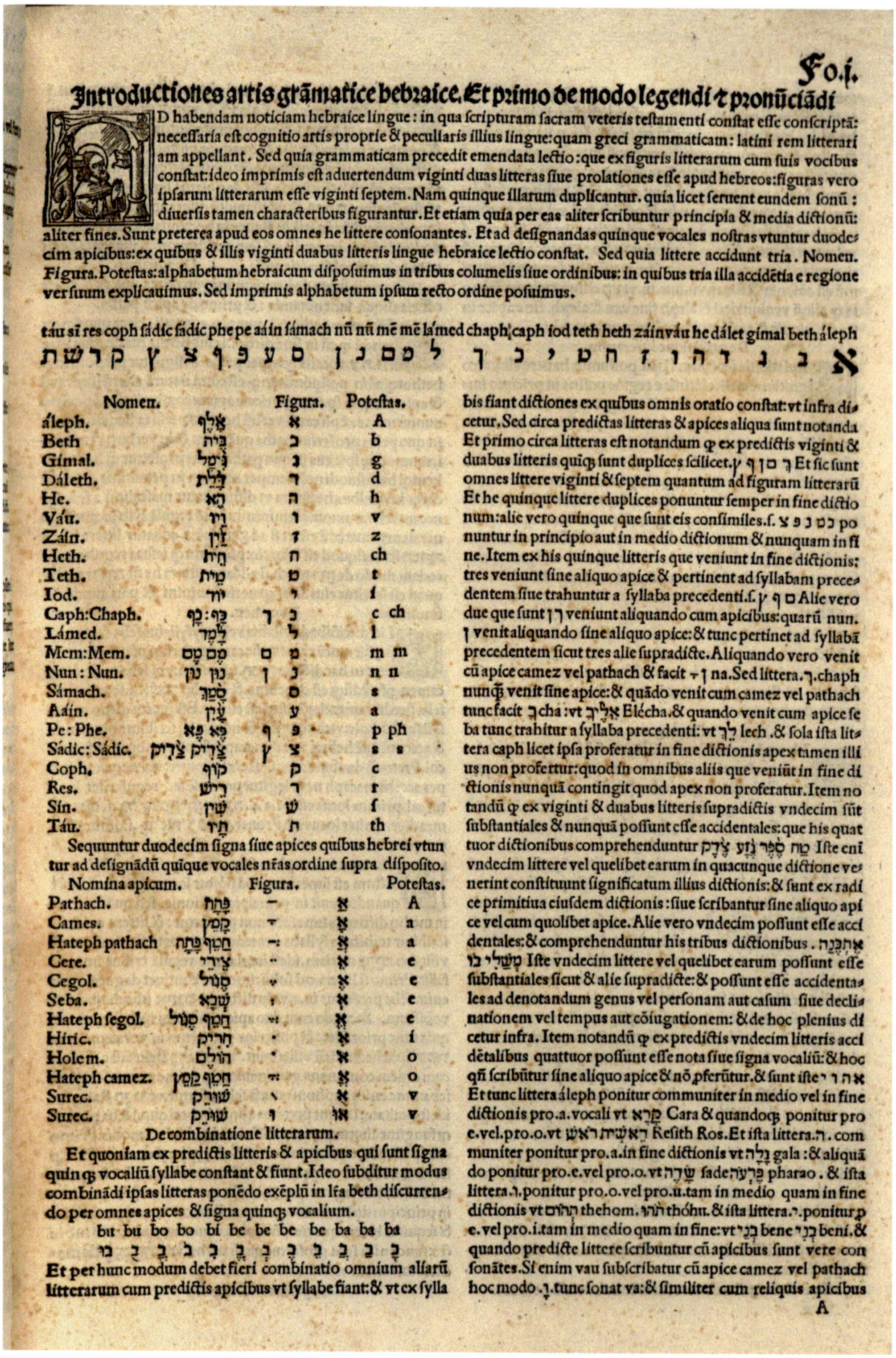

Fo.j.

Introductiones artis grāmatice hebraice. Et primo de modo legendi & pronūciādi

AD habendam noticiam hebraice lingue: in qua scripturam sacram veteris testamenti constat esse conscriptā: necessaria est cognitio artis proprie & peculiaris illius lingue: quam greci grammaticam: latini rem litterariam appellant. Sed quia grammaticam precedit emendata lectio: que ex figuris litterarum cum suis vocibus constat: ideo imprimis est aduertendum viginti duas litteras siue prolationes esse apud hebreos: figuras vero ipsarum litterarum esse viginti septem. Nam quinque illarum duplicantur. quia licet seruent eundem sonū: diuersis tamen characteribus figurantur. Et etiam quia per eas aliter scribuntur principia & media dictionū: aliter fines. Sunt preterea apud eos omnes he littere consonantes. Et ad designandas quinque vocales nostras vtuntur duodecim apicibus: ex quibus & illis viginti duabus litteris lingue hebraice lectio constat. Sed quia littere accidunt tria. Nomen. Figura. Potestas: alphabetum hebraicum disposuimus in tribus columelis siue ordinibus: in quibus tria illa accidētia e regione versuum explicauimus. Sed imprimis alphabetum ipsum recto ordine posuimus.

táu sī res coph sádic sádic phe pe aáin sámach nū nū mē mē lámed chaph caph iod teth heth záin váu he dálet gimal beth áleph

א ב ג ד ה ו ז ח ט י כ ך ל מ ם נ ן ס ע פ ף צ ץ ק ר ש ת

Nomen.			Figura.	Potestas.
áleph.	אָלֶף		א	A
Beth	בֵּית		ב	b
Gimal.	גִּימֶל		ג	g
Dáleth.	דָּלֶת		ד	d
He.	הֵא		ה	h
Váu.	וָיו		ו	v
Záin.	זַיִן		ז	z
Heth.	חֵית		ח	ch
Teth.	טֵית		ט	t
Iod.	יוֹד		י	i
Caph:Chaph.	כַּף : כַף	ך	כ	c ch
Lámed.	לָמֶד		ל	l
Mem:Mem.	מֶם מֶם	ם	מ	m m
Nun : Nun.	נוּן נוּן	ן	נ	n n
Sámach.	סָמֶךְ		ס	s
Aáin.	עַיִן		ע	a
Pe : Phe.	פֵּא פֵא	ף	פ	p ph
Sádic: Sádic.	צָדִיק צָדִיק	ץ	צ	s s
Coph.	קוֹף		ק	c
Res.	רֵישׁ		ר	r
Sín.	שִׁין		ש	ſ
Táu.	תָּיו		ת	th

Sequuntur duodecim signa siue apices quibus hebrei vtuntur ad designādū quīque vocales nr̄as ordine supra disposito.

Nomina apicum.		Figura.		Potestas.
Pathach.	פַּתַח	ַ	אַ	A
Cames.	קָמֵץ	ָ	אָ	a
Hateph pathach	חֲטֵף פַּתַח	ֲ	אֲ	a
Cere.	צֵירֵי	ֵ	אֵ	e
Cegol.	סֶגוֹל	ֶ	אֶ	e
Seba.	שְׁבָא	ְ	אְ	e
Hateph segol.	חֲטֵף סֶגוֹל	ֱ	אֱ	e
Hiric.	חִירֶק	ִ	אִ	i
Holem.	הוֹלֶם	ֹ	אֹ	o
Hateph camez.	חֲטֵף קָמֵץ	ֳ	אֳ	o
Surec.	שׁוּרֵק	ֻ	אֻ	v
Surec.	שׁוּרֵק	וּ	אוּ	v

De combinatione litterarum.

Et quoniam ex predictis litteris & apicibus qui sunt signa quinq; vocaliū syllabe constant & fiunt. Ideo subditur modus combinādi ipsas litteras ponēdo exēplū in lr̄a beth discurrendo per omnes apices & signa quinq; vocalium.

bu bu bo bo bi be be be be ba ba ba

בַּ בָּ בֲּ בֵּ בֶּ בְּ בֱּ בִּ בֹּ בֳּ בֻּ בוּ

Et per hunc modum debet fieri combinatio omnium aliarū litterarum cum predictis apicibus vt syllabe fiant: & vt ex syllabis fiant dictiones ex quibus omnis oratio constat: vt infra dicetur. Sed circa predictas litteras & apices aliqua sunt notanda Et primo circa litteras est notandum q̄ ex predictis viginti & duabus litteris quinq; sunt duplices scilicet. ך ם ן ף ץ Et sic sunt omnes littere viginti & septem quantum ad figuram litterarū Et he quinque littere duplices ponuntur semper in fine dictionum: alie vero quinque que sunt eis consimiles. s. כ מ נ פ צ ponuntur in principio aut in medio dictionum & nunquam in fine. Item ex his quinque litteris que veniunt in fine dictionis: tres veniunt sine aliquo apice & pertinent ad syllabam precedentem siue trahuntur a syllaba precedenti. s. ם ף ץ Alie vero due que sunt ך ן veniunt aliquando cum apicibus: quarū nun. ן venit aliquando sine aliquo apice: & tunc pertinet ad syllabā precedentem sicut tres alie supradicte. Aliquando vero venit cū apice camez vel pathach & facit ןָ na. Sed littera. ך. chaph nunq; venit sine apice: & quādo venit cum camez vel pathach tunc facit ךָ cha: vt אֵלֶיךָ Elécha. & quando venit cum apice seba tunc trahitur a syllaba precedenti: vt לֵךְ lech. & sola ista littera caph licet ipsa proferatur in fine dictionis apex tamen illius non profertur: quod in omnibus aliis que veniūt in fine dictionis nunquā contingit quod apex non proferatur. Item notandū q̄ ex viginti & duabus litteris supradictis vndecim sūt substantiales & nunquā possunt esse accidentales: que his quattuor dictionibus comprehenduntur טַח סֵפֶר גֶזַע צֶדֶק Iste enī vndecim littere vel quelibet earum in quacunque dictione venerint constituunt significatum illius dictionis: & sunt ex radice primitiua eiusdem dictionis: siue scribantur sine aliquo apice vel cum quolibet apice. Alie vero vndecim possunt esse accidentales: & comprehenduntur his tribus dictionibus. אֶתְכֶנָּה מֹשֶׁלִי בוֹ Iste vndecim littere vel quelibet earum possunt esse substantiales sicut & alie supradicte: & possunt esse accidentales ad denotandum genus vel personam aut casum siue declinationem vel tempus aut cōiugationem: & de hoc plenius dicetur infra. Item notandū q̄ ex predictis vndecim litteris accidētalibus quattuor possunt esse nota siue signa vocaliū: & hoc qn̄ scribūtur sine aliquo apice & nō pferūtur. & sunt iste א ה ו י Et tunc littera áleph ponitur communiter in medio vel in fine dictionis pro. a. vocali vt קָרָא Cara & quandoq; ponitur pro e. vel. pro. o. vt רֵאשִׁית רֹאשׁ Resith Ros. Et ista littera. ה. communiter ponitur pro. a. in fine dictionis vt גָלָה gala: & aliquādo ponitur pro. e. vel pro. o. vt שָׂדֶה sade פַּרְעֹה pharao. & ista littera. ו. ponitur pro. o. vel pro. u. tam in medio quam in fine dictionis vt תְּהוֹם thehom. תֹהוּ thóhu. & ista littera. י. ponitur pro e. vel pro. i. tam in medio quam in fine: vt בְּנֵי bene בְּנִי beni. & quando predicte littere scribuntur cū apicibus sunt vere consonātes. Si enim vau subscribatur cū apice camez vel pathach hoc modo. וָ. tunc sonat va: & similiter cum reliquis apicibus

A

Figure 18.1. Alfonso de Zamora, *Introductiones artis gra[m]matice hebraice* [*Complutensain Polyglot Bible*, vol. 6] (Alcalá de Henares: Arnao Guillén de Brocar, 1515). Madrid, Biblioteca Histórica de la Universidad Complutense de Madrid, BH FOA 106.

of the Bible, which began with the edition of the *Complutensian Polyglot Bible* and the foundation of San Ildefonso College by Cisneros. Alfonso de Zamora was undoubtedly the most notable Spanish Hebraist of the sixteenth century, combining as he did the intellectual heritage of the Jews of Sefarad and the Christian contribution to Spanish Renaissance Hebraism.

First Commissions on Hebrew Grammar

During this same period, as an authority on the Sefardi tradition of Hebrew grammar with considerable rabbinical and exegetical training,[9] Alfonso de Zamora began to receive commissions related to the study of the Hebrew language. These came from clerics in Cisneros's circle who were members of the Church elite or arose out of the need for reference and study materials for instruction at the University of Alcalá. Thus, in 1516, while he was still working on the *Polyglot Bible*, the university, with Cisneros's permission, asked Zamora to produce a manuscript that would embrace copies of *Sefer mikhlol* ('Book of the Epitome [of Hebrew Grammar]') and *Sefer ha-shorashim* ('Book of the Roots [of Biblical Hebrew]') by David Qimhi (Radaq); *Mahalakh* ('Course [of Hebrew Grammar]') by Moses Qimhi; *Masoret seyag la-torah* ('Final Masorah to the Torah') by Meir ha-Levi ben Todros Abulafia (Ramah); and other, minor grammatical works. This manuscript (Salamanca, Biblioteca General Histórica de la Universidad, MS 6)[10] includes an interesting note by Zamora:

דע כי בזמן הזה דון פרהיי פראנסישקו כהן גדול של טליטלה והוא הנזכר בסוף ספר השרשים ברוב עשרו וברוב חשקו להבין בכל הלשונות צוה לחבר ולדפוס לשון רומיי שהוא לאטין ספר השרשים של ר׳ דוד קמחי מלשון התורה וכל תרגום ודניאל ועזרא ובעבור שלא נמצא בספרד ספרים שיחברו מהם אלא ספר אחד לבדו והוא מוטעה על כן חסרו המחברים דברים מעטים ואלה הם הדברים החסרים שמצאתי בחיבורם.

(Know that at the time Don Fray Francisco [Jiménez de Cisneros] was the Archbishop of Toledo — he is the one who is cited at the end of the *Sefer ha-shorashim* — and in his great wealth and great desire to understand all the languages, he commanded Rabbi David Qimhi's *Sefer ha-shorashim*, in the language of the Torah, and all the Targum, [and the books of] Daniel and Ezra, to be copied and printed in the Roman language, which is Latin, and because there were no books in Spain from which to copy except one book alone, and it was flawed, therefore the copyists missed a few things, and this is what I found missing in their copy.)[11]

This reference to a Latin translation of *Sefer ha-shorashim* ordered by Cisneros is extremely interesting — firstly, because it reflects his keen interest in having tools available for teaching Hebrew at Alcalá; secondly, because this translation, if it was ever completed, has not been preserved; and thirdly, because it is not clear if it ever went to a printer.[12] It seems that Zamora had access to the translation, perhaps in the

---

9 While still a Jew, he was trained at the famous yeshiva in Zamora once led by Isaac Canpantón: see Muriel Sastre, p. 127, and Ho, pp. 9–10.

10 Described in José Llamas, 'Los manuscritos hebreos de la Universidad de Salamanca', *Sefarad*, 10 (1950), pp. 263–79 (pp. 274–78), and *Catálogo de manuscritos de la Biblioteca Universitaria de Salamanca*, ed. by Óscar Lilao Franca and Carmen Castrillo González (Salamanca: Ediciones Universidad de Salamanca, 1997), pp. 29–30: Ho, pp. 121–85.

11 Salamanca, Biblioteca General Histórica de la Universidad (BGH), MS 6, fol. 368ᵛ: see Ho, p. 159.

12 See Valle Rodríguez, 'Notas sobre Alfonso de Zamora', p. 177.

form of a (partial) draft prior to printing or as a collaborator serving as a reviser or an editor.

Another question that arises from the previous note is: Which manuscript was this 'one book alone' that was used for the translation of the *Shorashim* and that Zamora also consulted. There are two manuscripts of *Sefer ha-shorashim* at the Complutense University of Madrid that Zamora actually consulted and amended. One of them (Madrid, Biblioteca Histórica Marqués de Valdecilla de la Universidad Complutense, MS 17)[13] is from the second half of the fifteenth century, copied by two scribes, the second of whom wrote a colophon that reads as follows:

אני אהרן הכהן סימתי זה הספר לבחור הנחמד
המעולה המשכיל הנכבד יוסף נ׳ חביב בן כבוד
הנכבד דון ישקי נ׳ חביב נ״ע האל ברחמיו יזכהו
להגות בו הוא ובניו וכל זרעו אחריו וידבק בלבו
תורתו וירחיק מלבו רעות כוזבות לאמתו

(I, Aaron ha-Cohen, finished this book for the pleasant, extraordinary, intelligent and honourable man, Joseph ben Haviv, the son of the honoured and honourable Don Isaac ben Haviv, may he rest in paradise. May God in his mercy give [the power] to meditate with it [i.e., the book] to him and his children and all their descendants, and may he heartily adhere to His Law, and may he expel evil and falsehood from his heart by His truth.)[14]

This manuscript has numerous marginal notes in Hebrew and Latin in Zamora's hand, most of which identify biblical quotes (Figure 18.2). Ahuva Ho contends that this manuscript was the one used as the source for the Latin translation ordered by Cisneros, pointing out that the terms noted by Zamora in MS 6 from the University of Salamanca as being absent from the draft of the Latin translation are exactly the same ones that are missing from this manuscript.[15] She also notes that this book was part of a group of five acquired by Jorge Baracaldo, Cisneros's secretary, in July 1508.[16] Therefore, as the book was then in Alcalá, it was probably the manuscript that Zamora used as one of the sources for his own treatise on Hebrew grammar, which was printed in 1515 with Volume 6 of the *Polyglot Bible*.[17]

The Complutense University's other manuscript containing *Sefer ha-shorashim* (Marqués de Valdecilla, MS 21)[18] was copied on the Iberian Peninsula at the end of the fourteenth century or the beginning of the fifteenth. Zamora did not make marginal notes in that manuscript; rather, he replaced sixteen missing folios, almost all of which were at the beginning or the end of the work, with his own copies.

Zamora was careful to do the same whenever he came across incomplete manuscripts: he copied and inserted the missing text in order to be able to use the manuscripts in his classes and so that the students and other professors could consult complete versions of the works in the

---

13 Described in José Llamas, 'Los manuscritos hebreos de la Universidad de Madrid', *Sefarad*, 5 (1945), pp. 261–84 (pp. 276–77), and Javier del Barco, *Catálogo de manuscritos hebreos de la Comunidad de Madrid*, 3 vols (Madrid: Consejo Superior de Investigaciones Científicas, Instituto de Filología, 2003), I, p. 221. An updated description can be found in *Catálogo de manuscritos medievales de la Biblioteca Histórica Marqués de Valdecilla (Universidad Complutense de Madrid)*, ed. by Antonio López Fonseca, Marta Torres Santo Domingo, and Elisa Ruiz García (Madrid: Ediciones Complutense, 2019), pp. 121–24. The manuscript has also been explored in Ho, pp. 43–49.

14 Madrid, Biblioteca Histórica 'Marqués de Valdecilla' de la Universidad Complutense, MS 17, fol. 252ʳ.
15 Ho, p. 43.
16 Ho, p. 43.
17 This is also Ahuva Ho's assumption: see Ho, p. 43.
18 Described in Barco, I, p. 222; a more recent and updated description in *Catálogo de manuscritos medievales*, pp. 137–40; Ho, pp. 185–88.

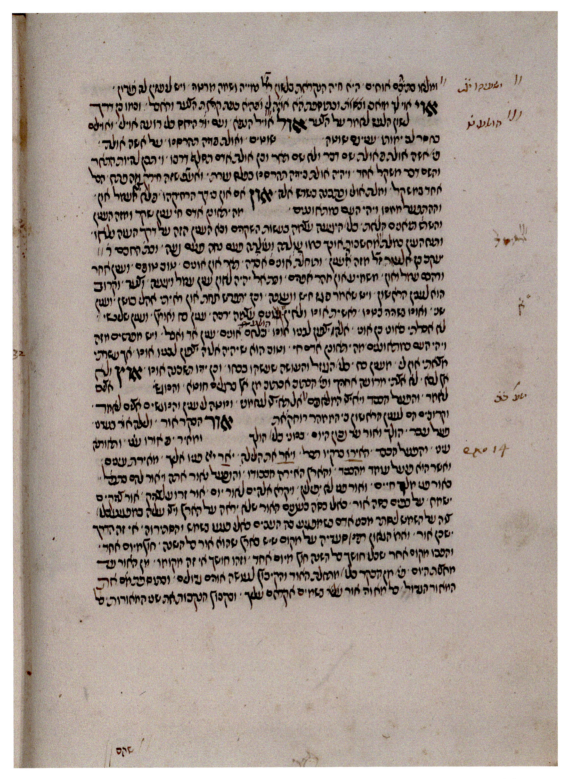

Figure 18.2. David Qimhi, *Sefer ha-shorashim*. Iberian Peninsula, c. 1475–1492. Madrid, Biblioteca Histórica de la Universidad Complutense de Madrid, BH MSS 17, fol. 4ᵛ.

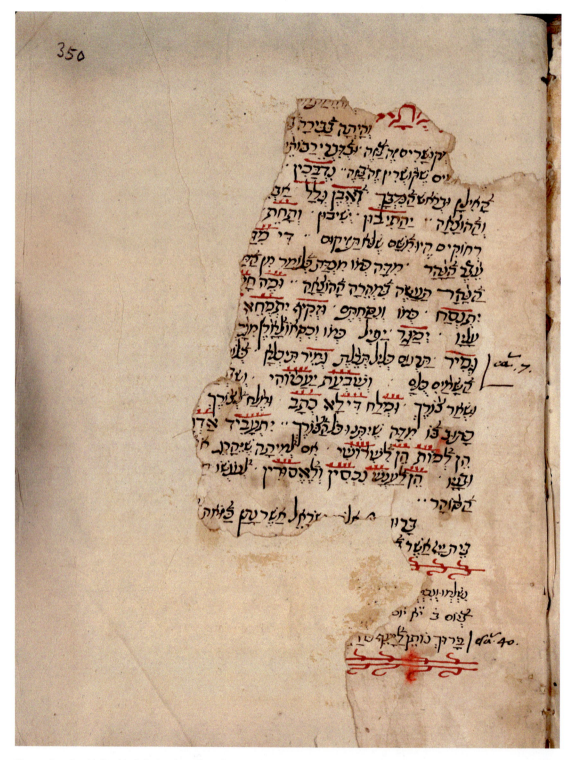

Figure 18.3. David Qimhi, *Sefer ha-shorashim*. Iberian Peninsula, c. 1350–1450. End and colophon by Alfonso de Zamora, c. 1516 or shortly thereafter. Madrid, Biblioteca Histórica de la Universidad Complutense de Madrid, BH MSS 21, fol. 350ʳ.

library. In almost every manuscript for which he did this, Zamora would write notes at the end mentioning the number of folios that he supplied and the date that he completed them. However, in this specific case, the notes are incomplete (Figure 18.3), and we do not know the dates that he worked on this particular manuscript.[19]

Nonetheless, Ho suggests that the manuscript may have been amended after it was acquired in the second half of 1516, so that a supplementary copy of Qimhi's *Shorashim* that was more complete than MS 17 would be available.[20] Incidentally, folio 1 of this manuscript is a stray sheet that has the title of Qimhi's *Sefer mikhlol* and the beginning of the work's introductory poem. This is unquestionably a folio that Zamora added to a copy of the *Mikhlol* (Marqués de Valdecilla, MS 20) that eventually got detached from the cover and was bound by mistake with this copy of the *Shorashim* at the beginning of the seventeenth century, when all the manuscripts at the University of Alcalá were inventoried, examined, and rebound.[21]

There is a third manuscript of the *Shorashim* with Zamora's annotations kept today in the Biblioteca Nacional de España in Madrid (MS 5454),[22] in which Zamora included an interesting note:

נאמר לכהן קוריא שישמני פירושי הנביאים שהם
בלי נקודות כדי שיתפאר על שאנג׳יז וחבריו שאינם
יודעים לקרוא בלי נקודות ויש לו פירושים בלי
נקודות כמו מלאכת אדון גדול ויהיה לי יותר נחת רוח

(We told the bishop of Coria[23] to study the commentaries of the prophets without vowel points, so that he could boast before Sánchez and his companions, who do not know how to read without vowel points, since he [the bishop] owns commentaries without vowel points, as befits a great lord. For me [doing so] would be easier and would require less effort.)[24]

Jesús de Prado identified this bishop of Coria as Francisco de Mendoza y Bobadilla, first bishop of Coria and then of Burgos, who studied Latin,

---

19 Alfonso de Zamora's note reads (Marqués de Valdecilla, MS 21, fol. 350ʳ): ונכת[בו...] ביום ב׳ י״א יום [...] ברוך [ולאין אונים עצמה ירבה] נותן ליעף כח ('Finished [...] on Monday, eleventh [...] blessed be He who "gives power to the faint, [and strengthens the powerless]", [Isaiah 40:29]').

20 She also gives other possible dates when the eleventh of the month fell on a Monday, ranging from 1515 to 1522: see Ho, p. 185.

21 MS 21 has two notes that read 'Visto 1614' ('Seen [Revised] 1614'), attesting to the fact that the manuscripts were examined at that time: one on fol. 3ʳ and the other on fol. 1ᵛ, which refers to MS 20.

22 Described in Mariano Gaspar Remiro, 'Los manuscritos rabínicos de la Biblioteca Nacional [I]', *Boletín de la Real Academia Española*, 5 (1918), pp. 601–17 (pp. 604–10); Carlos del Valle Rodríguez, *Catálogo descriptivo de los manuscritos hebreos de la Biblioteca Nacional* (Madrid: Ministerio de Cultura, 1986), pp. 31–33; Barco, II, pp. 171–72; Ho, pp. 317–29.

23 The Hebrew words כהן קוריא have been interpreted in different ways. The traditional reading is 'the priest Correa', in Neubauer, p. 205, and after him in Pérez Castro, p. lvii: Valle Rodríguez, *Catálogo descriptivo*, pp. 31–33, and Arturo Prats, '13. Sefer ha-shorashim [Diccionario de raíces]', in *Biblias de Sefarad – Bibles of Sepharad*, ed. by Esperanza Alfonso and others (Madrid: Biblioteca Nacional de España, 2012), p. 233; Ahuva Ho, pp. 317–18, understands the words as a title, reading them as '[the priest of] the Curia', i.e., the officials who assisted in the governance of a particular church. Jesús de Prado interprets them as 'the bishop of Coria' and provides compelling arguments in support of this reading in 'Los humanistas políglotas hispánicos, comitentes de códices en el siglo XVI: el cliente como factor de supervivencia del libro manuscrito en la Edad Moderna', in *Memorias del Congreso Internacional Las edades del libro*, ed. by Marina Garone Gravier, Isabel Galina, and Laurette Godinas (Mexico City: Instituto de Investigaciones Bibliográficas, Universidad Nacional Autónoma de México, 2012), ebook: http://www.edadesdellibro.unam.mx/edl2012/files/EdadesDelLibro.epub [accessed in July 2021], pp. [127–55].

24 Madrid, Biblioteca Nacional de España (BNE), MS 5454, fol. 1ʳ.

Greek, and Hebrew at Alcalá.[25] The annotation makes it clear that he was interested in learning to read the commentaries on the Prophets in Hebrew and that Zamora advised him to do so using unvocalized texts, such as the ones that appear in medieval Hebrew manuscripts. In 1541, Mendoza provided further proof of his interest when he commissioned Zamora to produce a copy of David Qimhi's commentary on Psalms.[26] The reference to Sánchez, whom Jesús de Prado identified as Diego Sánchez de la Fuente,[27] one of Zamora's former students, together with the reference to the bishop of Coria (appointed 1533), allows us to date this annotation to about 1534.[28]

This same manuscript contains another, earlier annotation by Zamora dated to 16 August 1526 confirming that by then he had access to this manuscript of the *Shorashim*. This is relevant information because it was in precisely that year that Zamora published the stand-alone edition of his treatise on Hebrew grammar, *Introductiones Artis Grammaticae Hebraicae*, which suggests that he may have consulted this manuscript, in addition to the ones discussed above, in preparing this edition.

Some years earlier, just after Cisneros's death in 1517, Zamora had received a commission from one of his collaborators on the *Polyglot Bible*, Diego López de Zúñiga,[29] to make a copy of a compendium of Hebrew grammar similar to MS 6 in Salamanca's Biblioteca General Histórica, mentioned above. This manuscript, which was completed between 1518 and 1519 (MS G-II-5 at San Lorenzo de El Escorial, Real Biblioteca),[30]

---

25 Prado Plumed, 'Los humanistas políglotas hispánicos' (p. [133]), stresses his role as a commissioner of books: 'El futuro cardenal de Burgos, todavía obispo de Coria y antes arcediano de Toledo, tuvo un papel relevante en la difusión de la actividad libraria de élite en España desde el mismo inicio de su carrera' (The future Cardinal of Burgos, still Bishop of Coria and before that Archdeacon of Toledo, played an important role in spreading elite book activity in Spain from the very beginning of his career). See also Jesús de Prado Plumed, 'The Commission of Targum Manuscripts and the Patronage of Christian Hebraism in Sixteenth-Century Castile', in *A Jewish Targum in a Christian World*, ed. by Alberdina Houtman, Eveline van Staalduine-Sulman, and Heans-Martin Kirn, Jewish and Christian Perspectives Series, 27 (Leiden: Brill, 2014), pp. 146–65 (p. 155).

26 The manuscript is Naples, Biblioteca Nazionale, MS Branc. IV-F-2: see Ho, pp. 633–45. The most complete study on this manuscript is Giancarlo Lacerenza, 'Il commento ai Salmi di Dawid Qimhi in un manoscritto di Alfonso de Zamora', in *Hebraica Hereditas: Studi in onore di Cesare Colafemmina*, ed. by Giancarlo Lacerenza (Naples: Università degli Studi di Napoli 'L'Orientale', 2005), pp. 67–93.

27 See Ho, p. 489.

28 Sánchez is mentioned in documents from the University of Salamanca in 1534 and 1536, where he taught Hebrew despite Zamora's low opinion of his proficiency in the language: see Ho, pp. 487–90, and the bibliography cited there.

29 The theologian Diego López de Zúñiga (d. *c*. 1531) edited the text of the Greek New Testament for the Polyglot Bible, which was printed in 1514, two years before Erasmus published his *Novum Instrumentum*, though López de Zúñiga's edition was not marketed until 1522. It is known that there was a prolonged dispute between López de Zúñiga and Erasmus regarding the latter's new Latin translation of the text of the New Testament: see Henk Jan de Jonge, *Desiderii Erasmi Roterodami, Apologia respondens ad ea quae Iacobus Lopis Stunica taxaverat in prima duntaxat Novi Testamenti aeditione* (Amsterdam and Oxford: North-Holland Publishing Company, 1983), pp. 3–49; Marcel Bataillon, *Erasmo y España: estudios sobre la historia espiritual del siglo XVI*, 2nd Sp. edn (México, Madrid: Fondo de Cultura Económica, 1979), pp. 91–102; César Chaparro Gómez, 'Erasmo de Rotterdam y Diego López de Zúñiga: una polémica áspera y prolongada', *Ágora. Estudos clássicos em debate*, 16 (2014), pp. 157–87; William B. Jones and Thomas B. Deutscher, 'Diego López Zúñiga', in *Contemporaries of Erasmus*, ed. by Peter G. Bietenholz, 3 vols (Toronto, Buffalo, and London: University of Toronto Press, 1986), II, pp. 348–49; Henk Jan de Jonge, 'Four Unpublished Letters on Erasmus from J. L. Stunica to Pope Leo X (1524)', in *Colloque Erasmien de Liège: Commémoration du 450e anniversaire de la mort d'Erasme*, ed. by Jean-Pierre Massaut (Paris: Les Belles Lettres, 1987), pp. 147–60.

30 Described in José Llamas, 'Los manuscritos hebreos de la Real Biblioteca de San Lorenzo de El Escorial [II]', *Sefarad*, 1 (1941), pp. 279–311 (pp. 308–09), and Barco, I, pp. 219–20; Ho, pp. 196–204.

includes David's Qimhi's *Sefer mikhlol*, Moshe Qimhi's *Mahalakh*, and a *Sefer diqduq*, which Zamora attributed to Abraham ibn Ezra.³¹

A few years later, in 1523, another cleric from Alcalá, Juan de Azcona, hired Zamora to produce a copy of Qimhi's *Mikhlol* with translations into Spanish and Latin. The manuscript, held today in the Biblioteca Nacional de España, MS 4188,³² actually contains a part of the *Mikhlol* translated into Latin (fols 1–79 and 160–83) and another part translated into Spanish (fols 80–159 and 184–304), the latter being the first translation of the *Mikhlol* into a European vernacular. Although the Spanish translation was copied (and presumably produced) by Zamora himself, the Latin translation seems to be in another hand.³³ The colophon to this manuscript, written in Hebrew and Spanish, reads:

נשלם ספר המכלול הזה ביום ששי חמשה ימים לחדש ג'וניו שנת אלף ות"ק וכ"ג ללדת מושיענו ישוע משיח על יד אלפונשו די סאמורה עבדו בכאן במתא אלכאלה די אינאריש לחסיד גמור פראי ג'ואן די אזקונה לרוב חשקו להבין דברי שפר³⁴ הנסתרים בספר

Fue acavado este libro del miclol este en el dia sesto cinco días del mes de juño. año de mil y quinientos y 23 al naçimiento de nuestro salvador ιηυ χρς por mano de alonso de çamora su siervo aquí en el lugar de alcalá de enares. para el rreligioso perfecto fray juan de azcona por la muchedumbre de su buen deseo de entender las palabras de hermosura que son escondidas en el libro.

(This book of the *Mikhlol* was finished on Friday, the fifth of June of the year 1523 from the birth of our saviour Jesus Christ, by the hand of Alonso de Zamora his servant, here in the place of Alcalá de Henares, for the irreproachable friar Juan de Azcona, because of his abundant desire to understand the words of beauty hidden in the book.)³⁵

Following the copy of the *Mikhlol*, the manuscript has the 613 precepts in Hebrew (fols 312–41), arranged in the same two-column page layout as the rest of the text. Zamora also copied these folios and the text is partially accompanied by a Spanish translation (up to fol. 318). Juan de Azcona may have also asked Zamora to produce the copy and the translation of the 613 precepts, as this text was, along with grammatical and exegetical works, one that Christian Hebraists frequently sought in the first half of the sixteenth century.³⁶ However, we cannot altogether discard the possibility that the 613 precepts were not part of this manuscript from the beginning, but that they were copied for somebody else to serve a different purpose. Jesús de Prado suggests that the copy of the 613 precepts in

---

31 This attribution has been questioned by both Pérez Castro, p. li note 4, and Carlos del Valle Rodríguez, 'Un *Sefer Diqdûq* atribuido a R. Abraham Ibn "Ezra"', *Sefarad*, 56 (1996), pp. 401–22.

32 Described in Valle Rodríguez, *Catálogo descriptivo*, pp. 27–30, and Barco, II, pp. 169–70; Ho, pp. 212–17. See also Sáenz-Badillos, pp. 24–25.

33 There are different opinions on this issue: see Ho, p. 212, and note 410.

34 These words recall the biblical אמרי שפר from Genesis 49:21.

35 BNE, MS 4188, fol. 304ᵛ.

36 Prado Plumed, 'Los humanistas políglotas hispánicos', explains: 'El estudio de las 613 *miswot* fue un tema predilecto de los eruditos cristianos del s. XVI'. See also Prado Plumed, 'Al lasso, fuerça', p. 184: 'En esa misma década [1530], en el norte de Europa, obra de Münster, se podía leer en *otra* traducción latina los mismos 613 preceptos, los mismos que 12 años antes había dado a la imprenta el converso Paulus Ricius y que 10 años más tarde se podrán leer en alemán impresos en Ulm.' (In that same decade [1530], in northern Europe, one could read the same 613 precepts in another Latin translation by Münster, the same ones that the convert Paulus Ricius had given to the printer 12 years earlier and that 10 years later would be printed in German in Ulm).

MS 4188 may be related to another manuscript that has the 613 precepts translated into Latin (Vitoria-Gasteiz, Biblioteca de la Facultad de Teología, MS 17), which Alfonso Manrique de Lara y Solís, archbishop of Seville and grand inquisitor commissioned from Zamora in the 1530s.³⁷ However, the relationship between the two manuscripts, if any, and the identity of the commissioner of the 613 precepts in MS 4188 remain unclear.

Two years after Azcona's 1523 commission, Zamora received another request for a copy of the *Mikhlol* with a Latin translation from Edward Lee, prebendary of York and Westminster, who was appointed English ambassador to the Spanish court of Charles V in 1525. That manuscript is now in Paris (Bibliothèque nationale de France, hébr. 1229).³⁸ Lee may have commissioned the copy and translation of the *Mikhlol* when he met Zamora during his stay in Castile. It seems, moreover, that the intermediary between the two was none other than Pablo Núñez Coronel, one of Zamora's collaborators in editing the Hebrew and Aramaic texts for the *Polyglot Bible*. Zamora himself said that Núñez Coronel encouraged him to accept the commission.³⁹

Again, the question arises as to which manuscripts Zamora could have used as the models for his copies. The Marqués de Valdecilla Library has three manuscripts that include the *Mikhlol* that Zamora consulted and annotated; in two of them, he also supplied missing material, as he did for other incomplete manuscripts.

The one to which Zamora did not have to add missing material as it was complete is Marqués de Valdecilla, MS 19, written in a semi-cursive Italian script, probably sometime in the fourteenth century.⁴⁰ It has numerous marginal notes in at least three different hands, one of which is certainly that of Zamora (Figure 18.4). These notes are proof that Zamora read and used this manuscript, whether to make a copy or in writing his own treatise on Hebrew grammar.⁴¹ The manuscript does not have any notes that would allow us to determine when Zamora used it. Yet, the scribe wrote a rhymed colophon mentioning his name, Isaiah, that reads (fol. 109ᵛ): האל אשר נותן ליעף כח יתן לישעיה עוז כבן מנוח והקורא פקח קוח ומעניינו ילכו שחוח ('God, that "gives power to the faint" [Isa. 40:29], may He give Yeshayah [as much] strength as to the son of Manoaḥ,⁴² and [may He give] the reader "release" [Isa. 61:1], and may our oppressors go "bending low" [Isa. 60:14]'). This colophon seems to have inspired Zamora when he copied the *Mikhlol* commissioned by Azcona, as we find there, before the colophon, annotation that reads: האל הנותן ליעף כח יתן לאלונשו הכותב מנוח ופקח קוח ('God, that "gives power to the faint" [Isa. 40:29], may He give

---

37 Prado Plumed, 'Al lasso, fuerça', pp. 183–84, esp. note 92.
38 Described in Hermann Zotenberg, *Manuscrits Orientaux. Catalogues des manuscrits hébreux et samaritains de la Bibliothèque Impériale* (Paris: Imprimerie impériale, 1866), p. 225, and Colette Sirat and Malachi Beit-Arié, *Manuscrits médiévaux en caractères hébraïques: Portant des indications de date jusqu'à 1540*, I: *Bibliothèques de France et d'Israël: Manuscrits de Grand Format*, [1] *Notices*, [2] *Planches* (Paris and Jerusalem: Centre National de la Recherche Scientifique and Israel Academy of Sciences and Humanities, 1972), no. I, p. 178; Eleazar Gutwirth, 'Alfonso de Zamora and Edward Lee', *Miscelánea de Estudios Árabes y Hebraicos*, 37–38 (1988), pp. 395–97, and Ho, pp. 332–37.
39 Paris, Bibliothèque nationale de France, MS 1229, fol. 241ᵛ: בעצת החכם השלם מאשטרי פאבלו נוניז קורוניל איש תם וישר ירא אלהים וסר מרע ('By the advice of the upright scholar Master Pablo Núñez Coronel, who is "blameless and upright, one who feared God and turned away from evil" [Job 1:1; 1:8; 2:3]'). This

acknowledgement is absent from the Latin colophon; on this matter and the reasons for the discrepancy between the two colophons, see Gutwirth, p. 297; Ho, pp. 335–36; Prado Plumed, 'Al lasso, fuerça', pp. 175–76.
40 Described in Llamas, 'Los manuscritos hebreos de la Universidad de Madrid', p. 278; Barco, I, p. 214; a more recent and updated description in *Catálogo de manuscritos medievales*, pp. 129–32; Ho, pp. 702–05.
41 Ho, p. 703, notes that here 'Alfonso's work is mostly an intense editing'.
42 That is, Samson, known for his proverbial strength.

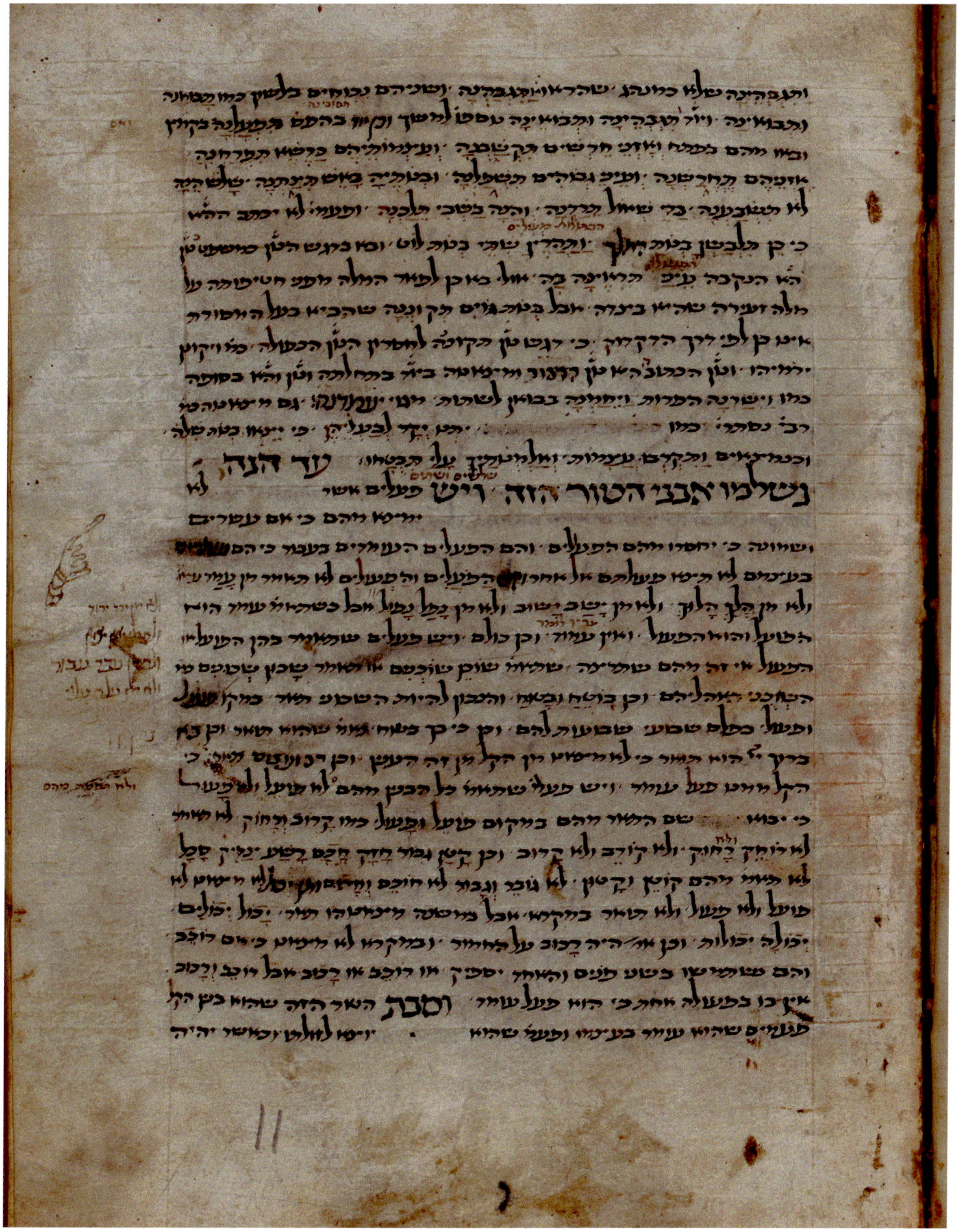

Figure 18.4. David Qimhi, *Sefer ha-mikhlol*. Italy, 14th c.? Madrid, Biblioteca Histórica de la Universidad Complutense de Madrid, BH MSS 19, fol. 11ʳ.

Alonso the scribe rest[43] and "release" [Isa. 61:1]').[44] Thus, if we accept that MS 19 was used for the copy of the *Mikhlol* commissioned by Azcona in 1523 and probably also for the production of Zamora's 1526 treatise on Hebrew grammar as well as the copy of the *Mikhlol* commissioned by Lee, we can date Zamora's first use of this manuscript to no later than 1523.[45]

A second copy of the *Mikhlol* in the Marqués de Valdecilla is MS 18, produced on the Iberian Peninsula in the first half of the fourteenth century.[46] Here, Zamora replaced the missing text by adding two quires at the beginning and three at the end, for a total of forty folios. Two of them (fols 140 and 141) are blank, which is why Zamora wrote (fol. 141ᵛ), 'son 19 pligos' ('there are 19 bifolia [added with written text]'), in other words, thirty-eight folios were added with written text (fols 1–12 and 114–39). This manuscript contains another note in Zamora's hand in which he informs us of the date he completed the replacement of the folios in the manuscript, as well as his reason for doing so:

נשלם חסרון ספר המכלול הזה והוא הנקוד על יד
אלפונשו די סאמורה במתא אלכלה די אינאריש
לשום אותו בבית הספרים אשר שם יעיינו בו
החכמים והמורים כדי להבין סתרי הספרים כ"ד
מאירים כספירים בשנת אלף וחמש מאות ושלשים
וארבע למנין ישועתנו ביום שני[47] שני ימים לחדש
אוטוברי ברוך נותן ליעף כח ולאין אונים עצמה
ירבה תהלה לאל

(The parts that were missing from this book of the *Mikhlol* have been completed, with [vowel] points, by the hand of Alfonso de Zamora in the city of Alcalá de Henares, in order to put it in the library, where sages and professors might peruse it in order to comprehend the secrets of the twenty-four books, which shine like sapphires. In the year 1534, reckoned from our salvation, on Monday, the second day of the month of October.)[48]

We do not know exactly when this manuscript was acquired for the use of teachers and students at the University of Alcalá de Henares, yet the fact that Zamora added the missing materials in 1534 inclines me to think that it was a late acquisition, so that this manuscript could not have served as a source for Zamora's 1523 and 1525 commissions to copy the *Mikhlol* with Latin/Spanish translations.

There is a third copy of the *Mikhlol* in the Marqués de Valdecilla (MS 20),[49] one which was produced in the Iberian Peninsula or in North Africa probably in the second half of the fourteenth century. In this manuscript, Zamora supplied a total of five folios, four of which are still in their places, while the fifth is the stray sheet that is found as folio 1 of Marqués de Valdecilla,

---

43 Here, using the same word as the name of Samson's father, Manoaḥ.
44 BNE, MS 4188, fol. 304ᵛ.
45 Llamas, 'Los manuscritos hebreos de la Universidad de Madrid', p. 278, claimed that this manuscript was used much earlier in the production of the Hebrew-Latin dictionary included in the *Complutensian Polyglot Bible*. On this and other possibilities, see also Ho, pp. 704–05, and note 1427.
46 Described in Llamas, 'Los manuscritos hebreos de la Universidad de Madrid', pp. 277–78; Barco, I, p. 213; a more recent and updated description in *Catálogo de manuscritos medievales*, pp. 125–28; Ho, pp. 576–80.

47 Ho, p. 580, warns that the date is wrong, as 2 October 1534 fell on Friday rather than on Monday. Alfonso de Zamora might have written the word שני twice, either from שני ימים, and then the date is Friday, 2 October, or from יום שני, and then it was on a Monday in the month of October.
48 Marqués de Valdecilla, MS 18, fol. 139ʳ.
49 Described in Llamas, 'Los manuscritos hebreos de la Universidad de Madrid', p. 278; Barco, I, pp. 215–16; a more recent and updated description in *Catálogo de manuscritos medievales*, pp. 133–36; Ho, pp. 700–02.

MS 21, which includes a copy of the *Shorashim*, as I recounted above. Moreover, Zamora filled in the illegible text on one of the manuscript's original folios (fol. 145). He referred to this emendation as a clarification, as we can see in a note on fol. 145ᵛ: '*son tres pligos enmendados* con lo aclarado'[50] ('there are three emended bifolia, *including the clarification*') — in other words, five folios that were replaced plus one folio on which he 'clarified' text that could no longer be read making six folios or three bifolia altogether.

Zamora also wrote a note stating that he copied the folios that were missing in the manuscript with vocalized text, but on this occasion he did not include the date.[51] It is thus very difficult to know if the manuscript was used for his treatise on Hebrew grammar or for the copies of the *Mikhlol* that he was commissioned to produce. We have to consider that the fact that it has very few annotations in his hand might indicate that this manuscript was not used for those projects.[52]

The Anti-Erasmian Movement

In 1526, while Zamora was finishing his commission from Lee, his *Introductiones Artis Grammaticae Hebraicae* was published by Miguel de Eguía's press.[53] Marcel Bataillon has pointed out that Eguía belonged to a group of Erasmians in Alcalá and collaborated on the publication and dissemination of Erasmus's works in Spain.[54] The year 1526 also saw the first of a series of codices of the interlinear Hebrew-Latin Bible with grammatical annotations that Zamora produced, probably with the collaboration of the theologian Pedro Sánchez Ciruelo for the Latin text,[55] which were executed between 1526 and 1537.[56] The volume containing the text of Genesis, now held in the Marqués de Valdecilla (MS 11),[57] was copied in 1527 and dedicated to the humanist and follower of Erasmus Alfonso de Fonseca y Ulloa, archbishop of Toledo, whose coat of arms must have been drawn on the cover

---

50 The emphasis is mine.
51 MS 20, fol. 145ᵛ: אלפונשו די סאמורה כתב כל הנקוד בספר המכלול הזה ('Alfonso de Zamora wrote all that is vocalized in this *Sefer ha-mikhlol*').
52 Ho, p. 700, contends that 'Its restoration work, either for teaching purposes or for augmenting the newly established Complutensian University Library or both, may categorize it with books handled before 1523'. However, the restoration work in this manuscript, apart from Zamora's addition of missing folios, was done in the eighteenth century. See *Catálogo de manuscritos medievales*, p. 136.
53 Miguel de Eguía (1495–1546) was the University of Alcalá's printer after Arnao Guillén de Brocar, who was famous for having printed the *Complutensian Polyglot Bible*.
54 Bataillon, pp. 212, 282, 341. On the connection between the Erasmians, Spanish humanism, and biblical studies, see Natalio Fernández Marcos and Emilia Fernández Tejero, 'Biblismo y erasmismo en la España del siglo XVI', in *El erasmismo en España*, ed. by Manuel Revuelta Sañudo and Ciriaco Morón Arroyo (Santander: Sociedad Menéndez Pelayo, 1986), pp. 97–108.
55 Ho, pp. 315, 386, 736, thinks that the Latin translations were not the work of Pedro Ciruelo, but rather that of Zamora, but admits that on some occasions Ciruelo might have helped Zamora with the Latin (Ho, pp. 234, 299). Pérez Castro, p. xxxviii, states that, at least for San Lorenzo de El Escorial, MS G-I-4, Zamora translated the Hebrew text into Latin and was responsible for the copying of both, the Hebrew and the Latin, while Ciruelo acted as a kind of consultant for the theological and doctrinal part derived from the translation.
56 These manuscripts were not all part of a single project but commissions from different patrons. As a result, some volumes have copies of the same biblical books: El Escorial, MS G-I-4 (1526); Marqués de Valdecilla, MSS 11 (copied 1527), 12 (1528), 13 (1530); BGH, MSS 589 (1536), 590 (1537), 2170 (1529–1530). There were no more volumes copied after 1537; Ho, p. 329, suggests that the appointment of Juan de Tavera, who was suspicious of the conversos' loyalty to the Church, as archbishop of Toledo in 1534 might have been the reason that these bilingual editions were cancelled.
57 Described in Llamas, 'Los manuscritos hebreos de la Universidad de Madrid', pp. 268–69; Barco, I, pp. 133–34; a more recent and updated description in *Catálogo de manuscritos medievales*, pp. 95–98; Ho, pp. 329–32.

of the manuscript, although it was subsequently cut out of the folio.⁵⁸

In 1527 an event took place that would have far-reaching consequences for the development of Spanish humanism and, indirectly, for Zamora's career. A theological conference was held in Valladolid to debate supposed doctrinal and philological errors in Erasmus's writings.⁵⁹ The Dutch humanist's orthodoxy had been called into question by prominent members of the mendicant orders, which he had satirized in his works.⁶⁰ Though the conference came to no definitive conclusions,⁶¹ during the 1530s anti-Erasmian conservatives gained in influence and power, and the Inquisition began to crack down on the best-known of the Erasmians. The printer Miguel de Eguía was interrogated in 1530, and in 1533, Juan de Vergara, a collaborator on the *Polyglot Bible* and a professor of philosophy at Alcalá, was arrested.⁶² Vergara was also the secretary of the archbishop of Toledo, Alfonso de Fonseca, who tried to protect him during the short period between his arrest in June 1533 and Fonseca's own death in February 1534.

In the copy of Abravanel's commentary on the Latter Prophets printed in Soncino in 1520, now in the Marqués de Valdecilla,⁶³ Zamora added the vowel points to the text of the entire commentary and added several annotations in 1531 and in 1534.⁶⁴ According to Carlos Alonso Fontela, in one of these annotations, he seems to be positioning himself against the Erasmians.⁶⁵ Alonso Fontela suggests that the legal dispute between Zamora and Eguía caused by a disagreement on the profit sharing coming from Zamora's treatise on Hebrew grammar might be the cause for this positioning against the group of Erasmians, including, among them, Vergara, as he speaks of 'the administrators of the archbishop of Toledo' who had been arrested by the Inquisition.⁶⁶

Opinions about Zamora's ideological stance on this issue are mixed. Alonso Fontela enumerates several possible reasons why Zamora may have resented the Erasmians, one of which was his desire for retribution for the financial harm some of them had done him, particularly Eguía for the legal dispute mentioned above, another his friendship with Sánchez Ciruelo, a known anti-Erasmian.⁶⁷ However, it is also possible that Zamora, given his status as a convert and his vulnerability after Archbishop Fonseca's death in 1534, decided to feign hostility towards the Erasmians and other heterodox thinkers and to strengthen his ties of friendship and collaboration

---

58 His coat of arms is still to be seen in the copy from 1526 held at El Escorial (MS G-I-4).
59 See Lu Ann Homza, 'Erasmus as Hero, or Heretic? Spanish Humanism and the Valladolid Assembly of 1527', *Renaissance Quarterly*, 50 (1997), pp. 78–118.
60 Alonso Fontela, pp. 231–32.
61 The conference was suspended when the plague struck Valladolid in early August, and it never resumed. See Homza, p. 78. Prado Plumed, '*Al lasso, fuerça*', p. 184 note 93, thinks that grand inquisitor Alfonso Manrique de Lara, who mostly supported Erasmus's ideas, took this opportunity to suspend the conference, as he realized that anti-Erasmus opinion was gaining traction in the debate. Homza, p. 109, argues that 'endorsement or rejection of Erasmus's ideas was neither as extensive nor as profound as we have been led to believe'.
62 Alonso Fontela, p. 232, citing Bataillon, pp. 432–93.
63 *Nevi'im aharonim 'im perush don Yitzhaq Avravan'el*, 2 vols (Soncino: Gershon Soncino, 1520); Marqués de Valdecilla, BH DER 686 and 687.
64 See the transcription and study of these annotations in Alonso Fontela.
65 Alonso Fontela, p. 231.
66 Alonso Fontela, pp. 232–33.
67 Alonso Fontela, p. 233: 'Alfonso de Zamora, bien por convicción personal, o bien por enemistad con los erasmistas complutenses, o por amistad con [Pedro Sánchez] Ciruelo, se unió al grupo anti-erasmista de Alcalá'. (Alfonso de Zamora, either out of personal conviction, or out of enmity with the Erasmians from Alcalá, or out of friendship with [Pedro Sánchez] Ciruelo, joined the anti-Erasmian group in Alcalá).

with figures who were beyond suspicion, such as Sánchez Ciruelo.[68]

Later Commissions on Polemics and Biblical Exegesis

The anti-Erasmian movement and Zamora's position in regard to this matter is of interest here. Once the Erasmians began to be persecuted around 1530, Zamora stopped receiving commissions for copies of David Qimhi's *Mikhlol* and *Shorashim* and other grammatical texts by Sefardi and Provençal authors. His new projects focused instead on works of polemics and biblical exegesis in Hebrew, along with further commissions for biblical texts and the Targum.[69] This change might have been due to the fact that commissioning grammatical works after 1530, whether Hebrew or Greek, could have been seen as a suspicious activity connected to the Erasmians or, in the case of Hebrew works, to Judaizers.[70]

Thus, in 1532 Zamora finished a commission from Juan Álvarez de Toledo, bishop of Cordoba, Burgos, and Santiago de Compostela for the manuscript now in El Escorial, MS G-I-8, a work in Hebrew entitled *Sefer hokhmat 'elohim* ('Book of Godly Wisdom'). Federico Pérez Castro studied the codex in the 1950s and identified it as a compilation of the Hebrew and Aramaic texts used by Ramón Martí in his classic polemic *Pugio fidei* ('Dagger of Faith').[71]

El Escorial also houses another manuscript (MS G-II-18) copied by Zamora, which includes David Qimhi's commentary on Isaiah in both Hebrew and Spanish, the latter up to Isaiah 26:12, preceded by a section of allegorical commentary on Genesis.[72] The manuscript does not offer any information as to when it was copied, but

---

68 The collaboration between Pedro Sánchez Ciruelo and Alfonso de Zamora lasted for more than a decade, starting prior to 1526. According to Valle Rodríguez, 'Notas sobre Alfonso de Zamora', p. 174: 'Probablemente éste [Ciruelo] aprendió el hebreo junto a Alfonso de Zamora. En efecto éste le asiste en la empresa de la traducción literal de la Biblia hebrea y aquél fue el máximo propiciador de la publicación de la gramática hebrea de Alfonso de Zamora' (Probably this [Ciruelo] learned Hebrew with Alfonso de Zamora. Indeed, the latter assists him in the business of the literal translation of the Hebrew Bible and Ciruelo was the greatest promoter of the publication of Alfonso de Zamora's treatise on Hebrew grammar), citing Llamas, 'Los manuscritos hebreos de la Universidad de Madrid', pp. 268–69, and the Hebrew epilogue of Zamora's Hebrew grammar, where we read: ויותר מכולם המורה וחכם גדול פידרו סירואילו כי הוא עזרני בכל כחו וכוונתו השלימה ('The one [who helped me] more than anyone else [in publishing the treatise on Hebrew grammar] is the teacher and great sage Pedro Ciruelo, for he has helped me with all his strength and entire devotion'). See also Ho, pp. 242–45.

69 This statement refers to new commissions and not to restored manuscripts. Zamora continued restoring and completing Hebrew manuscripts of all kinds.

70 Grammatical and philological studies at Alcalá, including the study of Hebrew and Greek, and the *Complutensian Polyglot Bible* project were initiatives funded and promoted by the Erasmian group in Alcalá, led first by Archbishop Cisneros and then by Archbishop Fonseca. Archbishop Juan de Tavera, appointed 1534, was not in favour of fostering similar initiatives; Valle Rodríguez, 'Notas sobre Alfonso de Zamora', p. 177, suggests that Tavera's lack of support might be the reason why Zamora never published a Latin translation of Qimhi's *Shorashim* and *Mikhlol* or the Latin edition of the Targum in print form.

71 Described in Llamas, 'Los manuscritos hebreos de la Real Biblioteca de San Lorenzo de El Escorial [II]', pp. 301–03; Barco, III, pp. 161–62; Pérez Castro and Ho, pp. 409–19.

72 Described in José Llamas, 'Los manuscritos hebreos de la Real Biblioteca de San Lorenzo de El Escorial [I]', *Sefarad*, 1 (1941), pp. 7–43 (pp. 32–33); Barco, I, pp. 191–92; Ho, pp. 689–92. On the tradition of copying the allegorical commentary on Genesis before Qimhi's commentary on Isaiah, as well as the text in this manuscript, see Ho, pp. 689–90. Chapter One from the commentary on Isaiah in this manuscript has been recently edited in Amalia del Rocío Martín Sides, 'Estudio codicológico y paleográfico del Ms. G-II-18 de El Escorial: Capítulo 1 del comentario a Isaías de

according to the paper's watermarks,[73] it must have been produced in or after 1540, that is, around the same time as the copy of Qimhi's commentary on Psalms, mentioned previously, that the bishop of Coria commissioned from Zamora in 1541.

There are two manuscripts with Qimhi's commentary on Isaiah in the Marqués de Valdecilla that Zamora used and amended which might have served as sources for the manuscript of Qimhi's Isaiah commentary with Spanish translation, in addition to printed copies of this commentary that he might have also used.[74] The first is MS 9, copied in 1390,[75] where Zamora supplied seven folios in 1534, as attested in a note on folio 173^v (Figure 18.5).[76] The second is MS 10, a manuscript that also includes Qimhi's commentary on Ezekiel,[77] which was finished in 1446 or a bit later.[78] In this second manuscript, Zamora supplied the complete first quire, although the first folio on which he penned the introductory poem and the beginning of the commentary was lost. There is no annotation in this manuscript attesting to the date of Zamora's addition, but it is likely that he amended this and MS 9 at around the same time.

Conclusions

From the above it is clear that most of the polemics and works of Jewish exegesis, particularly David Qimhi's commentaries, for which Zamora received the commission were made after 1530. Thus, I believe that the waning influence of the Erasmian group in Alcalá after the Valladolid conference and the appointment of Juan de Tavera as archbishop of Toledo may have created a situation in which any activities related to the copying of Hebrew grammatical works *per se* were considered suspicious. Therefore, the Church's intellectual elite and the nobility stopped commissioning works of this type, inclining rather towards works on polemics and exegesis that provided arguments in favour of Catholic doctrine.

These same elites were behind the founding and development of the University of Alcalá de Henares and the *Complutensian Polyglot Bible* at the beginning of the sixteenth century. However, Spanish Hebraism was not limited to these endeavours. As Zamora's manuscripts on Hebrew grammar and exegesis show, during the first half of the sixteenth century there were other commissions and editorial projects beyond the edition of the *Complutensian Polyglot Bible*, and there were other individuals at both Alcalá and

---

David Quimhi y la traducción de Alfonso de Zamora' (unpublished MA thesis, Universidad Complutense de Madrid, 2020).

73 See Martín Sides, pp. 21, 23. Ho, p. 690, suggests 1530 as the possible date of the copy, but without compelling arguments to support her hypothesis.

74 There were printed versions of Qimhi's commentary on Isaiah going back to 1481, when his commentary on the Latter Prophets was published (*Perush nevi'im aharonim*, Guadalajara: Shelomo Alkabetz, 1481).

75 Described in Llamas, 'Los manuscritos hebreos de la Universidad de Madrid', pp. 272–73; Barco, I, pp. 189–90; a more recent and updated description in *Catálogo de manuscritos medievales*, pp. 85–88; Ho, pp. 568–71.

76 The note reads: אלפונשו די סאמורה כתב חסרוני הספר הזה והם נקודים ונשלם בשנת אלף ות״ק ול״ד למנין ישועתנו במתא אלכאלה די אינארייש ('Alfonso de Zamora copied what was missing in this book, with vowel points, and he finished it in the year 1534 of the count of our salvation, in the city of Alcalá de Henares').

77 Described in Llamas, 'Los manuscritos hebreos de la Universidad de Madrid', p. 273; Barco, I, pp. 187–88; a more recent and updated description in *Catálogo de manuscritos medievales*, pp. 89–93; Ho, pp. 692–95.

78 The manuscript reflects the handwriting of three different scribes — one who copied Isaiah and left it incomplete; another who copied Ezekiel and also left it incomplete; and a third scribe, Solomon ben Abraham Saruq, who completed the copy of both commentaries and wrote a colophon at the end of Isaiah (fol. 179^r). This colophon dates the end of the copy of Isaiah to the 27 of *Shevat* 5206 (25 January 1446). If the commentary of Ezekiel was completed after Isaiah, it must have been finished at a later date.

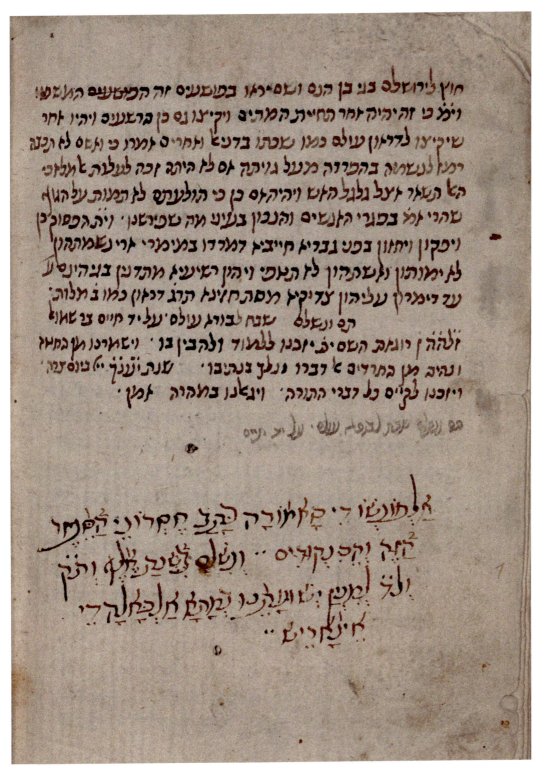

Figure 18.5. David Qimhi, *Commentary on Isaiah*. Iberian Peninsula, 1390. Colophon by Alfonso de Zamora, 1534. Madrid, Biblioteca Histórica de la Universidad Complutense de Madrid, BH MSS 9, fol. 173ᵛ.

Salamanca who studied, taught, and sometimes wrote on Hebrew grammar and the Hebrew Bible. As Stephen G. Burnett noted in 2000,[79] the comprehensive history of early modern Spanish Hebraism is still to be written.

According to Jesús de Prado, 'Christian Hebraism is often associated with the Reformation, in a fundamentally ahistorical and essentialist reading in which the study of Judaic scholarship by Christians and for Christian reasons would have almost exclusively been pushed by Protestantism and liberty of conscience'.[80] In light of the demand for works in Hebrew and for their translations among members of the nobility and the Church elite in Spain in the first half of the sixteenth century, it is very difficult to accept that Christian Hebraism was promoted almost exclusively by the religious transformations that occurred in northern Europe as a result of the Reformation. At least on the Iberian Peninsula, the same elites who eagerly sought out works from classical antiquity in Greek and Latin also demanded Jewish literature in the original languages. Thus, Christian Hebraism has to be framed within the context of humanism and the European Renaissance rather than solely within the context of the Reformation.

---

79 Burnett, p. 33: 'Apart from the accounts of the team which produced the Complutensian Polyglot of Alcalá, the story of the Spanish and Portuguese Christian Hebraism has yet to be told'.

80 Prado Plumed, 'The Commission of Targum Manuscripts', p. 158.

On the Beginnings of Christian Hebraist Bibliography in the Sixteenth Century

Introduction

On the binding of one of his manuscripts, the Christian Hebraist Johann Albrecht Widmanstetter (1506–57) recorded some of the observations he had made when reading this text (Figure 19.1):

לקוטות כל בו Collectanea expositionum variarum in libros Mosis. [...] Author collectaneorum est recentior, quadoquidem R. Salomonem et Abraham Aben Ezram saepissime citat. Desunt sectiones ultimae sex more Hebraeorum distinctae, quas פרשיות vocant.

(*Lequtot kol bo* ['Anthology of everything within']. A miscellany of different explanations of the Books of Moses. [...] The author of the collections is younger, because he frequently cites R[abbi] Solomon [ben Isaac] and Abraham ibn Ezra. The latter six parts, which according to the Jewish custom are separate, are missing and they are called *parashiyot*.)[1]

With a keen eye for textual details, from the quotations from the earlier authors Solomon ben Isaac (1040–1105) and Abraham ibn Ezra (1092–1164) in this Bible commentary, Widmanstetter surmised that it was authored sometime later. Modern scholarship agrees with Widmanstetter's placement of the text in the chronology of Jewish literature, dating *Lequtot kol bo* to the fourteenth century, although the identity of the author is a matter of some dispute.[2]

Similar title inscriptions in which Widmanstetter summarized the contents of his books on

---

1 Munich, Bayerische Staatsbibliothek (BSB), Cod.hebr. 252, binding. Between the words 'Mosis' and 'Author' one or more words have been expunged.
2 See the assessment of this work in Leopold Zunz, *Der Ritus des synagogalen Gottesdienstes, geschichtlich entwickelt* (Berlin: J. Springer, 1859), pp. 32, 179–80. However, this praise requires some qualification, as his characterization of this text is off the mark. *Lequtot kol bo* is not a commentary on the Bible in the sense of Rashi's commentary but rather deals with the ritual laws that are derived from the Pentateuch.

Maximilian de Molière • University of Munich / University of Halle-Wittenberg

Premodern Jewish Books, Their Makers and Readers in an Era of Media Change, ed. by Katrin Kogman-Appel and Ilona Steimann, Bibliologia, 67 (Turnhout: Brepols, 2024), pp. 429–446.

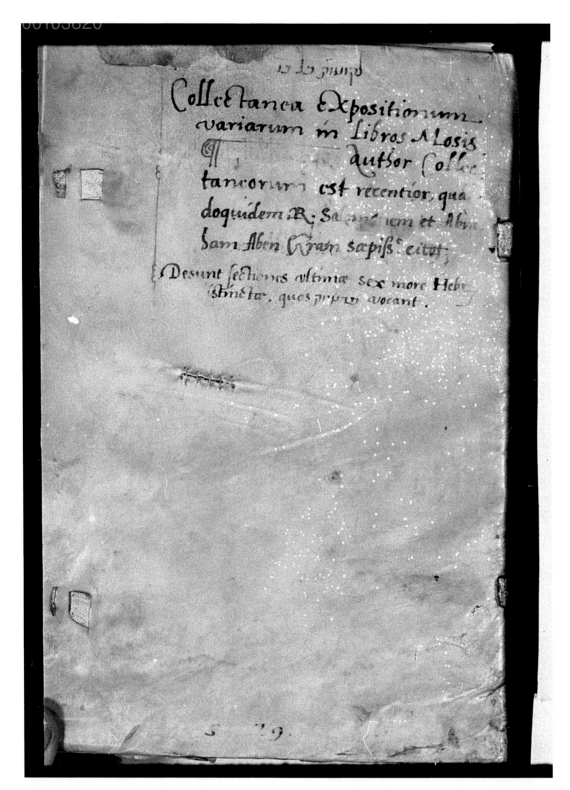

Figure 19.1. Munich, Bayerische Staatsbibliothek, Cod.hebr. 252, binding, Courtesy of Bayerische Staatsbibliothek München.

the bindings or on the flyleaves are preserved for more than two-thirds of his library, which comprises some 190 volumes. It can be assumed that the number of title inscriptions had originally been higher, but several of the books lost their original bindings and with them Widmanstetter's remarks. It is likely that he leveraged these title inscriptions to compile a catalogue of his library, which has also been lost.[3] The existence of this catalogue is attested in statements by several scholars who worked in the library during Widmanstetter's lifetime and shortly after, but it has not survived. It would seem that Widmanstetter first wrote a title and author into the book itself as a draft and then, once he was satisfied with his description, copied these data onto the binding. From the binding he would have copied a title inscription into a catalogue with each volume probably forming one entry.[4]

These inscriptions elucidate the bibliographic elements of books that this early modern scholar deemed useful and reflect the methodology he used to extract relevant information from the material objects in his possession. By calling attention to these essential steps in organizing a Christian library of Jewish books, we can add an important facet to the way Christians made sense of them in a larger context.

Johann Albrecht Widmanstetter began collecting Jewish books as a young man in Italy, where he studied halakhic and kabbalistic texts with various Jewish and Christian scholars, including the renowned Christian Kabbalist Cardinal Egidio da Viterbo (1472–1532).[5] After Egidio's death, Widmanstetter was able to copy some of the cardinal's valuable manuscripts, such as the Zohar, and appropriated others.[6] He acquired most of his Jewish books before returning to Germany

---

3 By examining all the books in his Hebraica collection, it becomes evident that Widmanstetter sometimes wrote these notes several times in different versions. In the case of BSB, Cod.hebr. 91, the title inscriptions occur twice inside the book and once more on the binding. Cod.hebr. 91, binding: '*Expositio introductionis Abamesis Euclidis libri XV interprete Thabuno. De motibus caelaestibus. Averrois in libros physicorum*' ('The exposition and introduction of Abamesis' [commentary] on Euclid's fifteenth book translated by Thabunus. On the celestial motions. Averroes on Physics'); fol. 2ʳ: '*Euclides cum figura terrae et caeli et aliis ad astronomian pertinentibus et commentum Averrois super duobus libris physicae Aristotelis*' ('Euclid with the figure of the earth and of the heavens and other things relevant to astronomy, and the commentary of Averroes on the two books of Aristotle's Physics') and fol. 2ᵛ: '*Jacob ben rabi Mechir*'. Multiple title inscriptions can be found in thirty-four volumes of the library. This number is far off the mark of the total number of 190 volumes that Widmanstetter's Hebraist library holds, but it is still large enough that the question appears pertinent whether the title inscriptions are the remnant stages of Widmanstetter's method of compiling a catalogue of his library.

4 The process could have included as an intermediary step the cutting and pasting of slips of paper as described by Ann Blair. That means he would have copied his descriptions onto slips of paper which he would then have sorted before writing the fair copy for the catalogue. For early modern techniques of organizing knowledge, see Ann Blair, *Too Much to Know: Managing Scholarly Information before the Modern Age* (New Haven: Yale University Press, 2010), esp. pp. 210–29.

5 The most thorough account of Widmanstetter's life remains Max Müller, *Johann Albrecht v. Widmanstetter 1506–1557: sein Leben und Wirken* (Munich: K.b. Ludwig-Maximilians-Universität München, 1907). A first survey was published in Hans Striedl, 'Die Bücherei des Orientalisten Johann Albrecht Widmanstetter', in *Serta Monacensia. Franz Babinger zum 15. Januar 1951 als Festgruß dargebracht*, ed. by Hans Joachim Kissling and Alois Schmaus (Leiden: Brill, 1952), pp. 201–44. For a book-length study of Widmanstetter's Hebraist library see, Maximilian de Molière, *Confronting Kabbalah: Studies in the Christian Hebraist Library of Johann Albrecht Widmanstetter* (Leiden: Brill, 2024)

6 On these manuscripts and the relationship between the libraries of the two men, see Maximilian de Molière, 'Johann Albrecht Widmanstetter's Recension of the Zohar', *Kabbalah: Journal for the Study of Jewish Mystical Texts*, 41 (2018), pp. 7–52 and Maximilian de Molière, 'Ex Bibliotheca Aegidiana: Das Fortleben der Bücher Kardinal Egidio da Viterbos in der hebraistischen Bibliothek Johann Albrecht Widmanstetters', in *Die Bibliothek – The Library – La Bibliothèque*, ed. by Andreas Speer and Lars Reuke, Miscellanea Mediaevalia, 41 (Berlin: De Gruyter, 2020), pp. 775–92 (pp. 779–86).

in 1539. Apart from his library, Widmanstetter is known today for his two major published works: a polemical commentary on the Quran, *Theologia Mahometis* (Nuremberg, 1543) and the *editio princeps* of the Syriac New Testament, *Liber sacrosancti Evangelii de Jesu Christo* (Vienna, 1555). After Widmanstetter's death, in 1558 Duke Albrecht V of Bavaria-Munich acquired his library for his nascent court library, the nucleus of the modern Bayerische Staatsbibliothek in Munich.[7]

In this chapter I offer a comparative survey of three Christian Hebraist bibliographies, those by Sebastian Münster (1488–1552), Conrad Gessner (1516–1565), and Andreas Masius (1514–1573), and Widmanstetter's inscriptions. These works were available in print around 1550, which was a time that Widmanstetter was active. In this survey, I also consider Jewish reference texts that could have served as models or sources for the bibliographic interests of Christian Hebraists and integrate their sources and methodologies into the overall discussion. Prior to the sixteenth century, Christians knew very little about the history of Jewish literature.[8] Throughout the Middle Ages, one of the few Jewish books Christians had come to know intimately was the Hebrew Bible in St Jerome's Latin translation. Central texts such as the Talmud were only known to small groups of specialists.[9] The scope of Jewish texts studied by Christians only began to expand when they discovered that many other Jewish texts could be leveraged to elucidate events in the Hebrew Bible and the life of Jesus Christ. In this period, textual critique became more sophisticated and scholars slowly began to realize that texts and books had a history that could be harnessed to understand the chronology of authors and the relationships of texts.[10] Moreover, intellectuals of the early modern period were forced to meet the challenge of a growing corpus of books by organizing knowledge by way of reference texts such as catalogues, book lists, and bibliographies.[11] These two developments in tandem paved the way for the bibliographic reference works that Christian Hebraists prepared in the sixteenth century.

Bibliographic texts authored by Christian Hebraists have received renewed attention over the last years through the research of Theodor Dunkelgrün and Fiammetta Sabba, whose studies explored their subjects against their respective

---

7 On the foundation of the ducal court library, see the seminal work that discusses many of the original sources Otto Hartig, *Die Gründung der Münchener Hofbibliothek durch Albrecht V. und Johann Jakob Fugger* (Munich: Verlag der Königlich Bayerischen Akademie der Wissenschaften, 1917). A more recent study by Helmut Zedelmaier has reassessed the duke's motivation for founding the library: Helmut Zedelmaier, 'Staatsräson und Repräsentation: Die Gründung der Münchener Hofbibliothek', in *Die Anfänge der Münchener Hofbibliothek unter Herzog Albrecht V.*, ed. by Alois Schmid (Munich: Beck, 2009), pp. 96–111.

8 See Moritz Steinschneider, 'Die hebräischen Handschriften der k. Hof- und Staatsbibliothek in München ein Beitrag zur Geschichte dieser Bibliothek', in *Sitzungsberichte der Bayrischen Akademie der Wissenschaften, Philosophisch-Philologische Classe* (Munich: Franz, 1875), pp. 169–206 (p. 175).

9 For a recent account of this field, see Alexander Fidora, 'The Latin Talmud and Its Place in Medieval Anti-Jewish Polemic', in *Studies on the Latin Talmud*, ed. by Ulisse Cecini and Eulàlia Vernet i Pons (Bellaterra: Universitat Autònoma de Barcelona, 2017), pp. 13–22.

10 For a comprehensive account of the humanists' philological toolset and its use, see Leighton D. Reynolds and Nigel G. Wilson, *Scribes and Scholars: A Guide to the Transmission of Greek and Latin Literature*, 3rd Ed. (Oxford: Clarendon Press, 1991), pp. 122–63. On Valla's exposure of the *Donation of Constantine* and his analysis of Scripture, see Alastair Hamilton, 'Humanists and the Bible', in *The Cambridge Companion to Renaissance Humanism*, ed. by Jill Kraye (Cambridge: Cambridge University Press, 1996), pp. 100–17 (pp. 104–05).

11 On the growth of reference works in this era and their methodologies, see Ann Blair, 'Organizations of Knowledge', in *The Cambridge Companion to Renaissance Philosophy*, ed. by James Hankins (Cambridge: Cambridge University Press, 2007), pp. 287–303 and Blair, *Too Much to Know*, pp. 161–66.

historical backgrounds and discussed their sources and methodologies.¹² The reference works of Münster, Gessner, and Masius differ from Widmanstetter's title inscriptions in that they were published in print, whereas the title inscriptions were only available to the person holding the respective volume in his hands. Another important difference is the distinct context which prompted the compilation of the bibliographic texts and the title inscriptions. Widmanstetter intended to reference the titles of the individual volumes, whereas Münster and the other authors also expressly included texts that were unavailable to them but which they considered noteworthy. The analysis of this survey, then, is founded on contextualizing the specific frame of reference of each bibliographic text that was formative in its creation. At the same time, I focus on those elements that are in fact comparable: the bibliographic data Widmanstetter inscribed in his books which portray texts and authors.

On the most basic level, catalogues, book lists, and bibliographies reference information such as the name of the author, the title, the publisher and so on. In semiotic terms, they are copies of these signs found on the title page and elsewhere in the book and are often organized according to a certain structure. Taken to an extreme, the bibliographer is not even required to understand these signs, as long as he can reliably transcribe them. Apart from these basic data, many bibliographic texts include supplementary information that may be specific to its author and his bibliographic methodology. Title inscriptions such as Widmanstetter's and similar bibliographic sources can thus help us to understand the bibliographic methodology Christian Hebraists applied to Jewish books and to better appreciate their methodologic achievements and the extent of their dependence on earlier authors. Another focal point is the way these sixteenth-century humanists described the history of Jewish literature and the Jewish book as a material object.

Jewish Historiography and Book Lists

Jewish authorities developed a rich and comprehensive tradition that systematically expounded the history of Jewish literature as early as in the medieval period.¹³ In his responsum, today

---

12 See Theodor Dunkelgrün, 'The Hebrew Library of a Renaissance Humanist Andreas Masius and the Bibliography to His *Iosuae Imperatoris Historia* (1574), with a Latin Edition and an Annotated English Translation', *Studia Rosenthaliana*, 42–43 (2011), pp. 197–252; Fiammetta Sabba, 'Eredità e futuro della tradizione scritta ebraica attraverso l'opera bibliografica di Conrad Gesner', *Bibliothecae.it*, 7 (2018), pp. 105–49; Fiammetta Sabba, 'Testimonies of Jewish Literature and Culture in the Bibliographic Work by Conrad Gessner', in *Conrad Gessner (1516–1565). Die Renaissance der Wissenschaften/ The Renaissance of Learning*, ed. by Urs B. Leu and Peter Optiz (Oldenbourg: De Gruyter, 2019), pp. 3–14. Research on Jewish bibliographies is referenced below.

13 An extensive, if dated account of the history of Jewish bibliography and its connections to Christian efforts in this field can be found in Julius Fürst, *Bibliotheca Judaica, bibliographisches Handbuch der gesammten jüdischen Literatur, mit Einschluss der Schriften über Juden und Judenthum und einer Geschichte der jüdischen Bibliographie* (Leipzig: Engelmann, 1863), III, pp. ix–civ. Another, more concise survey is offered by Abraham Meir Haberman, 'Bibliography', in *Encyclopaedia Hebraica*, ed. by Joseph Klausner and Benzion Netanyahu (Tel Aviv: Encyclopaedia Publishing Company, 1969) [in Hebrew], VIII, pp. 261–70. More recent publications that discuss individual Jewish and Christian Hebraist bibliographers include Saverio Campanini, 'Wege in die Stadt der Bücher: Ein Beitrag zur Geschichte der hebräischen Bibliographie (die katholische bibliographische "Dynastie" Iona-Bartolocci-Imbonati)', in *Reuchlin und seine Erben: Forscher, Denker, Ideologen und Spinner*, ed. by Peter Schäfer and Irina Wandrey, Pforzheimer Reuchlinschriften, 11 (Ostfildern: Jan Thorbecke, 2005), pp. 61–76; Reimund Leicht, 'Moritz Steinschneider's Concept of the History of Jewish Literature', in *Studies on Steinschneider: Moritz Steinschneider and the Emergence of the Science of Judaism*

known as *Iggeret Rabbi Sherira Ga'on* ('The Epistle of Rabbi Sherira Gaon'), the tenth-century Babylonian rabbi and head of the Academy of Pumbedita outlined the development of the Talmud beginning with the Mishnah and its additions, such as the Tosefta, and the various generations of sages who worked on it (Tannaim, Amoraim, Savoraim, and Geonim) until his own time. R. Sherira's successors published even more extensive accounts of Jewish literary history. Abraham ibn Daud (*c.* 1110–1180) in his *Sefer ha-qabbalah* ('The Book of Tradition') repudiated the attacks by Karaites on the legitimacy of the Oral Torah, tracing the chain of transmission of the Law from the revelation to Moses on Sinai to his own time.[14] Moses Maimonides (1138–1204), the philosopher and halakhist, contributed to this tradition with his *Iggeret Teiman* ('Epistle to Yemen'). The expression *shalshelet ha-qabbalah* ('chain of transmission') gave this literary genre its name. In the early modern period this tradition was continued by Abraham Zacuto (1452–c. 1515), the author of *Sefer yuhasin* ('The Book of Genealogy'), printed 1566 in Constantinople, and Gedaliah ibn Yahya (16th c.), who authored *Shalshelet ha-qabbalah* ('The Chain of Tradition'), printed 1587 in Venice. Both titles built on the foundation of earlier works by R. Sherira and others and expanded on points that in their authors' minds warranted further clarification.[15] Books concerned with the *shalshelet* tradition provide invaluable accounts of the transmission of Jewish literary traditions and were widely read by Jews and later by Christians. These works offer accounts of the literary production of delineated periods and systematic discussions about the relationships between them. The texts belonging to this tradition reference the earlier accounts and were designed to supplement books that had been published in the meantime. This finding indicates that compilers both reused accounts of authors and texts that had been published by earlier writers and leveraged the original texts that had not been previously transformed into such accounts. From a technical point of view, the *shalshelet* genre has little in common with the list format of catalogues and bibliographies. This genre would also influence the accounts of Jewish literary history by the Christian bibliographers under discussion.

The earliest precursors of what later became Jewish book catalogues and bibliographies are the booklists that were discovered in the Cairo Genizah.[16] Many of these lists were compiled from the eleventh to the thirteenth century in

---

in *Nineteenth-Century Germany*, ed. by Reimund Leicht and Gad Freudenthal (Leiden: Brill, 2012), pp. 151–74; and Avriel Bar-Levav, 'The Religious Order of Jewish Books: Structuring Hebrew Knowledge in Amsterdam', *Studia Rosenthaliana*, 44 (2012), pp. 1–27.

14 Ibn Daud's work was available in the sixteenth century in one edition, printed in Mantua in 1513, that also included *Seder 'Olam, 'Olam Zuta*, and *Megillat Ta'anit*: see Marvin J. Heller, *The Sixteenth-Century Hebrew Book: An Abridged Thesaurus* (Leiden: Brill, 2004), p. 53.

15 On these two later works and their printed editions, see Heller, pp. 585 and 751. When considering these texts, one should keep the debate surrounding them

in mind. Yerushalmi alleged that these works were not historiography in the strict sense as they sought to strengthen the authority of the Oral Torah and that few genuine works that fit the bill were written before the early modern period: Yosef Hayim Yerushalmi, *Zakhor: Jewish History and Jewish Memory*, 2nd Ed. (Seattle and London: University of Washington Press, 1999), esp. pp. 31–75. Bonfil challenged this view: see Robert Bonfil, 'Jewish Attitudes Toward History and Historical Writing in Pre-Modern Times', *Jewish History*, 11 (1997), 7–40. On this genre and on the debate about Jewish historiography in general, see Eva Haverkamp, 'Historiography', in *The Cambridge History of Judaism. Volume 6: The Middle Ages: The Christian World*, ed. by Robert Leon Chazan (Cambridge: Cambridge University Press, 2018), pp. 836–59, 902–03.

16 These lists were published in Nehemiah Allony, *The Jewish Library in the Middle Ages – Book Lists from the Cairo Genizah* [in Hebrew], ed. by Miriam Frenkel and Haggai Ben-Shammai (Jerusalem: Ben Zvi Institute, 2006).

a variety of contexts with different descriptive methodologies, which rendered their interpretation somewhat problematic. One group of these materials was compiled by booksellers who kept records of their available stocks and tracked the titles they had sold, including the asking prices. Occasionally, we even find references to the production of new books by scribes in the employ of these booksellers, elucidating the ebb and flood of supply and demand of certain titles and authors.[17] The lists, many of which were gathered by Nehemia Allony, shed light on a wide range of situations in which book lists were compiled. As a result, the motivations and the methodologies of recording books differed from, say, inventories listing books from legacies. For this reason, we also find in these descriptions references to material features such as the ornate covers in which some manuscripts were bound.

Similar features can be found in Italian Jewish booklists which were compiled by the owners of libraries.[18] Jean-Pierre Rothschild published and analysed dozens of Jewish booklists that he had discovered inside Italian manuscripts on flyleaves, then used his results to further the understanding of the cultural history of Italian Jewry. Some of these lists were inventories that Jews compiled to help keep their books in order and others were part of sales' contracts which listed the items being sold. Rothschild used these lists to investigate the literary tastes of the period. In his view, they provide a necessary corrective instrument for researchers to counter the heavy losses suffered by Jewish libraries at the hands of Christian persecutors and against the distortions that have resulted from the preferences of modern scholarship.[19] Moreover, the book owners who compiled these lists often recorded descriptions of their books, revealing the kinds of material features that medieval and early modern authors considered distinctive. In the booklist Moses of Norzi compiled in 1514, he described the first book as א׳ מקרא שלמה כתיבה מרובעת בקלף מכוסה עור אדום ('one complete Bible in square script, in parchment, covered with red leather') and then continued to outline fifty-five items in this detailed fashion.[20] Thus we find in many of these lists specifications about the colour of the book's bindings, its size, and sometimes even the script style (the contemporary descriptions usually distinguished between rounded and square script). Such descriptions of materiality in the lists were necessary for the compilers to reliably identify the artefacts, as some of these lists were part of sales' contracts, although the vast majority are records of private libraries assembled by the lists' compilers or inherited from their fathers.[21] Jewish booksellers and compilers of booklists thus

---

17 For instance, Allony, no. 40.
18 Jean-Pierre Rothschild edited and analysed the Italian booklists in a series of articles: Jean-Pierre Rothschild, 'Deux bibliothèques juives comtadines vers 1630', *Revue des Études Juives*, 145 (1986), pp. 75–102; Jean-Pierre Rothschild, 'Quelques listes de livres hébreux dans des manuscrits de la Bibliothèque nationale de Paris', *Revue d'histoire des textes*, 17 (1989), pp. 291–346; Jean-Pierre Rothschild, 'Listes de livres hébreux en Italie: nouveaux documents pour une typologie', *Revue d'histoire des textes*, 19 (1990), pp. 291–339; Jean-Pierre Rothschild, 'Les listes de livres reflet de la culture des Juifs en Italie du Nord au XVe et au XVIe siècle?', in *Manoscritti, frammenti e libri ebraici nell'Italia dei secoli XV–XVI: atti del 7 Congresso internazionale dell'AISG, S. Miniato, 7-8-9 novembre 1988*, ed. by Giuliano Tamani and Angelo Vivian (Rome: Carucci, 1991), pp. 163–93; Jean-Pierre Rothschild, 'Les bibliothèques hebraïques médiévales et l'exemple des livres de Léon Sini (vers 1523)', in *Libri, lettori e biblioteche dell'Italia medievale (secoli IX–XV)*, ed. by Guiseppe Lombardi and Donatella Nebbiai-Dalla Guarda (Rome: ICCU, 2001), pp. 229–61.

19 See Rothschild, 'Quelques listes', p. 340.
20 Rothschild, 'Quelques listes', list no. I.
21 See Malachi Beit-Arié, *Hebrew Codicology: Historical and Comparative Typology of Medieval Hebrew Codices Based on the Documentation of the Extant Dated Manuscripts until 1540 Using a Quantitative Approach*, trans. by Ilana Goldberg (Jerusalem and Hamburg: The Israel Academy of Sciences and Humanities, 2022) https://www.fdr.uni-hamburg.de/record/9349 [accessed in May 2023], pp. 99–100.

met the challenge of indexing material features of the books before them using a terminology that allowed themselves and others to compare these references with the original object and with similar lists.

Christian Hebraist Bibliographies

Christian scholars began to think systematically about Jewish texts in the sixteenth century. One of the first Christians to do so was the German Sebastian Münster, who published a bibliography of Jewish texts when he edited Elijah Levita's textbook on Hebrew grammar in a Latin translation as *Grammatica Hebraea*, supplemented with his own observations. He republished it several times during his lifetime, adding new material with each printing.[22] For a new printing of the book in 1543 he appended a list of Jewish books he called '*Nomenclatura hebraeorum quorundam librorum*' ('Title List of Certain Hebrew Books'),[23] which is subdivided into three sections. The first part consists of a list of the books authored by Elijah Levita, whose grammar Münster had translated into Latin. Münster then gave a list of his own publications pertaining to Hebrew grammar and lexicography on the page opposite Levita's publications.[24]

The third and most extensive list is titled '*Catalogus quorundam librorum sacrae linguae, qui hodie extant*' ('Catalogue of Some Books in the Holy Tongue Now in Existence').[25] Here, Münster compiled a broad array of titles: Bible, Talmud, rabbinic commentators, and others. The list leans towards textual bibliography, as Münster attempted to furnish concise characterizations of the more prominent authors and texts. The Talmud is described somewhat vaguely as '*ingens opus, varia complectens*' ('a large work that comprises different subjects'). Out of the entire body of the Talmud, Münster characterized only the Mishnah as '*potior pars Thalmud*' ('the most formidable section of the Talmud').[26] The entries in the remainder of Münster's list describe authors and their various works in some detail. The entry on Abraham Ibn Ezra is a fair example of Münster's imprecision in describing the listed authors:

> Sapiens Aben Ezra: hoc est, Abraham filius Ezrae, plurima scripsit: extant solummodi commentaria in Mosen et prophetas: fuit grammaticus, philosophus, astrologus, et theologus magnus.
>
> (The sage Ibn Ezra: that is Abraham son of Ezra, he wrote much: only the commentaries on [the books of] Moses and the Prophets are in existence. He was a great grammarian, a philosopher, an astrologer, and a great theologian.)[27]

---

22 Karl Heinz Burmeisters, *Sebastian Münster: Versuch eines biographischen Gesamtbildes* (Basel: Helbing & Lichtenhahn, 1963) is still the most extensive biography on Sebastian Münster.

23 The index is found in Sebastian Münster, *Grammatica Hebraea Eliae Levitae Germani* (Basel: Froben, 1543), pp. t4^r–t7^r. Steinschneider traced the changes Münster made to his book over the years and identified this text as the earliest attempt to compile a bibliography of Jewish books: see Moritz Steinschneider, *Bibliographisches Handbuch über die theoretische und praktische Literatur für hebräische Sprachkunde* (Leipzig: Vogel, 1859), pp. 96–97. Although Burnett briefly mentions Münster's list, he does not discuss it beyond a general remark about 'Münster's vague listing of Jewish authors and titles' (Stephen G. Burnett, *Christian Hebraism in the Reformation Era (1500–1660): Authors, Books, and the Transmission of Jewish Learning* [Leiden: Brill, 2012], p. 139).

24 This juxtaposition appears like a deliberate attempt to present himself as superior to the famous Jewish grammarian, especially since the list of Münster's books is markedly longer than that of Levita's books: see Münster, pp. t4^v–t5^r.

25 Münster, pp. t5^v–t7^r.

26 Münster, p. t5^v.

27 Münster, p. t6^r.

Münster was unable to follow through with this bibliographic paradigm to the end. The final part of the catalogue evolves into a bare enumeration of authors for whom Münster provided no explanations as to the fields to which they contributed nor are the names of their works given. Münster's lists often do not provide sufficient information, such as the exact title, to enable readers to acquire the book in question, making it unsuitable for collectors. Owing to the brevity of Münster's entries, it is difficult to determine if he gathered the bibliographic information from the texts themselves or if he drew on an earlier, possibly Jewish tradition. Widmanstetter, who had studied Hebrew under Münster, was apparently unfamiliar with this list, as he owned a copy of an earlier edition published in 1537, which does not contain the lists.[28]

The next reference book of Jewish texts by a Christian, which followed soon after Münster's list, was a revolution in the scope of the texts it covered and in the richness of its descriptions. In his multi-volume *Bibliotheca universalis*, the Swiss humanist Conrad Gessner ventured to compile a bibliography of all published works in Latin, Greek, and Hebrew. This monumental work, published between 1545 and 1555, includes about 3000 authors and some 12,000 titles listed alphabetically in twenty-one subject classes.[29] One list that Gessner included in his work was based on the sales' catalogue of the bookshop of the famous bookseller and printer Daniel Bomberg from the year 1543.[30] This list provides information on the printed editions that were available at this time in the Bomberg bookshop. The entries typically consist of the transliteration of the Hebrew title into Latin characters followed by a translation. There are no explanations of the texts nor characterizations of their authors. Additional information in the Bomberg list pertains to the sale of books: the number of volumes that comprise a given text and the price of each volume in Bomberg's shop. This list, then, is typical of catalogues handed out by booksellers in this era to attract customers.[31] Hebraist specialists would have found this list helpful, even if it dispensed with the rigorous classification that Gessner applied to other Jewish books.

The volume of Gessner's work titled *Partitiones theologicae* ('Theological Divisions') features more extensive bibliographic information on Jewish books than found in the Bomberg catalogue, both in the number of titles and the type of information it conveyed. Gessner included Hebrew books into a larger list of titles that he subsumed under the category 'Theology'. First, the beginning of this list is structured according

---

28 Widmanstetter's copy is BSB, L.as. 162. On Widmanstetter's studies under Sebastian Münster, see Müller, 13.

29 For the Jewish books in Gessner's work, see the diligent analysis in Sabba, 'Eredità e futuro'; Sabba, 'Testimonies of Jewish Literature'. The most important study of Conrad Gessner's *Bibliotheca* is to this day Helmut Zedelmaier, *Bibliotheca universalis und bibliotheca selecta: das Problem der Ordnung des gelehrten Wissens in der frühen Neuzeit*, Archiv für Kulturgeschichte, 33 (Cologne: Böhlau, 1992). A recent analysis of the Hebrew section can be found in Burnett, pp. 140–45. The fundamental study on Gessner's work in general remains Zedelmaier, *Bibliotheca universalis*. An instructional analysis of Gessner own library can be found in Urs B. Leu and others, *Conrad Gessner's Private Library*, History of Science and Medicine Library, 5 (Leiden: Brill, 2008).

30 See volume 2.1 of the *Bibliotheca*: Conrad Gessner, *Pandectarum Sive Partitionum Universalium Conradi Gesneri Tigurini, Medici et Philosophiae Professoris, Libri XXI: Secundus Hic Bibliothecae Nostrae Tomus Est* (Zurich: Froschauer, 1548), pp. 41b–42b. This booklist is published and commented on in Aron Freimann, 'Daniel Bombergs Bücherverzeichnis', *Zeitschrift für Hebräische Bibliographie*, 10 (1906), pp. 38–42. It will be analysed in more detail and compared to Widmanstetter's library of Jewish books in my upcoming study on this collection.

31 On the catalogues published by booksellers from that period, see Angela Nuovo, *The Book Trade in the Italian Renaissance*, Library of the Written Word, The Handpress World, 26 (Leiden: Brill, 2013), p. 331.

to the books contained in the Hebrew Bible and the New Testament. Under each biblical book, the relevant titles are listed, meaning that Hebrew titles are integrated among books by Latin and Greek authors. The data given in the list itself largely consist of the title and the author and additional information on the text's origin or important points. Gessner also devoted dedicated sections to the more prominent authors. Concerning Moses Maimonides, for example, he remarked among other things on the main points of the author's major works and the fact that most of them had been translated from the Arabic.[32] In the same vein as the theological works, Gessner also sorted Hebrew books into the subject heading 'Grammar,' which reflects less extensive commentaries on its titles.[33]

The list of theological works also includes a longish section on the two Talmuds with a concise description of all six *sedarim* ('orders'), lists of different editions, and a history of their composition.[34] Thanks to the diligent analysis of Fiametta Sabba, we know that Gessner drew much of his information from the works of numerous Jewish sages and Christian Hebraists. For example, he referenced Abraham ibn Daud as the author of *Sefer ha-qabbalah*.[35] In addition, he may have been able to access the catalogue of Cardinal Domenico Grimani's collection, compiled by Abraham de Balmes, when he visited the Sant'Antonio di Castello Library near Venice in 1543.[36] Among the many sources in this work, one that stands out is the catalogue Conrad Pellikan compiled during his tenure as librarian of the Bibliotheca Tigurina. Gessner succeeded Pellikan in this position but *Bibliotheca universalis* expanded the number of details about the included authors and texts.[37] Moreover, Gessner explained in the introduction that he cited extensively from Johannes Reuchlin and Pietro Galatino and arranged their works to form a learned discussion:

> Quis fuerit Talmud author, quando editus sit: in quot partes dividatur: et quibus de rebus praecipue tractet, ex Petri Galatini de arcanis catholicae veritatis lib. 1. cap. 5. Colloquuntur Capnion et Galatinus.
>
> (Who authored the Talmud? When was it published? Into what parts it is sectioned? And on some of the particular subjects discussed — [these subjects are taken] from Pietro Galatino's *On the Secrets of the Catholic Truth*, Book One, Chapter Five. — Capnion[38] and Galatino discuss [the matter].)[39]

Bibliotheca universalis provided for the first time extensive information about Jewish books and

---

32 '*Audio hunc authorem Arabice sua scripsisse, quae deinde ab aliis in Hebraicam linguam translata, non parum elegantius et purius quam reliquum Talmud legantur*' ('I hear that this author wrote in his Arabic which others thereafter translated into the Hebrew language so they could be read in a little more refined elegant and purer manner than the rest of the Talmud'), in volume 2.2 of the *Bibliotheca*: Conrad Gessner, *Partitiones theologicae, pandectarum universalium Conradi Gesneri, liber ultimus pandectis nostris sive secundo bibliothecae tomo* (Zurich: Froschauer, 1549), pp. 18a–b.

33 See Gessner, *Pandectarum*, pp. 38b–41b.

34 See Gessner, *Partitiones theologicae*, pp. 15b–17b.

35 '*Rabbi Abraham filius Levi scripsit Kabala Hebraice. Liber excusus est*' ('Rabbi Abraham the son of Levi wrote Kabbalah in Hebrew. The book is printed'), in volume 1.1 of the *Bibliotheca*: Conrad Gessner, *Bibliotheca uniuersalis, sive catalogus omnium scriptorium* [...] *quae omnis generis authorum nomina cum lucubrationibus* (Zurich: Froschauer, 1545), p. 2a.

36 See Sabba, 'Eredità e futuro', pp. 107–10. On Grimani's library and its fate, see also Giuliano Tamani, 'I libri ebraici del cardinal Domenico Grimani', *Annali di Ca' Foscari*, 24.3 (1995), pp. 5–52. Another account of Gessner's process can be found in Burnett, pp. 140–45.

37 For this assessment, see Sabba, 'Eredità e futuro', pp. 127–28.

38 The humanist name used by Reuchlin.

39 Gessner, *Partitiones theologicae*, p. 15b.

their history for a Christian readership. Gessner's chosen methodology, which involved compiling his bibliography using existing catalogues, was surely developed because of the enormous corpus that he had to process. The magnitude of Gessner's project only allowed for transposing existing textual bibliographic information on Jewish books from his sources to his own work.

Yet another attempt to organize Jewish literature is the bibliography Andreas Masius compiled in the 1570s. The Dutch Hebraist had corresponded with Widmanstetter and they had collaborated in the publication of the *Syriac New Testament*.[40] Masius conceived of this list after the burning of the Talmud in 1555 and the confiscation and destruction of many other Jewish books by the Inquisition. He tried to convince his Christian coreligionists of the harmlessness of these texts by informing them about the contents and history of Jewish literature. In line with this goal, Masius prepared his itemized list using a textual bibliography approach. A typical entry includes the title in the original Hebrew script, followed by a translation and in many cases a brief summary. When the author's name was known to him, Masius added it; otherwise, he tendered his own conjectures as to the author's identity. As a contributor to the *Antwerp Polyglot*, Masius was qualified to write many of these accounts of texts and authors himself. Nonetheless, he was also content to lean on the information provided by the *shalshelet* tradition. As Theodor Dunkelgrün has shown, Masius lifted some of his characterizations of texts from Abraham ibn Daud's work on the chronology of Jewish tradition, *Sefer ha-qabbalah*, and used this source extensively for background information. Owing to ibn Daud's work, for example, Masius was able to give the following characterization of *'Otiyot de-Rabbi Aqiva* ('The Letters of Rabbi Aqiva'):

> Floruit ille tempore Adriani Imperatoris cuius iussu dilaniatus est, cum fautor atque adiutor fuisset secessionis, quam apud Iudaeos fecerat בר כוזיבא, Bar-Cosba.
>
> ([R. Aqiva] flourished in the time of Emperor Hadrian, upon whose command he was torn to pieces, for he was an adherent and an accomplice of the uprising which *Bar Koziba*, Bar Cosba, had instigated among the Jews.)[41]

This penchant for the history of texts notwithstanding, Masius occasionally included descriptions of materiality into his bibliography, such as the observation that his own kabbalistic books were manuscripts.[42] His sincerity and rigor make Masius' bibliography a foundational contribution to the systematic study of Jewish texts by Christian scholars in the sixteenth century.

With this brief survey of bibliographies, lists, and catalogues the following trends among Jewish and Christian reference books emerge: Whereas the former displayed a more comprehensive interest in textual and material features, which varied according to the particular work's intended purpose, the latter were primarily concerned with the history of Jewish literature. Thus, we can now turn our attention to Widmanstetter's title inscriptions.

---

40 This text has been recently edited, translated, and commented on in Dunkelgrün's 'The Hebrew Library'. On Andreas Masius more generally, see Wim François, 'Andreas Masius (1514–1573)', *Journal of Eastern Christian Studies*, 61/3 (2009), pp. 199–244. One letter from Masius to Widmanstetter is published in Joseph Perles, *Beiträge zur Geschichte der hebräischen und aramäischen Studien* (Munich: Ackermann, 1884), pp. 203–04.

41 Dunkelgrün, pp. 235, 243.

42 '*Sequuntur libri cabbalistici manu scripti aliquot, eiusdem Andreae Masii*' ('There follow some kabbalistic books written by the hand of the same Andreas Masius'), cited from Dunkelgrün, pp. 235, 243.

Widmanstetter's Title Inscriptions

Most of the title inscriptions Widmanstetter prepared follow the same basic paradigm, consisting of the name of the author and the title, which is similar to the lists surveyed so far. As mentioned above, Widmanstetter probably used these inscriptions as the bases for a catalogue that has been lost since the 1570s. Still, the individual entries on the bindings and on the flyleaves elucidate the extent of his knowledge of Jewish texts as well as his bibliographic methodology.

Among Widmanstetter's title inscriptions, we can discern tendencies towards material descriptions and textual history. Particularly remarkable are those notes that touch on the materiality of his Jewish books. In Cod.hebr. 77 of the Bayerische Staatsbibliothek (BSB), he likely drew on the information in the colophon to write out the date of production, allowing him to conclude: '*Codex scriptus est Bononiae 5011*' ('The codex was written in Bologna in 5011').[43] The year 5011 of the Hebrew calendar corresponds to 1251 CE. This note is a paraphrase of the colophon, which reads כתבתיו פה בולונייה בחדש אייר שנת ה"א ואברהם ז'ק'ן' בא בימים ('I wrote it in Bologna in the month of Iyyar in the year "and Abraham was old (*zaqan*), well stricken in age"').[44] The Hebrew colophon indicates that the consonants of *zaqan* (*zayin*, *qof*, and *nun*) of the biblical verse Genesis 24:1 are to be understood in their numerical value, 157, which equals the year 1397 CE. Widmanstetter's mistake in calculating the common era date put his dating off by 150 years from the manuscript's actual date of production.[45] In total, he copied or computed the dates of production from the colophons of eight manuscripts and one printed book.[46] What appears on the surface as a simple task of transforming one set of signs in the original colophon into another set of signs in the inscription was in fact a complicated process that involved an understanding of *gematria*, the numerical value of the Hebrew letters, and of calculating Arabic numbers from the *gematria* of a biblical verse.

Interestingly, Widmanstetter did not devote the same attention to printed books as he gave to manuscripts. The antiquarian streak of humanism might have prejudiced his appreciation of his books in favour of manuscripts. It was only for the printed edition of *Yalqut Shim'oni* that Widmanstetter wrote down the date of production, '*Thessalonicae impressus anno 5286*' ('Printed in Salonica in 5286'),[47] while the bindings of all other printed books show only the authors and titles. Information about the books' origins based on his own reading of texts made up the building blocks by which Widmanstetter slowly mapped the landscape of Jewish book culture.

The history of Jewish textual transmission is another concern that can be detected in Widmanstetter's title inscriptions. A sizeable number of works in his library are translations of philosophic and scientific texts from the Greek and the Arabic into Hebrew, for example, Euclid's *De elementis* and Averroes' commentary on Aristotle's *Physica*. Many of these translated works were not available in any European language in the sixteenth

---

43   BSB, Cod.hebr. 77, fol. 1ᵛ.
44   BSB, Cod.hebr. 77, fol. 68ʳ.
45   Hebrew dates were often given according to the short reckoning, that is without the value for the millennia. The numerical value of eleven in the short reckoning would thus correspond to 5011 in the long reckoning. It seems that he calculated the numerical value of the two letters following *shenat* ('year'), misreading the letter *heh* for *yod* to arrive at the numerical value eleven (= 5011).
46   See BSB, Cod.hebr. 77, Cod.hebr. 81, Cod.hebr. 97 (colophon), Cod.hebr. 117 (colophon date of sale), Cod.hebr. 127, Cod.hebr. 119 (colophon), Cod.hebr. 207, and Cod.hebr. 285. In another case, Widmanstetter was mistaken in misreading a sale's contract as a colophon referencing the origin of the manuscript, see BSB, Cod.hebr. 207, fol. 101ʳ.
47   BSB, 2 A.hebr. 245, titlepage.

century,⁴⁸ and it was only through a knowledge of Hebrew that scholars were able to access these texts. In contrast to earlier Christian Hebraists, such as Egidio da Viterbo, Widmanstetter was not only interested in Hebrew because it allowed him to read kabbalistic texts and understand Jewish commentaries on the Bible, but it also gave him access to texts that were otherwise unavailable in sixteenth-century Europe.⁴⁹ In his title inscriptions, Widmanstetter took note of the transmission of texts from Arabic to Hebrew, remarking on the names of the translators and taking the information from the colophons of the manuscripts themselves. Thus, in BSB, Cod. hebr. 91, he remarked on Jacob ben Mechir, who had translated Euclid: '*Jacob ben rabi Mechir*' ('Jacob ben Mechir translated Euclid from the Arabic').⁵⁰ Widmanstetter wrote out the name of the translator in seven manuscripts,⁵¹ of which three also include the date of translation,⁵² and one merely mentions the fact that its text had been translated.⁵³

In one title inscription on BSB, Cod.hebr. 108, Widmanstetter identified the relevance of a Hebrew translation, as the text was no longer available in the original Greek: '*Themistii paraphrasis in XII metaphysica qui apud graecos non extat*' ('The paraphrase of Themistius's commentary on the twelfth book of [Aristotle's] *Metaphysics* is not found among the Greeks').⁵⁴ Indeed, Widmanstetter's assessment is corroborated by modern philology⁵⁵ and demonstrates a high degree of concern about the chain of transmission of Jewish culture. By modern standards, Widmanstetter did not identify a substantial number of translations, but in light of the limited resources at his disposal in the sixteenth century, such systematic considerations adumbrated the influences on Jewish learning in the Middle Ages.

Another set of title inscriptions sheds light on Widmanstetter's reasoning in dealing with chronology and authorship based on philological data. Even though he left only a small number of marginal notes inside his books that allow us to trace his reading, he added some of his own assessments on the texts in his title inscriptions. I cited one of these notes for *Lequtot kol bo* at the beginning of the chapter. In the context of another inscription, he correctly identified the Christian Arab Hunayn ibn Ishaq as the author of the *Book of Introduction* and traced its relationship to another text:

> Introductio ad medicinam Haninae filii Isaac, per quaestiones. Ex hoc libro puto Ioannitii Isagogen excerptam. Et Ioannitius ex Iohan Isac factum.

---

48 On translations from the Arabic, see Steven Harvey, 'Arabic into Hebrew', in *The Cambridge Companion to Medieval Jewish Philosophy*, ed. by Daniel H. Frank and Oliver Leaman (Cambridge: Cambridge University Press, 2003), pp. 258–80; Gad Freudenthal, 'Science and Medicine', in *The Cambridge History of Judaism*, ed. by Robert Chazan (Cambridge: Cambridge University Press, 2018), VI: The Middle Ages: The Christian World, pp. 702–41, 899–900. A chronological survey of translated texts is available in Mauro Zonta, 'Medieval Hebrew Translations of Philosophical and Scientific Texts', in *Science in Medieval Jewish Cultures*, ed. by Gad Freudenthal (Cambridge: Cambridge University Press, 2012), pp. 17–73. The DARE-project page (Digital Averroes Research Environment) offers comprehensive search options for all known translations of Averroes into Hebrew including the manuscripts, see https://dare.uni-koeln.de/app/works [accessed in May 2023].

49 This difference of interests is explored in Molière, 'Ex Bibliotheca Aegidiana', pp. 786–91.

50 BSB, Cod.hebr. 91, fol. 2bisʳ.

51 He lists the names in BSB, Cod.hebr. 91 (thrice), Cod. hebr. 213 (twice), Cod.hebr. 241, Cod.hebr. 256, Cod. hebr. 263, Cod.hebr. 289, and Cod.hebr. 297.

52 See BSB, Cod.hebr. 241, 256, 289, and 297.

53 See BSB, Cod.hebr. 106.

54 BSB, Cod.hebr. 108, fol. [IIIᵛ].

55 See Alfred L. Ivry, 'Themistius', in *Encyclopaedia Judaica*, ed. by Michael Berenbaum and Fred Skolnik, 2ⁿᵈ Ed. (Detroit: Macmillan Reference USA, 2007), pp. xix, 691.

(The [Book of] *Introduction* to medicine by Hanina the son of Isaac by the way of questions. I believe that the *Introduction to Medicine* of Joannitius is taken from this book. Joannitius was made from of Johan [i.e., Hanina] the son of Isaac.)⁵⁶

Widmanstetter transcribed the Arabic form of the author's name into Latin from the beginning of the Hebrew text. From there, he also gathered the information that the text was written in the form of questions and answers: ספר המבוא למלאכת הרפואות חברו חנין בן יצחק על דרך השאלה ותשובת המענה ('The *Book of Introduction* to the art of medicine, its author is Hanin ben Isaac [who lays out his material] by way of questions and answers').⁵⁷ Widmanstetter also posited that another work by the same author, the *Introduction to Medicine*, had used material from the *Book of Introduction*. His observation was a major creative feat, as he had to compare the *Introduction to Medicine* and the *Book of Introduction*.⁵⁸ However, he did not leave any remarks on the relationship between the two texts in this second manuscript — the title inscription consists merely of an itemized list. His ability to date a text based on quotations demonstrates the sophistication of his philological toolkit.

The names of the authors noted by Widmanstetter provide both a hint of his philological skills and his concern for bibliographic clarity. In the case of *Introduction to Medicine* vs. the *Book of Introduction*, he recognized the reason behind the similarities between the two texts that were in fact both written by Hunayn ibn Ishaq, who was referenced with two transcriptions of his name in Hebrew characters: The first manuscript gave a Hebrew rendition of the Arabic name, *Hunayn ibn Ishaq* to *Hanin ben Yitzhaq*, and the second transcribed the Latin form of his name, *Joannitius*, into Hebrew as יואניסיי (*Yoanisii*) — the final *yod* indicates that the Hebrew translator transcribed the genitive form of the name.⁵⁹ It seems that Widmanstetter did not catch onto to the identity of the author immediately. In the title inscription of the second manuscript, he used both forms next to one another, suggesting that he understood that both names referenced the same person only after he had recognized the similarities between *Introduction to Medicine* and the *Book of Introduction*. The inscription in this case is a record of the way he came understand the author's identity.⁶⁰ The ability to connect these two names with one author shows Widmanstetter's prowess as a bibliographer. He did not merely transfer the author's name as it was written in the manuscript into his title inscription but his knowledge of the author behind the two names allowed him to provide a robust form for indexing the name. He was well enough versed in medical texts to compile a more concise title inscription.

Unlike Gessner's and Masius's bibliographies, there is no detectable *shalshelet*-tradition influence in Widmanstetter's title inscriptions. This does not mean, however, that he was unfamiliar with these texts as the example of Moses Maimonides' *Iggeret Teiman* shows — the only text belonging to this tradition that was found in Widmanstetter's library. In a note that is part of the title inscription at the beginning of the book, Widmanstetter lamented that certain anti-Christian remarks in *Iggeret Teiman* were deleted in an attempt to take the sting out of a passage that was offensive to Christians:

> Epistola Theman, R. Maimonis, in qua deleta sunt ea quae pro Christianis facere visa sunt a perfidis Iudaeis, librum emi ab Abrahamo Scacciotio Hebraeo Romae XVIII Februario 1544.

---

56 BSB, Cod.hebr. 250, fol. [IIIᵛ].
57 BSB, Cod.hebr. 250, fol. 1ʳ.
58 See BSB, Cod.hebr. 270, fols 1ʳ–11ᵛ.
59 See BSB, Cod.hebr. 270, fol. 11ᵛ.
60 '1 Isagoge Joannitii. 2 Questiones et responsa Hanan filii Isaac ad introductio medicinae. 3 Aphorismi Hippocratis'. BSB, Cod.hebr. 270, fol. [Iᵛ].

(*The Epistle to Yemen* by R. Maimonides in which those things are expunged by the unbelieving Jews in order to show it to Christians. I bought it from Abraham de Scazzocchio the Jew in Rome on 18 February 1544.)[61]

The Italian Jew from whom Widmanstetter bought the manuscript was R. Abraham ben Aaron de Scazzocchio.[62] Widmanstetter realized that the deletions in the manuscript were anti-Christian polemics. Maimonides had penned this letter in the 1170s in response to a request by the Jews of Yemen, who had been under pressure to convert to Islam. In order to encourage his Yemenite coreligionists to resist conversion, Maimonides refuted Mohammad's claim of being a prophet and underscored his reasoning by also dismissing the Christian claim of Jesus's messiahship, because from a Jewish point of view it amounted to the abolition of the Divine Law.

The individual who deleted the explicit mention of Jesus from the manuscript may simply have intended to preclude an indictment for blasphemy. Although this measure would have been sufficient to avert legal repercussions, Widmanstetter's note shows that it was still possible to discern the work's anti-Christian thrust from the remaining text,[63] which suggests that the text was censored as a technical precaution to avert harm to the Jewish owner of the text.[64] Many Christians were motivated study to Jewish texts by the suspicion that Jews had falsified the Hebrew text of the Bible in order to delete references to the messiahship of Jesus. Widmanstetter refuted these charges in his *Commentary on the Quran*: '*Sed impossibile est eos, omnes omnium gentium et linguarum codices sacros corrumpere potuisse, quorum sensus aptissime congruunt.* (But it is impossible for them [the Jews] to have corrupted all the Scriptures of all peoples and in all languages, the contents of which are in perfect harmony)'.[65]

The remark Widmanstetter made over Jewish self-censorship clearly shows that he had studied *Iggeret Teiman* and would likely have noticed the discussion about earlier Jewish writers. However, apart from this single note at the beginning of the manuscript, he did not record his thoughts about the contents of *Iggeret Teiman*, leaving it unclear as to what impression Maimonides' concern for authoritative commentators had made on him.

Widmanstetter's title inscriptions not only reveal some of his strengths in analysing Jewish

---

61 BSB, Cod.hebr. 315, fol. [III[v]].
62 On Scazzocchio, see Kenneth R. Stow, 'Abramo Ben Aron Scazzocchio: Another Kind of Rabbi', in *The Mediterrannean and the Jews II: Society, Culture and Economy in Early Modern Times* (Ramat Gan: Bar Ilan University Press, 2002), pp. 85–97, and Hermann Vogelstein and Paul Rieger, *Geschichte der Juden in Rom* (Berlin: Mayer & Müller, 1895), pp. 97–100.
63 Here is sample from the text passage in Widmanstetter's manuscript, the deleted incriminating passage is indicated with curly brackets: מאמיניו להאמין כי הוא שלוח מאת האל בעבור שיבאר ספקות התורה וכי הוא {...} המובטח כן על ידי כל נביא ופירוש התורה יביא לבטל התורה כולה וכל מצוותיה ('His believers believe that he is sent by God so that he would burn the doubts of the Torah and for he

is [...] promised by every prophet and commentator of the Torah will lead to the annulment of the entire Torah and all its commandments', BSB, Cod.hebr. 315, fol. 14[r]).
64 Some ten years after Widmanstetter acquired the manuscript from Scazzocchio, the burning of the Talmud would lead Jews to practice self-censorship of some books that the rabbinic leadership deemed problematic. On Jewish self-censorship, see Joseph R. Hacker, 'Sixteenth-Century Jewish Internal Censorship of Hebrew Books', in *The Hebrew Book in Early Modern Italy*, ed. by Joseph R. Hacker and Adam Shear (Philadelphia: University of Pennsylvania Press, 2011), pp. 109–20 (pp. 114–20); Amnon Raz-Krakotzkin, *The Censor, the Editor, and the Text: The Catholic Church and the Shaping of the Jewish Canon in the Sixteenth Century* (Philadelphia: University of Pennsylvania Press, 2007), pp. 61–63.
65 Johann Albrecht Widmanstetter, *Mahometis Abdallae filii theologia dialogo explicata, Hermanno Nellingaunense interprete. Alcorani epitome Roberto Ketenense Anglo interprete* (Nuremberg: [Otto], 1543), *Epitome*, no. XXIII.

texts, but they also delineate the limitations of his knowledge in this field. For instance, he erred when describing the contents of a talmudic commentary in his library. On the binding of BSB, Cod.hebr. 75, he wrote '*Intellectus novi tractatus Babae posteris per Maimonem*' ('Novellae on the tractate *Bava Batra* by Maimonides'). In fact, the author of these novellae was none other than Moses Nahmanides. This mistake can probably be explained by the fact that the manuscript provided neither a title nor an author at the beginning of the text.⁶⁶ Owing to this lack of bibliographic information, Widmanstetter had to guess the identity of the author. Similarly, on another binding he wrongly attributed Jacob ben Asher's *'Arba'ah turim* ('Four Rows') to Moses Maimonides.⁶⁷ In the autobiographical notes that he published for the trial against the cleric Ambrosius von Gumppenberg, Widmanstetter claimed that he had studied halakhic texts under David ben Joseph ibn Yahya in Naples. Even so, this and several other lapses indicate that Widmanstetter had only a superficial knowledge of Jewish law.⁶⁸ For Widmanstetter, Maimonides simply was the halakhic authority par excellence.⁶⁹

The mistakes Widmanstetter made in his inscriptions and their informative value have been discussed at various points. In this context it is worthwhile to elaborate on some systematically recurring features that can be gleaned from the summary descriptions he provided in cases where he apparently did not feel competent to give a description. For instance, he characterized a collection of many different texts as '*Hebraica varia*' ('Various Hebrew Texts')⁷⁰ and gave the same title to BSB, Cod.hebr. 358, an anthology of halakhah, grammar, and midrash. He similarly titled his printed editions of *Meshal ha-qadmoni* ('Fable of the Ancient') and *Ruah hen* ('Spirit of Grace') by Moses Maimonides as '*Libri Hebraici*' ('Hebrew Books').⁷¹ In a small number of cases, Widmanstetter was either apparently unsure how to translate a title into Latin or he felt that a translation was not feasible and opted to copy the Hebrew title. The printed edition of Immanuel of Rome's *Mahbarot* ('Exercise Books') in BSB, 4 A.hebr. 283 thus remained simply in the original Hebrew script: ספר מחברות עמנואל ('The Exercise Books by Immanuel'). Looking back at the title inscription of *Lequtot kol bo* at the beginning of this chapter, I suggest that it is noteworthy that Widmanstetter was able to date it based on the quotations by Solomon ben Isaac and Abraham ibn Ezra. However, he did not translate the title but instead copied it verbatim, thus characterizing the book as '*Collectanea expositionum variarum in*

---

66 See BSB, Cod.hebr. 75, fol. 1ʳ.
67 See BSB, Cod.hebr. 255.
68 Similarly, Widmanstetter erroneously ascribed a text by Nahmanides in BSB, Cod.hebr. 112 to Maimonides: 'Harambam Porta retributionis' ('The Gate of Retribution by Rambam'). In BSB, Cod.hebr. 242, but he identified Nahmanides as the author of a *Commentary on Job*, binding 'Commentarii. In Threnos Hieremiae. Esther Job, authore Harambano' ('Commentaries on the Lamentations of Jeremiah, Esther, and Job authored by Rambam') and fol. [1ᵛ], 'In Threnos Hieremiae. In Esther. In Job, Harambani' ('On the Lamentations of Jeremiah, Esther, and Job by Ramban'). For Widmanstetter's account of his halakhic studies, see Müller, p. 18.
69 The marginal notes Widmanstetter added to his nine-volume Bomberg Talmud, BSB, 2 A hebr. 258 make it clear that he was primarily guided by a historical interest in the names of the rabbis rather than the contents of the halakhic debates.

70 BSB, Res. 4. A.hebr. 310. This volume holds a collection of different works, including *Sefer hasidim* ('Book of the Pious') by Judah he-Hasid, *Sefer 'or 'ammim* ('Light of the Nations') by Obadiah Sforno, *Kuzari* by Judah ha-Levi, *Sefer sha'ar ha-shamayim* ('Gate of the Heavens') by Gershom ben Solomon, *Sefer mivhar ha-peninim* ('Assortment of Pearls') and *Behinat ha-'olam* ('Examination of the World') by Jedaiah ben Abraham Bedersi Penini, and *'Even bohan* ('Testing Stone') by Qalonymus ben Qalonymus.
71 BSB, 4 A.hebr. 391.

libros Mosis' ('a miscellany of different explanations of the Books of Moses').⁷²

Christian Hebraists' Methodologies and Interests

Although the reference texts of Widmanstetter, Münster, Gessner, and Masius may seem different in their scope and thematic interests, they are still remarkably similar in their methodologies and reveal how Hebrew books were received and handled by Christian users. Looking at the surveyed bibliographic texts by Jewish and Christian authors, we can discern two main categories of bibliographic methodology that in some cases are reflected together in the same reference text and sometimes separately: one is concerned mainly with the materiality of books and the other is focused on the texts' history and transmission.

The first methodology can be described as material bibliography, which devotes a great deal of attention to the year of production and to features that are not part of the text, for example, the size and colour of the binding and the type of script used by the scribe or printer. Among the bibliographic texts that were surveyed, this approach was employed most often in connection with the medieval and early modern Jewish book lists, especially those from Italy that were used to reliably identify books based on the type of script and binding. Bomberg's catalogue in Gessner's bibliography limits material descriptions to the number of volumes, which was pertinent information in connection with the sale of books. Widmanstetter noted the date of production of a given manuscript in his title inscriptions if it was part of the scribe's colophon, which indicates an awareness of the history of the material object. Similarly, Masius noted that his kabbalistic books consisted of manuscripts. Recording the title, name, and date enabled the bibliographer to read them simply in the manner of an index, that is, they only had to copy the signs that made up the index terms. However, describing material features such as the distinction between a print and a manuscript required the bibliographer to creatively transform his own perceptions into signs that allowed himself and others to identify the object subsequently and to compare them to signs created by others. In short, bibliographies of this kind were concerned with finding a suitable vocabulary to portray the materiality of a book.

The second bibliographic methodology was characterized by attention to textual history. Lists, catalogues, and other sources often highlighted features related to the text such as the date of composition, the relationship of the author to other writers, and translations into other languages. These bibliographies, in essence, were designed to depict the histories of the texts they listed. The requirements for providing textual information were completely different from those for a material bibliography, as the bibliographer had to choose from a large repository of information. He could have mined the original text he was representing for useful data — a task that could have been daunting if time was short but might have yielded new information that he could use to create a new representation. As an alternative to exploring texts on his own, a bibliographer might have resorted to reusing representations that had been prepared by others before him, that is, older lists or bibliographies. The awareness of Jewish textual history was understandably far more advanced in the Jewish *shalshelet* tradition than in the writings of Christians Hebraists. This type of bibliographic methodology was the more prevalent one among the Christian Hebraist sources in this survey. Münster provided such information for some authors, but we do not know if he compiled it himself. Gessner freely

---

72 Other examples for this type of title inscription may be found on: BSB, Cod.hebr. 224, 236, 252, 264, 283, 297, 305, and BSB, 4 A.hebr. 411.

admitted to having drawn on the catalogues and references prepared by others, thus giving his reference book an unmatched comprehensiveness. Masius, too, relied on information by previous authors, but he also integrated his own observations. In sum it can be said that in the sixteenth century bibliographic methodology reflected the specific interests and possibilities of the Christian Hebraist author.

Compared to the trend of drawing on the textual information by previous Christian authors, exemplified here especially by the bibliographic reference texts by Gessner and Masius, Widmanstetter's title inscriptions stand out through his reliance on his own observations about the books' material and textual histories. The title inscriptions showcase his ability to distil textual information on Jewish texts from his own books. Sometimes the title inscriptions reflect his interest in philological details, such as the names of translators from Arabic to Hebrew and the dates of these translations. This emphasis on the textual history demonstrates Widmanstetter's high degree of concern about the chronology of Jewish literature and the textual transmission within Jewish culture, while the information regarding material features underscores his interest in the history of the individual artefact. Taken together, the material and textual bibliographic data in the title inscriptions disclose Widmanstetter's comprehensive view of the history of Jewish literature and of the Jewish book as a material object.

Manuscript Index

Cologny-Genève, Fondation Bodmer, MS 81 (Bodmer Haggadah): 23 n. 20, 26 n. 42, 53, 56, 58

Jerusalem
  Israel Museum
    MS 181/60 (First Nuremberg Haggadah): 22, 34–36, 50
  National Library of Israel
    MS Heb. 4°790 (Damascus Keter): 228–29
    MS Heb. 4°1384 (Moskowitz Mahzor): 23 n. 21 and 22, 34, 36 n. 57, 63–64
    MS Heb. 4°6130 (Rothschild Haggadah): 50, 59 n. 21, 60
    MS Heb. 8°2221 (Abrahm of Butera Bible): 234–35
    MS Heb. 8°6527 (Catalan Micrographic Mahzor): 88 n. 4, 230, 231 n. 13, 236 n. 24

Leiden, Leiden University Library, MS Leiden Or. 4720: 347–48

London
  British Library
    Add. MS 14762 (London Ashkenazi Haggadah): 22 n. 16, 40 n. 68, 44–45, 51 n. 11, 58, 159–61
    Add. MS 21160 (Jonah Pentateuch): 231 n. 15, 234 n. 21, 242–48
    Add. MS 26957 (Maraviglia Siddur): 22 n. 15 and n. 16, 24, 26–28, 30–31, 33–34, 36 n. 58, 37, 40
    MS Royal MS 2 A XXII (Westminster Psalter): 357

Collection David Sofer, MS 24087 (Second Nuremberg Haggadah): 164 n. 30
Lambeth Palace, MS 435: 354 n. 2, 367

Madrid
Biblioteca Histórica Marqués de Valdecilla de la Universidad Complutense
  MS 9: 426
  MS 10: 426
  MS 11: 432
  MS 17: 414
  MS 18: 422
  MS 19: 420
  MS 20: 417, 422, 423 n. 51
  MS 21: 417 n. 19 and n. 21, 423
Biblioteca Nacional de España
  MS 4188: 419–20, 422
  MS 5454: 417
Manchester, John Rylands University Library, MS heb. 6 (Rylands Haggadah): 231, 236 n. 24
Munich, Bayerische Staatsbibliothek
  Cod. 2 A.hebr. 245: 440 n. 47
  Cod. 2 A.hebr. 258: 444 n. 69
  Cod. 4 A.hebr. 283: 444, 445 n. 72
  Cod. 4 A.hebr. 391: 444
  Cod. 4 A.hebr. 411: 445
  Cod. Hebr. 67: 187
  Cod. Hebr. 75: 444
  Cod. Hebr. 77: 440
  Cod. Hebr. 81: 440 n. 46
  Cod. Hebr. 91: 441
  Cod. Hebr. 95: 190 n. 79, 312 n. 47, 313–14, 337

Cod. Hebr. 97: 440
Cod. Hebr. 106: 441 n. 53
Cod. Hebr. 108: 441
Cod. Hebr. 112: 444 n. 68
Cod. Hebr. 117: 440 n. 46
Cod. Hebr. 127: 440 n. 46
Cod. Hebr. 119: 440 n. 46
Cod. Hebr. 207: 440 n. 46
Cod. Hebr. 213: 441 n. 51
Cod. Hebr. 224: 445 n. 72
Cod. Hebr. 236: 445 n. 72
Cod. Hebr. 241: 441 n. 51 and n. 52
Cod. Hebr. 242: 444 n. 68
Cod. Hebr. 250: 442 n. 56 and n. 57
Cod. Hebr. 252: 429 n. 1, 430
Cod. Hebr. 255: 444 n. 67
Cod. Hebr. 256: 441 n. 51
Cod. Hebr. 263: 441 n. 51
Cod. Hebr. 270: 442 n. 58, n. 59, and n. 60
Cod. Hebr. 285: 440 n. 46
Cod. Hebr. 289: 441 n. 51
Cod. Hebr. 297: 441 n. 51
Cod. Hebr. 358: 444
L.as. 162: 437 n. 28
Res. 4. A.hebr. 310: 444 n. 70

New York, Jewish Theological Seminary
MS 4481 (First New York Haggadah): 50, 51 n. 9, 53, 55
MS 8279 (Second New York Haggadah): 33, 51–54, 56–58, 60
MS 8892 (Rothschild Mahzor): 32–33, 63–64

Paris, Bibliothèque nationale de France
hébr. 20: 236
hébr. 113: 6, 353–68
hébr. 1229: 420

Parma, Biblioteca palatina
MS Parm. 2998 (Parma Haggadah): 40–41
MS Parm. 3144 (Parma Tefillah): 22 n. 16, 31 n. 46 and 47, 50

Salamanca, Biblioteca General Histórica de la Universidad
MS 6: 413 n. 11, 414
MS 589: 423 n. 56
MS 590: 423 n. 56
MS 2170: 423 n. 56

San Lorenzo de El Escorial, Real Biblioteca
MS G-I-4: 423 n. 55 and n. 56, 424 n. 58
MS G-I-8: 425
MS G-II-5: 418
MS G-II-18: 425

Strasbourg, National and University Library, MS Strasbourg 4.099: 186 n. 64 and n. 65

Turin, Biblioteca Nazionale Universitaria, MS A. III. 14 (Turin Mahzor): 50–51, 58, 59 n. 21

Vatican, Biblioteca Apostolica
cod. Urb. ebr. 1: 232–33
cod. Ebr. 14: 265
cod. Ebr. 133: 348

Vitoria-Gasteiz, Biblioteca de la Facultad de Teología, MS 17: 420

Washington
Library of Congress, MS heb. 1 (Washington Haggadah): 21 n. 11, 22–24, 31 n. 44, 33 n. 51, 40, 42–43, 49 n. 1, 60, 159 n. 13, 166 n. 41
Museum of the Bible, MS ex-Valmadonna 1: 357

General Index

Abigail: 166, 168, 170, 278 n. 10
Abraham Abulafia: 393, 398, 407
   Gan na'ul: 393, 407
Abraham bar Hiyya: 109–11, 115–20, 123, 126
   Tzurat ha-'aretz: 109–12
Abraham ben Jacob: 51
Abraham ben Moses ha-Kohen: 104 n. 33
Abraham ibn Daud: 434, 438–39
   Sefer ha-qabbalah: 434
Abraham ibn Ezra: 74, 165 n. 38, 239, 323 n. 76, 419, 429, 436
Abravanel, Isaac: 68, 71 n. 28, 73 n. 42, 83, 85, 141, 411 n. 6
Abudarham, *see* David Abudarham
Abulafia, *see* Abraham Abulafia
Acculturation: 31, 69, 84, 137 n. 11, 279 n. 12
Adam: 180, 335
Adelkind, Barukh: 199, 257
Adelkind, Cornelio (Israel): 103 n. 27, 199 n. 24, 257 n. 27, 325, 398
Adversus Iudeorum inveteratam duritiem, *see* Peter the Venerable
Aemilius, Paulus: 183, 189, 190 n. 77 and n. 78
Agobard of Lyon: 335
Ahasuerus, King: 329
Alami, Solomon: 72
Alantansi, Eleazar: 77
Albeck, Shalom: 100 n. 13, 108 n. 58
Albrecht V, Duke of Bavaria-Munich: 370–72, 379–80, 432
Alcalá de Henares: 411–12, 419, 422, 426
Aldus Manutius: 200

Aleppo Codex: 238, 276
Alexander Süsslin ha-Kohen of Frankfurt: 102–03
   Sefer ha-'agudah: 102–05, 108 n. 58
Alfasi, *see* Isaac Alfasi
Alfonsi, Petrus: 308, 335
Alfonso de Fonseca y Ulloa, archbishop of Toledo: 423–24
Alfonso de Zamora: 15, 409–428
Alfonso Manrique de Lara y Solís, archbishop of Seville and grand inquisitor: 420, 424
Allony, Nehemia: 435
Alonso de Alcalá (la Real): 411
Alonso Fontela, Carlos: 411 n. 6, 424
Alphabet: 353, 361, 363–64, 367, 382, 385
   Greek: 364
   Hebrew: 363–64, 382, 385
   Runic: 353, 364
Amalek: 406
Amman, Caspar: 399
Anglo-Norman: 353, 356, 362
Annales school: 10
Anthology of the Talmud, Latin: 305, 309
anti-Christian polemics: 100 n. 14, 443
Antonio de Nebrija: 409, 411 n. 8
Antwerp: 153 n. 9, 177 n. 12, 193, 199, 209 n. 73, 221 n. 101, 238, 320, 366, 410, 439
Antwerp Polyglot Bible: 410, 439
Approbations: 93
Arabic: 90 n. 14, 101, 144, 253, 254 n. 13, 317 n. 57, 381, 438, 440–42, 446
Aragon: 71 n. 71, 307–08
'Arba'ah turim, *see* Jacob ben Asher

Arcangelo da Borgonovo: 394
Aristotle: 431 n. 3, 440–41
Arzei Ha-Levanon Adirei Ha-Torah: 315
Asher ben David: 401
Asher ben Yehiel (Rosh): 26 n. 42, 72, 100 n. 13, 138, 206 n. 59
Ashgara: 237
Ashkenazi, Isaac ben Aaron Samuel: 100
Ashkenazi, Yehiel of Jerusalem: 198
Astruc de Toulon: 67 n. 10, 82–83
Athens: 303
Athias, Yom Tob: 80
Audience: 14, 19, 21, 24, 38
Augsburg: 14, 38 n. 59, 159, 162–63, 175–91
Augsburg Haggadah (Augsburg 1534): 162 n. 18, 180
Augsburg, Zalman: 186, 188
Augustus: 303
authorship: 6, 69 n. 18, 197, 239, 275, 278, 441
'Av ha-rahamim: 319
Averroes: 431 n. 3, 440, 441 n. 48
Avignon: 302
'Avodah zarah 18a: 315
Axelrad, Bendit: 196

Ba'al Haturim, see Jacob ben Asher
Bahya ibn Paquda: 344
Balaam: 407
Basel: 99 n. 11, 101 n. 16, 103, 109–11, 115, 117, 119, 181, 191, 240 n. 46, 257, 278 n. 9, 296, 322 n. 72, 330, 372 n. 19, 381, 410 n. 2, 436 n. 23
Bataillon, Marcel: 418 n. 29, 423
Beit Yosef ('House of Joseph'): 94 n. 29, 198, 223 n. 104, 330
Beit-Arié, Malachi: 10 n. 2, 21 n. 9, 22 n. 13 and n. 18, 49 n. 1, 58, 63 n. 30, 78, 88 n. 3, 90 n. 15, 91, 97, 98 n. 2, 159 n. 13, 195 n. 6, 210 n. 76, 237 n. 27, 253 n. 8, 262, 265 n. 70 and n. 72, 353 n. 1, 377 n. 49, 399 n. 30, 420 n. 38, 435 n. 21
Ben Asher tradition: 238
Ben Asher, Jacob, *see* Jacob ben Asher
Ben Gershon, Aaron: 330
Ben ha-Qanah: 393
Benedict XIII: 302

Berakhot: 78 n. 73, 92, 100 n. 15, 167 n. 45, 168 n. 49, 173 n. 68, 237 n. 29, 319–21
bet midrash: 68 n. 16, 251
Béziers: 301
Bible française du 13e siècle (Bible de Paris): 256
Bible Moralisée: 310
Bibliography: 7, 9, 10 n. 3, 20 n. 4, 21 n. 11, 22 n. 17, 31 n. 46, 33 n. 53 and n. 54, 49 n. 1, 67 n. 6, 76 n. 59, 159 n. 14, 180 n. 31, 191 n. 84, 221 n. 103, 252 n. 2 and n. 6, 272 n. 96, 303 n. 5, 305 n. 13, 316 n. 52, 322 n. 72, 323 n. 75, 324 n. 77, 333 n. 121, 399 n. 29, 410 n. 3 and n. 4, 418 n. 28, 429, 433 n. 12 and n. 13, 436–37, 439, 445
Bibliography school: 9
Bibliotheca Tigurina: 438
Bibliotheca universalis, see Gessner, Conrad
bilingual manuscripts: 354 n. 3
binder's waste: 371
binding: 134, 221, 251, 255, 353–54, 358, 364–68, 377 n. 50, 380, 429–31, 435, 440, 444–45
Black Death: 372
Blaise de Vigenère: 394
Blanche of Castille: 307
Blanis, Mordekhai ben Yehudah: 343, 344 n. 13
blasphemy: 309–12, 326–27, 329, 335, 443
Boccaccio, Giovanni: 397
Boehm, Samuel: 103
Bohemia: 151, 159 n. 15, 162 n. 19, 176, 370, 371
Bologna: 78 n. 76, 104 n. 33, 134 n. 2, 190, 252, 258–59, 263 n. 65, 264–66, 267 n. 76, 270, 277 n. 9, 278 n. 9, 281–82, 298, 302, 393, 403, 440
Bomberg, Daniel: 72 n. 35, 101, 183, 190, 193, 199, 209 n. 73, 221 n. 103, 238, 255 n. 21, 257, 276, 278 n. 9, 279, 282, 284, 291, 320–21, 345, 348, 398–99, 437
Bonfil, Roberto: 196 n. 8, 197
Book illumination: 20 n. 8, 36, 46, 69, 230 n. 7 and n. 11, 236 n. 24
Book of Introduction, see Hunayn ibn Ishaq
Book of Psalms: 14, 258, 263, 281, 359, 385 n. 93
book trade, Jewish: 11–12
book-burning
    Christian texts: 303
    copies (as opposed to originals): 339
    Greco-Roman literature: 303 n. 4

Maimonides's works: 330
Talmud: 303–04
Bragadin, Alvise: 295, 324
Breu, Jörg (the Elder): 182
Brinkley, Richard: 367
Burgau: 189–90
Burgos: 228, 417, 418 n. 25, 425
Burnett, Stephen: 332
Bury St. Edmunds: 367
Busi, Giulio: 60 n. 27, 394 n. 6, 398, 406

Cairo Genizah: 134 n. 2, 137 n. 9, 434
Campo de' Fiori: 302, 325
Canpanton, Isaac: 70 n. 26, 73
Canterbury: 367
Capsali, Elijah: 196
Capsarii: 309, 327
Carafa, (Cardinal) Gian Pietro: 325
Castile: 70, 76, 78, 307, 418 n. 25, 420
Catholicism: 183
censored books: 271
censoring: 271–74, 297
censorship: 268 n. 80, 271 n. 92, 272–74, 295, 297, 304 n. 11, 312, 322, 326, 333, 405
Charles I, Duke of Münsterberg: 183
Charles V, Emperor: 403, 420
Chazan, Robert: 99 n. 7, 304 n. 11, 308 n. 25, 316 n. 53, 340 n. 2, 441 n. 48
Christian Hebraism: 252, 268 n. 82, 268, 332, 354–56, 368, 388, 409–11 n. 6, 418 n. 25, 428, 436 n. 23
Christian Hebraists: 12–14, 189, 239, 251, 255, 257, 267, 297, 324, 332–33, 353 n. 1–355, 362–64, 369, 410 n. 2, 419, 432–33, 438, 441, 445
Christological: 332, 382, 385–88
Church: 15, 68 n. 12, 97 n. 1, 261 n. 60, 295–96, 303, 305, 309–10, 312, 322 n. 72, 323 n. 75, 325, 327–28, 331, 333, 335, 340 n. 2, 343, 366, 370, 374, 381–82, 394, 410, 413, 417 n. 23, 423 n. 56, 426, 428, 443 n. 64
codicology: 9, 10 n. 2, 21 n. 9, 22 n. 13, 23 n. 21, 31 n. 47, 58 n. 17, 90 n. 15, 98 n. 2, 159 n. 13, 195 n. 6, 210 n. 76, 253 n. 8, 265 n. 70, 353 n. 1, 358 n. 18, 377 n. 49, 435 n. 21
Colbert, Jean-Baptiste: 357
Colchester: 358

Collegium Ducale: 373–75, 379–80, 382, 388
Collegium Trilingue: 376
Colodro, Samuel: 72 n. 36, 76
Cologne: 51, 53, 102, 220, 316 n. 52, 342
Colophon: 13, 22, 24–25 n. 33, 33, 49–51, 53 n. 15, 58 n. 16, n. 17, 58–61, 64, 72 n. 36, 76 n. 59, 78, 82–83, 87–88, 104 n. 33–105 n. 42, 151–53, 179, 186–87, 198–201, 209–10, 213, 221–22, 253, 258 n. 32, 263–65, 267, 347–49, 356, 363, 372, 377–78, 397, 399–400, 402, 407, 414, 416, 419–20, 426–27, 441, 445
Commentary (Bible): 257, 429
Consecration: 137–39, 145 n. 36, 219
Conservatism (Artistic): 70
Consolatio: 72–73
Constance: 20 n. 8, 183, 372
Constance, Council of: 372
conversion
    forced (Portugal): 320
    impact of print shops: 320
    Talmud as impediment to: 327
    Talmud as tool for: 327
converso, conversos: 71, 75, 80, 84, 410 n. 2, 411 n. 6, 419 n. 36
copying errors: 237
copyright: 91, 93 n. 25, 281, 320, 325
Counter-Reformation: 326–27, 333–34
Cracow: 87, 99 n. 11 and n. 12, 102–04, 325, 378 n. 54
Cremona: 50, 102, 223, 281 n. 15, 285, 302, 325 n. 83, 342 n. 8
Crusades
    Crusader lyrics: 318
    First: 98, 99 n. 7, 108, 319
Cuir-ciselé: 380
Cum nimis absurdum: 328
cup of blessing: 166–67, 168 n. 52, 170
customization: 13, 19, 21–24, 46, 68 n. 11

da Viterbo, Egidio: 6, 15, 393–96, 398–401, 408 n. 72, 431, 441
Damiano di Castiglia: 395, 397, 399
Dante: 397
Database: 91 n. 17, 139 n. 19, 237, 287, 289–91
    Graph: 288

David Abudarham: 77
David ben Joseph ibn Yahya: 68, 76, 444
David ben Solomon ibn Yahya: 68, 71–72, 74, 76
David, King: 386, 404
De arcanis catholicae Veritatis: 438
De articulis litterarum Papae, *see* Nicholas Donin
de Cordoba, Alfonso Fernandez: 77
de Heredia, Pablo: 407
de Mendoza y Bobadilla, Francisco, bishop of Coria and Burgos: 417
de Prado Plumed, Jesús: 410 n. 2 and n. 4, 411 n. 6, 418 n. 25
de Scazzocchio, Abraham ben Aaron: 443
De sphaera mundi (Heb. *Aspera* or *Mar'eh ha-'ofanim*): 112
De Thou, Jacques-Auguste: 357–58
de Toledo y Guzmán, Hernán Núñez: 411
della Volta, Gabriele: 395, 399–400
Delacrut, Matatiah: 113
diagrams: 82, 87, 111–13
Diaspora
   Portuguese: 13
   Sefardi: 5, 65–66, 84–85
Digital Humanities: 285, 287 n. 34
   distant reading: 286–87
divine names: 134, 136–38, 140, 143–44, 146, 148, 255 n. 20
Dominicans: 303, 311, 328
Donin, Nicholas: 305–06, 326
   De articulis litterarum Papae: 304 n. 11, 309, 335
donkey ascending a ladder: 50–51
dragon: 26 n. 42, 234
ductus: 227, 242, 247–48
Dunkelgrün, Theodor: 75 n. 56, 221 n. 101 and n. 103, 292 n. 44, 293, 323 n. 75, 333, 399 n. 29, 410 n. 4, 432, 433 n. 12, 439
Duran, Profayt: 74, 75 n. 52
Düren: 99, 102, 209 n. 71, 340

Ecclesiastes: 233, 255
Editing: 5, 9, 11–12, 14, 16, 94 n. 29–95, 101, 103 n. 25, 149, 193, 197 n. 18, 205, 207–08, 216, 222, 233, 238, 248, 291, 301, 312, 411, 420

Editio princeps: 72 n. 35, 83, 88 n. 7, 98, 99 n. 13, 102, 104, 108, 185 n. 56, 255 n. 19, 258, 281, 315 n. 49, 343, 345 n. 19, 347 n. 22, 348, 376, 432
Edward Lee, prebendary of York and Westminster: 420
Eidels, Samuel: 105
Einbinder, Susan: 316
El Pinciano, *see* de Toledo y Guzmán, Hernán Núñez
Elazar ha-Levi: 99 n. 8
Eleazar of Worms: 90, 101, 102 n. 22 and n. 23, 104
   Sefer ha-roqeah: 90, 101 n. 21, 102 n. 22 and n. 23
Eleh Ezkerah: 315
Elia of Pesaro: 345
Eliezer ben Ephraim of Cologne: 342
Eliezer ben Nathan: 98–99, 100 n. 13 and n. 16, 101 n. 17 and n. 18, 104–08
Elijah ben Solomon Zalman (Vilna Gaon): 394
Elqanah: 393
emblem: 59–61, 240–41
   Talmud as emblem for the Jews: 333
'Emeq ha-bakh'a, *see* Joseph ha-Kohen
England: 15, 307, 329 n. 104, 353 n. 1, 354–58, 360 n. 24, 361, 364, 368 n. 39, 381 n. 68
engraving: 24, 26, 31, 33, 38, 46, 135, 140, 181 n. 32, 292
Epistula de Secretis: 407
Epstein, Meir b. Jacob ha-Levi: 151
Erasmus of Rotterdam: 327 n. 93, 418 n. 29, 423–24
Erfurt: 102, 134 n. 2, 231 n. 15, 382 n. 74
   massacre of 1349: 102
eschatology: 403
Esther, Book of: 69 n. 21, 73 n. 39, 104, 255, 329, 444 n. 68
Euclid: 431 n. 3, 440–41
Eve: 180, 335
'Even ha-'ezer (Raven): 60, 98–100, 101 n. 17 and n. 18, 104–08, 114, 205 n. 57
Évora: 80, 81 n. 88, 84 n. 118
exegesis (biblical): 72–74, 276, 294, 381, 425
expulsion: 12–13, 15, 65, 68 n. 15, 71, 74, 80, 81 n. 89, 93, 176, 186, 188, 191, 312, 314, 316, 320, 353 n. 1, 354 n. 3, 356, 370–72, 380, 387
Extractiones de Talmud: 305 n. 11, 310 n. 37, 311

See also Thibaut de Sézanne
'Eyn Ya'aqov: 81–82, 325
Ezekiel, Book of: 330, 426

Faculty
   of Arts: 97, 105 n. 42, 374, 381
   of Theology: 373–75, 383
Fagius, Paulus: 183, 273
falconer: 231, 233 n. 19, 241 n. 49, 242, 244, 247
Fano: 80, 82–83, 90, 101 n. 21, 102, 135, 185 n. 57, 238 n. 29
Faro: 65, 72, 73 n. 42, 76, 77 n. 64, 78–80, 85, 252
Feibush (*See also* Joel ben Simeon): 24, 50, 53, 58
   Feibush Reiner: 51
Felice da Prato (Felix of Prato): 277 n. 7, 284, 291, 297, 398–401
Ferrara: 80, 189, 190, 277 n. 9, 302
Fez: 82–83, 85
filigree penwork: 36
Fine Manner: 26
Fisher, John: 367
foliation: 103 n. 25, 258 n. 37, 267 n. 76, 320
font: 263, 277, 280
Foucault, Michel: 329 n. 104
Fram, Edward: 204
France: 9, 26 n. 42, 67 n. 10, 69, 138, 145, 164 n. 30, 166 n. 41, 167, 201, 202 n. 37, 231 n. 17, 234, 241 n. 49, 248 n. 65, 262, 278 n. 9, 279–80, 302, 304 n. 11, 306–07, 309 n. 32, 312–14, 316 n. 51 and n. 52, 318–19, 322, 329 n. 104, 331 n. 115, 340–43, 353–54, 356–62, 364–68, 377, 380, 396, 400, 420
Franciscans: 328, 367
Franck, Sebastian: 177 n. 13, 178 n. 14, 179
Frankfurt am Main: 177, 181, 185 n. 56, 191
Friuli: 184

Gacon, Samuel: 78
Galatino, Pietro (Galatinus, Petrus [Colonna]): 328, 438
Gan na'ul, *see* Abraham Abulafia
Gans, David: 103 n. 27, 205 n. 54
Gedaliah ibn Yahya: 434
   Shalshelet ha-qabbalah: 434
Gedalya, Judah: 73 n. 39, 76, 81, 83

Gematria: 406–07, 440
German Lands: 14, 22, 36, 138, 145, 162, 169, 176, 188, 191, 204, 207 n. 62, 231, 234, 248, 279, 340, 378, 402
Gershom b. Solomon ha-Kohen: 151
Gessner, Conrad: 221, 432, 433 n. 12, 437, 438 n. 32 and n. 35
   Bibliotheca universalis: 437–38
   Pandectarum sive Partitionum universalium: 221, 437 n. 30
   Partitiones theologicae: 437–38
gezerot TaTNU, *see* Crusades, first
ghetto: 278 n. 9, 328, 331
Giustiniani, Marco Antonio (Marco Antonio Giustinian): 106, 322
Glossa Ordinaria: 320
Grace after Meals: 173
grammar
   Hebrew: 15, 74, 221, 354, 398, 409, 411, 413–14, 418, 420, 422–26, 428, 436
Grammatica Hebraea, *see* Münster, Sebastian
Gregory IX: 304 n. 11, 305, 307, 309 n. 32, 310, 312
Guerre d'Italia: 279
Gui, Bernard: 302
Guide for the Perplexed, *see* Moses Maimonides
Günzburg: 189–90, 302, 397
Günzburg, Isaac (Ayzek) Segal: 189
Gunzenhauser, Joseph: 74

Hadrianic period: 315
Hagiz, Moshe: 322 n. 74, 326
Halakha: 103, 106, 134–35, 137 n. 9, 142–43, 166–67, 193, 195 n. 5, 214–16, 220, 223, 444
ha-Levi, Joshua ben Joseph: 72
Ham: 335
Haman: 329
Hananiah Ben Teradion (Rabbi): 315
Hanau: 103 n. 25, 191
Hannah bat R. Isaiah: 51
Hayyim bar Shalom: 105
Hayyim ben Samuel ibn Gattegno: 400
Hayyim Joseph David Azulay: 398
Hayyun, Joseph: 69, 73, 81, 85
Hebraica: 59 n. 23 and n. 24, 92 n. 20, 189, 190 n. 76, 236 n. 24, 257, 269, 292 n. 45, 333, 362–63, 369–74,

376, 379, 386, 389–90, 392, 395, 399 n. 29, 410 n. 2, 418 n. 26, 423, 431 n. 3, 444
Hebrew-French glossaries: 256
Heddernheim: 177, 180–81, 185, 191
hegemony: 294–97
    cultural: 294, 296–97
Helicz, Samuel: 176
Hendel, Manoah: 113
heresy: 308 n. 25, 309–12, 325–27, 329 n. 104, 343
heretic: 303–04, 310, 312, 325, 335, 370, 424 n. 59
Híjar: 67, 77, 79, 82–83, 85
Hilgert, Markus: 10, 11 n. 6
Hirsch Qopa, Tzvi bar Manoah: 103
Hiyah Meir ben David: 193, 195–96
Ho, Ahuva: 411 n. 6, 414, 417 n. 23
Hofbibliothek (Vienna): 369, 371 n. 8, 375–76, 383 n. 80, 390
Holbein, Hans (the Younger): 181 n. 34, 182 n. 34
holidays
    Christian
        Lent: 68 n. 12, 307
    Jewish
        Ninth of Av (Tisha B'Av): 315–17, 330, 341, 380 n. 63
        Passover: 21 n. 10, 33 n. 53, n. 54–34 n. 55, 56, 73 n. 41, 82 n. 100–83, 151 n. 3, 158 n. 10–162, 166, 176 n. 4, 231 n. 14, 241 n. 49, 314, 319
        Rosh Ha-Shanah (New Year): 170 n. 65, 231 n. 13, 325
        Shavuot: 153–54, 157, 164, 166, 319
        Yom Kippur: 84, 186, 315
Homoearctons: 237
homoeoteleutons: 237
Hopfer, Daniel: 181
House of Converts (*domus catechumenorum*): 331
Hovot ha-levavot: 344
Hubhaus: 371
Humanism: 12, 68, 227, 280–81, 288, 324 n. 81, 332, 343 n. 12, 381 n. 68, 383 n. 81, 400 n. 34, 410, 423 n. 54–424, 428, 432 n. 10, 440
Humanist: 68 n. 17–69, 72–74 n. 43, 179, 183 n. 37, 197, 200, 221 n. 103, 239, 249, 252, 255, 261 n. 59, 268, 278, 281, 323 n. 75, 333, 349, 357–58, 368, 375, 393 n. 1, 395 n. 7, 399 n. 29, 409–11, 423–24, 432 n. 10–433, 437–38 n. 38

humash (liturgical Pentateuch): 180, 320
    Humash (Prague 1514–18): 183
    Humash (Oels 1530): 183
    Humash (Ichenhausen 1544–45): 183
    Humash (Lublin 1556–57): 183
    Humash in Yiddish (Constance 1544): 183
    Humash in Yiddish (Augsburg 1544): 183
Hunayn ibn Ishaq: 441–42
hunt scene: 153, 159, 162–65, 170 n. 66, 172, 231, 242
hurban: 329, 331
Hussite movement: 370, 372

Iberian Peninsula (Iberia): 67, 69 n. 18, 74, 78 n. 72, 84, 234, 236, 254, 393, 414–16, 422, 427–28
Ibn Yahya family: 68, 80
Ichenhausen: 177, 180–81, 183, 184, 189–90
Iggeret Rabbi Sherira Ga'on, see Sherira Ga'on
Iggeret Teiman, see Moses Maimonides
Immanuel of Rome: 274, 444
    Mahbarot: 444
Impresa: 227, 240–42
Imre shefer: 398
Incunabula: 67–68, 78 n. 73, 88 n. 3, 92 n. 18, 195 n. 6, 237, 252, 254, 255, 265 n. 72, 267, 268 n. 80, 277–79, 289, 293, 298, 315 n. 49
Index of Forbidden and Prohibited Books: 328
Innocent I: 311
Innocent IV: 309 n. 33, 310
Inquisition: 78 n. 72, 80, 332 n. 116, 424
    Congregation of: 325
    inquisitors' attacks on Jewish books: 185, 302, 325–28
Isaac ben Jacob Alfasi (Rif): 93, 100, 141 n. 26, 231, 307, 320, 326 n. 88, 330, 331 n. 112
    Sefer ha-halakhot: 307
Isaac ben Meir of Düren: 99
Isaac ben Moses ibn Zerah: 397, 399
Isaac ben Moses of Vienna: 99
    'Or zarua': 99, 205 n. 58
Isaac beRabbi Simeon ha-Levi: 231, 234, 242
Israel ben Petahya Isserlein: 203
Israel Bruna: 202, 208, 211
Israel, redemption of: 234, 242
Isserles, Moses of Cracow: 99, 103, 109 n. 25, 112–13, 325

Istanbul: 9 n. 1, 38, 67 n. 6 and n. 10, 73 n. 39 and n. 41, 74 n. 45 and n. 47, 77, 82–83, 85, 330
iyyun: 73

Jacob ben Asher: 14, 59, 77, 175, 220, 239, 444
   'Arba'a turim: 14, 59–61, 63–64, 82–83, 175, 187, 330, 444
   'Arba'a turim (Augsburg 1540): 175 n. 1
Jacob ben Hayyim ben Isaac ibn Adonijah (ibn Adoniahu): 238
Jacob ben Joseph: 108 n. 56
Jacob ben Mechir: 441
Jacob ben Meir – Rabbenu Tam: 342
Jacob Moellin: 207
Jacob Weil: 103
Jaffe, Mordecai: 105
Jerome: 335, 355, 362, 410 n. 2, 432
Jerusalem Temple: 315, 317, 329–31
Jesus Christ: 419, 432
Jewish-Christian relations: 12, 268, 276, 297, 305 n. 11
Jewish printing: 12, 65, 177 n. 7, 179 n. 23, 190–91 n. 84, 237–38
Jewish scribal art: 227
Jiménez de Cisneros, Francisco, Cardinal: 410, 413
Joachim of Fiore: 398
Joel ben Simeon: 5, 13, 19, 21, 22 n. 17, 23 n. 22 and n. 23, 24, 26 n. 43, 46–47, 49–50, 51 n. 7, 53, 58–61, 63–64, 159
   See also Feibush
Joel ha-Levi: 99, 100 n. 13
John XXII: 302
Jonah Gerondi: 72
Jonah son of Amitai: 247
Jonah, Book of: 242–43, 247–48, 283
Jorge Baracaldo: 414
Joseph ben Gedalya ibn Yahya: 68
Josef ha-Cohen: 99, 324 n. 81, 325 n. 83, 325 n. 85, 329, 331 n. 115
Joseph (Yoizel) ben Moses Ostreicher: 203
   Leqet yosher: 203, 204 n. 47, 206, 208 n. 66, 209 n. 70, 211–12, 219
Joseph Colon: 193, 198, 199 n. 23 and n. 25, 201–02, 205

Joseph ibn Waqar: 401
Joseph Sofer of Poznań: 100
Joshua ibn Gaon: 70 n. 23, 234
jousting knight: 246–47
Juan Álvarez de Toledo, bishop of Cordoba, Burgos, and Santiago de Compostela: 425
Juan de Azcona: 419
Juan de Tavera, archbishop of Toledo: 423 n. 56, 425 n. 70, 426
Juan de Vergara: 411, 424
Juda Leva ben Betsalel, the Maharal: 105 n. 44, 106 n. 44
Judah ben Gedalya ibn Yahya: 68
Judah ha-Levi: 80, 165 n. 38, 316, 317 n. 57, 444 n. 70
Judah ibn Tibbon: 90–91, 344
Judah Mintz: 196, 202
Judah of Pesaro: 102
Julius III: 325, 329

Kabbalah: 75, 87 n. 1, 94 n. 27, 97, 109, 238, 251, 281 n. 15, 288 n. 40, 318 n. 62, 324 n. 79, 331 n. 113, 332, 393 n. 1, 394, 398 n. 25, 399 n. 29, 400 n. 33, 401, 403, 407, 431 n. 6, 438 n. 35
   Christian: 238, 394–95, 398 n. 25, 401, 407, 431
Kafka, Franz: 323
Kanarfogel, Ephraim: 99 n. 6, 104 n. 38, 137 n. 10, 141, 145, 234 n. 20, 319, 341 n. 6
Karaite Jews: 306 n. 15, 335 n. 125, 434
Katz, Gershom: 33 n. 53, 39 n. 63, 176
Katz, Isaac ben Samson: 105, 106 n. 44
Katz, Joseph ben Mordecai Gershon: 103
Katz, Moses ben Betzalel: 98 n. 5, 101
Katznellenbogen, (Rabbi) Meir: 324
kavvanah: 134, 146–47
Kedar, Benjamin Z.: 309, 310 n. 34
ketiv/qere: 254, 258, 260–61
King's College: 367
Korets: 394
Krochmal, Menahem Mendel: 346
Kushnir-Oron, Mikal: 398

La Rochelle: 305
Lament: 315–17, 319, 330
Lamentations, Book of: 317

Landesjudenschaft: 188
law
   alia lex ('foreign law'): 309
   nova lex ('new law'): 309, 318, 327, 331
   Rabbinic: 147, 311
   Talmud as 'false' law: 309, 328
layout: 6, 14, 20–21, 38, 75–77, 78 n. 72–79, 84, 111, 251, 254–55, 258, 260, 262–63 n. 65, 265, 275–85, 287–93, 296–98, 320, 360, 363, 419
Le Fèvre, Nicolas: 357
Leipheim: 188
Leiria: 65, 71–73, 76–79, 283
Leo X: 255, 320, 332, 418 n. 29
Leon: 307
Leqet yosher, see Joseph (Yoizel) ben Moses Ostreicher
Lequtot kol bo: 429, 441, 444
Levi ben Gershom (Gersonides): 63, 72, 76
   Commentary on the Pentateuch: 63
Levita, Elijah: 183, 239, 240 n. 43, 260 n. 51, 410 n. 2, 436
   Sefer hatishby (Isny 1541): 190
Levush malkhut: 105
Libellus de litteris Hebraicis: 400 n. 34, 401
Liber sacrosancti Evangelii de Jesu Christo, see Widmanstetter, Johann Albrecht
Lichtenstein, Peter: 398
Lipton, Sara: 310
Lisbon: 65–85
Lisker, Hayyim: 111
liturgica: 254
liturgy: 53, 58 n. 17, 84, 97, 179, 184, 186–87, 189, 316–17, 335
Lombardy: 184
López de Zúñiga, Diego: 411, 418
Louis IX of France, King: 307, 311
Lublin: 95, 99 n. 11, 104 n. 34, 177, 180, 183, 191, 330
Luntschitz, Salomon Ephraim: 105 n. 44
Luther, Martin: 257, 394
Maclean, Ian: 98

Mafteah: 202, 216–17, 222
Maggi, Lucillo (Filalteus): 405
Mahbarot, see Immanuel of Rome
Mahzor (Augsburg 1536): 184

Mantua: 184–85, 257, 273, 281 n. 15, 434 n. 14
manuscript(s)
   illumination: 40 n. 68, 65
   scarcity of: 70, 103
Margoliouth, George: 24 n. 30, 228 n. 4, 398
Marian devotion: 307 n. 19, 318
Martí, Ramon (Friar): 327, 425
   Pugio Fidei: 328, 425
Martin, Francis Xavier: 395 n. 7, 396 n. 15
Martínez de Cantalapiedra, Martín: 409
Martyr: 304, 315, 318–19, 380 n. 63
martyrdom of Talmud: 319
martyrological texts: 315
Mary: 325, 335–36, 386
Masius, Andreas: 221 n. 103, 323 n. 75, 332, 398, 399 n. 29, 432, 439
Masorah: 14, 67 n. 10, 75 n. 55, 76, 227–28, 230–31, 234 n. 21, 237–42, 249, 251, 253, 255–57, 260–61, 265 n. 71, 279, 282, 284, 292, 361, 372 n. 13, 377, 378 n. 53, 392, 413
   text and annotation: 237 n. 26, 238, 240 n. 45
masora figurata: 14, 75 n. 55, 230, 240–41, 256, 227–28, 230, 233–34, 237, 239–42, 247–49, 269
masora finalis: 238, 257, 281
masora gedolah/magna: 228, 231, 234, 238, 240, 242, 247, 261, 281, 284–85, 372 n. 13, 377, 392
masorah qetanah/parva: 228, 231, 238, 240, 257, 260–61, 281, 284–85, 372 n. 13, 377, 392
Masorete: 6, 227–28, 231, 233, 239–42, 247–49, 265, 269, 292 n. 45, 377
masoretic
   Bible: 228, 236 n. 24–237, 238 n. 35, 240, 372
   lists: 227–28, 237, 239, 254
   notes: 76, 227, 239, 255, 262
Massoret ha-Massoret: 239, 250
Master of the Brick Background: 159
material
   history: 183 n. 44, 228 n. 4, 252 n. 6, 275–77, 348 n. 25
   object: 9–11, 15, 20 n. 4, 275, 340–41, 343, 346, 431, 433, 445–46
   text cultures: 277 n. 9, 288, 294
materiality: 6, 9–10, 15–16, 66–67, 75 n. 56, 275–76, 285, 292, 294, 339, 435, 439–40, 445

Maximilian I, Emperor: 403
McKitterick, David: 11 n. 7, 109, 195 n. 6
media: 1, 3, 5, 9–13, 17, 20 n. 2, 46, 89, 97–98, 109, 113
medicine: 194, 267, 395, 437 n. 29, 441 n. 48, 442
Mediterranean: 65, 78 n. 73, 80, 82 n. 107, 88 n. 3, 252 n. 7, 265 n. 72, 279 n. 13, 305 n. 11, 394
megillot (five): 182, 255, 392
Meir ben Barukh (MaHaRaM of Rothenburg): 316, 340–44, 346
   Sha'ali serufah ba-'eish: 316
Meir ha-Levi ben Todros Abulafia (Ramah): 413
Meiri, Menahem: 72, 76
memoria technical: 254
Menahem ben Benjamin: 347
Menahem Mendel of Shklow: 394
Meshal ha-qadmoni: 164 n. 34, 169, 170 n. 66, 444
Messiah son of David: 247
Messiah son of Joseph: 234
Metaphysics (Aristotle): 441
metatextual elements: 254
Michael, Heimann Joseph: 185
micrography: 14, 68, 70, 75 n. 55, 88 n. 4, 227–28 n. 6, 230–31, 233 n. 19–234, 236–37, 241–42 n. 53, 247–49
midrash: 68, 82, 247 n. 58, 251, 256, 276, 286, 305 n. 11, 310, 315, 345, 382, 444
Miguel de Eguía: 411, 423–24
minhag (prayer rite): 63 n. 31, 186, 188
minhagim (customs): 186, 188
miqdashyah: 331
Miqra'ot gedolot: 257
mise-en-page: 276
Mishnah: 72, 75, 83 n. 108, 141, 166 n. 42, 278 n. 9, 325, 434, 436
   Pirqei 'avot: 104
Mishneh Torah, see Moses Maimonides
Mithridates, Flavius: 401, 407, 408 n. 70
Mizrahi, Elijah: 109, 110 n. 64
   Qitzur ha-melekhet mispar: 110 n. 64
Mizrahi, Ephraim: 112 n. 72
Mohammad (Prophet): 443
Molkho, Solomon: 81
Montalcino, Cornelio da: 331
Montpellier: 303, 330 n. 110

Morawczyk, Yehiel bar Yedidyah Mikhl: 104
Mordecai ben Hillel ha-Kohen: 99 n. 13, 100 n. 15
Morinald, Robert: 358
Moses: 32–33, 56, 138, 306, 310 n. 37, 318, 335, 429, 434, 436, 445
Moses ben Shem Tov ibn Habib: 74
Moses Maimonides: 106 n. 46, 434, 438, 442, 444
   Guide for the Perplexed: 40, 73 n. 41
   Iggeret Teiman: 434, 442–43
   Mishneh Torah: 106 n. 46, 145 n. 35, 146 n. 41, 223, 281, 295, 324, 369 n. 2
Moses of Norzi: 435
Moses the Sefardi of Aragon: 308
mounted falconer: 231, 233 n. 19, 241 n. 49, 242, 244
mounted riders: 242, 247
Münster, Sebastian: 109, 111, 260 n. 51, 410 n. 2, 432, 436, 437 n. 28
   Grammatica Hebraea: 436
Murray, Alexander: 303
musar (genre): 72, 82

Nação Portuguesa (Portuguese Nation): 65, 85
Nahmias, David and Samuel: 82, 100 n. 15
Naples: 74, 82–83, 252, 273, 283, 302, 403, 444
Narbonne: 239, 280
Nathan ben Yehiel: 74, 376
Navarre: 307
Nedivot, Samuel: 82
Netherlands: 12, 97 n. 1, 367
network, rabbinic: 287
New Castile: 70
New Testament: 308, 318, 355 n. 6, 385, 399 n. 29, 418 n. 29, 432, 438
Nicholson, Segar: 354, 366
Nielsen, Bruce: 101, 324 n. 78, 399 n. 29
Noah: 335, 402–03
North Africa: 12, 71, 74, 78, 80, 84, 288, 323 n. 76, 422
Numa Pompilius: 303
Núñez Coronel, Pablo: 411, 420

oblong (book format): 84
Odo (Eudes) of Chateauroux: 304 n. 11, 307 n. 19, 311–12

Oels (Oleśnica): 176, 181 n. 32, 183
Offenbach: 110
Okhla ve-'okhla: 231, 242
Old Testament: 182, 308–310, 327, 331, 354
Oppenheim, David: 185
'Or zarua', see Isaac ben Moses
Ortas family: 77
orthography, plene or defective: 228
'Otiyot de-Rabbi Aqiva: 439
Otmar, Johann: 179
Otmar, Silvan: 178, 181–82
Otmar, Valentin: 179
Ottoman Empire: 12, 65, 80, 81 n. 88, 82, 85, 93, 330 n. 111
Owner/ownership notes

Padua: 185, 196, 279 n. 12, 324, 325 n. 82
palaeography: 22 n. 13, 58 n. 17, 253 n. 8, 353 n. 1
Palumbo, Margherita: 396
Pamiers: 302
Pandectarum sive Partitionum universalium, see Gessner, Conrad
papal schism: 372
Parashiyot: 255, 429
Paratext: 5, 12–14, 87–95, 101, 163–64, 172–73, 222, 276–77, 279, 281 n. 15, 282–86, 292
Partitiones theologicae, see Gessner, Conrad
Paul IV: 325, 329
Pérez Castro, Federico: 411 n. 6, 425
Pesaqim u-ketavim: 203, 206, 208 n. 69, 209 n. 70, 218, 219 n. 95, 220–23, 378 n. 56
Pesaro: 73 n. 41, 80, 82–83, 100 n. 15–102, 184, 238 n. 29, 255 n. 20, 257, 266–67, 283, 345
Peter Abelard, *Theologia*: 303
Peter the Venerable: 308, 309 n. 31, 335
    Adversus Iudeorum inveteratam duritiem: 308
Peterhouse: 366–68
Petri, Henricus: 109
petuha/setuma: 254, 263
Peuerbach, George: 112, 121–22, 124–25, 130
    Theoricae novae planetarum (Heb. *Teorika*): 112, 122, 124
Peutinger, Konrad: 179, 180 n. 24
Pfefferkorn, Johannes: 302

philology, Hebrew: 15
Piazza San Marco: 302
Pico della Mirandola, Giovanni: 401, 407 n. 68
Pighini, Sebastiano (Cardinal): 332
pilpul (analytical disputation methods): 73, 196, 345
Pirqei'avot, see Mishnah
Pisqei Mordekhai: 108 n. 56
Pithou, Pierre: 357
Pius IV: 333
piyyutim: 310
Place de Grève: 307
Poland: 105, 177 n. 10, 191, 196 n. 9, 205 n. 57
Poland–Lithuania: 184
Polemics: 15, 241, 305 n. 11, 306 n. 15, 335, 382, 425–26, 443
    anti-talmudic: 307 n. 21, 308
    medieval Christian: 308
    patristic: 308
    portentuosa bestia: 308
pollution
    book-burning as cleansing: 303
Porteiro, David: 80
Porteiro, Samuel: 78, 80
portentuosa bestia: 308
Porto, Menachem: 329
Portugal: 5, 13, 65–75, 77–78, 80, 82, 84, 254 n. 18, 278 n. 9, 307, 320
Posen: 330
Prague: 5, 21 n. 10, 33–34, 38–39, 94–95, 98–100, 103 n. 27, 105–07, 113 n. 77, 122, 124, 151–59, 162–67, 170, 173, 176–77, 180–81, 183–84, 191, 340 n. 4
Prague Haggadah (Prague 1526): 21 n. 10, 33–34, 38–39, 158 n. 10, 162 n. 22, 173, 176 n. 4, 180–81
prefigurative: 382, 385–87
print
    art of: 294–97
    invention of: 20, 33 n. 54, 238 n. 30, 281, 290, 293–94, 343
printers: 9 n. 1, 10, 12, 14, 79, 83, 85, 87–88, 91–93, 95, 98, 102–03, 104 n. 33, 144, 151, 153 n. 8, 158, 176, 178, 180 n. 25 and n. 29, 182 n. 35, 183 n. 45, 191, 196, 200, 221 n. 101, 223, 251, 255, 260 n. 51, 262, 267, 268 n. 86, 277, 280–81, 289, 291, 293–94, 296, 320, 345, 349, 410 n. 4

printing
  format of Talmud page: 324
  Hebrew Venetian: 324
  shops as social spaces: 323
proofreaders: 83, 238, 251, 265–66
Prostitz, Isaac ben Aaron: 99 n. 12, 103 n. 24 and n. 25, 104 n. 35
Protagoras, *On the Gods*: 303
Protestantism: 325, 428
Provenzali, Avraham: 344
Przemysl: 394
Psalter: 6, 15, 69, 84, 242 n. 50–253 n. 12, 353–64, 366–68, 377, 385, 398
Pugio Fidei, *see* Ramon Martí
puncta extraordinaria: 254

Qaro, Joseph: 94, 95 n. 30, 99 n. 12, 198, 223, 346
  Shulhan 'arukh: 94, 99, 107 n. 49, 138, 205 n. 56 and n. 57, 207, 223
qiddush: 5, 151–58, 160–61, 163–64, 166–68, 170, 172
Qimhi, David (Radaq): 9 n. 1, 58, 73 n. 39, 74, 76, 239, 255, 258, 267, 271 n. 91, 274, 280–81, 404, 413, 415–16, 418, 421, 425–27
  Commentary on Psalms: 58, 73 n. 39, 76, 258, 274, 280–81, 418, 425–27
  Sefer ha-shorashim: 67 n. 10, 74, 83, 269 n. 87, 404, 413–16, 417 n. 23
Qimhi, Moses: 73 n. 39, 413
Qitzur ha-melekhet mispar, *see* Mizrahi

Rabbinic Bible
  first: 276, 279–80, 324 n. 79
  second: 269, 276–77, 279–81, 284, 296–97, 323 n. 76
Raphael, Marco: 395
Raphelengius, Franciscus: 367
Raqah, David: 398
Raqah, Jacob: 398
Rashbam, *see* Samuel ben Meir
Rashi, *see* Solomon ben Isaac
Raz-Krakotzkin, Amnon: 261 n. 60, 323 n. 75, 326, 443 n. 64
redemption: 89, 100, 242, 248–49 n. 68, 319, 378, 402–03
  calculations of: 234

Reformation: 177–79, 252, 268 n. 82–269 n. 90, 326–27, 332–34, 343, 371 n. 12, 399 n. 29, 410 n. 4, 428, 436 n. 23
Regel, Jörg: 178
Regensburg: 31 n. 46, 107, 254 n. 14, 372 n. 16
Renaissance: 25–26, 38 n. 60 and n. 61, 49, 59, 71, 88 n. 6, 103 n. 32, 139, 181 n. 33, 185 n. 59, 196 n. 8, 197, 200 n. 29, 218 n. 94, 221 n. 103, 240 n. 47, 252 n. 3 and n. 6, 259 n. 43, 265 n. 70, 267, 276–77, 279 n. 12, 280 n. 14, 288 n. 40, 290 n. 43, 291 n. 43, 292 n. 44, 295–97, 323 n. 75, 324 n. 81, 329, 333, 343 n. 12, 344 n. 13, 354–55 n. 5, 358, 367 n. 35, 368, 381 n. 68, 393–94, 396 n. 10, 399 n. 29, 400 n. 34, 407, 410 n. 2, 413, 424 n. 59, 428, 432 n. 10 and n. 11, 433 n. 12, 437 n. 31
repetition: 33, 38–40, 46, 163–65, 223, 295
Reuchlin-Pfefferkorn controversy: 332
Reuchlin, Johannes: 269, 324 n. 79, 328, 369 n. 2, 387–88, 410–11, 438
revelation: 137 n. 9, 312, 317, 323 n. 75, 434
Rhineland: 13, 21, 141 n. 24, 146, 316, 372, 380
Ribeiro, Bernardim: 80
Robert of Naples and Sicily, King: 302
Rome: 197 n. 15, 240 n. 47, 252, 274, 277 n. 9, 302–04, 311, 319, 325–32, 334, 343, 394 n. 6, 395 n. 7, 396, 400, 403–05, 408, 443–44
Rothschild, Jean-Pierre: 435
Ruah hen: 444
Rudolph II: 105 n. 44
Runa: 364

Sabba, Fiammetta: 432, 433 n. 12
Sabbath: 5, 53 n. 14, 80 n. 87, 151, 153, 155, 157–59, 161, 163–66, 168, 172–73, 307
Sacrobosco, Johannes: 127–29
Sáenz-Badillos, Ángel: 230 n. 11, 409, 410 n. 4
Sages, Tannaitic: 239
Saint Andrews: 404
Salonica: 76, 80–83, 85
Samuel ben Meir (Rashbam): 108, 247, 248, 255
Samuel ben Solomon from Falaise: 340
Sánchez Ciruelo, Pedro: 411, 423–25
Sánchez de la Fuente, Diego: 418
Sanctio pragmatica: 375

Sarefield, Daniel: 303
Scaliger, Joseph: 357
Scechina: 400 n. 34, 401 n. 36 and n. 39, 403, 404 n. 49 and n. 50, 405
Schreckenfuchs, Erasmus Oswald: 109
Schrijver, Emile: 11, 90 n. 13, 238 n. 30
Scriniaria: 309
scriptio plene/defective, *see* orthography
Scripture: 72–75, 146, 228, 264, 276, 280–82, 285, 288–89, 292–94, 296–97, 308–11, 318, 335, 381–82, 385, 388, 432 n. 10–443
Sefaria: 286, 315 n. 49
Sefer ha-'agudah, *see* Alexander Süsslin ha-Kohen
Sefer ha-bahir: 394 n. 3, 408 n. 70
Sefer ha-halakhot, *see* Isaac Alfasi
Sefer ha-Mordekhai: 99–100, 103 n. 25, 108 n. 56, 380, 392
Sefer ha-peli'ah: 15, 393–400, 402–08
Sefer ha-qabbalah, *see* Abraham ibn Daud
Sefer ha-qanah: 394
Sefer ha-roqeah, *see* Eleazar of Worms
Sefer ha-shorashim, *see* Qimhi
Sefer ha-temunah: 394, 398, 401, 403–04
Sefer hasidim: 103, 104, 139–41, 444 n. 70
Sefer shorshe ha-qabbalah: 401
Sefer yuhasin, *see* Zacuto, Abraham
self-censoring: 312, 314–15, 405, 443 n. 64
Selihot (Augsburg 1536): 181, 186 n. 60 and n. 61
Selihot (Piove di Sacco *c.* 1475): 185
sermon: 68 n. 12–69, 73 n. 39, 80 n. 87–81, 142 n. 27, 204, 311 n. 41, 328, 382, 388
serpent of brass: 234
Sha'arei Dura: 99
Sha'ali serufah ba-'eish, *see* Meir ben Barukh of Rothenburg
shabbatot (special): 255
Shahor, Hayyim ben David: 175–76
Shalshelet ha-qabbalah, *see* Gedaliah ibn Yahya
Shamir, Avner: 332–33
Shekhinah: 317–18, 319 n. 62, 403
Sherira Ga'on: 434
Iggeret Rabbi Sherira Ga'on: 434
shorashim, *see* ShUT Maharyq
Shulhan 'arukh, *see* Qaro, Joseph

ShUM communities: 372
ShUT ha-Ramban: 197
ShUT Maharyq: 193, 196, 198–202, 204–05, 206 n. 59, 210, 213–14, 215 n. 86, 216, 217 n. 93, 222–23
ShUT Maharyq ha-hadashim: 202
siddur: 22 n. 15, n. 16, 24–26, 31, 33–34, 36 n. 58, 40, 63 n. 31, 67 n. 10, 104, 153, 179, 184
Siena: 345
Silesia: 176, 183 n. 45
Sirkis, Yoel: 205
Sirtut: 294
snake: 234
Solomon, King: 404
Soncino (Italy): 92, 100 n. 15, 237 n. 29, 252, 282, 319, 424
Soncino family: 9 n. 1, 237 n. 29, 277, 291
Gershom: 9, 80, 90, 100 n. 15, 101, 169, 185, 255 n. 20, 320, 324, 328
Joshua Solomon: 319
Soncino Press: 167 n. 45, 237
Sonne, Isaiah: 324
Spierinck, Nicholas: 354, 366, 368
St. Bartholomew's Night: 357
standardization: 19, 38, 40, 46, 237, 261
Steinschneider, Moritz: 90, 109, 111–12, 173, 176–77, 187, 203, 221, 307, 400, 432–33, 436
Stow, Kenneth: 301, 325 n. 84, 327
Studium generale: 381
subscriptions: 105, 106
Suleyman the Magnificent: 403
supercommentaries: 191, 255, 293
Superscriptio: 353 n. 1, 354 n. 3, 355 n. 7, 362, 385
Swabia: 175, 177, 189–91
synagogue: 31 n. 46, 80 n. 87, 97, 106, 184, 187–88, 239, 251, 253 n. 9, 262, 307–10, 316–17, 319, 325 n. 85, 330, 333, 356 n. 8, 378

Ta-Shma, Israel: 195 n. 5, 207, 393 n. 1
Taitazek, Joseph from Salonika: 346
Talmud
burning of: 6, 12, 15, 281, 295–96, 301–07, 310–12, 315–17, 319, 322, 324–34, 339–44, 439, 443 n. 64
Bomberg Edition: 280, 333 n. 121
Jerusalem: 88, 91, 340, 347–48

translation into Latin: 311
trial of: 304–07, 309–12, 324 n. 81, 326–27 n. 95
Targum
   Jonathan: 72, 76, 82 n. 100, 387–88
   Onqelos: 76, 82 n. 100–83, 279, 281, 284
Terumat ha-deshen: 193, 196, 198, 200–01, 203–16, 218–23, 378 n. 56
Tevel, David bar Ezekiel of Cracow: 104
Textualis Quadrata: 384
Themistius: 441
Theologia Mahometis, *see* Widmanstetter, Johann Albrecht
Theologia, *see* Peter Abelard
Theoricae novae planetarum (Heb. *Teorika*), *see* Peuerbach, George
Thibaut de Sézanne: 311
title inscription: 429, 431, 433, 439–46
title page: 9 n. 1, 13, 89–91, 93, 101, 103–04, 108, 179, 181–83, 186, 191 n. 84, 197, 199–200 n. 30, 209–10, 218, 221–22, 333, 433
Titulus crucis: 383
Toledano, Eliezer: 78
Toledo: 138, 220, 228–29, 411, 413, 418 n. 25, 423–26
Toledot Yeshu: 336
Torah
   Oral: 15, 141, 306, 317–18, 434
   scroll: 5, 13, 133–38, 141, 143–48, 234 n. 23, 257, 275–76, 315–17, 319, 378
   written: 148, 317–18
Tosafists: 107, 210 n. 76, 234 n. 20, 249 n. 68, 306 n. 15, 312
Tosafot: 82, 92, 141, 145, 167 n. 45, 234 n. 20, 247 n. 57, n. 58, 256, 320
Tosefta: 342, 434
Treves, Eliezer ben Naphtali: 101 n. 16, 191 n. 82, 278 n. 9
Treves, Naphtali Herz: 101 n. 16, 278
Troyes: 239, 247, 280, 358 n. 15
Tudela: 234, 236, 239
Turkey: 83, 322 n. 74, 326
Turnauer, Caspar: 181
Typesetters: 93, 193, 200, 251, 253, 255, 258 n. 38, 260–61, 264, 269, 323
typography, typographic(al): 10, 14, 67, 76 n. 59, 77–79, 81–85, 153 n. 9, 162 n. 19, 176 n. 6, 177 n. 10 and n. 12, 254, 258, 266, 277, 278 n. 9, 279–80, 282–83, 285, 292, 293, 295–96
Tzurat ha-'aretz, *see* Abraham bar Hiyya

Ulm: 159, 163, 177–79, 186, 188, 419 n. 36
Ulma Günzburg family: 190 n. 79
Usque, Samuel: 80

Valladolid: 424, 426
Vanni Fucci: 397
Veneto: 63 n. 31, 184, 395–96, 398 n. 27
Venice: 6, 68 n. 12, 70 n. 26, 73 n. 41–74 n. 47, 83, 88 n. 7, 92–93 n. 25, 99 n. 11, 103 n. 27, 105–06 n. 46, 141, 183, 185, 190, 193, 196–200, 203, 205 n. 55, 209 n. 70, 221, 223, 238–39, 251 n. 1, 255 n. 21–257, 268 n. 81, 271 n. 94, 277 n. 9–284, 291, 295, 297, 302, 304, 315 n. 49, 320–23, 326, 329–30, 339 n. 1, 343, 345, 376, 395, 397–99, 434, 438
Vienna: 15, 26, 29, 31, 99, 113, 129, 141 n. 23, 278 n. 9, 369–76, 378–84, 386, 390, 403, 404 n. 49, 432
   Österreichische Nationalbibliothek: 111, 129, 369, 372–73, 376–77, 379, 384, 386
   University of: 6, 15, 369–76, 378–79, 381, 383, 390
Vienna *Gezerah*: 370, 371, 374, 375, 376, 379, 380, 382
Vilna: 314, 315 n. 49, 394
Vizinho, Joseph: 78
vocalization: 78, 79 n. 79, 228, 239, 257, 266, 361, 362 n. 28, 377
von Gumppenberg, Ambrosius: 444
Vulgate: 324 n. 79, 355, 359, 362, 381, 383, 384–85, 386 n. 96, 388

Wakefield, Robert: 367 n. 35, 368
Werner, Thomas: 303
wheel charts (volvelles): 113
Widmanstetter, Johann Albrecht: 189, 400, 429, 431, 443 n. 65
   Theologia Mahometis: 432
Wind, August: 177
Wittenberg: 112, 429
Wolfhart, Bonifatius: 178, 179, 183, 190
Woodcut: 5, 20, 24, 31, 33–34, 38–39, 46, 77 n. 64, 151, 153, 158, 159, 162–64, 165–66, 168–70, 172–73, 180–82
Worms: 31 n. 46, 90, 101–02, 104, 187, 248 n. 65, 265 n. 72, 316 n. 52, 341, 372

Yaakov ben Meir (Rabbenu Tam): 342
Yafe, Kalonymos: 180
Yalqut Shim'oni: 440
Yehiel ben Yequtiel: 347
Yehiel of Paris: 305, 307, 341
Yehoel: 103
Yemen: 312 n. 47, 434, 443
Yerushalmi, Solomon Isaac (Zekil Ashkenazi): 330 n. 109, 344
Yuval, Israel: 204 n. 46, 319

Zacuto, Abraham: 78, 434
   Sefer yuhasin: 434
Zanwil, Samuel ben Israel of Worms: 104
Zion
   personification of: 317
   return to: 330
   Talmud figured as: 317
Zohar: 88, 91, 248 n. 63, 276, 281 n. 15, 288, 296, 400 n. 33, 431
Zorzi, Francesco: 394, 395, 396 n. 10, 398 n. 25, 399, 405, 406